SHENANDOAH
1862

CIVIL WAR AMERICA

Gary W. Gallagher, *Editor*

STONEWALL JACKSON'S

VALLEY CAMPAIGN

SHENANDOAH
1862

PETER COZZENS

THE UNIVERSITY OF NORTH CAROLINA PRESS
CHAPEL HILL

Designed by Courtney Leigh Baker
Set in Minion and Scala Sans
by Keystone Typesetting, Inc.
Manufactured in the United States of America

The paper in this book meets the guidelines for
permanence and durability of the Committee on
Production Guidelines for Book Longevity of the
Council on Library Resources.

The University of North Carolina Press has been a
member of the Green Press Initiative since 2003.

Library of Congress Cataloging-in-Publication Data
Cozzens, Peter, 1957–
    Shenandoah 1862 : Stonewall Jackson's Valley
Campaign / Peter Cozzens.
        p. cm. — (Civil War America)
    Includes bibliographical references and index.
I S B N 978-0-8078-3200-4 (cloth: alk. paper)
    1. Shenandoah Valley Campaign, 1862. 2. Jackson,
Stonewall, 1824–1863—Military leadership. I. Title.
E 473.7.C 69 2008
973.7′32—dc22
2008008849

12 11 10 09 08   5 4 3 2 1

University of North Carolina Press books may be
purchased at a discount for educational, business, or
sales promotional use. For information, please visit
www.uncpress.unc.edu or write to UNC Press,
attention: Sales Department, 116 South Boundary
Street, Chapel Hill, NC 27514-3808.

CONTENTS

ILLUSTRATIONS

MAPS

ACKNOWLEDGMENTS

My acknowledgments are few but most heartfelt. I would like to extend my deepest appreciation to Gary Gallagher, editor of the Civil War America series, and David Perry, senior editor at the University of North Carolina Press, for their confidence in me and their unbounded patience, as this manuscript took far longer to write than anyone had expected.

I also sincerely thank my dear friend, Rob Girardi, a superb editor of numerous Civil War titles, for his careful reading of the manuscript and his insightful suggestions.

Lastly, I offer my most profound thanks to my beloved Antonia Feldman for helping see this book to completion.

SHENANDOAH
1862

INTRODUCTION

The Shenandoah Valley campaign of 1862 evokes images of indefatigable Confederate infantry making rapid marches under the steady hand of Maj. Gen. Thomas J. "Stonewall" Jackson; of bold strikes against hapless Yankees whose commanders were inept fools, dangling from wires pulled in Washington, D.C.; and of a pre-orchestrated strategic plan that made Confederate victory inevitable.

There is truth in much of this. From his tactical defeat but strategic victory at Kernstown in March 1862 until his final two victories at Cross Keys and Port Republic in early June 1862, Jackson accomplished the broad goals that his immediate commander, Gen. Joseph E. (Joe) Johnston, and later Maj. Gen. Robert E. Lee, as general in chief and military adviser to Confederate president Jefferson Davis, set out for him. The first of these was to detain Federal forces in the Valley that might otherwise support Maj. Gen. George B. McClellan's army on the Peninsula, and the second was to relieve pressure on Fredericksburg, where 40,000 Union troops were concentrated to join McClellan's offensive against Richmond. Jackson accomplished these objectives in impressive style, making optimal use of interior lines to concentrate his small army, which never numbered more than 16,000 men, despite the fact that the total Union strength in the region fluctuated between 30,000 and 70,000 during May and June 1862, the months of his greatest successes.

How was this possible? The existing major works on the Shenandoah Valley campaign of 1862 provide only partial answers because they tell the story almost exclusively from the Confederate point of view. The sole modern work devoted to the campaign is Robert G. Tanner's *Stonewall in the Valley*, published in 1976 and reissued twenty years later. The single other study was undertaken in the 1880s by William Allan, a member of Jackson's staff, and titled *History of the Campaign of Gen. T. J. (Stonewall) Jackson in the Shenandoah Valley of Virginia*. Tanner gave as the stated purpose of both his original and revised book the "recounting of the campaign from the Confederate viewpoint, a task first undertaken by William Allan."[1] Apart from his own confession, the extent of Tanner's bias is demonstrated by the fact that every manuscript source he consulted and all but three printed primary sources are Confederate. Such a one-sided approach to a military campaign serves no good purpose; it is impossible to judge the true greatness, if indeed such a word is appropriate, of Jackson's accomplishments in the Valley without an equally thorough understanding of the campaign from the Union perspective.

Apart from the works of Tanner and Allan, the only other significant studies have been microhistories of one or more engagements of the Valley campaign. The best of these are Gary L. Ecelbarger's *"We Are in for It!": The First Battle of Kernstown*, and Robert K. Krick's *Conquering the Valley: Stonewall Jackson at Port Republic*. Both tell the story of these battles well, but neither approaches the campaign as a whole.

Most recently Gary W. Gallagher edited a series of essays, *The Shenandoah Valley Campaign of 1862*, for this press. The eight studies contained therein are excellent, but they do not seek to present a picture of the campaign in its totality. Topics range from the relatively esoteric—"Placed on the Pages of History in Blood: Reporting on and Remembering the 12th Georgia Infantry in the 1862 Valley Campaign," "Turner Ashby's Appeal," and "Maryland's Ablest Confederate: General Charles S. Winder of the Stonewall Brigade"—to two superb, groundbreaking essays that represent the first modern efforts at approaching the campaign from the Federal perspective—Gallagher's own " 'You Must Either Attack Richmond or Give Up the Job and Come to the Defence of Washington': Abraham Lincoln and the Shenandoah Campaign," and William J. Miller's "Such Men as Shields, Banks, and Frémont: Federal Command in Western Virginia, March–June 1862." But while excellent, both are by design only starting points to a fuller understanding of the Valley campaign.

It has been my purpose to write the first balanced, and I trust comprehensive, history of the 1862 Shenandoah Valley campaign, giving equal voice to both Union and Confederate sources. In no other manner can the degree of Jackson's success properly be judged. Fellow corps commander Lt. Gen. James

Longstreet addressed this question obliquely when he wrote long after the war that "Jackson was a very skillful man against such men as Shields, Banks, and Frémont, but when pitted against the best of the Federal commanders he did not appear so well."[2]

I find myself in broad agreement with William Miller in concluding that the Union generals sent to oppose Jackson—with the exception of Brig. Gen. James Shields, who was laid up with an incapacitating wound throughout the Battle of Kernstown, and then went on to embarrass himself in a tentative and confused march down Page (Luray) Valley in June 1862—performed reasonably well in view of the many factors working against them. Among these were the absence of an overall commander, chronic supply problems caused in part by persistent torrential rains, and well-intentioned but too often ill-informed meddling from Washington. President Abraham Lincoln did not, as Jackson biographers and earlier campaign studies would have it, panic at any stage in the campaign, but neither did he add positively to its conduct.

Lincoln played a far more active role in the management of the campaign on the Federal side than did President Jefferson Davis on the Southern side. Indeed, while Lincoln kept a keen eye on every detail during the critical last week of May and first week of June, at no point during the campaign did Davis apparently take anything but a passing interest in affairs in the Shenandoah Valley; the evidence suggests that he allowed Johnston and Robert E. Lee broadly to oversee Jackson's conduct of the campaign.

I begin my narrative with Jackson assuming command of the Valley District in the waning days of 1861 and look at the Bath and Romney winter campaign in detail. A knowledge of Jackson's shortcomings in the conduct of that ill-fated episode is critical to understanding how his army regarded him at the outset of the spring 1862 campaign, and to reveal early on flaws, or more charitably put, eccentricities in his command style. Among these, none were more damning, or potentially ruinous, than his determination always to keep his plans and objectives to himself, leaving his seconds-in-command to flail about in the dark.

But despite his faults Jackson did win the Valley campaign, and the impact of his victories was enormous, both strategically and psychologically. Jackson's audacious attack at Kernstown derailed McClellan's plans to have Maj. Gen. Nathaniel P. Banks's corps cover the approaches to Washington toward Centreville and caused Lincoln and his military advisers to look more closely at McClellan's dispositions for defending the capital while he embarked on his waterborne offensive against Richmond. What they saw troubled them. On

April 1 Lincoln stripped McClellan of his responsibilities as general in chief and created independent departments for Banks and for Maj. Gen. Irvin McDowell, who was to have threatened Richmond from Fredericksburg while McClellan moved up the Peninsula of Virginia. Retaining McDowell at Fredericksburg and taking direct responsibility for his movements as well as those of Banks, Lincoln and his secretary of war, Edwin M. Stanton, fractured the Federal command structure in the East.

The fatal impact of these decisions was felt during the last week of May 1862, when Lincoln reacted to Jackson's victory over Banks at Winchester by halting McDowell's long-delayed march on Richmond. Lincoln hastened him first to Manassas to cover Washington and then sent him on toward the Shenandoah Valley to combine with Maj. Gen. John C. Frémont, whom he ordered to move east from the Alleghenies, in order that the juncture of their forces would cut off Jackson's withdrawal up the Valley and destroy his small army. Lincoln's redirection of McDowell robbed McClellan of his force just as McClellan's plans for opening the final campaign for Richmond were at last maturing.

While it cannot be argued definitively that McClellan would have captured Richmond even with McDowell's large corps at his disposal, the lack of it made McClellan more cautious than ever and gave the Confederate army defending the capital much-needed breathing space.

Greater arguably than the strategic value of Jackson's victories in the Shenanoah Valley was the boost they gave to Southern morale, which in the spring of 1862 was at its nadir. Since the opening of 1862—from the eastern seaboard to the desert wastes of New Mexico Territory (where an abortive Southern effort to strike toward California had come to naught)—the war had been going the North's way.

Disaster had followed upon disaster. In February a combined-arms expedition under Brig. Gen. Ambrose Burnside steamed up Pamlico Sound, North Carolina, and after a sharp fight captured Roanoke Island. Burnside exploited his victory by seizing New Bern in mid-March. Farther down the coast, the Federals captured Fort Pulaski at the mouth of the Savannah River on April 11, permanently closing Savannah as a Confederate port. Then an expedition under Maj. Gen. Benjamin F. Butler, augmented by naval forces under David G. Farragut, occupied New Orleans on May 1.

Matters in the Confederate interior were just as grim. By late March the South had conceded all of Kentucky to the North except Columbus, and that city was about to be evacuated. Tennessee was effectively lost with the capture of Forts Henry and Donelson in February and the subsequent Southern evacuation of Nashville. In March, Ulysses S. Grant's army pushed to the southernmost reaches of Middle Tennessee along the Tennessee River and an army under Don Carlos Buell rushed from Nashville to join him near Pittsburg Landing. The overall Confederate commander in the West, Gen. Albert Sidney Johnston, gathered all available forces at Corinth, Mississippi, to strike back at the Federals in what for the South was an unprecedented concentration of forces. President Davis staunchly supported the move, concluding to abandon much of what remained of the seaboard "in order to defend the Tennessee line which is vital to our safety."[3] Pensacola and Mobile were stripped of troops, as was Arkansas (where the South had suffered a crushing defeat at Pea Ridge), and Columbus, Kentucky, was abandoned.

The grand concentration failed. The Confederates were defeated at Shiloh and Albert Sidney Johnston was killed. The remainder of the army, under Pierre G. T. Beauregard, limped back to Corinth, where during April and May an enormous Federal army under Maj. Gen. Henry Halleck advanced slowly but inexorably to evict Beauregard and seal off two of the best railroads in the Confederacy. Also in April, a Union force under Brig. Gen. John Pope demonstrated the bankruptcy of Confederate defenses along the Upper Mississippi River when he seized New Madrid, Missouri, and Island No. 10 in an almost bloodless campaign. In the East, McClellan had begun to squeeze Joe Johnston's much smaller army with his move to the Peninsula.

Amid these auguries of an early end to the Confederacy came the victories of Stonewall Jackson, first at McDowell on May 8, at Front Royal on May 23, then at Winchester on May 25, and finally at Cross Keys and Port Republic on June 8 and 9. Although small affairs, they demonstrated that Union armies and their commanders not only were not invincible, but also could be made to appear foolish through deft and daring maneuver. Countless letters from both the entire home front and from every Southern army attest to the seemingly inordinate psychological benefits derived from operations in the Shenandoah Valley.

Just as his victories heartened the Confederacy, so too they raised Stonewall Jackson from an obscure major general to a folk hero in both the North and the South, as well as in Europe. Songs were composed in his honor. Northern merchants hawked soap that Jackson purportedly fancied. As the Confederacy's only successful commander since First Bull Run, Jackson was especially praised by troops in the relatively inactive Southern army before Richmond, and Federals who had never even encountered him in battle feared him. Regardless of whatever contribution he might make thereafter, his name was secure.[4]

A final word is in order about the strategic and logistical significance of the Shenandoah Valley itself. The Valley provided an avenue by which either side might threaten the western flanks of Washington or Richmond. The threat was far greater to the Northern capital, as the Valley rolled to the northeast from the southwest, than it was to Richmond. But Federals moving southward through the Valley could cut critical rail lines supplying troops defending Richmond and threaten the left flank of a Southern army operating between the Occoquan and Rappahannock-Rapidan river line. The value of the Shenandoah Valley as a granary and source of livestock to the Confederacy cannot be overstated.

The harm inflicted on the Valley economy during the 1862 campaign has been overstated, except in places where the plundering Germans of Louis Blenker's division wandered. The damage done the civilian population was more psychological than physical—learning of loved ones killed within miles of home and, in Winchester, witnessing the brutality of combat up close. The loss of slaves impeded housework in the Lower Valley. White women in Winchester became brazen and foul in their treatment of the Yankees, even to the point of killing several during the Battle of Winchester, while the men generally remained submissive to authority—a sharp reversal for its time in the roles of the sexes. Federals and Confederates purchased livestock, wheat, and other provisions in large quantities from Lower Valley farmers, but the campaign scarcely touched the vast resources of the Upper Valley. Although Confederate commissary and quartermaster agents made heavy drafts on the region, bumper crops assured that the citizenry would not suffer.[5] It would be two years hence before the Valley learned the meaning of total war, when the Union's Maj. Gen. Philip H. Sheridan swept up it with express orders to lay waste to the region.

CHAPTER 1

THIS WAR IS A FARCE

Stonewall Jackson was angry. With "no other aid than the smiles of God," his brigade of Virginians had blunted the Federal advance and turned the fortunes of battle at First Manassas. But the rout of the Yankee army galled him as an empty triumph. The Confederate commanders, Gen. Joe Johnston and Gen. Pierre G. T. Beauregard, seemed content simply to hold the ground Jackson had won them. Fretting about at a field hospital just after the battle, Jackson unburdened himself on the surgeon who attended his broken finger. "If they will let me," he declared, "I'll march my brigade into Washington tonight!"

No one let him. As July slipped into August 1861, the Confederate army of 41,000 men sank into torpor in camps around the hamlet of Centreville, just twenty miles from the defenses of Washington, D.C. An inept commissary department and uncertain railroads kept the troops hungry in a rich harvest season. Measles and chronic diarrhea laid low thousands. The liberal granting of furloughs thinned the ranks in equal measure. A shortage of arms—the chief of ordnance had only 3,500 muskets, mostly antique flintlocks, on hand—impeded recruiting.[1]

Both the army and the civilian population of the South had expected that Johnston and Beauregard would advance after First Manassas at least as far as Alexandria. Sanguine spirits predicted the capture of Washington, D.C., and the defection of Maryland, Kentucky, and Missouri to the Confederacy. Some, beguiled by victory, considered the war all but over. A Virginia chaplain at the front recalled meeting a high-ranking officer just returned from Richmond who assured him: "We shall have no more fighting. It is not our policy to advance on the enemy now; they will hardly advance on us, and before spring England and France will recognize the Confederacy, and that will end the war."[2]

Stonewall Jackson disagreed. He argued that only by carrying the fight vigorously onto Northern soil could the South expect to prevail. Delay was fatal. "We must give [the enemy] no time to think," he wrote his wife Anna. "We must bewilder them and keep them bewildered. Our fighting must be sharp, impetuous, continuous. We cannot stand a long war."[3] Confederate inactivity after First Manassas was not simply a terrible blunder, Jackson believed, but also a dangerous repudiation of the will of God. In His divine providence, the Lord had given the Southern people a rare opportunity for securing the fruits of independence through decisive action in His name. "If the war is carried on with vigor," Jackson assured Anna, "I think that, under the blessing of God, it will not last long." Despite his deeply felt fears, both temporal and eternal, Jackson's sense of official propriety sealed his lips. When asked why the army did nothing, Jackson told his subordinates, "This is the affair of the commanding generals."[4]

Unknown to Jackson, the commanding generals also were impatient to strike a decisive blow, the more so as spies in Washington told them a reinvigorated, and hugely superior, Federal army under Maj. Gen. George B. McClellan might at any moment move against them. But without more arms and men, Johnston was loathe to advance beyond Fairfax Courthouse. At Johnston's request, President Jefferson Davis visited army headquarters on September 30 to review the situation. For two hours Davis, Johnston, Beauregard, and Maj. Gen. Gustavus W. Smith pored over maps and shuffled through ordnance and troop-strength reports. "No one questioned the disastrous results of remaining inactive through the winter," recalled Smith. "The enemy were daily increasing in number, arms, discipline, and efficiency. We looked forward to a sad state of things at the opening of a spring campaign."

Johnston pleaded for help. "Mr. President, is it not possible to increase the effective strength of this army and put us in condition to cross the Potomac and carry the war into the enemy's country? Can you not by stripping other points to the last they will bear, and even risking defeat in other places, put us in condition to move forward?"

How many more men would they need? Sixty thousand, said Johnston and Beauregard; fifty thousand, thought Smith. Out of the question, retorted Davis; the whole country demanded protection and arms and troops for defense. The generals were unrelenting. Better to risk almost certain defeat on the north side of the Potomac than watch the army waste away during the winter, at the end of which the terms of enlistment of half the force would expire. But Davis was adamant. Reinforcements were impossible; there was no course but to "await the winter and its results." As heartsick as his generals, Davis suggested a partial blow somewhere in the theater, perhaps a quick strike across the Potomac near Williamsport, Maryland, or Harpers Ferry, Virginia.[5]

Unaware that the issue had been decided, Jackson called on General Smith, who lay sick in his tent. Jackson apologized for disturbing him, but he had come on a matter of "great importance." Smith bade him proceed. Sitting himself on the ground at the head of Smith's cot, with a confidence perhaps borne of his October 7 promotion to major general in the Provisional Army of the Confederate States, Jackson offered up his war strategy. With his army of raw recruits, McClellan dare not make a move until spring. Now was the time to draw troops from other points and invade: Cross the Upper Potomac, seize Baltimore, destroy the factories of Philadelphia and play havoc with Pennsylvania, take and hold the shores of Lake Erie. It could all be done, expounded Jackson. We could live off the land; make "unrelenting war amidst their homes, force the people of the North to understand what it will cost them to hold the South in the Union at the bayonet's point." Smith must persuade Johnston and Beauregard of the correctness—and righteousness—of his vision.

Smith shook his head. Impossible, nothing he might say would do any good. But he must, countered Jackson. No, answered Smith, and to explain his reluctance he offered to "tell Jackson a secret."

"Please do not tell me any secret. I would prefer not to hear it." But Jackson must know. President Davis had ruled out an offensive; the South would wait for McClellan's advance, or for European recognition, as the case might be.

The passion left Jackson. "When I had finished," recalled Smith, "he rose from the ground, shook my hand warmly, and said, 'I am sorry, very sorry.' Without another word he went slowly out to his horse, a few feet in front of my tent, mounted very deliberately, and rode sadly away."[6]

UNION BRIGADIER GENERAL Frederick W. Lander was a restless spirit. Strong and fond of sports, Lander as a young man had parleyed an engineering degree from Norwich University into an assignment as a civil engineer on the Northern Pacific Railway survey of 1853. At home on the frontier, Lander returned to the Northwest the following year to lead a surveying expedition from Puget Sound to the Mississippi River. Over the next four years, he roamed the West as superintendent and chief engineer of the Overland Wagon Road, fighting Indians and bears in about equal measure, and earning from admiring Blackfoot guides the nom de guerre of "Old Grizzly." By the end of the decade, Lander had participated in five transcontinental surveys. When not challenging nature, he dabbled in poetry, writing with the same force and vigor that characterized his railroad work. In 1860 he married Jean Margaret Davenport, an acclaimed British actress.

At the outbreak of the Civil War, the Lincoln administration appointed Lander a civil agent and sent him on a confidential mission to Governor Sam Houston of Texas, with authority to order Federal troops in the state to support the governor. Later, as a volunteer aide on the staff of General Mc-Clellan, Lander distinguished himself in the engagements of Philippi and Rich Mountain. That won him a commission as a brigadier general of volunteers and command of a brigade in Brig. Gen. Charles P. Stone's Corps of Observation near Poolesville, Maryland, across the Potomac River from a small Confederate force at Leesburg, Virginia.[7]

Lander shared Jackson's yearning for action. In early October he traveled to Washington to lobby for a new assignment. Ambushing Lincoln and Secretary of State William H. Seward as they left the White House one evening, Lander promised the president he could do great things if granted a special force. With a handful of good men—loyal Virginians, whom he would raise himself—Lander would strike south and erase the "cowardly shame" of Bull Run, or die trying. Watching the rugged brigadier march off, a bemused Lincoln quipped to Seward: "If he really wanted a job like that, I could give it to him. Let him take his squad and go down behind Manassas and break up their railroad."

The commanding general of the army, Winfield Scott, took Lander more seriously. On October 13 he offered Lander, whom he once called the "great natural American soldier," command of a newly created Department of Harpers Ferry and Cumberland, which embraced a 120-mile stretch of the strategically critical Baltimore and Ohio Railroad. Thirty miles of the line cut through hostile territory.[8]

Lander accepted the assignment. He returned to Poolesville just long enough to tender his resignation from McClellan's moribund army, then hurried back to the War Department to consult with Scott. Confederate cavalry and local militia had burned railroad bridges and torn up much of the track in Virginia, but Lander was confident that he could reopen the line quickly.

Affairs in western Virginia certainly seemed propitious of success. McClellan's successor to departmental command, Brig. Gen. William S. Rosecrans, had swept poorly led Southern forces eastward toward the Allegheny Mountains. Reinforced and united under Maj. Gen. Robert E. Lee, the Confederates maintained a tentative presence in the Great Kanawha Valley, which Rosecrans threatened to disrupt. Nearer to Lander's new department, Brig. Gen. Benjamin F. Kelley commanded a brigade of Ohio and loyal Virginia regiments at Grafton in what was called the Railroad District of Rosecrans's department.[9]

Kelley was within striking distance of Romney, Virginia, a village of five hundred with an importance far beyond its humble size. From Romney, the excellent Northwest Turnpike ran east forty miles to Winchester, which was key to the Confederate defense of the Lower Shenandoah Valley. Romney was the principal town of the fertile South Branch Valley. Wide meadows on either side of the South Branch of the Potomac River yielded large crops of corn and offered ideal pasturage for cattle. Tucked among a patchwork of ridges, ravines, and low mountains on the east bank of the South Branch, Romney not only controlled the valley, but it also commanded the sixty-mile length of the Baltimore and Ohio Railroad most critical to Lander's new department. From Romney, the Confederates could reach the track in a short day's march. But with Romney in Federal hands, marauding Confederates would be hard pressed to operate against the railway. Lander understood this, and he urged General Scott to order Kelley to seize Romney and assume command of the Department of Harpers Ferry and Cumberland until Lander arrived. Scott complied, and on October 22 Lander repaired to his District of Columbia home to prepare for his new post.[10]

An unexpected clash the previous day involving his old brigade interrupted Lander's plans. General Stone had taken his Corps of Observation across the Potomac to do battle with a Confederate force at Ball's Bluff. In the ensuing fiasco Col. Edward D. Baker, a close friend of President Lincoln, was killed and the surviving Union troops were stranded. That evening a War Department courier delivered a short telegram from McClellan to Lander's E Street home ordering the general to return to his former command. Lander set out at once and the next morning took command of two thousand Federal troops on the Virginia shore at Edwards Ferry, ten miles downriver from Ball's Bluff. Lander was hit early in the day's fighting. A Rebel bullet smashed into his left leg, boring his bootstrap deep into the calf muscle. Refusing aid, Lander hobbled about in agony until the fight was over. A surgeon then cleaned bits of boot leather from the gaping hole, pronounced the wound "not at all dangerous," then remanded Lander to the care of his wife. Spitting epithets over the poor planning and wasted sacrifice of life that characterized Stone's sorry little campaign—"This war is a farce," he told a friend, "bloodless nerves ruin the roast"—Lander rode painfully back to his district home to convalesce. While he laid abed, his chief patron, General Scott, retired, and George McClellan replaced him as commanding general of the Northern armies. McClellan wanted a quiet winter. Undoubtedly concerned that the impetuous Lander would bring on a battle to reopen the Baltimore and Ohio as soon as he was healthy, McClellan terminated his new military department.[11]

INACTIVITY WAS ANATHEMA to Stonewall Jackson. Rebuffed in his calls for an offensive, Jackson devoted himself to improving his brigade, already the most efficient in Johnston's army. Other commands melted away, as troops took leave in large numbers to visit family or harvest crops, but Jackson granted no furloughs. His devotion to duty was absolute, and he expected nothing less from his officers and men. When Col. Kenton Harper of the 5th Virginia appealed to Jackson in late August for emergency leave to visit his terminally ill wife, he met with a harsh rebuke. "General, my wife is dying! I must see her!" implored Harper. A look of sadness betrayed Jackson's inner struggle, but he held firm. "Man," he asked Harper, "do you love your wife more than your country?" Harper's answer was a letter of resignation.[12]

Hypocrisy can sometimes catch the best of men unawares. While Colonel Harper journeyed home to Staunton to bury his wife, Mary Anna Jackson was on her way to Centreville to visit her husband. General Jackson commandeered an ambulance to meet her at the Manassas railhead, whisked her off to church services with the Stonewall Brigade, and then set her up in a farmhouse near headquarters. While Jackson drilled his brigade incessantly, Anna reveled in army life, entertaining high-ranking callers and generally enjoying her role as belle of the ball. Four times a day, in ninety-minute blocks, Jackson had the brigade on the parade ground. Their firm stand at Manassas had earned the Virginians and their commander the sobriquet "Stonewall." But tenacity on the defense was but one ingredient of military success; now they would learn to march and attack as one. Said an early Jackson biographer: "Shoulder to shoulder they advanced and retired, marched and countermarched, massed in column, formed line to front or flank, until they learned to move as a machine, until the limbs obeyed before the order had passed from ear to brain, until obedience became an instinct and cohesion a necessity of their nature." Amid the general apathy that had descended on the army, Jackson's men worked hard. When not drilling, they stood inspection, policed their camps, or picketed the perimeter. "Every officer and soldier," affirmed Jackson, "who is able to do duty ought to be busily engaged in military preparation by hard drilling, in order that, through the blessing of God, we may be victorious in the battles which in His all-wise providence may await us."[13]

It was not only his men who learned. Ever a close student of war, Jackson reflected on his actions at First Manassas, and from them derived tactical principles to guide him in the campaigns ahead. As a young lieutenant of artillery in the Mexican War, Jackson had learned how to deploy artillery to its best advantage. Running his section up to the walls of Chapultepec, far in advance of the infantry, Jackson had given shot for shot with the heavy guns of the castle until support reached him. His feat of daring inspired an assault that carried the works and won the battle. Just as the daring of a few well-served cannons might inspire the infantry, so too could their capture demoralize the ranks, as happened when Jackson's Virginians mowed down the gunners and horses of Ricketts's and Griffin's regular batteries at Manassas.

Jackson's ideas regarding the role of infantry were as aggressive as his artillery tactics. "I rather think," he said after First Manassas, "that fire by file [independent firing] is best on the whole, for it gives the enemy an idea that the fire is heavier than if it was by company or battalion [volley firing]. Sometimes, however, one may be best, sometimes the other, according to circumstances. But my opinion is that there ought not to be much firing at all. My idea is that the best mode of fighting is to reserve your fire till the enemy get—or you get them—to close quarters. Then deliver one deadly, deliberate fire—and charge!"[14]

No less important than controlling men in combat was the need to control oneself. Jackson knew himself to be imperturbable under fire, but some had mistaken his calm determination at Manassas for simpleminded indifference. Paying a call on Jackson three days after First Manassas, Capt. John D. Imboden asked him the secret of his equanimity in battle. "General," he inquired pointedly, "how is it that you can keep so cool, and appear so utterly insensible to danger in such a storm of shell and bullets as rained about you when your hand was hit?"

Perhaps because his battery had served Jackson faithfully at Manassas,

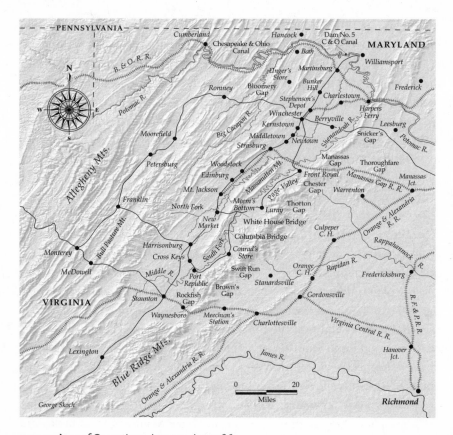

MAP 1. Area of Operations, January–June 1862

Imboden was at ease asking the reticent and intensely private Jackson so personal a question. And Jackson obliged him with an answer. "Captain," he said gravely, "my religious belief teaches me to feel as safe in battle as in bed. God has fixed the time for my death. I do not concern myself about that, but to be always ready, no matter when it may overtake me." Pausing, he looked the young captain in the face, then added, "That is the way all men should live, and then all would be equally brave."[15]

Although careful not to force his faith on them, Jackson had a profound concern for the spiritual welfare of his men. In late October he invited the Reverend Dr. William S. White, pastor of the Lexington Presbyterian Church, which Jackson had attended in peacetime, to preach to the command. For five days and nights White ministered to the Virginians, reserving time in the morning and evening to lead the worship service at headquarters. Jackson thrilled to these spiritual retreats with "a beaming face and warm abandon of manner." He prayed with uncommon intensity, remembered White. "He thanked God for sending me to visit the army, and prayed that He would own and bless my ministrations, both to officers and privates, so that many souls might be saved. He pleaded with such tenderness and fervor that God would baptize the whole army with His holy spirit, that my own hard heart was melted into penitence, gratitude, and praise."[16]

White unexpectedly found himself with more to do than spread the Gospel. On the morning of October 23, while White prepared for his daily ministrations, a troubled General Jackson handed him a letter he had just received. White studied it closely:

Richmond, October 21, 1861.
Major-General Jackson, Manassas:

SIR: The exposed condition of the Virginia frontier between the Blue Ridge and Allegheny Mountains has excited the deepest solicitude of the Government, and the constant appeals of the inhabitants that we should send a perfectly reliable officer for their protection have induced the Department to form a new military district, which is called the Valley District of the Department of Northern Virginia. In selecting an officer for this command the choice of the Government has fallen on you. This choice has been dictated, not only by a just appreciation of your qualities as a commander, but by other weighty considerations. Your intimate knowledge of the country, of its population and resources, rendered you peculiarly fitted to assume this command. Nor is this all. The people of that district, with one voice, have made constant and urgent appeals that to you, in whom they have confidence, should their defense be assigned. The administration shares the regret which you will no doubt feel at being separated from your command when there is a probability of early engagement between the opposing armies, but it feels confident that you will cheerfully yield your private wishes to your country's service in the sphere where you can be rendered most available.

In assuming the command to which you have been assigned by general orders, although your forces will for the present be small, they will be increased as rapidly as our means will possibly admit, whilst the people will themselves rally eagerly to your standard as soon as it is known that you are to command. In a few days detailed instructions will be sent you through the Adjutant-General, and I will be glad to receive any suggestions you may make to render effectual your measures of defense.

I am, respectfully, your obedient servant,

J. P. BENJAMIN Acting Secretary of War

The good reverend might have expected Jackson to welcome the news. But Jackson instead paced the ground in pained uncertainty. "Such a degree of public confidence and respect as puts it in one's power to serve his country should be accepted and prized," he conceded, "but, apart from that, promotion among men is only a temptation and a trouble. Had this communication not come *as an order*, I should instantly have declined it, and continued in command of my brave old brigade."[17]

Among his fellow generals, some thought it best that he decline. Beyond question he had shown his mettle as a brigade commander, but would he do as well in a larger role? Said one high-ranking skeptic, "I fear the government is exchanging our best brigade commander for a second or third class major general."[18]

General Johnston was reluctant to part with Jackson and perturbed that neither the president nor Secretary Benjamin had consulted him on the move. So he stalled, ignoring an October 28 War Department order directing the immediate reassignment of Jackson. Appeals for Jackson's service rang loudly from the Shenandoah Valley. "From the latest intelligence from that country I am inclined to think that it may be expedient to send Major General Jackson to his district," Johnston conceded halfheartedly to Samuel Cooper, adjutant general of the army. "It is reported that the enemy intend to repair the Baltimore and Ohio Railroad and put it in operation. It is of great importance to us to prevent it. For this I will send General Jackson to his district whenever there is a prospect of having such a force as will enable him to render service."[19]

November 4 brought a third set of orders for Jackson's reassignment. With or without troops, Jackson must go. In a letter to Anna that morning, he tried to put the best face on matters. "I am assigned to the command of the military district of the Northern frontier, between the Blue Ridge and the Allegheny Mountains, and I hope to have my little dove with me this winter. How do you like the program?" he asked playfully. "I trust I may be able to send for you after I get settled. I don't expect much sleep tonight, as my desire is to travel all night, if necessary, for the purpose of reaching Winchester before day tomorrow. My trust is in God for the defense of that country. I shall have great labor to perform, but, through the blessing of our ever-kind Heavenly Father, I trust that He will enable me to accomplish it."[20]

One painful task remained to Jackson before leaving. He must bid farewell to his old brigade. The regimental colonels came to his tent first to say good-bye. A deputation of regimental and company line officers filed through a little before noon. He cordially shook the hand of each. The last to enter the tent was Lt. Henry Kyd Douglas, a brash young Virginian with a high opinion of himself and an even higher opinion of his commander and the brigade he was leaving. Everyone wished him well, ventured Douglas, but the men of the Stonewall Brigade hoped he would not forget them. Jackson's lips tightened and his eyes brightened. "I am much obliged to you, Mr. Douglas, for what you say of the soldiers; and I believe it. I want to take the brigade with me, but cannot. I shall never forget them. In battle I shall always want them. I will not be satisfied until I get them. Good-bye."

An hour later, on his favorite mount, "Little Sorrel," Jackson rode out with his staff to the parade field, where the brigade stood at close column of regiments under a cold, slate-gray sky. Removing his hat, he offered his men thanks for their sacrifices and a "heartfelt goodbye." Then, rising in the stirrups and raising his arms, he exclaimed in his sharp, high-pitched western Virginia drawl: "In the Army of the Shenandoah you were the *First* Brigade; in the Army of the Potomac you were the *First* Brigade; in the Second Corps of the army you were the *First* Brigade; you are the *First* Brigade in the affections of your general; and I hope by your future deeds and bearing that you will be handed down to posterity as the First Brigade in this, our second War of Independence. May God Bless you! Farewell!"[21]

CHAPTER 2

DAUGHTER OF THE STARS

Governor Alexander Spotswood of colonial Virginia had been a man of action. A highly educated, gallant soldier imbued with the best of the liberal and progressive ideas of his day, Spotswood strove to further the interests both of his royal master and of the colony he governed. Those interests demanded room to grow, and on August 1, 1716, the restless governor set out from Williamsburg with fifty horsemen—gentry, servants, and rangers—to penetrate the terra incognita beyond the "high mountains," as the mystic Blue Ridge Mountains then were called. Hostile Indians dogged the footsteps of the party almost from the moment they left the tidewater. Thirty-six days and half a dozen skirmishes later, Spotswood and his party reached the brow of a winding, eleven-mile long pass though the mountains (known later as "Swift Run Gap"). Before them spread a vista of unrivaled magnificence. Rolling westward for twelve miles before bumping up against the blue background of a low, fifty-mile long ridge (Massanutten Mountain), and running to their right and left as far as the eye could reach, were vast prairies of bluegrass and clover. Silvery streams of serpentine coils laced the landscape, their banks fringed with forests of oak, cedar, locust, black walnut, and huge yellow pine. Here and there were cleared tracts, where the Native Americans—Susquehanough, Senedo, and Tuscarora mostly—grew tobacco, corn, and other vegetables. Game of every sort abounded. A wide Indian trail ran in almost a straight line the length of the valley, and numerous lesser paths crisscrossed the land. Beyond Massanutten, far on the horizon, was the hazy outline of the Allegheny Mountains.[1]

To the intoxicating effect of the scenery, the governor added a toast to the health of the king and another to the health of the royal family, then led the way down the slopes between the crouching hills. Pushing across the valley floor, through waving grass taller than the horses, Spotswood's party made camp beside a wide and lovely river that the governor named "Euphrates." (Spotswood's cognomen was quickly lost to history, and the Native American word, which came out "Shenandoah," or "The Daughter of the Stars," affixed itself both to the river and the valley.)

On the far side of the river, Spotswood buried a bottle with a paper claiming the land for His Majesty King George I. His party feasted on wild deer and turkey, and on the cucumbers, currants, and grapes that grew along the river. "We had a good dinner," recorded a member of the expedition, "and after it we got the men together and loaded all the arms; and we drank the King's health in champagne, and fired a volley; and the princess in burgundy, and fired a volley; and the rest of the royal family in claret, and fired a volley. We drank to the governor's health, and fired another volley."[2]

As they made their way back over the Blue Ridge, Spotswood and his well-lubricated explorers little could have imagined that a decade would pass before white men would return to settle the Shenandoah Valley, or that those who did so would not be fellow Englishmen of colonial Virginia, but rather German farmers from along the Susquehanna River in Pennsylvania. Crossing the Potomac River near what was one day to be Harpers Ferry, the first of these settlers founded in 1727 a village ten miles west of the junction of the Potomac and Shenandoah that they named "New Mecklenburg," later changed to "Shepherdstown." When it became clear that few Virginians cared to emigrate west of the Blue Ridge, the colonial government sent agents into Pennsylvania and Maryland to encourage further settlement from the north. The response was robust. Cheap land and a chance to practice their faiths unfettered drew German Lutherans, Mennonites, Dunkers, Scotch-Irish Presbyterians, and Welsh and English Quakers in large numbers. The Germans congregated in the northern half of the Shenandoah Valley, the Scots and Irish in the southern half. Relatively few blacks found there way to the Valley, either as freedmen or slaves. The Germans, as a rule, opposed slavery, as did the Quakers and Mennonites. What slaves existed there generally were the property of the English or Scotch-Irish. Because most settlers lived on small farms and did their own work, black house servants well outnumbered field hands, at least in the Lower Valley.

Early settlement benefited from the friendly disposition of the Native Americans of the Valley. The Quakers and Mennonites treated them fairly and paid them for the land they settled, but the tide of white migration eventually compelled the Valley tribes to cross the Alleghenies and join their kinsmen in the Ohio Valley. There, in the mid-1750s, they came under the influence of the French and with them returned to make war all along the border.[3]

Isolated farms fell prey to marauding Indians, but the conflict brought a tenuous prosperity to towns like Winchester, which became a staging area for British military expeditions into the interior. George Washington was a frequent visitor, first as a surveyor and later as an officer in the provisional army. His martial duties did not blind him to the great commercial potential of the Valley, which he judged "equal to the promised land for fertility, far superior to it for beauty, and inhabited by an infinitely superior people—choice but not chosen."

The French and Indian Wars ended in 1763. Men of the Shenandoah Valley served in the colonial army during the American Revolution, but the war left the region otherwise untouched. The Valley prospered, and by 1850 the economy, institutions, and physical improvements that were to see it through the Civil War years were firmly in place.[4]

WHAT, PRECISELY, CONSTITUTES the Shenandoah Valley? It is defined as the area drained by the Shenandoah River and its effluents, extending southwest from the Potomac River at Shepherdstown and Harpers Ferry for 140 miles. The first ranges of the Allegheny Mountains bound the Valley on the northwest. These came to be known respectively, from east to southwest, as the Little North, Shenandoah, and Bull Pasture Mountains. The Blue Ridge Mountains define the northeastern and eastern limits of the Valley. The average width of the Shenandoah Valley is twenty-five miles.

The northward flow of the Shenandoah River gave rise to terms of reference peculiar to the Valley. To travel north is to go "down" the Valley; to journey south is to go "up." Similarly, the northern portion of the region was known as the Lower Valley; the southern stretches, the Upper Valley.

The Shenandoah Valley comprised nine counties. The northernmost, Berkeley and Jefferson, became the eastern panhandle of West Virginia. Continuing southward were Frederick, Clarke, Shenandoah, Page, Rockingham, and Augusta counties. The southern boundary of Augusta County was considered the southwestern limit of the Valley.

Three streams heading in Augusta County—the South River, Middle River, and North River—unite at Port Republic in Rockingham County to become

The North Fork of the Shenandoah River and Massanutten Mountain, looking east from the vicinity of Strasburg. (John W. Wayland, *Art Folio of the Shenandoah Valley*, Staunton, Va., 1924)

the main divide, or South Fork, of the Shenandoah River. Continuing its northeasterly flow, the South Fork near Front Royal joins the North Fork, which has its head in the mountainous reaches of northwestern Rockingham County. Beginning gently, the North Fork from Edinburg to Strasburg follows a tortuous, winding course of seven huge horseshoe bends and a seemingly endless number of smaller turns. Of the many lesser watercourses in the Valley, that most worthy of the term "river" is Opequon Creek, which rises southwest of Winchester and flows first to the east and then to the northeast, entering the Potomac northeast of Martinsburg, Virginia.

Rising abruptly to a height of 2,900 feet from the Valley floor between the North and South forks of the Shenandoah, near Harrisonburg, and falling off just as sharply between Strasburg and Front Royal, is the spectacular Massanutten Mountain. At the time of the Civil War there was only one gap in the mountain capable of bearing traffic—a depression in the prevailing range six hundred feet above the Valley floor between New Market and Luray called "New Market Gap." The land east of Massanutten Mountain became known as "Page," or "Luray," Valley. Northeast of New Market Gap the Massanutten range splits into two parallel ridges. The western ridge was named "Tree Top Mountain," and the eastern ridge retained the name "Massanutten." Between these ridges runs Passage Creek, its isolated banks the antebellum home to a few dozen intrepid farmers and mill owners.

There are five natural gaps, or passes, through the Alleghenies. The old

Northwestern Turnpike was built through the gap northwest of Winchester. Cedar Creek descends from the second gap, which lies west of Strasburg. The North Fork of the Shenandoah River enters the Valley through Brock's Gap. West of Staunton stands Jennings's Gap and Buffalo Gap.

Passes through the Blue Ridge are more numerous, if less profound, than those through the Alleghenies. The most prominent of the Blue Ridge passes are Snicker's Gap, opposite Winchester; Ashby's Gap, seven miles southwest of Snicker's Gap; Manassas Gap, east of Front Royal; Chester Gap, southeast of the town; Thornton's Gap, east of Luray; Swift Run Gap, opposite Conrad's Store; and Brown's Gap, above Port Republic. Whereas the main passes through the Alleghenies are "water gaps" that drop to the Valley floor, those through the Blue Ridge are simple depressions, or "wind gaps," varying in elevation from six hundred to one thousand feet above the Valley floor.[5]

THE ANTEBELLUM SHENANDOAH Valley was a farm economy. In the counties of Warren, Frederick, and Shenandoah alone, the 1850 census recorded 2,006 farms, on which resided 36,350 people, or about eighteen persons per farm. Few Valley farms had more than one or two slaves or hired hands; children, grandchildren, maiden aunts, bachelor uncles, and other extended family members comprised the bulk of the farmer's circle. Wheat was the principal cash crop. In 1850 Warren, Frederick, and Shenandoah county farms yielded 652,732 bushels; ten years later, improved fertilizers brought the annual total to 751,761 bushels. In 1860 the Shenandoah Valley accounted for 18.6 percent of the wheat grown in Virginia.

Corn was the second crop of the Valley. At least 80 percent was consumed on the farm, mainly as animal feed. Distillers took most of the rest, as even "sober" farmers of the day drank a good deal. In 1860 the Valley accounted for 9.3 percent of the corn grown in Virginia.

Farmers generally gave the less fertile tracts of their land over to rye production, most of which went into whiskey. Although an incidental crop, in 1860 Valley rye production constituted 27 percent of the state total. Most farmers also raised potatoes, and many took an interest in fruit trees and grapevines. Orchards were small, and harvesting them was children's work.[6]

Livestock-raising complemented farming and was particularly important to the economy of the Upper Valley. In 1860 the Valley was home to 14 percent of the horses, 10 percent of the swine, 8 percent of the sheep, 11 percent of the beer cattle, and 9.5 percent of the milk cows in Virginia.

Not surprisingly, the farmers of the Shenandoah Valley enjoyed a standard of living considerably higher than that of most Virginians. Lower Valley farm-land was worth twice the state average per acre. In the decade before the Civil War, landowners saw the cash value of their farms climb by as much as a third. Nearly everyone in the Valley enjoyed a well-balanced diet. Valley farmers worked hard and ate heartily. Meat predominated; each adult consumed an annual average of 140 pounds of pork, 70 pounds of beef, 30 pounds of mutton and veal combined, and large quantities of chicken, duck, turkey, and geese. Breads and potatoes provided starch, and cabbage, beets, turnips, beans, carrots, celery, and asparagus rounded out a diet rich in vegetables.[7]

Demand for the agricultural products of the Valley came largely from the expanding markets of the Northeast, not the South. Getting products to ever distant customers required a reliable transportation network, and by the standards of the day, that available to Valley farmers was superior.

The South Fork of the Shenandoah River was an important artery for commerce from the Valley, and flatboats capable of carrying twelve tons in high water plied the river from Port Republic to Harpers Ferry in huge numbers. Unreliable water levels and the seventeen miles of horseshoe bends between Edinburg and Strasburg prevented navigation of the North Fork, but the Valley Turnpike, which ran generally parallel to the North Fork, more than compensated for the river's shortcomings.[8]

The Valley Pike, as the road was more commonly known, had been slow in coming. In 1817 the Virginia General Assembly issued a charter to construct a turnpike along the path of the old Indian road. The ruts of countless wagons had deepened and widened the native trail into what locals called the "Great Wagon road." Great in name only, the road was a trail of dust in dry weather and a long trough of mud in wet. Intersecting creeks and streams presented additional barriers to travel.

Apart from an occasional sprucing up of small stretches of the old wagon road, nothing came of the turnpike project until March 1834, when the state legislature chartered the Valley Pike Company, with authorized capital of $250,000, to build a thoroughfare from Harrisonburg to Winchester, a distance of sixty-eight miles. Valley residents subscribed to three-fifths of the stock, and the state board of public works financed the remainder. Three years later, the Harrisonburg and Staunton Turnpike Company was incorporated to extend the turnpike to Staunton. The two companies soon consolidated, and the entire ninety-three–mile road from Winchester to Staunton was placed under one management.

Minimum specifications for the turnpike were exacting. It was to be no less

The Valley Pike near Newton. (Author's Collection)

than twenty-two feet wide, eighteen feet of which were to be macadamized (a process of the day by which a layer of small broken stone was compacted on a convex, well-drained roadbed, using a bituminous binder for the mass). No grade was to exceed three degrees. Turnpike planners permitted deviations from the prescribed width as the road passed through towns, and at Woodstock it widened to seventy feet.

The turnpike companies also built bridges and culverts along the right-of-way. Good bridges already existed over Cedar Creek near Strasburg, Stony Creek at Edinburg, and Mill Creek at Mount Jackson, but Opequon Creek between Kernstown and Stephens City, Toms Brook, in the village of that name, and Narrow Passage Creek, midway between Woodstock and Edinburg, all were significant obstacles that had to be spanned.[9]

Yellow pines, which grew abundantly in the Valley until an insect plague in the last decade of the nineteenth century wiped them out, were used as timber. The bridges were covered with plank roofing and weatherboard sides and were strung on long wooden arches, made of timbers lapped, jointed, and bolted together—six or eight ply on longer expanses—and sunk into heavy abutments at either end of the bridge. Props placed at ten-foot intervals along each side and bolted to the arch gave the structures added strength.[10]

Work on the turnpike was completed in 1840 at a cost of $425,000. Fifteen tollgates—beginning with Hillman's Tollgate between Winchester and Kernstown—were built at five-mile intervals, and tolls of a penny a mile were collected from dawn to 10:00 P.M. daily to pay for pike maintenance. The

A typical covered bridge in the Shenandoah Valley. (John W. Wayland, *Art Folio of the Shenandoah Valley*, Staunton, Va., 1924)

tollgates were simple. Workers drove a forked post into the ground and bolted a pole to it. A wooden box filled with rocks weighted down one end, and the other end was tied to a hasp across the road, allowing the gatekeeper to raise and lower it easily. Gatekeepers earned ten dollars a month and lived rent-free in a house near their tollgate.[11]

Long rows of locust trees and fences of uncut stone removed from cleared farmland bordered long stretches of the Valley Pike; such fences also marked the boundaries of early Valley farms. When the stone ran out, farmers laid out split-rail fences in the oldtime "snake and rider" pattern. The stone fences were remarkably straight; the split-rail variety tended to zigzag across the land.

The Valley Pike was a remarkable achievement. "There was not a mud hole in it," marveled a Virginia volunteer in late 1861. A New England soldier conceded: "These pikes are superior as roadways to anything we have through the outlying country in the North, being graded macadamized roads from twenty-five to forty-feet broad, hardened with broken limestone, which crushes under the weight of wheels and cements." Nonetheless, the going could be hard. "This surface after a rain is almost as smooth, clean, and solid as a slate, and when dry a thin white coating, perhaps a quarter of an inch deep, makes dust under the constant grind of the wheels, which rises in clouds when disturbed by travelers and settles upon their clothing, making all look like millers. It grinds away shoes rapidly when a little wet, going through an army brogan in three days' marching." And the lack of mud holes came at a price, as the road was so hard it raised blisters on feet otherwise hardened to long marches.[12]

There were two other macadamized roads of note in the Valley: the Northwest Turnpike, which entered the Allegheny Mountains northwest of Winchester, and the Rockingham Turnpike, which ran from Harrisonburg to Richmond by way of Swift Run Gap.

Three railroads served the antebellum Valley. The most important of these was the Baltimore and Ohio line, which crossed the Lower Valley near the Potomac River and passed through Martinsburg and Harpers Ferry. Flatboats from the South Fork of the Shenandoah unloaded produce at Harpers Ferry for transfer to railcars. In 1836 the Baltimore and Ohio ran a branch (known as the Winchester and Potomac Railroad) from Harpers Ferry to Winchester, and the latter town became the northern terminus of much of the wagon traffic from the Upper Valley.

The Manassas Gap Railroad entered the Valley a mile north of Front Royal. Work on the road had been halting. Track was laid to Strasburg in October 1854; to Woodstock two years later; and to Mount Jackson in March 1859, which at last gave farmers of the Middle Valley ready access to markets along the Southern seaboard. The Virginia Central Railroad, which passed through Staunton on its eastward course to Richmond, offered farmers of the Upper Valley a similar outlet for products not shipped north.[13]

Although known principally for its agricultural wealth, the Shenandoah Valley by 1860 also was home to more than a dozen flourishing market towns and small cities, in which nearly a quarter of the Valley's population resided. The most prosperous antebellum town in the Upper Valley was Staunton. Situated in one of the richest agricultural regions of the state, at the junction of the Valley Pike and the Virginia Central Railroad, the town quickly developed into the leading transportation hub of the Upper Valley. Harrisonburg and Lexington also profited from ready access to the railroad, and Port Republic enjoyed a comfortable prosperity as the starting point for northbound river traffic. New Market and Mount Jackson west of Massanutten Mountain and Luray east of the range were the principal communities of the Central Valley. Among the main towns of the Lower Valley were Winchester, Front Royal, Strasburg, Woodstock, and Edinburg. Nearer the Potomac River, Martinsburg and Harpers Ferry had grown almost overnight into important railroad towns.

Winchester was the pride of the Lower Valley. In 1860 the town had a population of 4,403, of whom 3,040 were white, 655 black freedmen, and 708 slaves. Winchester stretched three miles south to north and two miles east to west at its widest point. As the hub of nine roads and the terminus of the spur line of the Baltimore and Ohio, Winchester commanded the commerce of the region, and the handsome, two-story brick Market House at the north end of town bustled with traffic. A brisk trade in cattle and flour existed between Winchester and Baltimore. Many of Winchester's leading citizens had family and business interests in the Maryland metropolis, and they regarded Baltimore—not Richmond—as their "city."

Residents of Winchester had much more than just a robust commerce to boast on. Gas lighting had been introduced in 1855, and by 1860 the streets of the town were paved and leveled. Scores of splendid brick homes, two large banks, the three-story Taylor Hotel, numerous fire houses, and at least fifty stores reflected the wealth of the community; a Masonic hall, lyceum, and several excellent private schools, among them the Valley Female College and the Winchester Medical College, attested to its cultural and civic refinement. The vigorous and varied religious life of the community found expression in twelve churches and a Quaker meeting house. Evangelical Presbyterianism was the dominant faith.[14]

Lesser communities developed niches of their own in the Valley economy. Newton boasted three dozen wagon-making shops. Middletown was noted for clock making and the manufacture of threshing machines. Columbia Furnace and nearby Liberty were home to ironworks. Pig iron from the twin furnaces was converted to steel at a forge near Union Forge Church and—when war came—sold to the Tredegar Iron Works in Richmond, a major arms manufacturer. Edinburg had two rifle factories, two gristmills, a sawmill, and a carding mill. Other important mills stood near Narrow Passage Creek and on Abram's (or Abraham's) Creek outside Winchester.[15]

Manufacturing establishments were small. For instance, in the Upper Valley county of Augusta the three most common enterprises were flour and meal mills, of which there were 62, employing only 89 hands, most of them slaves; sawed lumber mills, of which there were 22, with 48 employees; and distilleries, of which there were 18, with 37 employees. A total of 471 hands were employed in manufacturing in the county. Conditions were similar in the Lower Valley. In Frederick County, flour and meal mills were the most prevalent manufacturing concerns, with 37 mills employing 43 hands; 26 sawed lumber mills employed 29 people, and 9 leather shops, 29 hands. A total of 373 hands were employed in manufacturing in Frederick. Slave labor predominated in these enterprises.[16]

Not all the communities of the Shenandoah shared in the general affluence. As a New York lieutenant, otherwise enchanted with the beauty and richness of the Valley, observed early in the war:

> We cannot speak in terms of laudation respecting the villages, if they are worthy of the title. . . . Sometimes two or three houses, a tavern, and a tiny church constitute what is called a Southern village, and the buildings all have an air of antiquity, minus all associations of the beautiful and romantic. The chimneys, with few exceptions, are built outside of the houses, and the houses are mostly frame tenements that may have had a single coat of paint or whitewash, when first built, but age and weather have robbed them of everything of the ornamental, and they now look roughly beaten and worn out. One of the boys remarked, as he took a survey of these wooden tabernacles, that they had every appearance of being built when Adam was an infant.[17]

Slavery was incidental to the economy of the Lower Shenandoah Valley, but it grew in importance the deeper one journeyed up the Valley. Not only had the peculiar institution not taken deep root during the Lower Valley's first century, but also in the decade before the Civil War the number of slaves actually declined from 20 to 18 percent of the total Valley population.[18] Nearly every religious denomination in the Valley opposed slavery in principle, and the Mennonites prohibited their members from both holding slaves and hiring them without compensation.

In the Upper Valley, slaves worked principally in distilleries and mills. Mill owners owned an average of ten slaves, whom they spread out among several establishments. Because most slaves in the Lower Valley were house servants or worked side by side with their owners in the fields of small family farms, relations between master and slave tended to be closer there than elsewhere in the South, and the institution as a whole wore a softer aspect—or so the whites wished to believe.

The *Staunton Spectator* fed the prevailing white belief in the benevolence of slavery. The *Spectator* assured readers that "the intelligent, Christian slaveholder . . . is the best friend of the negro. He does not regard his bondsmen as mere chattel property, but as human beings to whom he owes duties."[19]

Slaves whose recollections endured painted a less rosy picture of their condition. Slave traders descended regularly on Upper Valley communities and broke up families. "Roty" Ruffin, an enslaved woman in Augusta County, credited her master for the fact that he "didn't buy nigger, didn't sell nigger."

But she recalled how another master in the county treated her aunt and uncle: "Whip 'em every morning before they eat mouthful." Notwithstanding such abuses, most Valley whites evinced a certain solicitude for at least the spiritual well-being of their slaves. Had it been otherwise, Stonewall Jackson would not have been able to conduct Bible classes for slaves in antebellum Lexington, openly and with the general approbation of his fellow Presbyterian parishioners. Neither would the white residents of Winchester have countenanced the sale in 1858 of the town's oldest house of worship—the Old Stone Presbyterian Church—to the Old School Baptists of Color. And certainly, had the yoke of bondage been as oppressive in the Shenandoah country as it was in the Deep South, there would have been unrest among Valley slaves in the wake of abolitionist John Brown's October 1859 raid on nearby Harpers Ferry, the news of which spread like wildfire among communities both black and white. But aside from "a few instances [of] a slight degree of insubordination," said a Valley resident, "the effect of the Brown Insurrection upon the Negroes of our community was but transient."

Although the excitement subsided quickly, John Brown's raid left a subcutaneous wound on the Valley psyche. "A feeling of distrust arose between master and slave," said young Tom Ashby, "weakening the warm attachment that had previously existed." When the master began to doubt the loyalty of his slave and the slave began to doubt the kindness and confidence of his master a mutual distrust began to express itself. That much of the North looked upon Brown not as a wild-eyed sociopath, but as a martyr sent by God to smite an evil institution, did not help matters. "In our community," remembered Ashby, "it was generally believed that the Brown insurrection was the beginning of more serious political complications—that secession and civil war would soon be the final solution of the conditions that confronted the slave-owning states."[20]

Perhaps, but commitment to the Union ran deep, and few in the Valley sought secession. Loyalty to Virginia rivaled that to the Union, but before John Brown's raid there was little evidence of Southern nationalism in the Valley. And that which found expression after 1859 was moderate. Union meetings during the summer and fall of 1860 drew thousands, who heard local leaders such as Congressman Alexander R. Boteler reject secession categorically. Throughout the turbulent presidential campaign, Valley newspapers appealed to their readers to remain loyal. They did, voting heavily for John Bell's Constitutional Union Party and its platform of mutual concession as the antidote to disunion sentiment. Although the election of Abraham Lincoln disheartened them, the people of the Valley entered what Henry Adams called "the Great Secession Winter of 1860" still committed to the Union.

Mass meetings tried to keep alive the spirit of compromise. On December 14 residents of Winchester gathered at the courthouse "to consult together and adopt such measures as, in their judgment, will best promote the peace of the country and maintain the rights of the South." They concluded that, while certain acts of the Federal government had been deplorable, "there is no cause at this time to justify the secession of any state from the Union." Three weeks later a group calling themselves "the bold yeomanry of our town and county" met at the courthouse and declared themselves unequivocally opposed to secession. Their brethren in Martinsburg, most of whom worked for the Harpers Ferry Federal arsenal or the Baltimore and Ohio Railroad, met the following day to condemn secession as "a usurpation of power unwarranted by the letter and spirit of the Constitution." Their paychecks determined their politics; in the event of a national breakup, whoever controlled the Baltimore and Ohio would command the allegiance of its employees.[21]

The press shared the public aversion to disunion, be it violent or peaceable. The *Lexington Gazette* editorialized: "If the election of one candidate over another is sufficient cause for dissolution of the Union, then its existence, with as good reason, might have been endangered at every election that has taken place." The *Staunton Spectator* told its readers that secession "remedies no wrongs, relieves no evils, redresses no grievances. . . . It has neither of the virtues, wisdom, bravery, nor patriotism, but is foolish, cowardly, and treasonable." The *Staunton Republican Vindicator* was more circumspect: "We are for a continuation of the Federal Union, if the Northern people repudiate and abandon their unjust course, and afford us sufficient security that they mean to deal honestly with the South. We are for secession if this security is not given."[22]

As one state after another followed South Carolina out of the Union, sentiment in the Shenandoah Valley, as in the rest of Virginia, began to shift. In March, on the heels of Lincoln's inauguration, at least four Valley newspapers reversed their course and called for immediate disunion. But Valley politicians trod lightly. Congressman Boteler continued to work with House Republicans, and he introduced the resolution that created the ill-fated Committee of Thirty-three, whose task it was to reach a settlement agreeable to all parties. Boteler spoke optimistically in public; privately, however, he confessed his loss of hope in any adjustment of sectional difficulties such "as will be right for us to accept."

The nine counties of the Shenandoah Valley sent pro-Union delegates to a secession convention that the state legislature called to consider the issue. Winchester's Robert Y. Conrad, a leading Unionist, was elected chairman of the convention's committee on federal relations. From the opening gavel in February until the April 17 vote, which took Virginia out of the Union, Conrad held the Shenandoah bloc firm. The final vote of the convention was 88 to 55 in favor of secession; among the Valley delegation, the vote was 12 to 5 against secession.[23]

The votes of Conrad and his fellow Unionists not only were irrelevant, but they also ran counter to public opinion back home. Valley moderates interpreted President Lincoln's decision to resupply Fort Sumter and defend Federal property in the seceded states as a declaration of war against the seceded states. Newspapers that for months had editorialized against disunion now whipped up war sentiment. "Lincoln's peace policy has been a sham," said the *Staunton Republican Vindicator* on April 12. "We pray we may be mistaken, but we do not see a hope—a ray of light—a straw to grasp at—nothing but war will satisfy the intense hatred that is borne at the North to the institutions of the South. It is too late now to talk of compromise, conference, or commission. The golden hour, when all this train of horrors could have been avoided has been lost."[24]

War frenzy spiraled beyond control. Fort Sumter fell on April 14. The next day Governor John Letcher of Virginia received and rejected Washington's call for three regiments to put down the rebellion. "You have chosen to inaugurate Civil War," he told the secretary of war, "and having done so we will meet you in a spirit as determined as the Administration has exhibited toward the South." When the small Federal garrison at Harpers Ferry began setting fire to the U.S. arsenal on April 18, two companies of shabbily dressed and indifferently armed Virginia militiamen stormed the town, extinguished the flames, and drove the frightened Federals across the Potomac River. Calmness and moderation yielded to outrage and bloodlust. Everyone was "furiously indignant" at the "twin insults to Virginia," said Mrs. Cornelia P. McDonald, the wife of a Valley militia colonel. At Winchester, "every person I met was full of joy; those who a week ago were so violently opposed to secession had completely turned around, and were as ardent and exultant as anyone."[25]

On April 22 Governor Letcher called out the militia, not to fight for the Southern Confederacy, but rather to "repel invasion and protect the citizens of the state in the present emergency." The commonwealth came first, and it was "noble state pride and love of home," as one volunteer put it, that inspired Valley men to arms in April 1861.[26]

Volunteers descended on Harpers Ferry in disorganized droves. "I have never seen such an outpouring of popular feelings in behalf of the South. We are in the midst of a great revolution; our people are united as one man, and are determined to maintain their rights at every sacrifice," Capt. Absalom Koiner of the Augusta Rifles wrote home to Staunton.

Captain Koiner was guilty of hyperbole. Not everyone in the Valley capable of bearing arms answered the call. The Mennonites remained staunchly pro-Union. Nearly to a man they refused to enlist or to drill, their only contribution to the Confederate cause being the fines they paid in lieu of service. Valley Quakers also refused to bear arms for the Confederacy. The railroad workmen of Martinsburg made good their promise to follow the fortunes of the Baltimore and Ohio, and in company with hundreds of other Unionist refugees streamed across the Potomac River, where they joined Federal volunteer regiments forming in Maryland. Intimidation kept quiet the Unionists who remained at home. "The hotheads were in control," remembered a Valley Mennonite. "They were fired up awful and threatened that they would kill all Southern men who would vote for the Union."[27]

Enough Valley men came freely to Harpers Ferry to fill out forty-eight companies, which over the course of three months were organized into five regiments—the 2nd, 4th, 5th, 27th, and 33rd Virginia. In early July the five regiments—together with the Rockbridge Artillery, a battery from Lexington commanded initially by Episcopal rector William Nelson Pendleton—became the First Virginia Brigade. Confederate regulations prescribed a strength of 1,389 officers and men for a regiment, but none of the Valley commands—nor few other Southern regiments during the war—fielded a full complement. At its original muster the First Virginia Brigade numbered 2,611 officers and men, nearly all of whom had volunteered for twelve months' service.

They were a tight-knit group; kinship, heritage, and place bound them together. "I never saw so many persons I knew in my life," commented a new recruit; "every third person speaks to me." Another soldier dubbed the brigade a "cousinwealth." Regional affiliation was strong. The 2nd and 33rd Virginia contained companies drawn largely from the Lower Valley, with the towns of Harrisonburg, Winchester, and Charlestown most heavily represented in the ranks. The 4th regiment came from deep in the Upper Valley. The largest unit in the brigade, the 5th Virginia, drew six of its ten companies from Staunton and rural Augusta County; the smallest unit, the 27th Virginia, comprised companies from Lexington and the western reaches of the Upper Valley.

The soldiers of the First Brigade shared two other traits: they were young—three-fifths of the men were between eighteen and twenty-seven, with the most common age being nineteen—and they were unusually well educated. Students and alumni of the Virginia Military Institute (VMI), Washington College, and the University of Virginia were well represented in the officer corps and among the rank and file. One company, the Liberty Hall Volunteers, contained fifty-seven Washington College students, a quarter of whom were preparing for the ministry. There were twenty-eight college graduates, twenty-five theological students, and seven men with masters' degrees from the University of Virginia on the rolls of the Rockbridge Artillery. Among the occupations recruits gave at first muster, that of student figured third. Farmers and farm laborers were the most common callings, with scores of clerks, merchants, tanners, and shoemakers, and dozens of blacksmiths, masons, machinists, lawyers, and teachers rounding out the rosters.[28]

Officers and men were eager to prove themselves. "They are ready for a fight, and I believe are eager to show their courage in driving back any invading foe," boasted Capt. William S. H. Baylor of his Augusta County boys. "Great enthusiasm animates all, and should the vice-regent of the archfiend dare send his minions to Old Virginia, we will repel them, or leave the memory of brave men for our friends to revere."[29]

NOBLE INTENTIONS AND martial words do not an army make. Order and discipline are essential, and both were sorely lacking in the chaotic camps that sprang up in the hills around Harpers Ferry in the closing days of April 1861. To instill these soldierly qualities in the Virginia boys and to organize the town's defenses, Governor Letcher and the commander of Virginia state troops, Maj. Gen. Robert E. Lee, assigned Col. Thomas J. Jackson, recently of the VMI faculty, to command the post of Harpers Ferry.

Jackson stepped off the train at the Harpers Ferry depot on April 30 to no great fanfare. Few outside of Lexington and VMI knew him, and those who had been cadets under his tutelage had little complimentary to say of him. They had called him "Old Jack" and "Tom Fool." An uninspiring teacher and slow learner himself, he was blessed with a photographic memory of that which he did learn. Jackson recited from textbooks verbatim, marching his students down a single, rigid avenue of logic. If a cadet seemed slow to understand a lesson, Jackson's solution was to repeat it, word for word. "Teaching, in the modern sense of that term, was not Jackson's forte," remembered one who had sat through his lectures. "His silence was phenomenal, and sometimes portentous. He had no turn for explanation, no talent for putting things in various points of view, so as to adapt them to the various mental conditions of his pupils. During the war he was often and highly commended for keeping his plans to himself; but I doubt if he could have explained those plans if he had done his best." It helped little that Jackson delivered his material in a slow, high-pitched drawl that betrayed his mountain-country upbringing. Cutting letters home from cadets were common. "I find the studies this year a great deal more interesting than they have been heretofore, with the exception of one single one, which so counterbalances the rest as to throw all the good part into the shade," complained Cadet Charles M. Barton, a scion of Valley aristocrats. "The study I referred to just now was Optics, which from being so very difficult and taught by such a hell of a fool, whose name is Jackson, has suggested the following lines:

The VMI, Oh what a spot,
In winter cold, in summer hot.
Great Lord Almighty, what a wonder
Major Jackson, Hell and Thunder.[30]

Neither was Jackson's appearance particularly inspiring. At five foot eleven, he was tall for his day and because he carried himself ramrod straight, seemed even taller. Jackson's hair was brown and curled at the ends. His lips were compressed, his forehead high. " 'Old Jack was so plain in manner and attire, there was so little effort at show, his feet were so large and his arms and hands fastened to his body in such awkward shape, that the cadets didn't take much pride in him," recalled a student at nearby Washington College. Fellow instructors were equally unimpressed upon meeting him. Recalling his introduction to Jackson in 1851, future Confederate general Raleigh Colston wrote:

There was nothing striking about his exterior. His figure was large-boned, angular and even ungainly for his hands and especially his feet were very large. He had a heavy, ungraceful and lumbering walk, altogether different from the springy regular and soldier-like gait which is produced by early military training. He wore at the time the old style military side-whiskers, not lower than the corner of the mouth as prescribed by army regulations. This gave to his countenance a stiff and formal expression which his conversation by no means tended to remove, for he had but little to say.

But perceptive faculty members soon saw what boyish cadets missed. Continued Colston:

> It was not long before, through the appearance of coldness and reserve . . .
> which arose mainly from his own diffidence, we perceived in him the sterling qualities and the kindly disposition which marked his character. . . .
> There never occurred the least unpleasant word or feeling to mar the
> friendship that arose between us from the beginning of our acquaintance.
> Nor is it to be wondered at, for there was never a man with whom it was
> easier to keep on friendly terms than with him. He was not demonstrative,
> but was one of the most obliging of men, ever willing to do any favor that
> might be asked of him, without any regard to his personal convenience.[31]

Apart from a beard, little in Jackson's appearance, and nothing about his character, had changed in the decade since Colston penned that description. Jackson's former pupils had no trouble recognizing him; he arrived for war in the same dingy, ill-fitting blue uniform and blue forage cap in which he had strode clumsily about the grounds of VMI. But snobbish ex-cadets, green recruits, and easygoing militiamen and their pompous officers were in for a surprise. Jackson may have been an obliging man in pleasant society, but he was unyielding in an army camp. Governor Letcher had ordered that all militia officers above the rank of captain be decommissioned; Jackson made a clean sweep of it, dismissing not only the officers, but also their staffs. Everyone—be he volunteer or militiaman —was roused at 5:00 A.M. to begin a seventeen-hour day of drill, target practice, guard duty, and more drill. Capt. John D. Imboden of the Staunton Artillery, just returned from a brief trip to Richmond, was astounded at what greeted him. "What a revolution three or four days had wrought! I could scarcely realize the change. . . . The presence of a master mind was visible in the changed condition of the camp. Perfect order reigned everywhere. Instruction in all details of military duties occupied Jackson's whole time."[32]

Duty—and duty alone—to God and to his new country demanded no less. Jackson shared in none of the prevailing ardor. He deplored war. "If the general government should persist in the measures now threatened, there must be war," he told the Reverend William White in December 1860. "It is painful to discover with what unconcern they speak of war, and threaten it. They do not know its horrors. I have seen enough of it to make me look upon it as the sum of all evils. Should the step be taken which is now threatened, we shall have no other alternative; we must fight." But perhaps there was yet a chance to halt the march to war. "Do you not think that all the Christian people of the land could be induced to unite in a concert of prayer to avert so great an evil? It seems to me that if they would thus unite in prayer, war might be prevented and peace preserved." If prayer failed and the Union was dissolved, there would be no cause for grief. "Why should Christians be disturbed about the dissolution of the Union?" he asked a despondent White. "It can come only by God's permission, and will only be permitted if for His people's good."[33]

Jackson prayed, but the war came anyway. Providence had placed a malediction on the land that only bloodshed could wash away. Victory would come to the righteous. Convinced that God had ordained the Confederacy as the next step in the evolution of American Christianity, Jackson would do everything in his power to see that the Southern people—or at least the officers and men under his command—remained worthy of God's blessing. Jackson had embarked on a religious crusade from which there could be no turning back. He was a wall of stone long before victory at First Manassas accorded him the cognomen.[34]

CHAPTER 3

THEY AIN'T RIGGED OUT

LIKE UNCLE SAM'S MEN

War brought the Shenandoah Valley a strategic importance exceeding even its agricultural bounty. For the North, the Valley offered more problems than opportunities. Before it could take the war confidently to its opponent, the North had first to secure its own soil from outrage and its capital from insult. The Shenandoah Valley complicated both tasks. The national capital stood at the outer edge of the Federal domain, with only the Potomac River separating it from Virginia. The Shenandoah Valley offered Confederate armies a shielded avenue into the rear of Washington, D.C., and straight toward the fertile farmlands of Maryland and Pennsylvania; control of the Blue Ridge passes into the Valley would protect advancing Southern forces from interference. An invasion of the North, as improbable as that may have been at the time, brought with it the specter of European recognition of the Confederacy. At a minimum, possession of the Lower Valley would enable the Confederates to sever key Federal lines of communication and supply.

The Shenandoah Valley was no less crucial to Confederate defensive designs. With the Federals firmly in control west of the Alleghenies, by late autumn 1861 the Valley had become the strategic left flank of the defenses of Richmond. Even in a strategic defense, ownership of the region offered the South opportunities to assume the initiative. Confederate forces in the Valley might debouch through the passes over the Blue Ridge Mountains on the flank or rear of any Union army operating directly against Richmond. Any threatened push down the Valley to the Potomac undoubtedly would distract Federal authorities from their own offensive operations; the mere static presence of a Confederate command would oblige the Lincoln administration to detach at least matching forces to the Valley, thereby reducing the size of the army it could send against Richmond. And the Federals had nothing to gain by transferring their principal effort to the western side of the Blue Ridge, as the Shenandoah Valley offered only an indirect route to the Confederate capital.[1]

All of these considerations were apparent to Stonewall Jackson as he settled into cramped and noisy quarters in Winchester's Taylor Hotel, but they seem to have left others in the Confederate high command unmoved. Beyond a vague hope that Jackson might prevent the Federals from repairing the Baltimore and Ohio Railroad "whenever there is prospect of having such a force as will enable him to render service," General Johnston gave little thought to the Valley District. Jackson, on the other hand, was consumed both with the magnitude of the tasks before him and the paucity of resources with which to accomplish them. He was, in a word, a commander without a command. The only troops in the six thousand–square-mile district subject to his orders were three fragmentary brigades of state militia under brigadier generals J. H. Carson, G. S. Meem, and James Boggs—a total of 1,461 infantrymen and 225 cavalrymen, fewer than 500 of whom were concentrated at Winchester, the rest being scattered aimlessly throughout the Lower Valley. Col. Angus W. McDonald commanded 485 volunteer cavalrymen spread out along the Northwest Turnpike and near the railroad, but he reported directly to Richmond. By all accounts, the militia was worse than useless. Morale was low, as the better officers and men had quit the state service to join the Confederate army. Those who remained seemed more interested in bringing in the autumn harvest, protecting their families from marauding Yankees, or lounging about Winchester than in drill or combat. In their defense, the militiamen lacked the means of doing much more. Many were unarmed; many more had nothing better than antiquated flintlock muskets. Ammunition was scarce, and everything from haversacks to horses was in short supply. So dire were the needs of the militiamen, and so inclined were they to take matters into their own hands, that one Valley quartermaster urged his wife to send him a pistol—not to shoot Yankees, but to protect him from the militia.[2]

Jackson was quick to appraise Richmond of his needs. "Deeply impressed with the importance of not only holding Winchester, but also of repelling the invaders from this district before they shall secure a firm lodgment," Jackson—

on November 5, the day after assuming command—urged the War Depart-ment to order all troops remaining west of the Allegheny Mountains to Win-chester, as well as any other disciplined units of infantry, artillery, and cavalry that might be spared. Although he did not specify them, Jackson undoubtedly had the Stonewall Brigade in mind for duty in the Shenandoah Valley. He dispatched his close friend and former VMI colleague, Lt. Col. James T. L. Preston, to deliver his appeal and acquaint Richmond with "the defenseless condition of this place." Jackson made a similar entreaty to Governor Letcher through his friend and patron, Confederate congressman Alexander R. Bote-ler, the former Valley representative to the U.S. House of Representatives who had introduced the resolution calling for the ill-fated Committee of Thirty-three.[3]

Boteler was pleased to help. The war had made the thirty-seven-year-old Shepherdstown-area native a refugee, and he had spent much of the autumn shuttling between Richmond, Charlestown, and Winchester, urging the Davis administration to act. The Princeton-educated Boteler was charismatic and persistent, "the most accomplished gentleman I ever met," wrote a Virginia volunteer captain, and people listened to him. Not only were his entreaties instrumental to Jackson's appointment to the Valley command, but they also brought to the attention of the War Department the service of another eccen-tric but selfless Virginian, Turner Ashby.[4]

If ever there were an American knight-errant, it was Turner Ashby. Born in 1828 to John and Mary Ashby on a modest farm in Fauquier County named "Rose Bank," which barely qualified for the easily applied Southern cognomen of "estate," Ashby at age six lost even the semblance of genteel fortune when his father died and his mother squandered the meager family resources trying to keep up the pretensions of planter-class aristocracy to which the family's distinguished lineage entitled them. There was no money to send Turner to college, and in matters of the mind he fell considerably behind his peers. In 1853 Mary Ashby sold the farm and moved in with a married daughter. Turner's younger brother Richard bought a farm near his mother, but Turner lingered in the neighborhood of Rose Bank until he had money enough to buy an adjacent property. He called his new home "Wolf's Craig" and lived there as a bachelor until the war broke out, barely scraping by and finding himself periodically hauled into court to make good on his debts.

There was little prepossessing in Ashby's appearance. He was short and slight, somewhat sickly as a boy, and of a swarthy complexion, with dark-hazel eyes, jet-black hair, and a flowing black beard. "I thought he looked more like an Arab, or the common idea of one, than any man I ever saw," said a Confederate staff officer. Ashby swore little and drank less, and had a reserve about him that bordered on the effeminate. What separated him from other young men of the planter class was his excellence as a rider and his contempt for danger. In a region where the horse was practically an appendage, Ashby stood out, both for his passionate fondness for the animal and for his great skill in the tournaments and fox chases that were the staple of youthful entertainment. He also was a natural leader. When the Manassas Gap Railroad began to lay tracks across the Blue Ridge in 1855, Ashby organized a mounted company to keep ruffians among the road crews from molesting local citizens. The young men of the area found the work a pleasant diversion, and they kept up the company after the railroad was finished. With Ashby still in command, the company took part in the grand gathering of militia at Harpers Ferry during the trial and hanging of John Brown. When war came, Ashby and his men became part of the 7th Virginia Cavalry, under the command of the hopelessly superannuated Col. Angus McDonald.[5]

Born in Winchester before the turn of the century, the West Point–educated McDonald was a good and well-meaning man who had once been a fine soldier. But his day had passed, and no one knew it better than McDonald himself. From the start he leaned heavily on Ashby, who rose quickly to the rank of lieutenant colonel. Ashby conducted what little drilling there was, but he made small effort to instill discipline, preferring to lead his free-spirited young horseman by example—a wise choice, thought Col. Thomas T. Munford of the 2nd Virginia Cavalry, as "the want of thorough discipline was caused by the fact that you could not exact of men rigid compliance with orders when they were rarely supplied with what they were entitled to receive."

Ashby's troopers were armed largely with what they brought from home or could scrounge, and they were poorly uniformed, even by Southern standards. Said a Union prisoner of Ashby's cavalry, on studying his captors: "They ain't rigged out like Uncle Sam's men. I can assure you that they are clothed in all sorts, gray homespun overcoats, pants of all colors and grades; some have straw hats and caps, and a great many are in citizens' clothes; in fact, they look pretty shabby."

Not only did they supply their own arms and clothes, but Ashby's men also had to furnish their own mounts. "A dead horse cannot be replaced without money, which the man could not procure and the government failed to supply," noted Colonel Munford. "The man felt at any moment he was liable to lose his horse. Not the government's horse, which would be replaced, but his own horse, when he had no chance of getting another and no hope of being remunerated for his loss." (Ashby himself brought to war a powerful black stallion and a handsome milk-white mare, both of which elicited the admiration of friend and foe.)

Munford and Ashby understood what Stonewall Jackson, with his uncompromising standards of discipline, never could comprehend. "You order a cavalryman to be drilled: his horse is not fit for duty, he cannot do it. He appears to be skulking. You order him to go into battle: his regiment is ordered off at a trot, a gallop; it is impossible for him to go," observed Munford. "The more gallant he is, the worse he naturally feels. His comrades know his worth and deplore his lot—they know they may be at any moment in the same condition. The man cannot and the other men will not perform their duty under such circumstances—and for reasons like these, a whole arm of the service is weakened and demoralized, and the handful who could keep mounted had to do all the duty. Ashby labored under all of these disadvantages in every company in his command, every day he had to move."[6]

When Jackson saw him in mid-November 1861, Ashby was a bitter man, half-crazed with grief and possessed of an insatiable lust for Yankee blood. Five months earlier, while covering the retreat of a patrol sent to interrogate a Union sympathizer, his brother Richard had taken a saber blow that cleaved off part of his skull. As Richard lay writhing on the ground, a Yankee horseman ran his sword into his belly, then stole his horse and spurs. The rattle of gunfire reached Turner Ashby's headquarters, and Turner rode quickly to the scene of the fight. He found Richard near death, bubbling blood as he pleaded with Turner for water. Richard died a week later. Turner was devastated. To his sister and mother he vowed to give himself over completely to the Confederate cause, regardless of personal risk—in other words, to kill Yankees at every opportunity. When one of his men was wounded in a skirmish in September, Ashby boasted to his sister that he had "good [cause] to believe that I have killed twenty or thirty of them in return." Ashby's troopers were pleased to oblige his rage. After a skirmish near Harpers Ferry on October 16, 1861, the Virginians stripped four dead Yankees naked, one of whom, said Union brigadier general John W. Geary, "was laid in the form of a crucifixion, with his hands spread out, and cut through the palms with a dull knife."

Civilians also felt Ashby's wrath. When he learned that Lower Valley resident John H. Boltz was a tax collector for the pro-Union rump government in western Virginia, Ashby yanked him from his bed and told his men to "shoot the infernal scoundrel or hang him to the first limb you come to and don't fetch him here." Fortunately for Boltz, Ashby calmed down before the order was carried out. For the remainder of his short life, Ashby would wage an inner struggle between his essential good nature and his almost maniacal desire for revenge.[7]

Ashby was balanced enough to earn the admiration of the gentlemanly Boteler, and the Confederate congressman took with him to Richmond both Jackson's appeal for men and arms and his own request that Governor Letcher promote Ashby to a full colonelcy and give him blanket authority to impose martial law on the "traitor-infested" river counties of the Lower Valley.

Letcher deferred action on Ashby's promotion, but he needed no prodding from Boteler to help Jackson. Well aware of the general's predicament, Letcher immediately called up the remaining militiamen of Boggs's, Carson's, and Meem's brigades and directed that 1,550 percussion muskets be sent to Winchester from the state armory. He also scraped together four pieces of artillery for Jackson—small six-pounder, "smooth-bore iron things, alleged cannon," quipped one Rebel. Jackson created a battery around them under the command of Capt. Joseph Carpenter of Company A, 27th Virginia Infantry, who had been a promising gunnery student in the vmi Class of 1858. The men of Carpenter's company went with him, and they quickly became adept gunners.[8]

Turner Ashby also recognized the need for cannons. Exercising the direct line he and Colonel McDonald had with the War Department, Ashby received permission to organize a battery of horse artillery. Another of Professor Jackson's former artillery students, eighteen-year-old Robert Preston Chew, commanded the battery, which consisted of three guns—a long-range Blakeley gun, a medium-range, three-inch rifled piece cast at Richmond's Tredegar Ironworks, and a stubby, short-range, twelve-pounder howitzer—and thirty-three volunteers, all of them good men. They had to be. Unlike regular cannoneers, who followed their gun limbers on foot, Chew's artillerymen would ride their own mounts, going everywhere the cavalry went. The young Chew proved just the man to command them. "I look upon Chew as the greatest artillerist of the war," recalled a battery member years afterward, "using as a basis of comparison his coolness under fire (for he was the only man I saw who could control his nerves and show no signs of danger). He made his gunners fire slowly and be careful to hit their mark. He could do more execution with fewer men and bring more out unharmed than any man in the service."[9]

Unquestionably the most welcome addition to Jackson's ranks was the Stonewall Brigade, which arrived in Winchester on the morning of November

11. The Virginians had had a rollicking good time getting there—too good a time for Jackson's liking. A number of "unmanageable Irishmen" from the 33rd Virginia fortified themselves with whiskey for the cold and bumpy railroad ride from Manassas to the Valley, raising hell along the way. When assigned a campsite beside a distillery, even the well-bred young men of the Rockbridge Artillery yielded to temptation. At roll call the next morning, remembered artilleryman Clement D. Fishburne, "it was hard to get enough sober men to harness and drive the horses. Some of the boys were put to driving that day who knew no more about it than they knew about steering a balloon. The situation was disgusting; so much so that it grew to be ludicrous." Capt. William McLaughlin and his lieutenants confiscated all the liquor they could find, but the men hid enough on their persons to stay drunk all day. That evening, continued Fishburne, "while we were delayed in crossing the Shenandoah at the ferry, the belligerent stage of drunkenness was reached, and there was a free fight in which one good soldier had his leg broken, and had to be left there till he recovered."[10]

The Stonewall Brigade was delighted to be back in the Valley; thoughts of home and the welfare of family had never been far from the men. Jackson had designated the fields and forests around Kernstown as their campsites, but neither the cold, drenching rain that greeted them nor memories of "Old Jack's" stern discipline could dissuade the men from striking out for Winchester to visit family and friends. Anticipating their antics, Jackson had circled the town with pickets, who had orders to let no one pass. The trouble was they were militiamen, for whom the Stonewall Brigade "regulars" had only contempt. "But, preferring peace to war with them, [we] devised ways and means to evade and avoid them," recalled Pvt. George C. Baylor of the 2nd Virginia. "Some flanked the posts, some deceived them with forged passes from General Jackson; but it was left to the ingenuity of our comrade Kim Frazier to obtain for us a wholesale entrance." Electing himself captain of a flanking party, Frazier ordered his men into line, marched them up to a militia post, and told the officer of the guard that he had orders from General Jackson to move his "company" to Winchester and arrest all Stonewall Brigade soldiers there without proper leave. The ruse worked. Once out of sight of the post, said Baylor, "we broke ranks, and each found friends and a comfortable resting place in hospitable old Winchester. I think it safe to say that fully half of the brigade visited Winchester that night."[11]

Jackson was furious. He issued new orders prohibiting even high-ranking officers of the Stonewall Brigade from entering Winchester without a pass from district headquarters, which must specify whether the officer's business was personal or official. Regimental commanders bristled. "That is an unwarranted assumption of authority and involves an improper inquiry into their private matters, of which, according to official usage and courtesy of the army the major general commanding has no right to require information." Quoting regulations to Jackson was a poor tactic. "The within-combined protest is in violation of the army regulations and subversive of military discipline," responded Jackson, who went on to give his colonels a well-merited lecture on discipline. They "either from incompetency [sic] to control their commands or from neglect of duty, so permitted their commands to become disorganized and their officers and men to enter Winchester without permission as to render several arrests of officers necessary." If the colonels expected to control their regiments, they had best stay with them and not wander off to Winchester themselves.[12]

Once again, hypocrisy crept into Jackson's comportment. His colonels must remain in their muddy camps, but that was no reason why Jackson himself should be miserable. After a few days in the crowded and noisy Taylor Hotel, Jackson accepted the offer of Lt. Col. Lewis T. Moore of the 4th Virginia that he move into Moore's unoccupied home at the northern end of Braddock Street. The elegant, two-story cottage made for an ideal headquarters and home. Jackson set up his office on the first floor and occupied a bedroom on the second. His staff slept across the hall. "Through the blessings of an everkind Heavenly Father, I am quite comfortable," Jackson wrote his wife in midNovember. Perhaps she might come stay with him. "The Rev. Mr. [James R.] Graham, our Presbyterian minister, lives in the second house from [here], his door being only about thirty yards from our gate. I have much work to perform and wouldn't have much time to talk to my darling except at night; but then there is so much pleasant society among the ladies here that you could pass your time very agreeably. I hope to send for you just as soon as I can do so." Anna needed no further encouragement. She set out for Winchester at once.[13]

The principal culprit for the poor behavior of the Stonewall Brigade when it arrived at Winchester had been the acting commander, Lt. Col. James Preston of the 4th Virginia. Though well-meaning, Preston was too old and too bothered by rheumatism to exercise command effectively. Col. James Allen of the 2nd Virginia, who replaced him as acting brigade commander in mid-November, fared little better. Even his own regiment was a hopeless case. "Its discipline is not such as its commander would wish it to be," confessed a company commander at the end of November, "particularly in the matter of absence without leave, which he [Allen] has labored hard to arrest, but which cannot be stopped without the most rigorous measures."[14]

Jackson appealed to Richmond for a competent brigadier general to lead the brigade, which further alienated the regimental commanders, who somehow felt that one of their number deserved the job. Jackson did not specify whom he wanted or what qualifications he sought for the post. Free to assign whom it pleased, the War Department sent him Richard B. Garnett, a proud but kindly scion of Tidewater aristocracy. Garnett was a West Point graduate who had done creditable service in the Seminole War and on the frontier, but somehow Jackson got it into his mind that Garnett's appointment had been base solely on political considerations.

Garnett may or may not have been the best man available to lead the Stonewall Brigade. But had Jackson known of the contretemps his original request for reinforcements had occasioned among the high command, he might have shown more gratitude at having his old brigade back, regardless of who led it. Acting Secretary of War Benjamin had concluded early on that Jackson needed help. He had decided to send the Stonewall Brigade to Winchester even before Colonel Preston called on him, and had issued the necessary orders on November 5. The trouble was, he had neglected to inform either the adjutant general, Samuel Cooper, or the losing commander, General Johnston, of his decision. Not surprisingly, Johnston protested the transfer, first to Benjamin and then, when that failed, directly to President Davis. But Davis declined to intervene. Rumors had reached Richmond that the enemy was planning to move against Winchester. Jackson needed troops, and the Stonewall Brigade, being composed of Valley men, was the logical unit to send.

In the same order that transferred the Stonewall Brigade to the Valley, Benjamin directed that six thousand men be detached from Brig. Gen. William W. Loring's small Army of the Northwest, then operating in the Allegheny country, to join Jackson's command by way of Staunton. Again, Benjamin neglected the chain of command. General Cooper assumed that Benjamin intended the troops for the army at Manassas and so informed General Johnston.[15]

So men were on the way—enough to bring Jackson's command to ten or eleven thousand when they arrived. That would still be far less than the forty thousand Federals that Jackson believed were threatening him from the north and west. What could Jackson do with his puny force in the face of such odds? He could attack.

CHAPTER 4

THE DAM[N] TRIP

Maj. Gen. Nathaniel Prentice Banks understood what the war was about. When he quit private life in April 1861 to accept the commission as major general of volunteers that made him the fourth ranking general in the Union army—standing behind only Winfield Scott, George B. McClellan, and John C. Frémont—it was with a clear sense of purpose. "Public affairs are in a desperate condition. Our government has lacked courage; first, to look its friends in the face and speak the truth; second, to look the rebels and quasi rebels in the face and speak the truth to them," he bluntly wrote his former employer, the president of the Illinois Central Railroad:

> Our people have been at fault in discrediting overmuch the condition and purposes of the Southern people. There are no fools in this world, according to my observation, to compare with those who cheat themselves, but it is all over now—and we are in for the war—a bloody and exterminating war. It might easily have been avoided without the slightest dishonor to the North, but now the North is *one* man, the South is another, and the fight is between them. In such position Shakespeare is a good counselor: "Beware of entrance to a quarrel, but being *in*, bear thyself that thy opposer may beware of thee."[1]

Whether Stonewall Jackson or anyone else would beware of Banks was an open question in the autumn of 1861. The forty-one-year-old Banks enjoyed great fame as a political moderate who had risen from the squalor and drudgery of a Massachusetts cotton mill to become speaker of the U.S. House of

Representatives and governor of Massachusetts, but he was a two-star military neophyte. That he had personal courage, strength of purpose, a keen intellect, and considerable personal charm, few doubted. Without these traits, this indifferently educated son of a cotton mill foreman never could have accomplished his miraculous public rise in Massachusetts. So novel was his background in the then largely agrarian United States that novelist William Makepeace Thayer, a famous creator of antebellum rags-to-riches legends, chose Banks's career as the subject of a novel, *The Bobbin Boy; or, How Nat Got His Learning.* Banks had gone to work at the age of eleven beside his father in the Waltham cotton mill of the Boston Manufacturing Company. His job had been to remove full bobbins from the spring frames and replace them with empty cylinders; hence the moniker, which followed him throughout his life.[2]

Banks worked in the factory until he was seventeen, leaving it to try his hand as an artisan in company machine shops. He also became a regular patron of the company library and organized a drama society among Waltham workers. An interest in temperance led him into politics in the 1830s, and his melodic voice and captivating appearance—he had what one contemporary called "a genius for being looked at"—led the Democrats to select him as a stump speaker in the 1840 presidential election. For the next two decades, Banks would make politics his business and livelihood.

To compensate for his lack of schooling, Banks cultivated a patrician image. He had a fine natural appearance—an athletic build, flowing hair arranged with careful carelessness, and penetrating black eyes. He stood erect and moved gracefully, which made him appear taller than his five feet eight inches. Banks convincingly camouflaged his working-class background with a studied air of dignity and deliberation. Although he would temporize on some issues to keep office—after all, politics was his bread and butter—Banks was at heart a good man who endorsed universal suffrage, the shorter work-hour movement, and other progressive reforms. He married for love, not status, taking as his wife a Waltham factory girl, "dearest, sweetest, fairest" Mary Theodosia Palmer, with whom he enjoyed a long and happy union. A political moderate by nature, Banks rejected radical abolitionism as too incendiary for the nation's good; he also opposed the Kansas-Nebraska Act, which cost him the backing of the national Democratic Party. Although as speaker of the house he continued to seek compromise on sectional issues—Georgian Alexander H. Stephens thought him "the most impartial Speaker I ever saw"— in late 1855 Banks joined Frank P. Blair Sr. and Salmon P. Chase in organizing the Republican Party, an irrefutable commitment to the antislavery movement. The following summer he helped John C. Frémont obtain the party's presidential nomination. Frémont lost the 1856 election but was ever grateful to Banks, his "first and foremost friend," for the lift to political prominence.

Banks kept private his doubts about the policies of the Lincoln administration in the first months of the war, and he retained the high regard of both the president and of Secretary of State William H. Seward. Lincoln, in particular, appreciated his loyalty. Rather than use his high army rank as a springboard to higher political office for himself, Banks did all he could to strengthen the president's hand.[3]

On July 25, 1861, Banks assumed command of the Department of the Shenandoah with headquarters initially at Harpers Ferry. His department embraced the Maryland counties of Washington and Allegheny and the Shenandoah Valley. On August 17 the Department of the Shenandoah was folded into the Department of the Potomac, and Banks's forces became a division in McClellan's Army of the Potomac. Mindful of the tactical weakness of Harpers Ferry, Banks withdrew across the Potomac River later that month, eventually setting up headquarters at Frederick, Maryland.

Banks worked hard to improve his command, regularly importuning the War Department for the artillery, arms, and cavalry he felt he had been shortchanged because of the relative isolation of his division. He prohibited the plundering of civilian property on either side of the Potomac and drove off the prostitutes and whiskey peddlers who preyed on his camps, but otherwise was an indifferent disciplinarian. He also struck his senior brigade commander, Brig. Gen. Alpheus S. Williams, as somewhat hesitant and uncertain. "He is not very communicative, even to those near him in command, and although always pleasant and courteous, he cannot be said to be a companionable person," Williams told his daughter. "I think he is oppressed somewhat with a position novel and untried, and full of responsibilities of a character so different from those he has had heretofore that he feels ill at ease. He is an officer of excellent judgment and good sense, but not familiar with military routine or etiquette."

Officers and men for the most part liked Banks. "Our commander, General Banks, is no great soldier," Brig. Gen. John P. Hatch told his father the following spring, "but he is a very good man. I admire him very much." The Reverend Horace Winslow, chaplain of the 5th Connecticut, thought him a "fine-looking man and cordial." Lt. H. Melzer Dutton of the same regiment agreed: "General Banks is a very stylish man and a polished and refined gentleman. He makes a fine appearance on horseback as he rides along the lines." The troops also appreciated the informality with which he greeted them, while at work or in camp. Even the young secessionist Belle Boyd found him charming and "one of the most affable gentlemen I have ever met."[4]

Of course, Banks would need more than charm and affability to defeat Stonewall Jackson. At a minimum, solid information on enemy strength and dispositions was necessary. This Banks had, thanks to the presence on his staff of David Hunter Strother. Born in Martinsburg in 1818 of prominent parentage, Strother had studied art in Philadelphia and later in Rome under Samuel F. B. Morse. On his return to America he began writing for *Harper's Monthly Magazine* under the pseudonym "Porte Crayon." His travel essays on Virginia and the South, which he illustrated with his own drawings, won him a national reputation and a readership greater than that of Herman Melville or Nathaniel Hawthorne. In 1857 several of his essays and 138 of his drawings were gathered into a pseudonymous volume, *Virginia Illustrated*. Of Strother, a contemporaneous literary critic said: "He imbued the Shenandoah Valley with synthetic and oral legends; he transcribed the dialect and individual character of the Virginia Negro and mountaineer . . . he delineated the common man with understanding and warmth, and throughout his work, he defined the tradition of Virginia's past."

In late 1861 the common man of Virginia loathed Strother. An ardent Unionist like his father, Col. John Strother of War of 1812 fame, Strother had offered his services to the North. "Let him go down to infamy doubly damned!" cursed Rebel captain Sam Coyner, expressing the common sentiment of Jackson's army. Strother cordially returned the feeling. Secession had turned his love for "Old Virginia" to scorn. Conversing with his new commander after tea one afternoon, Strother was delighted to find that General Banks's views of both politics and Virginia mirrored his own. "Speaking of Virginia, he [Banks] characterized our late public men as a very inferior set, both in manners and intellect, whiskey-drinking being the common ground on which they all met," remembered Strother. "I have myself considered the Old Virginia people as a decadent race. They have certainly gone down in manners, morals, and mental capacity. There seems to be nothing left of their traditional greatness but a senseless pride and a certain mixture of dignity and suavity of manner, the intelligence of a once great and magnanimous people. It was high time that war had come to wipe out this effete race and give this splendid country to a more active and progressive generation."[5]

Strother's intimate knowledge of the Shenandoah Valley and skill with the pen gained him a place on Banks's staff as assistant topographical engineer. He also proved an excellent intelligence officer. In the first of many intelligence reports he would submit, Strother assured Banks on November 18 that "if a strong demonstration was made on Winchester Jackson would either retire or be taken, and the position remain in our hands without further dispute." His informants correctly estimated the Rebel force at about four thousand men, composed mostly of militia "thought to be utterly worthless except for show." Strother's father was confident that an advance of five thousand men from Harpers Ferry would suffice to sweep the Valley clean of Confederates. Banks agreed with the elder Strother, and he told McClellan: "Nothing would delight this division more than to make the expedition to Winchester which is suggested by him and which I believe to be entirely feasible."[6]

The commanding general thought otherwise. Not only would McClellan not authorize an advance on Winchester, but he also refused to take even the minimal steps needed to reopen the Baltimore and Ohio (B&O) Railroad, an objective he regarded as "desirable but not vital. I had often observed to the president and to members of the cabinet," he later explained, "that the reconstruction of the railway could not be undertaken until we were in a condition to fight a battle to secure it." Crediting absurd reports that Joe Johnston's feeble army had been reinforced with 75,000 fresh troops and was preparing to attack Washington, the overly cautious McClellan ordered Banks to go into winter quarters around Frederick. To ensure that Banks lacked the means to defy his orders, McClellan instructed him to transfer the brigade reserved for duty under the convalescent Frederick Lander to Benjamin Kelley at Romney.[7]

Banks sulked, and the press fumed. "The Mississippi River being closed, the produce of the entire West is driven from that channel to the Eastern railroads," said the *Cincinnati Gazette*. "In addition to this, the Baltimore and Ohio Railroad is closed, and the Pennsylvania Central is largely occupied with government business. Thus railroad facilities have been reduced very nearly one half, while business has largely increased." The result was a twofold increase in freight fares.

The press also stressed military reasons for reopening the canal. The *Baltimore Evening Patriot* observed that Confederate possession of the Baltimore and Ohio "cripples the arm of the general government, adding millions to its expenses in forwarding troops, provisions, etc., and causing ruinous delays in the concentration of its troops."

With two thousand freight cars and two hundred locomotives lying idle, the president of the B&O, John W. Garrett, offered to bear the expense of rebuilding the road if the military would only offer his workers protection.[8] Brig. Gen. William S. Rosecrans, in command west of the Alleghenies, shared Banks's desire to oblige Garrett and to take Winchester in the bargain. Like Banks, he believed the town could be captured handily, particularly in light of General Kelley's easy seizure of Romney.

Kelley had approached Romney on the morning of October 22 with three regiments of infantry and a light cavalry screen. Six companies of Col. Angus McDonald's Virginia cavalry, a battery of artillery, and a detachment of militia garrisoned the town. No sooner had the Federals come into view than the militiamen broke and ran from their entrenchments, flinging aside rifles and packs in their haste to overtake McDonald's cavalry, which was fast disappearing into the hills east of Romney. "If the buggers would only stop and fight," said one disgusted Ohio private of the "Romney Race." The Confederate wagon train and artillery, along with all the military stores in town, fell into Federal hands.[9]

Kelley tried to make the occupation a gentle one. He placed few restrictions on the inhabitants and invited those who had fled to return without fear of punishment. Kelley's policy "is effecting great good among the people," his adjutant wrote the War Department. "The Union sentiment of this country is rapidly developing itself, and many of the citizens are coming in and availing themselves of the terms of [Kelley's] proclamation." Kelley himself was convinced that the entire South Branch Valley from Moorefield northward could be brought peaceably back into the Union fold if only enough Federal troops were made available to protect its inhabitants.[10]

Rosecrans quickly reinforced Kelley's command to division strength, with the treble purpose of solidifying Union control of the South Branch Valley, covering repairs to the B & O north of Romney, and facilitating an early winter march against Winchester.

The strategic situation impressed Rosecrans as especially propitious for offensive action. Behind Kelley's 5,000 at Romney, he had 22,000 troops concentrated along the railroad. Banks had 16,000 men at Frederick, with detachments guarding the Potomac River from Harpers Ferry to Williamsport. Both Rosecrans and Banks had reliable intelligence on Jackson's strength and dispositions throughout November and December, and their most generous estimates of his numbers never exceeded 7,000. They also knew that the only command near enough to reinforce him was a small brigade under Brig. Gen. Daniel Harvey Hill at Leesburg.

Rosecrans's calculations were worthy of serious consideration. A graduate of the West Point Class of 1842, Rosecrans had left the army to pursue a career as a civil engineer and architect. He had won the Battle of Rich Mountain in July 1861, a victory for which McClellan took credit. Possessed of great intelligence and seemingly boundless energy, his chief faults were a sharp tongue and an easy excitability. Although he lacked Stonewall Jackson's coolness under fire, Rosecrans equaled or excelled the Virginian in strategic vision and organizational ability. He also was persistent. When McClellan in late November began transferring troops from his command to the Western theater, Rosecrans left his Wheeling headquarters for Washington to gain approval for a winter campaign before McClellan cut his department "to a mere cipher."

But Rosecrans's arguments for launching an offensive against the Lower Shenandoah Valley impressed McClellan no more than had those of Banks. Little Mac was certain that if Rosecrans placed twenty thousand men in Winchester, the Confederates would reinforce Jackson with twenty thousand men to oppose them. If Rosecrans added more, the Confederates would counter with an equal number. And so on.[11]

On Capitol Hill, a convalescent Frederick Lander was making a case similar to that of Rosecrans before the Congressional Joint Committee on the Conduct of the War, created on December 10, 1861, to investigate the fiasco at Ball's Bluff and to examine McClellan's reluctance to advance his army. Lander did not know if a winter campaign could be undertaken with the pampered soldiers of the Army of the Potomac, "who are housed and buttered up about Washington and taught to believe that if they make a march of three miles it will get into the papers." But with the Ohio and Indiana boys on duty in western Virginia, he could whip Jackson at Winchester in any season, as could Banks, if properly supported. Lander urged that an advance of either or both commands be ordered at once.[12]

As he hobbled back to his E Street home after testifying on December 27, Lander looked forward to passing the New Year with his wife; his doctor had instructed him to rest his wounded leg at least another five days. Instead, he found the following special orders awaiting him: "Brigadier General Frederick W. Lander, United States Volunteers, will repair to Romney and assume command." Before setting out, Lander requested McClellan's permission to seize Martinsburg and Stephenson's Depot, three miles north of Winchester, as soon as practicable after his arrival at Romney. And he scribbled a brief note to Lincoln. "We need fighting men," he told the president. "Up to the present time [I] have seen so many shaking nerves in this war that I sometimes doubt my eyesight."[13]

THE ENFORCED INACTION of Banks and Rosecrans in the waning days of 1861 left the field open to Stonewall Jackson, and the promise of reinforcements from Loring's Army of the Northwest stirred him to grand plans. "Deeply impressed with the importance of absolute secrecy respecting military operations, I have made it a point to say but little respecting my proposed movements in the event of sufficient reinforcements arriving," Jackson told Secretary of War Benjamin on November 20, "but since conversing with Lt. Col. J. T. L. Preston, upon his return from General Loring, and ascertaining the disposition of the general's forces, I venture to respectfully urge that after concentrating all his troops here an attempt should be made to capture the Federal forces at Romney."

Any number of considerations suggested an attack on Romney as the best policy. It might lead McClellan to believe that Johnston's army had been so weakened as to induce him to advance on Centreville; should that occur, Jackson told Benjamin, he would march with Loring to reinforce Johnston at once. After helping dispose of McClellan, he would return to his own district and finish off Kelley at Romney. Not only would the occupation of Romney throw the Federals off balance and delay their own inevitable concentration in the region, but it would also allow his command to gather food and forage from the South Branch Valley before the Yankees picked the region clean. Jackson also wanted to move quickly so to dissuade people seduced by Kelley's benevolent policies from taking the oath of allegiance to the United States.

Anna Jackson thought her husband also wanted to undertake the march to keep his men healthy; he "remembered the saying of Napoleon, that 'an active winter's campaign is less liable to produce disease than a sedentary life by campfires in winter quarters.'" That might be so, but Jackson also understood the risks attendant to the enterprise. As he told Benjamin, "I know that what I have proposed will be an arduous undertaking and cannot be accomplished without the sacrifice of much personal comfort, but I feel that the troops will be prepared to make this sacrifice."[14]

Whether he would have the troops needed to conduct the campaign was uncertain. Unknown to Jackson, Secretary Benjamin had again muddied the strategic waters through his own inconsistency. In early November he had assured Jackson that Loring's troops—less 4,500 needed to guard the Allegheny

Mountain passes between Monterey and Huntington—were to be placed at his disposal. But Adjutant General Cooper thought the final disposition of Loring's troops would not be decided until they reached Staunton; at that time, he told Joe Johnston in late November, the War Department would either direct them to the Valley District or to the main army at Manassas. Johnston, for his part, thought that at least a portion of Loring's army should be detached to the Aquia District to reinforce his own vulnerable strategic right flank. And Benjamin gave Loring to understand that he, Loring, would have the final say on where his troops went. Benjamin offered only suggestions. "For several weeks [I have] been impressed with the conviction that a sudden and well-concealed movement of your entire command up the valley towards Romney, combined with a movement of General Jackson from Winchester, would result in the entire destruction, and perhaps capture of [the enemy force at Romney]," he wrote Loring on November 24. "If upon full consideration you think the proposed movement objectionable and too hazardous, you will decline to make it and so inform the [War] Department."[15]

Benjamin deferred to Loring in part because of that general's considerable reputation as a soldier. Indeed, Stonewall Jackson's martial accomplishments looked puny when stacked up alongside those of William W. Loring. Raised in St. Augustine, Florida, where his father ran one of the first sugar mills in the Florida Territory, Loring enlisted in the territorial militia at the age of fourteen to fight the Seminole Indians. For five years he slogged through the Florida swamps, winning distinction in combat and earning a second lieutenant's commission in 1837, until his parents pulled him from the militia and sent him to preparatory school in Alexandria, Virginia. Loring went on to study law at Georgetown College, and in 1842 he returned to St. Augustine to set up a practice. Five years later he was back in uniform with a direct commission as captain in a regiment of Mounted Rifles raised in Florida under the "Ten Regiment Bill," by which Congress expanded the regular army to help meet the troop needs of the Mexican War. Loring distinguished himself at the Battle of Chapultepec, then fell with a bullet in the arm while running with Lt. Ulysses S. Grant through the Belen Gate. He submitted to the inevitable amputation stoically. Said the operating physician: "Loring laid aside a cigar, sat quietly in a chair without opiates to relieve the pain, and allowed the arm to be cut off without a murmur or a groan. The arm was buried on the heights by his men, with the hand pointing towards the City of Mexico."[16]

Loring remained on active—and demanding—duty. In May 1849 he led his regiment on a grueling 2,500-mile march from Jefferson Barracks, Missouri, to the mouth of the Columbia River in Oregon Territory without losing a man. Two years of chasing Indians, protecting settlers and gold diggers, and tracking down deserters followed. "I had the pleasure to make the acquaintance of [Brevet] Colonel Loring and several of the junior officers of the regiment (having accompanied them to the Klamath River in the capacity of a guide)," recalled Oregon pioneer Jesse Applegate of one such expedition:

> Having left their quarters in haste in pursuit of deserters (attracted by the California gold mines), they were not prepared for so long a campaign and in consequence for several days were reduced to beef and boiled wheat as subsistence without a pipe of tobacco in camp. Notwithstanding disagreeable weather, muddy roads, high waters, and scarcity of food, the officers cheerfully underwent the fatigues and privation of the journey, performing all the duties of common soldiers. The colonel himself, though an invalid, set the example by taking his regular tour of three and a half hours every night as sentinel; thus undergoing in his own person these fatigues and privations, extraordinary for an officer of his rank, to capture men guilty of a high crime. Of the seventy taken, to all but two, who were incorrigible, he extended his pardon—a higher proof of the goodness of his heart or the soundness of his judgment could not be given.[17]

From Oregon, Loring and his regiment went on to the Texas and New Mexico frontiers for more rigorous duty. In June 1857 Loring, now a colonel, tracked the infamous Apache chieftain Cuchillo Negro far into the waterless recesses of the Mogollon Mountains, killing him and six of his warriors. On March 22, 1861, Loring assumed command of the Ninth District, Military Department of New Mexico. He was the youngest line colonel in the regular army. Not until June did he resign his commission to join the Confederate service. A month later, he was in the Alleghenies as commander of the Army of the Northwest.

Loring's long years of hard and varied service enabled him to weigh Benjamin's proposal knowledgeably. "I consider a winter campaign practicable if the means of transportation sufficient to move this army can be obtained, and especially in a country where supplies are abundant, which I am informed is the case in that section of Western Virginia where it is proposed to operate," he told the secretary on November 29. "With warm clothing, good tents, and proper attention by the regimental and company officers, there need be no suffering from the climate in that region." It would take him two or three weeks to get his troops in hand and secure wagons, but he would cooperate with Jackson "with a spirit to succeed . . . seconded by a command who will cheerfully endure all the hardships incident to a winter campaign."[18]

ON NOVEMBER 29 Brig. Gen. William B. Taliaferro's brigade, composed of the 3rd Arkansas, 23rd Virginia, 37th Virginia, and 1st Georgia regiments, bade farewell to their winter huts at McDowell and set off down the Staunton Pike under the first snowfall of the season. The snow was hard on the Georgians, who marched ignorant of their destination, but "buoyed with the hope of spending the winter under a warmer sun."[19] When he reached Staunton with Taliaferro's brigade on December 1, Loring was surprised to find a telegraph ordering the brigade to Manassas. "I came here today to carry into effect the proposed [Romney] campaign, and I find a telegram sending four regiments to Manassas," he wired Benjamin. "It is proper to state that, in consequence of movements made, in which I have been endeavoring to carry out your instructions, officers at a distance from my headquarters have been telegraphing without my authority to Richmond, the result of which has been a conflict of orders."[20]

Taliaferro's men camped at Staunton for three days while Loring waited for the War Department to sort matters out. For the 3rd Arkansas and 1st Georgia, it was an unpleasant introduction to their first Virginia winter. "Night settled down cold and cheerless, with our tents and blankets ten miles away, and we had to make the best of it" wrote Georgian Walter A. Clark of his regiment's first night on the outskirts of Staunton. "My bedfellow and I slept on an oilcloth, covered with an overcoat, and tied our four feet up together in a flannel shirt." Marching orders came on December 4, not south, as Clark and his comrades had hoped, or east, as Loring half expected, but by train from Mount Jackson to Strasburg, and from there by foot to Winchester, and "we reluctantly turned our faced northward again," remembered Clark. General Loring remained behind to shepherd the movements of the rest of the division.[21]

Four days later Taliaferro's men shuffled into Winchester, sore-footed and shivering. General Taliaferro, a Tidewater gentleman who had graduated from Harvard Law School and fought as an infantry captain in the Mexican War, reported to Jackson, whom he had not seen since the John Brown hanging two years earlier. Here now, at Winchester, "Jackson disclosed to me a trait which had not struck me before. There is a real difference in looking at a brevet major and a full major general. At the [Virginia Military] institute he was more than ordinarily passive. The fire was there, but he was a soldier in grain, and he believed it to be his duty, in his subordinate place, to execute, not to suggest. I had not noticed the saliency of his character—I will not say restlessness, but the desire to do, to be moving, to make, and to embrace opportunity."[22]

While waiting for Loring to come up with the remainder of his command, Jackson decided to do just that—move and make an opportunity. Casting about for something to attack, he settled on Dam No. 5 on the Chesapeake and Ohio Canal, seven miles above Williamsport, Maryland. Running parallel to the Potomac River along its northern bank, the C&O, as it was commonly known, took up a fair amount of the transportation slack left by the disabling of the Baltimore and Ohio Railroad. The canal also was vital for moving southwestern Pennsylvania coal to Washington; during October, 154 boats carrying 27,313 tons of it cleared the Cumberland mole. Heavy rains in November interrupted canal traffic, but by the beginning of December it was again open to navigation for its entire length. Coal, lumber, cordwood, hay, and oats cleared Cumberland by the ton-load.

Before the November freshet, President Davis had suggested that someone break up the canal. When the rains ceased, Jackson, believing as did Davis that a "boatable [canal was] of great service to the Federal army at Washington," acted to close it. Turner Ashby's cavalry had reported the continuous passage of empty canal boats upriver toward Cumberland; Jackson wanted to strike before their coal-laden return trip to Washington. Two dams—Nos. 4 and 5 of the canal network—lay within striking distance of Winchester. Both were built in the 1830s as log-cribbed, rock-filled dams, prone to leakage and in constant need of repair. After twenty years of wasted expense, the C&O Company decided to replace them with masonry dams. The new Dam No. 4 was built before Virginia seceded, but work on Dam No. 5 had languished. Given the choice between taking on a sturdy new masonry structure or a leaking rubble dam, Jackson opted for the latter. He detailed four hundred infantry, two hundred cavalry, and two sections of the Rockbridge Artillery, all under the command of the battery commander, Capt. William McLaughlin, to break the dam and reverse the flow of water.[23]

On the afternoon of December 7, McLaughlin's mixed command appeared on the icy, snow-draped Potomac Heights overlooking Dam No. 5. Wheeling their four cannons into battery along the bluff, the Rockbridge gunners took aim at the dam with solid shot and shell, while their infantry support peppered the far bank with rifle fire. The Rebels enjoyed the work as much as the bitter cold would allow. The Federals guarding the dam—one company of the 13th Massachusetts Infantry and two or three of the 12th Indiana Infantry —were armed with old short-range smoothbore muskets. Their bullets peppered the river harmlessly, leading Rebel infantrymen to slide down the bluff and from the water's edge hurl insults at their hapless opponents. But the Southern artillery proved as feckless as the Federal infantry, and when nightfall brought an end to the cannonade, the crib and rubble dam stood unscathed.

An angry Captain McLaughlin ran his guns up to the riverbank the next morning within point-blank range of the dam. But they never fired a shot. During the night, Col. Samuel H. Leonard of the 13th Massachusetts had sent a canal boat down to Williamsport to pick up a company of his regiment armed with Enfield rifle-muskets. Leonard posted them in the woods along the Maryland shore, with orders not to fire until he gave the word. As McLaughlin's gunners readied their pieces, Leonard yelled "Fire!" Two Confederates fell wounded, and the stunned cannoneers and their infantry and cavalry support scampered up the bluff, leaving four guns on the riverbank. After dark, the artillerymen sheepishly returned and dragged them off.

The Confederates were back at daybreak. Under cover of the artillery, now ensconced on high ground, a fatigue party worked its way down to the southern abutment of the dam, where its members captured an Indiana captain and seven enlisted men who had crossed the dam to "see if the Rebels were really over there." Hunched beneath the stone abutment, safe from Leonard's sharpshooters, the men set to work digging a ditch around the end of the abutment, hoping to divert enough water from the Potomac to wash away the dam. They finished at dark. Water rushed into the ditch, and a delighted Captain McLaughlin recalled his troops and at once headed home, confident that he had completed his mission.

He should have lingered a while. The Potomac River had been falling, and shortly after he marched away the flow into the ditch dropped off to a trickle, then ceased altogether. In a telegram to McClellan later that night, General Banks dismissed the affair at Dam No. 5 as inconsequential: "No damage done; no danger of attack."[24]

From his scouts Jackson learned of McLaughlin's failure. With Loring still a week or more away, he elected to try again. This time he would go himself, together with the Stonewall Brigade and all six guns of the Rockbridge Artillery. Ashby's cavalry and J. H. Carson's militia brigade would join the column on the march. Jackson intended to employ most of his force in creating diversions along the river or in protecting the work details at Dam No. 5. The dam-breaking itself was entrusted to small fatigue parties under the command of Capt. Raleigh Colston and his brother William B. "Bill" Colston of Company E, 2nd Virginia Infantry; the men hailed from Medford, a tiny hamlet a mile from the dam, and knew the ground intimately.

Jackson masked his intentions well. A few days before setting off for the dam, he sent scouts fanning out into the countryside to spread rumors that his objective was Kelley's brigade at Romney. The Federals took the bait. On December 16, the day Jackson's command set out from Winchester, the Northern War Department warned Kelley to expect an imminent attack and ordered Banks to be ready to reinforce him. Banks, in turn, directed Colonel Leonard at Williamsport to have his brigade ready to march to Romney "at the first call" for help, and he dispatched the 5th Connecticut Infantry from Frederick to replace Leonard's men or to join them in relieving Kelley, as Leonard saw fit. "You can call upon us for more troops, if they are wanted," Banks assured him.[25]

With high hopes to sustain him and a confused enemy before him, Jackson led the Stonewall Brigade out of Winchester at six o'clock on the bitterly cold morning of December 16. "If this plan succeeds," he assured Richmond, "as through the blessing of Providence it will—Washington will hardly get any further supply of coal during the war from Cumberland." Bill Colston thought otherwise. "In this instance," he later wrote, "I must confess that [Jackson's] zeal outran his discretion, as any damage we could do the canal would be only temporary, and winter had put an end to navigation of the canal."

Few besides the Colston brothers knew where they were bound. Remembered Alexander T. "Ted" Barclay, a member of Jackson's headquarters guard, the Liberty Hall Volunteers: "We were awakened by the drum at 2:00 A.M. and ordered to strike tents, pack baggage, eat as much beef and bread as you could stuff in you, and be prepared to march by four, to what place it was a mystery to us all, but we thought we were bound for Romney, so when we started in the opposite direction we were all puzzled."[26]

That evening, as the Stonewall Brigade, Ashby's troopers, and Carson's militia settled into camp two miles outside of Martinsburg—an "abolition hole which ought to be burnt as close to the ground as fire can get it," thought Ted Barclay—Bill Colston received a summons to headquarters. There he found his brother and Maj. Elisha Franklin "Bull" Paxton of the 27th Virginia, a trusted friend of Jackson from Lexington days, in consultation. A boast to Paxton that he knew "every foot" of the area around Dam No. 5 won Bill Colston a night hike to the bluffs overlooking the dam; he was to take four men and remain there until dark the following day. Colston led his party to a familiar spot on a towering cliff, where the men spread their blankets to watch and rest. Dawn came, and the day passed quietly, with only a handful of Federal pickets visible around the dam. But in the gathering winter twilight, Colston sensed danger. "Along toward sunset I heard a rustling in the leaves under the bluff, which sounded exactly like men marching in single file. I felt sure it was a reconnoitering party of Yankee soldiers and expected to see their heads pop up over the bluff," recalled Colston. "I cautioned my men to cock their guns but not to fire, only to halt the supposed soldiers and demand their surrender. I don't think I was ever more relieved in my life than when I discovered it was four calves that had caused the excitement. After dusk we went back to camp and reported to Major Paxton that there were no Yankees on the other side of the river, but did not say anything about the calves."[27]

To further confound Leonard and Banks, Jackson detached Carson's brigade to make a demonstration at Falling Waters, opposite Williamsport. On Colston's report he resumed the march to the dam with the Stonewall Brigade and Ashby's troopers, giving orders to leave behind tents and baggage. The Colston brothers went ahead with a three-company fatigue party from the 2nd Virginia to do what mischief they could before daybreak. The remainder of the command started at 3:00 A.M., December 18, and promptly became lost. "We took the road to Williamsport, went about five or six miles on it, struck to the left, got into the woods, and got lost completely," said Ted Barclay. "After a while we got on to the road again and took a bee line for the Potomac . . . by daybreak [got] within sound of the Potomac, took about an hour's sleep, and struck for the river when a bombshell hit us good morning and told us to right about. Having found where the Yankees were we went a little more cautiously."[28]

Colston's detail reached the bluffs above Dam No. 5 shortly after midnight. Laden with pickaxes, shovels, and crowbars, they made their way down to the riverbank, crept out onto the dam, slid waist-deep into the icy water halfway across, and set to work. Some began hacking away at the cribs, while others piled the loosened rocks into a crude breastwork perpendicular to the dam. The night air dampened the axe blows, and not until daybreak did Federal pickets on the Maryland bank realize what was happening. A heavy mist hung low over the water, and the Federals fired blind until it cleared.[29]

By then, Jackson had brought up two guns with orders to shell a brick house in which sharpshooters had taken cover. The cannons were unlimbered on a low hill overlooking the dam, and the Rebel gunners had a few minutes of fun. "After a few shots the Yankee sharpshooters ran from the house like rats, and while we were enjoying the sport, all at once a full battery opened on us from a wooded hill across the river," recalled Lt. William T. Poague of the Rockbridge Artillery.

What Poague thought to be an entire battery was merely a two-gun section of Battery E, 1st Pennsylvania Artillery. But the accuracy and rapid fire of the Yankee ten-pounder Parrotts panicked Captain McLaughlin. He frantically waved his and Robert Chew's gun crews and limber teams into a grove fifty yards to their right, less the cannons, which were left standing in the open. McLaughlin regained his composure sufficiently to order Lieutenant Poague to bring up the rest of the battery.

Poague exercised prudence on the return trip with the guns, detouring them onto a long ridge a little to the right of the enemy line of fire. In a large sinkhole to his left, Poague spied the limber team from Chew's abandoned gun, kicking and pulling to free the limber, which had wedged itself between two saplings. There too was Jackson, trying to coax the drivers from behind logs and trees. "Mr. Poague," he called out, "Can't you come and get those men and horses out of that place?" No, replied Poague, if the general could not, neither could he. "Well," said Jackson, "fetch your guns on to the top of the hill."

Poague did so and found himself again under fire. "Did I dodge?" Poague later asked rhetorically. "Yes: just as low as my saddle pommel would allow." Even Jackson, who had climbed out of the sinkhole to join him, ducked the screaming Parrott shells. "But who was that man out there walking slowly back and forth near the deserted guns in the open field, with arms folded, apparently enjoying a quiet promenade, totally indifferent to the hellish fire raining all about him," wondered Poague. "That was Turner Ashby—a man of the coolest courage and finest nerve I ever knew or saw in the army." Poague was delighted to find the enemy fire cease just before he wheeled his guns into line. Remarkably, no one had been hit in the shelling.[30]

The Federal fire stopped because Jackson, realizing the futility of hacking away at the dam in the daylight, had ordered the fatigue detail and demolition teams back up the ridge. "Our clothes froze stiff on us as soon as we came out of the water to return to camp," remembered Bill Colston, who was grateful for the respite, brief though it proved. Jackson organized new work parties from the 27th and 33rd Virginia regiments to assist Capt. Raleigh Colston's detail, and they were back in the frigid water that night. Before they went in, Jackson himself served out a cupful of whiskey to each man from a barrel brought forward for the occasion, along with an admonition to "pitch in the dam and tear [it] down." On the snow-covered bluffs above, the remaining soldiers of the Stonewall Brigade were content to wrap up in their blankets and watch the proceedings.[31]

There was plenty to see. The Yankees on duty at the dam were ready this time, and help was on the way. Carson's feint toward Falling Waters had backfired, serving only to convince Banks that Romney was no longer in danger. Deducing Jackson's true objective to be disruption of C&O Canal traffic, Banks hurried all available troops to the neighborhood of Williamsport. From there they could be shifted handily to Dam No. 4 or Dam No. 5, as the need arose. On the afternoon of December 18, Banks started three large regiments of infantry and a battery of regular artillery on the road from Frederick, Maryland, to reinforce Colonel Leonard.[32]

A terrific fire greeted the Confederate fatigue and demolition parties the moment they showed themselves on the riverbank. "The bullets came as thick as hail," recalled a 4th Virginia volunteer, who abandoned his pickaxe and took shelter behind a rock. The range was such that most Federal bullets fell short, said Pvt. John Garibaldi of the 27th Virginia, who had taken cover among the rocks as well, less from fear of being hit than to get a few well-aimed return shots at the Yankees. "After I got tired I got up and walked off," remembered Garibaldi, "and as I was going away from my hiding place there was no less than five or six shot at me, but none of them hit me, it was almost too far off to be killed by a ball, although there was several of the Yankee shot we could see laying on the ground and when they were falling."

The Pennsylvania Parrott guns, at least, rendered lethal service. Taking aim at a large abandoned mill just below the dam that the Rockbridge Rifles had appropriated, they blew apart the front wall, setting the interior ablaze and raining bricks on the Virginians, who fled up a towpath toward the bluff. One unfortunate man was torn to shreds by a shell as he emerged from the mill. Union marksmen crept down to the water's edge, marking their targets by the light of the burning mill. "The chit chat of musketry," said William T. Kinzer of the 4th Virginia, continued until dawn, when the hills again "reverberated with the report of cannon."[33]

Jackson brought forward McLaughlin's guns, but their fire did no more than ignite a few stacks of grain. In growing frustration, Jackson announced to any soldiers within hearing that they might go down to the riverbank and pitch in, as it was "a free fight." Even at that range no one hit much of anything. Edwin E. Marvin of the 5th Connecticut, which had arrived during the night, said his company fired perhaps thirteen rounds per man before giving up the effort, and "the Rebel bullets that came in return seemed to be so entirely spent, with a few exceptions, that it seemed to me useless to return the fire at all." The Federals fought from a low open hill near the water's edge. "I now think," said Marvin, "if we had climbed up the precipitous cliffs behind us a couple of hundred feet we could have done a good deal of effective work at that time."[34]

Colston's men returned to work at sunset on December 19, and just before dawn on the twentieth they succeeded in breaking apart a wooden abutment. Water from the pool behind the dam swept past them. Jackson watched the breach until mid-afternoon. Convinced it was wide enough to cripple the canal, he withdrew, ending what wags in the Rebel ranks called "the dam[n] trip."[35]

During the return march Jackson's staff got a good laugh at the general's expense. After riding some distance from the river, Jackson spotted a persimmon tree, a fruit of which he was particularly fond. Jackson had no problem climbing up the tree, or finding a good seat among the branches, where he ate in contented silence. But coming down proved a problem. Said Henry Kyd Douglas, "Attempting to swing himself from a limb to the main fork of the tree, [Jackson] got so completely entangled that he could move neither up nor down and was compelled to call for help." Amid general laughter, his staff fashioned a skid from fence rails, and Jackson slid to earth.[36]

Jackson rode into Winchester on the evening of the twenty-first. The last of his command trudged into town the next morning, delighted, so they thought, to be back in camp for the winter. "We built chimneys to our tents and made platforms to spread our beds on," said Lt. John N. Lyle of the 4th Virginia. "The officer's mess put its two tents together and made a double house, the outer room for dining and the inner for [a] sleeping apartment. This arrangement protected the door of the bed chamber from the cold wind, and a log fire in the fireplace made it as snug as could be desired."[37]

None were happier than Jackson to be back in Winchester. Just hours after he returned, a stagecoach deposited Anna in front of the Taylor Hotel. As she climbed the steps, a man in a heavy army coat, with his cap pulled down over his eyes, stalked her from behind. Hurrying on, she made it to the veranda before strong arms spun her about and engulfed her with a hard kiss. It was the general. Anna demanded to know why he hadn't met her at the stagecoach door. Jackson laughingly replied that he had not wanted to kiss "anybody else's *esposa*" by mistake. He whisked her off to the Moore cottage, where the two happily ensconced themselves.[38]

Jackson's radiance reflected itself in his overblown appraisal of the recent expedition. "There is reason to believe that the recent break in Dam No. 5 will destroy any vestige of hope that might have been entertained of supplying Washington with Cumberland coal by the Chesapeake and Ohio Canal," he reported to Richmond on Christmas Eve. In truth, apart from toughening his men to the cold, Jackson's expedition had been a rousing failure. As soon as the Rebels departed, Federal engineers scampered into the water to repair the breach to the dam. The damage proved negligible, and by nightfall on December 21 canal boats were running both ways.[39]

Jackson's expedition failed even to deter Banks from pressing his own aggressive agenda on McClellan. On December 19, while the fight for Dam No. 5 raged, or put more correctly, sputtered, Banks urged the general in chief to permit him to cross the Potomac in force and seize Martinsburg: "With sufficient artillery, the bridge and the rolling stock of the railway, and our men well entrenched in front of Martinsburg, I think we could hold and defend the line of the railway with our present force against any assaults of the enemy permanently posted at Winchester, Leesburg, or vicinity." But it was no go with McClellan, either for Banks or Rosecrans, and the initiative remained with Jackson.[40]

CHAPTER 5

OUR TRUE POLICY IS TO ATTACK

Christmas Day 1861 brought the opposing armies an odd mixture of revelry, homesickness, nostalgia, and license. Turner Ashby joined the Masonic Order over the holidays, becoming an apprentice in Martinsburg's Equality Lodge No. 136. Stonewall Jackson celebrated Christmas quietly with his wife and the family of the Reverend James R. Graham. Most everyone else raised hell. "We have had a right Merry Christmas," John Garibaldi of the 27th Virginia assured his hometown sweetheart. "We had plenty to eat, such as it was, and plenty to drink. The captain brought about ten or fifteen gallons of liquor and gave it to the company; he was right merry himself. The whole of the Twenty-seventh regiment was almost drunk, even the colonels, they were drunk too." The day passed much the same on the Maryland side of the Potomac. "Christmas came at last. Great excitement—fired a volley in honor of Christmas," a soldier of the 14th Indiana scribbled in his diary from camp near Frederick. "About half of our boys on a drunk; do not like to see it. It demoralizes [our] Company F, who bore a good name at all times."[1]

General Taliaferro's men enjoyed Christmas in camp, but the other two brigades of the Army of the Northwest spent the day on the march. Few relished the prospect of active winter service—under Jackson or anyone else. The early December order to abandon their comfortable winter quarters along the Greenbrier River had been "most unexpected," recalled Lt. Col. Thomas Garnett, whose 48th Virginia had "had more hard marches to make than any other." One hundred sixty-five men were absent sick; 153 of the 536 present were on the sick list. In the neighboring camp of the 42nd Virginia, only 60 percent of the men had overcoats. "It really does seem hard that we should be ordered at this inclement season through the snows of the Alleghenies on so long a march," complained Garnett. "It will place many a soldier in his grave."[2]

Loring and his staff reached Winchester on Christmas Eve. His Second Brigade, comprised of three Tennessee regiments commanded by Brig. Gen. Samuel R. Anderson, a tough fifty-seven-year-old who had been a lieutenant colonel of volunteers in the Mexican War, shuffled into Winchester amid a swirl of falling snow on Christmas Day. Loring's Third Brigade, consisting of the 21st, 42nd, and 48th Virginia regiments, arrived on December 26. Its commander was Col. William Gilham, a graduate of the West Point Class of 1840 who, as commandant of cadets at the Virginia Military Institute (VMI), had been Stonewall Jackson's prewar superior officer. As they filed through town, the more observant among Gilham's Virginians caught their first glimpse of the man who had summoned them from winter quarters. "We saw standing in the crowd on the sidewalk a man with full dark whiskers and hair, dressed in uniform, wearing a long dark blue overcoat with a large cape, his coat reaching to his boots, which were worn outside of his pants in regular military style, and on them were bright spurs," remembered John Worsham of the 21st Virginia. "His head was covered by a faded gray cap, pulled down so far over his face that between cap and whiskers one could see very little of it. That man was Stonewall Jackson."[3]

Jackson undoubtedly was preoccupied with matters other than the passing infantry. Conferring on Christmas Eve, he and Loring had agreed on the terms of their cooperation. Although he had hoped to integrate Loring's four brigades as the First Division of the Valley army, Jackson acceded to the North Carolinian's demand that his force retain its designation as the Army of the Northwest and that he, Loring, remain in command. From Loring, Jackson learned that Secretary Benjamin had permitted him to leave Edward Johnson's brigade at Monterey. Jackson's total force now consisted of 7,500 volunteers, 2,234 militia, and 664 cavalry—insufficient, he believed, to defend the Lower Valley. "If this place is to be held by us," Jackson wrote Joe Johnston,

> our true policy, in my opinion, is to attack the enemy in his present position before he receives additional reinforcements, and especially never to permit a junction of their forces at or near Martinsburg [precisely that for which Banks had argued unsuccessfully with McClellan]. I have given the subject much thought, and as the enemy appears to be continually receiv-

ing accessions, and as I may receive no more, it appears to me that my best plan is to attack him at the earliest practicable moment, and accordingly, as soon as the inspection of General Loring's forces shall be finished and the necessary munitions procured, I expect to march on the enemy, unless I receive orders to the contrary.

Johnston endorsed Jackson's plan, which he understood to be an attack on General Kelley's command at Romney. It is doubtful that he knew of Jackson's intention to move first against the small Federal garrisons at Bath and Hancock in order to cut off communications between Rosecrans and Banks and to isolate Kelley.[4]

As they emerged from their holiday hangovers to a bustle of martial preparation, the enlisted men of the Valley District passed along the prevailing rumor. "It is believed that we shall leave here and go to Romney to have a fight with the Yankees in a day or two," John Garibaldi wrote his sweetheart on December 30, before a general review of the army cut short his letter. On New Year's Eve artillery batteries filled their limber chests, infantrymen loaded up on cartridges, and everyone drew five-days' rations. Orders came for all units to march at 6:00 A.M. the next day.[5]

IN THE CONFEDERATE CAMPS outside Winchester, the long roll beat at 3:00 A.M. on January 1, 1862. The men rose easily; a warm, gentle rain had fallen the evening before, and in its wake came steadily rising temperatures. The lead elements of the Stonewall Brigade were on the road as scheduled at 6:00 A.M. Anderson's, Gilham's, and Taliaferro's brigades of Loring's army swung into march columns on separate country lanes shortly thereafter. By the time the sun rose at 7:13 A.M., temperatures had climbed to nearly sixty degrees. "The grass and limbs of the trees glistened, and everything betokened one of those freaks in the weather which are not uncommon in that latitude of Virginia and Maryland," said Sgt. Maj. Randolph Barton of the 33rd Virginia. In the Lower Valley they called such a morning a "weather breeder." Barton and other Valley natives understood that such unseasonably fine weather often portended a sudden freeze. But Loring's Deep South soldiers, along with far too many Virginia boys who should have known better, heaved their overcoats, blankets, and rations into supply wagons and set off in shirtsleeves. Spirits were high, and the men traded bets as to their destination—Romney, Bath, and Martinsburg being the principal guesses.[6]

Problems arose early on. Brig. Gen. G. S. Meem's militiamen, who were to have been ready with the remainder of the infantry at 6:00 A.M., were still packing knapsacks and striking tents four hours later. The Rockbridge Artillery had been ready as ordered at 8:00 A.M., but they were delayed another two hours while Captain McLaughlin sought marching directions from army headquarters, a consequence of the ignorance to which Jackson's secretiveness had relegated his subordinate commanders. The train of 160 wagons, with its freight of provisions, cooking utensils, medical supplies, overcoats, and blankets, did not start until 4:00 P.M.[7]

By mid-morning the Stonewall Brigade and Loring's three brigades had converged on the Romney Pike, five miles northwest of Winchester. "We are bound for Romney, for sure," laughed some. But at 2:00 P.M., about three miles beyond Pughtown, the column filed off onto a side road, which only Jackson and local boys in the ranks knew led to Bath. For the rest, all bets were off. "We were at wit's end" trying to divine the army's destination, remembered one of Loring's men.

Speculation about their objective gave way to concern for survival. A chilling north wind came up during the afternoon, growing fiercer and colder as the day wore on. By sunset, the thermometer had plummeted to near zero. Shivering infantrymen filed off the road and huddled for warmth in woods and ravines north of Pughtown. The more fortunate found their wagons not far behind. "When the wagons came up we made all haste to erect some shelter for the night," said Sergeant Major Barton, "and the adjutant and myself, by laying fence rails from the top of the span of fencing to the ground, and throwing over it an oil cloth or something of the kind, and under it some straw and our blankets, secured a delightful night's rest, which was not at all disturbed by a capital supper of fresh sausage and buckwheat cakes obtained at a nearby log cabin." The wagons of the 21st Virginia lumbered into camp at midnight, and it was past one before the men received their rations. Those of the 2nd Virginia never arrived, and the men bivouacked with neither food nor blankets. (Jackson's orders for each man to carry with him a day's cooked rations either had been ignored or the men had devoured the rations on the fifteen-mile march.) A dismal wind whipped down from the mountains. "I don't think I ever experienced a more windy time," recalled a Virginia militiaman. "We encamped on a piece of meadow ground which was rather low and wet. A great many of the men just lay on the ground."[8]

A brush with oblivion enlivened the evening for the Rockbridge Artillery. The battery bivouacked in a high field with good drainage, blanketed with dead grass and dotted with furze. It seemed an ideal campsite—that is, until the wind picked up. Sparks from nearby campfires blew into the field. Grass and furze ignited, and "we had quite an alarm," Pvt. Launcelot M. "Lanty" Blackford assured his mother. "The horses could not be immediately attached, so the men were ordered to guns and caissons which were with some difficulty drawn out of danger. In the limber and caisson of each gun there was an average of two hundred rounds of ammunition, comprising in all from 1,800 to 2,000 pounds of powder. You will readily infer from this that we had cause for alarm." Although the flames were soon beaten out, Captain McLaughlin thought it best to move a few hundred yards to a less comfortable, but better sheltered ravine.[9]

Reveille sounded at 5:00 A.M. on January 2, and the first units were on the march an hour later. The intense cold continued, and a light snow fell. The road was frozen hard most of the way to Unger's Store, and progress was slow. "If a man was at the head of the column he was alright," said Marcus Toney of the 1st Tennessee, "but after a few companies had passed over the snow became as slick as ice, and skating would have been good if a fellow had had skates." Several wagons rolled over and broke apart, causing the train to fall far behind the marching infantry. Part of Carson's militia brigade joined the column during the day, bringing the strength of Jackson's command to about 8,500.

The army encamped for the night among the steep hills surrounding the hamlet of Unger's Store, at the junction of the Bath and Martinsburg-Romney roads. Jackson made his headquarters in an abandoned log hut. Morale was mixed after the ten-mile march. Lt. John H. Grabill of the 33rd Virginia kept in good spirits. "We are located in a deep hollow in a thick grove. We have large fires, around one of which we are now sitting, while one of our number is rubbing music out of an old fiddle. The wind howls desolately around us," said Grabill, "but what care we for cold winds so long as we have a good fire and cheerful companions?" Tennessean Marcus Toney cared plenty. "I bivouacked on three cedar rails and built a rail fire on each side," he recalled, "and the red cedar popped sparks on the cape of my overcoat, and when I woke up I was afire." Artilleryman Clement Fishburne found the hillside on which his battery bivouacked so steep that it was all he could do to keep from rolling out of bed.[10]

Few were in worse humor than William Loring. During the day his command had been kept standing in the road for several hours so the Stonewall Brigade might remain in advance, and Loring made no secret of his disgust with the state of affairs. "Owing to the mismanagement, for which none of my command was responsible, the baggage wagons, with food, tents, and bedding, did not reach camp that night. It is quite possible," he confessed, "that my just indignation for this utter disregard for human suffering found expression in words." Jackson, on the other hand, remained serenely confident. That night, he penned Joe Johnston an update. Already he was situated so as to prevent a junction of Banks and Rosecrans, and on the morrow he hoped to recover Bath, after which he would destroy the railroad bridge over the Big Cacapon River.[11]

Jackson's knowledge of Bath and the surrounding country derived mainly from soldiers raised in the area, whom he quizzed on the evening of January 2. Bath rested at the eastern foot of a long ridge called "Warm Springs Mountain." As Lt. Samuel J. C. Moore of the 2nd Virginia explained it:

Bath, the county town, in which the warm springs are situated known as Berkeley Springs, lies in a basin, surrounded by high mountains, which slope down on all sides to form the valley in which the village is built. The place is a pretty one, having a number of neat houses, and a large and handsome hotel at the springs, formerly kept by Colonel Strother, father of the notorious David Strother, the traitor who has taken up arms against his native state and thrown himself into the arms of the infamous government of Lincoln.[12]

The road along which the army had been traveling paralleled the eastern base of Warm Springs Mountain. It continued beyond Bath to a small depot on to the B & O Railroad, passed through a gorge, and ended on the south bank of the Potomac River, opposite Hancock, Maryland. A back road ran along the western base of Warm Springs Mountain from Bloomery Gap to Bath, where it joined the main road to the Potomac.

Jackson's plan for taking Bath was simple enough. He would dispatch the militia across Warms Springs Mountain several miles south of Bath, with orders to push along its western base. Meanwhile, Loring would attack directly into Bath on the main road, herding the enemy north toward the Potomac or west into the militia. A company of cavalry would screen the march. The Stonewall Brigade would bring up the rear. Jackson intended for the fight to occur on January 3.

Simple or not, Jackson's plan failed on several counts. Jackson expected too much of both officers and men, the more so as he left everyone—Loring included—in the dark. Neither did he take into account the loose discipline and indifferent training of the militia, which rendered doubtful its ability to conduct any sort of independent maneuver. Lastly, he expected his men to go into battle in freezing weather on empty stomachs.

The results were predictable. To give the militiamen the time needed to cross Warm Springs Mountain and take up their parallel line of march, Jackson held Loring's brigades in camp for several hours after sunrise on the third. Not knowing the cause of the delay, Loring railed against Jackson's apparent callousness. Watching his men shiver in the stinging cold, Loring—who had endured unimaginable suffering himself on the frontier—barked at a staff officer from headquarters, "By God, sir, this is the damnedest outrage ever perpetrated in the annals of history, keeping my men out here in the cold without food!"[13]

Brig. Gen. Richard B. "Dick" Garnett was not about to let his men go hungry. For two days his Virginians had subsisted on scraps or fasted. So when the brigade train overtook them at mid-morning, Garnett understandably paused to draw rations. Observing his former brigade at rest, Jackson demanded an explanation.

"I have halted to let the men cook their rations," offered Garnett.

"There is no time for that," retorted Jackson.

Garnett persisted. "It is impossible for the men to march farther without them."

"I never found anything impossible with this brigade," snarled Jackson. He ordered the men to their feet at once.[14]

There was no need for haste. The Federal garrison at Bath consisted of just two cannons from the 4th U.S. Artillery under Lt. F. D. Muhlenburg and three companies—D, K, and I—of the 39th Illinois Infantry under Maj. O. L. Mann. The remainder of the regiment was scattered along the Potomac between Alpine and Sir John's Run, both stations on the B & O Railroad. Only two other regiments—the 13th Massachusetts, which was spread out between Cumberland and Hancock, and the 84th Pennsylvania, just arrived at Hancock—were within supporting distance. The remainder of Kelley's division was fifty miles to the west at Romney, and Banks's division was fifty miles to the east at Frederick.[15]

General Taliaferro also incurred Jackson's wrath. He had started out rearward rather than forward, withdrawing his brigade through a frosty bog in order to meet up with its wagons. The wade through the swamp left his men so chilled and exhausted that he felt compelled to rest them beside fires for two hours.

Notwithstanding Jackson's best efforts, no one marched more than ten miles that day. Recalled a soldier of the 4th Virginia: "We halted about every half mile along the road and would build rail fires, for we cared not for the country as all [was] owned by Union men." None in the ranks knew they were supposed to be advancing to the attack, nor understood why the march went so slowly. Lanty Blackford of the Rockbridge Artillery assumed the cause to be "egregious mismanagement on the part of somebody, for I never saw such apparently causeless delays, countermarching, stoppages, etc."[16]

O. L. Mann's Illinoisans had plenty of notice of the lumbering Confederate approach. That morning, a runaway slave had burst into the major's comfortable quarters near the bathhouses, urging him "in de name ob' de Lawd" to get out of town at once. He had traveled ten miles along the Winchester grade, explained the man, and no more than five miles back was Jackson with his entire army, making for Bath. A dubious Major Mann waited until mid-afternoon to organize a patrol. Calling upon Capt. Samuel S. Linton's Company K—sixty men strong—Mann set out at 3:00 P.M., supported by a mounted force consisting of himself, a lieutenant, and a half-dozen cavalry couriers. Once outside town, Captain Linton sent Lt. Austin Towner and ten men over Warm Springs Mountain to scout its western slope, while he marched with the remainder up the center of Bath Valley, on either side of the Winchester grade. Major Mann and his mounted party took the road.[17]

A few minutes before 5:00 P.M., as the sun set behind the forested and icy slopes of Warm Springs Mountain, Mann's patrol stumbled on eight Rebel cavalrymen, the advance guard of Gilham's brigade. The Yankees let go a ragged volley, and the horsemen wheeled and fled. Coming around a concealed bend in the road was the 21st Virginia. At the first sound of gunfire the Virginians froze in place. Gilham called up Company F from the rear of the column—the men of the company fancied that Stonewall himself had summoned them—and deployed them forward as skirmishers.

A sharp clash ensued between the Virginians, arrayed in loose order across the snowy fields, and Captain Linton's company, split into squads and well protected behind fences at the forest's edge. In the gathering twilight Linton's command loomed far larger than it was, and the Virginians felt their way forward. Pvt. William Exall of Company F fell mortally wounded—the first Southern casualty of the campaign—and Lt. James P. Payne dropped a few moments later. The Yankees held on until it was too dark to see, then retired to Bath, minus eight men caught in the open and captured.

A brisk snow began to fall. Gilham reined in the 21st Virginia, expecting to bivouac on the roadside. But Jackson wanted to keep on, and he dispatched

Colonel Preston with orders for Gilham to charge into Bath. An incredulous Loring countermanded the order. It was another of Jackson's outrages, he bellowed to all within hearing, to push half-starved men on in the dark, through a blinding snow toward an unseen enemy of indeterminate strength, and for a purpose unknown to Loring. Although second-in-command of the army, he knew little more of Jackson's plans than did the lowest private. If Jackson should be killed, Loring rightly complained to his staff, he would find himself "in command of an army of the object of whose movements he knew nothing."[18]

Here was an instance—the first of many in the coming months—in which Jackson took what might have been a commendable reticence to a hermetic extreme. Loyal staff officers then and later attempted to explain away—with considerable success to posterity—Jackson's fetish for secrecy. "I could relate many instances in connection with this habit of his, which had, in my opinion, much to do with his great success," averred Jedediah Hotchkiss. "He made his orders as few as possible and communicated them to as few persons as he could to ensure success in any movement. He frequently sent a staff officer to conduct a brigade or division commander to a position without telling that commander what road he was to take or anything else, except that he was to follow his guide. This very frequently provoked the wrath of successive officers." The Reverend J. William Jones recalled Jackson saying, "If I can deceive our own people, I will be sure to deceive the enemy as to my plans."[19] Perhaps, but one must wonder how deceiving his second-in-command could possibly contribute to success, or how much greater success Jackson might have enjoyed had his subordinates understood why he expected them to push their men beyond what prudence seemed to dictate.

Jackson joined Gilham and Loring and demanded that they resume the march. Loring refused, and "unpleasant words" passed between them before Jackson relented. It may have been a captured Illinoisan's lies, rather than Loring's protests, that convinced Jackson to call off the assault. Brought before General Jackson, the soldier, whom Major Mann praised as a "most accomplished liar," calmly "assured the Rebel chieftain that General Kelley had not over five thousand men at Bath, but that he understood before leaving camp that General Banks was crossing the entire army at Sir John's Run and at Hancock, and was expected at Bath that evening. The man knew that he was dealing out large lumps of 'taffy' to the general, but that it was also a 'military necessity.'"[20]

A night attack on Bath in any case would have gained Jackson little, as the militiamen had not only failed to close off the Federal routes of retreat, but also had taken themselves out of the picture altogether. The vanguard of Meem's brigade had encountered Lieutenant Towner's squad shortly before dusk, two miles outside of town. A frightened militia officer rode among the green Virginians, swearing that there were a thousand Yankees just over the hill. Meem deployed his lead regiment in line of battle, and it inched forward through the swirling snow, nervously trading volleys with Towner's ten men. When they came upon a small party of Yankees chopping trees across the road, Meem and Carson called a halt. Satisfied that they had done enough, at 6:00 P.M. they faced their brigades about, marched them a half mile, then allowed the men to break ranks and scrounge firewood for what was sure to be a long, cold night. Ration wagons were on the far side of Warm Springs Mountain, along with the brigades' knapsacks and blankets. Surg. Abram S. Miller of Meem's brigade was among the few to find food and shelter. "As we were going back I spied a house and went there and took up lodging for the night. The men not having anything to eat I brought some corn meal and a shoulder of meat, and after the general and his staff were done eating they stayed in the same house. They feasted on corn bread and onions." Miller understood his good fortune. Outside, "the men made fires and crept under pine bushes and slept the best that they could, the most of them having nothing to eat." The storm worsened as the night deepened, pounding the mountains with two to four inches of fresh snow and plunging the temperature into single digits.[21]

The only warmth in Loring's camp was in the oaths uttered against Jackson. The men went hungry, and Loring's displeasure trickled down to his lieutenants. That night, said a member of Jackson's staff, Loring's officers "did not hesitate to denounce Jackson openly and in unmeasured terms, as a madman for having marched them into the mountains at that season of the year, and for keeping them there in such tempestuous weather. They pronounced the expedition rash . . . and prophesized disastrous failure."[22]

THERE PROVED TO be an element of truth in the tale the audacious Illinois captive had told Jackson. Reinforcements did reach Bath, but they were scarcely of a caliber to inspire confidence. Shortly after midnight, Col. William G. Murray led the 84th Pennsylvania Infantry Volunteers into town. A regiment less prepared for battle could scarcely be imagined. The 84th was just four days removed from its training camp, and the men had only been issued weapons that morning. Those they were given—cumbersome, bent-barreled

.69-caliber Belgian muskets, caked shut with tallow—were "more dangerous at their butts than at their muzzles." No sooner had the men shouldered their worthless muskets than they were ordered into canal boats and ferried across the Potomac; two frantic couriers from Bath had brought Colonel Murray word of the impending attack.

Col. Thomas O. Osborn, commander of the 39th Illinois, greeted Murray, who assumed command by virtue of date of rank. The prospects for Murray's first combat command were poor. He and Osborn counted nearly two hundred enemy campfires in the fields south of Bath; how many more lighted the skies on the far side of Warm Springs Mountain, out of sight, was anyone's guess. Between them Murray and Osborn had fewer than 1,500 men. At best, they could expect two more regiments to arrive sometime on the fourth—the 13th Indiana from Romney and the 110th Pennsylvania, a regiment as green as the 84th, from Harrisburg's Camp Curtin. With slim hope for success, Murray ordered his men up the eastern face of Warm Springs Mountain at 4:00 A.M. to await the Confederate approach.[23]

Loring's command resumed the advance at dawn. The cold was intense, and Gilham moved at a snail's pace. "We crept along, freezing as we crept, pretty nearly all day," remembered a Virginian. No one in the ranks was particularly anxious to expose himself, as the danger of a bullet from behind seemed as great as one from in front. "We were furnished, in common with the rest of the army, with a battle badge, viz., a piece of white cotton tied around the right arm, receiving as an additional inducement for the wearing of it that orders had been issued that in the event of battle our men must shoot every man without one," explained Lanty Blackford. "The road was good but it was necessary to go very slowly, throwing out scouts and pickets all the while and going on 'hand over hand' fashion to avoid ambuscade."

Those in the rear of the column blessed the delays. "We would go a few hundred yards and then stop, sometimes an hour or two. Often we did not go more than fifty to one hundred yards without stopping," said a member of the Rockbridge Artillery. "Owing to the fact however that the whole line in front of us had to travel in the same fashion, and that we were among the last, we found at every point along these miles—at intervals of a half dozen yards, often on both sides of the road, excellent fires burning, by which we kept ourselves warm and reasoned and meditated on the excellence of the virtue called patience."[24]

Patience played no part in Stonewall Jackson's calculations that day. "So prematurely and repeatedly [did] General Loring permit the head of the column to halt," fumed Jackson, "that even his skirmishers were not kept within continuous sight of the enemy." Not until 10:00 A.M. did the 21st Virginia Infantry, once again in the lead, catch a glimpse of the Federals, strung out behind trees, rocks, and logs along the southeast side of Warm Springs Mountain, a mile and a half short of Bath. Muhlenburg's two guns boomed their greeting, and the 21st fell back. "It was too far for musket firing," recalled John Worsham, "but the men of each side engaged in much abuse of each other."

After enduring three hours of this apparent nonsense, Jackson took matters into his own hands. "General Jackson now arrived at the front and took the lead on horseback, a few couriers following him," said Worsham. "As he passed our company, he ordered us to double quick, and we soon ran. This was a grand sight . . . the Yankees in sight on the ridge to our left, running too."[25]

Jackson's display was anticlimactic. Loring had worked the 1st Tennessee Infantry of Anderson's brigade around the left of Gilham and up the ridge, which led Colonels Murray and Osborn to concede the fight even before Jackson made his appearance. The proximity of the militia on the western slope, coupled with the flanking movement of the 1st Tennessee atop the ridge and the presence in the valley of a force Osborn estimated at from ten to fifteen thousand, convinced the Federal commanders to fall back to Sir John's Run.

Once again, the militia had contributed nothing. Instead of blocking the Federal line of retreat, Meem's men had panicked and dispersed at the first fire of Northern skirmishers. The suddenness of the stampede stunned militia surgeon Abram Miller. Riding at the head of his regiment as it trudged along the snow-packed slope of Warm Springs Mountain, Miller caught sight of the Yankees, just as "they fired at our men and the regiment in front fired and most of the regiment took flight and ran off and left me on the top of the mountain with only a part of the regiment in front of me. . . . I jumped off my horse and followed after the regiment." While the militiamen on the ridge ran one way and the Federals the other, Stonewall Jackson galloped into Bath with a handful of Ashby's cavalry beside him and Gilham's skirmishers strung out in the rear.[26]

Two roads led from Bath to the Potomac—one in the direction of Hancock, six miles distant on the Maryland side of the river; the other to Sir John's Run, three miles away. A third road meandered over the mountains to the Great Cacapon River railroad bridge. Hoping to catch the fleeing Federals before they crossed the river, and perhaps to occupy Hancock himself, Jackson directed an immediate pursuit along all three routes. He personally ordered Gilham to find and attack the enemy at Sir John's Run, and detached the 3rd Arkansas Infantry to burn the bridge over the Great Cacapon. After leaving word for Garnett to occupy Bath, Jackson set off down the Hancock road with the remainder of Loring's command. Ahead of them galloped Ashby's cavalry companies. Bouncing along behind them were the gun carriages of the Rockbridge Artillery. "We dashed forward at a trot into the village," remembered Clement Fishburne. "In the center of the street leading toward Hancock lay a horse, smoking hot and bleeding, which had just been shot by some of the cavalry, who with General Jackson and his staff, had just preceded us. We had to make a slight deflection to pass the dead horse, at sight of which some of our animals were greatly excited." Battery mate Lanty Blackford was surprised at the stillness of the place. "There was not the smallest indication of welcome or the contrary given as we entered Bath. The former was not felt, the latter they dared not evince. I saw no faces at windows except at one house; indeed, the place looked deserted—which it was not, so far as I know, except by the enemy." As they hustled through Bath, Loring's troops could not fail to note that the Stonewall Brigade, which had trailed leisurely in reserve during the advance, now was permitted to remain behind and enjoy the spoils. Curses upon Jackson and his "Pet Lambs" peppered the ranks on the roads to Sir John's Run and Hancock.[27]

Left to their own devices, the men of the Stonewall Brigade launched an attack on the Strother family home. Shoving aside Colonel Strother, whom Lt. Sam Moore derided as "a driveling old Unionist," they ransacked "Porte Crayon's" library, rifling through manuscripts, upsetting easels and drawing tables, and "confiscating his fencing masks and foils as contraband of war." Garnett's Virginians also plundered the Berkeley Springs Hotel and nearby summerhouses belonging to the Strother family, while marveling at their grandeur. "To give you an idea of the size of the springs buildings," Ted Barclay of the 4th Virginia wrote home, "they quartered all of Jackson's brigades containing five regiments, and there was plenty of room too." While most bedded down on hotel mattresses, the more acquisitive among the brigade scavenged around town, finding but little for their trouble. "Some overcoats, shoes, and tents were taken, also two pieces of cannon," complained one man, but the Yankees had carried off everything else.[28]

Jackson had ridden far enough beyond town with "Old Gil" to prevent his former VMI colleague from "missing the way" to Sir John's Run, but not far enough to ensure that he would fight the Federals when he found them.

Nearing the depot at dusk, Gilham decried what appeared to be two Union regiments atop the intervening hills. Without attempting to develop their strength, he halted his brigade for the night. Had he pushed forward, Gilham would have enjoyed a turkey shoot and probably killed or captured every Federal in the area.

Colonels Murray and Mann had stumbled into the Sir John's Run depot just a few minutes ahead of Gilham. There they were delighted to meet up with Lt. Col. Robert S. Foster, just in by train from Cumberland with the 13th Indiana Volunteers. After a brief conference, the three commanders agreed to stand and fight; until, that is, Murray and Mann realized they had nothing with which to fight. The Indianans had only two rounds per man; Foster had been told to draw ammunition at Bath. Mann's Illinoisans had only a few rounds more, and the Belgian muskets of Murray's Pennsylvanians remained caked with tallow. The three agreed to withdraw while they were still able. Foster's Indianans boarded their train and returned to Cumberland, and the Illinoisans and Pennsylvanians made for the Potomac. Thanks to Gilham's timidity, the 39th Illinois was able to ford the river unmolested, along with the baggage wagons and artillery, which momentarily jammed the ford ahead of the 84th Pennsylvania. Not wanting to chance an encounter with Gilham, Murray changed course, leading his chilled and weary men east along the railroad tracks to Alpine Station, where, after a brief clash with a detachment of the 7th Virginia Cavalry, they waded the icy, chest-high water to the Maryland shore at Hancock. The frigid current swept away one man—a soldier named Pardee, the only Federal casualty of the day.[29]

Although he raged at Gilham's failure to bag the Yankees at Sir John's Run, Jackson himself had done little to prevent their escape at Alpine Station. After Murray repelled Ashby's cavalry, Jackson reined in Loring's infantry. From atop a high ridge the Confederates could see Murray's Pennsylvanians disappear across a field to their front and into woods near the riverbank. The Federals were safely on the far shore before Jackson reached the bluffs overlooking the Potomac.[30]

His humor hardly improved by the Federal escape, Jackson ordered his artillery to open fire on Hancock. There was no military justification for such action: the town was full of civilians, and Jackson had no intention of forcing a crossing. But he was angry because the Federals had shelled Shepherdstown, Virginia, on several occasions the year before, "while there were no troops in the place and it was not used as a means of defense." In Jackson's mind, such an outrage demanded retribution, even if it meant killing Southern sympathizers, of whom there were many in Hancock. At 6:00 P.M. the gunners of the Rockbridge Artillery reluctantly opened fire. "It seemed to me very barbarous to be firing away indiscriminately at the town," wrote Pvt. Randolph Fairfax, "but owing to the darkness of the night, I don't think we did much injury." The cannonade continued intermittently for five hours, blasting masonry from the homes along the waterfront, but injuring no one.[31]

As it happened, the people of Hancock had more to fear from the Federal reinforcements stumbling into town than from Rebel cannons. Shortly after midnight, the 110th Pennsylvania Volunteer Infantry made its appearance on the streets of Hancock, the men footsore from a twenty-six-mile forced march. Just two days out of their recruiting camp, the Pennsylvanians already had seen mortal combat; unfortunately, it had been an intramural affair. Four companies of the regiment hailed from Philadelphia; the remaining six had been recruited in the farm country and mountains of western Pennsylvania. Although country boys predominated in the ranks, the regimental officers were all Philadelphians. The smoldering resentment of the former turned violent when the regiment reached Hagerstown in the early morning hours of January 3. While Col. William D. Lewis and his officers disappeared into hotels to eat breakfast, the men broke ranks and headed for the saloons, drinking until, as the regimental historian put it, "half the regiment was tanked up full." A fistfight broke out when a party of country boys tried to yank the national flag away from the color guard of Philadelphians. The officers restored order sufficiently to march the regiment out of town. But the goose-egg sized limestone chunks of the freshly macadamized National Turnpike proved too tempting to the drunken soldiers, none of whom had yet been issued arms. Country companies squared off against city companies, and for twenty minutes they filled the air with limestone. The 1st Maryland Cavalry arrived to quell the riot, but not before three men had been killed and more than forty wounded, several mortally. When they reached Hancock, the Pennsylvania rabble busted into churches and homes, lying down to sleep where they wished.[32]

Far more welcome to the people of Hancock was the arrival several hours later of General Lander. He had left Baltimore that morning, intent on reaching his new command at Romney as quickly as possible. But when he entered Hagerstown late in the afternoon and learned of the attack on Bath, Lander changed his plans. He would go to Hancock and assume command, he wired General Banks; what was more, he intended to attack the enemy across the river, and he expected Banks to support him.[33]

CHAPTER 6

IS NOT WAR A GAME OF RISKS?

Sunday, January 5, dawned bitterly cold. The temperature had dropped to near zero overnight, where it would remain for seventy-two hours. By mid-morning the Stonewall Brigade was on the road from Bath to join Jackson, Ashby, and the Rockbridge Artillery opposite Hancock. The men welcomed the march as a means to keep warm, but their spirits sank when they reached their destination. Remembered General Taliaferro: "Along the river opposite Hancock there was neither tent nor camp equipage. No house was there, hardly a tree. The weather was intense, and a hard, crisp snow sheeted the landscape."[1]

Jackson never explained his reasons for lingering about Hancock. The Federal army stores gathered there were tempting prizes, but with the river high and large blocks of ice choking the fords, getting to them would be difficult enough even without opposition. But perhaps he might bluff the Yankees into leaving. At 9:30 A.M., while his infantry gathered along the heights, Jackson sent Turner Ashby across the river under a flag of truce. Ushered blindfolded into General Lander's presence, Ashby presented him with Jackson's ultimatum: Surrender Hancock, or he would shell the town, then come over and take it. Lander had two hours to evacuate noncombatants before Jackson opened fire.

"Colonel Ashby," interjected Lander, "give my regards to General Jackson and tell him to bombard and be damned! If he opens his batteries on this town he will injure more of his friends than he will of the enemy, for this is a damned secesh place anyhow!" Colonel Murray of the 84th Pennsylvania added a more balanced postscript. "As for destroying property," he told Ashby, "you will have to be responsible for that; and if you cross the river you will have to run your own risk. I have some men here who are determined to fight until the last man falls."

Ashby rose to leave. "Hold on! Take a seat Colonel Ashby," Lander said. "General Jackson has addressed me in a polite and soldierly manner and it demands a like reply." Wrote Lander: "I decline to accede to your request. If you feel justified in destroying the property and lives of peaceable citizens under the plea of crossing the Potomac at a particular point . . . which I dispute, you must do so on your own responsibility." As he handed Ashby the note, Lander remarked: "General Jackson and yourself, Colonel Ashby, are gentlemen and brave men, without a question, but you have started out in a God Damn bad cause!"[2]

While Ashby was rowed back across the Potomac, Lander prepared to receive Jackson's bombardment. He ordered all civilians to leave Hancock and posted the 84th Pennsylvania with water buckets along Main Street to douse flames from exploding shells. The rowdy 110th Pennsylvania drew the remainder of the stored, frozen Belgian muskets from the canal boats and took up positions in the warehouses, and Lt. F. D. Muhlenburg wheeled his two cannons onto a high hill behind the town.

An eerie silence reigned until 2:00 P.M., when the Confederate artillery belatedly opened fire. Muhlenburg replied briskly. No one was hurt in the ensuing exchange, which went on sporadically until dusk, but the Southern infantry seems to have suffered the most near misses. Said William Taliaferro: "It is a fact that the enemy literally snowballed us, for the missiles from their guns scattered in the hard snow and hurled the fragments upon us, almost as uncomfortable to us as the splinters from their shells."[3]

Under cover of the barrage, Jackson sent a detail two miles upriver to begin work on a bridge and another to Dam No. 5 to reopen the breach made the month before. Both efforts failed, but in the meantime Col. Albert Rust succeeded in wrecking the Big Cacapon River railroad bridge, a task that darkness had prevented him from completing on January 4.[4]

At nightfall a heavy snow replaced the cannonading. Hustling indoors, Federal soldiers wrought havoc on the abandoned houses of Hancock. The men of the 110th Pennsylvania outdid themselves that night, appropriating food, furniture, and fuel "without thought or decency," recalled Brig. Gen.

Alpheus S. Williams, who entered Hancock a few days later. "They knew nothing of camp, garrison, or other military duty, and were literally a mob firing their loaded muskets right and left and playing the very devil generally."

On the far bank of the Potomac, Southern soldiers thought only of keeping warm. A handful of wagons were able to make it up the narrow, frozen road from Bath with camp equipage, so most of the men bivouacked beneath the pelting snow with just small fires to console them. "The hardest night I ever spent was last night, by a fire with no blankets and snowing most of the time," Capt. Francis B. "Frank" Jones of the 2nd Virginia wrote his wife the next morning. "I ate my breakfast yesterday morning about sunrise, and from that time I could get not a single mouthful to eat." Daybreak on January 6 found Jackson's sleeping troops nearly buried in snow, their blankets too wet to carry. General Taliaferro saw some humor in the scene: "One officer [had] sent his servant back for his camp bed, and the next morning, covered with snow; it was an antique tomb, with the effigy of an ancient knight carved upon it."[5]

January 6 was harder yet on the Confederates. Some tried to entrench, more to keep warm than to protect themselves against Yankee shells, but the ground was frozen too hard. Most simply passed the long hours shivering in the ranks while the Rockbridge Artillery pointlessly lobbed shells over the river. If Jackson thought he could bombard the Federals out of Hancock, he was seriously mistaken. Far from contemplating retreat, General Lander was impatient to take the offensive. He begged Banks to cross the Potomac and take Jackson from behind, or to at least send him "five regiments by forced march and I will cross here and beat them." Something must be done, concluded Lander: "If I am to hold this place with four fords to attend to . . . the enemy will drive the men out in spite of me."[6]

Although unwilling to indulge Lander without McClellan's approval, Banks did order, on the evening of January 5, the brigade of Alpheus Williams to Hancock by forced march. In submitting Lander's proposals to McClellan, Banks argued that a precipitate crossing of the Potomac risked another Ball's Bluff; better to wait, he thought, until spring, when the Federals might "undertake the work at our own time and with full preparation." McClellan agreed. Lander tried to maintain his composure with Banks; after all, he had told a political confidant a few weeks earlier that, though not much of a soldier, Banks was a good and likable man. On the other hand, Lander's contempt for McClellan knew no bounds. Convinced that only Benjamin F. Kelley shared his aggressive spirit, Lander looked to extricate himself from Hancock and resume his journey to Romney at the earliest opportunity.[7]

As January 6 drew to a close, it appeared that Jackson would oblige him. After Lander had foiled a half-hearted Confederate attempt to ford the Potomac at Sir John's Run at sunset, the enemy opposite Hancock gave signs of withdrawing. With the element of surprise lost to him, Jackson had decided to abandon his efforts against the town, and on the morning of January 7 he turned his army. Although he had failed to capture the Union warehouses at Hancock, in burning the Big Cacapon Bridge and tearing up telegraph lines, Jackson had severed Federal communications between the Alleghenies and the Potomac. His rear was now secure for the march on Romney.[8]

That accomplishment brought little cheer to Jackson's freezing soldiers. Most would remember the march of January 7, 1862, as among the most harrowing noncombat experiences of their army service. The ordeal began at 4:00 A.M., when the drum beat assembly. Bending low against a harsh northwest wind, the men cooked their breakfasts by the uncertain flame of the campfire. Orders to pack up followed, and at 6:00 A.M. the troops fell in beside the road to Bath, where they stood for six to ten hours while the army supply train—160 wagons long—and the limbers and caisson of the artillery batteries lumbered past. The road was hilly but good. There had been a slight thaw the day before, and most of the wagon train got along all right. But as the day wore on and the wind blew harder, the tracks, worn smooth by so many wheels, froze hard.[9]

It was then the true suffering began. By a staff oversight, none of the army's horses had been rough shod. Lacking winter shoes, and almost half starved from six days of short feed, the horses proved more hindrance than help in hauling the wagons and cannons. "The men of each detachment were compelled to assist the horses to drag their guns and caissons up every hill, and were also required to assist in holding back the carriages and to prevent them from sliding sideways in going down hills," recalled Clement D. Fishburne of the Rockbridge Artillery. "There were many times when the horses would fall as they began to descend a hill, and the weight of the gun, or caisson, would push them in a heap to the foot. Then came the necessity of raising the poor horses to their feet again and of assisting them to pull their loads up the next hill." For the artillerymen, the agony of their battery horses was harder to bear than their own exhaustion. "Splotches and puddles of blood frequently marked the places where the horses fell," wrote another member of the Rockbridge Artillery; the horses "had fallen so often and had been so shoved by the carriages," said a third, "that many of them were badly scarred, and the blood had frozen over their wounds."

Although his battery was still two miles short of its assigned campsite, an appalled Captain McLaughlin called a halt at 2:00 A.M., some seven miles south of Bath. He damned Jackson's orders against dismantling fences for firewood and told his men to burn all the rails they could find. They appreciated the warmth, particularly as no one had eaten since daybreak. And with the wagon train far ahead of the battery and haversacks empty, there was no immediate prospect of a meal. All told, it was a wretched night. "I don't think I ever was more disgusted with war than then," the pious, patriotic Randolph Fairfax confessed to his mother. "We were on an exposed hill. We had no thermometers, but the cold was variously estimated at from twenty to forty degrees below zero," averred Fishburne. (The temperature never dropped below ten degrees, but the fierce northwester made for a horrific windchill factor.) "Sleep was impossible, but men sat about the fires nodding, faces begrimed with smoke, and with freezing backs. Many shoes were burnt out and many toes were frosted before daylight."[10]

Strung out along the road back toward Bath, the infantry had endured an equally agonizing day. "The march was a terrible one," remembered John Worsham of the 21st Virginia. "The road had become one sheet of ice from frequent marching over it, and the men would march in the side ditches and in the woods where it was practicable." Pioneer squads cut small trenches to give the soldiers better footing. Those who only had to march were fortunate; hundreds of infantrymen were plucked from the ranks to replace artillery horses and, with ropes and chains, haul cannons. Everyone from regimental commanders to the lowest privates cursed Jackson that day and hoped he had learned a lesson. As Maj. Frank Paxton of the 27th Virginia wrote his wife hopefully that night: "I am here in the woods, all hands froze up and waiting. I take it for granted the general will come to the conclusion from this experiment that a winter campaign won't pay, and will put us in winter quarters."[11]

But Jackson was uninterested in the hardships his men endured. He shared in the toils of the march and was often on foot, putting his shoulder to the wheel of a cannon, urging weary men forward, or rebuking officers wanting in energy. On the campaign, only the success of Confederate arms mattered; it mattered little to Jackson that the weak and sickly might succumb. As an early Jackson biographer put it, "The well-being of an individual or even of an army were as nothing compared with the interests of Virginia."[12]

And so January 8 was a day of continued suffering and confusion, as Jackson labored to consolidate his command at Unger's Store. "It was a desperate time," said acting chief quartermaster Michael C. Harman, who had to backtrack with the army trains to Unger's Store. "Sleet, snow, horses falling and braking their legs; wagons stalled and overturned, soldiers shrieking from painful, frozen wounds, men lying frozen dead in fence corners and straw stacks, with only the snow for a winding sheet—the very air breathed a frozen sound of death—all was gloom and despondency, while shoeless and bleeding feet tracked the snow."

Even Jackson recognized that men could not march indefinitely on empty stomachs in freezing weather, nor horses pull wagons without the proper shoes, and he called a halt at Unger's Store. Regiments and batteries were assigned campsites, mostly in miserable bottomland along Unger's Creek—the 5th Virginia christened its camps "Camp Mud" and "Camp No Better." Blacksmiths set to work roughening horseshoes, and teamsters to repairing their wagons. Soldiers picked lice from their filthy clothes and scrounged for food. Clement Fishburne and his battery mates of the Rockbridge Artillery robbed parched corn meant for their starving horses to make their first meal in thirty-six hours.[13]

A setback more chilling than the weather froze Jackson to Unger's Store for the next five days. As he shepherded his scattered command toward the crossroads hamlet on the night of January 7, Jackson learned from a dispatch rider that two thousand Federals from Romney had overwhelmed the seven hundred militia and cavalry stationed at Blue's Gap, the only Confederate outpost on the Northwestern Turnpike (Romney Pike). In taking the gap, the Yankees had marched fifteen miles in six hours under the same conditions that had slowed Jackson's march column to a crawl; there was no reason to doubt they could cover with similar speed the twenty-three miles that now separated them from Winchester—especially as not a single Southern soldier stood in their path.[14]

An ailing General Kelley had orchestrated the Blue's Gap raid from Cumberland. Although ill health had compelled him to remove his headquarters from Romney to Cumberland, it had not robbed him of his natural aggressiveness. When he learned of Lander's predicament at Hancock, Kelley directed Col. Samuel Dunning, in command at Romney, to move immediately against Blue's Gap in order to divert Jackson's attention and ease the threat along the Potomac.[15]

Dunning obeyed quickly. He received his orders on the evening of January 6; by one o'clock the next morning he had on the road a mixed force comprised of six companies apiece from the 14th Indiana, 1st West Virginia, and the 4th, 5th, 7th, and 8th Ohio infantry regiments, three sections of artillery, and five companies of cavalry. Opposing the Federals at Blue's Gap, or Hanging Rock Pass, as the passage through the Cacapon Mountains was also known, were three regiments of Virginia militia infantry under Col. J. Sencendiver, a handful of mounted militiamen, Capt. Wilbur E. Cutshaw's untrained Virginia battery, and a company of the 7th Virginia Cavalry under Capt. George F. Sheetz. The cavalrymen were posted ahead of the gap, with pickets thrown out beyond the west bank of North River. They passed their off-duty hours in the spacious and comfortable tavern of old "Colonel" Charles Blue, a prominent Hampshire County secessionist who also kept a mill at the gap bearing his name. The militiamen camped a few hundred feet up the road from Blue's Tavern in tents or log and brush shacks, nestled safely, so they thought, behind the steep rocky cliffs that guarded Blue's Gap. Apart from felling trees along the ridge north of the gap, the Southerners did little to improve their positions. "Blue's Gap was considered a strong position in a military sense and it was," said a trooper from Sheetz's company, "if the enemy had only kept in the road, but this, as it turned out, they failed to do."[16]

Dunning's demi-brigade gobbled up Sencendiver's advance picket posts and entered the North Mountain River Valley, opposite Blue's Gap, at daybreak. With the 4th and 5th Ohio regiments deployed as skirmishers, Dunning's command swept toward the bridge. The Yankees were across the North River before the stunned militiamen could react. Filing off the bridge and into a skirmish line again, the 4th and 5th Ohio started on the run for the ridge on either side of the gap, while the 8th Ohio led the remainder of the command up the turnpike in column.

At that moment the sole surviving picket stumbled into the militia camp gasping, "They're coming, the enemy are advancing." Colonel Sencendiver ordered the long roll beat and "to arms" sounded, but, as one of Sheetz's troopers recalled, "the fact was, few of them had arms and fewer ammunition." Panic ensued. "The bluecoats were coming down the road and through the fields in double quick, and the artillery rattling on the frozen grade like a train of empty wagons, drums beating and shouting added to the ferocity of the charge, and then came a demoralizing route that filled the timber south and east with refugees for days to come."[17]

So precipitate was the militia's flight that only two abandoned cannons and caissons, ten horses, and a few dozen discarded muskets greeted the 8th Ohio when it shoved through the gap. No Federals were killed in the affair. Perhaps half a dozen Southerners fell. Recalled William D. Landon of the 14th Indiana: "Sitting on a pine stump to rest and eat my breakfast, I caught sight of two dead Rebels lying a few yards off—one a large man, shot through the head—hole big enough to put your fist through, while the other's head was divided by a saber stroke."[18]

The courier who galloped to Jackson with news of the militia's defeat did not know that the Federals had failed to press their advantage. Colonel Dunning's orders were simply to clear Blue's Gap. Having done that, he allowed his men to take breakfast, gather spoils, and rest until early evening, then started back to Romney in the face of a fierce wind and a temperature near zero. Discipline disintegrated. "The boys got along as best they could, each on his own hook," recalled an Indiana volunteer. "Here a squad of infantry, with a knapsack or two each, strings of sausages, lengths of stove pipe, bed quilts, brooms, buckets full of honey, extra guns, chickens, turkeys, loaves of bread, and other articles too numerous to mention. I saw the skeletons of two female secesh (i.e., their hoops) dangling from the bayonet of a wild-looking volunteer."[19]

Colonel Dunning's questionable decision to burn Charles Blue's tavern and mill on the grounds that the family had harbored bushwhackers (the Federal euphemism for Virginia militia), encouraged wanton destruction on the return march. "Some crazy soldiers, encouraged by some of the officers, set fire to houses along the road, including the entire hamlet of Frenchburg—a piece of vandalism," wrote one disgusted Federal, "which should be punished with death, not only of the men who did it, but the officers who countenanced and encouraged it." General Kelley agreed, and he censored Dunning. Homeless civilians spread exaggerated tales of the destruction, claiming the poor had been burned alive in their cabins. Jackson's men assumed that the depredations represented Northern policy, and bitterness toward the "infamous defenders of the Stars and Stripes" entered their hearts. Jackson reached a similar conclusion. The Union commanders in western Virginia were reprobates, he told the Confederate War Department, "and have been apparently acting upon the principle of burning every house in which they ascertain that any of our troops have been."[20]

AT HIS HEADQUARTERS in the stately Washington Unger residence, which looked down on the Unger country store and surrounding countryside from a commanding knoll, Jackson battled anxiety and impatience in about equal measure. Although Sheetz's cavalry had reported Dunning's withdrawal from Blue's Gap promptly, Jackson could not be certain that the Federals at Romney had no designs on Winchester. Rather than withdraw, he wanted to move against Romney before Kelley was able to move against Winchester, but was constrained to wait nearly a week for his ferriers to rough shoe the horses.

Jackson availed himself of the delay to shake down his command, ridding it of officers and men whose conduct during the Bath expedition he deemed wanting. Particularly irksome to Jackson had been the timidity of the militia under fire and its lack of discipline on the march. And so on January 10 he sent General Meem off to Moorefield with 545 militiamen and General Carson to Bath with another 225. The wisdom of entrusting outpost duty to militia was doubtful. The Blue's Gap fiasco had demonstrated its reluctance to stand and fight, and Col. A. Monroe, commanding the militia detachment at Cacapon Bridge, warned Jackson that he feared he could not hold his men together much longer even in camp: "It is true that it may well be said that one's country is above all price, and that the inducements of the enemy are but a weak effort indeed toward seducing men's patriotism, but to those who are looking every day to see their houses and their all wrapped in flames and their wives and children left to perish in the snow, they are more powerful than Xerxes's armies."[21]

Jackson also faced the temporary loss of a considerable portion of his volunteer troops. Enlistments in the early months of the war had been of one year's duration; not until August 1862 would the Provisional Confederate Congress legislate three-year terms of service. Nearly a third of the volunteer regiments then in Confederate service, and all those of the Stonewall Brigade, were composed of one-year men, whose enlistments would expire in the spring. In an effort to induce reenlistments, the Confederate legislature on December 11, 1861 passed the Bounty and Furlough Act, under which one-year men willing to reenlist for two more years were offered a bounty of fifty dollars and a furlough of sixty days with transportation to and from their homes, or the money value of the trip if they did not go. In compliance with the act, Jackson authorized the granting of two-month furloughs to one commissioned officer, one noncommissioned officer, and two privates per company. He also furloughed indefinitely two popular officers of the 21st Virginia Infantry who had proved wanting—his old friend Colonel Gilham and Lt. Col. Scott Shipp, both of whom returned to the faculty of the Virginia Military Institute.[22]

Jackson sugarcoated the dismissals of Gilham and Shipp, and he wisely issued general orders praising the "courage and cheerfulness" of militiamen before sending them off. But there was no circumspection when it came to Brig. Gen. Richard B. Garnett. In a most unusual request, he asked the War Department to promote Lt. Col. Seth M. Barton of the 3rd Arkansas, a West

Point graduate whom Jackson thought "acquainted with the principles of his profession," to brigadier general and assign him command of the Stonewall Brigade. Of Dick Garnett, whose chief failing to date seems to have been a too-great solicitude for the well-being of his men, Jackson wrote:

> Whilst I am much attached to General Garnett as a gentleman possessing high social qualities, yet my duty to our country requires me to say that General Garnett is not qualified to command a brigade. Having myself been in command of his brigade up to the time of my assignment to this district, I feel justified in expressing the belief that it has no superior in our service. . . . And yet I do not feel safe in bringing it into action under the present commander, as he has satisfied me that he is not able to meet emergencies even in the proper management of his brigade in camp and on the march. Such being the case he cannot be expected to make proper dispositions of his command under fire, where unforeseen emergencies continually arise.

He added, somewhat sanctimoniously: "I am aware that in recommending that General Garnett be thus superseded, my conduct may be condemned; but I believe it to be my duty to report to the Department every change which in my opinion the interest of the public service requires."

Given the absence of specific allegations of misconduct, and the fact that Garnett had commanded the Stonewall Brigade barely a month—not to mention his standing among the Virginia aristocracy, the War Department chose to ignore Jackson's request. Garnett apparently knew nothing of Jackson's effort to unseat him.[23]

While Jackson sparred with higher authority, the officers and men under his command battled the soldier's twin enemies, filth and disease. "Due to the want of water," said a member of the Rockbridge Artillery, "or to a repugnance to the use of it, cold as it was," no one had bathed since leaving Winchester. "Many of the men had not washed even their hands and faces." A slight thaw while the army rested at Unger's Store gave the men the courage to strip off their filthy clothes. "Huge fires were built, and camp kettles full of water prepared, and though the thermometer still would have indicated a cold which was near the freezing point, a thorough cleansing was begun." As they shed their foul clothes, the men made a nauseating discovery—they were lousy. "Those parasites which the Confederate soldiers had dignified with the name of 'gray-backs' had taken up lodgings and reared families where they had never before been," wrote a disgusted Virginian. Lice had no respect for rank. "I thought it was a terrible disgrace when I found I was infected with them," recalled Captain Colston of the 2nd Virginia. "But when I found that all the other men were in the same fix, I got over that feeling." Disgust often overcame prudence. "The more provident among us scalded the offensive intruders and saved their garments for future use," Clement Fishburne remembered, "but some threw garments and intruders into the fire, trusting to the supremacy of luck for another supply of flannels."[24]

With the cold, dirt, and vermin came sickness. "This campaign is playing the wilds with us, and the sick are being carried off to the hospitals by the hundreds," a soldier of Taliaferro's brigade wrote home. "I really believe that the diseases produced by exposure since we left our camp will cause more deaths and produce more suffering than would have resulted from a hard-fought battle," Lt. Samuel J. C. Moore of the 2nd Virginia complained to his wife. "As for myself, you cannot imagine how very prudent I have become as regards taking care of my health. I spend a good deal of time in preparing my bed, so as to keep it as dry as possible; hardly ever leave my fire without wrapping up, and pay the greatest attention to keeping my feet dry."[25]

Few were as fastidious as Lieutenant Moore. Precisely how many men fell ill on the march or in camp at Unger's Store is unknown. Garnett's solicitude for his troops helped keep down losses from sickness in the Stonewall Brigade, while downright dereliction of duty nearly wrecked the brigades of Loring's army. Genuine illnesses were twice as common among Loring's men as in the Stonewall Brigade; feigned ailments were incalculably higher. Fed up with service under Jackson, an alarming number of Loring's officers encouraged their men to abandon their posts. The inspector general of the department later discovered that "hundreds who fell back to [Winchester] hospitals were found by the doctors to have nothing the matter with them at all, and they stated they were encouraged to come by their officers without medical certificates."[26] Those who remained on duty and endured the knee-deep mud, hail, sleet, and gray skies at Unger's Store—the sun had not shown since December —did so with grave misgivings. The common soldier gained no satisfaction in the knowledge that his commander was as ignorant as he was of the army's business. Lamented a Virginia private: "No one except General Jackson knows whether he accomplished the objects of the expedition or not, as he keeps his plans locked up in his own head and tells no one, not even General Loring."[27]

HAD HE KNOWN of the freedom of action his close-mouthed opponent enjoyed, General Lander undoubtedly would have sworn a blue streak of envious rage. McClellan kept him leashed tight, bringing him to heel each time he suggested an advance. When Jackson quit the Potomac on January 7, Lander beseeched General Banks to join him in pursuit of the Virginian, but Banks demurred; the risks in a winter operation were too great. Lander was incredulous. "Is not war a game of risks, are not fear and doubt states of nervous sentiment which embarrass leaders and prevent results?" he scribbled to himself. "Are we less able to penetrate the enemy's country than Jackson to penetrate ours?"

Lander laid aside these intemperate notes, but the telegram he sent McClellan, begging permission to start after Jackson, with or without Banks, was sufficiently immoderate to provoke McClellan's ire. "Say to General Lander that I might comment very severely on the tone of his dispatches but abstain," McClellan wired Banks. "Give him positive orders to repair at once to Romney and carry out the instructions I have sent already to fall back on the railway. It would be folly to cross the river at Hancock under the present circumstances." Banks forwarded McClellan's instructions to Lander, along with a parenthetical remark about Lander being "too suggestive and critical" that McClellan had not intended him to see.[28]

Lander was furious, the more so when he compared McClellan's lassitude with the pluck of General Kelley, who, in reporting the success of his Blue's Gap diversion to Lander, had asked him if he could not "be reinforced from Banks's column to any extent you may require to enable you to cross the river and act offensively?" Again Lander vented his anger at the lost opportunity in a note intended for no one, scrawling in the margin of McClellan's orders: "The country wants folly, asks for folly. . . . A demoralized enemy, starving and fearful, believing we are in force, a dark night, a snowy road, I would have stampeded the whole rearguard and burned his wagons." Instead, it became his duty to go to Romney and withdraw Kelley's victorious troops to the Potomac.[29]

CHAPTER 7

BE CAREFUL NOT TO BE CAUGHT

General Lander rode into Romney in the early morning hours of January 9, exhausted and in a foul mood. He had slept just fifteen hours in five days, had no staff, no decent maps of the area, and no real knowledge of the forces under his command. All he had were McClellan's orders that he "fall back in time [and] be careful not to be caught."[1]

Laboring mightily, Lander got the seven thousand men of his new command on the road the following evening. Their destination was the Patterson's Creek Station of the B&O Railroad, six miles east of Cumberland. A retreat seldom endears a new commander to his men, and the withdrawal to Patterson's Creek proved the rule. Bone-tired infantrymen slogging through knee-deep mud under a cold, hard rain might have endured the retreat better had there been a clear reason for it. During the night an occasional rocket seen cutting across the pitch-black eastern sky gave rise to speculation that Stonewall Jackson was about to attack in overwhelming numbers, which lent some sense to the march. But when cavalry scouts brought word at daybreak that there were no Rebels within a day's march, the men concluded that the cause of "this dilly-dallying and suffering in the flesh [was] a drunken brigadier general."[2]

Lander's actions did little to allay suspicions about his sobriety, or his sanity. He too was angry at having to inaugurate his command with a needless retreat. His anger, and the agonizing pain of his festering leg wound, triggered in Lander outbursts of gargantuan foulness. When the chaplain of the 14th Indiana inquired about arrangements to evacuate the sick, Lander snarled: "God damn you, the 14th Regiment, the whole army, everybody and everything! If I have forgotten anything, God damn it too!" Coming upon one of several swollen, swift-running creeks across the line of march, Lander whipped the Ringgold Cavalry Company, Pennsylvania Volunteers, into the torrent. Sixteen horses and four wagons were swept away in an effort to pontoon the stream. "The next time I undertake to move an army," roared Lander, "and God almighty sends such a rain, I will go around and cross hell on the ice!"[3]

Twenty-four miserable hours later, Lander's division traipsed into Patterson's Creek Station. A more woebegone site for a camp was scarcely imaginable. Three days of rain and moderating temperatures had churned the soil into paste. "It was a dreary prospect before us when we got there," said a member of the 7th Indiana, "the men tired and footsore, camp ankle deep in mud and snow, tents without floors, everything that could be imagined to render men uncomfortable." Sgt. Henry Hart of the 8th Ohio swore that "the mud which prevailed was at least six inches deep in the direst places." John W. Elwood of the Ringgold Company concluded: "This was the worst camp for man or beast that we had in all our four years and over of service. Mud is only a mild term to use in this instance."

Units unaccustomed to field duty fared poorly enough. The 29th Ohio and 67th Ohio, both of which had been guarding prisoners at Camp Chase, joined Lander's command in time to be "dumped into this camp, which was a sea of mud from torrential rains. We lived in rail pens chinked with straw." Veteran regiments nearly disintegrated. The soldiers of the 4th Ohio, which had been in continuous field service for six months, staggered about like beggars. Clothed in filthy rags, with hardly a blanket to their name, the Ohioans fell sick by the score. Parcels from home helped ameliorate the suffering; one civilian delegation contributed 134 blankets, 588 pairs of socks, 100 pairs of mittens, and 276 pairs of drawers to the regiment.[4]

NEWS THAT THE Yankees had abandoned Romney electrified Jackson. Clearly this was a miracle from God and, as such, must be acted on with all speed. Though hungry and bruised, the horses at last were rough shod, and at dawn on January 13 Jackson's army resumed its march on Romney. The Stonewall Brigade, in the lead, made nine miles before dark and bivouacked near Slane's Crossroads. Two inches of wet snow fell during the night. It continued into the day on the fourteenth, punctuated by sleet and blowing rain. Icicles formed on cap visors and hung from cartridge boxes and canteens. Wagons stuck fast in the muddy road, and morale sank lower than the wagon wheels. Epithets

Lander's command evacuates Romney. (Thomas Nast, *Harper's Weekly*, 1862)

against "Old Jackson" were freely spoken. A few Stonewall Brigade stalwarts were willing to give him the benefit of the doubt. "In the midst of the cursing and grumbling, along rides our general on Old Sorrel. Immediately the cursing stops, and all with one accord begin to cheer. He gallops by, his cap in hand and eyes to the front, his staff following him as best they can," said a Valley soldier. "Though the march was hard and toilsome, we felt that he knew what he was doing and that it was for the best."[5]

Even the most devoted must have questioned Jackson's judgment when the army reached Romney. "This place is one of the dirtiest holes any man ever came into," grumbled the normally cheerful Ted Barclay of the Liberty Hall Volunteers. "The Yankees have destroyed all the fences around the place and mined everything." "Of all the miserable holes in creation, Romney takes the lead," protested one Rebel infantryman. "[It is] a hog pen." Artilleryman Lanty Blackford concurred: "This is a dismal little place, and one which we will be happy to leave except to go upon another of these terrible marches."[6]

With no plans having been made for quartering the troops, and no one on hand to direct them, the men took it upon themselves to find shelter. Being first in town, the Stonewall Brigade got the best quarters, overrunning churches, private homes, and the courthouse. Bringing up the rear, Loring's men had to make do with stables or soggy fields outside town. "There was plenty of mud and slush," griped a soldier of the 37th Virginia. "The mountains were full of wet-weather springs, and we had to cut pine brush, pile them up over the water and mud, and then get on top to make our bed." The only consolation Loring's troops might take was in the knowledge that the Yankees had left the buildings of Romney laden with lice.[7]

For a time, it seemed that Jackson's army would leave Romney on an expedition seemingly more quixotic than the one that had just ended. Frustrated in his efforts to seize the Federal depot at Hancock, Jackson looked to capture the huge medical and other stores warehoused at Cumberland. Calculating the Federal force at Cumberland to be eleven thousand men, Jackson thought he could take the town with an additional brigade of infantry and regiment of cavalry. But Secretary of War Benjamin had no troops to send him, and so on January 17 Jackson altered his plans. Rather than move directly against Cumberland, he proposed to use Garnett's and Taliaferro's brigades to destroy the railroad bridges near New Creek Station, seventeen miles west of Romney, with the dual intent of disrupting Lander's communications west of Cumberland and threatening his flank and rear. Jackson issued marching orders for daybreak on January 18.[8]

The impracticability of the plan was apparent to the lowest private. Furloughs and illness had reduced the Stonewall Brigade to two-thirds of its former strength. Desertions had become so common that camp rumors credited entire picket details with going over to the Yankees, and the pervasive disgust with the whole Romney expedition won deserters sympathy even among those who remained true. Thoughtful chroniclers in the Stonewall Brigade such as Sgt. Maj. Randolph Barton of the 33rd Virginia and Lt. William T. Poague of the Rockbridge Artillery privately recorded their own wavering confidence in the commanding general.[9] Officers in Taliaferro's brigade, on the other hand, were outspoken in their criticism of Jackson. Maj. Frank "Bull" Paxton of the 27th Virginia, who nursed a grudge against Jackson for having first refused him a furlough and then declined his resignation, assured his wife that his men had suffered more from disease and the elements since leaving Winchester than they would have in two pitched battles. "I hope Jackson will have concluded by this time that a winter campaign is fruitful of disaster only, as it has been, and will put us at rest until spring." Capt. James K. Edmondson echoed his major's fears: "It does not become me to say so, but I am fully impressed with the belief that there is more danger of my falling prey to disease than there is of falling by the bullets of the enemy. I am fully convinced that winter campaigning will not pay. Victorious we may be. Yet after all victory is a defeat."[10]

With defeatism prevailing among the officers, Jackson could hardly expect much from the men. Reluctantly he canceled marching orders and prepared his army for winter quarters. "That Jackson was not popular with his officers and men, *even of his old brigade*, at that time is undeniable," General Taliaferro recalled years later, long after he had learned to esteem Jackson. "For the true secret of the power of the American soldier is his individuality, the natural result of American citizenship. Jackson's men thought, and thinking, did not think that the ends accomplished by the Romney campaign justified the sacrifices which were made."[11]

Had Jackson been more open about his plans and objectives, he probably would have won the support of Loring and his lieutenants, which undoubtedly would have quelled much of the dissent in the ranks. But such was not his nature. As staff officer Col. William Allan later explained: "Jackson, silent and reserved in manner, never taking counsel even with his next in command as to his plans, most rigid and exacting as a commander, had not yet acquired that wonderful control over his soldiers which a few months later would have rendered such murmuring impossible."[12]

Jackson himself was quite pleased with what he had accomplished during the campaign. "On the first of this month there was not a loyal citizen of Morgan County who in my opinion could with safety remain at home, and the same may be said respecting the most valuable portion of Hampshire County," he wrote Secretary Benjamin on January 20. "A kind Providence has restored to us the entire county of Morgan and nearly the entire county of Hampshire."[13] Expanding on the general's claims, Colonel Allan later asserted: "In two weeks, and with trifling loss, he had placed the troops opposed to him, while preparing for an aggressive movement, upon the defensive; had expelled them virtually from his whole district; had liberated three counties from their rule, and secured the supplies in them for the subsistence of his own troops."[14]

In truth, nothing Jackson had done influenced Federal plans for the region. McClellan had opted for a passive defense weeks before Jackson began the Romney expedition. Winter ice disrupted traffic along the C&O Canal far more effectively than did Jackson's "dam[n] trip." The subsistence he had secured in the South Branch Valley and the supplies he had seized in Bath and Romney were welcome but not critical to his army's well-being. Jackson had not driven the Federals from Romney; McClellan had intended for them to retire to the Potomac River for the winter. The loss of the Blue's Gap outpost to Colonel Dunning's Yankees, who showed themselves as capable of forced winter marches as Jackson's best, had partly offset the taking of Romney and demonstrated the uselessness of the Virginia militia, which constituted a third of Jackson's command. Had McClellan allowed Generals Kelley and Lander free rein, the Valley army might have ceased to exist on the wintry road to Romney. In no case were the Confederate gains worth the harm done the army's command structure.

Jackson compounded that damage when in the third week of January he decided to leave Loring's three brigades to garrison Romney and return with the Stonewall Brigade to Winchester to keep an eye on Banks. To secure Romney from surprise, Jackson distributed James Boggs's militia brigade, which had been recruited in the region, among outposts along the South Branch Valley as far south as Moorefield. (Apparently Jackson hoped that Boggs's men would perform better in their native valley than had the militia at Blue's Gap.) Three companies of cavalry under Captain Sheetz were also made available to Loring; presumably Sheetz had learned something of scouting and picket duty after his sorry showing at Blue's Gap. Carson's militia brigade was to remain at Bath, and Meem's brigade to take up post at Martinsburg. Ashby would patrol the Potomac River with the remaining companies of his command.[15]

Jackson's precautions for Loring's security ignored a fundamental consideration: Romney was all but indefensible. Jackson's own chief engineer, Lt. Col. Seth M. Barton, concluded as much. Not only the town must be held, he reported, but also the high ridges that dominated Romney on the west bank of the South Branch had to be defended, as did Fort Mill Ridge, an earthwork at the junction of the South Branch and Mill Creek, and the patchwork of hills and ravines that surrounded Romney on three sides east of the river. Barton estimated that twenty thousand men would be needed to defend Romney. As a war correspondent had observed during the Federal occupation the preceding October, "The place is so situated that it is not considered advisable to fortify it. The hills are thrown about in the wildest confusion, and no particular position will be held, as there is no one hill that is not overlooked by another." As General Lander was quick to discover, there were numerous roads by which an enemy might maneuver around Romney. Although Jackson set to work at once to establish telegraphic communications with Loring and had the high-grade Northwestern Turnpike at his disposal, at Cumberland Lander was fifteen miles closer to Romney than Jackson was at Winchester. The Potomac River was running high, but the bridges at Cumberland were intact.

Loring understood the odds against him. Scouts and spies provided him with a remarkably accurate estimate of the Federal strength in the neighborhood—6,000 troops near the depot at Patterson's Creek, eighteen miles distant; 1,500 at the Green Springs depot, nineteen miles from Romney; another

3,000 at the New Creek depot, eighteen miles away; and between 2,000 and 3,000 at Cumberland. The entire Yankee force, about 13,000 in all, could concentrate on the railroad within a matter of hours to move against Loring, who would be left to defend Romney with fewer than 5,000 men.[16]

For the Stonewall Brigade, the order to leave Romney came none too soon. At 8:00 A.M. on January 23, under dark skies that threatened snow, the men shuffled "out of little muddy Romney, no one shedding a tear," said Will Kinzer of Company L, 4th Virginia, "for none cared much for it, although to all Virginians it was 'My own, my native land.'" Ted Barclay of Company I felt sorry for those left behind. "Loring's army is very much dissatisfied with being left at Romney, and I cannot blame them, as of all the miserable holes in creation, Romney takes the lead."[17]

Months of occupation and changing hands indeed had left Romney a blighted and dreary sinkhole. Marching into town from their outlying camp-sites to occupy quarters the Stonewall Brigade had vacated, Pvt. Richard W. Waldrop of the 21st Virginia observed: "Romney looks very much as if it had been visited by an earthquake and pretty well shaken to pieces. The citizens, what few are here, don't seem to regret it much, and some of them say they hope the Yanks will burn it if they ever get here again." The foul odor of rotting beef rose from the courthouse, and the streets stank from a mix of raw sewage and "shin-deep mud." Being indoors did little to improve the humor of Waldrop and his companions. "I am at last gloriously fixed," Waldrop wrote his sister. "I am in a room with no glass in the windows, so I have to keep the shutters and door closed. There is a stove pipe-hole on each side; the stove smokes furiously, altogether rendering it so uncomfortable that loafers can't be prevailed to come near us. It suits admirably, all except the cold, smoke, and darkness."

With filth indoors and out, personal hygiene suffered in quarters as much as it had on the march. "I don't think you would know me if you could see me just now," Bull Paxton wrote his wife. "I think I am dirtier than I ever was before, and may be lousy besides. I have not changed clothes for two weeks, and my pants have a hole in each leg nearly big enough for a dog to creep through. I am afraid the dirt is sticking in, as I am somewhat afflicted with the baby's complaint—a pain under the apron." Sickness, real or feigned, soared, and during the last days of January a steady procession of coughing and feverish soldiers made their way along the Northwestern Turnpike to Winchester.[18]

Not everyone found Romney uninhabitable. John Worsham, also of the

21st Virginia, enjoyed the 25-cent buckwheat cake breakfasts at the Romney hotel and found his stay in town pleasant enough; Capt. William F. Harrison of the 23rd Virginia had a brick chimney and a good plank floor built for his tent and was "as comfortable as I desire." Good discipline could have salvaged morale among the rest, but most officers were beyond caring. Captain Harrison deplored their conduct. "Nearly all of our officers [have] left us and returned to Winchester, which is a disgrace to the Southern army. If officers fail to do their duty, what must be expected of privates?"[19]

Loring and his lieutenants saw their duty differently. Most of them considered Romney both indefensible and devoid of strategic value; many also foresaw disaster and ruin so long as they remained subject to the orders of a religious fanatic of questionable sanity and no common sense. Jackson's unwillingness to take him into his confidence continued to gall General Loring, the more so as he had joined his army to Jackson's voluntarily, and he freely expressed his displeasure to all who cared to listen.

Col. Samuel V. Fulkerson, commanding officer of the 37th Virginia Infantry, was the first to commit his doubts to paper. A conscientious and courageous leader, Fulkerson had conducted himself credibly during the disastrous western Virginia campaign the previous summer; his had been one of the few regiments to maintain good discipline and morale. A veteran of the Mexican War and former district judge, Sam Fulkerson was a man to whom people would listen. Having been a member of the Virginia Military Institute (VMI) Board of Visitors from 1852 to 1854 and again from 1857 to 1858, he also knew Jackson better than most in Loring's army. What he had seen of his former VMI colleague during the Romney campaign troubled him. And so, on January 23, as the Stonewall Brigade departed Romney, he asked Virginia congressmen Walter R. Staples and Walter Preston to use their influence to shake Loring's command free of Romney and Stonewall Jackson. "The terrible exposure since leaving Winchester has emaciated the force to almost a skeleton." And so long as the army remained in Romney, the chances of restoring it to its former vigor were nil. "We all must be impressed with the great importance of raising an army for the next summer," Fulkerson reminded the congressmen. "With the benefit of a short furlough for the men, I am satisfied that at Winchester I could have enlisted five hundred of my regiment for the war. With the present prospect before them, I do not know that I could get a single man. Still, if the men could yet be placed in a position where their spirits could be revived, many of them would reenlist for the war."

Fulkerson's brigade commander, William B. Taliaferro, added a postscript of his own to Fulkerson's letter to Staples. "I take the liberty with an old friend to state that every word and every idea conveyed by Colonel F. in his letter to you is strictly and unfortunately true. For Heaven's sake urge the withdrawal of the troops, or we will not [have] a man of this army for the spring campaign."[20]

Having thrown themselves in for a penny, Taliaferro and Fulkerson convinced their fellow officers to go in with them for a pound. On January 25 Taliaferro drafted a letter to Loring, repeating the essence of Fulkerson's arguments and enjoining him to "present the condition of your command to the War Department and earnestly ask that it may be ordered to some more favorable position." Fulkerson and six other regimental commanders cosigned the letter, as did Col. Jesse Burks, a VMI graduate who had replaced William Gilham as commander of Loring's Third Brigade. Although their men grumbled as much as did those of the Virginia regiments, neither Brig. Gen. Samuel R. Anderson nor the colonels of the three Tennessee regiments signed the petition. Loring endorsed the petition as reflecting "the true condition of this army" and asked that Secretary of War Benjamin give it every consideration. Loring not only forwarded the petition to Jackson, as protocol demanded, but he also took the highly irregular step of entrusting a copy to General Taliaferro, who was off to Richmond on furlough, to hand directly to President Davis.[21]

Taliaferro's reception at the capital was mixed. Congressman Preston gave him short shrift. Fed up with the allegations of Jackson's rashness, foolhardiness, and fanaticism already circulating in the halls of the Confederate Congress, he snapped: "It's a great pity, sir, that General Jackson has not bitten some of his subordinates on furlough and infected them with the same sort of craziness that he has himself."[22]

Taliaferro had better luck with the president, who already knew of the disaffection in the Army of the Northwest. Col. Albert Rust, whom Jackson had praised for his service at Bath, had come to Davis a few days earlier to request a transfer; he wanted nothing more to do with "that crazy preacher who marched us up and down the icy mountains to no purpose." Davis rebuffed his old friend but was more receptive when Taliaferro came calling. General Johnston, who thought Jackson should concentrate his command at Winchester, may have shared his concerns with Secretary Benjamin or the president. In any event, Davis not only accepted the petition from Taliaferro, an egregious breach of military protocol that he, as a former colonel of volunteers and secretary of war, must have understood, but he also asked Taliaferro to describe for him conditions in Romney and the location of Jackson's forces. "He did not hesitate to say at once that Jackson had made a mistake," recalled Taliaferro, "and he ordered the concentration of the troops at Winchester by telegraph that same morning."[23]

But not directly. Davis had Judah P. Benjamin transmit the orders under the latter's name. On January 30, 1862, Benjamin telegraphed Jackson curtly: "Our news indicates that a movement is being made to cut off General Loring's command. Order him back to Winchester immediately."[24]

Jackson complied—and resigned. "With such interference in my command," he wrote Benjamin the next day, "I cannot expect to be of much service in the field, and accordingly respectfully request to be ordered to report for duty to the superintendent of the Virginia Military Institute at Lexington. . . . Should the application not be granted, I respectfully request that the president will accept my resignation from the army."

In a letter to Governor Letcher, Jackson elaborated on his reasons for resigning:

> As a single order like that of the secretary's may destroy the entire fruits of a campaign, I cannot reasonably expect, if my operations are thus to be interfered with, to be of much service in the field. A sense of duty brought me into the field and has, thus far, kept me here. It now appears to be my duty to return to the institute, and I hope that you will leave no stone unturned to get me there. I desire to say nothing against the secretary of war. I take it for granted that he has done what he believes to be best, but I regard such a policy as ruinous.

Jackson mailed a similar letter to his friend, Alexander R. Boteler, Valley District representative in the Confederate Congress.[25]

Boteler hastened to Benjamin's office with the letter in hand. "In consequence of your order, Jackson has sent in his resignation," he announced.

"What! Jackson resigned! Are you sure of your information?"

"As sure as I can be of anything, for I have it here directly from himself, under his own hand and seal. Read this," said Boteler, handing him the letter.

Benjamin turned ashen. "You had better show that letter to the president." That was precisely what he intended to do, Boteler said.

"I'll not accept it, sir!" Davis told Boteler when presented with Jackson's resignation.

"I'm very glad to hear you say so, for I'm sure we cannot afford to lose him from the service. But you don't know General Jackson. When he takes a stand in accordance with his own ideas of duty, he's as firm as a rock."

Boteler called next on "Honest John" Letcher, who had not yet read Jackson's letter to him. The governor "swore a miscellaneous assortment of oaths" when Boteler told him that *his* general—for the governor had always considered Jackson as under his special care—was about to quit the army. Letcher convinced Benjamin and Davis to withhold action on the resignation until he had a chance to intercede with Jackson, and then dispatched Boteler to Winchester with a written appeal that he reconsider.

Boteler found Jackson at his new quarters in the home of the Reverend and Mrs. J. R. Graham on the evening of February 6. Outwardly calm, Jackson invited Boteler in for evening tea. While Anna Jackson sat sewing by his side, Jackson slowly read and then quietly pocketed Letcher's appeal. Later that evening, he and Boteler retired to the parlor to confer in private.

"I must resign," the general mused, "for my rule of life will not allow me to hold a position where I am no longer useful; and I am no longer useful here when what I do in the field is undone by the secretary of war. He ought to be made to understand at once that he cannot manage the details of a campaign sitting at his desk three hundred miles away." Benjamin's decision to evacuate Romney, added Jackson, enabled the Federals to bottle up the Confederates in the Shenandoah Valley. "When the spring campaign opens, the movement made in this direction will be on both flanks as well as from the front," he predicted. "They want this valley, and if the Valley is lost, Virginia is lost!"

Benjamin understood his error, interjected Boteler, and would not again meddle in Jackson's affairs. Protecting Virginia was precisely the reason Jackson must remain in command. "It is Virginia herself, through the governor, who asks you to continue in her service. It is our old mother state who makes the appeal! Will you turn a deaf ear to her solicitations?"

Jackson sat silently for a moment. Rising to leave, Boteler asked: "Well, what message am I to take back to our good friend, the governor, in answer to his letter?"

Boteler studied Jackson closely. The general's hurt was apparent. Too proud to retract his resignation directly, Jackson nonetheless yielded to the dictates of duty. Speaking slowly and pausing frequently, he said, "Tell him . . . that . . . he'll have to do . . . what he thinks best . . . for the state."[26]

It may have been well for the Confederacy that Jackson remained in the field, but it unquestionably was well for Jackson that Benjamin had ordered the Army of the Northwest out of Romney. Only a sudden, and for the Confederates fortuitous, breakdown in Frederick Lander's health had saved Jackson from perhaps irretrievable disaster.

GENERAL LANDER ASSUMED command at Cumberland determined to seize the offensive. He asked McClellan to direct Banks to cooperate with him against Jackson. Although his new command struck Lander as "more an armed mob than an army," and he was about to lose the capable Benjamin F. Kelley to convalescent leave, Lander nonetheless believed he could retake Romney handily and then join Banks, whose crossing of the Potomac he would cover from Bath in a combined movement against Winchester.

Lander appeared to have troops enough to accomplish his part of the plan. Of the 9,330 infantry available to him, 6,331 were concentrated near Cumberland on the Virginia side of the Potomac; most of the rest were parceled out in camps between Cumberland and North Branch Bridge on the Maryland side. Lander also had 1,114 cavalry at his disposal. Jackson's force was slightly smaller than Lander's. Except for the militia, which was scattered to outpost duty, it was about evenly divided between Romney and Winchester.[27]

Lander seemed fated to frustration. McClellan, rigidly adhering to the strategic defense, denied his request for a general advance on Winchester. Lander then submitted a more modest proposal, asking permission to concentrate his forces for a direct attack on Romney, while Banks made "only a show of force" at Shepherdstown to divert Jackson's attention. To this McClellan agreed, but heavy rains intervened and flooded the Potomac, preventing Lander from crossing his troops to the Maryland side. While waiting for the floodwaters to recede, Lander modified his plan further. The commander of the Maryland Home Brigade had prepared for him a new map of the region that revealed several roads of which the Federals had not been aware and by which Lander might circle around Romney and attack Loring's command from the east—an approach that Loring had feared and Jackson had ignored. McClellan approved this plan as well. To begin his movement Lander chose February 3—the very day that the first of Loring's brigades was to withdraw from Romney.

The auguries appeared to favor the Federals. Sunday, February 3, dawned clear. The temperature stood at thirty degrees—good marching weather. At noon Lander led his division out of Camp Kelley to board trains that would take it to the French's Store depot for the first leg of its march. A quarter mile out of camp, recall was sounded. General Lander had collapsed, wracked by intense pain and violent chills. While doctors struggled to diagnosis Lander's sudden illness, Loring slipped quietly out of Romney.[28]

LORING'S MEN MET with a cold reception at Winchester. The sick and malingerers who preceded them had slandered Jackson freely, and with effect. Recalled Lt. John N. Lyle of the 4th Virginia: "The untaught and unthinking among the citizens [of Winchester], listening to the malcontents, criticized Jackson, saying that he was insane, cruel, reckless, and full of inhumanity to expose his soldiers in campaign during the severity of winter." When the healthy troops of Loring's army strode into camp dispensing similar criticism, the men of the Stonewall Brigade responded with their fists; the Stonewall Brigade, said Lieutenant Lyle, "reserved to itself the exclusive right to cuss 'Old Jack.'" Jackson's abortive resignation added to their outrage. "There is but one feeling with us—that of perfect devotion to General Jackson. But if he is to be run down, our spirit is utterly broken," Capt. Hugh H. White told his father. "It was through the complaints of Loring's command that the secretary of war caused [Jackson's] resignation, and the men hated them," added Lieutenant Lyle. "So indignant were they at the prospect of losing their beloved commander that to fight Loring and his whole division would have delighted them as much as a battle with the Yankees." Loring's men gave as good as they got, especially the western troops. Said a soldier of the 21st Virginia, "The Jacksonians are terribly afraid of the Tennesseans, who suffer no opportunity of 'running' them to pass unimproved."[29]

As latecomers, Loring's troops were dealt the least desirable campgrounds. "It is not often in such a camp as ours that one can during winter find the time and place at which with even a little comfort to write at all," Virginian A. C. Chamberlayne scribbled to a friend. "There is but one chair in the regiment, one attempt at a table, and scarcely a half dozen tents that boast a stove or fireplace, so that we are much dependent upon the weather and at best must crouch around a pile of smoky logs in the open or shiver in a tent. During one windstorm four-fifths of the tents were prostrated and left us shivering."[30]

In a psychological sense, Loring's men were no closer to Winchester in their new quarters at Camp Zollicoffer than they had been in Romney. Captain Edmondson found the camp to be "one of the most lonesome places we have ever been at. It is stuck down under a large hill or mountain some distance from any public road, and although not more than five miles from town it seems, and I feel, to be a hundred miles from everywhere." Those five miles seemed insurmountable, the pious young Randolph Fairfax of the Rockbridge

Artillery told his parents, because headquarters had "a miserably restricted way of getting passes." Only five men a day per company were allowed passes to visit Winchester, and it took the better part of the morning to obtain the necessary signatures, including the countersignature of General Garnett, who attended to such business only between the hours of 9:00 and 10:00 A.M. Passes expired at 4:00 P.M.. "Considering that you have to walk four miles and back gives you very little time for enjoyment," complained Fairfax. "Really it seems to me that every obstacle is thrown in the way of the enjoyment of the poor private, and the few privileges they have seem to be surrounded with every possible difficulty. I am sure there is no field Negro that has not more liberty than we have, but I ought not to complain, as I suppose it is all a 'military necessity.' "[31]

Not that Winchester afforded much in the way of attractions. The town was awash in suffering. On January 30 the medical director of the Valley District, Dr. Hunter McGuire, reported 1,163 sick hospitalized in Winchester. Although he dismissed a fair percentage as healthy shirkers and calculated that the great majority of legitimate cases were "catarrhal and rapidly convalescing," the mere presence in Winchester of so many hospitalized men requiring at least a modicum of care exceeded the resources of McGuire's department and placed a tremendous strain on the town's economy. "Our town has become a complete hospital," the young Unionist Julia Chase recorded in her diary in late January. "If there is as much sickness where the soldiers are as in this part of the country, the whole South must become or is a complete hospital." Overburdened military authorities appealed to the citizenry for help. District headquarters took out advertisements in Valley newspapers asking "country ladies to send milk (sweet milk and buttermilk) for our sick soldiers in the hospitals. Those who have no other way can bring a jugful in their carriages on the Sabbath."[32]

The citizenry, however, had its own sick to look after. An outbreak of scarlet fever and typhoid ravaged Winchester during January and February, carrying off children and the elderly in large numbers. Julia Chase recorded the deaths of a half-dozen children a week from scarlet fever, which doctors told her was "raging like wildfire," and it seemed as if every family lost at least one loved one to illness. High prices and critical shortages compounded the misery. There was no gas for heating homes, and soldiers had stripped the forests of firewood. Competing for food with army contractors and with the scores of army wives who descended on Winchester, mothers found it hard to feed themselves or their children properly. Butter cost fifty cents a pound.

There was no tea, coffee, or molasses to be found at any price. A neighbor of Julia Chase sent off to Richmond for a pound of saffron and paid forty-five dollars. "Whoever heard of such prices," lamented Chase. "It is extravagant prices we are paying for everything a well man needs and ruinous prices for what the sick require. When our money fails, we will be in a terrible condition surely."[33]

The number of soldiers competing with the townspeople for food dropped sharply in mid-February, when the War Department intervened to separate the warring factions in Jackson's camp. On February 9 President Davis nominated William Loring for promotion to major general in recognition of his service in the Romney campaign and transferred him to Georgia. A week later the 1st Tennessee and 1st Georgia regiments were ordered to Tennessee, and the 7th and 14th Tennessee regiments were reassigned to Johnston's army at Manassas.[34]

Jackson had no regrets over Loring's departure but believed he should have been cashiered from the army, rather than promoted to a backwater command. Lest there be any doubt where he stood, Jackson preferred charges of neglect of duty and "conduct subversive of good order and military discipline" against Loring. Jackson's pique over the Romney petition was the driving force behind the charges. General Johnston thought the charges ought to be aired before a court-martial, but President Davis demurred; he could hardly sanction a court-martial against a general whom he had just recommended for promotion. Although he did concede that the Romney petition, which he had accepted from the hand of General Taliaferro, "should have been sent through the prescribed channel of correspondence," Davis ordered that the matter be dropped.[35]

Leaves of absence granted under the Bounty and Furlough Act reduced troop strength in the Valley District further. In the long term these furloughs were for the best, as they encouraged a brisk rate of reenlistment in the Valley regiments. John Hite of the 33rd Virginia recorded in his diary on February 9 that twenty members of his company had reenlisted; Thomas Smiley of the 5th Virginia wrote home two days later that ten men in his company had reenlisted for the duration of the war, "and more of them talk of doing so." An encouraging number of men from the Virginia regiments of Loring's former command also reenlisted. But in the short term furloughs threatened Jackson's capacity to maintain even a credible defensive posture. Furloughs, recruiting details, and absence for illness reduced most regiments to 50 percent strength. The February return for the 42nd Virginia, for instance, showed 131 officers and men absent on leave and another 176 in hospitals; the regiment counted just 345 troops present, as opposed to 344 absent. The total strength of the Valley District for February was 6,404 present and 7,355 absent.[36]

The probability of an early Federal offensive made those numbers particularly troublesome. Confederate scouts and spies brought word of troop buildups on the north bank of the Potomac, and reported that the Yankees had nearly completed repairs on the Big Cacapon railroad bridge. Banks had begun the month with 18,000 effectives and would end it with nearly 23,000. A seemingly recuperated Lander was shifting his forces from the mouth of Patterson's Creek twenty-two miles east to the Paw Paw railroad tunnel, leading Jackson to conclude that an advance of his and Banks's divisions was in the offing. Jackson told Johnston he needed at least 9,000 troops to hold the Lower Valley against a combined onslaught; where such troops might come from was anyone's guess.[37]

THE MALADY THAT struck General Lander so suddenly was not, as some uncharitable spirits in the ranks assumed, delirium tremens or drunkenness, but rather the onset of sepsis. Bacteria had invaded his body through his unhealed leg wound and penetrated the soft tissue of his bones. Lander was dying, and he knew it. From his sickbed he closed a rambling letter to Secretary of the Treasury Salmon P. Chase about his supply and transportation problems. "But as I am dying, my health gone, I fear, for all time—why complain?"[38]

Lander determined to make the most of his remaining days. Alternating between bed and the telegraph room, he oversaw the reoccupation of Romney by Col. Nathan Kimball's brigade on February 6. When he learned that Loring had escaped, Lander pulled Kimball back to Paw Paw Tunnel, where, on cleared and comfortably dry high ground, he intended to concentrate his division. The men welcomed the change from muck-ridden Camp Kelley, and Lander's spirits rose as well. "Now look at this campaign," he proudly wrote Secretary Chase (for whom he named the Paw Paw camp) on February 8: "I hold the Baltimore road to Big Cacapon Bridge. I hold the entire country south from Romney to [the] Big Cacapon."[39]

Having reopened the railroad in his district, Lander decided to test Jackson's strength. Colonel Dunning provided the first opportunity when he telegraphed Lander from New Creek Station requesting permission to march on Moorefield, forty miles south of Romney, and capture a large herd of beef cattle grazing there under the marginally watchful eye of the Hardy County militia. Lander concurred enthusiastically—a beef shortage had been among his complaints to Secretary Chase—and Dunning set out on February 10 with a mixed command of 1,400 troops to break up the "guerrilla haunt" at Moorefield. After some ineffectual skirmishing with Dunning's advance, the Hardy County militia—the same force that Jackson had counted on to protect Loring's left flank when he left that general to occupy Romney—fled into the hills beyond Moorefield. Dunning was disappointed to find that most of the cattle had been driven elsewhere the day before, but he and Lander were pleased to have cleared the South Branch Valley of Rebels.[40]

Lander wanted to do more, and quickly, before death overtook him. No longer did he care whom he offended. Caught in a downward spiral of fever, chills, and bone-snapping pain, Lander "goddamned to Hell" the souls of anyone under his command who displeased him and, when not sedated with morphine, scribbled blistering telegrams berating both his army colleagues and his superiors, civilian and military. The lassitude of McClellan, Banks, and Williams, coupled with the apparent indifference of the War Department to his ordnance and supply needs, infuriated him, and he told Secretary of War Stanton as much. "The orders of weak men" were a greater hindrance than the acumen of the enemy. "General Williams is an ass, General Banks is a failure. With faith in God and the American Republic I will beat the enemy forces with half their numbers. My enemy is your department, not in front. You will regard this as disrespectful; I hope you may. I am not here for promotion or emolument."

Perhaps he might shame Banks and Williams into action with another demonstration of his own aggressiveness. On February 12 he decided to eliminate the only remaining enemy presence in his district: four woefully understrength militia regiments under the luckless Col. J. Sencendiver (of the Blue's Gap debacle) posted at Bloomery Furnace, an iron-ore operation and hamlet tucked between two mountain passes on the Winchester Turnpike, fourteen miles south of Paw Paw Tunnel. The major pass, called "Bloomery Gap," was a water gap a mile west of the furnace. Through it the Little Cacapon River meandered on its northward course. A mile east of the furnace, "Bloomery Run Gap" cradled both Bloomery Run and the turnpike. Lander would be operating on Jackson's doorstep. Unger's Store lay only eight miles east of Bloomery Furnace; Winchester was another nineteen miles to the south. In clearing Bloomery Furnace, Lander would remove both a bushwhacking menace from his district (Federal commanders and their troops equated militia with guerrillas) and the only serious impediment to Williams crossing the Potomac. He would lead the expedition himself. "I detest the quibbles and fears of West Point always thrust under my nose," he wrote before setting out. "I go where the word can't is continuously introduced."[41]

At 4:00 P.M. on February 13, the six regiments of Colonel Kimball's First Brigade formed on the parade ground at Camp Chase, with blankets slung, two-days' cooked rations in their haversacks, and no idea of their destination. Lander rode out of camp with his staff and a two-company cavalry escort; four hours later, word came for the infantry to take up the march. Lander had summoned the remainder of his cavalry—the 1st Virginia (Union) regiment and three detached companies—from outpost duty along the Potomac the day before, but these units were still several hours away.[42]

For the infantry, the going was hard from the start. Temperatures in the mid-fifties had melted much of the snow blanketing the mountain country and muddied the Winchester Turnpike. Shortly after sunset the column filed to the left onto a miserable country road, barely wide enough for two men to walk abreast, that led to the Big Cacapon River. A three-and-one-half-mile climb through muck and over scattered patches of ice took them to the summit of Sideling Hill, high above the river. "An awful hill," remembered Capt. Marcus Spiegel of the 76th Ohio, "high rocks and scattered pine and spruce trees, and on the other side the grandest precipice down, down, as far as men could see, with an awful rolling of water . . . a romantic and fearful sight."[43]

Captain Spiegel had only a moment to contemplate the scene before Lander ordered his regiment and the 13th Indiana back to the turnpike. He wanted them to seal off Bloomery Gap from the west before dawn. The remainder of the command picked its way down the eastern slope of Sideling Hill, halting in the deep, dark river valley for a welcome respite while Maj. John Frothingham and his engineer corps puzzled over how best to bridge the swollen waters of the 180-foot-wide Big Cacapon. At 10:30 P.M. Frothingham reported the task impossible with the means at hand. Lander's reaction was predictable. Lounging beside their campfires, soldiers of the 8th Ohio eavesdropped as the general "stormed, swore, and out-roared the roaring flood." Lander had hoped to strike the Rebels before daylight. Seven miles of hard marching remained once they cleared the river; haste was imperative. Much to Frothingham's relief, John Fuller, wagon master of the 8th Ohio, stepped forward with a solution. He had done engineering work for a circus before the war and thought he could pontoon the river in an hour. Lander told him to try. Recalled an amused subaltern of the regiment who watched the proceedings: "[Fuller] hitched a good stout span of mules to a wagon tongue with plenty of ballast in the wagon, and drove through the river to the opposite bank, and then detaching the mules, another and another wagon hauled and left tandem, until the river was spanned, when boards were thrown on top." One hour stretched into four, but the troops got over and at 2:30 A.M. resumed the march, less the artillery, ambulances, and supply wagons, which Lander judged unable to negotiate the tortuous mountain path that led the rest of the way to Bloomery Furnace.[44]

Wading through knee-deep mud "as stiff as well-worked mortar," the infantry was two miles short of Bloomery Furnace at first light on February 14. Dimly visible on the horizon, tucked in a bend of Bloomery Run a few hundred feet east of the gap, was a cluster of shacks. In them, scouts assured Lander, the officers of the militia guarding the gap were quartered. Also visible were Southern pickets falling back toward the furnace, threatening to rob Lander of the element of surprise.

The timely arrival of the cavalry spared Lander's officers another of the general's outbursts. At the head of the column rode the colonel of the 1st (Union) Virginia Cavalry, Henry Anisansel. A Swiss immigrant who had taught music and dance in Pennsylvania before the war, Anisansel was derided by his American colleagues as "one of the foreign adventurers who so largely officered our army at its beginning and were absolutely useless for any purpose except to draw their pay and wear gold braid."[45]

And to exasperate their commanding officers. Swinging onto the road ahead of Anisansel, Lander led the cavalry galloping down the road—or so he thought. When he drew rein among the shacks, which were empty, Lander found himself alone except for his staff and a few troopers from his personal escort. A startled miller told him that Colonel Sencendiver had withdrawn to a spot two miles east of Bloomery Run Gap a few hours earlier. Anisansel came up. Lander barked him an order to charge through the gap after the Rebels and then retired to a nearby house to set up headquarters.

Anisansel's notion of a charge was a slow trot, followed by a dead halt at the gap, where a sharp bend in the road obstructed the view beyond. As he waved skirmishers forward, Anisansel told Capt. Nathan Menkin of the 1st Ohio Cavalry that he intended to wait for the infantry before pressing ahead with the main body. A disgusted Menkin sent a man back to Bloomery Furnace to apprise Lander of the holdup.

Lander erupted at the news. Riding with his staff to the head of the column, he bellowed at each company they passed, "Why in hell and damnation don't you charge?" Only the commanding officer of Company A, 1st Ohio Cavalry, responded, pulling his men from the column and falling in with Lander. Most company officers simply shrugged, and one startled captain gestured mutely at Anisansel. Ohio trooper Sam Gillespie overheard the exchange between Lander and Anisansel. "Why in the hell did you stop?" Lander demanded, ignoring the scattered firing of Confederate skirmishers just sixty yards away. Anisansel stammered that he was waiting for infantry support. He would not give one regiment of cavalry for ten regiments of infantry, Lander snarled. Firing his pistol in the air, Lander yelled that he would shoot any man who lagged behind. Calming a bit, he implored, "My men, my men, what are you staying here for? Come ahead and follow me! Charge!" Without tarrying to see the result of his appeal, Lander spun his horse around and galloped through the gap. Veering to the left, he spurred on toward Col. Robert F. Baldwin, who, with four other officers, was trying to deploy the 31st Virginia militia along a hillside four hundred yards away in order to enfilade the Union cavalry when it debouched through the gap. When just a few dozen yards from the cluster of Rebel officers, Lander realized that only five men had followed him, three of whom were members of his staff. Anisansel and his troopers remained glued to the gap.

Fortunately for Lander, Colonel Baldwin took him at his word when he announced, "Surrender, Gentleman, you are completely surrounded and cut off." As Baldwin and his companions handed their swords to the general, their leaderless militiamen peppered Lander's party from behind rocks and bushes. Gradually Company A, 1st Ohio Cavalry, worked its way through the gap. Taking heart, three other companies squeezed past the 1st (Union) Virginia Cavalry.[46]

Once again the militia demonstrated its unreliability, scattering the instant the Ohio troopers started up the hill. "I, lone-handed, took in six miserable guerrillas, who were huddled together behind a big stone, with their guns ready to fire," recalled John Dickey of Company A. "But I got the drop on them, when they stacked their arms, and Myram Judy and I marched them in to General Lander." Lander crisscrossed the slope, pausing here and there to help round up prisoners. An Ohio private waved the general down to help him disarm a recalcitrant militia officer. "He says he will never give his sword to a Yankee," complained the private. Lander dismounted and, shaking the officer by the shoulders, growled, "Then you'll give it to me!" The frightened Rebel unbuckled his sword and handed it to Lander. "If you find another man like this," Lander told the trooper as he remounted, "don't multiply words with him."

Lander had no compunction about shooting his own men either. Discharging a round at skulking cavalrymen, Lander warned, "The next time I'll hit you, and if you don't clear the road, this regiment shall deploy and fire upon you!"[47]

Whatever the wisdom of a division commander and five hangers-on charging two regiments of infantry, Lander's audacity delighted many. "General Lander is a trump," an Ohio infantry private wrote his parents. "He took a colonel and four other prisoners!" But not everyone agreed. Many in the truant cavalry thought Lander's histrionics were alcohol-induced. "Colonel Anisansel [had] halted his command in order to feel the enemy as a careful man should. While he was doing this, General Lander came up at full charge, drunk, cursing and damning, and put Colonel Anisansel under arrest for cowardice. There was no braver man than Colonel Anisansel. He simply did his duty to himself and men," asserted the historian of the Ringgold Cavalry. "I think Lander had snakes in his head when he made the attack," Pvt. Aungier Dobbs of the same company wrote home, "and Anisansel behaved general-like."[48]

At long last Anisansel got into the fight, coming upon the 51st and 89th Virginia militia regiments another three hundred yards down the road, only to suffer a fall from his horse that aggravated a hernia and knocked him senseless. His regiment retreated with a loss of two killed and three wounded. Colonel Kimball pushed past the cavalry with the 14th Indiana and 7th (Union) Virginia Infantry. Together they broke the Confederate resistance, gathering up several Rebel supply wagons that Anisansel's cavalry had overrun.

Indianan William D. Landon took stock of the carnage. The bitter wails of a small boy for his dead brother and captured father left Landon unmoved. "His brother, like all these bushwhackers, had fired on our men and then undertook to save his cowardly life by throwing away his gun and running into a house, but an Enfield bullet had overtaken him in his flight." Landon found the lamentations of two women no more compelling. "The wife and mother of a secesh captain of bushwhackers, [they] were filling the air with their cries of despair and grief over his body—refusing to surrender his weapons when twice called upon to do so. A cavalryman had nearly severed him in twain by a blow from his saber."[49]

While Landon jotted down his impressions (he was writing for his hometown newspaper), Col. Samuel S. Carroll came up with the 8th Ohio Infantry. Lander urged him to continue the pursuit. "Go on," he said to Carroll, "we need you now—clean them out and take their baggage." The Ohio colonel did just that, chasing the militia eight miles to Unger's Store, the limit of Lander's district. Carroll returned to Bloomery Furnace at 1:00 P.M. Two hours later Lander started his command, along with sixty-five prisoners, seventeen of whom were officers, on the return march to Paw Paw Tunnel. Weary troopers dozed in their saddles, and footsore infantrymen staggered through "the deepest mud you almost ever saw." By midnight they were back in camp. "You had better believe that we were a tired set when we stopped," said an Indiana officer. "Within a period of less than thirty hours the regiment marched forty-five miles, crossed the great Cacapon River on a bridge of wagons, broke up the Rebel camp, and helped capture nearly a hundred prisoners."[50]

None were more exhausted than General Lander. Before falling into a morphine-induced sleep, he wired McClellan news of both the Bloomery Gap action and Dunning's Moorefield raid. "As the work instructed to me may be regarded done and the enemy out of this department, I most earnestly request to be relieved. My health is too much broken to do any severe work." By way of postscript, Lander added, "General Williams can move over the river without risk."

McClellan admonished Lander: "Your conduct is just like you. Don't talk about resigning. If your health makes it necessary for you to be relieved, of course you shall be." He added, temptingly, "I advise, in view of probable movements, that you quietly rest at Cumberland and endeavor to recruit your health before making another move." Probable movements? Was McClellan tempting a dying man with false promises of an advance on Winchester? His record suggested as much.[51]

A congratulatory telegram from Stanton two days later gave Lander greater hope: "The president directs me to say that he has observed with pleasure the activity and enterprise manifested by yourself and the officers and soldiers of your command. You have shown how much may be done in the worst weather and worst roads by a spirited officer, at the head of a small force of brave men, unwilling to waste life in camp when the enemies of their country are within reach. Your brilliant success is a happy presage of what may be expected when the Army of the Potomac shall be led to the field by their gallant general."[52]

Stanton's telegram was as much thinly veiled criticism of McClellan as it was praise of Lander, but it delighted the ailing general just the same. Enjoying acclaim at McClellan's expense, Lander assured Stanton that he was ready to take the field again: "Give me, sir, men and means, orders to go on, without complimenting for minor successes. Hold me strictly responsible for failure. I am never so sick as when I cannot move."[53]

CHAPTER 8

DANGERS CLOSE US

ROUND ON EVERY SIDE

General Lander was correct in dismissing his victory as a "minor success." The Bloomery Gap affair hardly entered the consciousness of a Southern leadership preoccupied with calamities. The month of February saw a numbing string of strategic defeats that brought the entire Western theater to the verge of collapse. On February 6 Fort Henry on the Tennessee River fell. Outflanked, the Confederates evacuated Bowling Green, Kentucky, on the fifteenth. Fort Donelson on the Cumberland River surrendered the same day. Nashville was lost on February 26, and the evacuation of Columbus, Kentucky, began the next day. Sandwiched between these reversals were the Federal capture of Roanoke Island, North Carolina, and the Confederate evacuation of Lexington, Missouri. In three short weeks, Union troops had overrun Kentucky, Missouri, and the greater part of Tennessee. Along the Atlantic seaboard the North had demonstrated its capacity to carry out amphibious operations at places of its choosing with near impunity, while the blockade slowly choked the life out of the Southern economy. No European power had espoused the Confederate cause, and with only 40,000 troops near Manassas Junction to oppose the inevitable advance of McClellan's 155,500-man leviathan, it appeared to many thoughtful European observers that there might soon be no Confederacy to recognize. Faced with the prospect of imminent defeat, the Confederate Congress took up a measure that would have seemed unthinkable six months earlier; it was the supreme irony for a people in rebellion against centralized authority and enamored of states' rights—a conscription act to keep armies in the field past spring.

It was against this somber backdrop that President Davis wrote General Johnston on February 28, reminding him of his decision, taken in consultation with the cabinet and Johnston a week earlier, to withdraw the army closer to Richmond before McClellan began his spring offensive. With the reminder, Davis threw in a bit of gratuitous counsel: "Recent disasters have depressed the weak and are depriving us of the aid of the wavering; traitors show the tendencies heretofore concealed, and the selfish grow clamorous for local and personal interests. At such an hour the wisdom of the trained and the steadiness of the brave possess a double value." Continued Davis, "The military paradox, that impossibilities must be rendered possible, had never better occasion for application."

Davis intended that Jackson apply that paradox as well to the defense of the Shenandoah Valley, which in light of recent reverses had lost some of its former importance in the president's calculations. Davis had just received a request from Jackson for reinforcements, along with a warning that the Federals appeared ready to move against Winchester in force. "It is unnecessary for me to say that I have not the force to send, and have no other hope of his reinforcement than by the militia of the Valley," Davis told Johnston. "Anxious as heretofore to hold and defend the Valley, that object must be so pursued as to avoid the sacrifice of the army now holding it or the loss of the arms in store and in use there."[1]

Endless days of unrelenting hail, snow, and sleet—fourteen at one stretch—pounded the prevailing gloom into men's souls just as it pounded the Virginia countryside into paste. "Pitchy dark nights, dismal days, the whole earth one mud hole, wagons and teams rapidly going to wrack and ruin. There seems to be a more general feeling of despondency at this time than ever before since the war began." In Richmond, Robert G. H. Kean, the head of the Confederate Bureau of War, scribbled in his diary: "Dangers close us round on every side. The timid will begin to croak, the half-hearted to quail and suggest submission, the traitorous to agitate."[2]

In the Shenandoah Valley, civilians tried to make sense of the often conflicting but invariably discouraging news. To one Valley physician, the Western setbacks and the Roanoke Island fiasco seemed the only topics of conversation. The Valley press did its best to minimize the recent misfortunes, while also enjoining readers to greater efforts on behalf of the Confederacy. "To say that there is a possibility of our subjugation, we cannot believe," editorialized the *Winchester Republican*. "But if, sanguine of success, we slumber, while the enemy surrounds us on all sides, they may secure a foothold from which it may require years of toil and thousands of lives and treasures to dispossess them." The editors of the *Staunton Spectator* proclaimed: "We are not disposed to take a gloomy view of the seemingly sad reverses with which our arms have recently met. We do not feel discouraged by them; on the contrary, we believe that they will eventually result in good to the cause of the South. . . . These reverses are but the thunderclaps which are necessary to arouse the giant of Southern energy from its false repose."[3]

However much the manful words of newspapermen might cheer civilian readers, there were a considerable number of Valley soldiers on whom hopeful admonitions had no effect. Hundreds crossed the lines; so many, in fact, that General Banks found the cost of transporting them to Washington nearly prohibitive. Those who stood fast were wracked with doubt. "A considerable snowstorm has been blowing over the mountain last night and today," Cpl. James E. Hall of the 31st Virginia recorded in his diary on February 12. "The air is about as cold as they make it. We heard that our forces were defeated again, now at Roanoke Island. An opportunity was presented today to reenlist. I did not accept." Two day later Pvt. Richard W. Waldrop of the 21st Virginia told his father, "We have just had a muster to ascertain how many men of our company would reenlist, and the number is just none."

Some resolved to fight harder and complain less. Hugh A. White of the Liberty Hall Volunteers assured his younger brother that "the recent disasters have not discouraged but aroused the army, and they are more anxious to do something to redeem our cause than ever." Sandie Pendleton was "thoroughly disgusted, not disheartened. What could have possessed our generals at Fort Donelson? Are they demented? I hope we may hear of no more surrender, but of bloody fighting, deadly and worthy of the cause. What difference do a few hours more or less here of life make in comparison with the future destiny of the people?" John Hampden "Ham" Chamberlayne of the 21st Virginia was undismayed. He believed that the recent defeats, which stemmed from "overconfidence and vainglory," had come opportunely, "before the weather let the enemy avail himself of them in any quarters and in time to rouse our people, especially those who stay at home and wring their hands crying all is lost."[4]

The patriotic spirit of soldiers like Chamberlayne was contagious; a week after his downcast Valentine's Day letter home, Private Waldrop saw matters in a decidedly brighter light. "The Yankees seem to be having everything pretty much their own way at present, which I think is providential for us, as these reverses must have the effect of keeping most of the present army in the field and inducing a great many others to enter the field. If we put forth our whole strength and go safely through the approaching spring, I hope there will be some good reason for expecting an early termination of our troubles." As for himself, he would stay for the time being. "I begin to feel as it would be almost a disgrace for me to go home when my time expires, unless the tide of success should change and we win some important victories."[5]

There was little ambivalence of feeling among the thirty thousand Union soldiers camped near the Valley, most of whom thought the war all but won. "I think there is nothing more for us to accomplish here," Lt. David E. Beem of the 14th Indiana wrote his fiancée confidently from Camp Chase. "The recent success of our armies in Kentucky, Missouri, and on the Southern coast leads me to believe that the war will be ended before long." Celebrations were the order of the day. "Was not that a great victory at Fort Donelson?" a Michigan cavalryman with Banks's division asked his sister. "Our whole regiment came out by companies on their respective parade grounds with their revolvers loaded and fired six rounds in honor of the event. A few more such victories and the South will be subdued."[6]

President Lincoln meant to do everything within his power to see the war brought to the prompt and victorious close that the men in ranks expected. First and foremost, that meant getting General McClellan to move. When given command of the Army of the Potomac in October 1861, McClellan had agreed to a direct advance against Manassas, such as McDowell had attempted, as soon as conditions were favorable. But as the weeks passed, McClellan lost his nerve. Supposing Johnston to have 150,000 "well drilled and equipped, ably commanded, and strongly entrenched" troops at Manassas, rather than the 40,000 poorly trained and indifferently equipped volunteers then under arms, McClellan searched for an alternative. After his elevation to general in chief in November, McClellan began to talk vaguely of a grand turning movement to throw Johnston back upon Richmond, where he would fight one decisive battle to decide the outcome of the war. McClellan identified Urbana, a port near the mouth of the Rappahannock River, as his base of operations, from which he would march overland to seize West Point, the terminus of the Richmond and York River Railroad. McClellan expected to use the railroad to support his drive on Richmond. He also expected that the capture of Urbana and West Point would compel the Confederates to abandon the Lower Peninsula. That would open the York and James rivers to the Union navy, securing his flanks and ensuring him well-protected water and rail supply lines.

Actual planning did not match the grandeur of McClellan's strategic thought. He did little during the winter to assemble the ships needed to transport the army, and he neglected to keep either the president or the secretary of the navy apprised of his intentions. Confronted with uncertainty and fortified with the counsel of disinterested generals who favored the Manassas plan, President Lincoln on January 31 issued Special War Order No. 1, which instructed McClellan to march against Johnston at Manassas on or before February 22. When McClellan balked, Lincoln permitted him to submit arguments in favor of his Urbana scheme. In a long and meandering memorandum on February 3, McClellan finally provided details of his plan, which promised "the most brilliant result." While doubting he could beat Johnston at Manassas, McClellan regarded success on the Peninsula as "certain by all the chances of war." He concluded: "I will stake my life, my reputation on the result—more than that, I will stake upon it success of our cause." Lincoln relented. He laid aside his plan—or rather, the plan McClellan had agreed to implement in October—in favor of this new grand strategy.[7]

What all this meant for the Shenandoah Valley was unclear. Lander wanted to move (it had cost McClellan considerable effort throughout the winter to hold him in check), and in mid-February Banks signaled himself both ready and eager to advance. "On our side," he assured McClellan on February 11, "it may be said our men are healthy, well clothed, pretty well armed, with a sharp appetite for work." Six days later he repeated that assurance to Stanton, noting that his men had a "*very* sharp appetite for work . . . hard work."

Unlike McClellan, Banks was not deluded by false reports or his own fears into exaggerating the enemy's numbers. He and David Strother had assembled an excellent network of civilian spies, among whom were white Unionists and free blacks from the Lower Valley and the occasional runaway slave. Both Jackson's strength and the disaffection the Romney expedition had engendered were well known to Banks and Strother. As Banks assured McClellan:

> No important results whatever were obtained by him [Jackson] at any point on our lines to compensate for the suffering and loss of his men, and the consequence has been great discontent among men and quarrels among officers, ending in the tender of his resignation by General Jackson. The enemy was never in a feebler condition than at this time. His

force is chiefly in the vicinity of Winchester and beyond. The reports of large detachments near Charlestown and Harpers Ferry are greatly exaggerated, in my belief.

Banks was certain that he and Lander, working in concert, could occupy both Winchester and Leesburg before March 1.[8]

With his own preparations for the Urbana expedition lagging, and under growing pressure from the Lincoln administration to do something before the end of February, McClellan consented to Banks's request to cross the Potomac. Ever victim to his innate caution, McClellan decided to reinforce Banks with two brigades from the division of Brig. Gen. John Sedgwick, which would cross after him, and to limit the operation's objective to reopening the B&O Railroad in the neighborhood of Harpers Ferry. Even that would depend on the ability of the army's engineers to fashion a permanent bridge of pontoon boats across the river. Should the engineers fail, which McClellan thought likely, Banks was simply to occupy the Maryland shore opposite Harpers Ferry until the railroad bridge could be repaired, after which McClellan would consider an advance on Winchester. To ensure that there was no misunderstanding his intention, McClellan would supervise the crossing himself.[9]

McClellan took particular care to restrain Lander. He was to hold his command at Paw Paw until Banks's crossed the Potomac; keep his men "perfectly in hand, and be ready for a spring," as McClellan put it. "I wish to make this move carefully, and to ensure success," he added, which of course mitigated against any sort of "spring." Once Banks was over, Lander was to shift his division east of Hancock in order to cover repairs to the railroad from Hancock to Harpers Ferry.[10]

Banks assembled his forces promptly. Leaving Alpheus Williams's brigade temporarily at Hancock, he led the brigades of J. J. Abercrombie and Charles S. Hamilton on a cold, muddy march from Frederick to campsites behind Maryland Heights, opposite Harpers Ferry, where they were to wait, briefly it was supposed, until engineers assembled their pontoon bridge. But poor staff work disrupted McClellan's calculations, setting in motion five days of what a *Chicago Tribune* correspondent labeled "ridiculous and shameful blundering." No one had bothered to check the specifications for the pontoons—which McClellan had ordered built at Washington for the express purpose of spanning the Potomac River at Harpers Ferry—against the width of the locks on the C&O Canal.

Boarding the train for Harpers Ferry just as the first pontoons were laid into the canal, McClellan and his staff were unaware of what transpired when the engineers tried to float them north. "Arriving at the first lock above Washington," wrote the *Tribune* correspondent, "the master of pontoons found that they were all too large to go through the lock—contributing, in fact, to a 'dead lock.' Mac went on to the Ferry, but no pontoons!" The result, continued the *Tribune* man, was "inextinguishable laughter" among those with no reputations at stake and a scurrying about of McClellan and Banks, who "collected a lot of canal boats and scows and proceeded to rig a temporary concern, zigzag and rickety and entirely at the mercy of the swift current."[11]

With so many engineers delayed downriver, a detail of 150 former lumberjacks and boatmen from the 3rd Wisconsin Infantry was assembled to help lay the 1,300-foot makeshift span. Struggling under a cold drizzle and through a swift current, the Wisconsin men completed the structure at noon on February 26. Three hours later Hamilton's brigade started over. "We crossed in single file and then double, and files of four abreast, after which the artillery and horses crossed," wrote Josiah G. Williams of the 27th Indiana. "General Banks and McClellan were present. I was within ten feet of him, while he and General Banks were standing upon the massive wall underneath the Baltimore and Ohio Railroad Bridge, watching the crossing."[12]

The troops filed off the bridge onto the grounds of the old U.S. arsenal, past the engine house where John Brown had made his stand, and up the streets of Harpers Ferry. Their first footsteps on Virginia soil left most unimpressed. "The town of Harpers Ferry now has only twelve families in it," said Josiah Williams. "All around is desolation. Magnificent government buildings, nothing but the barren and twisted window frames of iron remaining."

A dismal, drenching winter rain began falling at dark. The crossing continued into the night, and at 10:20 P.M. McClellan was able to report to Stanton that he had 8,500 infantry, three batteries of artillery, and two cavalry squadrons across the river. Hamilton's brigade pushed a mile beyond Harpers Ferry and occupied Bolivar Heights, and Abercrombie's brigade took up position on Loudoun Heights. All but the unfortunate pickets were permitted to take up quarters in houses. "I have examined the ground and seen that the troops are in proper positions and are ready to resist any attack," McClellan assured the secretary, as if a Confederate assault were even remotely possible. "We will attempt the [pontoon] bridge tomorrow."

The morning of February 27 brought more of the "inextinguishable laughter" that the *Chicago Tribune* correspondent had carped about, as it was only then that McClellan learned the fate of the pontoons. As anxious to shift blame from himself as to complete the mission, McClellan protested: "It had always been represented to the engineers by the military railroad employees and others that the lock was large enough, and, the difference being too small to be detected by the eye, no one had thought of measuring it." To compound McClellan's woes, the storm worsened. Driving rain swelled the already dangerously high waters of the Potomac, and near gale-force winds rocked the rickety scow and plank bridge. Scores of wagons crowded the narrow, muddy approach beneath Maryland Heights, unable to cross, leaving the brigades on the Virginia shore without baggage or supplies. In a telegram to his chief of staff, Brig. Gen. Randolph B. Marcy, McClellan tried to put the best possible face on the farce. There would be no more talk for the moment of an advance on Winchester; he had "determined on the course I indicated to the president and secretary of war, viz., the opening of the railway and rebuilding of its bridges." And he would wash his hands of the mess. "In the meantime depots can be established which will make an advance easy. But I regard the other projected operations as too important for the time necessary to accomplish this, which can be done at any time hereafter." McClellan lingered until the evening of the twenty-eighth, just long enough to accompany a reconnaissance to Charlestown and to order Lander and Williams, who would now cross the river at Williamsport, to join forces and occupy Martinsburg. "I make other arrangements which render us secure," he told Stanton. "You will be satisfied when I see you that I have acted wisely and have everything in hand."[13]

"NOW WE MAY look for war in earnest," Jackson wrote Congressman Boteler when he learned that Banks had crossed the Potomac. "You ask me for a letter respecting the Valley. I have only to say this, that if this valley is lost, Virginia is lost."[14]

Outnumbered six to one, Jackson clearly could not defend the entire Lower Valley. Where to make a stand became the signal question. Jackson surrendered Martinsburg without a fight on February 27; would Winchester be next? That was the "all-absorbing question discussed in all circles," said Lieutenant Lyle of the 4th Virginia. "Go where you would, on the streets, in the places of business, in the parlor, at the table, anywhere that two or more were assembled, the talk was about whether Jackson would fight or evacuate." William T. Kinzer, also of the 4th Virginia, expected a fight for the town. Captain Edmondson of the 27th Virginia thought the Yankees would not move until the roads dried. The consensus among the townspeople, the young firebrand secessionist Kate S. Sperry recorded in her diary on February 28, was that Winchester would be evacuated in a few days.[15]

Many chose to leave rather than await developments. Former mayor Joseph H. Sherrard, whom one diarist thought "dreadfully scared," departed on March 1. The family of former senator John M. Mason, then Confederate commissioner to Great Britain, left town the same day. Dr. Hugh H. McGuire, father of Hunter McGuire, chief surgeon of the Valley army, sent his family away and announced that he would burn his house. Pro-Union diarist Julia Chase enjoyed the irony of it all: "The Virginians have always said never surrender; that they never ran. Pretty good numbers are running now fast enough."[16]

Not everyone who quit Winchester headed south. Numerous Northern sympathizers took advantage of the confusion and proximity of Federal troops to slip away toward Union lines. The brothers of Harriet Griffith set off before dawn on March 2 "for a country where they can do as they would like and not have to be drafted in this Rebel army." Two boys from Loudoun County stayed at the Griffith house the next night; they intended to swim the Potomac, if need be, rather than be drafted. From line-crossers Banks was able to obtain considerable intelligence on Jackson's strength and dispositions; after depositing his sons safely among the Federals, Harriet Griffith's father spent a night with Union officers briefing them on the situation at Winchester.[17]

Undoubtedly he told them that all signs pointed to an evacuation. On February 23 Jackson's chief commissary, Maj. Wells J. Hawks, redirected army food shipments to Strasburg and began work on a commissary depot at Mount Jackson. Three days later all units were ordered to keep one day's cooked rations on hand until further notice. Some of the quartermaster and commissary staff packed up and left, and on February 28 Jackson detailed a battalion to maintain order in Strasburg. Amid the bustle, Jackson found time for God's work. Loosely disciplined militiamen had made a shambles of the Market Street Methodist Church; on the twenty-eighth Jackson also ordered his overworked chief quartermaster, Maj. John A. Harman, to see to it that damages were repaired immediately.[18]

That day Valley residents got their first taste of Union occupation. At dawn, General McClellan and a large retinue of staff officers set out for Charlestown with the 2nd Massachusetts Infantry, the 3rd Wisconsin Infantry, two sections of the 1st New York Light Artillery, and a detachment of the 1st Michigan Cavalry. The day broke clear and cold, just brisk enough to be invigorating.

Talking war and politics with McClellan as they rode, David Strother enjoyed himself immensely. "The sun was high; the movement of our brilliant caval-cade was exhilarating. The view of these lovely scenes, the homesteads of friends I had loved, of spots endeared to youth and manhood by pleasant memories touched me deeply. To the land from which I had been exiled for seven months I was returning in armed triumph. It was glorious."[19]

Few civilians were on hand to greet the conquering host. Fear of pillage and rape kept most indoors. Residents had good cause to expect retribution from the "Northern Vandals." Every Union soldier knew Charlestown as the site of John Brown's trial and hanging and, abolitionist or not, was prepared to condemn the entire population as "rank secessionists." The presumed arro-gance of Valley inhabitants contributed to an atmosphere of tense expectation. Opinions were fixed before the first encounters. "For real thoroughbred aris-tocracy, the 'First Families of Virginia' can lay over, or think they can, all the 'bluebloods' of the North or South. They have a well-grounded opinion of their superiority to other mortals in this world, with anticipation of a similar rank in the next," averred a Massachusetts corporal. "It happened after we crossed the river into Virginia that, knowing little about them, we sought every opportunity of exciting mirth or provoking ridicule at their weaknesses."[20]

On the north end of town Strother met his brother-in-law, Horace Riddle, one of the only Unionists in Charlestown. Along Main Street the soldiers of the 3rd Wisconsin and 2nd Massachusetts paraded to salute. The 1st Michigan Cavalry had galloped into Charlestown a short time before, bugles blowing and sabers drawn but, as Pvt. Delevan Arnold put it, "the birds had flown, so we took possession of the town." In truth, the two dozen Virginia troopers on outpost duty in Charlestown had loped away in the direction of Winchester, well ahead of the charging Michiganders.[21]

At noon the weather turned savage. A hard, cold rain mixed with snow drove the Federals to find shelter in the courthouse and churches. Hurrying through the downpour to check on his Presbyterian church, the Reverend W. B. Dutton braced himself for the worst. Strother fell in with him, and to-gether they found the sanctuary overrun with soldiers from the 3rd Wis-consin, some of whom were rolling up the carpets. Dutton implored Strother and the regimental commander, Col. Thomas H. Ruger, to spare the pulpit, Bibles, and candelabras. Glancing toward the organ, Dutton "saw a platoon of rugged-looking fellows fumbling with the music books of the choir. He looked in agony at the prospective destruction and desecration," recalled Strother. "A moment after, the books were all open, and fifty accordant voices rose in a thrilling anthem that filled the church with solemn music. The alarmed clergyman paused a moment. His face became calm and solemn. He turned to the officer in command, 'You need not move the furniture from the pulpit, Sir. It will be safe, I feel assured.' "[22]

Things got a little rowdy after Strother and Dutton left. The 2nd Massachusetts had marched into Charlestown bellowing the strains of "John Brown's Body." Setting aside their hymnals, Ruger's Wisconsin lumbermen tried to outdo the New England dandies. "The boys determined to keep that song going constantly during our stay in Charlestown, and they came near keeping good the resolve," said Lt. Edwin E. Bryant, adjutant of the 3rd Wisconsin. "The song and the throats of the singers were rather worn out and ragged for sometime after."[23]

While part of the regiment annoyed the townspeople with their singing, many of the rest joined in a general roundup of Charlestown poultry. "I must tell you that in less than an hour after we broke ranks all of the chickens, turkeys, and also beehives came running into our camp, declaring themselves to belong to the Union," one man wrote home. "I cannot account for this, unless it was because they were headless." Slaves who were "mighty tickled" with the Yankee occupation helped soldiers find hidden stores of food. One smiling twelve-year-old led Private Arnold of the 1st Michigan Cavalry home, saying, "Massa's got right smart of flour in de cellar, hidin' it from you northern fellers."[24]

Slaves not only betrayed their masters in small matters; many also took advantage of the Northern presence to break the chains of bondage. Owners invented tales of Yankee atrocities to frighten their chattel, but to no avail. In less than a week, one of Charlestown's leading citizens lost a third of his farmhands, including the family seamstress and her husband, who took with them a wagon, two horses, and two mules. A prominent resident who expected greater loyalty from his slaves entreated Wilder Dwight, the urbane and immensely popular major of the 2nd Massachusetts, not to take his corn or grain. "I've a large family of Negroes dependent on me, and I must have enough left to feed them and to take care of my horses and cows till spring. My poor servants will starve." Dwight saw the man again a week later. All he had left were a cow and a horse. "His dependent servants have taken care of themselves, and Mr. Ransom is rubbing his eyes over the abrupt lightening of his burdens."[25]

Officers enforced orders against unauthorized foraging with varying degrees of enthusiasm. Livestock and poultry vanished along the line of march, but there were no wanton acts of destruction. "The sight of this beautiful valley, its rural wealth and improvements," said Strother, "seemed to have softened the hearts of officers and men."[26]

The men of Charlestown largely resigned themselves to Federal occupation, but not the women. The general overthrow of established order intoxicated ladies of Southern sympathy, many of whom found themselves acting and speaking with a coarse bluntness they would never have imagined possible. Their demeanor caught the occupiers off guard. "The women were most indignant and most outspoken," said Lieutenant Bryant. "They took such revenge as their bitter tongues and prayers that we might be exterminated could afford them." Their hostility was not directed merely at the uniformed military. A Northern war correspondent in search of lodging on Main Street was told by the lady of the house that she would "sooner die than allow one of the vile mercenaries of the North to pollute her hearthstone for the night." Pointing to her fourteen-year-old son, she snarled: "This is the last that is left at home. Six of his brothers are with our army, and every one of my male relatives who is capable, and I live in the hope that when this last one is old enough, he too will go forth, and I hope that he will plunge his sword deep into your hearts." With that she slammed the door.[27]

Martinsburg fell next. On March 2 Williams's brigade took it without opposition. General Williams had rousted his men out before dawn two days earlier for the twenty-three-mile march from Hancock to Williamsport. It was good marching weather—clear and cool—but the macadamized turnpike played hard on the feet of soldiers who had idled about all winter. "We were getting quite effeminate," confessed a Connecticut volunteer. Fewer than half the men of the brigade wore army brogans; the rest either marched in boots of their own purchase or drawn from state allocations, or in a few instances were left behind barefooted.

Alpheus Williams was beside himself over quartermaster inefficiencies. "I have had requisitions for thousands of shoes and have received but five hundred for two months," he complained to a family member. "I have written and cursed, and pleaded and begged, and in return have had promises that they should be sent forthwith. But they came not. Just fancy in this age soldiers left without shoes in this war for the Union, and that in midwinter and in a campaign!" Tents, axes, and entrenching tools also were in short supply, and Williams had been unable to obtain bugles for skirmishing drills. Banks's attitude in the matter exasperated him. "If I were General Banks, with his political influence, I should understand in a few days where the fault lies. He seems to take it easy and make abundant promises."[28]

A mere handful of Williams's troops reached Williamsport before nightfall; sore-footed stragglers lined the road for miles to the rear. It was just as well, because only a single scow, capable of holding one company of soldiers or a wagon and a four-horse team, and a towline were available for ferrying his six regiments across the Potomac.

The operation began at dawn on March 2. A heavy, blowing snow began falling at noon, and by nightfall only two regiments had gotten over. Two more days would be required to cross the remaining four regiments of infantry, one battery of artillery, two companies of cavalry, and the regimental and brigade trains.

Williams started the first two regiments for Martinsburg as soon as they were over the river. Shuffling through snow four inches deep, the 28th New York led the march into Martinsburg at 11:00 P.M. "When we arrived we found everything in a state of utmost confusion," recorded the regimental historian. "Places of business had been closed by the proprietors, who had fled, and every place so left had been plundered. Everything—clothes, groceries, and provisions—bore enormous prices." Bankrupt shopkeepers told Rufus Mead, the commissary sergeant of the 5th Connecticut, that the slackly disciplined Virginia militiamen who had garrisoned the town over the winter had plundered shops and private homes liberally, "whether secesh or not." Farmers who had been unable to slaughter their pigs for lack of salt to dress the meat begged Mead to sell them even a peck of the precious article.[29]

Undoubtedly the pro-Union reputation of Martinsburg had encouraged the Virginia militia in their plundering. Most of the younger Union men— railroad workers and merchants primarily—had gone into hiding or fled across the Potomac to Williamsport to avoid conscription in the Confederate service; many had been gone for ten months. Left behind, their wives and daughters had shown considerable enterprise and courage in providing for themselves and their children. In order to smuggle groceries from Williamsport, numerous women of the town regularly "ran the blockade" of militia pickets. Charles W. Boyce of the 28th New York met one young lady who had been in the habit of running pickets before dawn and walking on to Williamsport, where she would procure such groceries or other goods that she could conceal on her person. Spending the night with her father, a refugee in Williamsport, she would return the next day, being careful to cross the lines after dark. Boyce recorded her final trip:

> She had nearly reached home when she came rather unexpectedly on to the guard, but fortunately for her they were in a drunken sleep. The sentinel on duty saw or heard her after she had passed his post and raised an alarm, but his companions were too drunk to assist him, so she escaped from this danger to run immediately into another one. She had just entered the village when she was met by the patrol. She discovered them in time enough to dodge into an alley, but she was seen and was ordered to halt, and one of the party pursued her. She ran from one street to another, all the time running toward her home. When near home she found she was headed off in that direction; she could neither advance nor retreat. There was only one alternative left, she must hide or allow herself to be taken. She was near the ruins of the railroad bridge, and she succeeded in reaching them and crawling in, so they were unable to find her. She lay there for three long hours, when she got out and reached home in safety.[30]

An Indiana soldier boarded at the home of a woman who had been captured on her one attempt at blockade-running. She had walked twenty miles through the snow and crossed the Potomac to buy salt, but the pickets caught her on the way back. She was held a week in the Martinsburg jail and only released on the petition of sympathetic "secesh" neighbors.[31]

There were far fewer doors slammed in the faces of Union soldiers in Martinsburg than in Charlestown. When Rufus Mead and a teamster from the 5th Connecticut asked to spend the night on the kitchen floor of one home, they were fed a full dinner and given the guest room. A squad of Massachusetts men detailed to guard the farm of an elderly couple outside town instead found themselves pampered guests. They tried to set up their tattered wedge tents on the front lawn, but the old farmer insisted they sleep indoors. He would patrol the farm for them; if any trespassers appeared, he would let them know. The fortunate soldiers passed their days lounging on the piazza, their nights drowsing by the fire, playing chess, and sleeping between clean sheets. When finally summoned back to town, they left the farm laden with cakes and biscuits that the farmer's wife had baked for the regiment.[32]

Unfortunately, the kind attentions of the citizens were not always reciprocated. Soldiers of the 5th Connecticut quartered in the German Reformed

Church wreaked havoc. "The property we had cared for with so much interest was most sacrilegiously treated," read the church record book. "Mock religious services were held, the pulpit desecrated, the Communion table, around which the congregation had so often gathered to commemorate the dying love of Him who came on a mission of peace, was strewn with playing cards, the walls and ceilings defaced, pews broken, and the floors covered with filth."[33]

The people of Martinsburg were fortunate that only the five thousand men of Williams's brigade had descended on them; Lander's twelve thousand were to have been there ahead of Williams, but neither Williams, Banks, nor McClellan knew what had become of them. It was from fear that Lander had taken the direct road to Bunker Hill and precipitated a fight with Jackson that McClellan had caused Williams to hurry his lead regiments on to Martinsburg. "I have endeavored to recall [Lander], but fear it may be too late," McClellan wired Banks on the morning of March 2. "I still hope the order of recall will reach him in time."[34]

In fact, Frederick W. Lander was beyond the reach of any earthly orders. At 5:00 P.M. the day before, he had collapsed in delirium while preparing to join the brigades of Cols. Erastus B. Tyler and John Mason, which had set out from Camp Chase in the face of a blinding snowstorm an hour before. Capt. Simon F. Barstow, the division assistant adjutant general and an old friend, put Lander to bed—heavily sedated with morphine. Barstow waited for twenty hours, hoping Lander might once again recover, before recalling Tyler and Mason. But infection had at last conquered his body. After a brief rally and a few moments of lucidness, Lander slipped into a deep coma. He died at 5:00 P.M. on March 2.

"General Lander has just died without suffering," Barstow telegraphed McClellan before turning over division command to Colonel Kimball. "This campaign killed him, for he held on in spite of failing health and strength to the last."[35]

CHAPTER 9

WE ARE VERY HARD

PRESSED NOW

Sandie Pendleton had been on Stonewall Jackson's staff since May 1861, long enough to understand that staff officers were among the last to know Jackson's intentions. Writing his mother from Winchester on March 2, Pendleton could only speculate in the most general terms on what lay ahead:

> The activity just infused into the various departments and the sending of surplus stores and sick to the rear has set speculation all agog here. People do not reflect that spring is opening and the game of chess beginning, and that the pieces must go from spot to spot as occasion demands, to enable us to checkmate the enemy. What will be done I have no idea. That Winchester will be left, I doubt not, for it ought, but I am equally certain this part of the state is not to be abandoned, and that General Jackson will not leave without some fighting. When or where this fighting is to take place I know no more than you.[1]

In this instance, Jackson's taciturnity was not to blame for Pendleton's ignorance; the commanding general was as uncertain as his young aide of the army's next move. Strategic considerations seemed to dictate a retreat. Johnston's impending withdrawal from Centreville to Culpeper Courthouse, behind the Rappahannock River, would uncover the Manassas Gap Railroad, rendering any position Jackson might take north of Front Royal or Strasburg vulnerable from the rear. Nevertheless, Jackson had neither concluded to abandon Winchester nor decided on a line of retreat. (He did, however, send his wife Anna home to Lexington.) All his planning was conditional. If a withdrawal became necessary, and the roads were dry enough, he might fall back through Page Valley; otherwise, his only line of retreat would be the Valley Pike. His objective in either case, unless Johnston wanted him to come east of the Blue Ridge, would be Mount Jackson, where he had directed that his principal supply depot be established. If necessary, he wrote Johnston on March 3, he might retire another eight miles to New Market, which would put him roughly on the same east-west line as Johnston at Culpeper.[2]

Jackson also was having trouble getting reliable information on the enemy. He could tell Johnston only that some 4,500 Federals apparently were in Martinsburg, and that a large force of cavalry was rumored to be coming from Williamsport. The reported accumulation of Federal army stores in Cumberland "looks ominous," and the lack of news from Daniel Harvey Hill at Leesburg, who had been writing regularly, disturbed Jackson as well. Perhaps most irksome was the complacency of his own cavalry. Turner Ashby's pickets on the Charlestown road had been found asleep at their posts on March 6. Although most of his freewheeling troopers presumably were watching the Yankees, they were keeping their observations to themselves. Exasperated, Jackson told his staff to instruct Ashby to report on enemy movements every morning at a minimum and to send a daily dispatch giving the location of his headquarters; all dispatches were to include the hour they were written and the hour they were sent.[3]

Irresolution at headquarters had a bad effect on the army, and in particular on the disaffected regiments of Loring's former command. Colonel Fulkerson was disgusted with the whole state of affairs. "We are very hard pressed now, and it depends upon the spirit of our people whether we bear up against it, or give way under it. When I see so many men and especially officers shirking duty, and who seem to make it a study as to the best manner in which they can get around duty, I almost despair." Few reenlisted. James Edmondson thought his depleted company could only be filled by the draft, if at all. Hugh White decided, after "no little anxious thought, with prayer for divine guidance," to reenlist on March 3, but only because Jackson had promised him a discharge to return to divinity school if the fortunes of the Confederacy improved during the summer. Few of his comrades in the Liberty Hall Volunteers were yet prepared to commit themselves.[4]

BY MARCH 8, General Banks had a clear idea of what he wanted to do and what he was up against. His major difficulty lay in convincing McClellan to approve an advance. Dropping by headquarters on the afternoon of March 2, David Strother had found Banks "perplexed at hearing nothing from Winchester" and inclined to credit rumors that Jackson had been reinforced. Strother reiterated his firm belief that Jackson had no more than five thousand men and no intention of resisting an advance, then turned to leave. Banks followed him into the street. In the gathering darkness Strother spotted a squad with fixed bayonets leading a prisoner. As the squad passed by, the prisoner whispered Strother's name; he was a Federal spy just returned from Winchester. Strother and Banks ushered him into the general's private chamber, where to the visible delight of the commanding general the spy confirmed Strother's analysis. "We went to bed with a sense of relief," recalled Strother. The next morning Strother interrogated the man further, making notes and a sketch map of all that he said. Banks shared Strother's report with General Hamilton and on the strength of it pledged to redouble his efforts with McClellan.[5]

Intelligence received over the next six days corroborated, and fleshed out, the information Strother's agent had provided. On March 7 General Williams conducted a reconnaissance in force up the Valley Pike from Bunker Hill. Seven miles north of Winchester the Federals ran into a company of Ashby's cavalry drawn up in a deep wood. A sharp skirmish ensued between the Virginians and two companies of Yankee cavalry, in which Ashby's poorly equipped troopers—one man, Ashby said, went into the fight bareback and armed only with a club—were soundly thrashed, losing six men killed and seven wounded. An officer of the 46th Pennsylvania, which together with the 5th Connecticut had been forming line of battle when the Rebels broke contact, thought they might have "surrounded and captured the entire body, had it not been for the impetuosity of whiskey. . . . As it was, we were satisfied having for the first time witnessed firing and 'smelled powder.'" General Williams, for his part, returned to Bunker Hill confident that Winchester was his for the taking.[6]

Evidence of an imminent Rebel withdrawal mounted. On March 8 a Unionist civilian slipped a note through the lines telling Banks that Jackson intended to evacuate Winchester soon, perhaps within twenty-four hours. Prisoners and deserters spoke freely of Jackson's reduced numbers. The chaplain of the 2nd Virginia, T. J. McVeigh, seized near Berryville while looking for his servant, assured his captors that only ten regiments of infantry defended Winchester. Arthur S. Markell, a twenty-year-old lieutenant in the 5th Virginia who had deserted both his regiment and his boyhood home of Winchester, confirmed McVeigh's estimate, adding that supplies had already been sent south. Pvt. Jacob Poisel of the 2nd Virginia gave himself up on March 9; pressed into the service before the Romney campaign, the disillusioned eighteen-year-old wanted nothing more than to return to his family home near Hedgesville. He not only corroborated the accounts of McVeigh and Markell, but also provided Banks with the name of every regiment and regimental commander in the Stonewall Brigade. Not the least bit reticent in the presence of the Federal commander, Poisel pointed out to Banks the map locations of brigade camps and earthwork fortifications around Winchester. He told him that the average company numbered just thirty men, and that his company was armed with old smoothbore muskets. Grateful for such exact information, Banks permitted the boy to take the oath of allegiance and return home.[7]

As he had promised Hamilton, Banks importuned McClellan for permission to move on Winchester. "Our troops are in good health and spirits, eager for work," he assured the commanding general on March 8. Lander's former division was expected at Martinsburg within twenty-four hours, which would give the Federals overwhelming superiority in numbers. Banks's staff and Strother's spies were carrying out an aggressive deception plan, letting it be known that the Federals had no designs beyond reopening the Baltimore and Ohio (B&O) Railroad. "Our troops are, however, pressing forward in the direction of Winchester," Banks interjected, "and will gradually press upon Winchester." Although the momentum of a reconnaissance-in-force might carry his command into Winchester, Banks clearly preferred explicit orders. "Beyond the point we now occupy I have received no instructions from the commanding general—whether we are to move on as a force destined to effect a specific object by itself or to perform a part in combined operations. I shall be glad to receive more specific instructions. If left to our own discretion, the general desire will be to move on early." McClellan, whose major concern at the moment was to make sense out of reports that Johnston had abandoned Centreville and Manassas, gave Banks no orders, suggesting merely that he ascertain whether any portion of Johnston's army might be en route to Winchester. In the absence of orders to the contrary, Banks would continue to edge toward Winchester.[8]

Despite the evident need to do so soon, Jackson was not yet ready to concede Winchester. "I greatly desire to hold this place so far as may be consistent with your views and plans, and am making arrangements, by constructing works, removing forests, etc., to make a stand," he wrote Joe Johnston on March 8. While acknowledging Johnston's instructions that he fall back simultaneously with the withdrawal of D. H. Hill's brigade from Leesburg and the main army from Centreville and Manassas, Jackson also cited the commanding general's admonition of March 5 that he "delay the enemy as long as you can" to justify his continued presence in Winchester. "And now, General, that Hill has fallen back, can you not send him over here? The very idea of reinforcements coming to Winchester would, I think, be a damper to the enemy, in addition to the fine effect that would be produced on our own troops."[9]

Jackson's wish to strike the Yankees a blow at Winchester by no means blinded him to his larger obligations to preserve the Valley army intact and to support Johnston in whatever manner the commanding general saw fit. Preparations for an evacuation proceeded with marked efficiency. On March 8 Jackson's indefatigable chief quartermaster, Maj. John Harman, saw the last of the army supply train out of town. Harman had positioned 250 teams of horses and numerous cooking and feeding stations between Winchester and Strasburg, and over the course of eight days had shepherded army stores out of Winchester at the rate of 500 wagonloads every twenty-four hours. Not to be outdone, the ordnance department removed the first of thirteen siege guns from Winchester on March 9 and the remainder on the tenth. The rolling stock of the B & O was doused with oil and stuffed with wood shavings, to be ignited on evacuation. Tents were packed up and shipped off, and the men shivered away the night of March 9 wrapped only in their blankets. Most ominously for the frightened townspeople, on the evening of March 10 Jackson declared martial law. "The people are all crazy, perfectly frantic for fear this place will be evacuated and the Yanks nab them," recorded pro-Northern diarist Julia Chase. The Confederate majority, however, undoubtedly took pleasure in the general roundup of Unionists, which began that night when the provost marshal arrested several dozen men holding a Union meeting. Prominent Quakers and others of doubtful loyalty were brought in from the countryside and placed in the guardhouse. Most of those detained were elderly and seemingly harmless, but Jackson had good cause for his actions. He knew about old man Griffith's trip through the lines on March 3 and of similar incidents that threatened to compromise operational security. A suspicious fire on the night of March 8, attributed to arson, emphasized the danger of sabotage by Unionist provocateurs. As Colonel Fulkerson observed, "There are a good many here who sympathize with the Yankees, and will be rejoiced if they get possession of Winchester."[10]

That the Federals would seize Winchester seemed a foregone conclusion by sunset on March 10. Brig. Gen. Willis A. Gorman's brigade of John Sedgwick's division and J. J. Abercrombie's brigade of Banks's division were on Jackson's right flank at Berryville, just ten miles east of Winchester, and might move unopposed into his rear. Sedgwick's other two brigades were within easy supporting distance of Gorman and Abercrombie. In Jackson's immediate front stood four Union brigades—Hamilton's at Smithfield, Williams's at Bunker Hill, and Kimball's and Sullivan's brigades of Lander's former division, temporarily under the command of Col. Nathan Kimball, at Martinsburg. Erastus B. Tyler's brigade and the division's trains were eleven miles in the rear at the Back Creek railroad depot. At least thirty thousand Yankee troops were within a day's march of Winchester. To oppose them, Jackson mustered fewer than five thousand of all arms.[11]

The noose grew tighter on March 11. The evening before, Charles S. Hamilton, as senior officer on the field, had asked Banks to allow him to make a midnight forced march against Winchester's defenses. Banks, who remained at Charlestown, denied him permission; there were plenty of officers who wanted to attack Winchester, Banks told the overeager Hamilton, but he intended to postpone an assault until Sedgwick's entire division had closed up on Berryville. With McClellan now securely in possession of Manassas and Johnston withdrawing rapidly toward Culpeper, there was no cause to fear "an enemy in the rear." Feeling "perfectly safe" to devise plans for Jackson's discomfiture at his leisure, Banks contemplated pushing Sedgwick south to Millwood in order to outflank Jackson and, with luck, compel him to quit Winchester without a fight. Evidently overestimating the quality of Valley back roads, Banks thought Sedgwick also might move laterally and get astride the Valley Pike at Strasburg in time to cut off Jackson's escape south. Meanwhile, Hamilton was to conduct only a reconnaissance toward Winchester with his brigade and those of Williams, Kimball, and Sullivan.[12]

Among the eager officers of whom Banks spoke was the new commanding general of Lander's division, Brig. Gen. James Shields. Like Lander and Banks, Shields was a self-made man of remarkable and varied talents, and justly famous. Born in County Tyrone, Ireland, in 1806, Shields lost his father at age six. He nonetheless obtained a good classical education, partly from his paternal uncle James, a Revolutionary War veteran and professor of Latin and Greek who returned to Ireland for a number of years after his brother's death to help care for his young nephew. Shields also became proficient in French. Before again leaving Ireland, Shields's uncle promised to bring him to the United States when he came of age and make him his heir. Mindful of his uncle's alluring offer, Shields—now aged sixteen—sailed from Liverpool for America, but his ship was wrecked off the coast of Scotland. Shields was one of just three survivors. In Scotland he found work as a tutor to a wealthy family. After four years he again embarked for America, only to find when he reached New York that his uncle had died. Shields took to the sea as purser on a merchantman until an accident sent him to a New York hospital for three months with two broken legs. On recovering, he set off for Kaskaskia, Illinois, where he taught school and read law. Admitted to the bar in 1832, Shields enjoyed the patronage of U.S. district judge Nathaniel Pope and the friendship of the leading men of the county. Although a Democrat in an overwhelmingly Whig district, the popular Shields won election to the Illinois legislature in 1836. Three years later he was elected state auditor. In that capacity he helped correct the disordered finances of the state, which had been brought to the verge of bankruptcy by the panic of 1837. He instructed state revenue collectors to accept tax payments in silver or gold only, rather than the nearly worthless bank notes then in circulation. The credit of Illinois was maintained while that of neighboring states was ruined.[13]

Unable to abide a successful Democrat, Shields's former Whig friends began a smear campaign against him. Egged on by his fiancée Mary Todd and her friend Julia Jayne, the future wife of Republican senator Lyman Trumbull, Abraham Lincoln did his part, penning an anonymous letter to the *Springfield Journal* that hinted at peculation by Shields. Mary and Julia followed up with an unsigned letter of their own, which was even more scurrilous than Lincoln's. To be called "a fool as well as a liar," and to have it claimed in the press that his personal habits were such that the writer was right in saying, "If I were deaf and blind I could tell him by the smell," was more than honor could bear. When Lincoln shouldered responsibility for both articles, Shields challenged him to a duel. Their seconds dithered over the choice of weapons—at one point it appeared that the duelists would meet with heavy broadswords, a grossly unfair advantage to Lincoln, who was eight inches taller and far stronger than the slightly built Shields—and exchanged insults of their own, until Lincoln surrendered the identity of the lady authors and apologized for his own letter. Shields accepted Lincoln's apology, and the two men became fast friends.[14]

The incident forgotten, Shields rose steadily in public office. In 1843 he was appointed justice of the Illinois Supreme Court to replace his friend Stephen A. Douglas, who had been elected to Congress. Two years later President James K. Polk named him commissioner of the General Land Office in Washington. So highly did Polk regard him that at the outbreak of war with Mexico he commissioned Shields a brigadier general of U.S. Volunteers. Shields proved a firm disciplinarian and gallant leader. While leading his Illinois brigade at Cerro Gordo, he took an iron grapeshot through the lungs but refused to quit the field. Four months later, after stumbling a bit early in the fight, he led the decisive charge at the Battle of Churubusco. Shields was wounded again at Chapultepec, this time by a musket ball that fractured his right wrist.[15]

After the war Shields won election to the U.S. Senate. Scrupulously neat, urbane, and courteous, graceful and humorous in debate, Shields took his place confidently—somewhat too confidently for the taste of strict-party Democrats—beside the senior senator from Illinois, Stephen A. Douglas. Candid in speech and independent in action, Shields spoke out against the extension of slavery and for a free California. Shields's vanity, which former state supreme court justice Gustav Koerner thought so inordinate as to be "rather amusing than offensive," grated on his Whig opponents, but "his mind, while eccentric, sometimes erratic, was essentially of a lofty nature." Defeated for reelection in 1855, Shields promoted Irish immigration to Minnesota for four years, then moved to California, where he prospered in business and, at the age of fifty-four, married Mary Ann Carr, the daughter of an old family friend from Ireland. The couple wed on August 16, 1861, setting out by steamship the same evening for Mazatlan, Mexico, where Shields was part owner of a profitable silver mine. Their Mexican sojourn was brief. Shields had offered his services to President Lincoln upon learning of the attack on Fort Sumter, and in the late autumn his appointment as brigadier general of volunteers, to date from August 19, reached him at Mazatlan. Concluding business rapidly, he reported for duty to Washington and was assigned command of Lander's division on March 7, 1862. At fifty-six, Shields was among the oldest volunteer generals in the Union army.[16]

Shields was on hand to greet Tyler's brigade as it marched into Martinsburg on the afternoon of March 11, bands playing and colors flying. He made a good impression on the men of his new division, who, for reasons known only to themselves, stuck him with the moniker, "Dirty Dick." Shields's Mexican War reputation preceded him, and officers such as Capt. Marcus Spiegel of the 67th Ohio, the immigrant son of a Jewish rabbi, preferred his pleasant manner and temperate language to the volcanic coarseness of Lander. Few held Shields's Irish heritage against him. A Philadelphia war correspondent said the troops affectionately described their new commander as "an Irishman by birth, an American by choice, and a patriot because he could not be otherwise." It would be several weeks before Shields's darker side—what Nathan Kimball later described as "a peculiar imagination, equaled only by terrible egotism, vanity, and impudent assurance"—emerged to chill early good feelings for him.[17]

While Shields became acquainted with Tyler's brigade, Charles Hamilton pushed the four brigades under his temporary command up the Valley Pike. Williams's brigade led the march, skirmishing with Ashby's cavalry all day long and occasionally hurling artillery shells into the woods ahead of them. Williams halted for the night at Stephenson's Depot, five miles short of Winchester, and Hamilton closed up the remaining brigades behind him. In the gathering twilight the Rebel earthworks were dimly visible a mile distant, but whether or how strongly they were defended, no one could say. The men bivouacked in line of battle, and most lay down expecting a hard fight in the morning. Seemingly credible reports suggested that sixty-four cannons and twenty thousand men stood behind the Rebel fortifications, ready to contest a Federal advance. Notwithstanding the wildly exaggerated estimates of the enemy's strength, or the fact that Banks had authorized only a reconnaissance, Hamilton, Williams, and Shields agreed among themselves to stage a general assault on Jackson's line in the morning.[18]

Winchester's defenders passed March 11 in expectation of a fight at any moment. Reveille awoke the camps south of town at 5:00 A.M. An hour later orders came to strike tents, load wagons, and be ready to move. Artillery batteries rolled through town and took position among the low hills north and northeast of Winchester. Picket firing sounded on the horizon, and by noon, said a Virginia rifleman, "things looked fightish." At 2:00 P.M. the regiments of the Stonewall Brigade swung onto the Valley Pike, then shuffled north along Loudoun Street toward the shooting. Burks's brigade followed, and Taliaferro's brigade hurried northeast along the Berryville road to meet a rumored threat from that direction. Filing into the ragged line of half-dug rifle pits and behind the knee-high parapets that constituted the Confederate fortifications, Garnett's Virginians caught a glimpse of Yankee skirmishers bent low in the fields far to their front, and beyond them blue-clad regiments deploying from column into line of battle.[19]

Back in town, frightened civilians struggled to make sense of the commotion, while at the same time hiding valuables and anything—letters, flags, cartes de visite, weapons—that might identify them as secessionists. Few wished for a battle on their doorstep. Even the Rebel matron Mary Greenhow Lee, sister of the infamous Southern spy Rose Greenhow, hoped that Jackson, "unless he intends to hold Winchester, will not fight, as it will only draw on us poor helpless ones the fury of a defeated army, or the additional insolence of a victorious one." As one of the town's leading citizens, Mrs. Lee was on intimate terms with many of Jackson's senior officers, including his affable and plain-spoken inspector general, Col. William S. H. Baylor, who boarded with her family. But that familiarity availed her little. Trying to divine the meaning of the disconcerting chorus of loud cheers, muffled curses, and cadenced tread of infantry that sounded outside after dark, Mrs. Lee was astonished to find Colonel Baylor on her doorstep for evening tea. He knew no more than she did. Several regiments had retired through town to get supper from their provision wagons, Baylor told his host, and Jackson himself was at that moment dining with J. R. Graham and his wife. Baylor himself was to report to headquarters later that night, as he supposed for a council of war, "but whether they are to leave tonight, or have a battle tomorrow, no human being knows, save our general."[20]

Rather than cause him consternation, the Federal approach had stirred Jackson to a reckless spiritual ecstasy. He was God's instrument and as such must prevail. Though superior in numbers, the Yankees must be inferior in spirit. He would allow his soldiers to slip away from the earthworks north of town after dark just long enough to draw rations from the quartermaster wagons parked on the south side of Winchester and rest awhile. Then they would march back through town, and, in the black stillness before dawn, Jackson would throw them against the unwary Northerners. He intended to present his plan to "smite the sinful invaders," as a recent Jackson biographer phrased it, at the council of war to which Baylor had been summoned. But first, he would refresh himself with a light meal and fervent prayer at the home of the Reverend Graham.

The good reverend found himself knowing more of the general's intentions than did Jackson's staff or senior commanders. Jackson "was really joyous in spirit," remembered Graham, "speaking with glee and delight at the conduct and eagerness of his men to engage the enemy." He left for the council of war "full of spirits and completely relieving us of all our fears" for the safety of Winchester.

Jackson's mood soured as one after another of his lieutenants rejected his proposal for a night attack. "At first his commanding officers appeared not to have much confidence in his strategy," recalled Col. Robert P. Carson of the 37th Virginia. "Knowing him so well at V M I, I must confess that I was fearful he would lead us into some inextricable trouble." Jackson was shocked to learn that, instead of halting on the south side of Winchester, the ration wagons had continued five miles up the Valley Pike, the infantry following them in search of their supper. Not being privy to the general's intentions, no one had thought to halt either the wagons or the troops. A march of ten miles would be needed to bring the army into contact with the enemy. Jackson broke off the meeting and returned to the Grahams' house, angry and uncertain. Once again, Jackson's hermetic nature had confounded his plans.

"A sadder, more dejected countenance I never saw," said the reverend, who looked on as Jackson battled with himself in the family parlor. First he told Graham he must surrender Winchester without a fight. Then, as if that notion were too painful to contemplate, Jackson exclaimed, "This I grieve to do! I must fight!" Eyes flashing, he drew his sword halfway from the scabbard. For a moment he stood motionless. Then his shoulders slumped. Returning his sword to its place, he stammered, "No, it will cost the lives of too many brave men. I must retreat." Turning to the Grahams, he said: "I am compelled to say goodbye. Nothing but necessity and the conviction that it will be for the best induces me to leave." With bowed head and a muttered hope that "a good Providence will permit me to return and bring deliverance to the town," Jackson departed.[21]

It was midnight before Jackson could bring himself to issue the superfluous order to evacuate Winchester; by then, the head of the column was seven miles south of town, and some units already had bivouacked for the night. Jackson left Winchester with Surg. Hunter McGuire, who, grieved at having to abandon his family and home to the enemy, sobbed weakly. Jackson was too furious for tears. Pausing on a low hill south of town, he snarled, "That is the last council of war I will ever hold!" Then, wheeling his horse, he galloped off toward the head of the column. Bathed in the light of a full moon, Jackson cast a memorable shadow. "He came riding furiously like the driving of Jehu, and looked as if the thunderbolts of Jupiter were pent up in him, and [he] would like to hurl them on Banks and his army," said Lt. John N. Lyle. At 3:00 A.M., overcome with fatigue, Jackson lay down in a fence corner near Newton and went to sleep. Sandie Pendleton kept watch beside him.[22]

The demoralization of the army was complete. "It was with sad hearts that the college boys retreated from Old Winchester, leaving its splendid citizens to the mercy of the abolition invaders," Lieutenant Lyle recalled. "They felt like a gang of burglars sneaking out of a town they had just looted." Maj. Frank Jones of the 2nd Virginia rested beneath a large locust tree in a fence corner beside the Valley Pike only a short distance from "Caryesbrooke," his now deserted family estate. "I sleep in the open air and am now a refugee from my wife and children and native land. When shall I see them again? God alone knows, but to Him I trust it all, that if I go to him in trust and prayer he will not cast me off."[23]

In Winchester, the townspeople also prayed. "Oh! It is terrible to be listening for the cannon, now in the dead hours of the night, when everyone save myself is asleep," wrote Mary Greenhow Lee. "I am in my lovely little room, and every sound startles me; horsemen are dashing by continually; why do they ride as if the enemy were pursuing them? May the God of battles have mercy on us."[24]

BRIG. GEN. ALPHEUS S. Williams was a kind man and a conscientious officer. Although he had never heard a shot fired in anger (Williams was appointed lieutenant colonel of a Michigan regiment in the Mexican War but reached the theater of operations only after hostilities ended), his troops expected great things of him in battle. On the morning of March 12, 1862, he tried his best not to disappoint them.

As commander of the lead brigade in what most assumed would be a bloody assault on the Winchester defenses, the fifty-two-year-old former judge understood his duties well. He had his brigade under arms two hours before dawn. Blanketing his front with eight hundred skirmishers, Williams ordered the brigade to advance "with great, caution, as the hills showed entrenchments," in line of battle, four regiments abreast.

The day broke mild, the sky clear as crystal. The temperature climbed steadily, to near seventy by midday. Williams could scarcely contain his excitement as, through his field glass, he watched the skirmishers, "looking in the distance like a swarm of ants crawling up a hillside," approach the Rebel fortifications. Climbing over the four-barrel gabions and board fence that constituted the first line of works, the skirmishers edged toward the principal earthwork astride the turnpike. Word came back that it was occupied, and Williams directed his skirmishers to "feel them cautiously." The long line went forward. "Soon we saw them tumbling over the parapets, the bayonets brightly glaring in the morning sun. We knew then that the town was ours."[25]

While Williams closed his brigade into column of fours, Hamilton ordered the 1st Michigan Cavalry to sweep into Winchester. A few minutes before

8:00 A.M. the Michiganders galloped up Market Street, rounding up Rebel stragglers as they rode. Few of the Southern soldiers who remained in town had intended to surrender; so sudden had been the Valley army's nocturnal departure that many a man had been left behind at the home of a girlfriend or host family. Probably the last Confederate to depart Winchester was Turner Ashby, who sat quietly on his horse until convinced that the Yankees were coming in force, then, apparently in plain view of the Michigan troopers, turned and trotted methodically out of town.[26]

Hiding behind locked doors and drawn curtains, most townspeople were unaware of the Yankee presence. Cornelia McDonald, wife of Col. Angus McDonald, awoke at their home on the outskirts of town "thankful that we were still free." The morning seemed so peaceful that "a hope dawned that our men would come back." McDonald sat down to breakfast with her children, "feeling happy in proportion to my former depression," when suddenly a strain of music caused everyone to pause. Her boys clapped their hands and jumped from the table. "Our men have come back!" they yelled, rushing to the door. McDonald stopped them. The music grew louder. "Sure enough that music could not be mistaken, it was the 'Star Spangled Banner' that was played." A servant burst in, crying, "They are all marching through the town, and some have come over the hill into our orchard." McDonald ushered her children back to the breakfast table. "I began to eat my breakfast, but felt as if I should choke with anger and mortification."[27]

Two miles away, at her home on Market Street, McDonald's friend Mary Greenhow Lee also "felt depressed and abased when I first heard their hateful music." She recorded her impressions of the entry of the Yankee columns into Winchester in a letter to the editor of the *Richmond Enquirer* that she later smuggled through the lines. "On some streets there was a deathlike silence— doors and windows closed, and not a face to be seen, excepting a few servants on the sidewalks. On other streets, a few handkerchiefs were waved, Union flags hung out, and a few cheers raised by servants and some of the lower classes; but I have not heard of a single one of our more prominent citizens who welcomed the Northern horde to the Valley of Virginia."[28]

That was because there were few Union men left in town. Before quitting Winchester, Jackson's provost marshal had rounded them up, old men mostly, and marched them off with the army. Julia Chase's father Charles had been "lying sick on the sofa" when the provost guard came for him. Those able to pay were allowed to ride the stage south; the rest were compelled to walk with the troops. Charles Chase was incarcerated in relative comfort for six weeks in

Harrisonburg before being permitted to return home, but two of his companions died in prison. One of them, Job Throckmorton, a devout and "harmless man," as even the provost marshal admitted, had been seized while on his way to the Hopewell Quaker Meetinghouse. He died of typhoid fever in a Staunton prison six weeks later. To Julia Chase and her fellow Unionists, such a death was tantamount to murder.[29]

Among Federal troops, impressions of Winchester varied according to the fervency of their patriotism. To abolitionists in the ranks, Winchester was just another "secesh hole." Those able to set aside their animosity generally were quite taken with the place. The fine roads and "splendid country residences" such as the McDonald home particularly impressed Lt. David Beem of the 14th Indiana. The area reminded him of the "older and richer portions of Indiana. It makes one feel more like he was in a civilized land and gives more life and spirit and pleasure to all of us soldiers." Fellow Hoosier Lt. Frank Ingersoll found the streets too narrow but otherwise liked Winchester. The well-traveled Capt. Marcus Spiegel thought the town "has a regular Old Country appearance, like Worms." A soldier of the 60th Ohio praised Winchester to his hometown newspaper as "a very pretty town. The streets are lined with beautiful shade trees, and great care and pride is taken by the citizens to keep them in good order. The people are bountifully supplied with the best of water from a reservoir, and on every square are one or more public hydrants, besides fire plugs."[30]

Although barred doors, drawn blinds, and sullen faces were the order of the day, there was just enough Union feeling left in Winchester to temper any reciprocal ill will on the part of the soldiers. Oscar Kimberly, regimental bandleader of the 3rd Wisconsin, told his parents how on entering Winchester he was

> astonished to see such a Union sentiment manifested; it is estimated that two-thirds of the citizens are as great Union people as our town, but have to succumb to the Rebels. One man, who had been quite wealthy, but who was a good Union man, was pillaged and robbed of nearly all the necessities of life, determined he would not give up. He had in his possession a fine flag (Stars and Stripes), which he buried. The day after our arrival he took it up and said he "thanked God that it could again wave in defiance of those that had once threatened it." He had also two barrels of wine which he took out and told the soldiers to drink to the Stars and Stripes.

Rufus Mead, commissary sergeant of the 5th Connecticut, found "a great many men who profess Union sentiments." Among them, however, were a good number of shopkeepers, who, overburdened with depreciated Confederate currency, were anxious for greenbacks. The sincerity of their convictions might therefore be questioned.[31]

There could be no mistaking the feelings of the upper-class female clique, composed principally of the wives, daughters, mothers, and sweethearts of Confederate officers. In sheer mean-spiritedness, they outdid the secesh women of Charlestown. "We found ourselves in another atmosphere here," wrote John M. Gould, a Maine volunteer. "We had already seen Rebel women, but in all our travels we never saw any so bitter as those of Winchester. They were untiring in their efforts to show how they hated us. If we sat upon their doorsteps a moment, they would send out their servants to wash up the spot that was supposed to be made filthy by our presence." Innocent, simple kindnesses were rebuffed dramatically. "A lady of one of the very 'First Families' dropped her bible or prayer book on going to church," continued Gould. "It was instantly picked up by one of the boys, who stood near, and handed it to the lady, who scowled at him and refused to take it."

When mute scorn failed to evoke a response, the women resorted to cursing. Mary Greenhow Lee delighted in running off a Yankee who had wandered into her kitchen with a trail of oaths "as fearlessly as if I had been an armed man." He left, stammering, "I did not know we were so obnoxious to you." Some of the younger female firebrands went so far as to spit in the face of Yankees they passed on the street.

Not all Federal soldiers accepted the taunts in silence. A member of the 46th Pennsylvania witnessed a fine rejoinder from a member of General Banks's Zouave guard. Walking down the street on which Banks had his headquarters, Kate Sperry and several of her friends stopped short when they saw the Stars and Stripes waving out of a window over the pavement. "Kate, do you intend to walk under that dirty rag there," asked one of the girls as she pointed to the flag. "No never," exclaimed Sperry, and they struck out across the street to avoid it. Overhearing them, the Zouave sentinel paused in his beat to remark, "Misses! I think you have a dirtier rag under the skirts of your dresses." "They of course blushed and no doubt thought, 'ain't that a monster,'" recalled the Pennsylvanian, "but I say bully for the Zouave." A Massachusetts soldier, strolling past a well-dressed secessionist woman, poked the small Union flag he was carrying at her. She snatched it from him and threw it in the street. That was a little too much for the New Englander. Approaching her, he said coolly, "If you were not a woman, I would knock you ass over kettle for your damned impudence."[32]

Fortunately for the "she-devils" of Winchester, the Federal high command was more amused than angered by their ill-mannered displays. Every evening at dinner, James Shields endured epithets from Mary Tucker Magill, at whose home he boarded. "Mary allows her tongue full license and says all kinds of bitter sarcasms to General Shields," said Mary Greenhow Lee. "She told him that if they killed all the men of the South, the women would fight, and that when they were destroyed the dogs would bark at them; she never eats in his presence, and [when Shields] asked what she lives on; she replied, 'On the hopes of soon seeing our army back'; she has cut her hair off and said she did it because it was less painful than tearing it out by the roots." The benevolent General Williams, who boarded at the McDonald residence, believed that "all that is needed is kindness to make all these people return to Union love." General Hamilton simply thought the women of Winchester insane. Regardless of their personal feelings, each of them, as well as General Banks, guaranteed their secessionist hosts that private property would be respected and that any soldier who insulted a lady would be shot.[33]

Officers and men of the Valley army with family at risk appreciated the forbearance of the Federal high command. The chaplain of the 25th Virginia conceded that a "kindly feeling" developed for General Banks, as "he treated the people of the Valley much more leniently than his successors in command there." Bull Paxton assured his wife that the Yankee policy,

> so far as I can learn, has been, in Winchester and the counties which they occupy, to conciliate the people. I am glad they indicate their purpose to carry on the war on the principles of civilized warfare, as it exempts the women and children left at home from the savage barbarities of their vengeance. If the fate of war brings my own home with their lines, it will be some consolation to know that you and our dear little children are not subjected to insult and injury. While it is a sad thought to give up one's home to the enemy . . . it is utterly impossible to defend every section.[34]

As the Confederates continued their southward trek, not a few in the ranks wondered whether Jackson intended to defend any section of the Lower Shenandoah Valley. On the evening of March 12, the Valley army made camp between Cedar Creek and Strasburg. It was a poor location. The water was bad, and men fell sick in large numbers. Concerned also that Banks might outflank him, Jackson decided on March 14 to withdraw to the neighborhood of Red Banks, an enormous homestead four miles northeast of Mount Jackson. Built in 1803 by Lawrence Pittman Sr., the estate had, for nearly fifty years, hosted illustrious travelers such as Andrew Jackson and Madame Jerome Bonaparte en route to the healing waters of White Sulphur Springs. Retiring at a leisurely pace, with Ashby's cavalry screening the rear, the army reached Red Banks on the afternoon of March 16 and settled into what Maj. Frank Jones of the 2nd Virginia termed "a beautiful wood on a hill a short distance from the Shenandoah River." The Confederates named the spot "Camp Buchanan." Jackson took up quarters in the Pittman mansion, one of the largest and most impressive homes in the Valley. Three of Pittman's grandsons served in the Stonewall Brigade.[35]

As the army enjoyed a brief rest, Jackson pondered the difficulties of his situation. Notwithstanding Jackson's decidedly inferior numbers, General Johnston had made it clear that he expected the Valley army to keep Banks too busy to reinforce McClellan. Not merely the disparity in troop strength rendered Jackson's task problematic. In order to hold Banks's attention, he had to remain west of Massanutten Mountain and the Blue Ridge as long as the Federals did. That left Page Valley unguarded, endangering his communications with Johnston. A Federal force in that region could easily deny him the Blue Ridge passes he might need if summoned to join Johnston. The best Jackson could do was to retire far enough from Banks to retain freedom of maneuver, but not so far as to cause Banks to think he had left the Valley. Red Banks served his purpose well. Apart from its virtues as a camping ground, the Pittman estate lay only a short day's march from New Market Gap and a hard day's march from Winchester.[36]

Jackson could take solace in the knowledge that morale in the Valley army was surprisingly good. The men understood the logic of the retreat from Winchester and applauded its execution. "Surely our retreat has been conducted in the most masterly manner," Sgt. George W. Peterkin of the 21st Virginia assured his mother. "We have now more men than we had when we left Winchester, owing to recruits and reenlisted men coming in, and our army is in better spirits, and better organized and prepared in every way. No demoralization at all has taken place; we are more capable now than we have been for two months." Although perplexed by the continued withdrawal beyond Strasburg, most were willing to give Jackson the benefit of the doubt. Pvt. Richard W. Waldrop, also of the 21st Virginia, was confident that " 'Old Jack' knows what he is about, and when he does strike, will give a blow that will be felt."[37]

CHAPTER 10

KEEP THAT ARMY IN THE VALLEY

President Lincoln and the nation were fast losing confidence in George B. McClellan. The president had set a deadline of February 22 for a general advance of the armies. When that date came and passed with no movement of the Army of the Potomac, indignant newspaper editors began to question McClellan's loyalty. Calls for his dismissal arose from the halls of Congress. Cabinet support for the general in chief faltered when word of the botched crossing of the Upper Potomac reached Washington. Secretary of State William Seward decried the "imbecility" of McClellan's management, and Secretary of the Treasury Salmon Chase, referring to the farce of the oversized pontoons, said the expedition had "died of lockjaw." Attorney General Edward Bates was convinced that McClellan had "no plans but is fumbling and plunging in confusion and darkness."

Lincoln had expected much more than a reconnaissance to Charlestown to come out of the Harpers Ferry endeavor. At a minimum he had looked to a speedy reopening of the B & O Railroad. As presidential private secretary John Hay observed, his "slow anger was thoroughly roused by this ridiculous outcome of an important enterprise." Lincoln's displeasure was apparent in Presidential War Order No. 2, issued March 8, which dictated the immediate reorganization of the Army of the Potomac into five corps, its commanders to be drawn from the army's brigadier generals according to date of rank. The slight to McClellan was unmistakable. Over the winter Lincoln had informally urged him to establish a corps structure, but McClellan had demurred, preferring to wait until "some little experience in battle should show what general officers were most competent. It was therefore with as much regret as surprise that I learned of the existence of this order."[1]

McClellan was equally surprised at the cool personal reception Lincoln accorded him when he returned to the capital, but the general did little to redeem himself. Instead of bringing him glory, the grand advance of the Army of the Potomac against the Confederate works at Manassas on March 10 yielded merely another public embarrassment when it was discovered that the fortifications not only were empty, Johnston having successfully decamped, but also that what had appeared to be formidable-looking cannons behind them were in fact logs painted black.

The next evening Lincoln summoned Seward, Chase, and Secretary of War Stanton to the cabinet room to read to them Presidential War Order No. 3, by which he meant to relieve McClellan of his duties as general in chief. "Having personally taken the field," McClellan was limited to command of the Army of the Potomac. The three cabinet secretaries concurred, and the order was issued on March 12.

McClellan's first act in his diminished role as commander of the Army of the Potomac seemed to confirm the wisdom of his demotion: focusing his attention solely on the Virginia theater, he concluded that the Urbana plan was no longer viable. Characteristically, it was McClellan's timidity that led him to this conclusion. Still wrongly convinced that Johnston's woefully under-strength army outnumbered him (in actuality, he outnumbered Johnston nearly four to one), he attributed Johnston's withdrawal behind the Rappahannock to a leak of the Urbana plan. Undoubtedly Johnston was positioning himself to spring an ambush on him when he tried to disembark at Urbana. So far as McClellan was concerned, the only option was to shift the landing farther south to Fortress Monroe, which was already in Union hands. That would put his starting point seventy miles southeast of Richmond, on the peninsula created by the James and York rivers. McClellan's newly promoted corps commanders—McDowell, Sumner, Heintzelman, and Keyes—cautious men all, approved the plan, and on the morning of March 13 McClellan telegraphed it to the War Department. Lincoln's concurrence came the same evening. He had no objection to McClellan's proposed change of plans, provided that two conditions were met: McClellan must leave sufficient forces at Manassas Junction to "make it entirely certain that the enemy shall not repossess himself of that position and line of communication," and he must "leave Washington entirely secure." These conditions appeared simple enough to comprehend, but in the coming weeks McClellan was to underestimate the apprehension that lay behind the words "entirely secure," with grave consequences both to his own campaign and Federal fortunes in the Shenandoah Valley.[2]

PRESIDENTIAL WAR ORDER No. 2 meant greater responsibility for Banks, whose rank entitled him to command the newly constituted Fifth Corps of the Army of the Potomac. Banks named Maj. D. D. Perkins as chief of staff and Maj. R. Morris Copeland, a temperamental and self-serving New Englander, as assistant adjutant general. Williams assumed command of Banks's division, which was designated the First Division of the Fifth Army Corps; Shields's division was made the Second Division. Williams's First Division consisted of three brigades, the First under Col. Dudley Donnelly, who was promoted from command of the 28th New York; the Second, which remained under Brig. Gen. J. J. Abercrombie; and the Third, which Brig. Gen. Charles S. Hamilton, who was transferred to the Third Corps, yielded to Col. George H. Gordon, formerly colonel of the 2nd Massachusetts. Shields's division retained the same brigade designations and commanders: Kimball continued to lead the First Brigade, Col. Jeremiah C. Sullivan the Second, and Col. Erastus B. Tyler the Third. Not until March 28, when Brig. Gen. John P. Hatch joined the corps, was the cavalry consolidated under a single commander.

In the shakeup occasioned by the reorganization of the army, Sedgwick's division was transferred from Winchester to the Second Corps at Manassas Junction. Concluding that one division was sufficient to watch the retreating Jackson, McClellan on March 13 ordered Banks to send his other division to Centreville and to establish his corps headquarters at Manassas Junction. Two days later Banks set off for Washington to confer personally with McClellan. Their discussion—and Banks's apparently rosy appraisal of affairs in the Valley—resulted in a further modification of his orders. On March 16 McClellan directed him to leave in the Lower Valley just one brigade of infantry, which was to entrench at Strasburg, and two regiments of cavalry, which were to "thoroughly scour" the country beyond. Banks's principal responsibility was to rebuild the railroad from Manassas Junction back to Strasburg. The next day McClellan modified the order, telling Banks to hold Shields's division in the Valley until he had repaired the railroad.[3]

Prudence dictated that Banks first confirm that Jackson had withdrawn well beyond Strasburg. Before leaving for the capital he directed General Williams, the acting corps commander in his absence, to reconnoiter up the Valley Pike. Williams delegated the task to Shields.

It was the Irish general's first field test of the war, and his judgment left something to be desired. On the morning of March 17—the day McClellan began embarking the Army of the Potomac for the Peninsula—Shields told Col. John Mason to take two companies of his 4th Ohio Infantry and a squadron of cavalry, a woefully small force should serious opposition be encountered, and reconnoiter not only the Valley Pike toward Strasburg, but also the byroads. Shields had no notion of the unrealistic demands he had placed on Mason; David Strother found him at Williams's headquarters that cold afternoon "in high feather" and drinking punch. Fortunately Mason encountered nothing more than a handful of Turner Ashby's pickets, which he easily drove out of Newton, another of the "dilapidated-looking" secessionist hamlets of the Lower Valley. Careful not to press his luck, Mason turned off on to the Front Royal road, scouting it a short distance before returning to Winchester.[4]

Mason's inconclusive outing convinced Williams that a true reconnaissance in force was needed before he might safely leave with his division for Centreville. He left the details to Shields, who concocted a decidedly unrealistic plan for ensnaring Ashby's troopers. Mason would again take the Front Royal road out of Winchester, this time at the head of two regiments, the 8th Ohio and 7th Indiana; two sections of artillery; and the squadron of cavalry and two companies of his own 4th Ohio that had accompanied him on his first scout. He was to march south as far as Cedarville, then push west over a muddy back road to Middletown, in order to catch Ashby from behind. Shields, meanwhile, would lead the remaining 8,500 men of the division up the Valley Pike to take the Rebel cavalry from in front. Although impressed with the general's "pluck and enterprise," David Strother concluded that a bull had a better chance of catching a fox than Shields did of catching Ashby.[5]

And so it proved. Mason was on the road at 4:00 A.M. on March 18. Ten hours and twenty-four miles later he reached Middletown, only to find that Ashby had anticipated him by an hour and retired toward Strasburg. Swinging his command onto the Valley Pike, Mason pressed Ashby's skirmishers as far as Cedar Creek, where he found the bridge in flames and Ashby's entire force arrayed safely on the far bank. Under a taunting but otherwise harmless cannonade from Chew's battery, concealed among the trees of a low hill nine hundred yards away, Mason ordered his men off the road and into bivouac, intending to force a crossing in the morning.

Shields rode up to the head of his lumbering column at dusk, full of fight and ready to cross the creek at once. He waved the Ringgold Cavalry Company, Pennsylvania Volunteers, toward a ford just below the bridge, but the commanding officer, Capt. John Keys, hesitated, protesting that the burning timbers would fatally illuminate his troopers. Shields acquiesced, and the field fell silent. During the night he had planks thrown over the smoking ruins to fashion a temporary bridge for the morning. A lack of spirit on the part of officers and men had thwarted the Irish general, thought Strother, who, employing another metaphor also conceded that Shields's plan that day had been "as feasible as that of a child who tries to catch a bird by throwing salt on its tail."[6]

Dawn revealed that the bird had flown. Federal artillery fired at empty hills. The infantry waded the creek or hurried single file across the makeshift bridge. The Union artillery had scored at least one hit the day before. Near the turnpike, the lieutenant colonel of the 8th Ohio stumbled on a Rebel "literally cut in two by a cannonball."[7]

Shields entered Strasburg unopposed. There he halted long enough for the men to form a singularly unpleasant impression of the place. Capt. Marcus Spiegel described Strasburg as "a crooked-street, old-fashioned kind of town." Taverns outnumbered stores, thought an Indianan, who estimated the town as "one-mile long and two houses wide."[8]

From atop Fisher's Hill, a mile to the southwest, Chew's pesky gunners lobbed shells toward the Federals. Their rounds fell well short of target but near enough to disconcert Shields, who told his brigade commanders that he thought Jackson's whole force was before them and prepared for battle accordingly. With great fanfare he had his chief of artillery, Col. Philip Daum, place twenty cannons west of the turnpike, on high ground opposite Fisher's Hill. Behind the guns he stacked his three infantry brigades, less Mason's detachment, which drew the unenviable duty of advancing up the turnpike against Fisher's Hill with the 1st Michigan Cavalry.[9]

As it turned out, Mason had more to fear from his own artillery than from the Confederates. Opinion varied sharply as to the worth of Colonel Daum. Henry Capehart, the chief surgeon of the 1st West Virginia Cavalry, befriended the German immigrant and thought him an "artilleryman of great skill, unusual ability as a tactician, and indisputable pluck . . . a striking exception to the generality of foreign officers in our service." A soldier closer to the action, Pvt. Samuel W. Cass of Battery H, 1st Ohio Light Artillery, thought Daum's handling of Shields's artillery "ridiculous in the extreme." Daum, he said, was "the laughing stock of the boys," who set him down as "a Prussian fraud of the first class." On this occasion, Cass's estimation of Daum rang truest. Mason's infantry had no trouble clearing Fisher's Hill; Ashby had withdrawn his seven hundred troopers shortly after Shields completed what David Strother lamented as his "tardy maneuvers." But when they crested the abandoned hill, Daum, believing Mason's troops to be Confederates, directed his batteries to open fire on them. He also ordered guns turned on the troopers of the 1st Michigan Cavalry as they galloped out of a glen beneath Fisher's Hill. The commander of Battery E, 1st U.S. Artillery, Capt. Joseph C. Clark, remonstrated in vain that Daum was taking aim at Federals. The order was peremptory. Fortunately the range was long, and though the cannoneers unleashed what Strother called "a splendid volley [that] covered the country before us with bursting shells," only two Northern soldiers were wounded and three horses killed in the misdirected barrage.[10]

Shields pressed the pursuit for another five miles. From each hillock and ridge Chew's gunners contested the Federal advance, Ashby sitting beside them astride his distinctive white horse. Finally, at 5:00 P.M., an hour before sunset, Shields called a halt. Leaving a strong picket in his front, Shields marched the division under a chilling rain back to Strasburg, where, amid considerable grumbling over what seemed a wasted effort, the men camped for the night. Shields was satisfied with the result of the reconnaissance. He correctly deduced that Jackson's main body was well south of Woodstock, but the clear winner that day had been Ashby. As Strother grudgingly conceded, "Ashby played his part handsomely, displaying a great deal of personal boldness and military tact in checking so large a column as ours with his small force." Among the Yankees his performance assumed legendary proportions. "This Ashby was the terror and the wizard of the Shenandoah," wrote the lieutenant colonel of the 8th Ohio, which had borne the brunt of Chew's shelling. "He was represented as being always mounted on a white horse, of being everywhere present, and of wearing a charmed life; consequently, everything astride a white horse in front, in rear, along the mountains, near at hand, or in the distance, was at once conjured up in the minds of the soldier to be Ashby. His apparition had presented itself frequently during the day and still hovered about fitfully in the advance."[11]

At noon on Thursday, March 20, Shields marched the division back to Winchester. Rain had fallen steadily throughout the night and continued in spurts during the day. The turnpike was sloppy and the going hard. Shields permitted only one halt in twenty-two miles. "Tired and a little cross," men drifted from the ranks by the score, and fatigue drove one soldier of the hapless 110th Pennsylvania to suicide. The next morning only one hundred members of that regiment, or one man in five, were counted present for duty. But in the comfort of his headquarters, Shields bordered on the ecstatic. Calling together his brigade and regimental commanders on Friday afternoon, he announced to general approbation, recalled Colonel Mason, that "Jackson was off a long distance and that all we would have to do, until we had got things in readiness for an advance, would be to picket well in front." Banks, who had just returned from Washington in equally high spirits, agreed. He assured McClellan that Jackson was at Mount Jackson, twenty miles south of Winchester, and that he would set Williams's division in motion for Centreville the following morning. So confident was Banks that he had seen the last of Stonewall Jackson that he permitted Shields to make camp two miles north of Winchester and left only a corporal's guard with corps trains on the southern edge of town. A squadron of the 1st Michigan Cavalry watched the turnpike toward Kernstown.[12]

JACKSON HAD BEEN a long way off, but by the time Shields and Banks uttered their hopeful assessments, the Virginian was making ready to close the miles between the opposing commands. The stay at Camp Buchanan had done his small army good. Governor Letcher had ordered out the Valley militia on March 10, and ten days later four hundred members of the Augusta County contingent, loosely organized into three small regiments, joined the army at Mount Jackson. Encouraged by Letcher's proclamation, Jackson ordered three thousand muskets from the state arsenal to arm the expected reinforcements. The prospect of more fighting men allowed him to go easy on those who refused to take up arms on religious grounds. Quaker, Mennonite, and Dunkard men had been escaping through the lines in large numbers; those who remained behind might obey the governor's call, but many swore they would not shoot. "They can be made to fire, but they can very easily take bad aim," Jackson told the governor's military aide. Rather than dilute his fighting ranks with unreliable men, and to secure the loyalty of these conscientious objectors, Jackson wisely agreed to employ them as unarmed teamsters, organized into companies of one hundred men each. "If these men are, as represented to me, faithful laborers and careful of property, this arrangement will not only enable many volunteers to return to the ranks, but will also save many valuable horses and other public property in addition to arms."[13]

With the Augusta militia there came one man who would prove more valuable to Jackson than all the militiamen and teamsters of the Shenandoah Valley, thirty-three-year-old Jedediah Hotchkiss. A devout Presbyterian like

Jackson, the six-foot-tall, sleepy-eyed native New Yorker had made a name for himself in Virginia during the 1850s as a schoolmaster, geologist, and amateur cartographer. Hotchkiss offered his services to the Confederacy in June 1861, parleying his hobby into a staff position under Robert E. Lee in western Virginia, where he went to work making the general a map of Tygart's Valley. In August Hotchkiss contracted typhoid fever and returned home, but by March 1862 he considered himself again fit for service. He responded to the calling out of the militia in the hope of securing engineering duty with Jackson, an ambition that his friend Col. William S. H. Baylor of the general's staff encouraged. Jackson took to Hotchkiss instantly. Granting his request, Jackson assigned him to conduct a preliminary reconnaissance of Woodstock and vicinity. A delighted Hotchkiss spent March 21 mustering the Augusta County militia into Confederate service.[14]

Matters far graver than staff appointments occupied Jackson's mind that evening. A dispatch from Turner Ashby announcing Shields's withdrawal from Strasburg commanded his full attention. The day before Ashby had speculated that Shields, whose force he estimated at ten thousand men, intended to pursue Jackson as far as Staunton. His sudden departure from Ashby's front could mean only one thing: McClellan had elected to reinforce his army from the Valley for his push on Richmond, an eventuality that General Johnston had urged Jackson to forestall. "Would not your presence with your troops nearer Winchester prevent the enemy from diminishing his force there?" Johnston had asked him rhetorically on March 19. "It is important to keep that army in the Valley, and that it should not reinforce McClellan. Do try to prevent it by getting and keeping as near as prudence will permit."[15]

Jackson obeyed with alacrity. On the cool and sloppy morning of Saturday, March 22—it had snowed the previous morning, then thawed during the night—he put his army in motion for Winchester. It was an endeavor risky in the extreme; Jackson had fewer than 4,000 men with which to take on at least 10,000, and perhaps as many as 20,000, Federals. Fulkerson's small brigade, comprised of the 23rd and 37th Virginia Infantry and Shumaker's battery, set off from its camp near Woodstock. The Stonewall Brigade, encamped two miles below Mount Jackson, and Burks's Brigade, posted two miles above the town, hurried north to overtake it. By nightfall, at the expense of twenty-two to twenty-eight miles of hard marching, Jackson had reunited his command at Strasburg. What he would do next depended largely on what Ashby reported.[16]

Ashby had much to report. Reconnoitering down the Valley Pike on the outskirts of Kernstown shortly after 2:00 P.M., he ran into pickets from the squadron of the 1st Michigan Cavalry whom Banks had left south of Winchester. Ashby's 290 troopers drove the Yankee cavalrymen across Abram's Creek and past the Hollingsworth and Parkin's gristmills, almost capturing the Yankee commander, Maj. Angelo Paldi, who was lounging in a nearby house. Chew's three-gun battery unlimbered along a low ridge west of Hillman's Tollgate. Their first shots sailed into the Federal trains massed on the outskirts of Winchester. The train commander, Maj. Joseph Matthews of the 46th Pennsylvania, summoned the four companies comprising the guard under arms, then rode back to Banks's headquarters for orders.

Moments later he returned. Directing the wagons to hitch up and start north, he deployed his infantry in a long, open skirmish line east of the turnpike. At double-quick time they pushed Ashby's skirmishers back across Abram's Creek, then halted in a skirt of timber near the tollgate, two fields intervening between them and Chew's guns. Chew opened on the Matthews line with shrapnel, but the Yankees were too spread out for the rounds to have any effect. Though most of Ashby's cavalrymen retired behind the crest of the ridge, an intrepid handful dismounted and, with rifle or shotgun, worked their way down to an intervening fence for a clearer shot. "Though we learned pretty well the music of their missiles," recalled a Northern infantryman, "there was no damage done by them except to the trees and fences, which were badly splintered and battered with the fusillade."[17]

Matthews's quick thinking had saved the Federal supply train. Banks and Shields, on the other hand, displayed a singular lack of perspicacity in their reactions to Ashby's presence. Banks's sole apparent response to word of the Confederate approach was to send his unreliable assistant adjutant general, Maj. R. Morris Copeland, with Company L, 1st Michigan Cavalry—twenty-five men strong—to the front. On their way out of Winchester they were joined by Lt. Col. Joseph Copeland and the three remaining companies of the regiment, which Col. Thornton F. Brodhead, the chief of cavalry, had ordered out on learning from Major Paldi of his near brush with capture. It took three separate couriers, including one from Lt. Col. Franklin Sawyer, who with one company of the 8th Ohio had been on picket near Milltown, as the Hollingsworth and Parkin's mills and associated outbuildings were known, to convince General Shields that something was amiss. "With a part of his staff, he came galloping up to the cavalry headquarters and, still with an air of incredulity, demanded to know where the enemy was who had so disturbed the cavalry," said George K. Johnson, surgeon of the 1st Michigan. "Colonel Brodhead, a little nettled at the manner of the general, pointed to a range of hills three-fourths of a mile away, and running directly across the Valley Pike." Shields, still doubtful, set off for Milltown with Brodhead, Johnson, and his personal escort, the Ringgold Cavalry Company, to examine the situation.[18]

A glance through his field glass confirmed for Shields the correctness of Brodhead's report, and he summoned reinforcements. First on the field was Capt. James F. Huntington's Battery H, 1st Ohio Light Artillery. As Huntington unlimbered his six rifled pieces behind a row of willow trees on the west side of the turnpike near Parkin's Mill, the Ringgold Company, at Shields's behest, dismounted and tore down a fence blocking the artillery's field of fire. Right behind Huntington's battery came the six guns of Capt. Lucius N. Robinson's Battery L, 1st Ohio Light Artillery. At the first fire Robinson had harnessed and hitched up his battery in expectation of orders. "It was our first chance for a fight," explained Sgt. James Gildea, "and we did not want to miss it as it might end the war." After a delay that seemed interminable, orders came. With a cry of "Forward, follow me," Captain Robinson galloped down Loudoun Street. Following him proved an ordeal. Recalled Gildea: "The street was paved with limestone on edge and in keeping up with the captain's mad rush the gun carriage bounced almost four feet from the ground at every rut or projection which the wheels struck. Joseph Race received a rupture while riding on the limber chest, and I have often wondered since why we did not explode all our ammunition on that mad ride." Veering to the right off the turnpike, Robinson's limbers passed behind Battery H, already engaged with Chew's three guns, to take position on Huntington's right.[19]

The first infantry regiment to arrive was the 67th Ohio, temporarily under the command of the popular and capable Lt. Col. Alvin Voris. Shields directed him to wheel his column into line on the left of the turnpike and then deploy the regiment as skirmishers to keep Ashby's ubiquitous troopers at bay until other regiments could be brought up in support. Coming up the turnpike behind Voris, Col. Samuel S. Carroll similarly arrayed his 8th Ohio to the right of the road. Chew's three cannons fired on the Federals with remarkable rapidity but doubtful accuracy. "While we were deploying the enemy showered shell, grape, canister, and round ball among us," said Captain Spiegel of the 67th. "None of them did any damage, since they did not burst very near us, and the boys could dodge them."[20]

But one Rebel shell did grave harm. Just as the limber on which Sergeant

Gildea was riding bounced past the left gun of Huntington's battery, a shell exploded against a horse of his limber team, spraying fragments widely. One knocked General Shields from the saddle. Surgeon Johnson of the 1st Michigan Cavalry hastened to his side. "I found him limp, blanched, [and] senseless. A fragment of shell had struck his chest and made sad work with his left shoulder. In a moment he began to revive."

Surg. H. M. McAbee of the 4th Ohio joined Johnson just as Shields came to. "He said his arm would be dressed soon, and he would then take his horse." No sooner had Shields spoken those hopeful words than he fainted. Reviving, he asked for an open carriage to carry him around the battlefield. But when he tried to sit up to have his wound dressed, Shields again fainted. McAbee called instead for an ambulance to take the general back to Winchester. In the meantime, staff officers carried him to a house near Parkin's Mill to escape the rain of shot and shell. As they burst through the front door, a boy living there demanded to know the reason for the Yankee intrusion. Told that Shields's arm had been broken, the secessionist lad responded, "I wish it had struck him through his damned head."[21]

Command passed to Colonel Kimball, who met Shields's ambulance on the south side of town at sunset. Shields was lucid enough to describe affairs at the front accurately to Kimball, telling him that he thought the enemy's force consisted only of Ashby's cavalry and a battery of light artillery. Riding on, Kimball found the two sides locked in a stalemate. As the remaining regiments of his brigade arrived, Kimball fed them into line of battle on the right of the Valley Pike, consolidating the 8th and 67th Ohio regiments to the left of the pike. Jeremiah Sullivan's brigade formed in reserve a short distance to the rear.

In the deepening twilight Kimball ordered a general advance. Hopelessly outnumbered, Ashby retired his command six miles to Newton. Sweeping over the men of Matthews's train guard, who had hugged the ground between the opposing lines for nearly two hours, Kimball's brigade pursued Ashby's troopers for two miles before halting among the orchards and fields of the Pritchard farm, eight hundred yards north of the hamlet of Kernstown. "Here we remained all night without blankets or camping equipment, haversacks or canteens," remembered Sergeant Gildea, "as in the excitement of our first fight we did not take anything with us. We suffered for it and it learned us a lesson ever after to always go prepared." No fires were permitted, which meant no hot coffee—only hardtack and raw bacon and a bed in the mud.[22]

Colonel Kimball later claimed to have been prepared for battle the next day; that he alone among the Federal commanders recognized that Jackson had not abandoned the Valley, but rather had returned to retake Winchester and cripple Shields's lone division. Perhaps Kimball had divined Jackson's intentions, but if he made known his fears, no one took them seriously. Indeed, Banks and Shields, to the extent that the latter was able to focus his thoughts, remained certain that Jackson was far away and on the defensive.

Conferring at Banks's quarters in the home of George Seevers, to which the wounded Shields had been carried, they discounted Ashby's attack as nothing more than another annoying but otherwise meaningless foray by the pesky Virginian. Not even the frank testimony of Rebel cavalryman John Kitchen, whom the Ringgold Cavalry had picked up after dark and whom Banks personally interrogated that night, altered their thinking. Kitchen told Banks that Ashby was "under the impression that our troops had left Winchester, and Jackson's forces were on the road from Strasburg under the same impression." Banks forwarded Kitchen's disclosures to army headquarters at 10:30 P.M. without comment, other than to say that the last brigade of Williams's division had departed for Manassas that morning. Banks went to bed intending to leave for Manassas himself on the twenty-third. Apart from dispatching a squadron of cavalry apiece to picket the Front Royal and Romney roads, neither Banks, Shields, nor Kimball made any dispositions to receive an attack. Kimball's brigade stood alone in the neighborhood of Kernstown. Sullivan's brigade bivouacked just north of Hillman's Tollgate, and Tyler's brigade remained encamped on the north side of Winchester.[23]

On the night of March 22, the fog of war was as thick at Jackson's headquarters as it was at Banks's. The fault rested with Ashby. He told Jackson that only four Union regiments and a battery or two of artillery remained in the neighborhood of Winchester, and that they were preparing for a hasty withdrawal to Harpers Ferry. If Jackson would give him a few companies of infantry, Ashby was certain he could take Winchester in the morning. How Ashby came to conclude that only a skeleton force of Federals held Winchester remains a mystery. If he had spies in Winchester, they failed him miserably. Some Ashby apologists later blamed scouts for the erroneous news. One of Ashby's troopers attributed the misinformation to the town's female secessionists. It seems improbable that Ashby would base his report to Jackson on tales told by civilians. In any case, there is no evidence that any of Winchester's prominent lady informants were deceived as to the Federal troop strength. That night Mary Greenhow Lee recorded in her diary that only one division had departed

Winchester during the day, and she was aware that the wounded Shields was still in town. Of course, Ashby had seen only four Yankee infantry regiments and two artillery batteries in his afternoon skirmish, but to surmise that nothing lay behind them would have been foolhardy.

In any event, Jackson accepted Ashby's report. His duty became clear: he must attack those Yankees still at Winchester without delay in order to draw Banks back into the Valley. The stage was set for a bloody comedy of errors.[24]

CHAPTER 11

WE ARE IN FOR IT

"Kernstown [is] of the same shape like most of these towns on the Pike," said Capt. Marcus Spiegel of the 67th Ohio, "as long as the moral law, only one street along the pike; the regular old-fashioned post town, two or three stage offices or hotels." Manmade landmarks in the area were few. Five hundred yards south of the village and twenty yards west of the Valley Pike was the two-story, red-brick home of Joseph P. Mahaney, one of the area's wealthier Irish inhabitants. Four hundred yards west of Kernstown stood Opequon Church, an old stone Presbyterian structure built in 1790. Six hundred yards north of the church, near the base of the oblong, largely barren knob that bore the family name, the Pritchard family had built its home, a three-story, red-brick residence with twin chimneys and a veranda graced with stone columns. Open fields intervened between the Pritchard farm and Opequon Church.

The village itself lay nestled on the south bank of Hoge Run, an inconsequential tributary of Opequon Creek named for the family of settler William Hoge. A mile northwest of Kernstown and a half-mile west of Pritchard's Hill rose Sandy Ridge, which ran northeast past the western outskirts of Winchester and southwest two miles beyond Kernstown. Open woods of oak and pine covered much of the ridge, which nowhere was more than one hundred feet high. Beside the Valley Pike, the principal thoroughfares were the Cedar Creek Grade, which left the turnpike at Hillman's Tollgate, and the Middle road, a muddy lane that intersected the turnpike three hundred yards south of the tollgate and followed the eastern base of Sandy Ridge. Most of the country west of the Valley Pike was lightly wooded and relatively flat. Fields were

A postwar view of Hillman's Tollgate. (Author's Collection)

under plough and saturated, and horses sank fetlock-deep in the heavy meadows. The prevailing muck made marching anywhere off the paved turnpike exhausting.[1]

SUNDAY, MARCH 23, dawned cloudy and chill in the Lower Valley. Kimball had his men awakened at 4:00 A.M. In the distance the church bells of Winchester sounded morning worship; otherwise, all was quiet. Supposing Ashby had retired far up the Valley, the groggy Federals took heart. There seemed time to pause and enjoy nature. "Spring is here, the birds are singing and the grass is starting, and the buds is a swelling, which makes it very cheering to us soldiers," a Ringgold cavalryman wrote his wife. It was a time also to think of family. At daybreak Col. Sam Carroll ordered the tents of his 8th Ohio brought forward, then started for Martinsburg to bring his wife and children to Winchester. North of Winchester, the soldiers of Tyler's brigade drew three days' rations and were told to be ready to move at a moment's notice to join the army at Centreville.[2]

The pain of Shields's fractured arm had eased a bit. Calling on the general just after breakfast, Col. John Mason found him alert and interested in matters at Kernstown. Shields asked Mason to make a personal reconnaissance of the front and report back to him the strength and disposition of the Confederates. He also directed Lt. Col. Joseph Copeland to gather up what cavalry remained around Winchester and report with it to Colonel Kimball.[3]

Kimball also was vigilant. Shortly after Colonel Carroll cantered off to meet his family, Kimball directed Lt. Col. Franklin Sawyer to reconnoiter west of the turnpike toward Kernstown with three companies of the 8th Ohio. Sawyer felt his way over Pritchard's Hill and across Hoge Run without incident, bringing his small command to rest in an open wood near Opequon Church. The clatter of horseshoes on stone drew Sawyer's gaze to the Valley Pike, where he saw a battery of Rebel horse artillery deploying along a rise behind the Mahaney house, four hundred yards away. After hurriedly marching his skirmishers by the left flank to confront the battery, Sawyer rode forward for a closer look. He came within forty yards of the gun—only one cannon and limber had left the column—before the sight of dismounted Southern cavalrymen and infantrymen tucked behind the low ridge sent him galloping off to withdraw his exposed force. Troopers from Ashby's 7th Virginia Cavalry chased Sawyer across Hoge Run as far as Pritchard's Lane, where they in turn formed a ragged skirmish line.[4]

The cannon that had caught Sawyer's eye belonged to Chew's battery. Ashby was back, reinforced with four companies of infantry under Capt. John Quincy Adams Nadenbousch of the 2nd Virginia. At 9:00 A.M. Captain Chew let go the first shot of the battle from his Blakely gun. The round exploded harmlessly, but it galvanized Kimball into action. He recalled Colonel Carroll from his abortive attempt at a family reunion, sending him east of the turnpike with the remainder of the 8th Ohio while Sawyer reconnoitered on the west side. Riding up Pritchard's Hill, Kimball instinctively grasped the importance of the elevation. "My position being an excellent one for defense and observation, I determined to remain on it until I could receive reinforcements," he later explained. "The position commanded the plain or valley, and village in front, and to the left, a small valley, the woods and hills to the front and right. No better position could be found to cover the approaches to Winchester with the forces I had."

Having settled on Pritchard's Hill as key ground, Kimball rapidly concentrated forces atop it. First up were the four rifled guns of Capt. John Jenks's Battery A, 1st West Virginia Artillery. Next came six ten-pounder Parrotts belonging to Captain Clark's Battery E, 4th U.S. Artillery. Two more rifled cannons from Battery B, 1st West Virginia Artillery, gave Kimball ten pieces capable of ranging the Mahaney house and anything that might come down the turnpike behind it. Kimball brought up the closest available infantry regiment, the 67th Ohio, which had never tasted combat, to clean a band of Ashby's Virginians from the strip of timber bordering the western base of Pritchard's Hill.

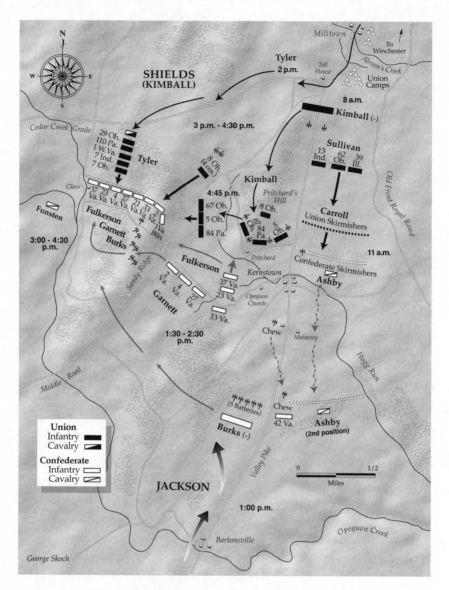

MAP 2. Battle of Kernstown, March 23, 1862, 8:00 A.M.–4:45 P.M.

The task almost proved lethal to the acting regimental commander, Lt. Col. Alvin Voris. "After passing one half mile, I soon heard the report of a rifle and the keen buzzing of a bullet directly over my head as I was leading my column forward. In a few minutes, bang and whiz, again awfully close to my ears. The boys told me that I was in the way of that fellow. Crack and whiz again so close to my head that I did dodge a little (well I do not like to be the target for a sharpshooter)," Voris confessed to his wife. "I cleared the woods of these sneaking sharpshooters, and then was ordered to support a battery of artillery." As Voris guided his men into close column behind Jenks's battery, Kimball advanced the 5th Ohio of Sullivan's brigade into position behind Clark's regulars. Confronted with this overwhelming force of Yankee infantry and artillery, Ashby's cavalrymen fell back across Hoge Run.[5]

Captain Nadenbousch's infantrymen enjoyed the discomfiture of their mounted comrades. Said one: "It was amusing to watch the maneuvers of a squad of our cavalry advancing boldly to the attack and then retiring in haste and disorder back through our lines concealed behind the fences."

Their amusement was short lived. The proximity of Chew's battery brought the counterbattery fire of Kimball's ten rifled cannons uncomfortably close, and a few minutes after the return of his overanxious troopers from Pritchard's Lane, Ashby ordered Nadenbousch's detachment to file to the right of the turnpike, form a skirmish line of two companies, with two companies in reserve, and probe northward. Leaving the Blakely gun at the Mahaney house, Ashby redeployed Chew's remaining two cannons in support of Nadenbousch. Ashby brought up the rear with his cavalry. Still convinced that the Federals had no more than four regiments in the neighborhood, Ashby evidently hoped to outflank the Yankees on Pritchard's Hill and sweep unopposed into Winchester.

Out on the Rebel skirmish line, the situation looked grim. Northern skirmishers—the advance guard of Carroll's seven companies of the 8th Ohio, together with three companies of the 67th Ohio that had picketed the area overnight—were plainly visible behind a stone wall three hundred yards north of Hoge Run. Three hundred yards north of the stone wall was a small wood. To reach the wall and the timber, recalled a soldier of the 2nd Virginia, "We had to advance through open fields in mud shoe-mouth deep and in the face of the fire of the skirmish line." At one hundred yards Nadenbousch ordered his men to fire a volley and charge. The audacity of the Southern maneuver sent Carroll's advance guard staggering back into the timber. Nadenbousch's men clambered over the wall in pursuit.

No sooner had the Virginians penetrated the woods than they ran head-long into Carroll's main line of resistance. A sharp volley sent the Confederates diving behind trees for cover. Carroll's troops followed suit, and, asserted a 2nd Virginia infantryman, "as high as eight or ten men could be seen strung out behind a tree." Sgt. Frank B. Nickerson of the 8th Ohio remembered the close-quarters clash—opposing lines were just fifty yards apart—as "pretty hot work." It was the Ohioans' first true test under fire, and few in the regiment—Colonel Carroll included—knew quite what to do. Riding a large gray horse thirty yards ahead of his men and with only a bugler at his side, Carroll took the brunt of the first Rebel volley. A half-dozen balls pierced his coat cape, but he escaped with only his pride wounded. Pvt. S. W. Drake of Company K was less fortunate. A Rebel bullet killed him instantly. Drake was the first fatality of the battle; for a moment, Sergeant Nickerson expected to be the second:

> I saw a man in gray standing in a path that the cows had made among the pines, and I was standing in the same path, loading my gun, and he aimed dead for my chest. I was green and didn't jump to one side, as we learned to do afterward, but thought I was a goner sure. Just then my ramrod slipped from my hand, and I stooped over quick and caught it before it reached the ground, and as I rose up I saw my enemy's gun smoking in his hand, and he staring at me in amazement. When I took my overcoat off I found that his ball has struck the coat just at the collar at the back of the neck and had cut a strip right down the back. He had made a center shot just as I caught my ramrod.[6]

The Confederate advantage in the skirmish was fleeting. From atop Pritchard's Hill, Colonel Kimball had an unobstructed view of the fight, and he responded decisively to Nadenbousch's advance. A few minutes before 10:00 A.M. he ordered his former command, the 14th Indiana Infantry, forward from its bivouac near Hillman's Tollgate to support Carroll. Mounted on horseback beside Chew's two guns on a low rise in the rear of Nadenbousch's detachment, Turner Ashby recognized the threat to his infantry, now outnumbered five to one. As the Hoosiers filed off the turnpike into line of battle behind Carroll, Ashby dispatched a courier to retrieve Nadenbousch. "In a considerably exhausted condition we reached Ashby," remembered a Virginia infantryman, "and found we had three men wounded, two of whom we had to leave on the field." Nearly a month of ceaseless scouting, short rations, and insufficient forage had left both men and horses of the 7th Virginia Cavalry equally exhausted, and the 150 troopers remaining in the saddle with Ashby were in little condition to resist the inevitable Federal counterattack. By 11:00 A.M. the commands of Nadenbousch and Ashby had been hurled back to a patch of woods a half mile southeast of Kernstown. Chew's battery fell back along the turnpike. Their Yankee pursuers—the 14th Indiana, 8th Ohio, and 5th Ohio, which Kimball had also thrown into the fray—kept a respectful distance, halting in the muddy meadows seven hundred yards north of Ashby's new line.[7]

An uncertain lull fell over the field, punctuated by an occasional cannon shot. Opposing commanders took stock of the situation, Colonel Kimball lubricating his deliberations with a few long draughts from his hip flask. Turner Ashby, though he had failed to take Winchester and had lost the tactically crucial Pritchard's Hill in the bargain, remained confident that only an inconsequential Federal rear guard stood between him and the town. How he reached that conclusion is a mystery. Two Yankee batteries were plainly visible on top of Pritchard's Hill, and a two-gun section of a third had wheeled into position directly opposite Ashby on the east side of the turnpike. Neither the gun crews nor the 14th Indiana, 8th Ohio, and 5th Ohio regiments made any effort to conceal their presence, and Ashby would have been foolish to assume that the batteries on Pritchard's Hill had no supporting infantry. His lack of vigilance was remarkable and would cost the Confederates dearly.

Having no reason to doubt Ashby, Stonewall Jackson pushed his column rapidly down the Valley Pike. The men were footsore and weary. Straggling was heavy, but spirits were high and "hearts were firm." A hopeful Jackson had written Joe Johnston at 6:50 A.M., a few minutes before breaking camp along Cedar Creek: "With the blessing of an ever-kind Providence I hope to be in the vicinity of Winchester this evening."[8]

It appeared that Banks and Shields would accommodate him. Returning to headquarters shortly before noon, Colonel Mason reported that his reconnaissance had turned up nothing more than Ashby's cavalry, in no greater strength than Shields had encountered the day before. Shields's assistant adjutant general, Maj. Harry G. Armstrong, had witnessed the opening action and agreed. On the strength of Mason and Armstrong's reports, Banks decided to leave for Washington, he and Shields having concluded that "Jackson could not be tempted to hazard himself so far away from his main support." Banks instructed his assistant adjutant general, R. Morris Copeland, to remain behind in the unlikely event that Jackson turned up.[9]

Shields had made up his mind about Jackson's intentions even before Mason returned with his reassuring news. Earlier that morning he had told

Colonel Sullivan that "there was no danger of Jackson's fighting again; that he knew him, and Jackson was afraid of him, and that I could go out and pick out a camp." Great was Sullivan's surprise, then, when a shell from Chew's battery nearly beheaded him as he crested a low hill east of the turnpike a few minutes before 10:00 A.M. At Kimball's behest, Sullivan advanced his brigade in line of battle—the 39th Illinois on the left, 62nd Ohio in the center, and 13th Indiana on the right—to the stone wall east of the turnpike and parallel to Pritchard's Lane, which Carroll had just vacated to pursue Nadenbousch's Rebels. There Sullivan remained, awaiting orders.[10]

None would come from Shields. The pugnacious Irishman wisely restrained himself from meddling too closely in affairs at the front. From his bed he read every message brought him from the field during the day and dictated replies to the 4th Ohio's Surgeon McAbee, whom he pressed into service as an informal aide-de-camp. But he issued no orders that were not discretionary. "I think he regarded himself to be in command of his division but not in active command on the field," surmised McAbee. "And I think that is the light he intended his orders or messages to be taken. That is, he did not propose to make the dispositions of the forces on the field. His messages were mainly addressed to Colonel Kimball, in the shape of suggestions or general instructions as to how this or that should be done; not as orders for the specific movements of this or that body of troops."[11]

Kimball disregarded Shields's first suggestion, which Major Armstrong delivered a little after 10:00 A.M., that he push a column up the Valley Pike to take Ashby from behind. Less certain than Shields that nothing greater than Rebel cavalry lay before him, Kimball opted to hold his ground and await developments. He strengthened his defensive posture by sending the poorly led but numerically strong 84th Pennsylvania (the regiment counted 503 officers and men present) to occupy a wooded tract beneath the eastern slope of Sandy Ridge, near the junction of Pritchard's Lane and the Middle road. But Kimball neglected to occupy the ridge itself, which left his right flank dangerously exposed, and he ignored Armstrong's repeated admonition that he advance against Ashby. Explained Kimball: "Now it was true the enemy's position, as represented by Armstrong, was as stated, so far as could be seen, but believing that [the enemy] had other forces near at hand, I did not propose to walk into the net."[12]

THE ONLY ONE walking into a net that raw and cloudy Sabbath morning was Stonewall Jackson. At noon the lead element of his march column, the Stonewall Brigade, reached Barton's Mill on the north bank of Opequon Creek, two miles south of Kernstown. The low rumble of artillery from Ashby's skirmish suggested to Jackson the wisdom of getting his infantrymen off the pike, lest they be exposed to Federal fire as they continued northward. He shepherded them into the southern reaches of Barton's Woods, a narrow, mile-long, boot-shaped stretch of timber northwest of the mill. Arriving over the course of the next ninety minutes, the brigades of Fulkerson and Burke similarly filed to the left into the forest.

The men welcomed the rest. Most had marched twenty-two miles the day before, and all had covered at least twelve miles that morning. Straggling had reduced Jackson's available infantry force to just 3,087 men. Twenty-nine pieces of artillery and their crews were on hand. The only cavalrymen present were Ashby's exhausted troopers. As the soldiers grabbed what rest they could among the trees, Jackson rode forward with aides George Junkin and Sandie Pendleton to reconnoiter the landscape. He intended to wait until the next morning to attack—offering battle on the Sabbath was repugnant to him, and, besides, fewer than six hours of daylight remained. But what Jackson saw on the horizon changed his thinking. Clearly silhouetted on Pritchard's Hill were the ten rifled cannons that Kimball had assembled; not visible were the three regiments of Union infantry standing in support on the far side of the knob. Neglecting to confer with Ashby, Jackson also was unaware of the nearly three thousand Federals east of the Valley Pike with whom his cavalry chief had earlier skirmished. Reasoning that the Federal gun crews on Pritchard's Hill could observe his army spread along the pike and readily gauge his strength, and fearful that, if left unmolested, they might either deny him a lunge at the Yankee rear guard or call for reinforcements during the night and compel him to give battle to a larger force, Jackson elected to attack at once.[13]

The Lord would forgive him for bathing the Sabbath in blood. "I felt it my duty to [attack], in consideration of the ruinous effects that might result from postponing the battle until the morning," he later told Anna. "So far as I can see, my course was a wise one; the best that I could do under the circumstances, though very distasteful to my feelings; and I hope and pray to our Heavenly Father that I may never again be circumstanced as on that day. I believed that so far as our troops were concerned, necessity and mercy both called for the battle. Arms is a profession that, if its principles are adhered to for success, requires an officer to do what he fears may be wrong . . . if success is to be attained."[14]

Jackson would try to minimize the slaughter by outflanking the Federals.

In keeping with West Point textbook tactics, he would seize the high ground (Sandy Ridge) west of Pritchard's Hill, turn the enemy line, and strike the Valley Pike in the Federal rear, allowing him to annihilate or rout the enemy and march unopposed into Winchester. As a preliminary measure, Jackson directed Colonel Fulkerson to sweep the length of Barton's Woods for Yankees.[15]

As he rode among the recumbent but animated soldiers of Fulkerson's and Garnett's brigades, Jackson thought he sensed not merely a readiness for battle, but also a keen desire to engage the enemy. The men, he later wrote, "were in good spirits at the prospect of meeting the enemy, [so] I determined to advance at once."

What Jackson assumed to be a bellicose display more probably was jubilation at the prospect of an early afternoon bivouac. When battle orders came instead, the mood darkened considerably. Col. Robert P. Carson of the 37th Virginia had a premonition of disaster. "I thought [Jackson] made a fearful mistake in leading us against a large force, expecting a defeat." Many Confederates hastily made peace with God. "It being evident that we would soon be engaged, we could see some of the tricks which the men's consciences were playing," observed a member of the Rockbridge Artillery. "Several well-worn packs of cards were thrown away, and men who had not been credited with a scrupulous knowledge of the difference between *meum* and *tuum*, were seen to draw out their pocket Testaments and go to reading diligently." Others, such as John H. Worsham of the 21st Virginia, tried to fill needs more mundane and immediate: "About noon it was ascertained we should have a battle. This had been so little expected that many had left their guns and cartridge boxes in the wagons. I borrowed cartridges from others and went on."[16]

Fulkerson's small brigade, composed of just the 23rd and 37th Virginia Infantry regiments, reached the northern extreme of Barton's Woods, some four hundred yards southwest of Opequon Church, without incident at 2:00 P.M. The Stonewall Brigade, less the 5th Virginia, which Jackson posted behind a fence near the turnpike, trailed Fulkerson through the timber. Jackson also detached the artillery batteries from their respective brigades, apparently without informing his brigade commanders, and grouped them as an artillery reserve in an open field northwest of Barton's Mill, subject solely to his orders. Jackson instructed Col. Jesse Burks to support the twenty-four guns with the Irish battalion and two of his three regiments, the 48th Virginia remaining in the rear to guard the army trains.

Garnett, Fulkerson, and Burks all complied with their orders, which they received through staff officers Pendleton or Junkin, but none of the three knew anything of Jackson's battle plan. Garnett, as second in command, had no more insight into Jackson's thinking than did the lowest private. As Garnett later commented on his predicament: "It is almost unnecessary to say that it was extremely embarrassing and dispiriting for my superior officer to withhold from me his confidence and the requisite information to guide and direct me in the intelligent dispatch of my duties, and whose position even I might by many accidents of service have been called on to fill."[17]

Colonel Kimball, on the other hand, freely shared his plans—such as they were—with both staff officers and subordinate commanders. By 2:00 P.M. he had at his disposal an integrated series of signal stations, which gave him rapid communication by signal flags with all commands on the ground and with division headquarters in Winchester. Couriers regularly passed from Pritchard's Hill to Shields's bedside; too frequently, in fact, for Kimball's taste. At 1:30 P.M. he had received a second discretionary order from Shields, again suggesting that he attack. Kimball again chose to ignore the Irishman's admonishment. He had glimpsed the advance of Fulkerson's Brigade through the Barton's Woods and knew it portended trouble. "Convinced that the general did not comprehend the situation, the strength of the enemy, nor the positions held by the respective forces, and satisfied that from his bed in the city five miles to the rear he could not properly conduct the movements which might be required by the exigencies of the situation, I determined to remain on the defensive."[18]

The rifled guns on Pritchard's Hill acknowledged Fulkerson's presence along the northern fringe of Barton's Woods with a rapid rain of shot and shell. The heavy Federal fire apparently unnerved Stonewall Jackson; at a minimum, it caused him to hurry his plans and deploy his forces piecemeal and recklessly. Galloping forward to the northern edge of Barton's Woods, Jackson directed Fulkerson to turn the flank of the batteries on Pritchard's Hill, hardly pausing to consider that in crossing the intervening three-quarter mile-wide meadow, Fulkerson's two regiments would be subjected to the full wrath of the Yankees guns. Jackson assumed that Garnett would follow him in support. Either Jackson momentarily scrapped his plan to occupy Sandy Ridge or Fulkerson misunderstood his objective, as he oriented his advance on a small grove of trees at the western base of Pritchard's Hill.

Fulkerson threw his command into column by division (that is, with a two-company frontage) at full distance, with the 37th Virginia leading and the 23rd

Virginia trailing. After skirmishers ripped apart a plank fence in the path of the column, he waved the six hundred Virginians into the open. Pritchard's Hill erupted in smoke and fire, remembered Fulkerson, as the enemy "instantly opened a galling fire upon us." Marshy soil and a patchwork of fences, dips, rises, and shallow ravines retarded the attack. Fulkerson's hope of finding a respite among the sheltering trees on the western slope of Pritchard's Hill was shattered when Capt. Lucius Robinson's Battery L, 1st Ohio Light Artillery, unlimbered at the junction of the Middle road and Pritchard's Lane, four hundred yards northwest of the grove, and took aim at the 37th Virginia. At the same moment Fulkerson noticed a heavy column of Yankee infantry—the 84th Pennsylvania—pass through the cannons of Jenks's battery and take position alongside the grove. Utterly exasperated, Fulkerson turned his column to the left and sought shelter in a tract of woods west of the Middle road. There, near the base of Sandy Ridge, the Virginians endured thirty minutes more of a fire "that might well have made veterans quail."[19]

Undoubtedly the absence of Garnett's supporting columns also helped convince Fulkerson to break off the assault on Pritchard's Hill. Lieutenant Junkin had delivered Jackson's order that Garnett support Fulkerson, but in doing so he had neglected to tell Garnett why Fulkerson was advancing, if Junkin even knew himself. Garnett, in turn, did a poor job of communicating Jackson's instructions to his regimental commanders. Garnett was riding with Col. Arthur C. Cummings, commander of the 33rd Virginia, his lead regiment, when Junkin found him, and so he was able to superintend the deployment of the regiment from line of battle into column by division. Garnett accompanied the 33rd Virginia into the meadow two hundred yards in Fulkerson's rear. But word of the movement never reached the commanders of the 2nd, 4th, or 27th Virginia, and they lingered with their men in Barton's Woods while the 33rd came under the same concentrated artillery fire that had caused Fulkerson to divert to the left. Ignorant of Fulkerson's objective and "feeling confident that if the regiment followed its present line of march it would suffer severely," Garnett likewise redirected his column westward, crossing the Middle road three hundred yards south of Fulkerson. With no timber in which to hide, Garnett hustled the 33rd Virginia to the far slope of Sandy Ridge. While Colonel Cummings and his 275 officers and men caught their breath, Garnett hurriedly assessed the situation. "I was in a wooded, rolling, and broken country [and] knew nothing of the strength of the enemy in front." The remaining regiments of the Stonewall Brigade were nowhere to be seen. Neither was Fulkerson's Brigade. Even if united, Garnett calculated, the 33rd Virginia and Fulkerson's two regiments could muster no more than eight hundred men to meet a possible counterattack. He decided to retrace his steps to Barton's Woods.[20]

Jackson, meanwhile, had taken charge of the stalled regiments of the Stonewall Brigade, dispatching Sandie Pendleton with orders to start them toward Sandy Ridge. Pendleton found the colonels of the 2nd and 4th Virginia regiments, and by 2:30 P.M. had them on their way. The two regiments marched by the left flank in column of twos out of Barton's Woods, which put them a good five hundred yards south of where Garnett had come under Federal artillery fire. The Yankee guns boomed their greeting as the 2nd and 4th came into the open, but the effect was more frightening than lethal. Said Hugh A. White of the Liberty Hall Volunteers: "As we moved from the woods, the enemy's artillery opened fire on us. Their shells passed very near us, but no one was struck. Some of the shells fired at us struck the ground and rebounded, forming a graceful curve and leaving a track of smoke behind them, exploded like rockets, thirty feet above our heads. But for the danger, the scene would have been beautiful." One round, at least, did good execution. A shell exploding nearby so terrified the horse of Lt. Col. Charles A. Ronald of the 4th Virginia that it ran away with him. Ronald lost his struggle to control the crazed animal, and it threw him hard on the ground a few hundred feet from the regiment, leaving the 4th temporarily without a commander.[21]

Just before the 4th Virginia emerged from Barton's Woods, Lt. John N. Lyle had caught a glimpse of Stonewall Jackson. "[He] was sitting on his horse nearby. What was remarkable, his countenance was pale and showed anxiety. But there was a set about his jaw that boded no good for the foe." Undoubtedly Jackson's anxiety stemmed for a concern that the Federals might surmise his intentions before he was able to concentrate enough force on Sandy Ridge to make a flank attack. To divert Yankee attention from the buildup there, Jackson ordered Turner Ashby to launch a diversionary attack against the Union extreme left. Although he had only 150 men, Ashby accepted the assignment with his customary zeal. Splashing across Hoge Run at about 2:30 P.M., he and his troopers galloped over a company of skirmishers from the 8th Ohio, taking seven prisoners before two companies, which Colonel Carroll sent to bolster his flank, repelled them. Ashby lost six men wounded and a fine young officer, Lt. Thaddeus Thrasher, killed, but he accomplished his mission. Fearing that Ashby's "spirited demonstration" presaged a general attack against his left flank, Colonel Kimball sent the 14th Indiana to support Carroll's 8th Ohio and kept three regiments of Sullivan's brigade in line of battle east of the Valley Pike.[22]

The piecemeal shuffle toward Sandy Ridge continued. Next to run the gauntlet of Federal fire was Capt. William McLaughlin's Rockbridge Artillery. Leading the eight-gun, 225-man battery into the meadows west of Barton's Woods was Maj. Frank P. Jones of the 2nd Virginia, whom Jackson a few minutes before had asked to serve as his aide for the day because of his familiarity with the ground; Jones's "Careysbrooke" estate lay just south and east of Kernstown. The Rockbridge Artillery debouched from the woods nearly three-quarters of a mile southwest of Pritchard's Hill "at break-neck speed," recalled Lieutenant Lyle. Again Daum's batteries overshot their mark. One lucky shot broke the trunnion off one of McLaughlin's rifled guns, but the Rockbridge Artillery passed over the open ground, behind a low rise, and into a wide belt of timber five hundred yards south of the 2nd and 4th Virginia regiments without a man or a horse hit. Gaining Sandy Ridge, McLaughlin swung his command northward. Garnett's infantrymen were happy to see the carriages and caissons of the Rockbridge Artillery careen past on their way into position, as they drew the Yankee fire from them. "During the cannonading we lay quiet," said Hugh White, "some talking and even laughing, while others were silent and thoughtful."[23]

Entering the meadows close on the heels of the Rockbridge Artillery—first at the double-quick, then at a run—were the 21st Virginia of Burks's Brigade, the 27th Virginia of the Stonewall Brigade, and the West Augusta Battery of Capt. James H. Waters. Again the Federal artillery thundered, majestically but harmlessly. "The enemy's guns were admirably served, their shells bursting in many instances at close quarters," conceded Col. John M. Patton Jr. of the 21st Virginia, "but fortunately with no loss to the regiment except one man slightly wounded and another stunned for a moment." In Waters's battery five men were knocked down momentarily by shell fragments, but the 27th crossed the field unscathed. Such was the nature of long-range artillery fire in the Civil War.[24]

Innocuous though the Yankee shelling from Pritchard's Hill was, Stonewall Jackson had no intention of allowing it to go unanswered. A few minutes before 3:00 P.M. he summoned a section of Capt. Joseph Carpenter's battery to the northern edge of Barton's Woods to return the fire, withholding the Irish battalion of Burks's Brigade to protect the guns. Before engaging in counterbattery fire, Carpenter's gunners trained their sights on the three supporting regiments of Union infantry, which had eased their way forward of Daum's line of cannons to Pritchard's Lane. Of special interest to the Southern artillery was the Pritchard barn, in which a crowd of Federals had sought shelter. Carpenter's first shot smashed through the barn door, scattering "them pell-mell to the four winds," remembered gunner C. A. Fonerden. Clapping his hands, Jackson exclaimed "Good, good!" Inspired by Jackson's presence, Carpenter's gun crews aimed carefully and fired deliberately, and within a few minutes had sent all three enemy regiments retiring for cover behind Pritchard's Hill.

It was an orderly withdrawal, as Carpenter's shells proved less deadly than Fonerden or Jackson supposed. An Ohio infantryman recalled the barrage more as sport than war. "The second shell they threw fell fair among the members of Company E, but by this time the boys had learned how to give a bomb a dodge, and we threw ourselves flat on the ground. The shell fell and exploded and threw soil in every direction. The whole company arose and answered the close call with a round cheer. We were not allowed to stand in this danger long, but were withdrawn behind the hill."

Apparently sharing the impression of Fonerden and his fellow cannoneers that they had "driven the enemy from our front," rather than simply compelled them to redeploy to safer ground nearby, Jackson fixed his attention on Sandy Ridge.[25] His presence there was much needed. The Southern forces on the ridge were scattered, their commanders confused. Fulkerson's Brigade lingered in the woods six hundred yards west of Pritchard's Hill. Garnett and the 33rd Virginia clung to the western slope of Sandy Ridge, six hundred yards south of Fulkerson, unaware that the 2nd and 4th Virginia had come to rest behind a low rise the same distance south of them. Neither Fulkerson nor Garnett were yet aware of the arrival of the 21st or 27th Virginia regiments. Neither did Garnett know that Jackson had sent McLaughlin's and Waters's batteries, both of which belonged to his brigade, to Sandy Ridge.

Garnett and Fulkerson found one another near the rear edge of the woods occupied by the latter's brigade. They must return with their commands to Barton's Woods, insisted Garnett, as they could accomplish nothing on Sandy Ridge with the small force available to them. Fulkerson disagreed, saying that he "was awaiting orders." Garnett insisted that he would withdraw the 33rd Virginia in any case. Fulkerson relented; he would retire in the same direction as Garnett. The two parted company to prepare their commands for the movement.[26]

Meanwhile, McLaughlin's and Waters's batteries had made their presence known, running their eleven guns into position along the treeless eastern slope of Sandy Ridge. A two-gun section of Carpenter's battery unlimbered northeast of McLaughlin and Waters. The thirteen Southern cannons deployed in full view of Daum's batteries, a mile distant and one hundred feet lower. The Yankee rifled artillery scored the first hit. Clement D. Fishburne of the Rockbridge Artillery witnessed the impact at close hand:

> We went into an open field through a gate in a stone fence. My gun was third, and as we passed through this gate one hub caught on the gatepost, and one of the hind traces broke. I dismounted and helped the driver to fix it by cutting a hole in the trace, and we moved on. The delay was but for a moment, but during that time a shell from the enemy struck the off-horse of the piece next behind me, passed through him into the saddle horse, taking off the driver's leg,[27] and then exploded in this horse, and one piece of shell took off the foot of a recruit named Gray who was standing nearby. The wounded men were carried to the rear, and in a surprisingly short time the guns were again in motion. The whole battery filed into the field and then through gaps torn in the stone fence.[28]

Cannon shells often followed strange trajectories. The lethal round that Fishburne thought had exploded in a horse had in fact passed through the animal. Lying with his regiment behind the Rockbridge Artillery, John H. Worsham of the 21st Virginia followed the final course of the shell. After eviscerating the battery horse, it "descended and passed through our ranks and struck a stump not far off, spinning around like a top, and before it stopped one of the company ran and jumped on it, taking it up and carrying it along as a trophy."[29]

Jackson rode up just after the Rockbridge Artillery opened an ineffectual return fire. "The greater part of the time we were engaged, we were engaged in an artillery duel," said Sergeant Fishburne. "I could see but indistinctly the point where the enemy were stationed, but ascertained that the shells from my piece, a twelve-pound howitzer, were not reaching the place." Jackson told Fishburne to reduce his fire to an occasional round, just enough to let the Yankees "know we were about." The men of Fishburne's detachment availed themselves of Jackson's order to take cover behind the stone fence, ten feet in the rear, while Fishburne stood by the gun. "Uncomfortably idle, [I] occasionally helped the next detachment to me to run up their gun after each recoil."[30]

Matters of graver concern than the short fire of a small howitzer demanded Jackson's attention. Sandie Pendleton had returned from reconnoitering beyond the batteries. From a high point on Sandy Ridge he had obtained a clear view of Pritchard's Hill and the country beyond, and the panorama unnerved him. Federal infantry regiments and artillery batteries seemed everywhere. At least ten thousand Yankees stood between them and Winchester, Pendleton told Jackson. "Say nothing about it," cautioned the general. "We are in for it."[31]

CHAPTER 12

IT SEEMS VERY MUCH

LIKE MURDER

Stonewall Jackson prepared for the worst. On the basis of Sandie Pendleton's startling report, he scrapped his plan for a general assault—a plan known only to himself, Pendleton, and perhaps two or three other staff officers. Sam Fulkerson and Dick Garnett remained ignorant of Jackson's plans for their commands, which were then assembled in a forested pocket of Sandy Ridge two hundred yards south of the exposed firing position of the Rockbridge Artillery.

Jackson's next action only added to the uncertainty. Pendleton had counted the flags of five Federal regiments marching in column down the Cedar Creek Grade road toward Sandy Ridge. Clearly, Jackson needed to protect his batteries on the ridge before the Yankees took them from behind. Bypassing Garnett, whom he later claimed was nowhere to be found (Garnett was at that moment conferring with Captain McLaughlin, who had asked him to ride forward to observe the same Yankee column that Pendleton had seen), Jackson personally ordered Col. John Echols to advance his 27th Virginia Infantry in support of Carpenter's exposed battery. Passing in the rear of Carpenter's guns, Echols's 170 Virginians continued up the rock-strewn field eight hundred yards to a shoulder-high stone wall that ran east to west for five hundred yards along a low spur of Sandy Ridge. Negotiating the wall, Echols's men entered a belt of open timber. There they halted. After throwing forward a company of skirmishers, Echols dispatched his second-in-command, Lt. Col. A. J. Grigsby, to find Garnett and relay Jackson's instructions. The time was 3:45 P.M.[1]

Neither Grigsby nor Garnett was yet aware of the Yankee designs on Sandy Ridge, which had been slow to materialize. Although the ridge commanded Pritchard's Hill and provided a concealed avenue into Kimball's rear, the Hoosier colonel had neglected to place a single soldier on it. That morning Kimball had rebuffed a suggestion from Colonel Mason that he occupy the ground. Ashby's brief mid-afternoon foray against the extreme Federal left further distracted Kimball from the far more ominous threat to his right—a danger evident even to the uninitiated among his retinue. "It occurred to me that the ridge afforded cover for a larger force than ours, and an attack organized from there could reach our flank and rear, and even interpose between our reserve and communications with Washington," said Surg. Henry Capehart. "I took the liberty of expressing such a possibility to the colonel, although disavowing any military knowledge; but his mind being occupied with the proceedings at the left, he somewhat coolly, and perhaps inattentively, merely answered, 'Oh, I have no fear of that,' and kept his attention in the direction of the firing with Ashby."[2]

Kimball also dismissed the concerns of Major Armstrong, who laughingly related the encounter to Colonel Mason. "Perhaps Colonel Kimball will say to me, as McClellan did to Lander, that I am too suggestive. I remarked to him that he better occupy that hill on our right." Mason agreed, "He better occupy it, or they will open a battery upon us." A moment later the Rockbridge Artillery opened fire, its two long-range rifled guns peppering Pritchard's Hill with shot and shell. That delivered Kimball from his reverie. "I must take that battery," he announced to all present shortly after 3:00 P.M., then sent Mason and his adjutant to bring up Tyler's brigade for the task of clearing Sandy Ridge of Rebels, together with the eight companies of cavalry under Lt. Col. Joseph T. Copeland that Shields had ordered forward that morning from Winchester. Despite Kimball's two-to-one superiority in numbers, the audacity of Jackson's flanking movement caused him to believe himself outnumbered as well as induced him to conform his movements to those of Jackson. Had Kimball used his numerical superiority to counterattack up the Valley Pike while containing Jackson's troops on Sandy Ridge, the result might have been a stunning Confederate defeat—perhaps even the annihilation of the Valley army—with little loss to the Federals. In a postwar letter, Kimball confessed his miscalculation of Rebel numbers: "His movements had been concealed by the woods. His force in my front did not appear to have been diminished and was equally as great as my own, so that any force moving around my right was in excess. Such was my conclusion."

Kimball relayed his decision to attack to Shields by courier and signal flag, giving the ailing Irishman his first intimation that Jackson was on the field in force. The knowledge availed him little; General Banks had departed for Harpers Ferry, and, apart from Tyler's brigade, Shields had no forces to send Kimball and no prospect of receiving more. The battle belonged to Kimball.[3]

COL. ERASTUS B. TYLER needed a victory. The thirty-nine-year-old Ohioan had risen to the rank of brigadier general in the state militia before the war, and at the outbreak of hostilities he had won election to the colonelcy of the 7th Ohio Infantry over future president James Garfield. Much was expected of Tyler, but in his first encounter with the enemy he had stumbled badly, allowing his regiment to be routed while breakfasting at Cross Lanes, in western Virginia, with a loss of over one hundred men captured. Tyler somehow survived the debacle with his reputation intact and in January 1862 was promoted to brigade command. Although he stood in good graces with his superior officers, Tyler had much to prove to his subordinates, particularly the officers of the 7th Ohio, who blamed him for the Cross Lanes fiasco.[4]

Kimball's attack order found the five regiments of Tyler's brigade dispersed. Kimball had summoned the 7th Indiana to shore up the Pritchard's Hill defenses, and the 7th Ohio lay in support of Robinson's battery. Tyler's remaining three regiments—the 29th Ohio, 1st West Virginia, and 110th Pennsylvania—were stacked in march column along the Valley Pike a few hundred yards to the rear.

Tyler responded to Kimball's summons with more enthusiasm than discretion. Recalled a sergeant of the 7th Ohio: "After we had lain an hour or so on the hill slope and had grown nervous at the noise of the shells, Tyler came riding up. He rose in his stirrups and shouted, 'Men, I have been asked whether my brigade can take that battery. I said you would take it if ordered. I have got the order. Men, will you do it?' Of course we all said we would and gave a cheer, though I doubt whether many of us really hungered for a nearer acquaintance with those shells."[5]

Tyler formed his reunited brigade in close column of divisions; in other words, the brigade showed a front of just two companies, perhaps seventy-five yards across, with the remaining forty-eight companies aligned like dominos in twenty-four lines to a depth of four hundred yards. The 7th Ohio led the column. Following it were the 7th Indiana, 1st West Virginia, 110th Pennsylvania, and 29th Ohio. Copeland's cavalry fell in behind the 29th Ohio. Removing knapsacks and fixing bayonets, the infantry started at double-quick time with weapons at trail arms across the broad fields between the Valley Pike and the Cedar Creek Grade road.

At a spot calculated to bring the Federals into action well behind the Confederate artillery, Tyler turned left off the grade road and plunged his command into the leafless timber. Here Tyler made an egregious miscalculation. Fearful of losing tactical control in the darkening woods—the sun was fast sinking behind the western hills, and slightly less than three hours of daylight remained—Tyler declined to open his column or to form line of battle. Instead, the brigade felt its way southward along Sandy Ridge, down tangled ravines and up wooded slopes, in the same dense formation with which it had begun the march. Tyler at least had the presence of mind to deploy skirmishers, and he did his best to maintain silence in the ranks. Commands were whispered or signaled, "no noise being made save the rattle of the dry leaves as we tread upon," said an Ohio infantryman.[6]

The stillness was shattered at 3:55 P.M., when Yankee skirmishers ran into skirmishers from the 27th Virginia, perhaps three hundred yards north of the east-to-west stone wall over which the Virginians had climbed ten minutes earlier. "It was a beautiful day, birds sang in the trees and the warm sun brought out all the aromatic odors of the forest," remembered twenty-one-year-old Virgil E. Smalley of Company D, 7th Ohio. "Suddenly spurts of fire seemed to come out of the tree trunks ahead of us, and we heard the sound of musket shots. We had struck the Confederate skirmish line. The orderly sergeant of one of our companies, a brave young Oberlin student, fell dead in the front rank. There was not a moment's halt. We marched steadily on for perhaps five minutes."[7]

As the Federals advanced, Echols wisely withdrew his regiment behind the stone wall. At 4:00 P.M., with the head of Tyler's column less than one hundred yards away, the 27th Virginia opened what Yankee survivors variously labeled a "withering volley," "blinding fire," or, as Virgil Smalley so vividly described the moment, "a terrific and indescribable uproar like a tornado ten times intensified. The whole air seemed filled with concussions and strange noises. Bark and branches from the trees came down upon our heads. At first the effect was so stunning that I did not realize what had happened. Some singular convulsion of nature appeared to be in progress. Luckily the effect was mostly on the trees."[8]

Although the initial Confederate volleys killed or maimed few, they revealed the folly of Tyler's double-column formation. "Amid the din of musketry and roar of artillery, no order could be heard by the men," said the lieutenant colonel of the 7th Indiana. Regiments disintegrated and companies splintered as officers and men, most of whom were facing fire for the first time, struggled to respond. The lead Yankee element, two companies comprising the first division of the 7th Ohio, charged a few dozen yards until the regimental commander, Lt. Col. William Creighton, had his horse shot out from under him. Grabbing a wounded man's Enfield rifle, he told those within shouting distance to take cover and return the fire as best they could—one of the few sensible orders issued in Tyler's brigade that afternoon.[9]

Companies D and F, comprising the second division of the 7th Ohio, had the misfortune to stumble within earshot of Colonel Tyler, who had been bellowing at his regiments to cease fire and deploy by the left flank into line of battle. At Tyler's behest, Maj. John Casement and Capt. George Wood of Company D, together with 1st Sgt. David D. Bard of Company F, led one hundred men to an open hillock three hundred yards to the east, expecting the remaining companies of regiment to fill in the interval to their right. But Sergeant Bard and his comrades found themselves alone in a "hot place." Everyone else had ducked into the ravine eighty yards north of the stone wall. "A continual shower of balls whistled with that fearful buzz that must be heard to know the disagreeableness of it," remembered Bard. "Two men were struck down by my side while several were wounded. A ball struck the ground in front of me and threw the dirt in my face." That was enough for Bard. "I got together about ten or fifteen of Company F's men that I found fighting by themselves. I marched them back to the right of the regiment, hoping to find our captain and the remainder of our company. I arrived at the hill and could not find any of the company or [its] officers."[10]

Virgil Smalley of Company D also ran the gauntlet to the exposed hillock and back:

The command to deploy to the left was given, and as the left guide of my company I led off through the woods and over a rail fence into a field, when finding nobody with me but the major, Jack Casement, and hearing bullets singing through the air and coming "zip, zip" through the dry weeds, we both fell back into the woods, the major with three holes through his cloak cape. The regiment appeared to be huddled in a little hollow in the woods, uncertain what to do. Instinctively I sought the shelter of a tree, but another man was ahead of me. A bullet struck him in the leg and he went limping off to the rear.[11]

The next regiment in column, the 7th Indiana, responded to the shock of battle much as did the 7th Ohio, the men hugging the ground or seeking protection behind trees. "The command to deploy was given," said Lt. Orville Thompson, "but companies were mixed together and measurably obliterated, and officers lost control of their men. There was no faltering, however; every man found a place, and it was in large measure the men's fight."[12]

Being farther removed from the fighting, though hardly immune from the swarm of bullets that whistled past or thudded into nearby trees, the 1st West Virginia held together reasonably well, its five divisions laying down one after the other like neatly falling dominos. Not so the undisciplined ruffians of the 110th Pennsylvania, who reveled in drinking and fisticuffs, but flinched from more serious work. A few stray bullets and tree bursts panicked them. Instead of obeying Col. William D. Lewis's order to charge, they fled through the ranks of the 29th Ohio. The Pennsylvanians "broke and scampered like sheep at the first fire," said the lieutenant colonel of the 29th, and in so doing cleaved the Ohio regiment in two. The six Buckeye companies on the right held fast, while the four companies to the left of the fleeing Pennsylvanians advanced to close the gap with the 1st West Virginia. Colonel Copeland summoned his cavalry to rally the 110th from its "shameful rout," but in vain.[13]

The conduct of the 110th caused Colonel Daum, who had left his batteries on Pritchard's Hill to accompany Tyler, to denounce the entire brigade as a mob of "tammed militia." Daum was overly critical, but the fact remains that Tyler's brigade had been stopped in the first five minutes of fighting. In the next five minutes the momentum of battle turned in favor of the Confederates, as Jackson rushed troops forward. Bypassing brigade commander Garnett, Jackson told Lt. Col. John M. Patton Jr. to advance his 21st Virginia to the stone wall. Patton maneuvered his regiment smartly. From his vantage point in the open field, Sergeant Bard of the 7th Ohio watched Patton's regiment take position on the right of the 27th Virginia "in beautiful order in line of battle. I distinctly saw that detestable three-striped flag." Crouched behind the wall, John H. Worsham of the 21st counted five Federal flags before his regiment's well-aimed opening volleys scattered the color guards, and the heavy, sulfurous smoke of battle obscured the view.[14]

Unable to deploy his brigade to the left, Tyler—at 4:10 P.M.—tried to extend his right flank, a maneuver that, if successful, would enable him easily to outflank the Rebels. Tyler chose for the task Col. Joseph Thoburn's 1st West Virginia. Thoburn's men had accomplished little in the opening moments of the fight, their initial volleys doing more damage to the 7th Indiana and 7th Ohio in their front than to the enemy behind the stone wall. But the regiment had remained intact, and Thoburn was able to extricate it from the brigade column in good order and form line of battle in a meadow. Placing his hat on the tip of his sword and bellowing, "Come on, Boys," Thoburn led his command in a mad dash for the unoccupied stretch of stone wall west of the 27th Virginia.[15]

With only one hundred yards of open ground between them and the vacant wall, Thoburn's 150 loyal Virginians felt confident of success. But their hopes proved fleeting. A double line of Confederate infantry suddenly appeared in their front, and the stone wall erupted in smoke and fire. Two bullets ripped through Thoburn's coat cape and pants without finding flesh, but a third dug into his upper arm, shattering the bone and knocking Thoburn to the ground. Thoburn's fall broke the momentum of the charge, and the remnants of the 1st West Virginia melted into the woods to their rear.

The Confederates who repelled Thoburn's flanking attack belonged to the 23rd and 37th Virginia regiments of Fulkerson's Brigade. Like Jackson, Fulkerson had responded decisively to the opening volleys along the stone wall. Riding to the head of his five-hundred-man brigade, he yelled "Men, follow me," and the Virginians started forward amid a shower of minie balls. Skirmishers from the 37th Virginia tore down a rail fence that blocked the line of march. The brigade spilled through the gap and broke into a run for the stone wall. George C. Pile of the 37th recalled the ensuing collision with the 7th Ohio: "We were armed with the old smoothbore muskets loaded with ball and three buckshot. The Yankees had now reached within fifty yards of the fence when we opened fire, and it appeared like every shot took effect, and what was left of them retreated to the wood from which they came. As there was only a space between us of two hundred yards, the ground looked like it was covered with the dead and wounded."[16]

Although neither the commanding general nor his aides knew his whereabouts, General Garnett reacted to Tyler's attack no less ably than did Jackson or Fulkerson. At the "first dropping shots of musketry in front," attested volunteer aide Lt. Elliott Johnston, Garnett interrupted his conversation with Colonel Grigsby to tell Johnston to get the 33rd Virginia, 275 men strong, then resting three hundred yards south of the stone wall, ready to move. Garnett joined the regiment a few minutes later, and within fifteen minutes of the first volley of the battle he had shepherded the 33rd into line to the right of the 21st Virginia.[17]

Next up was the 4th Virginia, which Garnett also personally led to the stone wall. He deployed the 203 Virginians so as to plug a two-hundred-yard gap between Fulkerson's right flank and the left flank of the 27th Virginia. It was a necessary maneuver, but the irregular terrain forced the two leftmost companies of the 4th Virginia—the Liberty Hall Volunteers and the Pulaski Guards— to deploy in a ravine. In so doing they became isolated from the rest of the regiment, which formed on high ground to their right, just out of sight.

The eight companies along the crest made short work of the enemy troops to their front, most of whom belonged to the badly chewed up 7th Indiana and 7th Ohio regiments. "After one volley from the 4th [Virginia] the Yankees broke and fled to the timber in their rear," said Lt. John N. Lyle of the Washington College Company. "Some of them fell flat to avoid the bullets, and undertake to wriggle to the rear, snake-fashion. Those furnished fine sport to our marksmen, as their slow movement gave time for taking good aim. Many of them were hit and turned up their toes to the daisies in evidence of the fact." Pvt. David G. Stein of the 7th Ohio affirmed the intensity, if not the accuracy, of the Rebel fire. His friend, George McKay, while lying on his back and capping his gun, had a ball strike the musket about midway up the stock. As the bullet glanced off, McKay looked back and remarked to his company commander, who knelt just behind him, that he had suffered a close call. "But the captain allowed that it was a close call for him, for had it not struck the musket, it would have taken the captain somewhere in the vicinity of the breadbasket, and thus a musket saved the life of Captain Crane." The national colors were less fortunate. "Our beautiful Star Spangled Banner was completely riddled with bullets; a portion of the spear was shot away, while the staff was so badly shattered that it broke off before the fight was over."[18]

From behind what cover they could find, the Federals returned the fire, each man an army of one. "After the first volley the officers did not amount to much. They could not do anything except to stay and take the fire. The confusion in the fight was beyond any movement that they might attempt to make," said Pvt. William S. Young of the 7th Indiana. "By indomitable pluck, coupled with the ignorance of the danger of our situation, and by utilizing every stone, stump, and tree as a shield, it became a free-for-all. The regiments [were] mixed up through and through, but we never ceased to get rid of our sixty rounds of cartridges as fast as we could load and shoot." Ohioan David Bard found his rifle so fouled by fast firing that he could scarcely ram home a cartridge.

At first the fight was fairer than may have been expected. Said Private

Young: "Fortunately for us we were in a depression of the ground, while the Rebels behind the stone wall were on a ridge, which caused them to overshoot, making our chances for success about equal." Sgt. Thomas Marsh of the 29th Ohio wrote his father that "in the excitement of battle I could aim at the Rebels when only forty or fifty yards from me as coolly as I ever did at a squirrel. But now it seems very much like murder. They would throw up their hands and fall almost every time we would get a fair shot at them, and we would laugh at their motions and make jest of their misfortune." Another Union survivor calculated that three-quarters of the killed and wounded on both sides were hit in the head, an estimate that squares with the reports of surgeons.[19]

Virgil Smalley of the 7th Ohio marveled at the slaughter and at the conduct of his comrades in the opening moments of battle. When his regiment— "a ragged line drawn up without much regard to company organization"— stepped out of the timber north of the stone wall, a startled rabbit darted past. Crying "Rabbit, rabbit!" a man near Smalley "actually left the ranks to chase the little animal." Sword-waving, swearing officers coaxed the command into the open. Smalley caught his first glimpse of the stone wall, two hundred yards distant. "I could see the heads or shoulders of gray-clad men amid the increasing smoke. Jets of flame seemed to leap from the top of the wall." Dropping down behind a knoll, Smalley threw himself into the fight, "lying on my back to load and partly rising on one knee to aim in the direction of the stone wall and the jets of flame." A nearby soldier from the 7th Indiana ceased firing and lay still. "Why don't you load your gun and shoot?" demanded Smalley. No reply came from the man, whose "eyes were open and [whose] face expressed the element of battle." Smalley yelled at him again. "Then I saw that there was a great pool of blood by his side. He had been shot through the heart, and death had seized him so suddenly that the look in his face had not changed. I got some cartridges from his box, moved a little further away from the pool of blood, and went on loading and firing."

Smalley kept his presence of mind amid the thunder. "What a fracas there was—a steady cracking and rattling of musket firing, penetrated by the loud reports of artillery. I remember to have listened with peculiar interest to the surging sound of the minie balls as they came close to my head. They made a vibrating, musical tone, something like a tuning fork. It was hard to realize that these little, swift, humming messengers, were bent on murderous errands." But nerves frayed, and good men broke. "Shortly after the steady work of fighting began a big, burly farmer boy, who was a sergeant in my company, stood on the knoll which served me as a shelter and kept shouting and waving his hands like an insane man. He was suddenly crazed for the moment with the excitement of the battle. He now ran along the ridge, screaming and gesticulating until I lost sight of him in the smoke." Reflected Smalley: "It is singular how differently men are affected by a battle. Some are frantic, some flushed and exhilarated[,] some pallid and nervous, but calm and plucky; some tremble with fear."[20]

Jackson continued to feed the fight against Tyler. At his command, the 2nd Virginia Infantry—320 strong—came into action on the right of the 33rd Virginia. That lengthened the Confederate line behind the stone wall to five hundred yards. A few minutes earlier the small 1st Virginia Battalion, better known as the "Irish Battalion," had joined the contest. At the direction of Colonel Grigsby, three companies squeezed into line to the right of the 27th Virginia to fill a gap opened when several dozen soldiers from the 21st Virginia slunk away from the stone wall. The two right-wing companies of the battalion marched due east into the field opposite the open knoll David Bard and his luckless comrades of the 7th Ohio had earlier held.

Despite their apparent advantage of position, the battle continued to prove costly to the Confederates. Sam Moore of the 2nd Virginia was hit twice: "I received a slight wound on the left side of the head from a minie ball, which tore my cap all to pieces, and a rather severe bruise on the right side of my backbone from a ball fired at me sideways. Neither is severe enough to render me unfit for duty." William B. Colston of Company E, who along with his brother Raleigh had been entrusted with breaching Dam No. 5 on the Potomac three months earlier, was shot as he scaled the stone wall to get a better aim at the enemy:

I was just ramming down my last cartridge when I was struck in the hip and tumbled over. It passed through my mind as I was falling that the bullet had either grazed the bone, broken my hip, or gone into the cavity of my stomach, in which case it would have been all over, so as soon as I touched the ground I whirled over on my hands and knees to see if my hip was broken, and finding it was not, I commenced to crawl back to the rear. In so doing I passed close to my brother, who called out to me to know if I was shot. I told him yes, in the hip. He ordered two men to take me off the field, and one took me by the head and the other by the heels, and started down the hill. They did not stand on the order of their going, but they went.[21]

Notwithstanding his prompt repulse of Tyler's assault, by 4:30 P.M. it was evident to Stonewall Jackson that his advantage on Sandy Ridge was transitory, and that the best he could hope for against Kimball's superior numbers was a stalemate. But the odds of a drawn battle looked good to him. He still had three regiments in reserve (the 5th, 42nd, and 48th Virginia), and less than two hours of daylight remained to the Federals to fashion a new attack plan. Jackson need only hold on until dark.

CHAPTER 13

GENERAL JACKSON WAS

COMPLETELY TAKEN IN

It had long been an axiom of war that a commander not reinforce failure. But Nathan Kimball was short on military education, and reinforcing failure was precisely what he set about to do after Tyler's attack on Sandy Ridge stalled. Rather than probe for weaknesses elsewhere along Jackson's attenuated lines, Kimball began a piecemeal redeployment of forces toward Sandy Ridge.

The four companies of the 8th Ohio Infantry under Lt. Col. Franklin Sawyer that had been supporting Robinson's battery on the knoll northwest of Pritchard's Hill marched into the fray first. Colonel Daum delivered the order to charge; Col. John S. Clark of Banks's staff came up a few moments later to point out the line of march—down the knoll, west across an open meadow, and up the timbered slope of Sandy Ridge. At 4:45 P.M. Sawyer led his men forward with fixed bayonets at the double-quick, which seemed more like the "quadruple quick" to one winded Ohioan. A three-quarters of a mile dash brought Sawyer's small command face-to-face with the two companies (C and E) of the Irish Battalion that had made their way beyond the stone wall. The ensuing close combat stunned Sawyer: "Cannon balls were crashing through the trees, and the ugly rifle and musket ball were whizzing fearfully close to us. The line struck the enemy at right angles with the stone wall, and a savage fight for a few minutes ensued. We were separated from the Rebels by a rail fence, which was nearly demolished by the line as it came up, leaving us absolutely among the Rebels. The fight was almost hand to hand, some of the men discharging and then clubbing their muskets." Sawyer waded in. His horse was twice struck as the Ohioans advanced, and Sawyer's sash was pierced with a ball. Dismounting at the fence, he tried to send his horse into a ravine to presumed safety. The animal refused to leave the colonel's side, instead following him wherever he went. Sawyer's men quipped that the horse thought "the safe place was with his master."[1]

There were precious few safe spots on that part of the field. Sgt. John H. Jack of Company E watched his second lieutenant, Alfred T. Craig, fall with a bullet in his side. Pointing to his wound, Craig asked his men "if they would revenge that." As the lieutenant spoke, twelve other members of the company went down; all the rest, recalled Sergeant Jack, "had the marks of bullets in their clothing."[2]

Several sharp volleys from the 2nd Virginia helped the Irish Battalion halt the 8th Ohio. A few minutes afterward three fresh Union regiments— the 84th Pennsylvania, 5th Ohio, and 67th Ohio—advanced from Pritchard's Hill past the left flank of Sawyer's stalled command to renew the assault on Sandy Ridge. None were in a condition to give a good account of themselves. The 67th Ohio, which struck the enemy first, went into action without its commander, Col. Otto Burstenbinder, who was under arrest awaiting court-martial. His absence as such was no loss. Burstenbinder was an inept coward— an "imbecile imposter and knave," said one regimental officer—and despised by all. During his tenure Burstenbinder had neglected to train the regiment to even minimal proficiency, and Lt. Col. Alvin C. Voris, who took the 350 men present for duty into combat that afternoon, feared for the result. Three weeks earlier he had confided to his wife: "If we were better instructed I would rejoice to go into a battle with the 67th. We have first-rate fighting material in the regiment, and properly handled would give a hard blow in an encounter with the enemy."[3]

Voris tried to remedy the regiment's shortcomings with a strong dose of personal courage. At the first fire he dismounted, grabbed the colors, and moved among the men, exhorting them to do their duty. His presence won him respect—"I cannot say enough in praise of Colonel Voris," one man wrote home after the battle—but could not compensate for a fatal disadvantage in position. Perched on the brow of the open ridge fifty yards east of the stone wall, the 67th took staggering casualties at the hands of the 2nd Virginia, which was tucked into the sheltered junction of the stone wall and long rail fence. In a letter to his mother, 1st Lt. Sheldon Colton of the 67th recalled both the general confusion and his own moment of horror:

During the action the lieutenant colonel came along and ordered our company to be moved a little to the left. In the meantime Captain Lewis had got hold of a rifle and was fighting on his own hook, so I took command and executed the movement. Just after this I concluded to see if my revolver would reach the enemy and had drawn it and was stooping forward slightly to get a look through a rail fence, behind which we were standing, when a ball struck the pair of scissors I have carried so long in my breast pocket, braking one point and bending the other. The force of the ball was partially broken by my pocket diary. It then glanced down, penetrating my body about two inches forward of the joint of the hip bone, passing around the bone in a semicircular direction, grazing it as it went along and lodging about two inches around the joint of the bone.[4]

Coming into action at 5:00 P.M. on the left of the 67th, the 5th Ohio was hampered by a similarly poor position, as well as by earlier meddling on the part of Colonel Kimball. Pvt. Mathias Schwab of the regimental color guard had found Kimball's original order to charge "strange . . . although the colonel's orders must be obeyed." His next command bordered on the criminal. Watching the 5th Ohio and 84th Pennsylvania descend Pritchard's Hill at double-quick time, Kimball regretted a decision that had stripped his artillery batteries of their infantry support. Collaring a nearby bugler, Kimball ordered him to blow recall just as the lead companies of the 5th Ohio entered the timber west of the Middle road. Only the five rear companies heard and heeded the recall. The regimental commander, Lt. Col. John H. Patrick, did not realize until he was in front of the enemy that he had only half a regiment with which to fight. What was equally damaging to Patrick's prospects, the 84th Pennsylvania had faltered in the timber, leaving the five companies of the 5th Ohio still with Patrick to enter the cleared field beneath the military crest of Sandy Ridge with their left flank exposed.[5]

Patrick made the best of the situation, yelling to those around him to "keep cool," "hold their ground," "stand solid," and "to remember Cincinnati, their homes, and their country." Unimpressed with the colonel's rhetoric, Lt. Hugh Marshall shouted at Patrick to drop back and stop exposing himself needlessly. An instant later the Ohioans surged over the brow of a small hill in the cleared field. Beneath them were the remnants of Companies C and E of the Irish Battalion and, another two hundred yards farther off, Waters's West Augusta Battery; beyond the Ohioans's right and nearly in their rear were the right-flank companies of the 2nd Virginia.

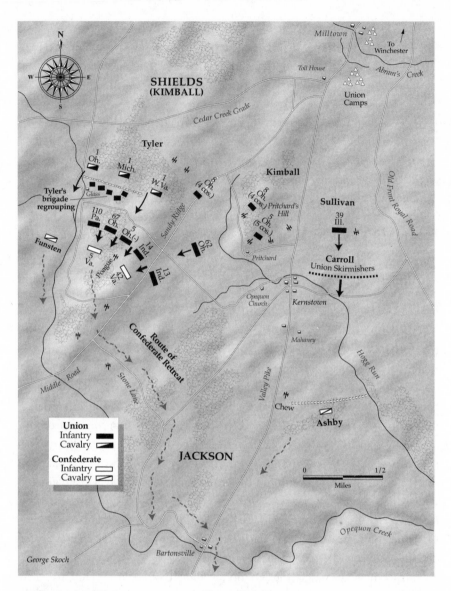

MAP 3. Battle of Kernstown, 4:45 P.M.–Close of Battle

The first Rebel volley downed both color-bearers of the 5th. Forty-eight bullets ripped through the national colors during the course of the fight, and ten pierced the regimental banner. The flagstaffs were splintered. Eight more men bearing the flags were struck. When the captain of the color company dropped with a bullet in the head, several dozen Southerners darted forward to seize the colors, and the struggle, said the acting adjutant of the 5th, became almost hand-to-hand. "The enemy were within ten yards of our regiment. The fire was galling, and a perfect whirlwind of balls were flying, as if the air had been suddenly filled with hissing snakes. It appeared to rage with increasing fury."[6]

Twice the 84th Pennsylvania tried to come up on the left flank of the 5th Ohio, and twice the regiment wilted into the timber. The 84th seemed a hopeless case. Recruiting service and special details had reduced it to 255 men. The lieutenant colonel, major, and several captains were absent. Moreover, two days before the battle, seventeen of the remaining regimental officers had handed the regimental commander, Col. William G. Murray, a letter demanding that he resign: "It is the opinion of the undersigned that though endowed with many traits which distinguish in civil life, you have yet failed to discover that peculiar genius which qualifies for martial command. The conduct of the regiment since its organization has been, it is respectfully submitted, not only unsatisfactory but criminal. Lives are not to be imperiled wantonly because of inefficiency ascribable to the incompetence of command." Eleven days earlier, the mutineers had sent a similar letter to the state capital.[7]

With his military future hanging in the balance, Colonel Murray placed himself in front of the regiment and led it into the open a third time. "On we went," wrote Lt. Harvey S. Wells of Company F, "the dead and wounded fast thinning the ranks. Several times we halted, the men throwing themselves flat on the ground for protection from the rain of shell and bullets, to be rallied again in the forward charge by the stentorian voice of the gallant colonel. Color-bearer after color-bearer had been shot down until six of them were killed or wounded, and the noble flag had been penetrated fifty-six times by bullets." Two-thirds of the way across the field, Murray gave the command "Fire!" At a range of forty yards, remembered Thomas Fowler of Company D, "we let them have the 'lead pills' as fast as we could work our Belgian rifles."[8]

The return fire was devastating. From higher ground behind the Irish companies, Waters's battery plowed the ranks of the Pennsylvanians, who had taken to the ground, with a steady discharge of canister. In what had become a turkey shoot, the 2nd Virginia peppered away at both the survivors of the 5th

Ohio and the right companies of the 84th Pennsylvania. The 21st Virginia, which had redeployed without orders from its place behind the main stone wall to another, somewhat shorter stone wall five hundred yards to the southeast, ravaged the left companies of the 84th at a distance of one hundred yards. A fine time was had by all on the Southern side, recalled John Worsham. "Some of Company F were kneeling down, firing from behind the fence, some were standing up; soon all were standing and taking deadly aim as they fired. As the excitement increased, they mounted the [stone] fence, and many sat on it, loading and firing until every cartridge was shot away." Within minutes, the Pennsylvanians found themselves confronted with what one dazed Yankee termed "a double line of fire [and] a partial crossfire, which no mortal regiment, unprotected, could withstand."[9]

At 5:45 P.M. Colonel Murray had reached the same conclusion. A third of his men lay dead or wounded. He shouted to adjutant Thomas H. Craig, "My regiment is all cut to pieces," gave the order to fall back, then stepped behind the colors, where a bullet found him. Striking the figures "84" in the embroidered bugle on the front of his cap, it drilled through Murray's head and lay open the brain. Death was instantaneous. Just as quickly, the regiment disintegrated.[10]

NINE UNION REGIMENTS floundered on Sandy Ridge in the gathering twilight. The 5th Ohio, 67th Ohio, and 84th Pennsylvania had done no more than oblige Carpenter's battery to displace five hundred yards to the west. But Jackson's role in halting these Federal regiments had been negligible. Not only had he not anticipated a direct assault from Pritchard's Hill, he also had done nothing to meet it when it came. Only the initiative of Colonel Patton in rallying the 21st Virginia to the threat had saved Garnett's Brigade from envelopment and near certain annihilation, and Waters's battery and the Rockbridge Artillery from probable capture.

Not one to give up while enough daylight remained to wreck another regiment, Kimball at 5:30 P.M. committed the 14th Indiana Volunteer Infantry —nearly 450 officers and men strong—to the battle. The numerical strength of the 14th was offset by the "troublesome nature" of its commander, Lt. Col. William Harrow, whose penchant for the bottle disgusted his subordinates. He apparently entered the Battle of Kernstown intoxicated. Elijah H. C. Cavins of Company D swore that "on the day of battle, Harrow was so drunk he didn't know anything," adding "a great many say that it takes a good deal of whiskey to get his courage up to the sticking point."[11]

A drunken colonel invited trouble, and the first mistake the 14th Indiana made was to unload a volley into the 5th Ohio. Horrified, Colonel Patrick ran back to meet the regiment. Ignoring Harrow, Patrick begged the adjutant, who appeared to be exercising command, to cease firing. The adjutant quieted his men and asked Patrick where he might find the "secesh lines." Patrick pointed south toward the blue smoke and stone wall that hid the 21st Virginia from view. Working its way to the left, the 14th Indiana deployed from column into line of battle three hundred yards behind and slightly to the left of the 84th Pennsylvania, just after Colonel Murray was shot. Watching the 84th collapse did little for Hoosier morale. "The 84th Pennsylvania whom we were sent to relieve were cut to pieces," said Capt. William D. Houghton of Company C. "They were almost panic stricken and many were running toward us. Their colonel was borne through the ranks of Company C with his brains dropping out of his broken skull."[12]

The gory spectacle froze several dozen Indianans in their tracks. Those who kept on understood what awaited them. "Ten or fifteen minutes rapid marching brought our regiment into the woods at the foot of the little hill, on the brow of which eternity would begin for many of us," remembered one. "We were protected by the hill, but the bullets rattled like hail in the treetops, and some of our men were wounded by the bullets striking the branches of trees and glancing downward. A few steps brought us to the top of the hill and a little clearing, across which not more than sixty yards distant stood the stone wall, decorated with a fringe of smoke." Out of the smoke, another Indianan recalled, "a line of fire flashed constantly. Between our line and this wall the dead and wounded lay in heaps, while clustered around the Stars and Stripes, a few heroic blue jackets still fought desperately—some standing, some kneeling, and others lying at full length; but all apparently determined to die right there."[13]

The Indianans delivered a volley and a "Hoosier yell," then hugged the ground, hoping the Rebels would give way. Instead, Sgt. Charles H. Myerhoff of Company E, the color company, noted despairingly, "they gave us blow for blow." Myerhoff's company had lost its first man in the woods when a glancing shot put out the left eye of James McQuill. Now men were hit with dizzying speed. The color guard vanished in the smoke. Myerhoff heard a call, "Please pull me down the hill far enough to keep the balls from whizzing so near my ears." It was the color-bearer, Cpl. Alexander S. Retan. Crawling to him, Myerhoff asked, "Alex, are you hurt much?" "I am shot through my body and my backbone is broken. Get me by the heels and pull me down quickly. My nerves are completely unstrung." Retan clenched his teeth, and Myerhoff did as he was told. He dragged Retan out of range as Retan alternated between shrieks of pain and cries of "Farther, farther!" Returning to the line, Myerhoff found that the second color-bearer had been wounded. He helped him off the hill as well.[14]

Fortunately for the 14th, the Rebels generally overshot their mark, and the Hoosiers were able to retain their toehold opposite the 21st Virginia. Here and there, a few men screwed up the courage to press forward. Acting color sergeant Joseph N. Schneider grabbed the regimental colors and almost single-handedly ran the Virginia Irishmen who had been troubling the 5th Ohio color company back to the stone wall. Most conspicuous among the enlisted men who turned the tide in favor of the Hoosiers was six-foot-six-inch-tall Paul Truckey, a thirty-four-year-old carpenter turned private of French descent. Springing to the front of the Company G battle line at 6:00 P.M., Truckey waved his Enfield rifle over his head, yelled "Come on boys!" and, "wild as a deer, ran headlong after the Rebels as a dog would chase a rabbit, loading and firing as he went." Spontaneous shouts of "Charge!" and "Forward!" rang along the regimental line, as common soldiers took matters into their own hands.[15]

The situation on the far side of the stone wall had turned grim. "The battle was a most desperate affair," remembered Sgt. George W. Peterkin of the 21st Virginia. "The firing was much heavier, and the fight fiercer and longer, than Manassas. We held our position against five or six regiments for more than an hour, until our ammunition was gone. During that hour the firing of musketry was uninterrupted; we were pouring volley after volley into each other at distances varying from forty to 150 yards. Colonel Patton behaved very gallantly, being always present in the thickest of the fight; his horse was wounded, and he had a ball through his coat."[16]

Finding that few of his men had any ammunition. Patton was relieved to receive an order at 6:00 P.M. from General Garnett to withdraw. Most of the 21st Virginia got away in good order. Several dozen men threw away their empty muskets to hasten their flight. What remained of Companies C and E of the Irish Battalion quit the field with them. Captain Waters limbered up his guns and also departed, losing a cannon that overturned when a minie ball killed one of the horses pulling it.[17]

The 14th Indiana was right behind the retreating Virginians. Helping two wounded color-bearers from the field had heated Sergeant Myerhoff "to the charging point." He grabbed one of the colors, waved it three times, and

The 14th Indiana pursues the Irish Battalion at the Battle of Kernstown. (Tradition Studios)

cleared the stone wall with his comrades. Overcome with nervous fatigue, Myerhoff planted the flagstaff in the wall and asked a comrade to look after the colors. When he regained his strength, Myerhoff retrieved his rifle and started after the enemy. Entering a strip of timber, he found himself alone with David Jenner, a member of his company. They were about to part when a ball, fired either by fleeing Rebels or overzealous Federals, ricocheted off a tree and struck Jenner midway between his knee and thigh. "He was a good-sized, fat boy, and when he fell he made a noise like a bawling calf. I sprang to him, and having thought I had heard the ball strike and fall to the ground, I did not understand why he looked so lifeless. I felt his limb and soon found the dent the ball made. I then came to the conclusion that the blow had stopped the circulation, and I began rubbing the limb strongly. Within a moment or two

Dave's eyes began to open, and he exclaimed, 'Dog gone, that feels good,' when again we started, still in view of those we were following."[18]

GENERAL GARNETT WAS five hundred yards removed from the fighting on the extreme right, but from an intimate knowledge of the sorry state of affairs on his own front he interpolated correctly the plight of the 21st Virginia. During "a heavy and incessant fire of musketry," from 4:30 P.M. until nearly 6:00 P.M., Garnett had moved up and down the line, pausing "in the ranks of every regiment of my brigade, encouraging and directing them as far as I possibly could." Colonel Grigsby of the 27th Virginia, among others, appreciated Garnett's leadership. The general, he noted, "stood coolly and calming surveying everything that was going on, [bearing] himself most gallantly throughout that field." Courage at the top was no substitute for bullets or company-grade leadership. Line officers were falling at an alarming rate, and an increasing number of men pushed past Garnett for the rear. The general felt for them; they left the ranks, he said, "some from exhaustion, and others because they had expended their ammunition."

By 6:00 P.M., casualties and defections had caused the fire from the Stonewall Brigade to slacken markedly, a fact not lost on Tyler's brigade, which was showing renewed life as soldiers of the 7th Ohio and 7th Indiana, having fired their last rounds, gave way to the better supplied 29th Ohio. More troublesome than the renewed fury of the Yankee fire to Garnett's front was the presence of Federal cavalry beyond his and Fulkerson's left. A detachment of the 1st Ohio Cavalry was roaming around the Glass farm, picking up Confederate infantrymen who had quit the ranks in that direction. Reports of Yankee numbers at the Glass farm were understandably vague; tired and frightened stragglers tell grand tales. But they were reliable enough to lead Garnett to conclude that he was about to be enveloped, which, he later explained, "would have resulted probably in the loss of part of our artillery, and also endangered our transportation." Under the circumstances, with no idea of Jackson's whereabouts or of his battle plan, Garnett took the only rational course of action—he directed an immediate withdrawal from the stone wall.[19]

Volunteer aide Elliott Johnston was pleased to deliver the order to regimental commanders. Passing among the uninjured officers and men who milled in the rear of the firing line a few minutes earlier, Johnston had asked why they did not fight. The answer was the same: "I haven't a round in my cartridge box—what can I do?" Not a man in the 27th Virginia had a single cartridge to his name. Johnston's conclusion? "We could not hold our position longer."[20]

The commander of the 33rd Virginia, Col. Arthur C. Cummings, also was grateful for Garnett's decision. He had lost all control over his regiment, which had become hopelessly intermingled with the right companies of the 27th Virginia and left companies of the 2nd Virginia; a handful of officers and men from the 21st Virginia also fought in his ranks. Cartridge boxes were empty or nearly so, and the men were bone tired. As the 33rd Virginia withdrew from the stone wall, Cummings felt proud of what his regiment had accomplished. "The brave and gallant manner in which the officers, non-commissioned officers, and privates of my regiment did their duty, under the most disadvantageous circumstances, being worn out by the fatigue of a long march over muddy roads, justly entitles them to the everlasting gratitude of their country."[21]

Capt. D. B. Bridgford of the Irish Battalion was short on gratitude; the withdrawal of the 33rd Virginia, which he thought was done "in great confusion," compelled his companies to fall back in disorder. If Colonel Grigsby is to be believed, the 27th Virginia and the battalion of the 4th Virginia on the spur broke from the wall in good order "after the men had fired their last round of cartridges."[22]

Down in the gully and on the left of the line, the other battalion of the 4th Virginia and Fulkerson's two regiments fought on, unaware that they did so alone. Colonel Fulkerson was having trouble enough just staying on his horse. "The day's work hurt my horse worse than anything which he has gone through," Fulkerson told his sister eleven days after the battle. "He was under the saddle from daylight till eleven at night and was greatly excited. The reports of the guns did not scare him, but the whistling of the balls and particularly the minie balls excited him to the highest pitch. He has not yet recovered."[23]

In the smoky twilight, the officers of Tyler's brigade were slow to understand that much of the stone wall had been vacated. Once they recognized their opportunity, it took time for them to organize their scattered commands for a pursuit. By then, twenty-one-year-old Virgil Smalley of the 7th Ohio was too tired to much care one way or the other:

Probably I lay behind that knoll firing for an hour and a half. I recall very few incidents of that time, yet I was in a state of high nervous tension and observed everything that went on, but the smoke grew thicker and thicker and shut out from view all objects a few rods away. It began to grow dark. My cartridges were exhausted. I got up and went down into the hollow in the woods to look for a fresh supply. Just then our lieutenant colonel,

[William R.] Creighton, ordered all the men back into the woods and put a tolerably good line forward. The command, "Forward, charge bayonets!" was given and repeated down the line.[24]

Despite the best efforts of Colonel Creighton and other officers, it was too dark, and the men were too tired, for Tyler's brigade to make a meaningful pursuit. Most troops slunk down beside the stone wall. But enough men remained on their feet to deliver an enfilading volley that put the left-behind companies of the 4th Virginia and Fulkerson's unsuspecting regiments to flight. The direction of the Federal fire caused many of Fulkerson's Virginians to run west toward the Glass farm and waiting Yankee cavalry, rather than south and out of danger. The deepening twilight, a millpond, and several stone fences across the line of retreat added to the confusion.[25]

Stories of anger, courage, despair, and sheer terror abounded among the stunned survivors of the Confederate left. "The command to fall back regardless of order was given, and we went in a hurry, every man for himself," said Lt. John Lyle of the 4th Virginia. "The retreat to the crest of the ridge was harder than the rush we had made for the stone wall. It was an uphill run, the ground had recently been cleared and was covered with brush and snags, and the enemy was making it warm for our rear." Lyle tripped over an exposed tree root and ended up in the rear of the retreating mass. Scrambling to his feet, Lyle topped the hill to find he had lost sight of his unit. "The sun in a clear sky was just disappearing behind North Mountain. I braced myself and started on a run for liberty down the open face of the hill."[26]

Matters were no better on the far slope. Remembered George C. Pile of the 37th Virginia: "As we retreated down the hill I saw one of our men rise up on his hands when the blood spurted out of his nose. He had been shot in the ear, and the bullet came out near his nose, yet he recovered. But the sight had a depressing effect, and a great number of the men retreated to the left toward a pond and were captured, while those who followed Fulkerson and went to the right escaped." Pile went with Fulkerson. During a pause in their flight, the Virginia private scrutinized his brigade commander for signs of wavering. A frightened officer asked Fulkerson, "Colonel, do you think the Yankees will capture us?" "Stay with me, and I'll get you out," replied Fulkerson calmly. "It was now nearly dark," continued Pile. "I saw many of our men who crossed the pond shot down as they were pressed close by charging cavalry and refused to surrender, many of them facing about shot the enemy. We lost heavily in the fight."[27]

At the eastern end of the stone wall, the 2nd Virginia also lost heavily. Col. James Allen never heard the withdrawal order, perhaps because he was busy saving the regimental colors. With the enemy only a few dozen yards off, he dismounted and grabbed them himself after a third color-bearer fell and the staff was shot away. By the time he gave the command to retire, the regiment was all but surrounded. Between forty and fifty men were captured.[28]

Where was Stonewall Jackson while his main line of resistance was crumbling? His whereabouts are uncertain, but the evidence suggests that he spent much of the two-hour fight near the Rockbridge Artillery, well removed from the struggle on Garnett's front. His probable location, lack of communication with Garnett, who it must be remembered knew nothing of the battle plan, and failure to inform his nominal second-in-command of his location implies that Jackson had entrusted Garnett with the defense of the stone wall and all decisions relating to it. Certainly that would have been a reasonable conclusion for Garnett to reach. But Garnett discovered that whatever authority he presumably possessed was illusory if it conflicted with Jackson's fantasies—for it was sheer fantasy that impelled Jackson in the closing hour of the battle.

Had Jackson placed himself nearer the action, he would have understand the uneven nature of the struggle along the stone wall. Shifting Fulkerson's largely unengaged 23rd and 37th Virginia toward the center of the line might have allowed the Stonewall Brigade to hold on long enough for the reinforcements on which he now counted—the 5th Virginia and the 42nd and 48th Virginia regiments of Burks's Brigade—to make their presence felt. But with circumstances as they were, Garnett could not wait for these one thousand fresh troops—which he had no idea were on the way—to enter the battle.

The first inkling Jackson had of trouble came shortly after 6:00 P.M., not from Garnett's front but from the far right, as soldiers of the 21st Virginia began to stream past the Rockbridge Artillery. Collaring a man from Company F, Jackson demanded to know where he was going. To the rear; he had shot up all his ammunition, the man answered. Rising in the stirrups, Stonewall thundered, "Then go back and give them the bayonet." With that he rode off.[29]

When he returned to the neighborhood of the Rockbridge Artillery a few minutes later, it was at the head of the 5th Virginia, which Maj. Frank Jones had brought up. A delighted Jackson waved his cap at the Rockbridge gunners and called out, "Cheer the reinforcements." Cannoneer Clement Fishburne found little cause for celebration: "We looked to see them and saw a fragment of a regiment, which had been hurried from the east side of the macadamized pike, and which came panting along in rear of us toward our left, in the direction from which our own brigade seemed to be falling back. We gave the best cheers we could and kept firing."[30] Evidently a considerable number of the 450 men reported present for action in the 5th Virginia had fallen behind during the cross-country sprint, not surprising in view of their combined thirty-five-mile march of that morning and the day before.

Jackson sent Major Jones and the 5th Virginia into the woods south of Garnett's position to reinforce the Stonewall Brigade, less one man—Hugh Barr, a drummer in Company A. In the first of several feckless attempts at rallying the 21st Virginia, Jackson had Barr beat a rally for all he was worth. But Barr's drumbeats were lost in the boom of artillery and cracking of rifle shots, and fugitives from the 21st Virginia continued to slip away.

A scenario far more alarming than the defection of one regiment greeted Major Jones and Col. William H. Harman, commander of the 5th Virginia, as they pressed northward. Riding ahead of the regimental column, Jones encountered General Garnett, who was riding rearward, in the open fields south of the stone wall. Jones explained that Jackson had directed him to guide the 5th Virginia forward to the wall. Garnett dismissed Jones abruptly: "I told him (seeing that there was but little probability of the troops being rallied) I thought the regiment [could] effect no good there, knowing it was only between 400 and 500 strong, and therefore could not successfully oppose an enemy, before which the main body had been obliged to retire."

Garnett encountered Harman moments later, in "great eagerness to carry out any order I might see fit to give him," but "in ignorance of the ground." Garnett told him all he could hope to do was to cover the retreat of the Stonewall Brigade and the artillery. Choosing the best available ground near at hand, Garnett told Harman to place his regiment in line of battle behind a stone fence below the wooded crest of a spur that ran nearly parallel to, and one-quarter of a mile in rear of, the original stone wall line. In front of Harman's designated position lay a huge field, through which Federals pursuing the 21st Virginia and Rockbridge Artillery would have to pass. Garnett told Harman to wait hidden until the moment was right to stage an ambush.[31]

It was a sound plan, but Jackson had other ideas. Coming upon the 5th Virginia filing into its ambush position, Jackson concluded—wrongly, and apparently without asking anyone—that Garnett had ordered the regiment to fall back. He was about to take action himself when he spotted Garnett withdrawing with his own troops. It was their first encounter since the battle had begun, and it left Jackson unimpressed with the conduct of his second-in-command:

He did not manifest any concern, and was not using any efforts to rally his men. I rode up to him and asked him why he did not rally his men, or try to do so. He told me he had done so, till he was hoarse. He then endeavored to rally his men; part of them made a stand in the woods for a few minutes. Could the troops have held their position five minutes longer before falling back, there is good reason to believe that we would not have been forced from that part of the hill, as they were in rear of the open space; it would have given time for the Fifth and Forty-second Regiments to have gotten into position before they were attacked by the enemy, and possibly for the last regiment, Colonel Campbell's [Forty-eighth], which was coming up to take part in the engagement.

Jackson either had a faulty memory or chose to lie. Five minutes would have made no difference in the outcome of the battle. The 42nd Virginia, then double-quicking across the Pritchard's fields under a heavy fire of artillery from the knob, was at least fifteen minutes away at the time Jackson and Garnett met. Moreover, the 48th Virginia, which was guarding the army trains three miles in the rear, was at least an hour from the battlefield, as Jackson well knew, having sent Sandie Pendleton just a short time before to retrieve it.[32]

Jackson lessened the chance that the 5th Virginia might influence the battle by ordering the regiment forward from its sheltered position. In the woods beyond the open space that Garnett had hoped to employ as a killing zone, Harman's Virginians walked into a hornet's nest. In their front and on their right was the 14th Indiana, along with portions of the 5th and 67th Ohio, which had rallied to the charge. Opposite their left flank was the 110th Pennsylvania, which Colonel Daum and Maj. R. C. Shriber had coaxed back into action; with the stone wall clear of Rebels, the timorous Pennsylvanians had finally shown a stomach for battle. Also in the path of the reinvigorated Federals was Lt. William T. Poague's two-gun section of the Rockbridge Artillery, which Jackson had ordered be moved two hundred yards forward of the battery's main position. Poague unlimbered his pieces behind a stone fence near a cluster of haystacks.[33]

Poague's guns attracted the attention of every Federal foot soldier within sight. Sergeant Myerhoff, whose small detachment of 14th Indiana men got caught up in the twilight clash, remembered:

Our forces were pressing on far to the right. Fearing my left flank not sufficiently protected, I began moving to my left to confront the two guns on the ridge. Soon I heard the command [emanating from the 5th Virginia],

"Ready-aim-fire!" I got down and hugged Mother Earth very closely and took a side glance out of the corner of my eye to see what they were going to shoot at, but saw no one near me. Just then there was a slight rustle in the leaves about, and here and there the bushes and trees were barked. Finding myself still a moveable body, I crawled along the ground quickly to get to the top of the ridge, then only one hundred yards distant. I succeeded in reaching the point, where I found a lieutenant of Company K and about ten men. The two guns at the stacks were not 150 yards distant, and they were giving us canister with a will. The stumps and trees we were using as a cover were badly scalped.[34]

Those blasts of canister masked a greater chaos among Poague's cannoneers. Pvt. Randolph Fairfax of Poague's section rued their position as "unluckily a bad one, as they were able to come too near under cover of the woods. Consequently our fire was not so effective as it otherwise would have been." When the 5th Virginia to his left broke for the rear after enduring only a handful of volleys, Lieutenant Poague found himself flanked and in need of retiring his guns with the utmost speed. Unfortunately, lamented Private Fairfax, "our drivers being raw hands we were so long limbering up that two of our men were wounded, one of our horses struck in three places, and his mate in one." Under a swarm of buzzing minie balls, the limber hauling Fairfax's gun slid off the ridge and into a narrow, wooded hollow, where its badly wounded horses fell dead across the limber pole. At the same instant a Union shell sliced off the leg of the gun commander. With no time left to swap horses, Poague ordered the men to unhitch and mount the other horses and save themselves. "That we did, in Bull Run style," said Fairfax. "I hated mightily to lose our old piece. It was taken at Manassas, and [was] one of the best of our six pounders."[35]

Battery commander Capt. William McLaughlin did a commendable job of removing the other two sections of the Rockbridge Artillery. Wheeling them to the left, he directed that the guns be withdrawn one at a time, while the others maintained a rapid fire of canister on the Federals then pouring into the field near Poague's position. Gunner Clement Fishburne obeyed the order as best he could: "I aimed my gun at an advancing column of infantry just as it reached a zigzag rail fence, as well as I could in the confusion and dim light, for it was getting dark. The fence was about 150 yards off. I fired at a fence corner, thinking to scatter the rails at least, and I saw that the shell did good work as far as the rails were concerned." McLaughlin lost one caisson when a spent minie ball slapped into a wheel horse just as the team was descending a sharp slope in the woods. The horse became hysterical, and the caisson ran into a stump and flipped over.[36]

Meanwhile, the 5th Virginia had withdrawn to the stone wall at the southern edge of the field, where Garnett had wanted the regiment in the first place. Colonel Harman counted six or seven Yankee regimental flags in the gathering darkness (it was 6:30 P.M., and the sun had set eighteen minutes earlier) and despaired of holding his ground. The timely arrival of Colonel Burks and the 42nd Virginia on Harman's right briefly stabilized the situation. With his small brigade scattered over the field, Burks had elected to lead the 293-man regiment into battle himself. While limbering his cannon, Pvt. Lanty Blackford of the Rockbridge Artillery caught a glimpse of Burks: "I saw Colonel Burks galloping on a hundred yards in front of his command, waving his sword and shouting in the most cheerful and inspiring tone, 'This way, Forty-second!' The men had been for some time at double quick but still pressed rapidly on and up the wooded slope."[37]

Out of the smoke appeared the 14th Indiana, or at least part of it. Five companies lingered around Poague's captured cannon, leaving Colonel Harrow to confront Burks and Harman with just half of his command. Sergeant Myerhoff guided his detachment back to the ranks just in time to be a victim of the first volley fired by the 42nd Virginia:

> A shot or shots struck my cartridge box, which I always placed in proper position for a barricade for my breadbasket, flanked by my canteen and haversack, while taking the position of aim. The cartridge box was badly tore up, the heavy tin apartments being forced in a wad, my watch smashed, the ball passing through my overcoat, blouse, and pants, and only giving me a slight wound above the hip. I was thrown down upon the ground and rolled over two or three times. For a moment I lay stunned. Soon I felt a dreadful vacancy about my body. In venturing to feel my bare backbone, you can judge my thankfulness when I found it was only my cartridge box that was disemboweled.[38]

As Myerhoff regained his feet, the 13th Indiana of Sullivan's brigade, which Kimball had summoned from the extreme left at 5:00 P.M., appeared on the field to tilt the balance back in favor of the Federals.

The 13th was a veteran regiment, well led. Declared Pvt. Lee Frazier of Company B: "Lt. Col. [Robert S.] Foster was a soldier by instinct, and a braver man never drew a sword. We had been supporting a battery all day. When finally called upon he marched us with our guns at right-shoulder shift to within thirty or forty yards of the enemy. We were impatient at restraint. Looking down the line, where the regiment was bulging forward, Foster, seeing their impatience, shouted, 'Damn it, go in then!' "[39]

With a cheer the 13th Indiana rose to its feet and, at 7:00 P.M., swept past the left flank of Harrow's command, striking the center and right-flank companies of the 42nd Virginia a fatal blow. The men of the 14th bore their fellow Hoosiers no resentment for their success. "No two regiments in the service think more of each other than the 13th and 14th Indiana," said William Landon of the 14th. He and other members of the companies that had gone ahead with Harrow appreciated Colonel Foster's gesture in galloping over to their adjutant to speak a few words of encouragement before leading his own regiment in the charge. Capt. William Houghton of Company C admired the "splendid style" with which the 13th "went in without a break, and I could not see that they even staggered under the first terrible volley that met them, as it had us. They moved over the stone wall and routed and sent flying from the field this last remnant of Stonewall Jackson's command."[40]

All but a handful of the 14th Indiana were too scattered to join their comrades in the 13th in pursuit of the enemy, a pursuit that Colonel Foster quickly halted for fear of firing into friendly troops in the darkness that now blanketed the forest. Privates Lee Frazier and Bob Owens of Company B kept up the chase long enough to bag one of Stonewall Jackson's aides, Lt. George Junkin, who had been flailing away with his sword at retreating Virginians. Mistaking Frazier and Owens for two more skulkers, he bellowed, "What are you running from the damn Yankees for?" Without a word Frazier grabbed the lieutenant's bridle on one side, and Owens on the other. When he recognized his error, Junkin surrendered.[41]

The 5th and 42nd Virginia fought until the artillery and most of the 2nd, 27th, and 33rd Virginia regiments, with Garnett and Jackson among them, made good their escape cross-country in the direction of the Valley Pike. But the spirited work of Union cavalry under Lt. Col. Joseph T. Copeland netted nearly two hundred prisoners, the majority from Fulkerson's Brigade and the 4th Virginia. Had the Federals been better horsemen, they might have captured many more. "They are splendidly equipped and very gay, but such bobbing up and down in the saddles is ridiculous to behold," young Kate Sperry had observed on watching Yankee cavalry canter through Winchester, "not one of them can ride fit to be seen." One of Jackson's staff officers thought their inability to jump fences or stone walls, as Ashby's cavalry was able to do, proved the salvation of many Confederate infantrymen that evening.[42]

The suddenness of their collapse actually worked in favor of the Confederate foot soldiers in their flight from the stone wall. Galloping up to the commander of Company A, 1st Ohio Cavalry, to deliver Copeland's order to charge, Maj. Benjamin Chamberlain of the 1st West Virginia Cavalry was surprised when the Buckeye captain asked him, "Which way?" "Anywhere—off to the right," stammered Chamberlain breathlessly. "Go in, Captain, charge them." "Please direct us, Major, where to go," remonstrated the captain. "No, I must go back and bring up my own men."

Left to their own devices, the Ohioans rode west along the stone wall for half a mile, looking for an opening, until they reached the Glass farm. With clear ground at last before them, they put spurs to the horses. Then, remembered bugler Samuel L. Gillespie, the fun began. They chased a company of Rebels into a field of freshly threshed straw. Most turned their guns and stuck the bayonet into the ground as a sign of surrender. Several begged for mercy, saying their ammunition was spent. A few had to be rousted out of straw piles at saber point. One Southern captain, "the bravest man I ever saw—a mere boy, weighing not over 115 pounds," recalled an Ohio trooper, stood his ground, threatening to shoot the first man to approach him. "He seemed to be the only unbeaten man in that entire army." The captain emptied his revolver until, surrounded by a dozen cavalrymen and wounded in the side, he lunged at his tormenters with his saber. Another bullet knocked him to the ground. Raising himself up on an elbow, he threw his sword at the man who shot him and started to reload his pistol. A compassionate Yankee disarmed him. Before falling into a faint, the captain handed his captor a ring, asking that he send it to his mother with his saber and the words, "I never surrendered."[43]

For Lt. Randolph Barton of the 33rd Virginia, the loss of his sword was nearly as mortifying as the loss of his freedom. Captured in woods in which he had played as a boy, Barton was compelled to surrender an heirloom sword. "It had been purchased by my uncle when a militia major, and for years had hung upon the walls of my grandmother's cottage. As a boy of ten I had time and again taken it down, strapped it on, and paraded around the yard with it, little thinking I would wear it in actual war."[44]

Lt. John Lyle of the Washington College Company tried to break rather than surrender his saber, and his temerity nearly cost him his life. Lyle and several of his men had made a determined, if ultimately fruitless, bid for liberty. Three hundred yards south of the stone wall, a squadron of the 1st Michigan Cavalry interposed itself between the members of Lyle's squad and the remainder of their company, forcing them to change course to the west. The darkness provided little protection. "Bullets hit men with a thwack like an impact with oilcloth on a frosty morning," said Lyle. "They sang about the ears like a swarm of angry bees; they whizzed between the legs; they grazed the body and knocked the dirt from under heels as they were lifted in flight." As his party neared Neal's Dam, Lyle spotted a seemingly deserted two-story frame house. He contemplated taking refuge in it, "but then, I reflected, they will hunt us out of that. So we kept going. Bullets were raining on that slope and pattering like hail against the house and plank fences. An old black mammy as I passed was chasing about the yard, her eyes as big as saucers, and she shouting, 'Oh, good Lawd, de jedgment day am sho'ly come!'"

Federal cavalry finally cornered Lyle and his men in a clover field west of Sandy Ridge. Unsheathing his sword, Lyle was about to snap it over his knee when a gruff voice called out, "If you break that sword I'll shoot you." Lyle glanced up and found himself gazing "into the muzzle of a six shooter that looked as wide as the mouth of a cannon. The trooper had the gun cocked, his finger on the trigger, and he was shaking with excitement like an aspen leaf and liable to pull the thing off accidentally. I concluded without further argument not to break that sword."[45]

Among some who should have set better examples, excitement yielded to hysteria. John O. Casler and several of his companions of the 33rd Virginia had paused at the edge of the woods south of the stone wall to decide what to do when a Southern officer galloped up and asked what regiment they belonged to. Casler answered. The officer exclaimed, in the saddest tones Casler had ever heard, "We've lost the day; we've lost the day." Looking about vacantly, he repeated the phrase, "We've lost the day; we've lost the day," then turned his horse toward the battlefield and dashed off at breakneck speed. "None of us knew him or his rank, as it was getting too dark to observe him well. But I thought then, and have since thought, that the man was shocked by a shell passing or exploding near him, for he appeared crazy, or bewildered." Casler's party elected to split up, each man to go it on his own in search of the Valley Pike.[46]

Many Confederates, among them officers, were too exhausted to care whether or not they were captured. When Federal cavalry had closed to within fifty yards of him, Capt. John Wade dropped down in a fence corner to rest, expecting to be taken any moment. But the cavalry rode past him, and Wade lay still until well after dark before setting off again. Maj. Frank Paxton and Capt. James K. Edmondson of the 27th Virginia had run so far, so fast, that a winded Paxton decided to surrender to the first Yankee troopers who might come in sight. Edmondson kept on. Paxton felt better after shedding his overcoat and canteen, and resumed his flight.[47]

A detachment of one hundred troopers from the 7th Virginia Cavalry that had been dispatched to the Confederate left earlier in the battle made no impression on the marauding Federals, harassing Company A of the 1st Ohio Cavalry only briefly as the Ohioans headed rearward with their trophies of captured ambulances and infantrymen. Not until 8:00 P.M., after the last of the retreating Rebel infantry and artillery were three-quarters of a mile from the battlefield, were these Virginians, under the command of Maj. O. R. Funsten, able to organize something approaching a blocking force.[48]

Jackson ordered the army to bivouac along the Valley Pike south of Newton, about five miles from the battlefield, but the order had little meaning. John Casler recalled seeing only one regiment, the 5th Virginia, intact that night. As for the men of his own regiment: "We all scattered, every fellow for himself, building fires out of fence rails and making ourselves as comfortable as we could after the fatigues of the day."[49] Jackson himself rode silently up the turnpike with his staff until in the darkness he lost all but his chief commissary, Major Hawks. Exhaustion and incredulity probably troubled him in equal measure. "I don't recollect having ever heard such a roar of musketry," he later wrote. Dismounting in an orchard beside the road, Jackson asked Hawks if he could make them a fire. "We will have to burn rails tonight." Pleased with the roaring fire and bed of rails Hawks had fashioned, Jackson murmured, "You seem determined to make yourself and those around you comfortable." Knowing Jackson had fasted all day, Hawks obtained some bread and meat from a nearby squad of soldiers. After sharing their meager meal, Jackson and Hawks went to sleep on the rail bed in a fence corner.[50]

Earlier that night, Jackson had paused beside a campfire belonging to some men of Carpenter's battery. One insolent young artillerist told the commanding general, "General, it looks like you cut off more tobacco today than you could chew," to which Jackson replied, "Oh, I think we did very well."[51]

They had done better than Jackson could have imagined. As will be shown, Jackson's aggressive attack at Kernstown tied up Banks's corps, which McClellan had counted on to guard the approaches to Washington east of the Blue Ridge, in the Shenandoah Valley, and led Lincoln and his advisers to look more closely at McClellan's entire stated plan for protecting the nation's capital. They would not like what they saw, nor would McClellan suffer the consequences easily.

Few shared Jackson's opinion of the battle. In a letter home, a captain of the 23rd Virginia snarled: "General Jackson was completely taken in. The wonder is why the Yankees didn't capture our whole army." General Garnett and Colonel Fulkerson believed that only nightfall had spared the army from destruction. Private Fairfax of the Rockbridge Artillery attributed the army's salvation to darkness and "the want of daring on the part of the Yankee cavalry. It seems to me it was the height of presumption and daring for so small a force to attack one so large and well equipped. Jackson must have been fooled by the Yankees." Turner Ashby's chaplain blamed superior enemy numbers and fortitude for the outcome. At Kernstown, he wrote after the war, the Federal troops "fought better than they ever did before or after—especially the Northwestern men." Lt. Sam Moore of the 2nd Virginia saw a divine hand in the defeat: "I trust we may never more have a Sunday fight in which we are the attacking party, for I believe that such a disregard of the Sabbath always meets with punishment. I don't know what General Jackson was thinking of when he made the attack on that day."[52]

Perhaps the most telling reproach of Jackson's generalship came from a mangled and delirious Southern captain, whom Sgt. James Gildea of Battery L, 1st Ohio Light Artillery, came upon while wheeling his gun into position on Sandy Ridge after sunset. The man had been shot in both legs, then had them crushed by the wheels of an escaping Confederate gun limber. When Gildea found him, he was engaged in a fevered dialogue with a phantom commanding general. As Gildea's crew lifted him out of the way, the captain babbled, "I tell you Stonewall, we want ten thousand more men or we are whipped."[53]

CHAPTER 14

VACILLATION IS OUR NAME

Colonel Kimball gave no thought to a pursuit of Jackson's beaten army on the night of March 23: "My men, though filled with spirited determination, were almost physically exhausted from the fatigue and exertions of the day, and they had not had any food or drink since the earliest hour of the morning; had been on the field and under arms since the day before. I therefore determined to halt, give the men and animals food and rest until morning." Colonel Tyler would have been of little help had Kimball decided otherwise; he had curled up beneath the captured Rockbridge Artillery cannon, with a tarpaulin thrown over it, enjoying what Surgeon Capehart called "the most sumptuous lodging on the field."[1]

Notwithstanding Kimball's good intentions or Tyler's selfish but practical example, few Federals on the battlefield ate or rested much that night. Shields's inexperienced commissary department was not up to the challenge of combat rationing, nor was the quartermaster staff inclined to cooperate in distributing food; they were niggardly even in providing wagons to the corps medical director for collecting the wounded.[2] It was after midnight before the first rations reached the field, and by then the soldiers were too tired to cook or consume them.

Nearly every able-bodied man was engaged at one time or another during the course of the night in combing the ground for wounded comrades. Search parties formed spontaneously or at the behest of company and regimental officers. Capt. J. E. Gregg and those members of his Company E, 8th Ohio, with enough strength left in them toiled until 2:00 A.M. hunting for and carrying their wounded to camp, two miles from the battlefield. The musicians of the 7th Ohio gathered that regiment's wounded, built fires to warm freezing limbs, and delivered water "to assuage the tormenting thirst," recalled bandsman Sam Marshall. Capt. Lucius N. Robinson asked Sgt. James Gildea to gather some men and return to the spot near Pritchard's Hill where the first member of Battery L, 1st Ohio Artillery, had been killed and build a pen around the body to protect it from scavenging hogs. Wrote Gildea: "I took the direct line over the ground which the 5th Ohio had charged. It was very dark and I, being in a great hurry to get back as soon as possible, did not notice very particular where I stepped when I slipped. I suddenly fell head first into a dead man, having fallen over him. The contact of a cold corpse startled me, and I started to run, but concluded that I was in more danger from living than dead men and continued on my way."

On his return trip, Gildea had the presence of my mind to gather an armful of straw, which he and Robinson placed under the captain's poncho. Calling over a third man, the three bunked together for mutual warmth. Brief, darkly comical scuffles interrupted their sleep. Cpl. Stephen Edmonds had crawled under a bush on the ledge of a nearby stone wall for the night. He slept well until awakened by a tug at his boots. Raising himself up, Edmonds demanded to know what was wanted. "Why, hell," came a voice in the dark, "I thought you were dead and did not want them boots any longer." Ordnance Sgt. A. J. Jackson had curled up beside a stack of straw, surrounded by wounded men. After he lay down, hospital orderlies arrived to carry the wounded to a field hospital, carting off a sleeping Jackson among them. Not until a surgeon making his rounds shook him sharply by the shoulder did Jackson awake. "This man is dead, try the next," he heard someone say—the next man being Jackson. Jumping to his feet, Jackson hurried away. "Hey, what's the matter with you? Come back here," called the surgeon. "Not much," answered Jackson. "You can't patch me up, I am all right."[3]

Few slept as soundly as Sergeant Jackson had. Death, suffering, and the biting cold conspired against slumber. Sgt. Frank B. Nickerson of the 8th Ohio organized a party to help a badly wounded Southern lieutenant, whose agonized refrain, "Oh, my poor wife and little boy!" kept everyone within a hundred yards of him awake. "We went to where he was," recalled Nickerson. "His leg was swollen frightfully; an ounce ball from one of those old Harpers Ferry rifled muskets had struck his leg half way above the knee, and it looked as though you could put a hen's egg right through the hole." Nickerson had his comrades cover the man with blankets and gave him hot coffee; he, in turn, offered them four hundred dollars in gold if they would carry him back to Winchester. The Ohioans declined his money but did the best they were able, carrying him to the nearest house on the battlefield.[4]

Sleeplessness and curiosity impelled many to wander the battlefield that night. "I lay down upon the cold ground without any supplies and tried to get a few moments' sleep, but the excitement through which I had passed made sleep impossible, so I took a stroll to see the effects of our fire," Sgt. John C. Marsh of the 29th Ohio told his father:

> It was terrible. The small bushes were cut to pieces, and every tree was filled with balls. The dead lay thickly in those woods and behind the stone wall, some torn all to pieces with shell, some badly mangled with canister, but by far the larger portion were killed with rifle balls. It was curious to note the different expressions on the faces of the dead. Some seemed to have died in the greatest agony; others wore a smile even in death. And still others seemed possessed of the very spirit of cruelty and revenge. I can think of nothing to express their look except, *Infernal*.

Wandering beyond the battleground in the predawn twilight, Marsh chanced upon three wounded Virginians tucked in a thicket of vines. "Their groans were heart rending; the cold night had so stiffened them that they were in the deepest agony. I built a fire, brought them some water from a mud hole nearby, and then went back to show an ambulance where to find them. One of them said that they had been sure in the morning they would take supplies in Winchester and enter the town at the heels of flying Yankees. Poor fellows, I can't help pitying them [even] if they are Rebels, for they have no doubt been deceived."[5]

No less deceived were the pro-Confederate citizens of Winchester, who assumed that Jackson had returned to deliver them of their Yankee occupiers. Intervening hills and forest shut out the sights but not the sounds of battle. An intrepid few slipped past Federal provost marshal patrols to catch a closer view of the struggle. Among these were two sons of Cornelia McDonald. "Thinking of no danger other than occurred every day," she had given them permission to set out in the morning, when only occasional, distant cannon shot suggested something amiss near Kernstown. But by midday she had repented her decision. "I sat all that fearful afternoon in terror for fear my boys had come to harm, with my baby on my lap and the four little ones clustered around, listening to the dreadful storm of battle, and feeling how bitterly that at each shot some one of the flower of our youth was perishing. And my little boys!

How could I have suffered them to go away from me so thoughtlessly when nearly every moment brought danger?"

With the darkness came silence. "All the turmoil had ceased, and in its place a dreary pattering rain was the only sound I heard. As I sat there in the dark my imagination painted the scenes behind those hills. The dead, the dying, the trampling horses, the moans, the ghastly forms of those that some of us loved." With a start she screamed, "Where are my boys?" and ran down to the kitchen. There she found her house servants, Aunt Winnie and Tuss, seated nervously by the fire. "Whey is dem boys?" repeated Tuss. At 9:00 P.M. they came home, "very grave and sad looking. Indeed they seemed not like the same boys, so sad and unnatural was their expression." As they told their stories, their aspect of aged weariness deepened. At the beginning of the battle they had sat on a fence near a line of Federals, but when a man's severed head rolled close to their perch, the boys withdrew to a safer spot. When the boys spoke of Jackson's retreat, said McDonald, "their anger and mortification found relief in tears, but they were tears of pity when they told of the wounded." The boys had lingered to give water to some, until Yankee sentinels shooed them off.[6]

The McDonald boys were perhaps the only Winchester residents on the battlefield that evening. Federal authorities kept townspeople from the ground for twenty-four hours after the battle so as not to impede the removal of casualties. That gave rise to rumors that the Yankees were purposefully allowing Southern wounded to expire on Sandy Ridge, but such was not the case. Overworked but well-intentioned Federal ambulance drivers brought wounded into Winchester without regard for the color of their uniform.[7]

The same could not be said of the secessionist ladies of Winchester who tended the casualties that fast filled the town. These women hurried to the courthouse and Union Hotel, both of which had been converted into hospitals, bearing baskets laden with food and drink and offering their services as nurses—but only for Confederate wounded. "They demanded admission to our hospitals to minister to the wounds and wants of their brothers and neighbors, and while there was no ministration of love or service for the suffering Rebels to which they did not willingly give themselves with the most untiring devotion, there was no need or want or suffering of any blue-coated soldier that in the least softened their rancor or approached their hearts," remembered one indignant Federal. He added with only slight hyperbole: "They were as indifferent to the groans of suffering of such as they would be to entangled flies buzzing for dear life in a spider's web in their gardens." That sat poorly with their enemy. "The people of Winchester have lost all our sympathy, and some are quite in favor of burning the town," observed a Union commissary sergeant. "I pity the inhabitants around as the men all feel at liberty to take all they can get and confiscate it, as they say."[8]

Cornelia McDonald negotiated the rows of dead men—their faces covered with great coats, to which had been pinned slips of paper identifying the remains—that lined the courthouse porch and slipped into the building to bring succor to Southern sufferers. But the theater of gore was more than she could bear. "I wanted to be useful, and tried my best, but at the sight of one face that the surgeon uncovered, telling me that it must be washed, I thought I should faint. A ball had struck him in the side of the face, taking away both eyes and the bridge of his nose." McDonald tried to compose herself as the surgeon explained how, and why, the man might be saved, but her gaze remained transfixed on the "fearful wound, still fresh and bleeding." Then the "awful, eyeless face" spoke, the mangled man raising his hand and, with a weak touch of his left temple, saying, "Ah, if they had only struck there, I should have troubled no one." When the surgeon asked McDonald to wash the wound, "I tried to say yes, but the thought of it made me so faint that I could only stagger toward the door." As she left the room, her dress brushed against a stack of amputated limbs. "My faintness increased, and I had to stop and lean against the wall to keep from falling."[9]

Other women found work counting and tagging the Southern dead and wounded, keeping records that they later smuggled through the lines to Confederate authorities.[10] For some, the afternoon of March 24 offered a brief reunion with friends and loved ones among the living. At 2:00 P.M. the provost marshal's guard led 234 Southern captives up Market Street to the Winchester and Potomac Railroad depot for transportation north. Women and girls lined the street, waving handkerchiefs and thrusting clothes and food into the arms of the prisoners, who returned the kindness with hearty cheers for Jeff Davis and the Confederacy. The parade grew so rowdy that one Union captain of the escort later told a friend that "he never was so troubled in his life as he was when they were bringing in the prisoners. He said he thought the women would tear him to pieces. They called him every name they could think of, as they felt sure Jackson would conquer and retake Winchester."[11]

Lt. Randolph Barton of the 33rd Virginia suffered the gut-wrenching experience of being marched past his family home, the doors of which stood open and beckoning. His father and mother stood on the pavement, shouting words of encouragement. Laura Lee's daughter rushed out with a colander full of biscuits, to which Barton and the other prisoners helped themselves. "The vessel being soon emptied, she waived it over her head, cheering most lustily," said Barton.[12]

Although much farther from home, Lt. John N. Lyle the night before had been offered a far better chance of escape than Barton, an opportunity that his sense of honor forbade him from taking. After he surrendered, a single Union cavalryman had shepherded Lyle down the Cedar Creek Grade road toward Winchester. Humiliation and nostalgia stalked the Virginian. "As I walked with that fellow riding after me, like a cowboy after a yearling, I would have given all I ever expected to possess to have been at home with the old folks." Meeting up with a group of fellow prisoners, Lyle's spirits rose, as he realized he had done all he could to avoid capture. Just then a trooper from the 1st West Virginia Cavalry rode by, "going from the rear toward the front after the battle was over." As he passed he took a swipe at Lyle with his saber, eliciting from the lieutenant's captor an unexpected response. "My Yankee swore at him fearfully and threatened to shoot him for his cowardly act of assaulting an unarmed prisoner." Continuing on their way, Lyle and his captor fell into conversation. "We became quite sociable, and on learning that I had marched fifteen miles and fought in the battle within two days, he carried me to Winchester on his horse behind him. As he and a companion rode to the city through the woods and darkness, his loaded pistol hung at his hip in touch with my right hand, and I might have gained liberty by quickly drawing it and sending a ball through him, but it would have been murder. My Yankee took me to the camp of the company in the fairgrounds and gave me supper."[13]

Riding over the battlefield at sunset on March 24, Col. George H. Gordon encountered a spectral figure who shared none of the sympathy Lieutenant Lyle's Yankee held for his enemy, dead or alive. Gordon and his brigade had just arrived in Winchester, recalled that morning from beyond Berryville with the remainder of Williams's division. Finding the crisis over, Gordon and his aide-de-camp went sightseeing on Sandy Ridge. A ragged red line of blood ran the length of the stone wall. Bullets and canister had shaved trees to within six feet of the ground. "To a novice the scene was awful. The wounded on both sides had been removed, but the dead still lay where they fell." A curiosity seeker from Gordon's brigade counted five dead Rebels clustered around an uprooted tree, each shot in the head. One had a plug of tobacco between his lips and a brass snuffbox at his side. The Yankee confiscated the box and the small squares of tobacco it contained. The chaplain of the 2nd Massachusetts also walked over the battlefield that evening. "I found the enemy's dead scattered in every direction. This was a new sight to me. The expression on the faces of the dead Rebels was horrible; they still seemed to look mad at the damned Yankees, as they call us."[14]

Gordon's apparition damned them right back. "Peering into the darkness, I saw a man on horseback, slowly moving towards me, with head bowed low, gazing sternly into the upturned ghastly faces, while denunciations fell from his lips, as without pity in his heart he rejoiced in this carnival of death."

At last the man drew near enough for Gordon to recognize him. It was David Strother, "a son of Virginia, here upon the soil of his native state, cursing with all the bitterness of his heart his dead kinsmen at his feet; a loyal Virginian, who had been driven from home, who had seen his aged father driven out of his house to die; a man maddened by outrages and gloating over this terrible retribution."[15]

Strother had been on a brief leave of absence visiting his wife in Charles-town when the battle was fought. He returned to Winchester only a few minutes ahead of Gordon's brigade. As Strother told it, a "horrid curiosity," rather than hatred, led him onto the battlefield. Whatever may have been his motive, Strother said he recognized no one familiar among the dead. He accompanied Gordon back to town for supper and a night's rest at Gordon's headquarters.[16]

Whether he did so with contempt or from mere curiosity, Strother found plenty of dead Rebels to view. Of the nearly 3,500 Confederates present at Kernstown, 139 were killed or mortally wounded; 312 were wounded (of whom a fair share later died), 253 captured, and 33 listed as missing (and presumed dead)—for a total of 737, or 22.4 percent of those engaged. Federal losses were considerably lower, both in absolute terms and as a percentage of Northern combatants. Official reports broke down casualties as 118 killed, 450 wounded, and 22 missing or captured—a total of 574, or 8.2 percent of the 6,352 Federals engaged.[17]

GENERAL BANKS RETURNED to Winchester from Harpers Ferry early on the morning of March 24 frightened and perplexed, both by Jackson's army and by the burden of his first trial in an independent command. He was not alone in his fear. During the night of the twenty-third, Lieutenants George Junkin of Jackson's staff and John Lyle of his headquarters guard had rattled their cap-tors with tall tales of their army's strength and their commanding general's intentions. Junkin swore that thirty thousand troops were momentarily ex-pected to reinforce the Valley army. Ushered into the provost marshal's office on the heels of Junkin, Lyle sensed the prevailing dread, which he was delighted to feed. Although the battle had ended two hours earlier, "the evidence of fright was visible at ten o'clock that night. The officers were nervous and asking silly questions of the prisoners. The provost had barely recorded my name when he asked me if I knew what General Jackson's intentions were, as if the general would confide his plans to anyone, though he ranked as high as a lieutenant of his army." The provost marshal must have recognized the absurdity of his question, because he quickly shifted the interrogation to the matter of Rebel reinforcements. Were the commands of James Longstreet and Gustavus Smith with Jackson? Assuming a mysterious air, Lyle replied: "You just wait till morning, and you'll find out. We were just skirmishing with you this evening." Mumbling that it had been a "pretty hard fight for a mere skirmish," the provost marshal dismissed Lyle.[18]

Banks was skeptical of the provost marshal's report in his communications with McClellan on March 24, but privately it gnawed at him. Before starting for Middletown to join Kimball's advance, Banks scribbled his wife what he confessed might be his last mortal letter. "I go out this morning and may not see you again. No one but myself can know how much I have loved you. Tell the dear children how much I have loved them. Good bye."[19]

Under great pressure himself to begin his Peninsula campaign, McClellan urged Banks to push Jackson hard—with infantry beyond Strasburg and, if possible, with cavalry as far as Mount Jackson. Vigorous action was to be the order of the day.[20]

Neither Shields nor Kimball needed prodding from above to go after Jackson. From his bed, the wounded Irishman issued Kimball "thundering orders to drive things through."

At first light on the twenty-fourth, a raw and overcast morning, Kimball set his infantry in motion. The cavalry, on the other hand, slept late. It was 1:00 P.M. before the scattered companies came abreast of the infantry, then closing on Middletown. Kimball shooed them forward to give eyes to his advance guard: three regiments and an artillery battery under the command of Colonel Carroll of the 8th Ohio. At 1:30 P.M. the Federal horsemen stumbled on Turner Ashby's cavalry, drawn up with Chew's horse artillery on the outskirts of Middletown, fifteen miles south of Kernstown. Carroll called up his battery, and a brief but spirited artillery duel ensued.[21]

The Yankees were moving too fast, and in numbers too great, for Ashby to make much of an impression on them, and his troopers spilled up the Valley Pike toward Cedar Creek in near panic. Maj. Frank Jones, just returned to the

2nd Virginia after his brief stint on Jackson's staff, was cooking his dinner when, from atop one of several high hills overlooking the creek, he saw Ashby's cavalrymen gallop in. The 2nd and 5th Virginia regiments and the Rockbridge Artillery were on rear-guard duty to augment Ashby's battalions. With them was much of the three-mile-long army train, which Jackson had permitted to trail his retreating command rather than travel securely ahead of it. It was a monumental error. Surprisingly, Jackson's capable and normally pugnacious chief quartermaster, Maj. John Harman, apparently raised no objection.

The vigor of the Yankee pursuit stunned Harman and Jones. Tossing aside his bread and uncooked meat, Jones formed the 2nd Virginia into line of battle. The 5th Virginia also assembled, and Harman hurried along the wagon train. The wagons of the 2nd Virginia bounced off up the turnpike before anyone was able to stow the regiment's tents or cooking utensils. Bidding farewell to his possessions, Jones helped usher the 2nd Virginia into the hills to the right of the turnpike.[22] Yankee shells burst overhead. No one was hit, but everyone understood they faced a danger greater than enemy shrapnel. Said Pvt. Lanty Blackford of the Rockbridge Artillery: "All of a sudden an order came for the wagons to be repacked and sent ahead, and then for the artillery and infantry in succession to withdraw and make the best of their way up the Valley. Before we got to anything like a place of security the enemy had their guns on the opposite hills a mile or two off and were trying to shell us out. There was criminal neglect somewhere in not letting us know sooner of the close advance of the enemy." A chance round sailed over the rear guard and fell among the ranks of the 27th Virginia, killing or wounding half a dozen men. Blackford saw "the poor fellows lying dead and mangled near the very place where, half an hour before, this company had been cooking and eating."[23]

Word of the Federal approach flashed the length of Jackson's army. Veterans took the news in stride, but it threw the raw Augusta militia into disorder. Chancing by as the battalion wavered, Jackson noted with satisfaction the conduct of its adjutant, Jedediah Hotchkiss, in suppressing the panic. He made a mental note to inquire further about the resourceful officer and then rode on toward Narrow Passage Creek. Behind its steep banks, Jackson hoped to fashion a line of defense.[24]

By 2:30 P.M. Colonel Kimball had the cavalry well in hand and his three brigades of infantry deployed to cross Cedar Creek. Ashby had burned the turnpike bridge during the first Confederate retreat two weeks earlier, but there were good fords, including one under cover of Kimball's guns that his cavalry might have splashed across and, as Lanty Blackford observed, "cut us to pieces." That was what the Virginian had expected. Before his battery withdrew, he had spotted "large bodies of the enemy's cavalry on the commanding hills on the other side of the turnpike, and I could distinctly see the U.S. flag floating over one of them." It also was what Kimball had intended. He was ready to cross at the turnpike ford in force and to send a strong flanking detachment along the back road from Winchester to Strasburg to intercept Jackson's trains. But just as he gave orders to set his command in motion, General Banks appeared with the vanguard of Williams's division and canceled the movement. "He deemed it prudent to await reinforcements," remembered Kimball, "and our army remained in camp at Middletown and Cedar Creek that night, while the enemy escaped."[25]

Kimball's mood darkened. Banks now had nearly twenty thousand troops. But beyond sending his cavalry gingerly forward to reconnoiter, Banks did nothing to molest Jackson for three days. Short on rations for both man and beast, and wary of contact with the dreaded Turner Ashby, the Union cavalry gave a sorry account of itself. Not until the evening of March 26 did the Federal horsemen succeed in planting outposts along Tom's Brook, a mere seventeen miles south of the Kernstown battlefield and six miles north of Woodstock. Kimball's and Williams's divisions crept along behind them at a pace that infuriated nearly everyone with shoulder boards but Banks. He halted Kimball five miles south of Strasburg and Williams on the outskirts of the town.[26]

Strasburg left the Federals singularly unimpressed. The abolitionist chaplain of the 2nd Massachusetts thought it the "dirtiest, nastiest, meanest, poorest, and most shiftless town I have yet seen in all the shiftless, poor, mean, nasty, dirty towns of this beautiful valley." A Wisconsin lieutenant who had admired Winchester called Strasburg a "miserable-looking hole [that] does not merit the importance which this war has given it." Indeed, agreed a private of his company, "Strasburg was a 'dirty town.' "[27]

Despite Banks's misgivings, his officers and men generally believed Jackson's army to be demoralized and to number less than a quarter of the strength of their own force. But they also recognized the superior Southern leadership.[28] In a letter home, Lt. Col. Wilder Dwight of the 2nd Massachusetts summarized the prevailing respect for Ashby and Jackson, as well as the exasperation with Banks. "The enterprising and clever Ashby, with two pieces of light artillery, is light, active, skillful, and we are tormented by him like a bull with a gadfly. [Jackson] keeps him in the rear. His game is a winning one, even when he loses." Continued Dwight:

> With his small force he detains twenty thousand men in this valley. It seems probable that his attack on [Kernstown] was in pursuance of a positive order from Johnston . . . to arrest and detain our force from its intended movement to Centreville. In this aspect it was a success. In my judgment our weakness was in turning back. The force left behind was large enough to take care of this valley. But, indeed, it seems as if we had no plan and no courage or decision. Vacillation is our name. My admiration and sympathy go with the gallant Ashby and the indefatigable and resolute Jackson.[29]

Banks saw matters differently. Yes, he told McClellan on the afternoon of March 26, "the enemy is broken, but will rally." Trusting to rumors and the lies of prisoners, Banks assured McClellan that Stonewall Jackson and James Longstreet were about to unite at New Market. From there, they would operate as necessary on either side of Massanutten Mountain to keep Banks away from Centreville. McClellan disagreed. "I do not attach much weight to the rumors of Jackson being reinforced," he responded. Banks must "push [Jackson] well."[30]

It was excellent counsel from the normally hypercautious McClellan. The trouble was, Banks was no more aggressive by nature than was the general in chief. He had built his political career largely on compromise and conciliation. Neither was he a risk taker, even if the risk was minimal. A pursuit was pointless, he wired McClellan nine hours after sending his "broken but will rally" telegram, because "the best informed Southern men say Jackson is moving to Staunton en route for Richmond; that we shall not see him again here." But his rear guard remained in strength near Woodstock, and the next day Banks promised to press it "further and quickly."

He did neither. Banks also ignored a demand from McClellan on March 29 that he "ascertain as soon as possible the intentions of the enemy, and if [Jackson] be in force, drive him from the Valley." March drew to a quiet close in the Shenandoah Valley. Only an occasional picket shot, or an artillery round lobbed across Tom's Brook, broke the tranquility of early spring.[31]

STONEWALL JACKSON FOUND little in his opponent's actions to tax his restless energy or fire his imagination. The Valley army made a leisurely march from Woodstock to Mount Jackson on March 25. During the course of the following week, Jackson methodically rotated infantry units between Mount Jackson and Woodstock to support Ashby.[32]

Jackson's dispositions were sound. By withdrawing up the North Fork of the Shenandoah River, he had enticed Banks farther from McClellan's army. Should Banks leave the Valley, or Johnston have need of Jackson, he was no more than a two days' march away. Jackson had placed Ashby's cavalry so as to perform two functions critical to the security of the Valley army. His presence along Tom's Brook prevented Banks from reconnoitering southward, and roving Confederate cavalry patrols combed the roads that connected Banks's command with the Mountain Department to give Jackson early warning of any attempt at a junction of Union forces from that direction. Scouts, spies, and deserters provided Jackson with an accurate count of Banks's troop strength, as well as of the general's muddled thinking. "The enemy at Strasburg believed that I had fallen back to Staunton en route to join you," Jackson wrote Johnston on March 27. "I will try and correct this error and then fall back, if necessary."[33]

While Banks remained dormant, Jackson occupied himself with administrative matters. His first priority was to improve on his knowledge of Valley topography. For that he needed reliable maps, as well as a topographer to produce them. Colonel Baylor knew just the man for the job—Jedediah Hotchkiss, whom Jackson had watched rally the Augusta militia on the march through Strasburg. Hotchkiss's résumé, as Baylor related it, satisfied Jackson. On the morning of March 26 he summoned Hotchkiss to the Stover house, his temporary headquarters at Narrow Passage Creek. After some slight conversation about Hotchkiss's topographical work in northwestern Virginia the year before, Jackson said to Hotchkiss: "I want you to make me a map of the Valley, from Harpers Ferry to Lexington, showing all the points of offense and defense in those places. Mr. [Sandie] Pendleton will give you orders for whatever outfit you want. Good morning, Sir."

Hotchkiss went to work at once. Leaving Jackson, he rode along the bank of Narrow Passage Creek, from the Stover house to Little North Mountain and back. The line was indefensible, he told Jackson. Two days later, Jackson withdrew the infantry brigade posted behind the creek to Woodstock.[34]

With temporal topography now in capable hands, Jackson looked for a guide to the spiritual plain. He offered the post of headquarters chaplain to Robert L. Dabney, a nationally prominent Presbyterian minister then on the faculty of Hampden Sidney College in Lexington. Dabney also happened to be the husband of Anna Jackson's cousin, and Anna thought him the most brilliant theologian alive after her father. Dabney had served briefly as chaplain of a Virginia regiment in 1861. Despite Dabney's inexperience, Jackson offered him the added inducement of a senior staff position should he wish to involve himself in military affairs.[35]

Jackson's next personnel action stunned the Valley army. On April 1 he relieved General Garnett from command of the Stonewall Brigade for "neglect of duty" at Kernstown and placed him under arrest pending convocation of a court-martial. Four days earlier, Jackson had asked Johnston to send him a new brigadier general. Garnett was hustled off under guard to Harrisonburg without knowing the specifications of the charge against him for several days.

Jackson consulted no one before acting against Garnett; neither did he gather evidence to support the charge or its seven specifications. But evidence would have held no sway with Jackson in any case. He had made up his mind that Garnett's decision to quit the field before nightfall had robbed the Valley army of victory at Kernstown, or at least of a drawn battle.[36]

Seldom during the Civil War was a general officer as gallant and as capable as Garnett treated so unjustly (the court-martial of Union major general Fitz John Porter on charges equally trumped up ranks with Garnett's dismissal on the scales of military infamy). By any objective standard, Garnett had done the best at Kernstown that could reasonably have been expected under the circumstances as they existed. Ignorant of Jackson's tactical blueprint, his brigade out of ammunition and outflanked, Garnett took the only sane course of action. In so doing he saved the Valley army. But Jackson, who generously accorded the Almighty credit for his victories, was reluctant to accept responsibility for his defeats. He had charged his old friend Col. William Gilham with "neglect of duty" after the incomplete victory at Bath; he had tried to make Brig. Gen. William Loring the scapegoat for the Romney fiasco; and now Garnett was to take the fall for Kernstown. Maj. A. Campbell Brown, the fair-minded aide to Southern division commander Maj. Gen. Richard Ewell, thought that "if Kernstown had been a victory, there would have been no charges against Garnett. Certain it is, if the court that tried him had ever reassembled, he would have been triumphantly acquitted." As it was, the court convened only briefly in the autumn of 1862, breaking up without rendering a verdict due to the press of field obligations on its members.[37]

Shock, disbelief, and anger greeted Garnett's arrest. Almost to a man, the Stonewall Brigade condemned Jackson for having deprived them of a popular and battle-tested commander. Frank Jones was dumbfounded at the news.

"Heard this evening General Garnett has been suspended from command," he jotted in his diary on the night of April 2. "It fell like a thunderbolt on our brigade, and officers hastened to [Garnett's] tent to express our astonishment and sorrow to lose so valuable and gallant an officer." Four days later, Jones was no closer to comprehending the matter. "General Jackson has arrested General Garnett and deprived him of his command," Jones told his wife. "We do not really know why, but General Garnett acted with great gallantry on the twenty-third. Our brigade was astounded at the order, and had it not been that our cause was too sacred to jeopardize, there would have been considerable commotion amongst us."[38]

Jackson's new aide-de-camp, Henry Kyd Douglas, was unable to find a single officer in the Stonewall Brigade who believed Garnett had done wrong in retreating at Kernstown. "It may be said that, for once, the officers and the men of General Jackson's old brigade almost unanimously differed with him. Their regret at the loss of General Garnett was so great, and their anger at his removal so intense and universal that their conduct amounted almost to insubordination." Whereas before Jackson's rides past the brigade had been greeted with wild cheers, for three weeks after Garnett's arrest they occasioned only "sullen and resentful silence."[39]

Garnett's replacement, Charles S. Winder, initially fared no better, either with the Stonewall Brigade or, ironically, with the commanding general. Jackson appeared constitutionally unable to trust his seconds-in-command or to use them properly. As Henry Kyd Douglas put it, Jackson "was not always in pleasant accord with officers next in rank to him and was apt to judge them harshly." The thirty-two-year-old Winder was a promising officer. At one time one of the youngest captains in the regular army, his career had been derailed by chronic poor health. Like Jackson, Winder was a strict disciplinarian and a man of strong will. "The two were in some respects very much alike," thought Douglas, but in "personal appearance and bearing, the exact opposite." Douglas also regarded the Maryland native as among "the most brilliant officers in the army," a quality no one would ever attribute to Jackson. Winder had expected—and wished—to be assigned to a brigade in General Longstreet's division, and he took the Valley assignment reluctantly. Winder's first encounters with Jackson were icy, and his relations with the commanding general, Douglas observed, "were not any more pleasant" than Garnett's had been.[40]

A day or two before Winder joined the Valley army, the field officers of the Stonewall Brigade met secretly and agreed to show their displeasure by not calling on their new commander. With one exception, they were true to their word. Maj. G. Douglas Mercer, the brigade quartermaster, broke with his companions and paid a visit to Winder for the express purpose of wagering his fellow Marylander that he would only last a few weeks in command before Jackson placed him under arrest for some cause or another.

The rank and file of the brigade, for their part, were loathe to transfer loyalty from the likable Garnett to a haughty non-Virginian. Winder's aide-de-camp, Lt. McHenry Howard, got an early taste of the brigade's hostility and of Winder's uncompromising rigidity in the face of it. "One day, when I was riding with General Winder past the encampment or bivouac of one of the regiments there was some faint hissing. I was not certain that the general heard it, but as soon as he reached headquarters he sent for the colonel and told him it indicated a bad state of discipline in his regiment, and if anything like it occurred again he would hold the colonel responsible."[41]

Dropping in on some friends in the 21st Virginia, one of the regiments that still proudly called itself "Loring's men," Howard found disgust with Jackson strong. "I sat on a log and talked with my friends for some time. They said they were glad to see me but were sorry for me to have come to serve under a crazy man. They told me much about Jackson's eccentricities, both personal and in his military operations, and predicted that some dire disaster would one day befall him and his army."[42]

STONEWALL JACKSON TOOK little notice of the Valley army's low opinion of him (if he even was aware of it; at the same time the Stonewall Brigade was hissing Winder and Loring's men were doubting the commanding general's sanity, Jackson was assuring a confidant that his army was "in fine spirits")[43] and did nothing to better it.

James Shields, on the other hand, appeared intent on ruining his own division's high regard for him. His fractured arm may have prevented him from exercising command at Kernstown, but it did not keep Shields from claiming the victory as his own. The politician displaced the general, and truth mourned the consequence. In a day when generals wrote their reports with a weather eye on public opinion, as newspapers invariably published them, Shields penned an account that stood alone for sheer fantasy and self-promotion. Placing a moratorium on outgoing mail in order to have the first word, Shields the day after the battle hurried off two telegrams to the War Department proclaiming his triumph against a numerically superior foe. He supplemented them with two private letters to Secretary of War Stanton, a sympathetic fellow Democrat.

On March 26 Shields wrote a friend in Congress, Democratic senator Milton S. Lapham of California, a fanciful narrative of Kernstown intended for publication. In the letter Shields claimed to have fixed Jackson's position and strength on his March 18–19 reconnaissance to Strasburg. He then had retired two miles north of Winchester to create the impression that he had abandoned the town and to lure Jackson into a trap. Evidence that the Confederate had taken the bait came in the form of signal fires from Ashby to Jackson, the meaning of which Shields somehow had "divined." Shields said he had responded to Ashby's March 22 reconnaissance with only a token force so as to increase the enemy's "delusion." Despite receiving a wound that had "prostrated him ever since," Shields assured Lapham that he had been lucid enough on the evening of March 22 "to make preparations for any emergency that might occur, that night or the next morning." Jackson's attack had come as no surprise. "Knowing the crafty enemy I had to deal with, I omitted no precautions." Shields said he not only had ordered Tyler's attack on Sandy Ridge from his bed in Winchester, but also had directed the movements of individual batteries of artillery. His efforts had been decisive. "The havoc which has been made in the ranks of the Rebels has struck a blow such as they have nowhere else endured since the commencement of the war. Jackson and his Stonewall Brigade and all the other brigades accompanying him will never meet this division again in battle."

Shields promised greater gifts to the republic—if he were promoted. "I hope to be able in a few days to ride in a buggy myself at the head of my command, but I have neither sufficient force nor sufficient rank to do that service to the country that I hope and feel that I am capable of." Lapham evidently shared Shields's letter with Stanton, because the secretary hastened to assure Shields that "every effort in my power will be made to place you in a condition worthy of your skill and courage, and secure to the country the benefit of your superior military talents. . . . You may confidently rely on my confidence and support to the fullest extent." Secretary of State William H. Seward delivered the administration's appreciation personally, visiting with Shields briefly on the night of March 28 accompanied by his son and daughter and Stanton's wife. The Sewards and Mrs. Stanton toured the battlefield the following day.[44]

Fawning politicians and accommodating newspaper editors may have taken Shields at his word, but most Federals in Banks's command—even those who had not been in the battle—knew a rat when they smelled one. Wilder Dwight wrote home: "I suppose you might have read General Shields's 'private' letter about the battle at Winchester. A more barefaced series of Irish romances I never read. The man actually has the effrontery to connect his fortunate blunders into a chain of shrewd stratagems, and with after-event wisdom to glorify himself. The idea of a man in bed with a broken arm, four miles from the field [and] not knowing of the enemy's force or positions till 4:00 P.M., directing and guiding a battle that commenced at once and closed in two hours. Pshaw!"[45]

Though Shields's gasconade and false claims left him hurt and perplexed, Nathan Kimball refrained from contesting them in public. He wrote a straightforward, self-effacing report of the battle and aired his grievances in a genuinely private letter to Indiana congressman James A. Cravens. "I had full command and directed the movements of the entire fight in person, and the commendations of the officers under me best attest the ability displayed," he informed Cravens. "You will not wonder therefore that I am annoyed at seeing the garbled and false accounts that have appeared in the newspapers. I am at a loss to understand how such patent misstatements ever found their way into these columns of respectable journals. The officers are coming forward in contradiction to render me the justice that is my due."

It took time for Kimball to appreciate the extent of Shields's mendacity, but eventually he was able to find humor in it. "From the evening of the twenty-second and up to the moment Banks arrived and took command, I received twelve orders [from Shields]," Kimball told an acquaintance two decades later. "Shields had a severe attack of note writing—suggestion diarrhea—which came upon him when he found that the battle was being fought and our forces managed without regard to him. Shields was thus preparing to claim the honors, as I have since become convinced. There was no suggestion made by him during the entire affair, either written or verbal, which was followed by me, except the order on the eve of the twenty-second to take command."[46]

Kimball's contribution to the Union victory at Kernstown did not go unrewarded. In April 1862 he was promoted to brigadier general for his conduct in the battle.

Erastus Tyler also was advanced. He gained his star through deceit and the generosity of superior officers. In his own report of the battle, Tyler neglected to mention his faulty attack dispositions. He attributed his failure on Sandy Ridge to the pressure of nine Rebel regiments, when in fact his brigade had been halted by a mere two hundred men from the 27th Virginia. Only two of Tyler's regimental commanders filed field reports, and neither contradicted him. General Shields lavished praise on Tyler, who "won my admiration by his fearless intrepidity." Kimball was too much the gentleman to say other than that "Colonel Tyler deserves the highest commendation for the gallant manner in which he led his brigade during the conflict."[47]

David Strother saw past the lies at headquarters. Of Kernstown, he wrote: "The strategy was feebly managed, but the men fought well and, as soon as permitted, made short work of it. Our troops had no leader but were commanded by a senior colonel. The superior fire and courage of the infantry won the battle for the government. Thus endeth the first lesson of the Valley."[48]

CHAPTER 15

NOW WE'LL HAVE WAR

IN EARNEST

East of the Shenandoah Valley the warm winds of spring carried the scent of coming warfare. On April 1 General McClellan left Washington for the Peninsula of Virginia to direct the opening moves of his long-delayed campaign against Richmond. The next day he set in motion his first two corps. Opposing them was a single Confederate division under Maj. Gen. "Prince John" Magruder, stretched thin behind seven miles of earthworks across the Peninsula near Yorktown that McClellan had not known existed. McClellan called a temporary halt as torrential rains pummeled the countryside. Meanwhile, Joe Johnston was hurrying to Magruder's aid with the main body of his army. He had left 8,000 men under Maj. Gen. Richard S. Ewell at Gordonsville to communicate with Stonewall Jackson in the Valley and protect the vital railroad connection with eastern Tennessee, and 2,000 troops under Brig. Gen. Charles Fields had been detached to watch Irvin McDowell's 32,000-man Federal corps, then dangerously near Fredericksburg.

For the Peninsula campaign, McClellan had counted on having at least 120,000 men to fight an enemy whose strength he continued to exaggerate. McClellan had done nothing in the closing days of March to regain the confidence of the president or secretary of war, and he now found the administration cleaving away at his command. Stonewall Jackson's antics in the Valley played a large part in what transpired between Washington and the Peninsula.

McClellan's corps commanders had conditioned their support for his Peninsula plan on him leaving a 25,000-man covering force in front of Washington, in addition to the city's garrison. That was an acknowledgment as much of Lincoln's preoccupation with the safety of the capital as of military prudence. McClellan had assigned the covering-force role to Banks's Fifth Corps. But the Battle of Kernstown upset his calculations. On April 1 McClellan told Banks to stay in the Valley and drive Jackson "well back," then assume "such a position as to enable you to prevent his return."[1]

Rather than weaken the Peninsula army to create a new covering force in northern Virginia, McClellan juggled numbers on paper. Before departing Washington on April 1, he reported to the War Department that he was leaving 18,000 men to garrison the city and another 55,000 in a covering force "in and about Washington." The trouble was, recognized Lincoln and Stanton, two-thirds of the supposed covering force were not in close proximity to the capital, but in fact represented Banks's command eighty miles away in the Shenandoah Valley. Moreover, McClellan had double-counted one of Banks's brigades and had overstated the strength of the Washington garrison by 6,500 men. Most of those on duty in the city were, in fact, raw recruits. "When the president became aware of this," remembered Senator Charles Sumner, "he was justly indignant."[2]

Lincoln and Stanton genuinely wished McClellan to have all the forces they reckoned he could use effectively on the Peninsula, but they were not about to expose Washington to accommodate him, nor idly abide the apparent contempt reflected in his disingenuous reports. The specter of Stonewall Jackson, whose numbers Shields had estimated at 15,000, loomed large in their minds. Alarming too was the phantasmagoric army of 150,000 that McClellan thought Johnston mustered. Finally, the superannuated but respected Mexican War hero Maj. Gen. John E. Wool, in command at Fortress Monroe on the tip of the Peninsula, assured Stanton that McClellan already had a force large enough for the work before him.

On April 3 President Lincoln clipped McClellan's wings. He countermanded embarkation orders for McDowell's corps and elevated that general to command a new Department of the Rappahannock, with headquarters at Fredericksburg. Lincoln also made Banks independent of McClellan, creating for him the Department of the Shenandoah, but left McClellan's April 1 order to him to drive Jackson unchanged.[3]

Lecturing McClellan on his de facto assumption of the role of general in chief, Lincoln said:

General Banks's corps, once designed for Manassas Junction, was divided and tied up on the line of Winchester and Strasburg, and could not leave it again without exposing the Upper Potomac and the Baltimore and Ohio Railroad. This presented (or would present, when McDowell and Sumner should be gone) a great temptation for the enemy to turn back from the Rappahannock and sack Washington. My explicit directions that Washington should, by the judgment of all the commanders of corps, be left entirely secure, had been entirely neglected. It was precisely this that drove me to McDowell.

McClellan had brought on his troubles himself. Scolded Lincoln: "I do not forget that I was satisfied with your arrangement to leave Banks at Manassas Junction, but when that arrangement was broken up, and nothing substituted for it, of course I was not satisfied; I was constrained to substitute something for it myself."[4]

The president already had taken a direct hand in matters west of the Shenandoah Valley. To placate Radical Republicans, he appointed on March 11 their tarnished idol, former presidential candidate and famed Western explorer Maj. Gen. John C. Frémont, to command the new Mountain Department in place of the immensely talented William S. Rosecrans. In contrast to Rosecrans's sterling early-war performance, the headstrong and mercurial Frémont had exhibited military and administrative incompetence of stunning magnitude while in command of the Department of the West the year before. But his political influence and martial ambitions remained formidable, and Lincoln felt compelled to make a place for him.

Lincoln also had created the Mountain Department to further a pet idea of his. He wanted Frémont to lead an offensive from western Virginia into East Tennessee, seizing the railroad at Knoxville and rescuing the Unionist population of the region from Confederate clutches.[5]

Before setting out for his new headquarters at Wheeling, Virginia, Frémont assured the president that he could accomplish both tasks with the 25,000 men he understood were assigned to the Mountain Department. Forty-eight hours on the ground showed him the folly of his ill-informed promise. Although the paper strength of the department was nearly 26,000, there were fewer than 22,000 present for duty—a formidable enough force, it seemed, but one indifferently supplied and scattered across a sparsely populated, mountainous backwater nearly eighty miles from north to south. The department comprised four territorial divisions: the Railroad District of Brig. Gen. Benjamin F. Kelley; the District of the Cumberland under Brig. Gen. Robert C. Schenck; the Cheat Mountain District under Brig. Gen. Robert H. Milroy; and the District of the Kanawha, commanded by Brig. Gen. Jacob D. Cox. The only organized Confederate opposition of consequence consisted of three thousand troops under Brig. Gen. Edward Johnson, posted at Camp Allegheny since the winter.

Frémont had four capable district commanders, but the difficulties confronting them were considerable. Wagons were scarce, as were good roads. At least five artillery batteries in the department had no horses. There were no pontoons with which to bridge the many deep and swift-running rivers of the region. In late March Frémont wired the president that his promise of swift action had been premature; all he could hope to do with his present force was maintain established communications and put down Rebel irregulars. He was not entirely sure how many more men he needed. "I can do work if you will let me have immediately twenty-thousand men," Frémont assured Stanton in the opening sentence of a brief March 30 telegram, only to close his appeal, "Pray let me have ten to twelve thousand men from the East, so that I may take the field immediately."[6]

Stanton obliged Frémont's lower estimate. On April 1 he detached from the Army of the Potomac Brig. Gen. Louis Blenker's division, which was about to embark for the Peninsula. Blenker's orders directed him to join Frémont by way of Harpers Ferry.

Lincoln told McClellan that he had approved the transfer "with great pain, understanding that you would wish it otherwise." He permitted McClellan to modify the instructions to the extent that Blenker was to join Banks while en route and remain with him for as long as Banks was able to make good use of him.[7]

There were now in April 1862 three independent Union commands between the Alleghenies and the Potomac River, each of which reported directly to Washington. McClellan exercised authority over only that portion of the Army of the Potomac operating on the Peninsula. In seeking to direct the specific movements of three widely separated forces, the president and secretary of war had taken on a mighty challenge. Time alone would tell whether they were equal to it.

MAJ. FRANK "BULL" Paxton of the 27th Virginia awoke on April 1 with an odd mix of emotions. It was a gorgeous morning, and he had had little to occupy his time since reporting with four companies for duty with Turner Ashby four days earlier, a part of the rotating infantry support to Ashby's mounted rear guard. "I go down occasionally to take a view of the enemy's pickets, but most of the time have been lying idle. The enemy are encamped around Strasburg and for some four miles this side, where they seem disposed to remain quiet for the present," he wrote his wife that morning. "The whole country bears the appearance of a funeral, everything is so quiet. Work on the farms seems suspended; many of the houses deserted. The soldiers alone seem to exhibit the appearance of contentment and happiness. A mode of life which once seemed so strange and unnatural, habit has made familiar to us, and if peace ever comes, many of them will be disqualified for a life of industry."[8]

A sudden boom of artillery and rattle of small-arms fire interrupted Paxton's ruminations. Banks was on the move. At sunrise Col. George H. Gordon's brigade of Williams's division, with the 2nd Massachusetts Infantry arrayed as skirmishers in the lead, splashed across Tom's Brook, and the fight was on. Ashby contested the Federal advance three times. He did the Yankees little harm but put on quite a show. Ashby's troopers and Paxton's infantry "shot very badly, most of their bullets going over our heads," said a Massachusetts lieutenant. Chew's guns also occasionally overshot their mark, but more often than not, it was the failure of their shells to explode that spared the Federals heavy losses, as Gordon learned to his relief when he took up Ashby's first challenge, on the outskirts of Woodstock. "As we were descending the hill that brought us into this picturesque little town, bang went a gun, and a shell whizzed about ten feet over our heads, grazing the neck of Colonel Brodhead's horse and striking the road a few feet in front of a company of the 2nd Massachusetts. Fortunately the shell did not explode. Perhaps a minute passed when there arose a puff of smoke, then a report, and a shell streamed along the ranks; but this, like its predecessor, did not burst."[9]

Gordon called up his own section's rifled guns, and a brief artillery duel ensued in which, said Gordon, "we gave a dozen shots to their four." Terrified civilians cowered indoors, waiting for the storm to pass. One shell flew into a house and blew up a cooking stove. Another passed through the tower of the courthouse, tearing off shingles as it went. A third perforated the stone walls of the jailhouse. Both sides caused about equal damage to the village, but the Rebel-hating David Strother laid the blame solely on Turner Ashby. "This reckless fire through a village filled with women and children seems to me entirely unjustifiable when we consider that [Ashby] was maintaining no position and fired with no other object than the spiteful hope of injuring someone of our advance." Captain Chew felt uncomfortable firing on the Yankees, but for a very different reason: "Ashby was with our guns when we were fighting from hill to hill. Upon several occasions I suggested to him that we were lavish in the expenditure of ammunition, but he said he believed in firing at the enemy whenever they showed their heads."[10]

Ashby also believed in burning every bridge, pulling up the planks covering every culvert on the turnpike, and making a nuisance of himself whenever possible—all evidence of what Gordon conceded was a "very skillful" perfor-mance. Gordon also admired Ashby's courage, what Captain Chew lamented "the reckless exposure of his person." Gordon maintained that "Ashby was as cool and brave as he was experienced. I think our men had a kind of admira-tion for the man, as he sat unmoved upon his horse and let our men pepper away at him as if he enjoyed it."[11]

But nothing Ashby did could stop or appreciably impede the Federal ad-vance. Gordon brushed aside his second challenge, which came at Narrow Passage Creek, as easily as he had the first. By 3:30 P.M. the 2nd Massachusetts had closed in on Edinburg, having traveled and skirmished nineteen miles in nine hours. "We almost caught them at Edinburg; the two bridges across Stony Creek had not been on fire fifteen minutes when we arrived," said Lt. Charles Morse of Company C. "The enemy, knowing we could not ford that stream, took up a position and shelled away at us, but our battery silenced them in less than a quarter of an hour."[12]

Redeploying from point to point along the wooded ridge on the south bank of Stony Creek after every round or two, Chew's gunners continued to lob shells at the Yankees until nightfall. Few paid them much notice; the rounds that went off generally burst hundreds of feet in the air, giving what General Williams called "the semblance of pyrotechnics got up for our enter-tainment." The spectacle turned deadly when one spinning and smoking chunk of iron cleaved open the skull of a Pennsylvania soldier who was seated on a railroad tie quietly eating his rations. He was the only man killed in the skirmishing on Stony Creek.

As the trailing regiments of his brigade came up, Gordon ushered them into line along the north side of the creek. Williams's Second Brigade biv-ouacked in town behind them, and Williams set up headquarters a mile north of Edinburg. Shields's division brought up the rear. Banks established himself in Woodstock, content to allow the deep waters of Stony Creek and the "utter exhaustion of our supplies" to dictate a halt. Most of Banks's supply wagons were still east of the Blue Ridge Mountains. It would be two weeks before he considered his command ready to move.

Reduced rations threatened morale and invited depredations. A recovered General Shields complained to Banks on April 4 that a "want of discipline" in Gordon's brigade had compelled his patrols to arrest several squads of men from the 3rd Wisconsin and 2nd Massachusetts found "scattered around and loitering" in the neighborhood of Edinburg. Nonsense, Gordon replied testily, his men were not loitering; the lack of rations had forced him to authorize foraging. Shields's men, he added, were guilty of the same infractions. Banks spent a good deal of his time replying to letters from angry civilians. Two months in the Old Dominion had strained his conciliatory nature, as shown in the sharp tone he assumed in a letter to a female complainant from Woodstock:

> Permit me to suggest in answer to your note that you are mistaken in supposing we come into Virginia for your protection. We come here solely to assist in upholding the government of the United States. In exercising this duty, we desire to avoid any interference whatever with the privileges or property of the people, except when exigencies of the service require it, and whenever property is taken for public use, receipts are given and compensation secured. In every case where property has been taken for public use, orders have been given to take the surplus only and to avoid distressing any person by a total deprivation of their forage or stock.[13]

While Banks's lieutenants sparred and his infantry scrounged for food, Northern artillerymen passed the time "playing target" with Captain Chew. "I call it playing target," said battery commander Capt. James F. Huntington, "because I imagine we did them about as much harm as they did us, which was just none at all. This immunity was due not so much to want of skill on the part of the enemy's as to the poor quality of their ammunition. Their powder was doubtless of uncertain value, a condition fatal to accuracy in firing beyond point-blank range. Their percussion shell very often failed to explode; many of them were so poorly balanced as to come end over end, striking butt first. We built quite a little pyramid of these unexploded projectiles."[14]

Stonewall Jackson made good use of the lull in operations. After reinforcing Ashby with the Stonewall Brigade to hold the Stony Creek line, he fell back on April 2 with the rest of his little army from Mount Jackson to Rude's Hill. Jed Hotchkiss, who had scouted and recommended Stony Creek as an ideal rear-guard line, identified Rude's Hill as "a fine position to hold; the next one [hill] above Stony Creek." Jackson also liked it, and he made his headquarters in the home of the Reverend Anders Rude at the foot of the hill.

Rude's Hill overlooked Meem's Bottom, a mile-and-a-half-wide plain formed by a sharp bend in the North Fork of the Shenandoah. The hill commanded the bridge at the northern end of Meem's Bottom and nearby fords, which melting snows had in any case rendered useless. Rude's Hill also offered an unobstructed view of the country for several miles in every direction.

Safe for the moment from the Yankees, Jackson set about recruiting and reorganizing the Valley army. He also allowed his men much-needed rest. Jackson was in good spirits, and he penned a decidedly upbeat report of the Battle of Kernstown. "Though Winchester was not recovered, yet the more important object for the present, that of calling back troops that were leaving the Valley and thus preventing a junction of Banks's command with other forces was accomplished. Under these circumstances I feel justified in saying that, though the field is in possession of the enemy, yet the most essential fruits of the battle are ours."

The Confederate Congress agreed. On April 8 it rendered its thanks to Jackson and his command for their "gallant and meritorious service in the successful engagement with a greatly superior force of enemy near Kernstown."

Eight days later, the Confederate Congress enacted legislation that would have a lasting impact on the Southern military structure. Consistent with a recommendation President Davis had submitted on March 28, the Rebel legislature passed the first conscription act in American history. It made all white men between the ages of eighteen and thirty-five subject to three years of military service, obliging those already in the army on a twelve-month enlistment to serve two years more. However, a drafted man could hire a substitute from among white men not liable to conscription.

Anticipating congressional approval of Davis's request, Governor Letcher on March 29 ordered that all Virginia militia then in service be drafted into existing volunteer companies in order to bring regiments as close to full strength as possible. It fell to Sandie Pendleton to implement Letcher's instructions in the Valley District, a task he found "laborious and intensely disagreeable, as the militia has sundry objections to make." Jed Hotchkiss sympathized with his former comrades, who saw their units broken up to feed the volunteer regiments; even Jackson doubted the need for the governor's order. "This will throw all the officers into the ranks as privates. I am sorry for some of them, for they are good men," said Hotchkiss. "I am glad that I have made my escape from the militia before this proclamation, and I should have been very sorry to have had to take part in disbanding them, as they wish to remain organized as they are. General Jackson regrets that the order has been issued, as he was more than pleased with the way in which the militia has conducted itself."

The overwhelming number of militiamen accepted their fate. "If I was certain that I would be drafted into a company I would volunteer and save them the trouble of drafting me," a Harrisonburg man wrote his wife. But a large part of the Rockingham contingent opted for armed resistance to the proclamation. While on their way to join the Valley army, two hundred members of the unit deserted into the mountains near Swift Run Gap. Fortifying themselves and placing a levy on neighboring farms, the deserters declared their intent to fight the draft.

Jackson moved swiftly to crush the mutiny. He sent four companies of the 33rd Virginia, three companies of the 27th Virginia, some cavalry, and a section of artillery into the mountain fastness to dislodge the Rockingham militia. "It required only a few shells to drive them from their position, bringing part of them to terms and frightening the other half to death, and causing them to scatter in every direction," said an artilleryman. Nearly all of the deserters were rounded up and shipped off to Harrisonburg. Within a week they found themselves reluctant members of the Valley army, many in the same companies of the 27th Virginia that had rousted them out of the mountains.[15]

Pro-Union sentiment had motivated a surprisingly large number of the Rockingham mutineers. Other Valley men sought to evade the general draft on religious grounds. Pacifistic convictions kept them from provoking an armed confrontation, but not from leaving, and Quakers, Dunkers, and Mennonites by the hundreds went underground or headed north. Mennonite Peter Hartman said that his cousin dug a shelter under his barn and remained in hiding for eighteen months. "Potter John" Heatwole set off for West Virginia armed only with the Mennonite *Confession of Faith*. He introduced it to people with whom he became acquainted during his sojourn. Quite a number took to what he taught. After the war, Heatwole organized a mission of Upper Valley Mennonites to bring these West Virginians into the fold. Abraham Good began ferrying the faithful across the Ohio River. He was caught once, said Hartman, but the captain of the Rebel guard was a boyhood friend, and he let Good go. Not so fortunate was a party of seventy-three Mennonites and

Dunker men from the Upper Valley detained at Parkersburg, Virginia, by five paroled Confederates. Somehow the parolees had acquired weapons, and they drove the civilians back into Southern lines.

Although at the time of the Valley campaign the Conscription Act caused a considerable spike in Confederate desertions, in the end it proved a success in filling Southern armies. Jackson apparently thought only of the long-term consequences. When John Harman brought Jackson his first news of the law, a mutual friend said the general had become "so elated that he slapped the major on the shoulder—a very unusual thing for him to do—and fairly shouted, 'Now, Major, we'll have war in earnest! Virginia has waked up!'"

The draft itself, enlistments by those preferring to avoid the stigma of conscription, and the return of veterans from furloughs granted under the December 1861 Furlough and Bounty Act doubled the strength of the Valley army in April 1862 to just over six thousand men. The experience of the 2nd Virginia Infantry was typical. Company H mustered 21 potential conscripts; another company netted 28 on a recruiting drive north to Mount Jackson. On April 16, the date the law was to take effect, 91 men volunteered for the regiment. All told, the 2nd Virginia gained 274 men—208 by enlistments and 66 by draft. A handful of veterans over age thirty-five elected to take honorable discharges, as provided for in the Conscription Act.

The new men and returning veterans found themselves in a miserable mud hole of a camp. The weather was unseasonably cold during the first half of April, and it rained or snowed constantly. Heavy wagon traffic churned the meadows of Meem's Bottom and the open slopes of Rude's Hill to muck. Everyone in the Valley suffered from the elements. The air was dense with chilling and penetrating moisture. Camps were saturated. Tall pine trees, weighted down with icicles, cracked and fell. Drilling was suspended. The unlucky shivered on sentinel duty, while those in camp huddled around sputtering fires. "Our encampment was worse than any barnyard, for in many places there seems no bottom," wrote Major Jones of the 2nd Virginia. "Our tent floors are deep in mud." Venturing from camp in search of cooking utensils, Jones and a companion had no luck until they reached New Market. "An oven could not be bought for love or money. In despair I heard of an old Irishman who had one, hunted him up on one of the backstreets, and found he had in his hog pen an oven which his wife had been using for the hogs. [I] gave him two dollars for it and went on my way rejoicing."[16]

The horrible weather caused Banks to drop for the time being any plans he may have entertained for pressing forward beyond Stony Creek. Banks's record to date suggested more promises than action, but when part of the supplies he had lacked reached Strasburg on March 31, he had moved the next day. After reaching Stony Creek, he had checked off for the War Department his reasons for not pressing on immediately. Reduced rations was foremost. Cavalry inadequate both in numbers and quality was a second reason. Only 531 were present for duty on April 4, and Banks found them barely fit. General Williams concurred. "The cavalry," he wrote, "is good for kicking up dust, doing foraging, capturing horses and stealing them, and for not much else. The material is good enough, but they are poorly drilled and poorly mounted. The horses have not been over half-fed during the winter, and of late have been severely handled. The Rebel cavalry seems much better drilled and have better horses. At any rate, they scale fences most beautifully and show themselves very fearless." Even the mean-spirited Colonel Gordon, who quarreled with superiors seemingly for the fun of it, would have been hard-pressed to differ with Banks and Williams. During the scrimmage along Narrow Passage Creek, Gordon had ordered the commander of his cavalry detachment to engage Ashby's troopers, only to have him decline. "I can't catch them sir," the officer explained; "they leap fences like deer."

For all their skill, Ashby's cavalrymen were not invincible. On April 16, acting on a tip from a Unionist refugee, a task force composed of two companies of Federal infantry and the Washington and Ringgold cavalry companies —120 men in all—captured between 50 and 65 of Ashby's men near the village of Columbia Furnace. The Virginians were holed up in two churches, trying to escape the rain and cold, when the Yankees fell upon them just after midnight. Their captors admired their appearance, if not their diligence. The commander of the Federal detachment thought that "these cavalrymen were well mounted and armed generally with sabers, Colt revolvers, together with some kind of rifle or gun for longer range shooting or carbine service. Among them were a few Colt revolving rifles, two Sharp's rifles, one or two Enfield rifles, but the prevailing arm was the double-barreled shot gun, mostly fine guns, and many of them of English make, all of which were loaded with buck and bull when we captured them. They were well uniformed in grey, and were native Virginians, about the best-looking Rebel soldiers that we came in contact with."[17]

A third reason Banks gave for postponing his advance was the poor state of his supply lines. The heavy April rains had ruined the roadbed of the Winchester railway. Banks's own wagon train had caught up, but Shields's division was badly in need of transportation, having no more than one hundred two-horse wagons to go around. A fourth reason, and one that every sore-footed soldier would endorse, was the lack of shoes. The colonel of the 29th Pennsylvania told Banks that nearly his entire regiment was barefoot. The 13th Indiana and 5th Connecticut were in similar straits. General Williams claimed that the shoddy shoes issued in Winchester just after the Battle of Kernstown had worn out in less than two weeks. "Such is the fraud that contractors are permitted to put upon poor soldiers! I can hardly conceive of a crime more fitly punished by death. We should be far in advance but for these constant drawbacks, which fairly unfit an army for marching."

A final cause for holding back was the absence of Blenker's division, which Banks had been counting on daily to augment his force, but which seemingly had disappeared from the face of the earth after setting off from Warrenton on April 6. After six days with no word from the all-German contingent, an exasperated Secretary Stanton instructed General Rosecrans, then in the capital awaiting assignment, to go out and find Blenker.

Rosecrans located him on April 15 near Paris, Virginia, on the east bank of the Shenandoah River, just twenty-five miles from Warrenton. The Germans had been there for four days, trying to find a way across the swollen Shenandoah. It was bad enough that the division was woefully short of ammunition, shoes, tents, food, and wagons, and that the men had to sleep in the snow and mud without shelter. "All this our men have borne without murmur," Blenker later reported. But after Blenker tried to negotiate the river without pontoon boats, even his brigade commanders protested. Blenker had had the men build rafts out of materials at hand. On April 12 he sent the first regiment of Brig. Gen. Henry Bohlen's brigade across without incident, but then a raft overloaded at his insistence overturned, drowning forty soldiers. "Never will I forget the moment the raft began to sink in the wild waters of the strong-pulling stream," recalled a member of the 45th New York Infantry. "The unfortunate victims, screaming for help, were endangering each other by holding and clinging to each other in the water. Even if it had been possible for some soldiers to save their lives, they were pulled underwater by their helpless, frightened comrades." Several officers had called Blenker's attention to the danger of the undertaking, and now General Bohlen stepped forward. He refused to allow another man across. Blenker relented, and the division returned to Paris while scouts searched for another crossing site.

Of Blenker's division, Rosecrans told Stanton: "They have been wandering without tents, shelter, or knapsacks, with but four wagons per regiment. Their clothing is worn, no pay since December. Not much wonder they stole and robbed." Stanton apologized to Blenker for the government's neglect of his "brave and patriotic" German soldiers, then ordered him to proceed directly to Frémont's department. Rosecrans accompanied him to make sure he found his way.[18]

Despite the hardships and inactivity, morale in Banks's command was high. Union victories in the West raised expectations of an early end to the war. "Why not enjoy my soldiering to the fullest while I am a soldier," Colonel Voris of the 67th Ohio asked his wife rhetorically. "Sixty days will substantially end the fighting. Just think of Island No. 10 and Pittsburgh Landing for one week's work. If General McClellan is successful where he is now fighting, Virginia will be cleaned out in a very short time. I am afraid I shall be compelled to go home with the honors of only the Winchester fight. It does appear to me that this part of Virginia is not disposed to do any more serious fighting."

Defections from the Southern ranks—a by-product of the Conscription Act—also boosted hopes for a rapid end to hostilities. "I hear desertions from the Rebels are a daily occurrence," wrote an Ohio sergeant. "They say that the force of Rebels at Mt. Jackson is not over seven thousand. Thirty left one day (deserted) in a body, taking their guns along. This division may have another fight with Jackson, but the fact is Jackson won't have men enough in six weeks for a rear guard unless he gets reinforcements."[19]

AFTER FIFTEEN DAYS of fretting over supplies and sundry other matters, General Banks at long last felt himself ready to test Jackson's strength. On April 16 he fashioned a plan—a good one—to get behind the Rebel rear guard, take both Ashby's cavalry and Mount Jackson in one fell swoop, and seize the bridges over Mill Creek, just south of Mount Jackson, and the North Fork before Jackson was able to burn them. Banks also hoped to drive the Confederates from their Rude's Hill stronghold, preferably without a fight. The objective for the march, which was to begin shortly after midnight, was New Market, fifteen miles beyond the Stony Creek line of departure. Col. Sam Carroll of the 8th Ohio was selected to lead a task force of one thousand men over the Middle road, which ran parallel to and from one to two miles west of the Valley Pike as far as Harrisonburg, and use it to get in Ashby's rear. Meanwhile, General Shields was to push directly up the turnpike with the bulk of his division as rapidly as possible. Williams would follow in reserve. Carroll's flanking column and Shields's main body were expected to reunite at Mount Jackson.

Carroll set out at 6:00 P.M. The march went poorly from the start. The route was found to be seven miles longer than represented. Mountain streams crossing it were badly swollen by recent rains and difficult to ford, and the road was muddy. Carroll was to have been at Mount Jackson before dawn on the seventeenth. Instead, he found himself still eight miles short of the town at 9:00 A.M. Although unproductive, the march was not without its moments of humor. Riding ahead of the column with one or two staff officers during the nightlong trek, Colonel Carroll encountered a Rebel cavalryman, who challenged him with, "Who come there?" "Friends," replied the colonel. "Friends to whom?" the man again challenged. "To ourselves," said Carroll. The Rebel mumbled something indistinct, to which Carroll answered, "Yes." That satisfied the Southerner, who came forward out of the darkness to find himself surrounded by "so many bluecoats he did not know what to make of it." The unfortunate Confederate had been on his way home to have breakfast with his family, which lived nearby. A few miles on, one of Carroll's cavalry escort came upon six of Ashby's pickets. Assuming an authoritative air, the trooper shouted, "If you have not the countersign, follow me." The Virginians meekly followed him, not realizing they were being led into Union lines until some of Carroll's troops foolishly cheered, enabling the Rebels to escape.

Shields's column splashed across Stony Creek at 3:00 A.M. on April 17. The crossing was unopposed. "As the enemy knew as well as we did what we were about, it was no surprise to us, when the advance arrived where the enemy's pickets had been posted, that nothing but expiring campfires were found." The Federal vanguard entered Mount Jackson at 7:00 A.M., flags unfurled and bands serenading "sullen inhabitants" with "The Star-Spangled Banner." The only sign of the enemy were the Confederate medical corps flags flying over three large abandoned hospitals. Black smoke hung over the village. The engine house was in ruins, and several railroad cars were still burning.[20]

A second pillar of smoke rose on the horizon a mile south of the village. Shields's cavalry—consisting of one company of the 1st Vermont, two companies of the 1st Ohio, and one company of the 1st Michigan regiments— galloped toward the flames. Eight dismounted Rebel troopers could be seen lingering on the near side of the river, trying to stoke the flames that licked the side timbers of the long covered bridge across the North Fork. Ashby was among them, astride his prized white charger, "Tom Telegraph." The remainder of his cavalry was already over the river on Meem's Bottom, riding hard for shelter behind Rude's Hill.

Ashby's men had stripped off the floorboards before setting fire to the bridge, which had the unintended effect of reducing the amount of combustible material on hand. Despite the best efforts of Ashby and his small party to hurry the destruction, the flames had not yet reached the roof, meaning the bridge might yet be saved. Appraising the situation in a glance, Cpl. George R. Maxwell diverted the Michigan company he commanded from the turnpike to the river. Filling their slouch hats with water, they doused the flames before much damage was done.

Ashby was the last Confederate to leave the bridge. Four Ohio cavalrymen challenged him to drop the torch he was applying to side timbers and surrender. As he wheeled his horse to escape, the Yankees discharged their pistols. One round cut into Ashby's boot, grazing his leg before burying itself into the side of Tom Telegraph. Ashby turned and slashed at the nearest enemy with his saber, then spurred his wounded mount across the bridge and over Meem's Bottom. The animal bore Ashby up the slope of Rude's Hill, where the crew of Chew's Blakely gun, along with the Rockbridge Artillery, Henry Kyd Douglas, and several other admiring Confederate staff officers, awaited the colonel. Douglas described the scene. It was one of Ashby's finest moments, a melodramatic highlight of his cavalier career:

> Having borne his master with unabated spirit until the danger was over, Ashby's splendid stallion sank to the ground, dappled with the foam of heat and suffering; his wound was mortal. The big-hearted cavalier bent over him, stroked his mane, stooped down and gazed affectionately into his eyes, and the excitement of the last hour was swallowed up in his sorrow for his dying companion. Thus the most splendid horseman I ever knew lost the most beautiful warhorse I ever knew.

After Ashby stepped away, troopers quietly surrounded the animal, cutting away tufts of tail and mane as souvenirs.[21]

Securing another mount, Ashby returned to the forward slope of Rude's Hill with Stonewall Jackson. Leading the file was J. S. Harnsberger, chief of the courier line from army headquarters to Swift Run Gap. Harnsberger was edgy. He had never been under a shelling before, and now federal cannons were booming away from along Mount Jackson Ridge, just beyond the North Fork Bridge. Suddenly Harnsberger spotted a cannon ball sailing straight for him. "It struck in the middle of the turnpike, bounced over my head, passed between the hind legs of General Jackson's horse, and then close along by General Ashby. I was surprised at the cool indifference they manifested."

Far more troubling to Jackson than the occasional shell was the blue tide forming below him on Meem's Bottom. Banks and Shields expected Jackson to make a stand on Rude's Hill, the consensus among Federal officers being that if Jackson would not fight with the advantages of terrain he enjoyed there, he would not fight anywhere. And so they deployed four brigades—two from Shields's division and two from Williams's—with great fanfare, as if for a frontal assault. At the same time, Banks sent Shields's remaining brigade, commanded by Col. Samuel H. Dunning, and Gordon's brigade of Williams's division on a flanking march along the Middle road. With Carroll nowhere to be found (Shields indulged in an expletive or two at the Ohioan's expense), Banks hoped instead to interpose Gordon and Dunning between Jackson's army and New Market, which lay seven miles to the south.

The sky was clear and the day unseasonably warm for April. Many thought it as hot as a mid-July afternoon. "Under a pelting sun Gordon's flanking column moved over a road all edges of rock and quagmires of mud," said the adjutant of the 3rd Wisconsin. "Dunning's brigade, in the lead, straggled fearfully, as the early start and the heat had much fatigued the men."[22]

The troops of the main body also found the going hard. Meem's Bottom was soaked from the rain and snow of the past two weeks, and in places men sank knee-deep. To those not struggling through the muck, the scene was most impressive. "We drew up our entire force on the broad river-bottom on both sides of the road, covering the columns by a cloud of skirmishers extending several miles. Cavalry and artillery were intermingled in masses amongst the infantry. The field from the high riverbank on the north could be overlooked for miles, and every corps could be distinctly seen. It was a splendid spectacle, the finest military show I have seen in America," said General Williams. "Indeed, I have never before seen a single plain upon which so many troops could be displayed this side of our western prairies."[23]

Capt. James F. Huntington lost his choice seat on Mount Jackson Ridge at 4:00 P.M. "I was admiring the martial scene, as with wavering banners and glittering arms the troops formed in battle array, when one of General Banks's staff gave me an order to cross the river, get in front of the line of battle, and follow the skirmishers." Huntington was perplexed. "The idea of skirmishing with a battery was new to me, but finding the order authentic I proceeded to obey." As he struggled through the mud, now well in advance of the line of battle, Huntington expected at any moment for a party of Rebel horsemen or infantry to come charging off Rude's Hill and capture his guns. But Jackson quit Rude's Hill without a fight. Riding forward, General Williams counted only two parting artillery rounds before the enemy vanished, and he and Huntington waited atop the abandoned hill for the Federal infantry to catch up.[24]

Pressing on, Shields and Williams reached New Market at nightfall. Carroll straggled in sometime after. Dunning and Gordon came up at 9:00 P.M. They had had to ford the North Fork to rejoin the main body, an experience the sun-baked men found a welcome diversion. A Wisconsin lieutenant recalled that "the water was up to the armpits, cold as ice and swift, but the men crossed with uproarious hilarity. Many stripped off their clothes and held the bundle high over their heads, and all roared with laughter when the current carried the legs from under some luckless comrade and ducked him, clothes and all."[25]

While his men rested for the night on the outskirts of town, General Banks penned Stanton a brief telegram announcing the capture of New Market without the loss of any of his own troops and with the capture of many Rebels (several dozen stragglers fell into Federal arms). The secretary wired back his thanks "for the brilliant and successful operations of this day." The news put Banks in "high spirits," said Maj. Wilder Dwight. "He complimented our march and said the secretary of war had telegraphed thanks to us, that when our movement was perceived the rear of Jackson's force fled hastily, etc. My own opinion is that the movement was all nonsense and pretty expensive silliness for us. Here we are, eighty miles from our supplies, all our wagons on the road, our tents and baggage behind, our rations precarious, and following a mirage into the desert. Jackson was ready to run and began to do so as soon was we began to move."[26]

Dwight guessed right. Stonewall Jackson had found nothing particularly troublesome in the events of April 17. He had been prepared to concede not only Mount Jackson and New Market, but also the entire Valley as far south as the North River. Johnston's redeployment to the Peninsula had made it imperative that Jackson keep in close communication with Richard S. Ewell, whose 8,500-man division then near Brandy Station represented the only organized Confederate force between him and Johnston, and that he also retain his freedom of maneuver so that he could unite with Ewell as necessary. The Confederacy might temporarily concede the Shenandoah Valley, but with McClellan's enormous army knocking at the gates of Richmond, it could ill-afford to lose the commands of Jackson or Ewell. The need to preserve their forces and keep them mobile was foremost in the mind of Gen. Robert E. Lee, who had rejoined the war effort in the East as military adviser to President

Davis. In the coming weeks, Lee would act as a conduit of information between Johnston and his distant subordinates, a sounding board for their sometimes conflicting desires and plans, and a source of suggestions, but never outright orders.

On April 10 Jackson opened communications with Ewell on the subject of his possible withdrawal up the Valley. Johnston had given Jackson discretionary authority to call upon Ewell in the event Jackson fell back, and on April 12 Jackson told Ewell to make ready to join him at Swift Run Gap if Banks were to advance. Ewell had ideas of his own. He wanted to attack Blenker's division as it floundered about east of the Blue Ridge, as much from antipathy for the Germans as for any valid military reason. Ewell implored Jackson to unite with him in the endeavor. "Blenker's troops are very much scattered and demoralized, are ill-treating the people, robbing and stealing, and wantonly killing all stock. They are Dutch," Ewell told Jackson on the thirteenth. "Were you to come through the mountains and attack Blenker's force we would find them scattered and cut up, and it would cause Banks to clear the Valley. Blenker's men are deserting; those I have seen are stupid, ignorant Dutch." Jackson ignored Ewell's request. "I am much obliged to you for the news" was all he had to say on the matter before repeating his instructions that Ewell come to Swift Run Gap when called upon.[27]

The forty-five-year-old Virginian found little inspiring in his initial communications with Jackson. Ewell was as willful as his younger compatriot and, in his own mind at least, a good deal more intelligent. Few would question his intellect. The grandson of Benjamin Stoddert, first U.S. secretary of the navy, and the son of Thomas Ewell, an accomplished physician who lost a battle with alcoholism and died at age forty, Richard Stoddert Ewell graduated thirteenth of forty-five in the West Point Class of 1840. He possessed Thomas Ewell's violent temper and love of alcohol but luckily escaped most of his father's excesses. From his mother he inherited a sharp tongue. He spoke his mind freely and was something of an agnostic. A childhood run-in with his Sunday school teacher, typical of Ewell, would have mortified Jackson. The teacher, a man named Nelson Lloyd, had made a gift of a Bible to Ewell. When he accepted it without a word, his mother felt obliged to speak up. "Aren't you going to thank Mr. Lloyd for it?" No, he would not. "I never asked him for it," retorted young Richard.

Ewell had demonstrated considerable bravery during two decades of service on the Indian frontier. As a general, his greatest liability to date seems to have been a tendency toward incoherence in the heat of battle. "His written orders were full, accurate, and lucid," remembered a subordinate, "but his verbal orders or directions, especially when under intense excitement, no man could comprehend. At such times his eyes would flash with a peculiar brilliancy, and his brain far outran his tongue. His thoughts would leap across great gaps which his words never touched, but which he expected his listener to fill up by intuition, and woe to the dull subordinate who failed to understand him."[28]

Fortunately for those under him, Ewell's rough exterior hid what was essentially a good heart. He cared for his men and their well-being, and was not given to needless effusion of blood.

In the spring of 1862, Ewell also was very much in love. The object of his affection was his beautiful cousin, Lizinka Brown. He had loved her as a teenager, and he loved her still. Now the widowed mother of a seventeen-year-old daughter and an adult son, Campbell Brown, who served on the general's staff, Lizinka had consented the previous December to marry Ewell. They kept the engagement a secret but could not hide their love.[29]

Ewell found Johnston more receptive to his plan for taking on Blenker's division, but by the time he received permission to attack, the Germans had crossed the Blue Ridge Mountains and were gone. Jackson's men, meantime, had done some hard marching to get there ahead of Ewell. The Valley army had fallen back from Banks's front to within twelve miles of Harrisonburg on the night of April 17. After a brief bivouac, the retreat was resumed at 4:00 A.M. on the eighteenth. The Confederates cleared Harrisonburg before noon, and Jackson made his headquarters at Peale's Crossroads, five miles southeast of town, that night. On April 19 the army passed beneath the southern tip of Massanutten Mountain and then swung to the northeast, crossing the South Fork of the Shenandoah at the hamlet of Conrad's Store before making camp in narrow Elk Run Valley, between the river and Swift Run Gap. The Valley army had made fifty miles in three days.[30]

Jackson's withdrawal caused considerable turmoil in Staunton. Rumors circulated on the night of April 17 that thirty-five thousand Yankees and one hundred cannon had bested him, and that he was in full retreat toward the town. In addition to ordinary quartermaster and commissary stores, Staunton was home to large stockpiles of ammunition, weapons, and uniforms for some twelve thousand soldiers. Not only the civilian population, but also much of the military personnel in town panicked. Convalescent patients were hurried away to Charlottesville, along with all the money in the town banks and the court records. Col. William S. H. Baylor watched the unfolding scene in bemusement: "Quartermasters and commissaries were seen running to and fro through rain and mud, begging and hiring passage to some other point of safety. It is said that the Virginia Hotel was so completely deserted as to require it to be closed up, and all this panic when the enemy was at least thirty miles from there." Two or three days were needed to restore a measure of calm.[31]

Although such tactical subtleties would be lost on the townspeople of Staunton and its rear-echelon military denizens, Jackson had chosen his position at Swift Run Gap in part to deter Banks from threatening Staunton. South of Harrisonburg the Valley widened to twenty-five miles. There was no strong ground suitable for a defensive stand between Harrisonburg and Staunton, and even if one had existed, with six thousand men Jackson could not have hoped to hold it long against a far stronger foe. On the other hand, even a small force in the Elk Run Valley was protected from attack. There the South Fork of the Shenandoah covered the Valley army's front. Steep, pathless, and densely wooded spurs of the Blue Ridge protected both flanks, while good roads led from Jackson's rear over the mountains into the open country around Gordonsville. Jackson held the South Fork bridge nearest him and was but a day's march from Harrisonburg, ready to hurl himself against the Federal flank and rear should Banks make a move on Staunton. Secure in his own position, Jackson more effectively barred a further enemy advance than if he had remained in Banks's front.[32]

Not that Banks had shown much of an inclination to move anywhere fast. Five days elapsed before Union cavalry proceeded from New Market to Harrisonburg. Williams's division entered Harrisonburg on April 25. It was the usual story of drawn curtains, closed blinds, and empty streets. But there any comparison with Winchester ended. Capt. Erwin A. Bowen of the 28th New York Infantry had been appointed provost marshal of the town, and he took his responsibilities seriously. Establishing himself in the county clerk's office, across from the imposing Bank of Rockingham building, where General Williams set up headquarters, Bowen made clear his intention to protect all the rights of the townspeople. He had guards posted at every intersection, saw to it that the streets and alleys were cleaned and the post office opened, permitted printing presses to operate, and closed the saloons.

Modest and gentlemanly in his demeanor, Bowen endeared himself to the citizenry with numerous acts of kindness. When he learned that the wife of a resident who had been arrested on some minor offense and sent down the Valley a prisoner was dangerously ill, he procured the man's release and escorted him back to her bedside. In another instance, he locked horns with

General Williams over the request of a Harrisonburg lady that she be allowed to retrieve the body of her husband, a Confederate officer killed outside the lines, for burial in the town cemetery. Bowen granted the permit, but Williams returned it disapproved, with the question, "Why in hell do you ask for such an order?" Bowen resubmitted the permit with his endorsement, "I did not enter the service to fight dead men, women, or children." This time Williams approved the order. Bowen not only saw to it that the woman was passed safely through the lines, but he also provided her with an escort and an ambulance.[33]

As word of Bowen's kindnesses spread, the citizens softened toward their occupiers. Seldom was anything more hostile than the occasional pursed lip or brazen glance of a female encountered; even the crusty abolitionist chaplain of the 2nd Massachusetts, Alonso Quint, found the inhabitants "decently courteous." Soldiers and civilians mixed at Sunday worship. Businessmen opened their doors to the enemy, sometimes at less-than-fair terms. "Virginia gentility is a humbug," said Samuel Sexton, assistant surgeon of an Ohio regiment. "I have never seen a Jew or Yankee peddler half so anxious to make a close trade. There are most exorbitant prices for everything they are willing to sell." Some Union soldiers were inclined to see only the worst in the Southerners. Chaplain Horace Winslow of the 5th Connecticut dismissed the entire population of the Upper Valley as "miserable, shiftless, dirty, and stupid . . . not worth saving." Lt. Melzer Dutton of the same regiment found the men cowardly and the women insolent, although he admitted that the ladies softened up in the face of pleasantries.[34]

The young Mennonite Peter Hartman was completely taken with the invaders. "They must have been about the most orderly army in the war. They did not molest anyone. They paid for the few things they wanted. They would come out to our house, sit down and talk, and get us to sing for them. One time my father sent me up to Landis's Mill. While I was going through town, some of them jumped on to my wagon and said they wanted to ride along to go fishing."[35]

On two things all of the Federal soldiers were seemingly in agreement: that Harrisonburg was the loveliest town they had yet seen in the Shenandoah Valley, and that the contraband slaves swarming into their camps were determined both to have their freedom and to work. "Many fine Negroes are leaving their Rebel masters and seeking employment in the army," said Surgeon Sexton. "Our quartermaster employs many, paying them good wages. The most reliable information we get is from these colored fugitives from the

Rebel lines. They will tell the truth, which is more than can be said of many of the white inhabitants." The Reverend Quint recalled a conversation with one former slave. "How is it with you, can you take care of yourself?" Quint had inquired. "Gosh a-mighty, massa; guess I can," answered the man. "Been take car' of myself and old massa dis twenty year. Guess 'an take car' of dis nig all alone."[36]

STONEWALL JACKSON SAID little on the march to Swift Run Gap. Chief courier Harnsberger rode near the general most of the way. At the end of the second evening Jackson asked him, "Have the troops water and wood?" "Yes general," replied Harnsberger. Those were the only words that passed between them. But once settled in his new headquarters in the Kite house, a spacious two-story residence near the gap, Jackson resumed his vigorous exchange of messages with Ewell, often writing him twice a day. His instructions initially were tentative. Jackson asked only that Ewell withdraw across the Rapidan River to Gordonsville, where he was to halt his command "and make it as comfortable as you can." At Gordonsville, Ewell would be within two days' march of either Swift Run Gap or Fisher's Gap. Ewell complied at once, and by the evening of April 21 he had his division encamped at Gordonsville astride the turnpike to Madison Courthouse.

General Lee insinuated himself into the proceedings the same day. Reports from General Fields of a Federal buildup at Falmouth and Aquia led him to conclude that the enemy intended to occupy Fredericksburg as a base of operations against Richmond. Relieving Fredericksburg now became a paramount concern. Lee thought that Jackson might accomplish this with a combined attack on Banks with his command and Ewell's division. But if Jackson considered Banks too strong to be approached, and if he felt himself able to hold Banks in check with the Valley army alone, it might be better if Ewell moved nearer Fredericksburg to reinforce Fields as necessary.[37]

Jackson replied on April 23. He wanted Ewell but would concede to any decision Lee might reach; indeed, he encouraged him to make one. His objective, he told Lee, had been to get in Banks's rear should he advance on Staunton. Without Ewell's division, Jackson doubted that he could create enough of a distraction to prevent Banks from taking the town. Johnston had wanted him to unite with Ewell near the top of the Blue Ridge and give battle there, but Jackson felt there was little chance of drawing Banks into the mountains. "I have given you my views respecting things here, but it may be that General

Ewell could render more service at Fredericksburg, and, if so, I hope that you will direct his movements accordingly."[38]

Lee declined to impose his preference. "I have hoped in the present divided condition of the enemy's forces that a successful blow may be dealt them by a rapid combination of our troops before they can be strengthened themselves," he told Jackson on April 25. "The blow, wherever struck, must be sudden and heavy. The troops must be efficient and light. I cannot pretend at this distance to direct operations depending on circumstances unknown to me and requiring the exercise of discretion and judgment as to time and execution." Jackson took Lee at his word. With reconnoitering Federal cavalry and infantry now only seven miles from Swift Run Gap, Jackson ordered Ewell to march to Stanardsville at dawn on April 27—whether to meet an attack from Banks or stage one of his own, he did not say.[39]

CHAPTER 16

A COUNTRY TO FIGHT FOR

The soldiers of the Valley army disliked their new surroundings. Shortly after they made camp, the weather turned miserable. Rain alternated with snow for several days. The gravelly soil of Swift Run Gap washed down the mountainside into the campsites, where the troops huddled around sputtering fires day and night and slept in the open. "We made ourselves as comfortable as we could in the shelter of brush and oilcloths," said John Worsham. "The day we reached here General Jackson ordered all the wagons containing tents and extra baggage to the rear, and so far that we never saw them again! This was a hard blow to us, since we had gotten in the habit of smuggling many articles into tents to avoid carrying them, and when our tents left, they had dress coats, underclothing, etc., in them. 'Old Jack' flanked us that time." Maj. Frank Jones recognized his good fortune in having kept his tent with him, but nonetheless disliked his situation. "This is a dull stupid life; all day long we are cooped up with nothing to do and everything to make life disagreeable." Adding to the prevailing gloom was a feeling that Jackson had given up the game. "We are out in the mountains of Rockingham in all probability on our way to eastern Virginia, having to all appearance given up the Valley to the enemy, which makes me almost now a refuge [*sic*] and most certainly will be entirely so in a short time," lamented Capt. James K. Edmondson of the 27th Virginia.[1]

Among the few distractions was the reorganization of regiments and the election of new company and regimental officers mandated under the Conscription Act. The results of the exercise were decidedly mixed. The 2nd

Virginia reelected James W. Allen as colonel, but Allen, who had lost all desire to serve under Jackson, sent in his resignation. To his mortification, it was denied, and he labored on. Frank Jones was again chosen major, enabling him to continue what he considered the dull, stupid army life. Arthur C. Cummings refused to stand for reelection as commander of the 33rd Virginia, and the colonelcy went to John F. Neff, the son of a Dunkard minister in Shenandoah County. At age twenty-seven, Neff became the youngest regimental commander in the Valley army. The highly esteemed William S. H. Baylor was unanimously voted colonel of the 5th Virginia, command of which he had been earlier denied. "But for the gratification of being thus returned to a position of which I was deprived so unjustly twelve months ago I do not know that I should not decline the honor," he told his wife. "It is no pleasant thought to have the care of the lives of one thousand men. I will use every effort to look after them, to be a father and leader, and I beseech you and all to pray to Heaven to give me the ability and assistance necessary for so hard a task and so responsible a position."

The 5th Virginia was lucky to have Baylor; the 21st Virginia fared poorly by comparison. The regimental election "was a great misfortune to us," said John Worsham of the 21st, "as many good officers were thrown out, and men who were popular were elected in their stead; in many instances men utterly unfit to fill the places to which they were elected." But popularity also brought some good men promotions. It earned William T. Poague the captaincy of the Rockbridge Artillery in place of the poorly regarded Capt. William McLaughlin. McLaughlin had left a mess, and Poague's strict brand of discipline, which General Winder demanded he impose, bred some dissatisfaction. "I had to require better attention to the horses," Poague recalled. "I had to haul up many delinquents in petty matters. I was directed to prefer charges of desertion against some who over-stayed their leaves. In fact, our new brigadier general required the regulations of war to be carried out in every particular."[2]

Also popular with the troops was William B. Taliaferro, the politically influential officer who had railed so bitterly against Jackson's conduct of the Romney expedition. Taliaferro was back with a star on his shoulder, reassigned to the Valley District in special orders from General Johnston dated April 6. It was a double blow to Jackson—not only was he stuck with Taliaferro, but also Taliaferro had returned to replace Sam Fulkerson, for whom an admiring Jackson had hoped to secure a brigadier general's commission. Jackson protested the assignment in and out of channels, but to no avail. Fortunately, Taliaferro's attitude had improved. He shared the discomforts of a forest bivouac with the men cheerfully and struck Lt. Col. E. T. H. Warren of the 10th Virginia, which had just been transferred to Taliaferro's brigade from Ewell's division, as a "nice gentleman."

The Second Brigade also had a new commander. Col. Jesse Burks had left the district on extended sick leave, and the senior regimental commander, Col. John A. Campbell of the 48th Virginia took his place. Campbell was popular and capable. An 1844 graduate of the Virginia Military Institute (v m i), he had been a judge before the war and had seen service in western Virginia before coming to the Valley District with Loring.[3]

For Turner Ashby, popularity came at a high price. To maintain it he had neglected discipline, and the consequences were now making themselves felt. On arrival at Swift Run Gap, Jackson had assigned Jedediah Hotchkiss the task of razing three bridges over the South Fork of the Shenandoah that lay just north of Conrad's Store in order to keep Banks out of Page Valley. The closest bridge was a gaudily painted wooden structure called "Red Bridge"; six miles to the north was a rickety covered expanse known as "Columbia Bridge." Both Red and Columbia bridges lay on roads leading eastward from New Market. North of Columbia Bidge and opposite the village of Luray stood White House Bridge.

At first the bridge burning went well. Calling upon three of Ashby's companies to accompany him, Hotchkiss rode first to Red Bridge, which he found undefended. He posted a strong picket nearby and then saw to it that the planks were taken up and fires set before riding on six miles to Columbia Bridge. There everything unraveled. Capt. Macon Jordan and nearly all the men of his company were a drunken liability to Hotchkiss. Capt. George Sheetz and his troopers were sober but of little use either. At Columbia Bridge, they ran into Yankee cavalry. The Federals charged, and Sheetz's company stampeded. Hotchkiss tried to coax the inebriated Jordan and his men forward. "Every attempt to rally was unavailing. Some actually threw away their guns, many of them their coats and blankets. I never saw a more disgraceful affair, all owing to the state of intoxication of some of the men and to the want of discipline among them. Our escape was providential." Hotchkiss and his unruly detachment abandoned Columbia and White House bridges, intact and in Northern hands.[4]

Word of the cavalry's embarrassment spread quickly. Just two days after joining the Valley army, Colonel Warren of the 10th Virginia had sized matters up enough to tell his wife that "the cavalry is in a perfectly disorganized and insufficient condition, and Colonel Ashby is rather a humbug."[5] Jackson agreed. For him, the fiasco at Columbia Bridge was the last straw. The reorganization of the army had swelled Ashby's command to twenty-one companies. Scores of infantrymen reenlisted in the mounted arm. Jackson quickly prohibited this, and after receiving Hotchkiss's report he also acted to impose order on Ashby's fragmented command, instructing ten companies to report to Taliaferro and the remaining eleven to Winder. They would hereafter be attached to the infantry brigades. Ashby was to command the advance guard of the army when on the advance and the rear guard when on retreat. He would have no troops of his own, but would have to apply to Taliaferro and Winder for whatever force he needed.

There was sympathy for Jackson's action among Ashby's officers. "There was still no regimental formation, and his large brigade with only two officers was an unwieldy body," said William McDonald. "It was more like a tribal band held together by the authority of a single chief. Increase of numbers rather diminished than increased its efficiency as a whole, and made it more unmanageable. Jackson saw the evil and tried to correct it." Chaplain Avirett understood that Jackson's intention was not to deprive Ashby of his command, but rather thought that "the sole object was to bring the large command of Colonel Ashby immediately under the eye of officers whom he thought better qualified to control the men in camp, while in the field the cavalry would still be under the control and lead of Ashby."[6]

But Ashby saw matters differently. Already in bad humor because of lingering illness, Ashby submitted his resignation, telling the bearer of it, Surg. Thomas L. Settle, that if Jackson and he were of the same rank, he would challenge him. Furthermore, he had obtained from the War Department authority to organize his command in any way he saw fit, and no one, not even Jackson, whom he estimated "a good man and a very valuable servant to the Confederacy," was entitled to interfere.

Settle delivered Ashby's resignation to Henry Kyd Douglas, who gave it to Jackson. After studying it for a day, Jackson told Douglas to summon Ashby to headquarters. Meanwhile, General Winder had ridden out to the cavalry outpost at McGaheysville to have a talk with Ashby. He promised to speak with Jackson if Ashby consented to withhold his resignation for the moment. Ashby agreed. Winder's good offices at first were unavailing. When Ashby arrived at headquarters on April 24, he and Jackson argued sharply. Jackson asked him to withdraw his resignation for the good of the Confederacy, just as he had withdrawn his after the Romney embarrassment. Ashby declined, telling him that "but for the fact that he had the highest respect for Jackson's ability as a soldier, and believed him essential to the cause of the South, he would hold him to a personal account for the indignity he had put upon him." With that he strode from the headquarters tent, declaring to all present his intention to raise an independent command in the Lower Valley.[7]

Cooler heads finally prevailed. Winder intervened again on Ashby's behalf. Sandie Pendleton and Henry Kyd Douglas also might have urged restraint. Recognizing that "if I persisted in my attempt to increase the efficiency of the cavalry, it would produce the contrary effect, as Colonel Ashby's influence, who is very popular with his men, would be thrown against me," Jackson revoked the order dividing Ashby's command after exacting from Ashby a promise to instill some discipline among his men. Ashby departed in fine spirits, remembered Chaplain Avirett, not realizing that Jackson intended to take up the matter with the War Department at a later date. In the meantime, he would be sure to issue Ashby exacting field orders that admitted of no misunderstanding.[8]

THE FEDERAL OCCUPATION of Harrisonburg proved brief. The same heavy rains that drenched the Valley army at Swift Run Gap during the last week of April washed away bridges in Banks's rear, causing him new fears for his attenuated supply lines. Although confident that Jackson had "abandoned the Valley of Virginia permanently," as he told Stanton on April 22, Banks had been reluctant to pursue him without adequate supplies and a better cavalry force. "We do not intend to lie still or wait, and want to move," he assured the adjutant general of the army the next day. But the secretary of war was satisfied with what Banks had accomplished and cautioned him not to push too far forward. President Lincoln felt he already had gone farther up the Valley than was prudent. Stanton told Banks on April 26 of his concern that the commands of Banks, Frémont, and McDowell were too widely separated. Stanton also warned Banks that Shields's division might be needed in the Department of the Rappahannock.[9]

That was fine by Banks. "You need have no apprehensions for our safety," he answered Stanton on April 30. That Jackson had left the Valley to join Johnson's army before Richmond, he had no doubt. "There is nothing more to be done by us in the Valley." With that all his officers concurred. "Nothing this side of Strasburg requires our presence." For a change, a Federal commander downplayed the enemy's strength. The Valley army was far smaller than represented in newspapers, Banks said, "not more than twenty thousand at the outside," and it was "reduced, demoralized, [and] on half rations." He foresaw no hazard in detaching Shields, who was anxious to go to where the fighting was, and asked that the remainder of the Fifth Corps be reassigned east of the Blue Ridge as well. A small garrison at Strasburg, thought Banks, would be sufficient to hold the Valley. Anticipating a recall order, Banks on April 30 began calling in his outlying detachments to Harrisonburg and New Market.[10]

Either Banks had lied to Stanton about the unanimity of opinion among his lieutenants or General Williams had kept his own counsel. While Banks assured the secretary that Jackson had fled, Williams confided to his daughter his belief that Jackson, whom he correctly placed "fifteen to twenty miles distant on the slopes of the Blue Ridge," had been "largely reinforced and intends to turn upon us here."[11]

Williams was right about Jackson's location but wrong about his plans. Jackson had briefly entertained the idea of attacking Banks, but General Lee, in one of his few decisive acts as pseudo general in chief, declined Jackson the reinforcements that Jackson believed necessary for offensive operations against Banks. Jackson had asked for five thousand men from the Peninsula, or for Fields's brigade, then watching McDowell's thirty thousand near Fredericksburg. Lee was long on sympathy but short on troops: "A decisive and successful blow at Banks's column would be fraught with the happiest results, and I deeply regret my inability to send you the reinforcements you ask." Perhaps Jackson might call upon Brig. Gen. Edward Johnson for an attack on Banks. "As he does not appear to be pressed, it is suggested that a portion of his force might be temporarily moved from its present position and made available for the movement in question."[12]

The next day (April 29) Jackson wrote Lee again to suggest three possible plans. Absent large reinforcements, he might leave Ewell at Swift Run Gap to threaten Banks's flank and himself move to join Johnson for a rapid attack on the forces in his front, namely Robert H. Milroy's Brigade of the Mountain Department. Alternatively, he might cooperate with Ewell to gobble up Sullivan's brigade, which Banks had thrown forward with Hatch's cavalry to hold the Columbia Bridge, and then strike at Banks's rear near New Market. Finally, he might pass down the South Fork of the Shenandoah with his army and Ewell's division to Sperryville and feint toward Winchester by way of Front Royal, thereby inducing Banks to withdraw down the Valley. Of the three plans, Jackson preferred the first, "for if successful I would afterwards only have Banks to contend with, and in doing this would be reinforced by General Johnson."[13]

Jackson's proposals showed real daring, as the situation hardly appeared propitious for any sort of Southern offensive in the Valley. Union forces outnumbered those of the Confederates two to one. Jackson had approximately 8,000 men at Swift Run Gap. Ewell, a day's march in his rear, mustered an additional 8,000 troops. Johnson, then encamped on the railroad at Westview, seven miles west of Staunton, counted 3,600 men, for a total of just over 19,000 Confederate soldiers in or near the Valley. Banks, on the other hand, had 19,000 men himself. Milroy had pushed forward from Monterey to McDowell with 3,000 men on April 27 to maintain pressure on Johnson, and Brig. Gen. Robert C. Schenck at Franklin was within supporting distance of Milroy with another 3,000 troops. Frémont was then preparing to join them with a force sufficient to give him a movable column of 15,000. If Jackson were to strike, he clearly must do so before Banks and Frémont were able to unite and oppose him with double his numbers.[14]

Lee replied to Jackson on May 1: "I have carefully considered the three plans of operations proposed by you. I must leave the selection of the one to be adopted to your judgment."[15]

It was good for Jackson that Lee did not impose a preference, because Jackson already had put in motion his plan to combine with Johnson for an attack on Milroy. He had directed Ashby to demonstrate toward Harrisonburg and had sent Jed Hotchkiss to the top of Peaked Mountain (at the southwest end of Massanutten Mountain) to report by rudimentary signals on Banks's activities. On April 28 he wrote VMI superintendent F. H. Smith confidentially to request the services of faculty member Col. Thomas H. Williamson for "an important movement in contemplation." He also had invoked the help of the Almighty. Jackson told Smith: "My prayer is that the proposed undertaking will receive God's blessing, for without it I can do nothing."

Williamson reported to Jackson on the morning of April 30 and received his mission: He was to proceed to Westview, obtain an escort from General Johnson, and reconnoiter the enemy lines with an eye toward finding a suitable site for a battle north of Staunton. "Now let that be as death with you," Jackson enjoined him.[16]

Jackson also had spoken with Ewell. He summoned him to his Swift Run Gap headquarters twice, once on April 29 and again on the morning of the thirtieth. How much of his plans he confided to Ewell is uncertain. Ewell learned that Jackson was about to move toward Staunton and that he was to take his place at Swift Run Gap; Ewell told Lee as much. Otherwise, Jackson appeared to have been his usual closed-mouth self. Ewell was not even sure whom Jackson intended to attack. They spoke in general terms about the threat Banks posed, but Jackson was short on specifics. A confused Ewell told Lee: "From the conversation held with General Jackson I inferred that he considered the force of General Banks too strong to be attacked with confidence by our combined commands." Certainly his two brief meetings with Jackson did nothing to give him any great confidence in the man. Col. Benjamin S. Ewell said that his brother led the division to Swift Run Gap "in obedience to orders, and not from choice, as at that time he believed Jackson to be a brave but very eccentric man."[17]

Richard Ewell, in turn, kept what little he knew to himself. His officers and men had expected to find Jackson's veterans when they reached the rain-swept pastures at the west end of Swift Run Gap on the evening of April 30. With hope in their hearts, they had marched up the Blue Ridge to the strains of "Listen to the Mocking Bird" and other popular tunes. Remembered a soldier of the 1st Maryland: "Nothing could have exceeded the joy of the troops at this unexpected order, for we had supposed ourselves destined to reinforce the army of Johnston in the swamps of the Chickahominy. To be in the beautiful Valley of Virginia was a pleasure unexpected, and it was with light hearts and elastic step that we left our camp. We marched to see Jackson, talk with his troops over the great battle they had so recently fought, and more than all, to discuss the prospects before us, and, if possible, to ascertain our destination."

Instead, Ewell's division encountered only vacant campsites. "Tired and worn out by the fatigues of the march, we went into bivouac, full of anticipation for the morrow's reunion," another Marylander recalled. "When the morning came there was left nothing, save the smoldering embers of the campfires of the night previous. Jackson had disappeared; whither no one seemed to know." A rumor circulated that Ewell "sat on the fence and cried because no one could tell him of Jackson's whereabouts," wrote a third member of the 1st Maryland. "We could get no tidings of Jackson; no one knew where to find him; all that was known was that he had moved rapidly in the direction of Staunton."[18]

In point of fact, Jackson's army had moved nowhere rapidly. His initial destination on leaving Swift Run Gap on the afternoon of April 30 had been the hamlet of Port Republic, just fourteen miles to the south. From Port Republic he intended to pass through Brown's Gap and march southeast to Mechum's Station on the Virginia Central Railroad. There the Valley army would board cars for the short ride west to Staunton. Jackson wanted to make the thirty-five-mile march over the Blue Ridge and to the railroad quickly but without any effort at concealment; he hoped to trick Banks into thinking his destination to be Richmond.[19]

Heavy rains disrupted Jackson's timetable. The route from Swift Run Gap to Port Republic was an unpaved country road running along the three-mile-wide sandy plain between the South Fork of the Shenandoah River and the foot of the Blue Ridge. April 30 dawned bright and pleasant, but around mid-afternoon the temperature dropped and the rain came in torrents. The Reverend Robert L. Dabney, who had joined the army a few days earlier as both spiritual adviser and chief of staff, graphically described the consequences: "The flat, treacherous soil was speedily converted by the trains of baggage and artillery into a quagmire without apparent bottom. If the teamsters attempted to evade this by turning aside into the woodlands, as soon as the fibrous roots of the surface were severed, the subsoil proved even more deceitful than the mire of the roads, and a few vehicles made the track impassable. The rivulets descending from the mountain were swollen into broad rivers, and the glades of the forest were converted into lakes." Jackson and his staff were able to cover thirteen miles that day, often at a gallop, and they passed the night at Lewiston, the estate of Charles Lewis on the outskirts of Port Republic. But the infantry and trains traveled only five miles.[20]

Matters improved little the next day. A hard wind whipped rain into the faces of the struggling soldiers. Pioneers toiled to repair damaged wagons and caissons. Nearly everyone agreed that the road was the worst they had ever seen. "Whole roadbeds formed of stones and brushwood sank into the quicksand, and others were placed above them, again and again," said Dabney, who got a taste of manual labor himself. "The general and his staff were seen dismounted, urging on the laborers; and he carried stones and timber upon his own shoulders, with his uniform bespattered with mud like a common soldier's." The cavalry cleared Lewiston during the day, and part of the infantry reached the estate at nightfall, but the trains and much of the artillery lagged far behind.

The struggle with mud and rain was repeated on May 2. Late in the afternoon the sun peeked through the clouds and "lit up this beautiful valley. Never did my eyes rest on so beautiful a prospect," said Maj. Frank Jones, whose 2nd Virginia had enjoyed a day of rest in the woods near Brown's Gap. "The larger fields were green with wheat. What a country to fight for! What a country to die for if need be!" May 3 dawned bright and warm. The army crossed Brown's Gap at daybreak and reached Mechum's Station before sunset by an easy march over a dry turnpike.[21]

Jackson had subjected his soldiers to three days of agony needlessly. From signal stations on Massanutten Mountain, deserters, and Sullivan's brigade at Columbia Bridge, Banks learned of Jackson's move to Port Republic and of his subsequent crossing of Brown's Gap, but he remained unaware of his march to Mechum's Station. Sullivan first reported movement up the river on the evening of May 1. By mid-afternoon the next day General Williams was able conclude with some certainty that Jackson was on his way to make a junction with Johnson, and he guessed that Ewell had come over the mountains from Stanardsville. Banks agreed with Williams. Jackson's carefully orchestrated ruse thus had gone for naught; he might just as well have marched all the way to Gordonsville over a good macadamized turnpike, taken trains from there to Staunton, and saved the wear and tear on his men and wagons.[22]

In the end it mattered little whether Banks divined Jackson's intentions or not; he was in no position to do anything to counter them. Taking Banks at his word that nothing remained to be accomplished in the Shenandoah Valley, President Lincoln on May 1 instructed him to withdraw to Strasburg. Orders directing Shields to join McDowell followed the next day.

Banks seemingly had gotten what he had requested. But Jackson's stirrings worried him. From Harrisonburg on May 4 he wrote his friend Congressman Schuyler Colfax of his concerns:

> We have driven the enemy out of the Valley, halting at this place by order of the government. If our force divides, the enemy returns again into the Valley, and all our work is lost. If we all move over the mountains altogether we can occupy him in conjunction with Frémont so that he cannot return. I do not know whether you speak with the president or secretary on army matters. If you do so, I should be glad of a word of explanation on the subject, not however by way of complaint. I feel perfectly secure that our force cannot divide without unfortunate results.

Banks made good strategic arguments, but he also recognized that garrison duty in Strasburg offered no chance for personal advancement. As he told Stanton, "I shall grieve not to be included in the active operations of this summer." And the public might easily misconstrue any movement rearward, regardless of the reason behind it, as defeat. Banks's own staff was talking that way. "There is a hope that our retreat on Strasburg will not be insisted on and that our column may yet be saved that disgrace," David Strother wrote in his diary. "All the news from Richmond goes to show that the enemy is caving in everywhere. Yet we are retreating."[23]

CHAPTER 17

GOD BLESSED OUR ARMS

WITH VICTORY

Edward "Allegheny" Johnson was a likable character, popular both with his men and with the ladies. Devoid of vanity or untoward ambition, warm-hearted and friendly, the forty-five-year-old Virginian had one disarming trait. As diarist Mary Chesnut observed: "He had an odd habit of falling into a state of incessant winking as soon as he was the least startled or agitated. He seemed persistently winking one eye at you, but he meant nothing by it. In point of fact he did not know it himself. In Mexico he had been wounded in the eye—and the nerve vibrates independently [*illegible word*] of his will" (italics in the original).[1]

Beside the eye twitch, Johnson also had acquired a reputation as a fine fighting officer in Mexico. He was brevetted captain for gallantry and meritorious conduct at the Battle of Molino del Rey, and again for gallantry at Churubusco and the storming of Chapultepec. After the Mexican War he served on the frontier, resigning his commission in 1861 to enter the Confederate service as colonel of the 12th Georgia Infantry.

Johnson also enjoyed the esteem of Stonewall Jackson, and their reunion at Westview on May 6 no doubt was a cordial one. Jackson was well fitted out for the occasion. While in Staunton he had gotten a haircut and had exchanged the tattered blue U.S. major's uniform he had worn at V M I and in the field for a new, full suit of Confederate gray. Thomas H. Williamson also was at Westview. He had little to report to Jackson, as woods and rolling mountains had thwarted his reconnaissance beyond the village.

The Valley army was at Staunton. Most units had traveled from Mechum's Station to Staunton by train on May 4 and 5 (a few unlucky regiments walked), and by Confederate standards the men were well fed and rested. Four companies of VMI cadets—two hundred boys in all—which had been attached for temporary service with the Stonewall Bridge, provided the veterans with a source of amusement.[2]

The jury was out on Jackson so far as the soldiers of Johnson's brigade were concerned. Said Pvt. John S. Robson of the 52nd Virginia:

> We had not heard much of [Jackson], apart from the record he made at Manassas, until reports of his crazy battle at Kernstown were received, and although it was the custom for both sides to magnify their victories and depreciate their defeats, we were pretty strongly impressed with the belief that Jackson had been pretty badly worsted by that fighting Irishman, General Shields, whom we rated always as a gentleman and a soldier; and when we learned that Jackson was retreating up the Valley before Banks, our faith was visibly weakened.[3]

The combined commands of Jackson and Johnson set out for McDowell at daybreak on May 7. The day was sunny and warm, the road dusty but good. The march was an easy one for everyone but Jackson's staff and the VMI boys. With the exception of Williamson and Hotchkiss, members of the general's official circle were "so totally ignorant" of the plan of campaign that a number of them took the wrong road and went twenty-five miles out of their way before rejoining the army.

The cadets simply were unaccustomed to marching and none too proud to admit it. Catching sight of General Winder, one young straggler asked, "Mister, won't you take me up behind?" Winder helped him up on his horse. As they rode along, the boy inquired, "Mister, what cavalry company do you belong to?"

"I don't belong to any," the general replied.

"Well, to what battery?"

"To none."

"Well, to what regiment then?"

"To none. I am General Winder of the Stonewall Brigade."

"Oh, General," said the young fellow, "I beg your pardon. I never would have asked you to take me up if I had known who you were," and he tried to slide off. But Winder prevented him, and continuing on, the two soon fell into an easy chat.[4]

Jackson accorded Johnson the advance because of his "familiarity with the mountain region and high qualities as a soldier." Taliaferro and Campbell followed. The Stonewall Brigade and the cadets brought up the rear. Approaching Shenandoah Mountain, fourteen miles west of Staunton, Johnson's vanguard ran into pickets from the 1st West Virginia Cavalry. Dusty and frightened, the Yankee troopers galloped through the camp of the 32nd Ohio Infantry, which Milroy had placed at the eastern foot of the mountain to protect foraging parties, shouting "The Rebels are coming." Throwing aside their breakfast of hardtack and coffee, the Ohioans struggled to the summit and formed line of battle just ahead of Johnson's advance. Left behind for the enemy were their newly issued Sibley tents and a considerable stock of sutlers' stores.

Stonewall Jackson was riding with Johnson. He motioned Colonel Williamson up the steep slope to the right of the 32nd Ohio Infantry in search of flanking trails and Jed Hotchkiss to the left. By the time they reached the top, the Federals had vanished down the western slope. Johnson pressed the advance toward Shaw's Ridge, the next elevation between Staunton and McDowell. There General Milroy had planted the 75th Ohio Infantry and the 9th Ohio Battery. A few quick shots from the battery drove the Rebels back over Shenandoah Mountain. Milroy also summoned the 73rd Ohio Infantry and 3rd West Virginia Infantry to reinforce the retreating 32nd Ohio. Before long, word reached him that the Confederates were feeling their way around his left flank, and Milroy withdrew his forces to McDowell before nightfall. Johnson made camp beside the headwaters of Shaw's Fork, at the base of the ridge, six miles east of McDowell. The Stonewall Brigade and the cadets bivouacked near Buffalo Gap, ten miles behind Johnson.[5]

The night of May 7 was an uneasy one for Milroy's command. Diary accounts reveal that the Yankee rank and file somehow knew Jackson and Johnson had combined forces against them. To drive the Federals from McDowell appeared simple. The village was nearly impossible to defend, particularly by a force outnumbered four to one. McDowell lay on the west bank of Bull Pasture River, one of the tributaries of the mighty James River. The principal dwellings included a store, log schoolhouse, sawmill, blacksmith shop, and the brick residences of Felix K. and George W. Hull. The Parkersburg and Staunton Turnpike passed through McDowell from east to west, and a thrice-weekly stagecoach was the only connection the townspeople had with the outside world. Opposite McDowell, Bull Pasture River was so narrow and shallow, said an early resident, that "of a hot summer's day the mild-eyed cattle stand and gaze as they cool themselves on the pebbly bed, over which the murmuring waters flow. The oaks and elms of the mountain bend over the stream, almost arching it with graceful gothic tracery done in green and brown." Nonsense, thought Sandie Pendleton. There was nothing remotely romantic about the region. It was "the meanest country I ever saw, but still it is old Virginia, and we must have it."

High ground commanded McDowell in every direction. Jackson's Mountain loomed just west of the village, and Bull Pasture Mountain rose up two miles to the east. A spur of Bull Pasture Mountain called "Sitlington's Hill" stretched south of the Parkersburg and Staunton Turnpike nearly to the east bank of Bull Pasture River. Its steep western slope towered five hundred feet above the river. Sitlington's Hill had a broad and rugged top, laced with sharp ridges and ravines. On the north side of the road, Hull's Ridge ran southwest like a pointed finger to the riverbank opposite McDowell. The southern extremity of Hull's Hill was known as "Cedar Knob."[6]

No matter that the situation appeared hopeless. Milroy knew Jackson was coming, and he was determined to make a stand. Two days earlier, he had told John Frémont he thought Jackson's move toward Port Republic "a feint for relief of Johnston. I shall not retire beyond this point, but in case of an attack by a superior force will await reinforcements." Should Jackson not come forward, he would advance on Staunton himself. Robert Schenck expected nothing less of his fellow brigade commander, whom he said was "always moved by undaunted and impetuous, though rather uncalculating, bravery." Neither did his men. They called the six-foot-four Indianan the "War Eagle" and delighted in his presence. Said one: "Imagine a large, gray-headed man with brown whiskers seated on an iron-gray horse of the corresponding proportions and speaking in a low, sharp, quick voice, and you have Milroy, one of the most impetuous, go-ahead, fearless men in the whole army."[7]

On May 8 Milroy had roll call sounded at 2:30 A.M. Tents were struck at 4:00 A.M., and the men were herded into ranks. Daybreak came, but no enemy. Milroy expected to be attacked both from the front and from North River Gap, fifteen miles beyond his left flank. He sent a squad of cavalrymen in that direction, but they turned up nothing. Milroy also deployed pickets from the 2nd West Virginia Infantry along Sitlington's Hill, and he pushed a squadron of the 1st West Virginia Cavalry out along the Parkersburg and Staunton Turnpike two miles to the gap through Bull Pasture Mountain.

At 10:00 A.M. Schenck arrived with 1,500 infantry, a battery of artillery, and a squadron of cavalry. His men had marched thirty-four miles in twenty-three hours and were bone-tired, but their presence did much to reassure Milroy and his men. As a lieutenant from the 75th Ohio said, "We now felt tolerable safe." Milroy shook Schenck's hand and thanked him for arriving "just in time."

The two conferred. Milroy wanted to make an attack with every man they had. Schenck disagreed. As senior officer on the field Schenck might have pressed his views, but instead he and Milroy struck a compromise that appeased Milroy's combativeness while also protecting their outnumbered forces. "We agreed," said Schenck, "that the better plan would be to send, that evening, whatever portion of our united forces was available for the attack up the side of the mountain to assault the enemy and deliver a blow, if we could, and then retire from his front before he had recovered from the surprise of such a movement."[8]

As yet there were no Confederates to attack. At 10:30 A.M. Capt. George R. Latham, in command of the detachment of the 2nd West Virginia atop Sitlington's Hill, reported seeing Confederate artillery moving toward him through Bull Pasture Mountain Gap. Otherwise, the front appeared clear. Milroy responded to Latham's report by sending Company B, 73rd Ohio Infantry, under Capt. Thomas W. Higgins, across the river and up the slope of Sitlington's Hill to reconnoiter ahead of Latham's right flank. Schenck deployed the 82nd Ohio Infantry on the eastern slope of Cedar Knob, where it commanded the turnpike approach to McDowell. For good measure Milroy had a section of Capt. Henry F. Hyman's 12th Ohio Battery line up alongside the 82nd Ohio, and it began to lob shells at the wooded heights across the turnpike at a rate of one every five minutes.[9]

Hyman's gunners fired blindly until noon, when a party of Southern horsemen and foot soldiers appeared on the crest of Sitlington's Hill. What Schenck and Milroy mistook for Southern skirmishers were in fact Generals Jackson and Johnson, their staffs, and a thirty-man infantry escort from the 52nd Virginia. A crucial member of the entourage was Jed Hotchkiss. Hotchkiss had examined the country around McDowell carefully the year before, and Jackson applied Hotchkiss's knowledge by making him commander of the advance guard on the morning march from Shenandoah Mountain to Bull

Pasture Mountain. Hotchkiss took the task seriously. He rode well ahead of the skirmishers, pausing at each bend in the road to signal the way clear.

Confident that his cartographer would not lead him astray, Jackson accompanied Hotchkiss to a rocky spur of Bull Pasture Mountain. There they had a clean view of the countryside around McDowell. With Jackson looking on, Hotchkiss sketched a rough map of the enemy's forces. Arrayed in line of battle along the western bank of Bull Pasture Mountain were the six regiments of Milroy's Brigade (the 82nd Ohio and Hyman's section had not yet ascended Cedar Knob), together with two of Schenck's three regiments. Schenck's third regiment, the 5th West Virginia, and the Yankee artillery were congregated on a low knoll behind the village.[10]

His sketch finished, Hotchkiss rode back to the turnpike with Jackson, who summoned General Johnson and their party for a ride up Sitlington's Hill. There, on the crest, they drew the attention of every Yankee in sight. Federal artillerymen stepped up the tempo of their barrage. With more enthusiasm than clarity of purpose, Milroy waved skirmishers across Bull Pasture River; Maj. Richard Long set out with two companies from the 73rd Ohio to support Captain Higgins. Two companies from the 32nd Ohio and a company from the 3rd West Virginia went with them. Company G, 75th Ohio, ranged toward a narrow eminence south of Sitlington's Hill.[11]

Jackson found nothing alarming in the Northern maneuvers. He neither expected nor intended to fight a battle that day. Before leaving the hill, Jackson asked Colonel Williamson and Hotchkiss to hunt for a road around the enemy's right flank, over which he could send artillery. Jackson told Hotchkiss that he wanted his batteries in place to shell the Yankees no later than 3:00 A.M. the next day. After giving orders to ration the army, Jackson told his staff to retire to his headquarters in John Wilson's hotel and tollhouse on Cow Pasture River for supper and rest. Johnson, meanwhile, called up his brigade, which was then under the direct command of Col. W. C. Scott, to occupy Sitlington's Hill.[12]

As Jackson and Johnson rode leisurely off Sitlington's Hill, opposing skirmishers clashed. Their escort met Latham's and Long's detachments on the hilltop, while the remainder of the 52nd Virginia hurried forward through a wide ravine to the crest of a lower eminence a half mile to the south. After a brief, winning clash with Company G, 75th Ohio, the 52nd Virginia deployed as skirmishers to protect the Confederate left. To the right of the 52nd, Colonel Scott placed the 44th Virginia Infantry in regular line of battle. Johnson intervened to modify Scott's dispositions. He ordered the men deployed in

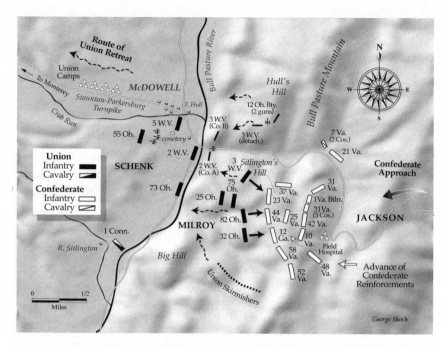

MAP 4. Battle of McDowell, May 8, 1862

pairs, with intervals of five paces between the pairs, and told the men to lie down to avoid the Union shells, which were coming faster and with greater accuracy. After helping drive off Latham and Long, the 58th Virginia similarly deployed along the northern crest of Sitlington's Hill, fronting west, with its right flank anchored on the turnpike. Coming up the ravine in support of the 44th and 58th Virginia regiments was the 12th Georgia Infantry. Organized in June 1861, the regiment had in its ranks the "flower of the young manhood" of the Georgia cotton belt, but Col. Z. T. Conner, elevated to regimental command only a month earlier, was unproven.

Sitlington's Hill was in fact a ridge, with a largely open crest that ran north to south. Between the positions of the 44th Virginia and the 52nd Virginia the crest dipped sharply. That Scott's brigade was spread thin was of no concern to Jackson. With a nearly three-to-one numerical advantage, the last thing he expected was a Federal attack.[13]

But that is precisely what came his way at 4:30 P.M. Milroy had obtained Schenck's consent to stage what he called a "reconnaissance-in-force" of Sitlington's Hill with five regiments, or just under 2,400 men. The proximate cause of the movement, to which Schenck and Milroy had agreed in principle that morning, was an erroneous report from Captain Latham that the Rebels were planting a battery on the summit of Sitlington's Hill. In response, Milroy directed two of his regiments—the 25th Ohio under Lt. Col. W. P. Richardson and the 75th Ohio under Col. Nathaniel C. McLean, with McLean in overall command—to advance against the presumed center of the Confederate line. Milroy ordered two other regiments—the 32nd Ohio from his brigade and the 82nd Ohio from Schenck's—to support McLean with an assault on the Southern right and rear. Apparently as an afterthought, Milroy sent the 3rd West Virginia Infantry forward along the Parkersburg and Staunton Turnpike.[14]

Atop Cedar Knob, "from whence I could see the whole combat on both sides like a map," General Milroy watched the attack unfold. From his vantage point, everything appeared "most splendid." But from McLean's perspective, matters looked grim:

> The enemy were in position on the top of the mountain, entirely screened from our view, and the conformation of the ridge permitted them to deliver their fire with only the exposure of a small portion of their bodies, and in reloading they were entirely protected from our fire by the crest of the hill. The side of the mountain up which I was compelled to make the attack was entirely destitute of protection, either from trees or rocks, and so steep that the men were at times compelled to march either to one side or the other in order to make the assault.

McLean's men evidently negotiated the difficult approach well. Former VMI instructor and major of the 52nd Virginia, John De Hart Ross, admired the Yankee advance: "The enemy's discipline is immensely superior to ours. I watched them well during the fight, or rather at the beginning of it, and I never saw cadets at drill march with greater precision and more regularly than did the Yankees under fire. Not a man shrank from his position but they all marched alike, true soldiers to the attack."[15]

The Confederates withheld their fire until the last moment. For that, Lt. George Fox of the 75th Ohio was grateful: "Up we went right in front of them, a place where I think they did not expect us, for I know if they had at one time come to the top and fired one volley or so it would have just more than raked us." Notwithstanding its apparent advantages, Scott's position had serious drawbacks. The Southerners could duck behind the ridge to reload, but in firing they were silhouetted against the clear evening sky. Conversely, the setting sun cast shadows that masked the Yankees.[16]

The 75th Ohio met the enemy sooner than expected. Johnson and Scott had thrown the 12th Georgia forward of the main line to a "large hilly old field" on a spur of Sitlington's Hill. The Georgians neared the spot as the Yankees clambered up the far slope. Wheeling by company into line of battle, the 12th opened and took fire simultaneously. The curvature of the open ground forced the regiment into an inverted *V* that vitiated the Georgians' fire. So too did their weapons, antiquated .69-caliber smoothbore muskets with a maximum effective range of just one hundred yards—nearly the distance separating the opposing lines.[17] McLean's Ohioans had modern rifled muskets, but it took them an hour to score their first hit. At 5:30 P.M. a minie bullet pierced the head of Orderly Sgt. Asa Sherwood. A cry went up to avenge his death, and company commander James G. Rodgers had a hard time preventing his men from "rushing madly at the foe." Casualties came more regularly after Sherwood's death. Said Captain Rodgers:

> Next to fall was W. S. C. Rogers. He had nobly done his work, and being much exhausted, he was lying on his side. I had just shot his gun for him, and handed it back to be reloaded, when he exclaimed, "Oh, Captain, I am shot and dying." I at once examined him and saw a hole in his coat between the neck and shoulder blade. I told him that perhaps he was only slightly wounded. My attention was drawn off for about ten minutes, and when I again turned to examine him, he was in the last agonies of death.
>
> The next to fall were the brave uncle and nephew, Joe Wilder and William Hurd, both shot through the head.
>
> Oh, I tell you, it was trying to a captain's heart to see his brave men being shot down all around him. Not enough to kill those brave boys named, I had still to suffer in the fall of my friend and [fellow] officer, Lt. W. A. Massey. For two long hours had he been in the thickest of the fight, cheering the men by deed and words. He had just said to me, "Don't the boys fight nobly!" and had given a loud cheer to Jeff Davis, when he fell by my side, shot through the side, [and] exclaimed, "Oh, Captain, I am a dead man; send me home to father; I am willing to die, for it is a righteous cause."[18]

By the time the 32nd and 82nd Ohio regiments came into musket range of Sitlington's Hill, the Southern line had tightened. Rebel fire grew more deadly. "The 82nd Ohio and 32nd Ohio obeyed the order with the greatest alacrity," said Milroy, "but the enemy, observing the design and having a much superior force, in a handsome manner changed his front to the rear." In point of fact, the Confederates had not changed front as Milroy supposed because there was no threat to their rear; the two Ohio regiments struck the right of Johnson's line head on. Instead, Colonel Scott had rearranged his defenses to accommodate reinforcements from Conner's brigade. He moved the 58th Virginia from the right to the center and pulled the 44th Virginia briefly out of the line to rest. General Johnson guided the 25th and 31st Virginia Infantry regiments into space the 58th had vacated and shook out one company of the 31st onto the turnpike to watch for enemy flanking maneuvers.[19]

The 32nd and 82nd Ohio regiments collided with the 25th Virginia moments after the Virginians took the field. Staff engineer Lt. J. K. Boswell looked at his watch and noted the time of the first volley as 6:15 P.M. The sudden crescendo of rifle fire brought the 44th Virginia to its feet, and the regiment surged forward without orders to fill the gap between the 58th Virginia and the 25th Virginia.

Col. George H. Smith of the 25th Virginia appreciated the help. "This was my first fight, and I hardly knew what to do," he confessed. Catching sight of the left companies of the 82nd Ohio ascending a brushy trail on his right flank, Smith panicked. He reported his observation to both Johnson and Jackson, "but I could get no reply at all and knew not what they would do."[20]

Smith's men took matters into their own hands. Said Pvt. George W. Sponaugle: "We were on a hill and had to shoot down at the Yankees, and there was a tendency to overshoot them, while they had us between them and the skyline, and we made a good mark. The timber had been cut down in front of us. This made it harder for them to get up to us, but at the same time it afforded them shelter." Nonetheless, Sponaugle and his comrades got in their fair share of good shots. "There was a long log about fifty yards away from us, parallel with our lines, and they were thick behind this log. They were about all killed too, shot through the head, when their heads would appear above the log."[21]

Alvid Lee of the 82nd Ohio attested to the Virginians' handiwork: "Happening to look to the rear, I saw some men lying on the grass. My first impression was that they had lain down to avoid being hit. But they were motionless. The truth flashed over me—they were dead! I had scarcely noticed, before, that anybody had been hurt, except that a bullet had struck the musket of a man next to me, and glancing had wounded him in the wrist."[22]

The Ohioans gave as good as they got. So many Rebels fell that the survivors piled up the bodies for breastworks. Their macabre defenses availed them little, said Ohioan E. M. Hutchinson, "as our men picked them off as fast as they would raise to shoot."

Private Sponaugle lost himself to the frenzy:

> The first one of our men wounded was shot in the mouth or face. I did not mind it much, though, once I was into it. I was a might good shot with a rifle, as I had used one ever since I had been big enough to carry one. I fired twenty-three rounds, and some of them were fired at mighty close range. Every time I saw a head, I shot at it. They were concealed by the timber, and it was not long until the hill was wrapped in powder smoke, like a thick fog, and it was hard to see them. I expect I came as near killing some of them as the next one, but it is better that one does not know for certain. It does not weigh so hard on one's mind.[23]

Weighing heavily on Colonel Scott's mind was the sorry showing of the 44th Virginia. Evidently its men had a dubious reputation; in a diary entry six months earlier, a corporal of the 31st Virginia had labeled them "the grandest cowards in the army." Despite their enthusiasm this day, Scott did not like what he saw:

> In firing, the front rank of my right flank, after delivering its fire, would retire some three or four paces to the rear and lie down and load, and, as they were shielded from danger while loading, I allowed this system to continue. But observing that some men retired farther to the rear than necessary, and were lying on their faces and taking no part in the battle, I attempted to rouse them by words, but finding that neither harsh words nor threats were of any avail, I commenced riding over them, which soon made them join the line of battle.[24]

While the 32nd and 82nd Ohio regiments grappled with the 25th Virginia and the right companies of the 44th Virginia atop Sitlington's Hill, and the 25th and 75th Ohio struggled to make headway against the 12th Georgia and the left companies of the 44th Virginia, a sharp fight erupted down on the Parkersburg and Staunton Turnpike. There, just beyond the Confederate right flank, the 3rd West Virginia collided with the detachment of the 52nd Virginia posted north of the turnpike and with skirmishers belonging to Company C, 31st Virginia, deployed on the road and southward up a rocky ledge. Company C had been recruited in Clarksburg, as had three companies of the 3rd West Virginia. All had served in the same antebellum militia company. Before the first volley, the West Virginians came close enough to the Virginia skirmishers to recognize and call out to them by name.[25]

Confederate reinforcements continued to appear, crowding the battlefield and giving the defenders a decisive numerical advantage over the attackers. Jackson directed the 10th Virginia of Taliaferro's brigade to form in reserve to the 58th Virginia on the Southern left, and during a lull in the fight with the 82nd Ohio he replaced the 25th Virginia with the 23rd and 37th Virginia regiments.[26]

There was no relief at hand for the 12th Georgia, which was getting the worst of its encounter with the 75th Ohio. For nearly three hours the Georgians withstood fire from three sides, as their assailants wrapped themselves around the open knoll. The sun set at 6:46 P.M. on a cloudless horizon. A brilliant half moon rose in its place. With nightfall came the cry, "We are out of ammunition." While his first lieutenant ran the gauntlet of Yankee fire to retrieve a hatful of bullets, Captain Rodgers ordered the men of his company to lie down. "How long seemed the hour we had to wait, quietly taking the enemy's fire and not returning it. This is more trying to a soldier than anything else—to [lay] still and almost feel the balls of the enemy flying over your head, and continually the peculiar 'zip' of the minies sounding in your ear." At sunset Martin D. Brett of the 12th received his first combat wound, a minie ball through the left arm:

> It was a new experience to me. Soon after being shot I was seized with the most intense craving for water I had ever felt. It seemed as though my insides were burning out. I stood several minutes watching other men fall near me. I heard others calling for water. I did so too, but there was no one to supply our wants. I watched the blood spout freely from my arm. Very soon the gray mountain rocks turned green. The mountains seemed to spin around in the air like a boy's toy top. My desire for water overcame all pain caused by the wound, and I staggered back about fifty paces to a little branch we had fought over about an hour before. The water was cool and refreshing, and I drank my fill.[27]

When the Georgians finally withdrew, first from the exposed knoll and then from the main line—exhausted and out of ammunition, but not broken—the 48th Virginia of Campbell's brigade was on hand to take their place. "They moved with perfect coolness in the face of a deadly fire, and never halted until they had swept back the Federals," said an admiring Georgian. "This was one of the handsomest affairs that I witnessed during the war."

Captain Rodgers was less complimentary of the efforts of the 48th: "During the engagement one regiment undertook to relieve us, as our ammunition was exhausted. They came up, fired one round, but could not stand it, so they fell back again." Colonel Scott happened to be standing nearby when the Virginians broke. "I used all my exertions to rally them, principally by appeals to their state pride, and after they had run back some twenty or thirty yards I succeeded in bringing them to a halt, and after loading they returned to the line of battle with great animation."[28]

In fairness to the 48th Virginia, a column of Federals creeping up a dark ravine had caught the regiment unawares. "Their flag was suddenly hoisted within fifty yards of our line of battle," conceded Colonel Scott. "Our men, so soon as they discovered the flag and enemy, received a deadly fire and simultaneously returned it, and then, with the exception of some fifteen or twenty, broke and ran back."[29]

In the end, the performance of the 48th Virginia was of no consequence. Exhausted and nearly out of ammunition themselves, the Yankees were in no condition to press the fight.

The force that stung the Virginians was the 32nd Ohio, which had moved laterally at the double-quick shortly after 7:00 P.M. in an attempt to re-invigorate the flagging Federal attack against the Southern left. At Milroy's direction, the 3rd West Virginia left the turnpike to join the 82nd Ohio in a final push against the Confederate right. Both assaults floundered (there were now eleven Confederate regiments and one battalion to oppose five attacking Northern regiments). Colonel McLean wisely told everyone within reach to break ranks, find what cover they could, and hold their ground.[30]

The shooting sputtered out at 9:00 P.M. By then, said Colonel Fulkerson of the 37th Virginia, "we could only see the outlines of the enemy, which was soon lost, and we had to fire by the flash of their guns." General Johnson had been wounded in the ankle an hour earlier and after a hurried conversation with Jackson moved on toward the hospital. Colonel Harman of the 52nd Virginia was carried past a few moments later. Jackson told the ever-present Jed Hotchkiss to find General Taliaferro, deliver Jackson's compliments, and tell him that he must hold on until Jackson could bring up the Stonewall Brigade. "I at once galloped down to where a steep log rollway led up to the field of the engagement," said Hotchkiss. "Finding there a soldier whom I knew, I gave my horse in his charge and scrambled up to the top of the mountain where the fighting had been going on, but which had then ceased but a short time. Everything was confusion—the men all mixed up and hunting for the wounded and reforming in anticipation of another attack." Hotch-kiss delivered his message and returned to Jackson's side. The two waited in the chill darkness for sounds of renewed fighting, but all was quiet. After a few minutes a courier appeared with word from Taliaferro that the battle was over. Countermanding the order to bring up the Stonewall Brigade, Jackson set off for headquarters.[31]

At 10:00 P.M. Milroy withdrew his regiments from Sitlington's Hill. "My boys were anxious to hold on and send for more [ammunition]," he told his wife proudly, "but I deemed it prudent in their exhausted condition to with-draw them down to camp, which was done in good order, bringing off all our dead and wounded."

Not quite all the dead. Recalled Alvid Lee of the 82nd Ohio:

> The wounded had all been carried to the rear, but there lay the dead, and
> it seemed too bad to leave them behind. So two of us picked up one of the
> bodies and endeavored to bear it away with the retreating line. But we had
> not realized until then how fatigued we were! The slain soldier was a
> young German, who had received a bullet full in the forehead. We laid
> him down gently by the stump of a tree, with his face upturned to the
> moonlight, and there we left him. A few minutes later I found myself try-
> ing to quench, in a muddy pool at the turnpike, the fever and thirst begot-
> ten of the extraordinary exertion and excitement.[32]

After an informal council of war, in which every field-grade officer in the two brigades agreed that McDowell was indefensible against an enemy whose superior strength they correctly estimated, Schenck and Milroy gave orders for a withdrawal toward Franklin.

There were 26 Union dead to be carried off Sitlington's Hill. Another 230 officers and enlisted men were wounded. Only 3 men were reported missing. Confederate losses were far higher, one of the rare instances in the war in which the defender suffered more than the attacker. Jackson lost 146 men killed or mortally wounded, 382 wounded, and 4 men captured. In the 12th Georgia alone, out of 540 men engaged, 52 had been killed and 123 wounded.[33]

A number of factors accounted for the low Federal losses. First was the superior range of the Enfield rifled muskets, which most of the Ohioans carried. Second, the Southerners, in firing downhill, tended to overshoot. They also fired fast, as they were exposed from the waist up when they deliv-ered their shots. Crouched among boulders and brush and aiming upward, the Yankees presented smaller targets. (Said Lt. McHenry Howard: "Uphill shooting is more accurate than down, which is apt to overshoot the mark, as every sportsman knows.") Third, the Confederates fired into the setting sun, while the Federals aimed into a clear, deep-blue horizon. Finally, Jackson was unable to employ his artillery. It "was not brought up," he explained in his report, "there being no road to the rear by which our guns could be withdrawn in event of disaster, and the prospect of successfully using them did not compensate for the risk."[34]

That Jackson imagined any risk of defeat at the hands of a vastly weaker foe (and Jackson could easily see all the Union forces on the field and across the Bull Pasture River) speaks well of Schenck and Milroy's tactics. They had accomplished their stated purpose of delaying an enemy attack and had inflicted heavy casualties in the bargain. By any reasonable calculation, McDowell was a tactical Union victory. But in a larger sense, the fruits of victory rested with the Confederates. Jackson was not prevaricating when he told Richmond the next morning, "God blessed our arms with victory at McDowell yesterday." The battle was of no strategic consequence to the Federals. But for the Southern people, who had come to know only defeat after defeat, Jackson's perceived tenacity at McDowell, and his subsequent pursuit of Schenck and Milroy, was a tonic they imbibed eagerly. The reputation of Stonewall Jackson was beginning to spread beyond Virginia, his exploits carried in Deep South newspapers as well as those of the Old Dominion.[35]

THE FEDERAL RETREAT began at 12:30 A.M., a sad and silent procession. "We filed through the village in the darkness, the baggage and sick in advance, weary, wet, cold, and sleepy," remembered a lieutenant of the 73rd Ohio. "We had had no rest worth speaking of for two nights." Another Ohio officer recalled: "You have no idea of the suffering our men went through that night. Without their wounds dressed properly they were crowded into ambulances, wagons, and on horses—any way to get them along, comfort or ease being but a secondary matter." Milroy remained behind with the rear guard until daybreak, as the Yankees burned provisions and threw excess ammunition into Bull Pasture River. By the time they left town, he told his wife, "I was so sleepy and wearied that I could hardly sit on Jasper."[36]

There would be little sleeping for Federals and Confederates alike. Determined to push Schenck and Milroy as far from a possible junction with Banks, or perhaps get in Banks's rear himself, Jackson began a pursuit on the afternoon of May 9. The Federals put thirteen miles between themselves and their pursuers before Jackson got started, but Schenck halted on a high ridge commanding the road to Franklin, defying the Confederates to give battle. Jackson declined, and the Federals resumed their retreat to Franklin, where Schenck presumed Frémont would meet him.[37]

On May 11 the brigades of Schenck and Milroy shuffled into Franklin. There was no sign of Frémont. The shabby state of Blenker's division, which had reached him at Petersburg forty-eight hours earlier, had delayed the Path-finder. But the rugged ridges dominating the way into Franklin gave Schenck confidence, and he deployed his forces astride and above the road. Before reaching the town he had set fire to the forest on either side of the road as he passed. The flames retarded Jackson's approach more effectively than could a clash of arms. Jackson felt his way to the outskirts of Franklin, but "having other and more important plans," as John Worsham put it, withdrew toward McDowell on the morning of May 13.[38]

Those plans were to join Ewell for a push down the Valley after Banks, whom Jackson had deduced from irregular message traffic with Ewell was retiring on Winchester. General Lee had approved of Ewell's decision to re-main at Conrad's Store pending Jackson's return. Johnston went a step further and suggested he and Jackson unite against Banks, calling on the brigade of Brig. Gen. Lawrence O'Bryan Branch, then near Gordonsville as needed.[39]

Jackson kept Ewell regularly apprised of his progress toward Harrisonburg and of his intention to strike a blow at Banks. Jackson was vague on specifics. On May 16, as the Valley army rested in observance of a national day of prayer and fasting that President Davis had decreed in order that the South might reflect on its recent reversals, he wrote Ewell from a hamlet eleven miles short of Harrisonburg, "I design moving, via Harrisonburg, down the valley, and it may be that a kind Providence will enable us to unite and strike a successful blow."[40]

CHAPTER 18

ON YOUR COURSE MAY DEPEND

THE FATE OF RICHMOND

Ewell was mightily frustrated. Jackson had given him no indication of how or precisely when he intended to attack Banks, who was busy digging in his reduced command at Strasburg. All he knew was that Jackson wished him to encamp north of New Market no later than May 21. Meanwhile, Ewell's superiors in Richmond were sending him conflicting instructions. On May 14 General Lee told him: "Unless Banks leaves the valley entirely, you must remain in present position until General Jackson's safe return is secured or until otherwise ordered." On May 17 Ewell received new instructions from Joe Johnston, penned four days earlier. Johnston advised Ewell: "I have written to Major General Jackson to return to the valley near you, and if your united force is strong enough, to attack General Banks. Should the latter cross the Blue Ridge to join General McDowell at Fredericksburg, General Jackson and yourself should move eastward rapidly to join the army near Fredericksburg, commanded by Brig. Gen. J. R. Anderson, or this one." Also on May 17, Col. Thomas T. Munford confirmed that Shields was east of the Blue Ridge, evidently headed for Catlett's Station.

Although Johnston's orders were not discretionary, neither did they reflect the true situation on the ground. They summoned Jackson and Ewell east in the event Banks quit the Valley altogether. But only half of Banks's army had left; the other half, entrenched or otherwise, was vulnerable to attack. Contemplating the possibilities, Ewell made a bold decision. He got his brigades on the road but told them to go no farther east than the crest of the Blue Ridge, and he instructed Lawrence O'Bryan Branch to retire no farther than Gordonsville. Ewell also sent Campbell Brown to Gordonsville with a telegram for Lee seeking clarification of Johnston's orders. While he awaited a reply, Ewell would go and have a talk with Jackson.[1]

WITH LITTLE ELSE to occupy his attention, General Banks passed the early days of May chasing phantoms and rewriting history. Ashby's cavalry screened the country south of Harrisonburg so well that Banks knew nothing of Jackson's whereabouts. He was aware only of the Confederate march from Elk Run Valley to Port Republic that had so frightened Jeremiah Sullivan, whose brigade watched the White House and Columbia bridges from the west bank of the South Fork of the Shenandoah. To calm Sullivan, Banks sent Col. George H. Gordon's brigade, which had just trudged twenty miles from Harrisonburg to New Market as part of the first phase of Banks's withdrawal to Strasburg, on a midnight forced march over Massanutten Mountain. But the alarm proved false, and "we reached the end of our long and toilsome night march to find no enemy, no prospect of any fight," said Gordon. "So we fell down to deep slumbers. I had not closed my eyes for two nights."[2]

What Gordon's march did accomplish was to bring forth the dregs of Valley society from their crude mountain aeries. "There were in the Valley many wives of poor men who had been forced into the Confederate ranks. These poor women, often with large families of children, were left in destitution and were the pictures of wretchedness," a Wisconsin lieutenant remembered. "There were many Dunkards. They hid in the mountains during Jackson's occupation, but came from their hiding places when our forces appeared, only to flee again as soon as we fell back." The pointless midnight trek, and contact with the displaced poor, contributed to a growing resentment in Gordon's brigade with service under Banks, a feeling the irascible Gordon did little to discourage. "We found the alarm a false one," snarled Maj. Wilder Dwight, "owing to the stupidity of General Shields's division. Our work has been awful and useless utterly. My soul is weary; so, indeed, is my body."[3]

Banks too was weary, and despondent. Apparently forgetting that he had recommended a withdrawal to the Lower Valley and had acceded cheerfully to the detachment of Shields, Banks wrote Secretary of War Stanton on May 9 in support of Frémont's supposition that Jackson and Johnson had united to fight Milroy, and obliquely to complain about the carving up of his command.

He observed, presciently but too late to change his fate, "Jackson and Johnson will concentrate against any small force left in the Valley." Banks also wrote Brig. Gen. John W. Geary, whose demi-brigade patrolled the Manassas Gap Railroad east of Front Royal: "We are to fall back to Strasburg. We were within a few miles of Staunton when ordered to halt. I only wish that with my whole force I could have held that place and cooperated with Frémont, who was then coming down from the mountains. The Valley would have been cleared of the enemy from the Manassas Gap Railway to the Virginia Central between Staunton and Gordonsville. But that is not in the line of our orders."

In obedience to orders, Shields's division left Banks at New Market on May 12 to join McDowell. Shields's route of march led through New Market Gap to Luray, then north through the Luray Valley to Front Royal, where his division bivouacked for two days before continuing on to Catlett's Station and finally to Falmouth. That morning Banks also put what remained of his corps—two understrength brigades and a smattering of cavalry—in motion for Strasburg. The day was bright and warm, the turnpike dusty. Banks and Strother rode in an ambulance. "We passed the marching army with its spoils of horses, dogs, niggers, and cattle," Strother said. "It reminds me of the advent of a party of mad sailors into a heathen village."[4]

The last of Banks's small force straggled into Strasburg on the evening of May 13. No sooner was camp made than the simmering discontent in Gordon's brigade boiled over. Good news from other fronts had created a general impression that the war would soon end. "In camp," recalled Lt. Julian Hinkley of the 3rd Wisconsin, "bets were freely offered, with no takers, that the regiment would be back in Wisconsin by September." Some welcomed the prospect of loafing around in a scenic backwater district, but those with an itch for action or a reputation to make wanted out. "Soldiering grew tame," said the adjutant of the 3rd Wisconsin. "We seemed likely to remain simply as a guard. All were discontented." Lt. Edward G. Abbott of the 2nd Massachusetts complained: "To give Banks so small a force shows the estimation in which he is held. Now while we are sitting quietly here at our ease, other Massachusetts men are fighting, doing what we should do. We are no better than a home guard. When the war is over, other regiments will laugh and sneer at us—'Oh, you were in General Banks's army.' What I came out for was to fight, not fool away my time here." Lt. Charles Morse snarled: "I never expected to write another letter from this place during the war, but so it is. After ten days marching and countermarching, crossing the mountains into the other valley and coming back again, we have got here again, after an absence of nearly two months, without having accomplished the first thing during the whole of that time." Abbott, Morse, and their fellow line officers of the 2nd Massachusetts drew up a petition to the secretary of war and to the governor of Massachusetts asking to be transferred to another division.[5]

Gordon made a nuisance of himself. The Massachusetts colonel, who after the war showed more than the usual tendency of former generals to alter the record to enhance their contributions, claimed to have "taken the liberty" of advising Banks to move his force from Strasburg to Front Royal, as the latter seemed a more defensible location to him. "I besought him to apply for a change of orders to enable him to do this, and Major Perkins, his adjutant general, joined me in my intercession. But Banks was unmovable."[6]

General Williams privately criticized the withdrawal to Strasburg and the administration policies that he said had dictated it. "You will see that we have made a retrograde movement," he wrote his daughter on May 17. "I cannot explain the reason, because I really don't think there is any. If there be one, it is unknown to us here and is confided to the authorities at Washington. We regard it as a most unfortunate policy and altogether inexplicable, especially as we had the game all in our hands, and if the moves had been made with the least skill we could easily have checkmated Jackson, Ewell, and Johnson, instead of leaving them to attack and drive back Milroy."

Williams trembled at the probable consequences of their retreat: "Here we are with a greatly reduced force, either used as a decoy for the Rebel forces or for some unaccountable purpose known only to the War Department. The worst part is that we have put ourselves in a most critical position and exposed the whole of this important valley to be retaken and its immense property of railroads and stores to be destroyed."[7]

Unless Banks failed to share with him his late April telegrams to Stanton, Williams's bewilderment over the withdrawal is inexplicable. Or perhaps Banks and Williams both had had a change of heart. Banks did say to Stanton that all of his generals had concurred in the proposed retrograde. But once he was settled in Strasburg, Banks apparently forgot that his predicament had been of his own making. Instead, he cruelly—and wrongly—blamed General McDowell (the bogeyman of choice since First Bull Run) for depriving him of Shields's division and the chance for glory against Jackson's and Ewell's divided forces. In his diary, Colonel Strother recorded a May 18 meeting at headquarters:

I found the general [Banks] and Colonel Clark looking over the map and discussing the position of the troops before our retreat from New Market. The mistakes and confusion on this line are attributed to McDowell's cowardice or jealousy. It has been through his representation that the authorities in Washington have been alarmed in regard to an advance on that city by the Confederates. He has kept forty thousand men idle near Fredericksburg, thwarting McClellan's plans, weakening and discouraging the government and its defenders. His conduct has been most contemptible and explains Bull Run.[8]

Colonel Gordon was right, either in hindsight or, as he claimed, at the time. Strasburg was vulnerable to a flanking movement by way of Page Valley. But relocating their forces to Front Royal would have done no more than permit a more hasty retreat from the Shenandoah Valley. The ideal position from which to hold the Lower Valley, secure Banks's flanks, and also deprive Jackson of much of the element of surprise, was Winchester. Jackson and Ewell understood that, and they were determined to make the most of the enemy's lapse in judgment.

GENERAL EWELL RODE into Jackson's camp at daybreak on May 18. He had covered nearly fifty miles during the night. Jackson at once ushered him into an old clapboard mill on the bank of Mossy Creek for a private discussion. Ewell was anxious to talk; breakfast could wait. Both he and Jackson agreed that Johnston's orders did not fit the present situation, but Ewell was loath to disobey them, even though they were based on a false premise. "Then Providence denies me the privilege of striking a decisive blow for my country, and I must be satisfied with the humble task of hiding my little army about these mountains, to watch a superior force," lamented Jackson.

By nature Ewell was a follower, not a leader. Reluctant to challenge authority, he generally kept his opinions to himself. As Campbell Brown told his mother later that year: "I wish that one defect in the temper of our chief could be remedied, but it is one common to all his family, and I suppose is past all cure. He sees very plainly the good that might be done by a little more common sense in the control of our movements, but having formed an idea that his advice will be ungraciously received, and perhaps his interference rebuked; he refuses to interpose in any way."[9]

On this occasion, however, Ewell took a stand. He still harbored doubts about Jackson's sanity, but he shared his desire to strike the Federals a decisive blow. Although his division officially was part of Johnston's army, he was in the Shenandoah Valley under Jackson's authority. Jackson had written Johnston the evening before asking for new instructions in light of the changed circumstances on the ground. An answer could not be expected for three days, as Johnston insisted on transmitting messages by courier, rather than telegraph. Ewell told Jackson that he would stay and fight under Jackson until Johnston replied, so long as Jackson assumed responsibility for their actions. Jackson agreed. He asked Ewell to put his dilemma in writing, to which he would respond in kind. Ewell did so then and there. Falsely dating his letter, "Near Columbia Bridge—May 18, 10:00 A.M." and saying nothing of his nocturnal ride to Jackson or of their meeting, Ewell restated Johnston's orders, summarized his dispositions, and related reports of Shields's departure for Fredericksburg. He closed: "I have now sent you to show just how matters are. On your course may depend the fate of Richmond." Jackson wrote out and handed Ewell the following reply:

HEADQUARTERS VALLEY DISTRICT,
Mount Solon, May 18, 1862.

Maj. Gen. R. S. Ewell,
    Commanding Third Division, Army of the Peninsula:
GENERAL: Your letter of this date, in which you state that you have received letters from Generals Lee, Johnston, and myself requiring somewhat different movements, and desiring my views respecting your position, has been received. In reply I would state that as you are in the Valley District you constitute part of my command. Should you receive orders different from those sent from these headquarters, please advise me of the same at as early a period as practicable.

    You will please move your command so as to encamp between New Market and Mount Jackson on next Wednesday night, unless you receive orders from a superior officer and of a date subsequent to the sixteenth instant.

T. J. Jackson,
Major-General[10]

Having obtained Ewell's pledge to remain in the Valley, Jackson explained his plan for defeating Banks. It was a simple one. He and Ewell would concentrate their forces between New Market and Mount Jackson on the evening of May 21. Jackson would march down the Valley Pike. Ewell, with two of his three brigades, and Branch were to cross Massanutten Mountain at New

Market Gap. To avoid congestion in Page Valley, as Branch tried to catch up with Ewell, Jackson asked that Richard Taylor's Louisiana brigade, which was camped near the southern exit of the valley, proceed around the southern tip of Massanutten Mountain and fall in behind Jackson's command for the march north. Once united, the commands of Jackson, Ewell, and Branch would drive down the Valley Pike and overwhelm Banks at Strasburg.

One other item of business remained. Brig. Gen. George H Steuart, a Marylander with more political influence than military skill, had come to the Valley District with special orders from Richmond to organize an all-Maryland brigade, to be known as the "Maryland Line." Jackson had no Maryland units of his own, so he directed Ewell to detach the 1st Maryland Infantry and Brockenbough's Baltimore Battery from Brig. Gen. Arnold Elzey's

Strasburg under Federal occupation, May 1862. (*Frank Leslie's Illustrated Newspaper*, 1862)

brigade to form the nucleus of the Maryland Line. As that would leave the capable Elzey with only one regiment, Jackson had the 12th Georgia, 25th Virginia, and 31st Virginia regiments from Allegheny Johnson's Army of the Northwest reassigned to Elzey.[11]

Their business concluded, Jackson invited Ewell to breakfast. Afterward Ewell joined Jackson and his staff for Sunday prayer and a sermon by the Reverend Dabney at the camp of the 12th Georgia. Ewell was back in the saddle before noon for the return trip to Columbia Bridge, which he made in the face of a hard afternoon rain shower. Ewell had not slept in twenty-four hours.[12]

Nor was he to get much rest. On May 19 Jackson had everyone up in his camp at 3:00 A.M. and on the road to Harrisonburg before dawn. He expected and received the same promptitude from Ewell. At daybreak, after sending an order to General Branch directing him to resume his march to Madison Courthouse, Ewell led his own division off the Blue Ridge and back into Page Valley. Ewell's men marched thirteen miles under a broiling sun to Columbia Bridge. There the grateful infantrymen were permitted to rest.

They had enjoyed the return march across Page Valley. "We passed many pleasant homes and well-stocked farms," said a chaplain. "The people received us everywhere with the liveliest demonstrations of joy and supplied us abundantly with food of every description."[13] And they reveled in the late afternoon halt. "As soon as we had stacked arms there was a break for the Shenandoah, where hundreds of men were soon to be seen all along the banks standing on the water's edge or in the water, washing themselves or their clothes," remembered Randolph H. McKim of the 1st Maryland. "The river was in flood, and no one dared to attempt to swim across, till Redmond, the athlete of our mess, plunged in and struck out for the opposite shore. He was watched with breathless interest by almost the entire regiment, and when at length he accomplished the feat and stood safe on the other bank, a great shout went up from hundreds of throats."

Not willing to be outdone, McKim also took the plunge. He made it across, but at a considerable cost. Stepping out of the water to the acclaim of the crowd, McKim was seized with a chill. "When I tried to swim back, my strength left me after a few strokes, and I was at the mercy of the current. I made up my mind that my end had come and said my prayers accordingly but, the river making a sharp curve just there, I was carried by the current near to shore, and by a desperate effort succeeded in making a landing." Fortunately for McKim, the division did no more marching that day.[14]

A good number of Jackson's men also got wet on the nineteenth, though not by choice. Early in the afternoon, eight miles southwest of Harrisonburg, they ran up against the North River. On the far bank stood the hamlet of Bridgewater. Here the North River, a tributary of the South Fork of the Shenandoah, had a width of nearly two hundred feet. Ashby had burned the bridge to prevent the Federals from swatting at Jackson's right flank during the march to McDowell, and Jackson now found himself with no way across. Jed Hotchkiss suggested an expedient—a temporary bridge made from the big four- and six-horse wagons common to the region. Jackson agreed and ordered staff engineer Capt. Claiborne R. Mason and his corps of black pioneers to gather up wagons and push them into the river, one behind the other, closed up, with tongues upstream and planks laid from one wagon to the next.

The job was done before dusk. Jackson's advance guard felt its way across the swaying structure, with a good many men getting dunked in the bargain, and after wading two or three small streams, bivouacked for the night at Dayton, four miles short of Harrisonburg. The remainder of the Valley army got no farther than Bridgewater.[15]

The energy of Jackson and Ewell left Branch singularly unimpressed; he took their peregrinations and orders to him to be sure signs of lunacy. And not without reason. Ewell's commands over the past three days had been a study in contradiction. On May 15 Ewell had told him to march from Gordonsville to Luray. On the evening of the sixteenth, Branch received orders from Ewell to halt. Ewell then instructed him to resume the march at noon on the seventeenth, but after three miles he countermanded that order and told Branch to return to Gordonsville. Not a man in Branch's brigade had set foot in Page Valley, and rumor had it that they were not going to reinforce Ewell after all, but rather had been marching in circles within sight of the Blue Ridge to trick the Yankees into believing that to be their purpose. Unaware that Ewell's orders were the product of crossed communications with Richmond, Branch complained to his wife: "I think this foolish ordering and counterordering results from rivalry and jealousy between Generals Jackson and Ewell. It is very unfortunate that our government is under the necessity of suddenly transforming so many lieutenants and captains of the old army into brigadiers and major generals."[16]

The last straw for Branch proved, in fact, to be the last word on his participation in the Valley campaign. On May 20 a courier brought Ewell a most unwelcome message from Johnston. Dated May 17, the same day Jackson had pleaded from Mount Solon that he and Ewell be allowed to attack Banks, Johnston's dispatch notified him that he had written Branch, ordering him to march forthwith to Hanover Junction, on the line of the Fredericksburg and Potomac Railroad, to help Brig. Gen. Joseph R. Anderson's tiny command fend off McDowell's forty thousand troops, which that day had begun their long-feared march southward toward the capital.

Worse yet, Johnston instructed Ewell to rejoin the main army or Anderson's covering force, as circumstances might dictate. "If Banks is fortifying near Strasburg the attack would be too hazardous," wrote Johnston. "In such an event we must leave him in his works." Johnston told Ewell to pass the dispatch along to Jackson, "for whom it is intended as well as for yourself."[17]

The day had begun well for Ewell. He had his division, less Taylor's brigade, which was marching with Jackson, across Columbia Bridge and up Massanutten Mountain with the rising sun. Brig. Gen. Isaac Trimble's brigade reached New Market before nightfall, and Elzey's brigade camped on the eastern slope of Massanutten. That put Ewell ahead of the schedule Jackson had set for him and guaranteed their rendezvous between New Market and Mount Jackson, planned for the twenty-first.

Now badly shaken, Ewell set out for Jackson's headquarters late in the afternoon of May 20, dispatch in hand. Ewell found Jackson at Tenth Legion, a village on the Valley Pike between Harrisonburg and New Market. Jackson was having a good day, so good, in fact, that he hardly noticed Ewell's ill-humored expression. Marching fast and comfortably over the finely graded turnpike, Jackson's troops too were ahead of schedule.

"General Ewell, I'm glad to see you," said Jackson with surprising bonhomie.

"You will not be so glad, when I tell you what brought me," snarled Ewell.

"What? Are the Yankees after you?"

"Worse than that. I am ordered to join General Johnston."[18]

Ewell dismounted, and Jackson ushered him into a grove of trees out of earshot of his staff. Sandie Pendleton watched the generals intently, and as he did so, he wrote his mother: "General Ewell and General Jackson are now in close conclave, and what the result may be, I do not know. I surmise that Ewell is ordered to take his force which joined us today over the [Blue] Ridge tomorrow."[19]

Jackson at first was undecided. Johnston's orders were clear, but both Jackson and Ewell recognized the great opportunity that would be lost in obeying them. If, as was reasonable to conclude, Johnston's intention was to prevent more Federal forces from reaching McClellan, a rapid attack on Banks, followed by a strong demonstration toward the Potomac River to draw Shields back to the Valley, seemed more likely than Ewell's slinking off toward Fredericksburg to accomplish that end. Fed up with the three days it took to get answers from Johnston, Jackson appealed to Robert E. Lee to intercede. He wrote: "I am of the opinion that an attempt should be made to defeat Banks, but under instructions just received from General Johnston, I do not feel at liberty to make an attack. Please answer by telegraph at once." A courier galloped to Staunton with Jackson's message; from there it was flashed by telegram to Richmond. Jackson handed Johnston's order back to Ewell with an insubordinate endorsement, directing him to "suspend the execution of the order for returning to the east until I receive an answer to my telegram."[20]

Jackson had his answer sooner than expected. That night a courier from Richmond delivered Johnston's reply to Ewell's May 18 telegram to Lee, which

Lee had passed to Johnston. Conceding the game, Johnston told Ewell: "The whole question is whether or not Generals Jackson and yourself are too late to attack Banks. If so, the march eastward should be made; if not (supposing your strength sufficient), the attack. At such a distance a commanding officer can receive only general instructions." The courier also brought a postscript from Johnston, who advised Ewell, "The object you have to accomplish is the prevention of the junction of General Banks's troops with those of General McDowell."[21]

Which is precisely what he and Jackson intended. Conferring again on the morning of Wednesday, May 21, the two generals settled on a new plan for besting Banks. Colonel Munford had alerted Ewell to the presence of a small Union garrison at Front Royal. Instead of continuing their direct march against Strasburg, Jackson and Ewell would cross over to Page Valley and, by a concealed approach, take Front Royal, with its Yankee occupiers, and turn Banks's position in the bargain. Not only would that place their commands between those of Banks and McDowell, but it also would compel Banks to withdraw toward the Potomac to preserve his lines of communication, without the carnage that would attend a frontal assault on Banks's works at Strasburg. Before they parted, Capt. John D. Imboden reported in from Staunton with Johnston's brief reply—this time by telegram—to Jackson's telegraph to Lee. It gave them yet further confirmation of Johnston's new attitude. "If you and General Ewell united can beat Banks," Johnston wrote Jackson, "Do it."[22]

THE FEDERAL FORTIFICATIONS at Strasburg that had caused Johnston so much anxiety were, in fact, the object of ridicule by their builders. Aside from a long line of simple breastworks on the south side of town, the only other fieldwork was an earthen redoubt on a high hill on the northwest edge of Strasburg, called "Banks' Fort." Banks' Folly would have been a more suitable name for the fort, which was never completed. One company from each regiment of Donnelly's brigade drew construction duty, a task that Colonel Gordon said "furnished, with speculations upon the fall of Richmond, the whole staple of amusement." A Vermont cavalry lieutenant told his parents: "There is quite a large fort being built at Strasburg. It will command the whole valley between the mountains, Blue Ridge and Shenandoah. I do not think the fort will ever amount to much, but as the government has got so much money, they may as well put it into forts in the Valley as to spend it anywhere else."[23]

Stonewall Jackson was well briefed on Banks's defenses. On the morning of May 20 he had sent Jed Hotchkiss and Lt. J. K. Boswell of his staff down the

Valley to reconnoiter. Hotchkiss was no more impressed with the Federal fortifications than was the Vermont subaltern. Watching progress on them from atop Signal Knob, Hotchkiss reported: "Banks' earthworks only covered and closed the Valley Pike. They did not command either the middle or the back roads, [nor] closed the Valley from the North Mountain to the Massanutten."[24]

Hotchkiss also gazed upon enough potential loot to supply the needs of the Valley army for months. As Gordon observed: "The amount of public property at Strasburg was enormous. Since we had first passed through it, a bountiful government had piled up stores for clothing, feeding, moving, healing, and killing, until the ware-rooms positively groaned with the burden. Here too had been deposited, as a safe depot, all the superfluous transportation which Shields had abandoned."[25]

Far from the "safe depot" that Gordon termed it, Strasburg was becoming, in General Banks's estimation, a serious liability. He feared for the safety not only of the vast government stores, but also of his small command. While obeying every administration order, Banks also made clear his doubts regarding their wisdom. On May 16 Secretary Stanton directed him to detach two regiments to relieve General Geary at Front Royal. Banks complied with the intent of the order, sending his largest regiment, Col. John R. Kenly's 1st Maryland Infantry, nearly one thousand strong, to the Blue Ridge town the next day. But, he warned Stanton, "this will reduce my force greatly, which is already too small to defend Strasburg if attacked."[26]

Kenly's departure left Banks with only 4,476 infantry, 1,600 cavalry, ten Parrott guns, and six smoothbore Napoleons at Strasburg. Five companies of the 1st Maine Cavalry patrolled the countryside. Company G, 3rd Wisconsin Infantry, and one company of the 27th Indiana watched the Manassas Gap Railroad from Strasburg to Buckton, a distance of six miles. Companies B and G of the 29th Pennsylvania guarded the railroad bridge over the South Fork of the Shenandoah, one and a half miles north of Front Royal. To the Pennsylvanians, it seemed choice duty. Remembered David Mouat of Company G: "When we were located our adjutant, who accompanied us, he said, 'Boys, this will be a nice job for you, and if you behave yourselves you can stay until the war will be over. I guess we'll all be home next Fourth of July.' We had a fine easy time, only guarding the bridge, fishing in the river and living off the fat of the land."[27]

Spirits also were high among the men in Strasburg. New Yorker Charles Boyce recalled celebrating his regiment's first anniversary of service on May 22 with a wager that the unit, which had seen no action, would end the war without ever having fired a volley. "Some were anxious to stake quite large sums that we would be mustered out of service—the war closed—before the Fourth of July. The reasons given for such a belief were the great success that had attended our arms."[28]

Banks shared none of his troops' optimism. With each passing day, his worries mounted. He had positive orders to hold Strasburg, and his warnings to the War Department had gone unheeded. Deserters correctly placed Ewell on May 17 at Swift Run Gap, where Banks expected him to stay until Jackson returned to the Valley. His information on Jackson's whereabouts was sketchy and outdated, but Banks had little doubt that he and Ewell would unite against him. On May 22 he told Stanton:

> From all the information I can gather—and I do not wish to excite alarm unnecessarily—I am compelled to believe that he [Jackson] meditates attack here. I regard it as certain that he will move north as far as New Market, a position which commands the mountain gap and the roads into the Department of the Rappahannock, and enables him also to cooperate with General Ewell. Once at New Market, they are within twenty-five miles of Strasburg with a force of not less than sixteen thousand men. Our situation certainly invites attack in the strongest manner. At present our danger is imminent at both the line of the [Manassas Gap rail] road and the position at Strasburg.

Banks also was getting to know his opponent. "To these important considerations," he warned, "ought to be added the persistent adherence of Jackson to the defense of the Valley and his well-known purpose to expel the government troops from this country if in his power. This may be assumed as certain."[29]

INDEED, IT WAS. Armed now with Johnston's consent, Jackson and Ewell lost no time in pushing offensive preparations. It mattered nothing to Jackson that his men were exhausted. From camp near New Market on the night of May 20, Cpl. James E. Hall of the 31st Virginia had scrawled in his diary: "We are very much wearied by the march, in fact, virtually worn down. A night's rest appears to do us no good—just as sleepy and languid in the morning as when we stop in the evening." On the evening of May 22, artilleryman Lanty Blackford told his mother that the battery had been marching twenty-three days straight, with only three days of rest. "We are about as nearly broken down as men well can be to get along at all. An order has just come to cook rations for

New Market Gap. (John W. Wayland, *Art Folio of the Shenandoah Valley*, Staunton, Va., 1924)

three days and rise at 2:30 A.M. tomorrow to continue the march. This caps the climax, and we are really disconsolate." But at least the weather was good. Said Corporal Hall: "The air is so soft and mellow that it forcibly reminds me of those beautiful days when I used to wander over the blue hills of home."[30]

The mood was particularly grim in the 1st Maryland Infantry. Companies organized the year before at Harpers Ferry had been mustered into the volunteer service for twelve months; those mustered in Richmond had entered the Confederate States army for the duration of the war. On May 18 the term of Company C expired. Despite entreaties from the temporary commander of the Maryland Line, Col. Bradley T. Johnson, and from brigade commander Arnold Elzey, the men quit the regiment. "They wanted their rights," said Johnson. "They wanted to go into the cavalry, they were tired of trudging. So off they went." Four days later the term of the Harpers Ferry companies expired. Though they were then within an easy march of the enemy at Front Royal, most of the men stacked their arms and refused to budge. That was mutiny. Colonel Johnson had the arms promptly packed in wagons and the mutineers placed under guard of the Richmond companies. Johnson then asked the color sergeant to find out how many of the disaffected men were willing to defer their grievance until after the campaign. About half agreed, and they had their arms returned to them. What they might do under fire was anyone's guess. Hoping for the best, Johnson and Elzey were careful to keep word of the affair from Jackson.[31]

Richard Taylor had had his first encounter with Jackson the evening before.

After bedding down his brigade alongside the Valley army, Taylor went looking for the enigmatic Virginian. Someone pointed him out, "a figure perched
on the topmost rail of a fence, overlooking the road and field." Taylor approached him, saluted, stated his name and rank, then waited for a response.
Before it came, the Louisianan sized up his new commander: "a pair of cavalry
boots covering feet of gigantic size, a mangy gap, with visor drawn low, a
heavy, dark beard, and weary eyes—eyes I afterward saw filled with intense but
never brilliant light." Softly, gently, Jackson asked how far and by what road
Taylor had marched that day.

"Six-and-twenty miles—Keezletown road."

"You seem to have no stragglers," Jackson commented.

"Never allow stragglers," retorted Taylor.

"You must teach my people. They straggle badly."

Taylor bowed in reply. Nearby a regimental band of Taylor's Louisiana
Creoles broke out with a waltz. Sucking contemplatively on a lemon, Jackson
remarked, "Thoughtless fellows for serious work." Taylor bristled. "I expressed a hope that the work would not be less well done because of the
gayety." A return to the lemon was Taylor's queue to depart. Late that night,
Jackson came to Taylor's campfire. "He said we would move at dawn, asked a
few questions about the marching of my men, which seems to have impressed
him and then remained silent. If silence be golden, he was a 'bonanza.'"[32]

Jackson and Ewell moved with a will. Leaving two companies (those of
Captains George W. Myers and Edward H. McDonald) of Ashby's cavalry
south of Strasburg to watch Banks from that direction, Jackson on May 21
passed with the Valley army and Taylor's brigade from New Market to Luray
by way of New Market Gap. The next day, with Taylor in advance, the commands of Jackson and Ewell marched north from Luray to within twelve miles
of Front Royal. Screening the march were the 2nd and 6th Virginia Cavalry.
Both regiments had crossed the Blue Ridge into Page Valley on the twenty-
first. In the absence of Colonel Munford, who was away on official business,
Col. Thomas S. Flournoy of the 6th assumed overall command. At nightfall
came the order to cook rations, preparatory to a predawn departure, that
Lanty Blackford had found so repugnant. But cavalryman William L. Wilson
saw matters in a brighter light. "Everything is excitement. Really this looks like
going down the Valley!"[33]

CHAPTER 19

GO IT, BOYS!

MARYLAND WHIP MARYLAND!

Front Royal, Virginia, was the kind of place that induced languor in both residents and military occupiers. "Sleepy" and "quiet" were the words Union troops most often used to describe it; "strongly secesh" was how they generally characterized its seven hundred inhabitants. Nestled between Massanutten Mountain and the Blue Ridge, Front Royal was the picture of bucolic tranquility. Only the presence of two large, well-built Confederate hospitals near the courthouse and a well-behaved Union garrison encamped on the outskirts of town hinted at the larger strife looming beyond the mountains.

The village lay at the center of a patchwork quilt of rivers, railroads, ridges, and bridges. The North and South forks of the Shenandoah met two miles north of town. A 450-foot-long trestle bridge carried the Manassas Gap Railroad over the South Fork of the Shenandoah River parallel to and just south of the junction of the two rivers. East of town a minor stream called "Happy Creek" meandered through a valley of the same name before emptying into the North Fork just north of its confluence with the South Fork. A bold, flat-topped ridge with a heavily forested crest and sharp sides separated the two forks of the Shenandoah. Other prominent ridges included Guard Hill, located on the north bank of the North Fork opposite the railroad bridge, and Richardson's Hill, a 150-foot-high flint-rock ridge one mile north of Front Royal.

Good roads connected Front Royal with Strasburg to the west and with

Winchester to the north. There were two ways into town from the south—the Luray road, also known as the River road because it ran under the bluffs of the South Fork for three miles, and the less frequented Gooney Manor Grade, which traversed the bench of Dickey Ridge. A steep, barely passable trail connected the River road with the Gooney Manor Grade two miles south of Front Royal. Four miles southwest of Front Royal a better route, called "Spangler's Crossroads," left the River road at the Spangler place and joined the Gooney Manor Grade at Boyd's Mill, seven miles south of town. Maps that Hotchkiss sketched show the Gooney Manor Grade departing the Valley through a minor pass in the Blue Ridge called "Gravelly Spring Gap."[1]

In May 1862 the most notorious civilian in Front Royal was not an inhabitant, but an eighteen-year-old female visitor from Martinsburg. Belle Boyd may not have been the "accomplished prostitute" a Northern war correspondent claimed her to be, but she did use her good looks and easy morals to curry favor with officers Union and Confederate. War seems to have been a game with her; seducing men who wore shoulder boards the object. That she was promiscuous seems certain. Thomas Ashby, an adolescent resident of Front Royal, said decent people scorned her. "She played the game of flirt and lowered the dignity of her sex. She was a young woman of some personal beauty and a skilled rider of spirited horses. Nor was she wanting in energy, dash, and courage. But she had none of the genius, inspiration, and religious fervor of the true heroine. She loved notoriety and attention, and was as far below the standard of the pure and noble womanhood of the South as was a circus rider. Her own sex in the South repudiated her, and the true manhood of both armies was suspicious of her character." About all Belle had to recommend her to the Confederate army was an antebellum friendship with young Henry Kyd Douglas and familial ties to Dr. Hunter McGuire.

Her questionable reputation extended well beyond Front Royal. Kate Sperry of Winchester pitied whoever might marry her, "for of all wild, reckless, fast girls she beats all." David Strother thought her ill-treated. When he encountered her in Front Royal on May 21, she was "looking well and deporting herself in a very ladylike manner. She sported a bunch of buttons despoiled from General Shields and our officers and seemed ready to increase her trophies." Belle Boyd's chances for plunder were good; during his brief stay in Front Royal, Shields made his headquarters in her uncle's house, and Colonel Kenly of the 1st Maryland (Union) visited it often thereafter.

Neither Jackson nor Ewell had need of whatever intelligence Boyd might pick up through her flirtations with Yankee staff officers. Jackson derived timely and detailed information on Federal strength and dispositions in and around Front Royal from members of Ashby's cavalry who had resided there before the war and now acted as scouts. One of the most comprehensive reports came from a descendant of the first chief justice of the U.S. Supreme Court. Even youngsters such as twelve-year-old Thomas Ashby provided reports as reliable as any Belle Boyd might dish up.

The young Ashby counted two companies of the 1st Maryland Infantry (Union) posted in town as a guard to the provost marshal, whose office was in Front Royal's only hotel. He and his playmates noted the outposts and picket posts along the main roads into town. They got along well with the Maryland Yankees, who Ashby said were "well behaved, orderly, and kind to our people; they created a good impression." Ewell had some fine scouts from the 16th Mississippi who traversed the entire length of Massanutten Mountain, carefully examining both Banks's and Kenly's positions.[2]

FRIDAY, MAY 23, dawned sunny and warm. The soldiers of the Valley army and Ewell's division were up at daybreak. Twelve miles remained between them and Front Royal.

The 350 members of the 1st Maryland Infantry (Confederate), mutineers and faithful alike, watched Ewell's division and Jackson's veterans—minus the Stonewall Brigade, which was back in Luray—shuffle past their camp onto the River road. The troops of the Valley army were "cheering and in the best possible spirits," remembered Capt. John E. Post. "Even up to that time they had fought several battles, and many were barefooted, carrying their boots in their hands, their feet being blistered from long and continued marching." Setting of at a brisk pace, the Confederate vanguard covered seven miles in two hours without a halt. Meanwhile, large intervals opened up between units in the main body. The Stonewall Brigade, which did not leave Luray until 5:00 A.M., was too far away to be counted a part of Jackson's effective force that day.

Jackson had intended to split his command at Spangler's Crossroads, with Ewell taking the Gooney Manor Grade into Front Royal and the Valley army pushing straight down the Luray road. But once at the crossroads, he elected to concentrate his forces on the grade and strike Front Royal along a single axis. An approach over the Gooney Manor Grade had the added advantage of giving him enough troops with which to cut off a Yankee retreat east along either the Manassas Gap Railroad or the wagon road through Chester Gap.

At Spangler's Crossroads the cavalry left the march column on a lightning mission to destroy telegraph and rail communications between Strasburg and

Front Royal, intercept Federals fleeing west from Front Royal, and delay reinforcements from Strasburg. Crossing the South Fork at McCoy's Ford, the Southern troopers cantered as one body along the west bank, over one of the oldest roads in the Valley, until they reached the Strasburg–Front Royal road. There the cavalry separated. With three hundred men (eighteen of his twenty-six companies were on detached service elsewhere in the Valley), Turner Ashby rode west toward Buckton Station. Colonel Flournoy moved cross-country with the 2nd and 6th Virginia Cavalry, striking the railroad a half mile west of the North Fork Bridge. His men tore up track and cut telegraph wire until 2:00 P.M., when they galloped off to rejoin the infantry.

Two miles outside of Front Royal, Jackson again halted. From atop Dickey Ridge his scouts had sighted Kenly's picket posts and had captured several stray soldiers from the 1st Maryland (Union). From them, Jackson learned the identity of the Federal regiment in Front Royal. Unaware of the discord within his own 1st Maryland, Jackson summoned the regiment from the rear of the column so it might enjoy the honor of meeting the enemy first. At 1:00 P.M. Jackson's ironic summons reached Bradley Johnson by courier.[3]

The colonel saw Jackson's call as a providential opportunity to regain control of his regiment. Already the mutineers were having second thoughts. On the march that morning Johnson had observed that "many men were greatly mortified at what had occurred, so injurious to the reputation of the 1st Maryland [Confederate], which had always been without a blemish, and many were uncertain whether they were right or wrong. Thus they plodded along, silent, lifeless, and without spirit."[4]

Turning now to his men, his voice "tremulous with suppressed anger and with a face flush with mortification and shame," Johnson called the regiment to attention. There followed a harangue "most scathing in denunciation, and yet most fervent in appeal." Began Johnson: "I have just received an order from General Jackson that very nearly concerns yourselves, and I will read it to you." Holding high the dispatch, he read: "Colonel Johnson will move the 1st Maryland to the front with all dispatch, and in conjunction with Wheat's Battalion attack the enemy at Front Royal. The army will halt while you pass. Signed Jackson."

"You have heard the order," continued Johnson, "and I must confess are in a pretty condition to obey it. I will have to return it with the endorsement upon the back that the 1st Maryland refuses to meet the enemy, though ordered by General Jackson. Before this day I was proud to call myself a Marylander," Johnson went on,

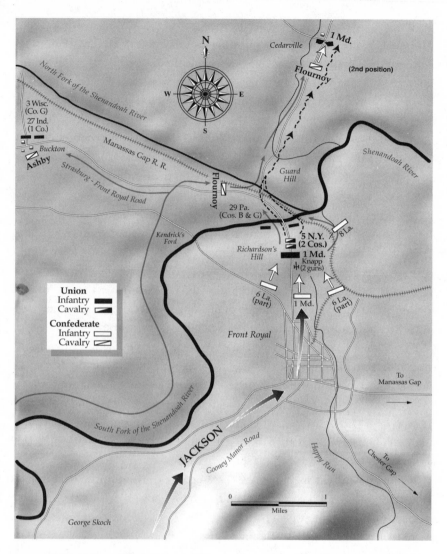

MAP 5. Affair at Front Royal, May 23, 1862

but now, God knows I would rather be known as anything else. When you meet your fathers and mothers, brothers, sisters, and sweethearts, tell them it was you who, when brought face to face with the enemy, proved yourself recreants, and acknowledged yourselves to be cowards. Tell them this, and see if you are not spurned from their presence like some loathsome leper and despised. You will wander over the face of the earth with the brand of coward, traitor indelibly imprinted upon your foreheads, and in the end sink into a dishonored grave, unwept, uncared for.[5]

Johnson's words had the desired effect. Scarcely had he concluded when a wild yell broke the painful stillness that had greeted his address. Shouts of "We won't leave you," "We will not disgrace the state," "We don't want to dodge," rose from the ranks. "Give us back our guns, and we will show you if Maryland is to be put to shame," cried a mutineer, and with a mad rush he and the others made for the ordnance wagon.[6]

As they double-quicked in column to the front, the Marylanders became almost manic in their delight, singing, "Baltimore, Ain't You Happy" to mark their cadence. Along the northern face of Dickey Ridge the 1st Maryland (Confederate) formed line of battle. To their left and rear lined up Maj. Robideaux Chatham Wheat's 150-man battalion of Louisiana Tigers, an unruly and sordid agglomeration of Crescent State cutthroats, drunks, and criminals. Himself a former soldier of fortune who had seen action with William Walker in Nicaragua and Garbaldi in Italy, the six-foot-four, 240-pound Wheat was the only man able to control the Tigers. The Tigers were as impatient as the shamed soldiers of the 1st Maryland (Confederate) to close with the enemy, and a good deal more impetuous; several Tigers tossed aside their muskets and charged only with bowie knives.[7]

A little before 2:00 P.M., the 1st Maryland (Confederate) started down the slope at quick time, their enthusiasm tempered with caution, said Captain Post, "as we knew not at what moment Yankees might open upon us from some ambush."

The danger did not bother General Ewell, who reconnoitered personally along the Gooney Manor Grade ahead of the 1st Maryland (Confederate). With him rode Generals Taylor and Steuart, and Colonel Johnson. Turning a bend in the road, the high-ranking scouting party chanced upon a Yankee sentinel. The man, said Colonel Johnson, "was taking his ease at full length under a rail shelter. The group of horsemen appeared somewhat to puzzle him. He looked, and looked again, as if he could not believe his eyes; at last, lazily getting up, he reached over for his musket, and all at once quickly raised it, fired, and ran for his life. The truth had suddenly flashed on his benighted brain that the Rebels were upon him." Johnson waved forward Companies D and G of the 1st Maryland (Confederate), and in a few minutes the entire picket post was captured. "What regiment do you belong to?" Johnson asked a German whom a Virginia cavalryman was shepherding to the rear. "I pelongs to de 1st Maryland [Union]," answered the man. "There's the 1st Maryland," shouted Johnson, and his own Maryland boys dashed on in a run.[8]

Wheat's battalion advanced a few minutes after the 1st Maryland (Confederate). Campbell Brown happened to be standing in the road with Generals Ewell and Jackson when the Tigers passed to the front. "I shall never forget [their] style. [Wheat] was riding full gallop, yelling at the top of his voice—his big sergeant major running at top speed just after him, calling to the men to come on, and they strung out according to their speed or stomach for the fight, all running—all yelling—all *looking* like fight. Their peculiar Zouave dress, light-striped, baggy pants, bronzed and desperate faces, and wild excitement made up a glorious picture." Behind Wheat's rowdy band, atop Dickey Ridge, the remainder of Taylor's Louisiana brigade stood in reserve, its well-disciplined ranks and "perfectly uniformed" men the envy of the army. "Each man was wearing white gaiters and leggings," said an admiring Georgian, "while the blue-gray uniforms of the officers were brilliant with gold lace, their rakish slouch hats adorned with tassels and plumes."[9]

LOUNGING IN HIS tent a mile and a quarter north of town, Lt. George W. Thompson of the 1st Maryland (Union) was startled by the cries of a frightened black man, who galloped into camp at 2:30 P.M., shouting that the Rebels had taken Front Royal and were about to "surround you and cut you off." Thompson joined a group of enlisted men who had gathered to make fun of him, for the man "was frightened nearly to death." Thinking the trouble no more than a picket skirmish with guerrillas whom the Marylanders knew to be lurking in the mountains around town, Lt. Col. Nathan T. Dushane and the regimental surgeon rode off to have a look. In a matter of minutes they returned, as terrified as the civilian whose alarm they had disparaged. Rebel infantry in line of battle had rolled through the town, reported Dushane breathlessly, scattering pickets and routing the provost marshal guard. Dozens had been captured, and gunshots fired from the windows of homes had killed several men.[10]

Colonel Kenly ordered the "long roll" beat, and the six companies of the 1st

Maryland (Union) then in camp, joined by survivors of the picket and provost companies, formed line of battle on Richardson's Hill. On their way out of camp, the men burned what camp equipment and stores lay within reach. A section of two ten-pounder Parrott rifled guns of Capt. Joseph Knapp's Pennsylvania battery on duty with the 1st Maryland (Union) wedged itself into line to the right of the Front Royal–Winchester Turnpike (Front Royal road). In front of Kenly's position was a broad meadow, which the enemy must cross to reach the railroad bridges.[11]

"We had scarcely been placed in position," said an incredulous Lieutenant Thompson, "when the Rebels were seen advancing in great force." A few of Johnson's troops were troubled at having to fight friends and neighbors in blue, as many men of both Maryland regiments had been recruited from the same neighborhoods. But most of the attacking Confederates were in high spirits because the Yankees had given up Front Royal almost without a fight. "Firing one volley, they wheeled about, every man for himself," remembered a Louisiana Tiger. "They scampered out of town like a flock of sheep." In the midst of the shooting, Confederate Marylander Randolph McKim recalled, "a lovely girl of about fifteen years ran out of one of the houses and, waving a Confederate flag, cried, 'Go it, Boys! Maryland whip Maryland!' She was much excited and seemed unconscious of her danger."[12]

Far more self-conscious, particularly of the exulted role in the unfolding drama that she later arrogated herself, was Belle Boyd. At the first crack of rifle fire, she appeared. Jackson's and Ewell's staff officers were clustered on horseback astride the Gooney Manor Grade south of town, "gossiping with that queer idleness that sometimes preceded any expected severe contest," when Henry Kyd Douglas called Campbell Brown's attention to her. Brown was thunderstruck. Coming toward him, clad in white and waving a bonnet, was a young woman, "very pleasant and ladylike in appearance." She was "running like mad down from the hill on our right, keeping a fence between her and the town and gesticulating wildly to us."

Douglas and Sandie Pendleton rode forward to meet her. Catching her breath, Belle said in gasps: "I knew it must be Stonewall when I heard the first gun. Go back quick and tell him that the Yankee force is very small—one regiment of Maryland infantry, several pieces of artillery, and several companies of cavalry. Tell him I know, for I went through the camps and got it out of an officer. Tell him to charge right down, and he will catch them all. I must hurry back. Goodbye. My love to all the dear boys—and remember if you meet me in town, you haven't seen me today." Douglas tipped his hat. Belle blew a kiss and was gone. Jackson quizzed Douglas about the odd young woman with the white bonnet. Although she told him little or nothing about the Yankee force he did not already know, Jackson evidently appreciated Belle's intrepid spirit; certainly every man who saw her appreciated her lithe form, gliding unexpectedly across the fields before them.[13]

Young Tom Ashby was bathing with some friends in Happy Creek north of town when the first picket shots rang out. Hastily dressing, the boys split up and made for their respective homes. All was well with Ashby until he left Main Street for a curved cross street that ran in the direction of his house. As he turned the curve Ashby ran into the Yankee provost marshal guards, retreating in disorder, their pursuers following in equal disorder, "firing their guns in the most irregular manner, and yelling and shouting like wild Indians. No one was hurt, and the disorder was more like a police riot than a fight between soldiers." A stray bullet whizzed just inches past Ashby's head, striking the house against which he was leaning. Ashby ducked indoors until the soldiers were no longer in view. Then he again set out for his house, which lay five hundred yards south of the village proper. A Confederate on horseback, whom Ashby recognized, urged him to run home and get into the cellar as fast as possible, as the enemy surely would bombard the village. No sooner had Ashby started running than he heard the thunder of artillery fire coming from both sides. Shells exploded so near that he felt "each gunner was looking for me."

A friendly Confederate, crouched behind a large locust tree alongside the last house in town, beckoned Ashby to join him. "I was so badly frightened that I was glad to accept the soldier's offer. In the house lived a widow with some five or six small children, all crying in the greatest alarm," remembered Ashby. "For over an hour—and it seemed a week—I sat behind that tree, believing in my childish fear that every shell was directed at the old house and tree. While in this state of alarm I saw one shell strike a nearby tree, a fragment of another shell wounded a cow grazing in a meadow close to my home, and eight or ten shells fell in the yard surrounding my home. One large oak tree in front of our house was perforated by a shell that went entirely through it and then exploded." When the shelling stopped, Ashby hurried inside to find his family unhurt but his mother terrified at what might have befallen her son.[14]

The Yankee Parrotts caused Jackson's recently appointed and as yet untested chief of artillery, Col. Stapleton Crutchfield, nearly as much consternation as they did the young Ashby. For some time the Federals had the field to themselves, as Crutchfield struggled to find rifled pieces of his own to match their range. The first Confederate battery to report to Crutchfield consisted of only smoothbore six-pounders and twelve-pounder howitzers. Waving them off the road, he pulled a rifled gun from the next battery to come up and opened fire on Richardson's Hill. Capt. John Brockenbrough's Baltimore Light Artillery then appeared, and from it Crutchfield drew two more rifled pieces. A brisk fifteen-minute cannonade ensued. The firing stopped, said Crutchfield, "with no injury to ourselves and no apparent damage to the enemy." Crutchfield thought he had compelled the Yankees to cease fire. In fact, section commander Lt. Charles A. Atwell merely had shifted his fire to meet the 1st Maryland (Confederate) and Louisiana Tigers, then spilling into the fields between Front Royal and Richardson's Hill. Atwell's fire, averred a Rebel infantry captain, "came very close but did no execution."[15]

On Richardson's Hill, matters looked grim. Kenly was doing everything possible to buy time for Banks at Strasburg. He maneuvered his 773 men with an eye toward deceiving the Rebels into thinking his force was much larger than it was. Kenly directed Colonel Dushane to protect the right flank with two companies, pushed forward a company under Maj. John W. Wilson to engage in skirmishing, and moved Lt. Thomas Saville's company and the camp guard farther to the left to cover the railroad.[16]

Kenly received a measure of help from the two companies of the 29th Pennsylvania tucked between the rivers to guard the railroad and wagon bridges. Their commander, Lt. Col. Charles Parham, had been lying in bed in great pain from a fall he had sustained a couple of days earlier when word reached him of the Confederate attack on Front Royal. "I ordered my horse to be saddled, and although I could not stand a moment before nor get on my boots, I put on an old pair of shoes, intending if not successful in so doing to mount in stocking feet." Once in the saddle, Parham placed Company G and a fifty-six-man pioneer detachment under Capt. William H. H. Mapes along the southern slope of the flat-topped ridge between the rivers, a half mile behind Kenly. Company B lined up on a bluff nearer the railroad bridge.[17]

Help of a more direct sort came from two companies of the 5th New York Cavalry under Maj. Philip G. Vought, which Banks had ordered out from Strasburg that morning to give Kenly better communications with his own distant picket posts and with Buckton and Strasburg. The New Yorkers reported first to Parham, who directed them over the South Fork to Kenly's assistance. Before doing so Parham ordered two of the cavalrymen to return to Strasburg with news of Jackson's attack.[18]

Wild cheers greeted Vought's appearance on Richardson's Hill at about

4:00 P.M. The New York troopers galloped far enough forward to drive off the skirmishers of the 1st Maryland (Confederate), then retired to the hill. There Kenly moved them about in sight of the enemy infantry to give the impression that he was being continually reinforced.[19]

Kenly knew his ruse was weak, as "it was painfully apparent that I was being surrounded." Generals Ewell and Taylor and their staffs had kept just behind the advance and were thus in a good position to direct reinforcements. The 6th Louisiana joined the fray first, easing its way in line of battle in a tract of woods opposite Kenly's right flank. To the right and rear of the 1st Maryland (Confederate) and the Louisiana Tigers, which by now had become hopelessly intermingled, the remaining regiments of Taylor's Louisiana brigade swept along the railroad tracks toward Kenly's left. Through the fields west of town Trimble's brigade edged forward.[20]

Kenly could see all this, but he was determined to hang on until the last possible moment. What finally convinced him to yield was news that Confederate cavalrymen were thundering down the Manassas Gap Railroad in his rear. Astonished, Kenly left the hill to confirm the report himself. Finding it true, he made ready to retire at 4:30 P.M. Colonel Parham also spotted the Rebel troopers, which he calculated at two thousand strong. Although they presented a more immediate threat to his own right flank than to Kenly's command, he gave orders for his men to hold their ground until the Marylanders were safely across both forks of the Shenandoah.[21]

The menacing Southern cavalry were Flournoy's 2nd and 6th Virginia regiments, which had made their way toward the fight. Fortunately for the Federals, Colonel Flournoy elected to pause well west of Parham's line to await the outcome of the expected infantry action.[22]

But there would be no clash of infantry. Kenly got his men across the two bridges spanning the South Fork in good order, well ahead of the enemy. After ushering them, the two companies of the 29th Pennsylvania, and finally the 5th New York Cavalry squadron over the North Fork, Kenly ordered Captain Mapes and his pioneers to burn the bridges. Undoubtedly terrified by the long lines of yelling Rebel infantry nearing the river, Mapes's detail botched their job. That much of the wood was green also hindered their efforts. Only the North Fork Bridge sustained serious damage, and that to only one span.

Meanwhile, on the far side of the North Fork, Kenly fashioned a new defensive line. He positioned Lieutenant Atwell's Parrott rifles on Guard Hill, and his own and Parham's infantry on the slope of an adjacent ridge. Major Vought drew up his troopers in reserve. Watching the enemy retreat unmolested across the bridges, when long-range guns could have broken them, Jackson moaned, "Oh, what an opportunity for artillery!"[23]

Had it not been for the rapacity of the Louisiana Tigers, much of Kenly's command might have been trapped on the south bank of the South Fork. But the lure of plunder was too great, and the Tigers dispersed when they reached Kenly's abandoned camp. Confederate Marylander Washington Hands looked on in disgust as the Louisiana ruffians ignored the "threats and entreaties of their officers. When they were at length prevailed upon to move forward, it was found the enemy in their front had escaped." Hands and his comrades, on the other hand, could take pride in having bagged several dozen Yankee Marylanders at the riverbank. Unquestionably, a fair share of the 1st Maryland (Confederate) joined in the looting of their homestate nemeses's camp, and Trimble's brigade lost its stride when passing among the Federal tents as well. Said David Holt of the 16th Mississippi: "As I ran over one of their small fires, I picked up a hot frying pan which was still on the fire, threw the hardtack in it, placed my little finger over the spout of the coffee pot, and carried the [dinner] of that Yank for over a mile before I got a chance to eat a mouthful."[24]

Kenly had held the Confederates at bay from Richardson's Hill for nearly two hours; from Guard Hill, he delayed their advance another hour. Atwell's Parrotts kept Flournoy's troopers at a respectful distance west of Kenly's position, and they nearly took the life of General Ewell after he and a detail of couriers occupied Richardson's Hill for a better look at the enemy. As one well-aimed round howled savagely close, Ewell turned to the commander of the couriers, Lt. Frank Myers, and demanded, "What do you mean, sir, by making a target of me with these men?"

Myers replied sharply, "Why, General, you told me to stay near you, and I'm trying to do it."

"Clear out, Sir, clear out," roared Ewell. "I didn't tell you to get all your men killed and me too!"

That was enough for Myers. He led his men off the hill and into the Federal camp. There the men pitched in for plunder, trading double-barreled shotguns and civilian saddles for new sabers, pistols, and carbines.[25]

By 6:00 P.M. the tide had turned decisively against Kenly. Riding off Guard Hill to check the progress of the flames that licked the floorboards of the North Fork Bridge, the Maryland colonel was startled to see the river just a few hundred feet west of him alive with horsemen: Flournoy had found two fords, and in a few more minutes he would have men on the north bank. But a greater threat loomed against Kenly's left. While the men of the 1st Maryland

(Confederate) and Wheat's battalion were struggling to extricate themselves from the Yankee camps and from one another, Lt. Col. Henry B. Kelly had led his 8th Louisiana Infantry across the smoldering railroad bridge in the face of a plunging fire of musketry from Guard Hill. Once over, Colonel Kelly urged his men on toward the wagon bridge over the North Fork with the cheer, "Come on, boys! We will yet have them!" Finding the bridge in flames and directly under the fire of Atwell's Parrotts, Kelly followed a set of horse tracks to the river's edge, hoping they led to a ford. They did, and Kelly plunged into the swift-flowing water at once. Behind him came the strongest swimmers in the regiment. As soon as enough men were over to provide a covering fire, Kelly waved a detachment onto the bridge to extinguish the blaze. General Taylor urged the rest of his brigade to Kelly's support in a wild surge for the burning span. "My horse and clothing were scorched," said Taylor, "and many men burned their hands severely while throwing brands into the river." But the flames were doused.[26]

Kenly's position was now untenable. Detaching one company to hold the 8th Louisiana in check, Kenly—with the remainder of his regiment, Parham's two companies, and Atwell's artillery section—started down the Front Royal road toward the hamlet of Cedarville, two miles away. Major Vought shook out his small squadron to protect Kenly's rear.[27]

Colonel Flournoy appeared at the bridge moments after Kenly decamped. Only a handful of his troopers had forded the North Fork, and he endeavored to cross the rest of his command over the charred span. Fresh planks were laid on the smoldering floorboards, and Flournoy's men started over, one horse and rider at a time.

General Jackson was on hand. After watching four companies from the 6th Virginia Cavalry feel their way across, Jackson grew impatient. Gesturing north in the direction of Cedarville, he told Flournoy, "Colonel, they have two pieces of artillery, go and take them." Flournoy obeyed and set off with 250 riders at a gallop. Companies A and K charged through fields to the right of the road and Company E to the left; Company B thundered down the thoroughfare itself.[28]

Two miles to the north, Colonel Kenly struggled to reach the crossroad that led from Middletown to Cedarville. There he hoped to make a final stand. It was nearly 6:00 P.M. Just over an hour of daylight remained. "All had so far gone well, and I commenced to indulge a hope that I might yet save my command, when the sudden appearance of cavalry galloping through the fields on my left satisfied me that I was lost."

Just then his own cavalry commander, Major Vought, galloped up to say his squadron was closely pressed. Determined to make a fight of it, Kenly told Vought he would order Atwell to halt his two Parrott guns in the road and would deploy the infantry on either side of the road near the Fairview estate of Thomas McKay; Vought, meanwhile, was to return to his command and charge the enemy, "so as to check, if but a few minutes, their advance."

He rode back," said Kenly, "as if to comply with the order." Instead, the good major lost his nerve and cravenly told his men to make a run for it, the devil take the hindmost. Vought and his sergeant major hid in a thick wood beside the road while Flournoy's troopers galloped by. There they remained until 11:00 P.M., when, convinced that the danger had passed, they mounted their horses and started for Winchester.[29]

After dismissing Vought, Colonel Kenly and his lieutenant colonel maneuvered the right-wing companies of the 1st Maryland (Union) from column into line in a field and orchard near the McKay house, tearing away a panel of fencing through which the men squeezed. Glancing back at the road and finding no sign of Atwell's section, Kenly left the troops in the field to Colonel Dushane and "dashed forward to learn why my orders had not been obeyed." As Kenly wheeled his horse onto the road, "the discharge of firearms and the rush of cavalry caused me to turn in time to see that the cavalry had not charged the enemy, but were running over my men, who had not yet left the road, and were closely followed by the enemy's horse."[30]

Company B, 6th Virginia Cavalry, turned sharply off the road and charged the breach in the rail fence four abreast. Dushane's companies greeted the tightly packed horsemen with a volley that toppled twenty-three of thirty-eight riders and twenty-one horses. The color-bearer, eighteen-year-old Dallas Brown, fell with fourteen bullets in him. Flournoy's other three companies hacked and sliced their way through the fast-scattering ranks of Parham's Pennsylvanians and the left-wing companies of the 1st Maryland (Union) before closing on Dushane's band in the orchard from three sides.[31]

Few Federals escaped. Colonel Parham, whose contusions had compelled him to dismount at Guard Hill and ride a caisson, thought that nearly three thousand Rebel horsemen had descended on the McKay place. He nearly had his head cleaved in by a saber, but an opportune bump in the road cause the side wheel of his caisson to come off, throwing the Confederate trooper aside and Parham under his mount. Dozens of cavalrymen galloped over and around him before Parham was able to drag himself out of the road. No sooner had he collapsed beside a fence than four Southerners demanded he stand up and deliver his pistol. Parham said he did so "good-naturedly," taking some satisfaction in having tossed his sword under the caisson wheel. "They demanded my scabbard and belt; took off my coat to see what I had underneath, they at the same time threatening to shoot, but I deemed it prudent to be as pleasant as possible, so I laughed them out of the notion and actually engaged in conversation with them until an opportunity presented itself for me to escape." In the meantime, Parham stretched out in the grass as several dozen of his men were deposited beside him under guard. Noticing that some of the Rebel cavalrymen who occupied the road in front of them were repeatedly looking over their shoulders, Parham suddenly sprang to his feet, shouting, "Here come our reinforcements boys; we're good for another fight."

The ruse took. In one body the Confederates put spurs to their horses and fled into the fields. Parham made for a riderless horse, unhitched him, mounted, and left, shouting for his men to break for the woods, "a large number escaping before the Rebels discovered the trick. They fired after me, but I had no time to stop."[32]

Pennsylvanian David Mouat of Company G was not among the escapees. He had been captured while hiding with his sergeant, a man named White, in a wheat field. "Here's two of the sons of bitches. Surrender, you damned Yankee," called out a mounted Rebel.

Sergeant White jumped up and said, "I surrender. I'm a sergeant. Here's my sword."

Mouat stood up. "Where's your gun," inquired the Rebel. Mouat said he'd lost it.

"What regiment do you belong to?"

"The 29th Pennsylvania," answered Mouat.

"Damn you," snarled his captor. "It's a good thing you do not belong to the 28th Pennsylvania. I am going to kill every son of a bitch I come across of them fellows; they stole all my old woman's pigs."

"I'm damn glad I don't belong to them," Mouat hastened to assure the man. "Oh, no, I belong to the 29th. Pardner, give us a drink."

"Drink hell," the Southerner yelled. "Get back to the rear." Leveling his revolver, the man yelled, "Quicker." Mouat and White went as quickly as their tired legs would carry them.[33]

Lieutenant Atwell escaped by running a limbered Parrott right through the Rebel cavalry. Either the horses or Atwell's courage gave out, however, as two privates of the 6th Virginia Cavalry stumbled on the abandoned gun the next morning just outside the Yankee picket lines, four miles short of Winchester. Commandeering two plow horses from a neighboring field, they hauled the piece back to Front Royal. "A piece of cool daring," commented General Ewell, "hard to match."[34]

In the melee on the Front Royal road, Colonel Kenly went down with a saber slash to the back of his head, a slight cut on the neck, and a grazing wound to the head from a pistol ball discharged point-blank, together with numerous bruises about the face and chest sustained when he fell from his horse. "Colonel Kenly was fighting hand to hand with the Rebels," remembered Lt. George Thompson of Company D. "He called our men to rally around their colors, which was the last order I heard from him."

A rumor started that Kenly had been gunned down in cold blood while stretched out helplessly in an ambulance. In truth, he spoke quite highly of the care he received from his captors and was paroled in early June. His kind treatment of Southern noncombatants while in command at Front Royal had won him equally good care. Tom Ashby recalled that during Kenly's brief captivity his father and several other citizens brought the Marylander numerous fine meals and sincere condolences.[35]

The Confederate victories at Front Royal and Cedarville were complete. At a cost of 36 killed and wounded, Stonewall Jackson had inflicted 773 casualties on the Federals, of which 691 were prisoners of war. He had taken a large amount of quartermaster and commissary stores in Front Royal, and had come away with two fine Parrott rifled guns. Most importantly, he had turned Banks's flank and opened the way to Winchester.[36]

TURNER ASHBY HAD suffered a stinging repulse at Buckton Station that afternoon. Two of his most promising officers, Captains George Sheetz and John Fletcher, were killed in a reckless and unnecessary charge on the garrison.

To have had any chance of success against defenders who were better armed and only slightly outnumbered, Ashby needed the element of surprise. But there had been hints of impending trouble. Southern patrols had captured two members of the Wisconsin company the day before. The captain of the Indiana company had gone to Strasburg early on the twenty-third and not returned; he, in fact, was taken prisoner between Strasburg and Buckton Station that afternoon. Colonel Parham had ordered the post commander to Front Royal to confer about their respective defenses. Fearing attack, he instead sent two lieutenants down the track to talk with Parham.[37]

Even with surprise and superior numbers, Buckton Station was a tough nut to crack. The Manassas Gap Railroad bridge, which gave the place its military importance, crossed a small stream less than one-half mile south of the North Fork of the Shenandoah River. The railroad grade was high enough to form a good breastwork, and with the river so close in the defender's rear, an attacking force was obliged to make a frontal assault over open ground. Solidly constructed of brick, the Buckton Station depot, which lay behind the embankment, made a formidable blockhouse. South of the track and east of the stream lay a large wheat field, and beyond that a large tract of timber. The camp of the Indiana company stood in the wheat field; that of the Wisconsin company rested on the west side of the stream. Ashby might have prevailed had he had artillery support. But Chew's battery was on detached service.[38]

At 2:00 P.M. Ashby's three hundred troopers thundered out of the timber where they had formed unseen for the charge. They came, said the adjutant of the 3rd Wisconsin, "with a whoop and yell, two or three officers in front swinging their sabers," toward the company camps. Neither company flinched. Both formed line of battle in front of their tents quickly enough to deliver a volley before the cavalrymen came near enough to use their pistols or sabers. Captains Sheetz and Fletcher toppled from their horses dead, along with at least eight of their men. The survivors fled into the timber in confusion and, said a Union officer, "at breakneck speed."[39]

Capt. E. L. Hubbard redeployed his companies behind the railroad embankment in anticipation of another charge. While they waited for it, the men did a curious thing. From their vest pockets and haversacks they pulled wads of currency—facsimile Confederate bills that an enterprising Northern printer had made up and circulated throughout Banks's army. The soldiers had passed hundreds of the counterfeit bills off on unsophisticated Virginians as genuine money. When the Confederate government learned of the fraud, it declared that any Yankee caught with bogus notes on capture would be treated not as a prisoner of war but as a counterfeiter and sent to state prison. After reloading their guns, the men hastily buried their fake money in the railroad bank; wags among them called it "putting their money in the bank."[40]

The second Confederate charge was repulsed as easily as the first. Only a handful of Rebel horsemen reached the embankment, and they were shot down. Ashby gave up and retired down the railroad toward Front Royal. Before opening the action at Buckton Station, Ashby had sent a detachment to cut the wires and destroy the railroad between the station and Strasburg, which it did. That closed Hubbard's communications with Banks as effectively as his defeat would have. Ashby's frontal attacks had been a waste of lives, entirely in keeping with the Virginia cavalier's concept of warfare as a stand-up contest of gallant gentlemen.

ASHBY'S BUNGLING WAS forgotten in the self-congratulatory atmosphere of the evening. Flournoy's exploits at Cedarville, all the more remarkable because Kenly had outnumbered him four to one, were the principal topic of headquarters conversation. Ewell lauded Flournoy's charge as "one of the most gallant affairs he had ever witnessed"; Jackson expressed a similar view to his staff.

Jackson and Ewell lingered at the front well into the evening, supervising the roundup of Kenly's men. Although he had advocated an attack on Front Royal, Ewell claimed no credit for the victory. "The decided results at Front Royal," he wrote, "were the fruits of Major General Jackson's personal superintendence and planning." For Ewell, Jackson had emerged in a new light. No longer was he the half-demented wagon master, but rather a skillful tactician who just might pull off the decisive grand triumph for which Ewell had waited nearly a year.[41]

CHAPTER 20

WE MUST CUT OUR
WAY THROUGH!

Nathaniel Banks had his shortcomings as a military commander, but lack of nerve was not among them. At a moment when many a man would have panicked, on the night of May 23 Banks kept his head, sifting as calmly as possible through fragmentary and sometimes contradictory information. He provided authorities with unexaggerated estimates of the enemy's strength and probable intentions (one can merely imagine the hyperbole with which McClellan would have greeted such an upset), and he never asked for more men than he thought he needed to set matters right.[1]

The first word from Front Royal reached Banks shortly after 4:00 P.M. Cpl. Charles H. Greenleaf of Company D, 5th New York Cavalry, bore the news. Colonel Kenly had sent Greenleaf for reinforcements while he yet held Richardson's Hill. Greenleaf stopped first at the headquarters tent of Colonel Gordon, who was lolling away the afternoon with Brig. Gen. John P. Hatch. "The day was intensely hot, the air positively stifling under canvas," said Gordon. "A general languor was manifested in the drowsy way in which the sentinels dawdled along their posts, or in the aimless sleepy air in which the troops addressed themselves to such amusements as were suggested by time and place."

Corporal Greenleaf interrupted Gordon's reverie and asked for Banks. Gordon pointed the way to headquarters. Watching as Greenleaf galloped off without revealing his message, Hatch remarked, "This man, I think, may have information that will solve our doubts." "I believe he brings news of an attack upon our outposts," speculated Gordon.[2]

Greenleaf arrived at Banks's headquarters exhausted. Obliged by Ashby's cavalry to take a wide detour from Front Royal to Strasburg, he had ridden seventeen miles in fifty-five minutes. Banks took Greenleaf's news calmly. He saw to it that the corporal had a fresh mount for the return ride and then retired to his room to consult with Brig. Gen. Samuel Crawford, a general without a command who happened to be visiting headquarters. At 5:30 P.M. a messenger from Colonel Parham arrived. The news he provided was sketchy, and Banks admonished Parham by return courier: "Our information is brief —in substance only that you are attacked; nothing of the strength of the enemy or of the extent of reinforcements needed." Nonetheless, Banks assured Parham: "We will aid you all in our power. Let us know the condition of affairs immediately."[3]

The reports of Greenleaf and Parham led Banks to order one infantry regiment and a section of artillery to reinforce the Front Royal garrison. The task fell to the 3rd Wisconsin, which started down the Manassas Gap Railroad before sunset. Without clarification of the enemy's strength and likely intentions, Banks was reluctant to do more.[4]

News continued to trickle in. A contraband came to headquarters after dark, saying that he had left the scene of the fight at 5:00 P.M. and that Kenly was falling back across the river. From Winchester came a report from a captain of the 1st Maryland Cavalry (Union) who claimed that Kenly's regiment had been annihilated and the colonel killed, and that ten thousand Confederates had crossed the North Fork. Banks handed the message to Colonel Strother for his opinion. The Virginian dismissed it as the babbling of a coward "who had ingloriously fled the field and covered his ignominy by monstrous lying." A little later a teamster from Company B of the 27th Indiana reported in from Buckton Station with a note from the post commander, which read: "I was attacked this afternoon about 4:00 P.M. by three or four hundred cavalry and some infantry, who dashed upon me and attempted to burn the bridge. I defended it successfully and saved it with a loss of several killed and quite a number wounded. The enemy was close by and will probably renew the attack in the morning. I would like to be reinforced." A message from Col. Thomas H. Ruger of the 3rd Wisconsin, then five miles from Strasburg, confirmed the Buckton Station report and, ominously, noted an absence of communication between Buckton Station and Front Royal. At 10:00 P.M. a lieutenant from the 1st Michigan Cavalry telegraphed reports from teamsters, pioneers, sutlers, and cavalrymen then stumbling into Winchester that Front Royal had fallen, that Kenly had been killed, and that some fifteen to twenty thousand Rebels were on the march for Strasburg.[5]

None of these reports, either separately or in the aggregate, were conclusive. Yet prudence dictated that Banks, exposed as he was at Strasburg, assume the worst and make preparations accordingly. Notwithstanding later claims by the querulous Colonel Gordon to the contrary, that is exactly what Banks did.[6] Wagon trains started for Winchester around 10:00 P.M. Regiments encamped south of Strasburg were ordered to pack their trains and fall back into town, and regimental trains began rolling out of Strasburg at midnight.[7]

Also at midnight the first reliable confirmation of the Union disaster at Front Royal reached headquarters in the form of a telegram from Major Vought, then safe at Winchester. Evidently Vought had recovered his balance, as Colonel Strother deemed his report a "cool" one. "He said his command had been taken, killed, and dispersed, and that he had remained concealed in his bushes," recalled Porte Crayon. "He saw the Rebel force fall back on Front Royal, five or six thousand strong he supposed. He also overheard some scouts say they were only going to scour the country and then fall back to town. This story seemed truthful and reassured us to the movement. General Banks went to bed, and I sat up the remainder of the night."[8]

Before retiring, Banks reevaluated matters: "The extraordinary force of the enemy could no longer be doubted. It was apparent also that they had a more extended purpose than the capture of the brave little band at Front Royal. This purpose could be nothing less than the defeat of my own command or its possible capture by occupying Winchester, and by this movement intercepting supplies or reinforcements, and cutting off all possibility of retreat."

Just whom he faced remained uncertain. Calling upon Banks at 1:00 A.M., the commander of Williams's First Brigade, Col. Dudley Donnelly, found the consensus at headquarters to be that Ewell was in their front and that Jackson, whom Federal scouts still placed near Harrisonburg, was coming down the Valley Pike to "push upon us in our rear, placing us between two fires, each doubtless larger than the little command which remained to General Banks after the withdrawal of so large a portion of it to reinforce other *less exposed* divisions of the army." After conferring with Donnelly, Banks ordered his brigade to overtake its trains on the Valley Pike and march as far as Middletown. Additional orders would come at dawn.[9]

Banks resumed his study of the situation. It was bad, but not irretrievable. He had three options. They were, as he later explained them:

First, a retreat across Little North Mountain to the Potomac River on the west; second, an attack upon the enemy's flank on the Front Royal road; third, a rapid movement direct upon Winchester, with a view to anticipate his occupation of the town by seizing it ourselves, thus placing my command in communication with its original base of operations in the line of reinforcements from Harper's Ferry and Martinsburg, and securing a safe retreat in case of disaster.

To remain at Strasburg was to be surrounded; to move over the mountains was to abandon our train at the outset and subject my command to flank attacks without possibility of succor, and to attack the enemy in such overwhelming force could only result in certain destruction. It was determined, therefore, to enter the lists with the enemy in a race of a battle, as he should choose, for the possession of Winchester, the key of the Valley, and for us the position of safety.[10]

Banks had sent the War Department his first appraisal of the situation shortly before 11:00 P.M. He calculated the Rebel force at five thousand and asked that reinforcements be sent him "if possible." An hour later Banks forwarded the report of the hysterical Maryland cavalry captain who had placed the enemy's force at fifteen to twenty thousand. General Crawford had debriefed the man and found him credible. Still, Banks thought the captain's estimate of the enemy's strength "much overestimated. But the enemy's force is undoubtedly very large and their possession of Front Royal complete."[11]

While waiting for the War Department to respond to his appeal for reinforcements, Banks took the liberty of asking Col. Dixon Miles, in command at Harpers Ferry, to send whatever forces were available to him to Winchester. Miles was charged with protecting the Baltimore and Ohio Railroad and the Chesapeake and Ohio Canal, and his small command was spread thin. Two weeks earlier Miles had released the 1st Maine Cavalry for temporary service with Banks. He had little more to offer, and what he could scrape together would be slow in appearing. For the moment, Banks was on his own.[12]

ON MAY 24 GENERAL Banks was up before dawn, if he had slept at all. The morning was raw and chilly. A light rain fell, mixed briefly with hail. Everything was in readiness to abandon Strasburg. Military hospitals had been evacuated of all but sixty-four patients deemed too critically ill or wounded to move. At the Cedar Creek commissary and quartermaster depot, orders had been received after midnight to load up the division wagons, along with those

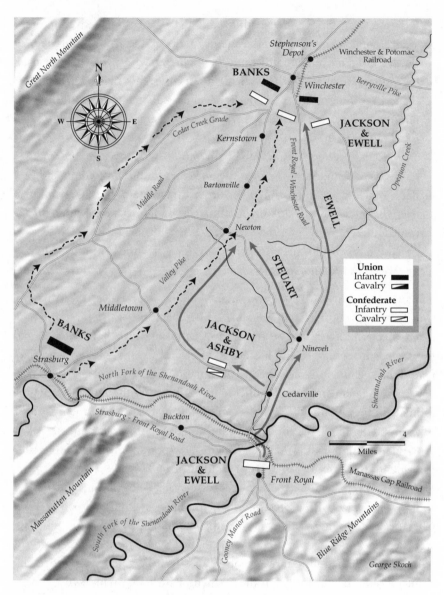

MAP 6. Jackson's Pursuit of Banks, May 24, 1862

that Shields had left behind. The three-hundred-man depot guard was to hold the place as long as possible and then burn what supplies remained to prevent their capture. Colonel Donnelly's brigade trains were parked on the Valley Pike between Strasburg and Cedar Creek; those of Colonel Gordon were rolling north past Donnelly's brigade, which was in line of battle on the northern edge of town fronting south, to fall in behind his trains. Gordon's brigade, less the 3rd Wisconsin, which had begun the return march from Buckton Station at 7:00 A.M., was in town—packed, rationed, and ready to march. To facilitate communications between the front and rear of the march column, Banks had three-man signal stations set up on high ground along the route from Strasburg to Winchester.[13]

Banks accorded Hatch's cavalry command—consisting of the 5th New York Cavalry, the 1st Vermont Cavalry, five companies of the 1st Maine Cavalry, five companies of the 1st Maryland Cavalry (Union), Battery F, Pennsylvania Light Artillery, and one howitzer detached from Battery F, 4th U.S. Artillery—the mission of rear guard, with the added responsibility of assisting the depot guard in burning supplies. But first, Banks wanted Hatch to reconnoiter the turnpike and the Middle road above Woodstock in case Jackson was approaching from the south. At the same time a task force comprising the 29th Pennsylvania Infantry, three companies of the 1st Michigan Cavalry, and a section of artillery were to reconnoiter an obscure lane known as "the Chapel road" from Middletown to Cedarville, over which Ewell could be expected to advance in order to cut off Banks's line of retreat to Winchester. In the event of contact, they were to hold their ground "at all hazards."[14]

Col. Charles H. Tompkins had the 1st Vermont Cavalry on the road before 5:00 A.M. As he felt his way south along the Valley Pike in the cool and misty gray dawn, two companies of the 5th New York Cavalry paralleled him on the Middle road. Neither command found any trace of the enemy, and both returned to Strasburg before 9:00 A.M. Banks could at least be reassured that no immediate danger lurked in his rear.[15]

The threat to his front remained unclear. The 29th Pennsylvania Infantry and its cavalry escort had done a miserable job, advancing just three miles down the Chapel road before a few carbine shots from the woods to their front sent them scurrying back to Middletown. They had seen nothing and so could report nothing. David Strother found their conduct despicable. Had they done their duty, said Strother, "we should have immediately known our position, but the troops sent, through timidity, utterly failed in their duty."[16]

Banks ordered another reconnaissance of the Chapel road be done at once.

The task fell to five companies of the 1st Maine Cavalry under Lt. Col. Calvin S. Douty, then encamped at Toms Brook, together with a squadron of the 1st Vermont Cavalry, just returned from its patrol toward Woodstock, under the command of Maj. William D. Collins. After pausing at department headquarters for instructions, Douty and Collins hurried down the Valley Pike to Middletown. It was nearly 8:00 A.M.[17]

There was no time to await the results of Douty's reconnaissance. Taking his place at the head of Donnelly's brigade, at 9:00 A.M., Banks issued orders for his small command and its huge wagon train to move out.[18]

Contributing to a sense of impending dread and near chaos was the large number of contraband and their families who took flight with the retreating army. "There were half as many Negroes as soldiers, some drivers and some refugees, wagons loaded with Negro women, waiting on some officers, mess kettles, pans, and chickens," marveled a Connecticut lieutenant. "Then there were droves of loose horses branded U.S. going along independently, and hundreds of beef cattle belonging to the commissary department, ambulances with sick, all hurrying in one direction."[19]

Charles W. Boyce of the 28th New York studied the former slaves and their odd conveyances closely:

> The road in the direction of Winchester was crowded with every kind of vehicle. There was the ponderous Virginia market wagon, fashioned after Noah's Ark, drawn by six horses and loaded with a heterogeneous mass of articles pitched in promiscuously, bureaus and bedsteads, tables, chairs, and stoves; the whole machine drawn by an immense Negro with protruding eyes and widely distended nostrils, his every appearance reflecting the very extremity of fear. Now to the smaller fry that came in the way of this prodigious turnout. There were four-horse teams, two-horse teams and wagons, and carts with only one horse or mule attached, all hurrying in the same direction, all actuated by the same motive—fear. Troops of women and children, black and white, were following the wagons on foot. Some of the loads were topped out with children of both races, who were the only ones that showed no symptoms of fear; they were joyous as though the cavalcade of hurriedly loaded teams were racing along for their special amusement.[20]

Nearly five hundred army wagons and an untold number of civilian vehicles set off from Strasburg and Cedar Creek. How many might reach Winchester was anyone's guess.[21]

THERE HAD BEEN a festive air in Front Royal the night of May 23, a gaiety that soldiers and civilians alike had shared. Young Tom Ashby said his house had been filled with Confederate officers and distinguished citizens, all "as bright and as happy in spirit as it was possible for men to be, predicting glorious results from the campaign. Indeed, one or two were so optimistic as to predict that Jackson would be in Washington before the end of another week."[22]

Everyone in Front Royal ate well that night. "At that early stage of the war our people had the greatest abundance of food supplies, and many of the luxuries of peace," explained Tom Ashby. "In my own home the smokehouse and pantry were filled with meat, flour, sugar, coffee, eggs, butter, and milk. We had Aunt Susan in the kitchen, and other women servants to assist her. These Negroes went to work . . . to cook food for the soldiers as fast as the men came for it. My mother estimated that she had fed over three hundred men."[23]

The men were tired but as anxious as their officers to maintain the momentum of victory. "Many of the boys are broken down," a soldier of the 4th Virginia wrote his father on the morning of May 24. "We marched twenty-five miles yesterday and can do the same today, if thereby we can only drive out the invader." While most thought only of rest and food, the irrepressible Louisiana Tigers looked for fun—the more dangerous, the better. Raiding Yankee quartermaster stores, several Tigers threw off their Zouave uniforms and donned fresh Union blue. They then fired up a locomotive and, with a couple of cars attached, steamed down the track to Markham, where there was a small Union outpost. The Yankees had not yet received word of the fall of Front Royal. Taking the Tigers for their own men, they accepted the Louisianans' invitation of a ride back to Front Royal, hardly suspecting that it would be a one-way trip. Others among Ewell's veterans found a more productive outlet for their energy, combing the Federal camps and stores for new rifled muskets. Said an Alabamian who traded up, "Next morning the fence corners were filled with guns our boys had exchanged and got the best kind."[24]

Neither Jackson nor Ewell shared in the merrymaking. Both made their bivouac at Cedarville. Before retiring, Jackson conferred with Ewell. Jackson had come to trust Ewell far more than any of the seconds-in-command—Loring, Garnett, or Winder—with whom he previously had been saddled, but he had little to offer in the way of a plan for the next day. "In the event of Banks leaving Strasburg he might escape toward the Potomac," Jackson later wrote, "or if we moved directly to Winchester he might move via Front Royal toward Washington City." Jackson's experience with Banks to date, particularly Banks's snail-like pursuit after Kernstown, suggested that the Massachusetts politician-turned-general would act cautiously and fall back to Winchester. But until Banks's intentions became clear, the best Jackson could do was to begin a tentative march from Front Royal toward Winchester. He was not fearful enough of Banks to withhold a large force at Front Royal, nor contemptuous enough of Banks's martial skills to think he would remain at Strasburg and permit himself to be outflanked.[25]

Jackson hoped his cavalry might give him an early indication of Banks's intentions, as well as any Federal moves to reinforce him. He directed Turner Ashby to send one company east from Front Royal to observe the Shenandoah River ford leading to Ashby's Gap in the Blue Ridge, and a second company to attack the small Union garrison on the railroad at Linden. One or more companies were ordered out to watch Banks at Strasburg.

A larger reconnaissance mission went to the 2nd and 6th Virginia Cavalry regiments. Jackson wanted them to start from Front Royal at daylight over the Front Royal road ahead of the infantry, then cut cross-country from a point three miles north of Nineveh to Newton on the Valley Pike. If Banks was there, the cavalry could delay him until Jackson brought up the infantry; if not, they could advise Jackson accordingly. Jackson decided to give the two regiments to Brig. Gen. George Steuart, who as commander of only the 1st Maryland Infantry and Baltimore Light Artillery had little to do befitting his rank. Besides, Steuart had a good antebellum record as a cavalry officer in the Regular army.[26]

After speaking with Ewell, Jackson paused beside the campfire of Richard Taylor. "He mentioned that I would move at dawn, and then relapsed into silence. I fancied he looked at me kindly, and interpreted this into an approval of the conduct of the brigade." From Taylor's bivouac, Jackson and his staff made their way to Fairview. At the McCoy house they enjoyed a good supper before bedding down for the night in the front yard. The nearest friendly troops occupied picket posts. "As it turned out afterwards," said Jed Hotchkiss, "we were actually on an outpost." Not at all troubled with that thought, Jackson lay down to sleep. "He had nothing with him but his overcoat," Hotchkiss remembered. "I arranged his saddle and mine side-by-side, and having a rubber-lined blanket I spread it on the ground, riding up over the saddles, and invited him to occupy it with me. This he did, each of us covering himself with his overcoat."[27]

General Ewell bivouacked near Isaac Trimble's troops. He and Campbell Brown shared a tree with Trimble. Brown had enough corn for his horse and Ewell's, and his couriers had enough for their own mounts. Brown had just retired when Ewell's manservant whispered to him, "Mas's Campbell, look at that gentleman stealing the corn from your horse."

"Who is it, Willis?" asked Brown.

"It's Gen'l Trimble, Sir."

Brown called to Ewell, "General, look at that old rascal stealing my corn."

Ewell motioned to Willis. "Willis," he said, "Go and give my compliments to that gentleman and ask him to put back the corn he took from that horse."

Willis did so. Trimble mumbled a reply and glanced over at Ewell. Brown feigned sleep but looked out of one eye to see what Trimble would do. "The inimitable old scamp bowed politely, said 'Very well' and coolly put down three ears—then walked on to a courier's horse and helped himself to some more! At the time he put down these ears, he had on his arm five or six more, and I expect his horse got the largest feed that night."[28]

No one recorded how well General Steuart's horses were fed that night, but at 6:00 A.M. on Saturday, May 24 (seventy-three minutes after sunrise), they started down the Front Royal road from Cedarville carrying the troopers of the 2nd and 6th Virginia Cavalry regiments. Ashby's companies apparently had set out on their various assignments at 3:00 A.M. Ewell's division took up the march at 6:00 A.M., with Trimble's brigade and the 1st Maryland in the lead. Elzey's and Taylor's brigades marched behind Trimble. The Valley army got a comparatively late start. The Stonewall Brigade did not move until 8:00 A.M., and Taliaferro's brigade, temporarily under the command of Sam Fulkerson, started the day four miles south of Front Royal. Not until 10:00 A.M. had the last of Jackson's command crossed the two forks of the Shenandoah.[29]

Jackson and Ewell began the march with the vanguard. The absence of information on Banks's whereabouts played hard on Jackson, and after two hours he halted the head of the column three miles beyond the hamlet of Nineveh, dismounted at a farmhouse, and asked for breakfast. Three hours were lost as Jackson fretted and the trailing brigades of the Valley army closed up on Cedarville. At 11:00 A.M. a sweating courier brought Jackson the first definite news of the enemy: General Steuart had reached Newton shortly after 10:00 A.M. to find the Valley Pike packed with wagons. He had attacked, said the man, and was raising hell with the Yankee trains.[30]

Steuart had confirmed the fact of Banks's retreat, but he had missed a unique opportunity to stop it and to destroy much of the Federal trains. Everything about his assault bespoke poor leadership. On the approach to Newton, Steuart had failed to keep his column closed up. His advance guard, perhaps thirty troopers in all, burst forth from the wooded crossroad at Newton ahead of the main body of the 2nd Virginia Cavalry, well before the 6th Virginia Cavalry had caught up. The attackers fell upon the Yankee hospital train, which had stopped in the hamlet to get water. They had an easy time of it. Only a handful of the Federals—invalids and the walking ill—put up any sort of resistance, and they were readily persuaded to surrender. Said a Virginia trooper: "I rode up to a stonewall fence. There were seven bluecoats hid behind the fence. I presented my pistol to them and ordered them over the fence. To my great relief they soon hopped over. I marched them back to headquarters." About seventy Federals were gathered up, among them Pvt. E. M. Suppler of the 29th Ohio. "After unhitching and cutting the mules loose from the wagons, which were left, we were hustled off to the mountains," said Suppler. "Being still weak from the effects of the measles, and the others in no better condition for such a race, we were all used up. Finally, through the guards' great kindness, we were ordered to mount the mules." Only one Union soldier was killed, a sick man from the Sixty-sixth Ohio allegedly shot down in cold blood—the only shot fired in the affair.[31]

With or without accompanying gunfire, the presence of Rebel cavalry was enough to cause a panic among the teamsters, many of whom were hired former slaves and, unaccustomed as they were to warfare, easily frightened. But even seasoned drivers fled. As General Williams explained in a letter to his daughter: "Wagoners [sic] are proverbially scary, and on the first alarm they cut their traces, mount horses, and decamp. This is often done when not an enemy is within miles."[32]

Within moments of the Rebels' appearance, several score of wagons stood deserted. At least three were in a ditch, upset when their drivers tried to turn back.[33] With both his regiments at hand, now was the moment for Steuart to consolidate his gains and burn the Yankee wagons en masse. Miles of flaming wagons would have posed an impassable blockade to Banks's column and most certainly would have caused its destruction, or at least dispersed his infantry over the countryside so completely as to eliminate Williams's division as an effective fighting force. Instead, Steuart led his troopers on a wild ride up the Valley Pike toward Middletown, leaving the wagons undisturbed in their wake.

Banks and his staff were near the Cedar Creek Bridge when a terrified wagon master told them of the fiasco at Newton. Several field officers rode past and confirmed the presence of enemy cavalry at the head of the trains.

"This was a shock," said David Strother. "I had to that moment been tenaciously incredulous of an enemy in our rear. This seemed proof positive."[34]

Banks told staff officer Capt. James W. Abert to take charge of the headquarters guard, Captain Collis's Zouaves d'Afrique, and prepare to burn the bridge over Cedar Creek in order to prevent an enemy pursuit from that direction. Proceeding to a neighboring barn, Abert gathered up a tar barrel, straw, some greasy commissary pork, and other inflammable materials, lit a fire close to the bridge, and stood guard.[35]

Banks and Strother rode on in silence, "each heart manning itself for the death struggle." They met mounted teamsters rushing back in terror, beheld the deserted line of wagons stretched out before them as far as the eye could see, but heard no firing. "I rode close to the general summing up our position," said Strother. "I had till this time stoutly denied the possibility of an enemy in our rear. I was mortified at the utter failure of my judgment. I saw little way for any of us but an honorable death, for with Ewell in our front, Jackson must of course be close in our rear." Banks said nothing against Strother but remarked kindly, "It seems we were mistaken in our calculation." Lowering his head, Strother answered, "It seems so."[36]

As they neared Middletown, the signs grew hopeful. The master teamster rode by, "cursing furiously at his underlings for stampeding the trains, threatening and ordering the fugitives back to their places." Humiliated wagon masters planted themselves in the road and rounded up the frightened. The panic ceased, and the teamsters turned back with their teams toward their deserted wagons, each blaming and accusing the other of cowardice. The black drivers were another matter. Their fears were not so easily quieted. As a New York officer observed:

> They were not so ignorant but what they knew that they had everything to lose in being captured. There was some excuse for them to act as they did, seeing the example set by those whose fortune it was to be born white. They did not return so readily to the charge. The wagon masters set themselves at work to hunt them out and whip them back to their places. It seemed that they were used to this kind of persuasion, for after all was restored to order, and the train again in motion, they could be heard talking and laughing over the affair and inquiring of each other how many cuts they got.[37]

Taking heart in the example of the master teamster, Generals Banks and Williams rode among the soldiers of Donnelly's brigade, encouraging them forward and receiving in turn "manifestations of pleasure and confidence." At Middletown, Donnelly deployed the men of the 46th Pennsylvania as skirmishers to the right of the turnpike with a section of Battery F, 4th U.S. Artillery, in close support and started the line forward. Behind them in column came the 28th New York and the 5th Connecticut infantry regiments. In the distance could be seen Steuart's cavalry, also deployed on the east side of the Valley Pike. Between them and the Pennsylvanians were three companies of the 1st Michigan Cavalry under Maj. Angelo Paldi. At the first sign of trouble Paldi had set out from Middletown for Newton. He fought a delaying action to within a mile of Middletown, when he passed through the ranks of the 46th Pennsylvania to allow the infantry to take over. Paldi brought to Banks and Strother a prisoner he had caught during the skirmish. The soldier, a well-educated youth from Bedford County, openly confessed the disposition and strength of the force before them. Feeling even better now that he knew Ewell had not interposed himself astride the Union line of retreat, Strother urged Banks to sacrifice none of the army stores at Strasburg. Banks agreed, but the precautionary orders to Abert stood.[38]

A few rounds from the Federal rifled guns dispersed Steuart's cavalry. Unslinging knapsacks and "loading at will," the 46th Pennsylvania charged at the double-quick for four miles, Rebel horsemen scattering before them. As the enemy fell back into the woods east of Newton a little before noon, the 46th Pennsylvania again took its place in the march column, and the retrograde was resumed. General Banks was well pleased with the work of Major Paldi and Colonel Donnelly. "This episode, with the change of front, occupied nearly an hour, but it saved our column. Had the enemy vigorously attacked our train while at the head of the column it would have been thrown into such dire confusion as to have made the successful continuation of our march impossible."[39]

STONEWALL JACKSON TOOK the news of Steuart's engagement as evidence that Banks was in headlong flight for Winchester and probably strung out along the Valley Pike. On the strength of the report and this assumption, he decided to split his army. He ordered Ewell to stand fast near Nineveh with Trimble and Elzey while he backtracked to Cedarville. There he would pick up Taylor's brigade and lunge across the Chapel road, hoping to sever Banks's column at Middletown. The brigades of Winder, Campbell, and Fulkerson, then south of Cedarville, were to fall in behind Taylor.[40]

To satisfy himself beyond any doubt that Banks had quit Strasburg, Jackson asked Jed Hotchkiss to take a small cavalry escort and ride out the Chapel road ahead of the troops. Hotchkiss had gone no more than a mile and a half when he ran into videttes belonging to the 1st Maine Cavalry, which Colonel Douty had sent forward after reaching Providence (or Union) Church with five companies of his regiment and Collins's squadron of the 1st Vermont Cavalry. It was nearly noon. A drenching rain beat the dirt road into mud. After exchanging a few ragged volleys with the Yankees, Hotchkiss and his band fell back.[41]

Hotchkiss galloped to Jackson with news of his encounter. Jackson was pleased but wanted Hotchkiss to push harder in order to determine the size of the Yankee force. Dutifully Hotchkiss returned to the front at the head of two or three companies of the 8th Louisiana Infantry that happened to be resting near Jackson. The added firepower of the Louisianans broke the Federal vidette line. Hotchkiss pressed on until he came to an open field opposite Providence Church, where Douty had formed line of battle, half of his command on the brow of a low hill to one side of the chapel, the remainder tucked in a grove on the opposite side. Again Hotchkiss paused for reinforcements.[42]

Jackson obliged him quickly, sending up Ashby with all available cavalry, Chew's battery, and the two rifled guns of Capt. William Poague's Rockbridge Artillery. Ashby's cannons opened on the Federal cavalrymen, hitting no one but compelling Douty to order a withdrawal. The four-mile retrograde was deliberate and consumed nearly two hours, time vital to the passage of the Union trains along the Valley Pike. "Stubborn as mules" was how Ashby later characterized the resistance of Douty's troopers. They retired at a walk in column of fours, deploying when the ground permitted and always keeping beyond artillery range. Ashby's cavalry and guns maintained a respectful distance throughout, and not a single Union cavalryman was hit.[43]

Emerging from the timber-lined crossroad onto the Valley Pike at Middletown at 2:30 P.M., Douty chanced upon Lt. William Rowley, the signal officer who had been posted there to relay messages up and down the turnpike. He told Douty that the trains and infantry had passed, along with Generals Banks and Williams and their staffs. General Hatch, who had been left behind to organize the rear guard, was expected momentarily. Lacking orders, Douty elected to wait for him. He turned his command to the left off the Chapel road and then led them into the village of Middletown, which sat south of the crossroads. There they halted on the east side of the Valley Pike in column of fours.[44]

Hatch arrived a half hour later. The 5th New York Cavalry and remaining companies of the 1st Vermont Cavalry had been delayed on the south bank of Cedar Creek. Unable to fight their way through the throng of wagons, they had fallen back to Strasburg. The 1st Michigan Cavalry was near the head of the column with Donnelly's brigade. For the moment, Hatch and his escort constituted the entire Union rear guard. Delighted to find the companies of Douty and Collins on hand, he ordered them deployed into the side streets and fields east of the turnpike in case Ashby should appear. As the horses had been under saddle since daybreak without forage or water, Hatch permitted them to be removed from the line and watered by companies.

Ashby appeared an hour later, but not from the direction Hatch or Douty had expected. Recalled Major Collins: "I had been scanning the field through my field glass in the direction of the [the Chapel road], when suddenly his artillery was seen to debouch from the woods in our rear, which fact I instantly communicated to Lieutenant Colonel Douty, who was mounted near me, at the same time handing him my glass. The order to mount was quickly given by him, and the rear guard drawn in." Before departing to look after his own men, Collins caught sight of Rebel infantry—one hundred soldiers from the 8th Louisiana detailed to Hotchkiss—hurry into line behind the stonewall on the right side of the turnpike north of town. He also glimpsed the familiar field pieces of Chew's battery wheel into position alongside them. The guns opened fire at once and "would have told with fearful havoc were it not for the buildings behind which our troopers were directed to take cover." Collins got his men into column and then tracked down Hatch and Douty on the corner of a cross street. The general, said Collins, "with his customary coolness, deliberately surveyed the enemy for a few moments, when, it being evident our position was no longer tenable, he gave the order to move down into the principal street on the pike." A trooper within earshot overheard Hatch warn Douty, "We must cut our way through!" Hatch took his place at the front with his escort. Collins's squadron lined up in column behind him. Douty's four companies brought up the rear.[45]

Up to that moment the Rebel guns had fired frequently but without effect. An instant before Hatch gave the order to charge, a well-aimed Parrott shell ripped through the right arm of a Captain Cilley of Company B, the rearmost element of the 1st Maine Cavalry. Cilley had been sitting at the head of his company near an orchard. Shells were bursting among the trees uncomfortably close. But there was Cilley, said the regimental historian, "assuring his men that the sound of shell and canister was much worse than the actual danger." Down the captain went, falling from his horse "in much the same deliberate manner in which a squirrel falls to the ground when shot." The sight of their captain writhing in agony, his arm connected to the body by only a thin slice of skin and integuments, panicked the green troopers, and Douty hastened to the rear of the column to steady them.[46]

In the meantime Hatch bellowed the order to charge, and down the pike went the cavalrymen by fours at a gallop. The rain had stopped. Rising dust from the macadam surface choked rider and horse alike and obscured the enemy from view. The Federals had covered just one hundred yards before the Louisianans behind the stone wall opened fire at a range of thirty feet. Chew joined in with his entire battery and Captain Poague's two Parrott guns. The effect was horrible. Company B of the 1st Maine Cavalry was spared; it had re-formed too late to take part in the charge, but three of the other four companies were decimated. In Company E, 61 horses were lost and 42 men reported missing—most presumed dead or wounded; in Company M, 47 horses and 33 men were lost; and in Company A, 55 horses and 44 men. Many of the horses escaped unscathed and were impressed into the Confederate service; Jed Hotchkiss recalled rounding up sixty or seventy fine mounts. A good number of the men ran behind houses or into cellars and were captured. But the slaughter was real enough. Some found it diverting. "The Federal cavalry would tumble off their horses, roll over, scream, and scramble to the roadside in the most amusing manner," a Rebel cavalryman said. Henry Kyd Douglas showed more compassion: "It was a sickening sight, the worst I had ever seen, and for a moment I felt a twinge of regret." So did Turner Ashby. After watching the tumbling of men and horses, remembered Hotchkiss, the general remarked that it looked "too bad to see so many of them disposed of at once." Hotchkiss disagreed. "I am not vindictive," he told his wife, "but I really did not feel sorry to see the horse and his insolent rider laid low. It seemed a just retribution for the evils they had inflicted on an innocent people." Stonewall Jackson, who watched the affair from a nearby knoll, observed sympathetically in his report: "In a few moments the turnpike, which had just before teemed with life, presented a most appalling spectacle of carnage and destruction. The road was literally obstructed with the mingled and confused mass of struggling and dying horses and riders."[47]

At first Colonel Douty was unaware of the slaughter: "The dust was so thick I could neither see nor tell anything in particular, except close by me. I passed over the bodies of men and horses strewn along the road till I had come up to near the center of Company M, the third company from the rear, where I found the bodies of men and horses so piled up that it was impossible to proceed." Falling back into Middletown, Douty led the survivors of the 1st Maine Cavalry west along a muddy side road to the Middle road; from there they made their way to Winchester, arriving at daybreak on May 25. Hatch and Collins kept on along the turnpike and ran square into the rear of their own baggage train, which had gotten a late start from Strasburg. The wagons, said Collins, "being deserted by the drivers, [were] tumbling down the pike."[48]

Southern shells hurried along the Yankee wagons. Captains Chew and Poague had limbered their guns after the surviving Federal cavalry galloped out of range. As the artillery limbers bounced into an open field nearer the Valley Pike, Jed Hotchkiss called Ashby's attention to the fact that a bend in the road a few hundred feet away "had placed the crowds of wagons that were on it in a line so that we could enfilade it. [Ashby] at once ordered the batteries to open on this double line of wagons with solid shot, which they did, giving them a raking fire for nearly a mile and throwing them into the wildest confusion."[49]

At that moment Stonewall Jackson took charge. It was 4:00 P.M., and less than four hours of daylight remained. Time was of the essence if he were to catch Banks before dark, but Jackson had no way of knowing how much of Banks's wagon train had passed Middletown. Neither did he know the location of the Federal infantry. In short, Jackson had no idea at what point he had severed Banks's march column. His instinct was to head north and hope for the best, and in that spirit he had the Reverend Dabney write the first message to Ewell since the two generals had parted company that morning near Nineveh. It read: "The enemy has retreated en masse toward Winchester. Major General Jackson requests that you will move on Winchester with all the force you have left as promptly as possible." No sooner had a courier left with the message than a clash of arms on the edge of Middletown suggested that Jackson had guessed wrong. At least a portion of the Yankee fighting force had been cut off south of the village, and so, as quickly as they marched into Middletown off the Chapel road, Jackson turned his brigades toward Strasburg. He also had Dabney write Ewell a second order at 4:30 P.M., requesting that he send Elzey's brigade to Middletown and suspending Ewell's advance on Winchester until further notice.[50]

The sharp skirmish that disrupted Jackson's plans had been precipitated by Captain Collis's approximately one hundred Zouaves and several dozen soldiers from the depot guard, all of whom Banks had left with Captain Abert of his staff to burn the bridge over Cedar Creek after the last troops and wagons had passed. Abert had lit a bonfire beside the bridge in readiness to execute the order, but after noticing that the nearest ford was in better condition than the bridge, he elected to leave the structure intact and, with Collis's company and the depot guard, set off down the Valley Pike at 3:30 P.M. Crossing Cedar Creek, they ascended a long hill three-quarters of a mile southwest of Middletown in time to witness the ambush of Hatch's cavalry. Abert and Collis also spotted a Southern infantry regiment—probably the 9th Louisiana —marching along the main street in column by company. Thirty-five baggage and supply wagons, cut off from the remainder of the train, were tearing up the pike toward Cedar Creek. As the last surviving Federal troopers vanished into the fields west of the village, Collis hurried his company across the plain east of the Belle Grove estate and into line behind a stone wall that ran perpendicular to the turnpike on the south side of town, within 150 paces of the enemy.

Collis's men timed their first volley perfectly. Remembered Pvt. Henry Handerson of the 9th Louisiana: "As we jumped over the stone wall into the pike, a vicious volley of bullets whistled through our disordered ranks, splintering the rails of the neighboring fence and wounding several of my comrades, and, looking down the road towards Strasburg, I saw a company of Zouaves firing vigorously upon our advance." The 9th Louisiana abandoned the turnpike and rushed around houses, through yards, and over fences to outflank them, but after delivering two more volleys Collis extricated his men from the wall in good order and fell back toward the ridge beyond Belle Grove.[51]

As Abert and Collis withdrew up the hill, they met Capt. R. B. Hampton at the head of Battery F, Pennsylvania Light Artillery. "By the greatest good fortune," said Abert, "By an intervention of a generous God," agreed Collis, their small command gained a thirty-minute respite behind Hampton's four Parrott guns. The thirty-five wagons that had escaped Ashby's marauding cavalry line up behind the ridge.[52]

Joining the little conclave on the hill was Col. Charles H. Tompkins with five companies of the 1st Vermont Cavalry and, a few minutes later, Col. Othneil De Forest with six companies of the 5th New York Cavalry. Both Tompkins and De Forest had received orders to destroy residual public property in Strasburg. Of the two, De Forest had performed his duties better. He emptied the largest church in town of ordnance stores and burned them, as well as cleaned out the freight depot of clothing and fired it, along with a large outbuilding containing tents and accoutrements. Tompkins claimed, unconvincingly, that Hatch had countermanded his orders.[53]

While his cannoneers held the enemy at bay in back of Belle Grove, Hampton, Tompkins, and De Forest hastily conferred. Tompkins offered to lead them all out of their fix by way of a mountain road west of the Valley Pike, saying that he had a captain in his command who could guide them. De Forest agreed and rode off to organize the wagons. He returned to find no sign of Tompkins or his squadron; the Vermont colonel had deserted, De Forest later alleged, taking with him the only guide they had.[54]

Meanwhile, Richard Taylor's brigade had formed a line of battle and was advancing. Campbell's and Taliaferro's brigades had turned off the Chapel road and were following up the Valley Pike in column. The scene in Middletown was briefly festive. "Everything in Middletown turned out to greet us," declared a Virginia artillerymen, "men, women, girls, children, dogs, cats, and chickens, and nobody corrected the frequently repeated mistakes when some pretty girl would take some young man for her brother."[55]

Taylor's well-disciplined Louisiana regiments had deployed with their usual crispness. And, as usual, Major Wheat's battalion had gone astray. Taylor found it among some abandoned Yankee wagons. "The gentle Tigers were looting right merrily, diving in and out of wagons with the activity of rabbits in a warren—an occupation abandoned on my approach—and, in a moment, they were in line, looking as solemn and virtuous as deacons at a funeral." Taylor marched his brigade straight for the hillcrest, on which were drawn up "a body of Federals—cavalry, artillery, and infantry, with some wagons. Their number was unknown, and for a moment they looked threatening." Hampton's Parrott guns did good service. "A shell knocked over eight men of the 7th Louisiana," said Taylor. "Another, as I rode forward to an eminence to get a view, struck the ground under my horse and exploded. The saddlecloth on both sides was torn away, and I and Adjutant Surget, who was just behind me, were nearly smothered by earth, but neither man nor horse received a scratch."[56]

Hampton waited until the Louisianans were near enough for canister to have an effect. That checked the enemy long enough for everyone to vacate the hill and splash across Cedar Creek. This time Abert burned the bridge. Falling back on Strasburg, the Federal infantry formed on Hupp's Hill, determined, Captain Collis said, "to make a final struggle." De Forest gathered his troopers and the wagons in town. George Brooks of Company D, 46th Pennsylvania, was among the defenders. "Well do I remember those moments of suspense as our little band of perhaps three hundred men, representing all branches of the army, were gathered in the earthworks. Each and every man was aware that nothing he could do would prevent our capture, but we were anxious to make a show of resistance."[57]

As it happened, none was needed. The Confederates broke off the pursuit at Cedar Creek. Abert and De Forest led both their men and the wagons west from Strasburg to the Cedar Creek Turnpike. Back roads took them to the Romney Pike and away from both the enemy and their own forces. At 2:00 P.M. on May 26, after marching 141 miles in forty-seven hours and fording the Potomac River, the party arrived at Hancock, Maryland, exhausted but without the loss of a wagon or a man.[58]

The Federal stand south of Middletown cost Jackson nearly two hours. At 5:45 P.M. he turned his four brigades north and set out after Banks. Haste was imperative if either he or Ewell were to overtake the Yankees before they reached Winchester or before nightfall drew a curtain on their operations. The brief order he now dictated to Dabney reflected the urgency. "Major General Ewell: Major General Jackson requests that you will at once move with all your force on Winchester," Dabney scribbled. "Please acknowledge the receipt of this by return of courier and the hour of your movement."[59]

Ewell already was on the march. Being told to start and then to stop did not sit well with him. He had set out for Winchester from Nineveh at 5:00 P.M. on receipt of Jackson's 4:00 P.M. order (it took an hour for couriers to travel between the two generals). A half hour later he halted in response to Jackson's 4:30 P.M. order and sent Elzey backtracking to Cedarville to join Jackson at Middletown.

Ewell grew impatient. The sound of artillery and small arms fire clearly was advancing down the Valley Pike toward Winchester. At 5:45 P.M. he wrote Jackson suggesting he be permitted to march with Trimble—the only brigade left to him—to Newton. An hour passed with no reply. With sunset just an hour off, Ewell took matters into his own hands. "Without instructions my situation became embarrassing," he later explained, "but I decided after consultation with General Trimble and Major Brown of my staff to move on to Winchester."[60]

Disobeying a direct order from Stonewall Jackson was a risky proposition, but Ewell's good judgment was confirmed fifteen minutes after he gave the order to march. A courier handed him Jackson's 5:45 P.M. dispatch affirming his decision to advance on Winchester. Events continued to outpace orders. At 7:00 P.M. Jackson received Ewell's 5:45 P.M. dispatch suggesting he march to Newton. Jackson approved it and issued Ewell the necessary orders. By the time Ewell received them, he had gone too far on the Front Royal road to turn back. He ignored the order, sent a return courier to notify Jackson of his action, and continued on toward Winchester. Ewell also called up Steuart, whose cavalry was then scouring the countryside between Newton and Nineveh for Federal fugitives.[61]

Ewell reached the outskirts of Winchester at 10:00 P.M., well before Jackson. Along a hilltop three and a half miles southeast of town his lead regiment, the 21st North Carolina, ran into Yankee pickets consisting of one company from the free-wheeling 1st Maryland Cavalry (Union), whose captain had reinforced himself that afternoon with a little Valley whiskey, and two companies from the spit-and-polish 10th Maine Infantry, their trademark white gloves a source of derision. Four companies of the 10th Maine had been on provost marshal duty in Winchester since early May; four other companies had just arrived from the Harpers Ferry area.

At the first fire the Marylanders broke. In the darkness the Maine infantrymen, posted several hundred feet to the rear, waited in anticipation. "A crackling of pistols was heard first, then something decidedly like a yell, which made every man's heart thump and his knees shake," confessed the historian of the 10th Maine. "Then came that wild jargon of sounds so indescribable and terrible—the rush and clatter of horsemen. Then with the increasing whirr of the approaching mass, that most dreadful of all sensations increased which one feels in the opening of battle. And at last, just when the fears of the men were excited to the utmost, the horses of our friends went rolling up the road."

After a pause to settle their nerves, the Maine men rose up from the hillcrest, fired a volley, and then ran rearward faster than the double-quick prescribed by tactics manuals. Two North Carolinians were wounded. An angry Col. William W. Kirkland called up the entire regiment to reinforce the skirmish company and pursued the Federals as far as the tollhouse at the junction of the Front Royal road and Millwood Pike, just over a mile south of Winchester. There the opposing lines traded fire until midnight, neither knowing the strength of the other. The remaining regiments of Trimble's brigade halted along the Front Royal road a half mile behind the 21st North Carolina. Steuart caught up before midnight with the 1st Maryland Infantry (Confederate) and Brockenbrough's Maryland battery; the 2nd and 6th Virginia Cavalry were too hopelessly scattered to recall in the dark.[62]

The temperature dropped sharply during the night to near freezing. Trimble's soldiers had left their coats, blankets, and knapsacks at Front Royal that morning to be brought up by wagons that never appeared, and they suffered acutely now from the cold and a sharp, piercing wind. The men evidently endured additional discomfort due to stupidity in high places. Said Capt. William C. Oates of the 15th Alabama: "We stood in the road all night. We were not permitted to sit down, but were kept standing all night. It was a precaution wholly unnecessary and a cruel punishment. Two or three men and a trusty officer from each company would have been enough to have kept standing and on the alert. Not a word was spoken above a whisper. The men shivered and their teeth chattered with the cold, and they would stack up and brace against each other fifteen or twenty in a group to keep from freezing."

Captain Oates may have exaggerated their predicament; Pvt. William Mc-Clendon of the same regiment recalled huddling on the ground with his messmates often enough to catch a few catnaps. At least one company of the 16th Mississippi became fed up and marched off, their captain with them, to a house a few hundred yards behind the lines, lit a huge bonfire, and bedded down for the night.[63]

Ewell's men at least were able to rest in place or steal an occasional moment of sleep; Jackson's veterans were on the move, marching and fighting, from the time they turned north at Middletown until nearly dawn on May 25. Jackson was in a foot race with Banks, and he pushed his tired troops unsparingly. Jackson hoped to at least seize the chain of hills that stood a half mile southwest of Winchester before morning. At 5:45 P.M., twelve miles of turnpike and a determined Yankee rear guard stood between him and his objective.[64]

The affair south of Middletown had disordered Jackson's march column of the morning. When Jackson countermarched his command north from Belle Grove, the Stonewall Brigade became the lead infantry command, following directly behind Ashby's cavalry, Chew's battery, and Captain Poague with his two Parrott guns. Three regiments—the 4th, 5th, and 2nd Virginia Infantry—already had filed to the left off the Chapel road toward Strasburg. These General Winder halted while the 33rd and 27th Virginia infantry regiments filed off the Chapel road to the right. Winder placed the four guns of the Rockbridge Artillery not with Ashby behind the 33rd Virginia. The 4th, 5th, and 2nd Virginia regiments countermarched and took the brigade rear. When all were in place, Winder led his command down the road at a grueling double-quick time. Campbell's brigade came next, then Fulkerson. Taylor's Louisianans brought up the rear.[65]

Even without an enemy to challenge the Confederates, the going was hard. Said a member of the Rockbridge Artillery: "The road was strewn with guns, blankets, oil cloths, sutlers' stores, cartridge boxes, and a long line of abandoned wagons stretched for more than a mile towards Newton." Other vehicles were smashed or overturned, their contents scattered over the turnpike. "I wish," artilleryman Lanty Blackford wrote his mother, "I could give you an adequate idea of the immense variety of their contents and of the evidences they afforded of the almost luxurious manner of living among the Yankee soldiery. Lemons, oranges, dates, hermetically sealed fruits and vegetables, candies, jellies, pickles, tea, coffee, sugars, etc." Battery mate Randolph Fairfax told his sister that he found several sticks of "delicious cream chocolate. If you only knew how completely like a child a soldier is, in his eagerness for sweet things, you might perhaps form some idea of the promiscuous scramble that ensued upon the discovery of anything good to eat. Officers, Yankees, and everything were forgotten then."

Sweetness came in many forms; women and girls emerged from farmhouses to cheer Jackson's progress and pass out edibles. Captain Poague said that most of the infantrymen and cannoneers behaved themselves reasonably well in the face of temptation material and moral, pausing only to peep into the wagons, embrace a girl, or pick up an occasional oil cloth or blanket (apparently Poague was unaware that two of his men had climbed into a sutler's wagon, knocked the heads off some gingersnap barrels, and poured the contents onto the turnpike). Lt. McHenry Howard contented himself with an officer's broad red silk sash, "which helped to give to my plain dress evidence of my being a commissioned officer; I wore it almost through the rest of the war." But Ashby's troopers lost themselves entirely in the plunder. They "were looting wagons and capturing horses, utterly undisciplined," Poague complained.[66]

Stonewall Jackson simmered at the spectacle, but with Ashby helpless—Poague found him following his guns alone and seemingly bereft—Jackson could do nothing but lament a fast-fading opportunity. "From the attack upon Front Royal up to the present moment every opposition had been borne down, and there was reason to believe, if Banks reached Winchester, it would be without a train, if not without an army; but in the midst of these hopes I was pained to see that so many of Ashby's command, forgetful of their high trust as the advance of a pursuing army, deserted their colors and abandoned themselves to pillage to such an extent as to make it necessary for that gallant officer to discontinue further pursuit."[67]

If Henry Kyd Douglas is to be believed, and quite often he is not, Jackson himself briefly succumbed to temptation:

I was riding with the general and a small party of staff and couriers along the road. He was in good spirits but silent and thoughtful. Once he dismounted and took from an overturned wagon a cracker, hard and not too clean, and attempted to eat it, for he had eaten nothing since early morning. Riding along in a meditative way, thinking over some social movements I intended to execute if Banks let us into Winchester, I was startled when he suddenly called across the road to me, "Mr. Douglas, what do you think of the ladies of Winchester?" A blush mantled my cheek before he continued with a quiet smile, "I mean the ladies generally. Don't you think they are a noble set, worth fighting for? I do. They are the truest people in the South." He drew his cap down further over his eyes, moved "Little Sorrel" into a rather better pace, and relapsed into silence.[68]

General Banks found nothing humorous in his predicament or his prospects. Approaching Winchester with General Williams and their staffs near sundown, he was unsure if that town even remained in friendly hands. To find an answer he accepted the offer of Col. Thornton Brodhead, who was desperately ill and should have been in an ambulance, to ride on ahead with five companies of his 1st Michigan Cavalry and reconnoiter. They covered the six miles rapidly and were able to give Banks his first bit of good news that day: although full of frightened teamsters and runaway wagons, Winchester was still theirs. The 10th Maine Infantry and five companies of the 8th New York Cavalry, just arrived from Dixon Miles's command, kept order over the unruly and expectant populace.[69]

With the road before him now certain, Banks turned his attention to his imperiled rear. A mile north of Bartonsville he waved down Colonel Gordon, riding at the head of his old regiment, the 2nd Massachusetts Infantry. Banks had with him the 28th New York of Donnelly's brigade, which he had ordered to face about and return to Newton to protect the disintegrating supply and baggage train that Hatch had been expected to escort to safety. After announcing to all within earshot that Brodhead had found the way to Winchester clear, Banks ordered Gordon to take the 28th New York and 2nd Massachusetts, along with a section of Battery F, 4th U.S. Artillery, and of Cothran's New York Battery, and save the train. The last Gordon saw of Banks, he was trying to disentangle several wagons near the rear of Donnelly's brigade.[70]

Two miles south of Newton, Col. Silas Colgrove was busy deploying the 27th Indiana across the Valley Pike to check the Confederate advance. Who ordered him there is uncertain. In his postwar memoirs, Gordon said that before meeting Banks he had ordered the 27th and a section of Battery F, 4th U.S. Artillery, to countermarch from Newton in response to pleas for help from the train. In his official report, he wrote that the regiment had been sent back with a section of artillery but did not take credit for the order. Probably the order came from General Williams. In any event, Colgrove and his Hoosiers answered the call in fine style. Filing at the double-quick into a wheat field on the west side of the Valley Pike north of Newton, the men unslung their knapsacks, piled them in windrows—never to see them again— and moved off toward the rear of the train on the run. "As we approached the scene of trouble, more and more commotion was in evidence," said the regimental historian. "The four- and six-mule teams were all in a furious gallop, drivers were lashing with their whips, shouting and swearing like mad men, wagon masters and other mounted men responsible for public property were joining in the uproar, and all were making a supreme effort to hurry themselves to a place of safety."

As soon as his men cleared the rear of the train, Colonel Colgrove formed the regiment in line of battle behind a fence on the east side of the Valley Pike, just south of the Crisman (Chrisman) place, which stood west of the road. The two cannons from Battery F, 4th U.S. Artillery—"popguns," a lieutenant of Company I called them—unlimbered in the road. In the distance, out of sight, there was a yell. A bugle sounded, and the Hoosiers made ready to meet a cavalry charge. Instead, a lone horseman appeared on the horizon, whether drunk or delusional, no one ever knew. "He rode at a steady lope, waving his saber and cheering. We could easily see that he was a Rebel officer, but when we saw that he was alone an order was passed down the line not to shoot him," the regimental historian recorded. "So he rode unmolested, plum up to our men on the pike. Halting and exchanging a word or two with those near him, he seemed to comprehend the situation." Ignoring the dictates of reason and Yankee pleas, he refused to surrender; rather, reining his horse around, he started back up the pike. One or two men fired at him and missed. "Then, without orders but by a common impulse, a large part of the right wing of the regiment fired, in a well-timed volley, and one of the brass pieces was fired at the same moment." The shell sliced off the strange Rebel's head, and his body fell to the ground, "a quivering mass, riddled with holes." His horse stopped, came back, and was caught by soldiers of the 27th Indiana.

An instant later the Hoosiers heard a rumble of wheels. Occasionally a man's head popped up over a rise in their front. Continued the historian of the

27th: "Before we had fairly time to think of what it might mean, a thin line of smoke shot up in the air. Our colonel commanded, 'Lay down!' and as each man fell deftly forward on his face, boom! went a cannon, followed instantly by a shell passing over us with the swish of an immense sky rocket. Others followed in quick succession."

They came from the Parrott guns of the Rockbridge Artillery, which Captain Poague, abandoned by Ashby's plundering cavalrymen, had run up unsupported to within rifle shot of the 27th Indiana. The Hoosiers' own artillery support failed them. At the first Rebel shot, the lieutenant in command limbered up his section and galloped off. "Go to hell with your popguns, they are no account anyway," shouted Colonel Colgrove.[71]

As soon as he was able, Colgrove moved one company to the opposite side of the pike and gave the order for the remaining nine companies to fall back slowly in line of battle. As the regiment drew out of range of Poague's guns, Colgrove detailed men to burn the seven or eight abandoned wagons of clothing and provisions that they passed on the way through and beyond Newton.

South of the village, Captain Poague edged his guns forward through the wheat fields on the west side of the pike. General Winder had come up and deployed three regiments in line of battle behind Poague.[72]

While the Hoosiers were falling back and firing wagons, the 2nd Massachusetts appeared in a field north of them. Poague fired at the regiment, as did the remaining four cannons of the Rockbridge Artillery, which Winder had brought up and placed on the east side of the pike. The 2nd Massachusetts responded with a volley that cut into the ranks of the 27th Indiana. Shoving their way past the flotsam of the shattered wagon train, the soldiers of the 27th emerged from the flames cursing and yelling. Then they re-formed ranks sharply, filed past the 2nd Massachusetts, and left the fighting to the Bay Staters. Lt. Col. George L. Andrews deployed his regiment, his artillery support unlimbered in the road, the 28th New York drew up in support, and the battle resumed at long range. The two sides traded artillery salvos until dark, when the Federals—well assured that what was left of the depot trains had escaped—pulled back into the night.[73]

Entering Newton with the Stonewall Brigade, which had resumed a column formation, Jed Hotchkiss observed "how peculiarly the streets were lighted up by the burning of a commissary train, especially the flames from burning bacon and from wagonloads of rice." John H. Worsham of the 21st Virginia noticed an oddity of a different sort: "Some of the wagons had been fired. As we passed, one thing struck the writer about the contents of those wagons as singular. In every one that had articles in sight, I could see portions of women's clothing; in one wagon a bonnet, in another a shawl, a dress in the next, and in some all of a woman's outfit. I never saw the Yankee soldiers wearing this kind of uniform, and why they carried it was beyond my knowledge. Some of our men suggested that it had been confiscated from citizens of the Valley." The village of Newton itself wore a weird aspect. "Here again the people met us as they had done in Middletown, with the same uproarious and delighted greeting, illuminating their houses with bits of candles stuck in the inner sash, while the people broke out into the street," said Pvt. Robert T. Barton of the Rockbridge Artillery, a resident of the area. "While they gave me good things to eat, nobody kissed me, and I was not a bad-looking lad then, although rather slender."[74]

The Confederate column felt its way slowly forward in the darkness. Turner Ashby had managed to round up a handful of his cavalrymen and with them again led the march. Poague followed with his battery, now reunited. Chew's three guns probably were tucked in the column behind Poague. General Jackson and his staff rode ahead of the infantry. In the main body the Stonewall Brigade retained the lead. The 33rd Virginia came first, followed by the 27th, 2nd, and 5th Virginia regiments; the 4th Virginia brought up the brigade's rear. General Winder and his staff rode behind Jackson. Following the Stonewall Brigade were the brigades of Campbell, Taliaferro, Taylor, and—at a distance too great to be considered part of the march column proper—Elzey.[75]

At Bartonsville, on a hill just north of Opequon Creek, the 2nd Massachusetts paused to rest. There the men had dropped their knapsacks before going into action three hours earlier, and now they set about reclaiming them. Maj. Wilder Dwight moved down to the creek with Company I to keep watch while their comrades gathered up their knapsacks. Company B formed in a clover field in support of Dwight's detail. The men of Company D acted as flankers on either side of them, those on the west side of the pike forming behind a lilac hedge that bordered the Springdale estate. Colonel Gordon had continued north with the 27th Indiana, the 28th New York, and the artillery, leaving Colonel Andrews to manage things alone.

General Hatch appeared briefly at the head of five companies of the 5th New York Cavalry and the squadron of the 1st Vermont Cavalry that he had brought with him from Middletown by side roads. Hatch bore lurid tales of defeat and lurking disaster. While riding toward Kernstown, high up on the Cedar Creek Grade road, he had seen silhouetted against a backdrop of burn-

ing wagons seemingly endless columns of enemy infantry and artillery marching down the Valley Pike. Hatch remained just long enough to pass along his
grim news, then set off with the 27th Indiana.[76]

The Hoosiers found Hatch's presence unsettling for reasons that had nothing to do with his bitter tales. "We will always remember the conduct of our
cavalry that night. It was a good thing for them that we had not then heard of a
reward being offered for a dead cavalryman, as we did afterwards; otherwise,
we surely would have killed a few of them," averred the historian of the 27th:

> There seemed to be an effort to have a small force of cavalry remain with
> the rear guard, but in the darkness they could easily rein their horses out
> of ranks, put spurs to them, and go speeding away. So there was a constant
> procession of them galloping through our ranks. We were in mortal terror
> of our lives. Look out! someone would shout, and the word would be
> passed along the line of tired, sleepy men, followed by the clatter of horse
> hooves and the clink and rattle of sabers. Men crowded each other into
> ditches, or over stones or logs, in their efforts to get out of the way. There
> could not have been one cavalryman with the rear guard when it arrived
> at Winchester.[77]

Hardly had Company I of the 2nd Massachusetts taken up its post than
Dwight heard voices on the far bank of Opequon Creek giving orders. Not a
word was spoken among the Federals; Dwight made his dispositions to receive
an attack quickly and silently. From across the run someone cried out, "There
they are! There they are! In the road." Another yelled, "Charge!" Dwight
formed his little band into a square. No shot was fired until the Rebel horsemen were within fifty yards, when Dwight barked the orders, "'Rear rank,
aim! Fire! Load! Front rank, aim! Fire! Charge bayonets!' But bayonets were
not needed," remembered Lt. Charles Morse. "Men and horses were rolled
over together, breaking the charge and sending them back in confusion."[78]

In their flight, Ashby's frightened troopers thundered past Poague's and
Chew's limbered guns and headlong into Jackson and Winder and their staffs.
The two generals were barely able to draw themselves and their retinues aside
before the cavalrymen galloped heedlessly past them. Private Barton remembered the moment when Dwight's detail opened fire: "General Jackson and his
staff and a company of cavalry had gotten down to the bridge that crosses the
Opequon, while we were close behind them coming down the hill. Just then
the darkness was illuminated by a brilliant flash of fire, and bullets fell all
around us, hitting our wheels and a few scraping the sides of the horses."[79]

Neither Jackson nor Winder was able to slow the troopers. They rode over the front ranks of the 33rd Virginia, injuring several officers and men and, said Col. John F. Neff, "creating for the moment a scene of most mortifying confusion." Neff and his lieutenant colonel got the regiment off the pike, and the 27th Virginia charged past, formed a firing line, and opened what Dwight termed "a galling and severe infantry fire" on the Massachusetts men. Lieutenant Morse and several other men had fallen asleep before the cavalry charge and only now awakened. While the 27th Virginia kept up its volley fire, General Winder had one company each from the 2nd and 5th Virginia regiments, companies composed largely of men from the area, deployed on either side of the pike to cross the stream and drive the enemy back. Robert Barton's older brother Strother commanded one of the companies chosen.

Major Dwight pulled back before the Rebels delivered their assault, having lost ten men killed or wounded. Colonel Andrews called in the flankers, and the 2nd Massachusetts resumed its march. At nearly every stone wall between Bartonsville and Milltown a company or two dropped back to deliver a volley at their pursuers. At 2:00 A.M. the 2nd Massachusetts stumbled into Winchester, the last Federal unit to enter the town that night.[80]

Young Robert Barton was just a few hundred yards from home, and he took advantage of the momentary lull following the withdrawal of the 2nd Massachusetts from Bartonsville to stop at the gate of the Springdale estate to beg a glass of milk or water, "which I needed very much to help me in this long march [that] had continuously kept up since five o'clock in the morning, and it was then one o'clock the next morning." The overseer and his family were standing in the yard, and Barton tried to open the gate. He shoved but found it obstructed. "Looking down I discovered a dead Federal soldier with a bullet through his head, and his head against the gate. Later I found the hole made by the bullet, which had gone through a panel of the gate and had evidently been fired by one of General Jackson's escort in return for the first volley from behind the lilacs. I made no further effort to get in but hurried on to join my slowly moving company."[81]

The humiliating brush with the 2nd Massachusetts at Bartonsville caused General Jackson to change his tactics. Advancing with Ashby's demoralized troopers and a battery of artillery in the lead had been rash; now, five miles short of Winchester, Jackson elected to play it safe. He knew that the 5th Virginia had been raised in Winchester and, bypassing Winder, ordered it to the front. Next he called for Capt. George W. Kurtz, who had spent his life in the area. After quizzing Kurtz about the Valley Pike and adjacent roads to satisfy himself that the captain knew the ground well, Jackson said: "Captain, take Company A with your own company and push on towards Winchester. You can drive in all their pickets if you move cautiously."

Kurtz did so. Every time he encountered a company of the 2nd Massachusetts he reported to Jackson, who with Winder was walking only a short distance behind. Each time the answer was the same. "Captain," said Jackson. "Move cautiously. I am confident you can drive in every picket."

In that manner the Valley army inched forward through the night toward Winchester, the men in the ranks reeling from exhaustion. Dozens collapsed at every stop. At 3:00 A.M. the army halted north of Kernstown while Captain Kurtz cleared the road around Parkin's Mill. That was the last step Capt. Hugh A. White of the Liberty Hall Volunteers took that night; he sank down onto the dusty macadam and fell instantly asleep. The stamina of youth failed Robert Barton as well: "When we got a little beyond Kernstown we turned a little to the left in a field and parked our guns, and as the column came up it formed in a sort of line of battle, the men falling down where they stood and going to sleep. I remember how chilly and damp the dewy grass felt to me, but how soon my weariness overcame the thought of cold and I was fast asleep."[82]

The plain-spoken Colonel Fulkerson also had had enough. Stepping from the blackness he told Jackson frankly that he must either grant the army rest or he would have nothing more than a skirmish line left by dawn. Jackson tried to remonstrate. After what Fulkerson had endured from the Yankee batteries on Pritchard's Hill two months earlier, he surely must understand the importance of seizing the high ground first; reaching the hills overlooking Winchester tonight would save lives in the morning. That was true enough, conceded Fulkerson, but it no longer mattered. Jackson yielded. The men would have two hours' sleep.

Before closing his eyes Henry Kyd Douglas caught a glimpse of Jackson and Ashby pacing before him, their gazes fixed on the shadowy forms of the Milltown hills, just a few hundred yards away on the far side of Abrams Creek. Apart from Captain Kurtz's skirmishers, Douglas thought before sleep overcame him, there was no one else between the Valley army and Banks.[83]

CHAPTER 21

THIS IS A CRUSHING BLOW

May 24, 1862, was a day of reckoning not only for Nathaniel P. Banks, but also for the architects of the Union war effort, Abraham Lincoln and Edwin M. Stanton. Each reacted to Jackson's surprise offensive in keeping with his character: Banks as the pragmatic, guarded optimist; Stanton as the sometimes bullying but supremely efficient bureaucrat; and President Lincoln as the captain of calculated risk, ever with the master politician's eye for opportunity in adversity.

General Banks had reason to be satisfied that night. He had kept his composure on the retreat and had displayed considerable personal courage. Tying his fate to that of the trains, Banks had remained with the column every step of the way, exhorting jittery teamsters, unsnarling traffic jams, and caballing together a reliable infantry rear guard to replace the useless cavalry at precisely the right juncture. By and large, the officers and men retained confidence in him. Of Banks's leadership, Lt. Charles W. Boyce of the 28th New York said: "Such was the unbounded confidence placed in him by the men under his command that they considered him equal to the task of extricating them from almost any difficulty." In his diary that evening Capt. Warren W. Packer of the 5th Connecticut recorded the prevailing sentiment when he wrote that "the whole thing during the afternoon was exceedingly well managed, and no regiment was very severely handled while holding the rear guard, except the 2nd Massachusetts." And the losses in the 2nd Massachusetts, it should be added, were light. Watching Banks's weary but well-ordered infantry shuffle into Winchester after dark—"not sandwiched, not demoralized, not whipped, the worst off not so badly used up as to be unserviceable"—Lt. John Mead Gould of the 10th Maine observed, "It seems singular that a retreat like this should have caused so little excitement." Only the cavalry had wavered, becoming by nightfall more of a liability to Banks than an asset. Behaving more like mounted ruffians than Federal soldiers, on the pretext of finding forage and shelter for the animals, Hatch's troopers dispersed throughout Winchester, shooting off their pistols in the air, threatening to kill any woman who dared exhibit delight at their predicament or cheer Jackson's approach, and otherwise terrifying the populace.[1]

Banks's infantry was too hungry and tired to terrify anyone. Between marching and countermarching, the regiments of the rear guard—the 2nd Massachusetts, 27th Indiana, and 28th New York—had covered nearly thirty miles during the day. No one had eaten in nearly twenty-four hours, and the prospects for obtaining rations that night were slim to nonexistent. Among the wagons destroyed during the retreat were several containing rations and cooking utensils. Even those regiments fortunate enough to have brought off their regimental trains had trouble getting access to them. Those with rations were unable to cook them, as fires were prohibited. Not even a cup of hot coffee was to be had. Most lay down for the night with little more than a cracker or two in their stomachs.

Sleep too was hard and brief. No one went into bivouac before 9:00 P.M., and the 2nd Massachusetts did not bed down until at least 2:00 A.M. Three of Banks's seven infantry regiments—the 27th Indiana, 5th Connecticut, and 28th New York—had lost their blankets, overcoats, and knapsacks in the course of the retreat.

The night was cold and the ground wet. Both brigades bedded down in soft clover fields south of town. "With everything gone except what we had on our persons," said the historian of the 27th Indiana, "there was nothing for us to do but lie down in the rank clover, thoroughly soaked as it was with a mountain dew. As there was nothing under us but wet grass, neither was there anything over us but a limitless expanse of murky fog."[2]

A murky fog momentarily clouded the otherwise clear thinking of General Banks that night. At 8:00 P.M. he telegraphed the president to explain his actions and report on the day's events. "I was satisfied by the affair at Front Royal yesterday that I could not hold Strasburg with my force against Jackson's and Ewell's armies, who I believed intended immediate attack. Though I might have saved my command, it would have been impossible to secure the vast stores and extensive trains accumulated there. . . . I concluded that the safest course for my command was to anticipate the enemy in the occupation of Winchester. My advance guard entered this town at five this evening, with all our trains in safety."

There Banks was guilty of forgivable hyperbole. A good number of wagons had indeed been lost. Confederate sources bragged that deserted wagons littered the way at the rate of one every fifty yards, certainly an exaggeration. But the department quartermaster later reported between 55 and 58 large wagons, 17 two-horse conveyances, 11 ambulances, 1 spring wagon, and 19 four-horse wagons lost in the two-day retreat from Strasburg to Williamsport, Maryland, for a total of not more than 106 vehicles. Nearly all of these were lost on May 24, and that coincides with more reliable Southern estimates of 100 wagons counted as abandoned on the Valley Pike that day. (Twenty-one of the wagons reported lost belonged to the 1st Vermont Cavalry, giving support to Colonel De Forest's charges that Colonel Tompkins had been guilty of gross negligence on the retreat.) But nearly all of the division and brigade trains, and most of the depot trains—at least five hundred wagons in all—were indeed brought off safely, no mean achievement in view of the marked superiority of the Confederate cavalry, both in numbers and in quality.[3]

Having made clear his reasons for falling back to Winchester, Banks closed his dispatch with the strange promise, "I shall return to Strasburg with my command immediately." Banks hardly could have meant that; he knew when he sent the telegram that he was outnumbered at least three to one. Perhaps fatigue, or false elation at having survived the day, momentarily obscured his thinking. Whatever the reason, it was a promise that Banks neither repeated nor explained when a surprised Stanton called him on it. "In your dispatch of this evening to the president you say that you intend to return with your command to Strasburg. The question is suggested whether you will not by that movement expose your stores and trains at Winchester," Stanton pointed out with uncommon restraint. "The president desires therefore more detailed information than you have yet furnished respecting the force and position of the enemy in your neighborhood before you make a movement that will subject Winchester or Harper's Ferry to danger from sudden attack. You will please report fully before moving."[4]

Banks did not so report because he could not. He knew only that Jackson and Ewell were somewhere in his front in overwhelming numbers, ranging from 25,000 to 30,000. All sources available to him at Winchester—"secessionists, Union men, refugees, fugitives, and prisoners"—concurred in that estimate. Nobody placed the number at less than 15,000, said General Williams.

Both he and Hatch agreed with Banks that the true total was 25,000 and that Jackson intended to attack in strength at dawn. To meet him, Banks had a paper strength of about 6,400. But that included nearly 1,500 worthless cavalry. Subtracting from the total another 300 to represent Collis's missing Zouave company and the Cedar Creek depot guard, and allowing for 200 stragglers—a conservative guess—Banks had no more than 4,400 men ready for battle. Williams guessed that he had about 3,500 infantry, along with twenty Parrott guns and "six useless brass pieces." The only positive offset were the 856 well-rested soldiers of the 10th Maine Infantry.[5]

Outnumbered or not, Banks knew he had to stay and fight. At midnight he asked Brig. Gen. Samuel Crawford, then without a command, and "a bevy of staff officers" to track down Generals Williams and Hatch for a council of war. Williams had just gone to bed at the Taylor house when a "terrible rapping" startled him out of "the deepest sleep" and returned him to the cares of command. "The general must see me at once to arrange the program for the morning. Of course I was obliged to lose my second night's sleep." Williams and Hatch agreed that they must "make a fight as we were, in front of the town." As Banks put it, "I determined to test the substance and strength of the enemy by actual collision." Expectations were low. "That we should all be prisoners of war I had little doubt," said Williams, "but we could not get away without a show of resistance, both to know the enemy's position and to give our trains a chance to get to the rear. I hurried up my own wagons and sent them off to get the advance, if possible, and after sundry preparations and a hurried cup of coffee found the daylight coming on."[6]

Secretary of War Stanton's measured query about Banks's plans for retaking Strasburg reflected the generally balanced tenor of his communications that day. While the president mulled the proper response to Jackson's thrust, Stanton busied himself marshaling reinforcements for the Shenandoah Valley and gathering what information he could on the state of affairs there. Greatly complicating Stanton's efforts to get at the truth were alarmist reports from Brig. Gen. John Geary. Though tall in stature at six foot six, Geary was short on judgment and on troops. He had one regiment of infantry, the 28th Pennsylvania, to guard the Manassas Gap Railroad from Manassas Gap to Thoroughfare Gap and a battalion of the 1st Michigan Cavalry to patrol south of the road. Geary also was a defeatist. Six days before Jackson set out on his offensive, Geary had told his wife: "Unless I receive the reinforcements I have called for we must have hard times here. I have no troops to do anything with, nor have I any rally point behind; we must take what we get, and there is no help for us. I place my trust in the God of Battles and feel that he is all powerful to deliver us, if it is His Divine Will, as He has done heretofore."[7]

Geary's cavalry was as unreliable as that of Banks. From it he obtained, and then forwarded to Stanton, false reports of an enemy buildup east of the Blue Ridge. The only Confederates in his sector were one company of Ashby's cavalry, yet on the night of May 23 he had warned Stanton that "there are still bodies of Rebel cavalry south of us, and I have no doubt they are supported by infantry. If my position be attacked," Geary added dramatically, "I will hold it to the last extremity." He assumed the objective of the nonexistent foe to be the capture of Thoroughfare Gap.[8]

On May 24 Geary became completely unhinged. As an officer of the 1st Maine Cavalry put it, he allowed himself to be "sadly misled by that most unreliable of all creatures, the intelligent contraband." Two runaway slaves told him that there were ten thousand Southern troops approaching him from the west and another ten thousand from the south, the latter already at Orleans. Surely they were right, Geary assured Stanton, because they had "sought my headquarters breathless and evinced sincerity in their manners." They were wrong. Everything Geary learned that day and the next from contrabands was false, but he reported their uninformed ramblings as gospel truth. After one company of his cavalry was bested in a skirmish with a more or less equal number of Southern horsemen near Linden, Geary became convinced that he was surrounded. Again he informed Stanton: "Finding that bodies of the enemy are moving north of me and others in the south to cut me off on the flanking road, I have ordered my command back to White Plains—only practicable method of preventing them and securing a position I shall be enabled to hold."[9]

President Lincoln had just concluded a conference with Generals McDowell and Shields at Falmouth when news of the Front Royal debacle reached him. Lincoln had exacted from both a promise that they would move down the line of the Richmond, Fredericksburg, and Potomac Railroad toward the Confederate capital on May 26.[10] With 40,000 men between them, brushing aside the brigades of Joseph R. Anderson and Lawrence O'Bryan Branch seemed a simple enough matter. Once they crossed the Pamunkey River, McDowell and Shields would belong to McClellan. Nearly 160,000 Federals would then be poised before the gates of Richmond, with only 60,000 Southern soldiers to oppose them. Even with his penchant for greatly exaggerating the enemy's strength, McClellan would be hard-pressed to fail; Joe Johnston could not oppose both McDowell and McClellan without exposing the slimness of his numbers at the first clash of arms. Union prospects in the Eastern theater had never looked better.

The thunderclap from the Shenandoah Valley upset everyone's calculations. The crisis was genuine. In the event Banks were defeated, Harpers Ferry and railroad communications with the West would be imperiled. Until Jackson's strength was known, a Confederate dash on the Federal capital could not be ruled out. And until the whereabouts of J. R. Anderson's command, which had vanished from McDowell's front, was confirmed, neither could Geary's reports of a simultaneous Southern buildup east of the Blue Ridge be discounted.

The question before Abraham Lincoln—who was directing armies at the time, through necessity rather than inclination—was clear: What should he do with McDowell? Should he be permitted to join McClellan, or should he be used against Jackson and the force (not yet exposed as chimerical) confronting Geary? There was no panic in Lincoln's decision; no blind reaction to, nor even mention of, a possible Confederate descent on Washington. Lincoln's intentions were aggressive; he would redirect McDowell in order to trap Jackson. Shields's division, still footsore from its march to Falmouth, was to return to the Shenandoah Valley at once. At 4:00 P.M. on May 24 he telegraphed McClellan his decision: "In consequence of General Banks's critical position I have been compelled to suspend General McDowell's movements to you. The enemy are making a desperate push upon Harper's Ferry, and we are trying to throw Frémont's force and part of McDowell's in their rear."

McClellan's brief reply was as manly as it was unexpected: "Telegram of 4 P.M. received. I will make my calculations accordingly."

Stanton had given McDowell a warning order of sorts at 11:12 A.M., telling him that he must leave one more brigade at Fredericksburg than he had planned before setting off toward Richmond. At 5:00 P.M., an hour after advising McClellan of the new plan, President Lincoln wired McDowell his new instructions. After telling him that Frémont had been ordered to march from Franklin to Harrisonburg to relieve Banks and engage Jackson and Ewell, Lincoln gave McDowell a mission emphatically clear: "You are instructed to lay aside for the present the movement on Richmond to put twenty thousand men in motion at once for the Shenandoah, moving on the line or in advance of the Manassas Gap Railroad. Your object will be to capture the forces of Jackson and Ewell, either in cooperation with General Frémont or in case want of supplies or of transportation interferes with his movement, it is believed that the force with which you move will be sufficient to accomplish the object alone." Lincoln told McDowell not to count on help from Banks, either.[11]

McDowell's response was hardly one to inspire confidence. In reply to Lincoln's telegram, he wrote Stanton: "The president's order has been received and is in process of execution. This is a crushing blow to us."[12]

Clearly McDowell needed bucking up. Lincoln had to be sure there was no misunderstanding of orders, nor want of energy in carrying them out. So he sent a messenger to McDowell—not a low-ranking officer or even a general, but Secretary of the Treasury Salmon P. Chase. The secretary boarded a boat for Falmouth at 5:30 P.M. While Chase steamed down the Potomac, Lincoln offered McDowell a sympathetic shoulder. At 8:00 P.M. he told the disappointed corps commander: "I am highly gratified by your alacrity in obeying my orders. The change was as painful to me as it can possibly be to you or anyone. Everything now depends upon the celerity and vigor of your movement."[13]

That Lincoln had not underestimated the depth of McDowell's dismay is evident from the message he sent the president at 9:30 P.M. He had obeyed Lincoln's order at once, "for it was both positive and urgent, and perhaps as a subordinate there I ought to stop." But he could not. Casting heavy doubt on the president's plan, he observed that considerations both of distance and supply rendered cooperation with Frémont problematic at best. (Apparently he disagreed with Lincoln's conclusion that his command alone was enough to best Jackson and Ewell.) Also, Jackson's line of retreat up the Shenandoah Valley was far shorter than McDowell's line of approach against him. McDowell thought that ten days would be needed to get twenty thousand men into the Valley over the route Lincoln had indicated. "I shall gain nothing for you there, and shall lose much for you here. It is therefore not only on personal grounds that I have a heavy heart in the matter, but that I feel it throws us all back, and from Richmond north we shall have our large masses paralyzed and shall have to repeat what we have just accomplished." Nonetheless, he had directed Shields to begin the movement west by sunrise on the twenty-fifth. A second division would follow in the afternoon. McDowell closed, "I hope to see Governor Chase tonight and express myself more fully to him."[14]

Chase would have to talk with Shields as well. Skipping channels, the feisty Irishman that afternoon had expressed to Lincoln his opinion that the whole matter in the Valley was nothing more than a panic. "In any event, no help would reach [Banks] in time from here, and a panic there ought not to paralyze this movement just now prepared on the eve of execution. Banks has enough troops, if well handled, to defend himself against everything that can by any possibility be in the Valley of the Shenandoah."[15]

Only Frémont's answer to his orders seemed unequivocally positive. "Your telegram received at 5:00 o'clock this afternoon," Frémont wired from Franklin, deep in the West Virginia mountains. "Will move as ordered and operate against the enemy in such a way as to afford prompt relief to General Banks." He directed the members of his staff to have their "house in order" by 5:00 A.M. the next morning in preparation for the march.

Taking Frémont at his word, Lincoln, at 7:15 P.M., wrote back: "Many thanks for the promptness with which you have answered that you will execute the order. Much—perhaps all—depends upon the celerity with which you can execute it. Put the utmost speed into it. Do not lose a minute."[16]

That the execution might not match the promise should have been apparent from a long, frankly timorous letter that Frémont had sent Stanton at 2:30 P.M. Banks had informed him of Jackson's attack and requested reinforcements. After asking Stanton if he could expect support, Frémont begged not to be called upon to help Banks. Within his own department, the enemy seemed "everywhere reinforced and active. Under the circumstances my force cannot be divided, and if I abandon this line and move eastward to the support of General Banks this whole country to the Ohio would be thrown open." Frémont was not sure he could move anywhere. "Want of supplies has kept this force at Franklin. Beef is now secured, but during the last eight days there has been but one ration of bread, two of coffee and sugar, and nothing else. There is nothing but beef now in camp. This want of food has been nigh to produce disorder and rendered advance hazardous." Heavy rain had flooded the region and was still coming down in torrents. His cavalry was useless for lack of mounts; he needed immediate approval to purchase four hundred horses; would Stanton give it?

Lincoln answered for the secretary. With exasperation apparent in every word, he had told Frémont, at 4:00 P.M., to "purchase the four hundred horses or take them wherever or however you can get them." Lincoln was so flustered he referred to himself in the third person: "You are directed by the president to move against Jackson at Harrisonburg and operate against the enemy in such a way as to relieve Banks. This movement must be made immediately. You will acknowledge the receipt of this order and specify the hour it is received by you."

Frémont had responded in less than an hour with his short "Will move as ordered" telegram. He delayed an answer to Lincoln's word of thanks until the next morning. Dating his message "*On the march*, May 25, 1862," Frémont assured Lincoln his army would do "the best to answer your expectations." Only time would tell for sure whether the croaker or the courageous would prevail in the Pathfinder.[17]

CHAPTER 22

ATTACK AT DAYLIGHT

Dawn came chill and dreary on May 25. A heavy fog blanketed the clover fields and pastures along Abram's Creek east of the Valley Pike. The sun rose at 4:48 A.M., but the mist made it hard to tell just when daylight began.

What light there was revealed a horrible flaw in Banks's lines. The four regiments of Gordon's brigade were spread along an elevation called Bower's Hill on the west side of the Valley Pike, with Winchester behind them and a ridge four hundred yards in front of them. Even a military neophyte like the Reverend Dabney could see the bankruptcy of their defenses. He painted a vivid image of the battleground:

> The town of Winchester is seated upon ground almost level; and such also is the surface south and east of it, through which the great roads from Strasburg and Front Royal approach. The former especially passes through smooth fields and meadows, by a smiling suburb and millhouse [Milltown], a mile from town; after which it surmounts a gentle ascent [Bower's Hill] and enters the street. But towards the southwest, a cluster of beautiful hills projects itself for a mile toward the left, commanding the town, the turnpike, and the adjacent country. They were then enclosed with fences of wood or stone, and covered with luxuriant clover and pasturage, with here and there a forest grove covering the eminences farthest west.

Speculated Dabney: "Why the enemy did not post their powerful artillery upon the foremost of these heights, supported by their main force, can only be explained by that infatuation which possessed them, by the will of God, throughout these events."[1]

There was precious little to infatuate the Union soldiers who, with empty stomachs and aching limbs, shivered their way into line of battle. They knew what was coming. "Long before daylight the beating of drums and the rumble of wheels in their front advised our outposts that the enemy was again on the move," recalled the historian of the 27th Indiana. Col. Thomas Ruger deployed his 3rd Wisconsin where it had slept, with its left resting on the turnpike. Lt. Col. George Andrews aligned the 2nd Massachusetts on Ruger's right. Two sections of Battery M, 1st New York Light Artillery, unlimbered on a knoll to the right of the 2nd. The 27th Indiana and 29th Pennsylvania regiments formed in reserve. A two-gun section of Battery F, Pennsylvania Light Artillery, set up astride the turnpike with a squadron or two of cavalry in support.

The regimental commanders had picked their positions themselves. At sunrise there was no Federal general on the field. Gordon, Williams, Hatch, and Banks were all in town, doing one thing or another. In search of ammunition, Maj. Wilder Dwight of the 2nd Massachusetts had found Gordon still in his hotel room. Leaving Gordon, he met a courier from Colonel Andrews with word that an attack seemed imminent. Hurrying back to the regiment, Dwight ran into Williams and Hatch and gave them the message. On the field he came upon Colonels Andrews and Ruger. Through the parting mist all three eyed the ground ahead. "Ought we not to take possession of that ridge," asked Dwight. "I have already selected it, but where is Colonel Gordon?" snarled Andrews. Until he arrived, there could be no forward movement.[2]

Col. Dudley Donnelly was at the front and had his brigade up and in line well before dawn. Reveille sounded early enough in the 28th New York for Col. Edwin F. Brown to have his regiment formed neatly behind a stone wall by 4:00 A.M. The New Yorkers occupied the extreme left of the Union line, with their right on the Front Royal road and their left flank resting near the Hollingsworth house. Built in the 1754, the handsome two-story stone structure was the oldest house in Winchester. It stood on a slight rise of the west bank of a narrow stream called "Town Run." The 5th Connecticut took position in a field in front of and a little to the left of the 28th New York. The 46th Pennsylvania drew up on the right of the 5th Connecticut and to the right of the Front Royal road. Battery F, 4th U.S. Artillery, and the remaining section of Battery M, 1st New York Light Artillery, unlimbered on a rise called "Camp Hill" a quarter mile south of town. Capt. Macon Jordan's battalion of the 10th Maine was still out in front on the Front Royal road near the tollhouse. It withdrew after skirmishing with Rebel pickets at first light and marched back to its quarters in town, where it rejoined the regiment. Remarkably, Col. George L. Beal and his 856 officers and men of the 10th Maine Infantry found themselves forgotten. Not a single order was issued to them that morning.[3]

General Banks understood the disadvantage both in position and numbers under which he labored. But he had not changed his mind overnight; to save his trains he had no alternative but to fight. At first light, he gave General Williams oral orders identical to those Williams had received four hours earlier: Williams was to "offer such resistance to the Rebels as would develop with more certainty their strength and give time for our transportation wagons to move clear of the route of our retreat."[4]

A MILE SOUTHEAST of Winchester, General Ewell read a dispatch from Stonewall Jackson. It was a single sheet of paper, on which were delineated the roads, streams, woods, and houses around Winchester, along with Jackson's position on the Valley Pike. Beneath the map were the words "Attack at daylight."

With the ground before him blanketed in fog, Ewell's first moves were necessarily tentative. The skirmishers of the 21st North Carolina had rousted Jordan's Maine battalion from the tollhouse, but the fog caused Col. William Kirkland to halt his regiment behind a stone fence and nearby wheat stack on the southern bank of Abram's Creek. To Kirkland's left and rear Col. Bradley T. Johnson's 1st Maryland (Confederate) ran into similar difficulties. Advancing cautiously along the Millwood Pike toward the tollhouse, the Marylanders engaged some of Jordan's retreating pickets but could not follow them. "The fog now had become so dense as to make it impossible to see twenty steps in any direction, and Colonel Johnson therefore thought it advisable to assemble the skirmish line, as we had entirely lost sight of our line of battle and did not know but we might be enveloped by the enemy," said Washington Hands. "Quietly the men were drawn in, and the regiment lay down in an orchard and concealed itself behind a board fence to await the lifting of the fog."[5]

The scattering of Jordan's battalion cleared a commanding hill at the junction of the Millwood Pike, a mile from town. The batteries of Captains A. R. Courtney and John Brockenbrough unlimbered in the wheat field that crowned the hill and at once opened fire on the shadowy ranks of Donnelly's brigade. The Union guns on Camp Hill responded. From west of the Valley Pike the two Parrott guns of the Rockbridge Artillery joined in.

Making his headquarters just behind his batteries, Ewell had as good a

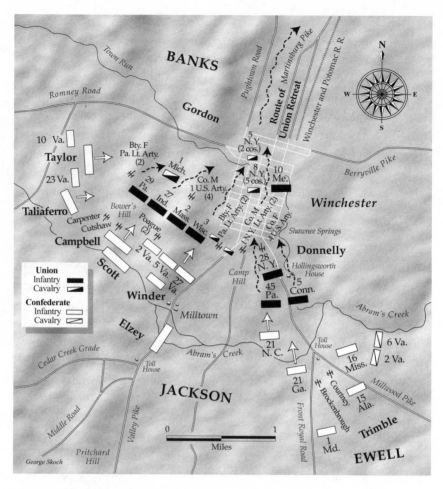

MAP 7. Battle of Winchester, May 25, 1862

vantage point of the artillery exchange as the fog permitted. The sound of Jackson's guns reassured Ewell of his commander's aggressive intentions, and he rode forward with a rifled cannon and the commander of Courtney's battery, eighteen-year-old Lt. Joseph W. Latimer, and told Kirkland to press the attack.

The North Carolinian responded with more enthusiasm than good sense. Leaving his skirmishers to catch up, Kirkland set off across Abram's Creek and down the Front Royal road at 5:40 A.M. with his regiment marching by the flank at double-quick time—a long column presenting a front of just four men. Stone walls on either side of the turnpike allowed for no lateral movement. It was a most unmilitary maneuver for a West Point graduate, thought an officer of the 21st Georgia, which had stood behind the North Carolinians. Kirkland recognized the risk but went on anyway. As he later explained: "Knowing nothing of the topography of the country and having no time to reconnoiter the approaches to the town, I had no alternative but to advance along the main turnpike." Perhaps not, but there could be no excusing his failure to deploy skirmishers. Kirkland neglected even to have the men ground their knapsacks.[6]

Ironically, the barrage of Courtney's and Brockenbrough's batteries, most of which was fired blind into the fog, helped perfect the ambush into which the 21st North Carolina was about to stumble. The first shots fell near the 5th Connecticut as the men were rising from their sleep and boiling coffee. No one was hit, but the third shot struck a stack of rifled muskets, scattering the guns and causing the soldiers spontaneously to seize their weapons and form ranks. Col. George D. Chapman sent a courier back to ask Donnelly whether he should advance or hold his ground; impatient of a reply, he ordered the regiment to fall back by column of companies to a hollow in a wheat field. There, amid tall standing grain and wet fog, the 5th Connecticut dropped entirely out of sight.[7]

The artillery fire also drove the 46th Pennsylvania to cover. Redeploying the regiment from line to company columns at half distance, Col. Joseph F. Knipe withdrew it behind a small rise and into the same depression as the 5th Connecticut. The regimental front of the 46th formed an acute angle with the road. On higher ground 150 yards in rear of the 5th Connecticut, the 28th New York remained safely tucked behind a stone wall.[8]

The mist lifted just enough for the soldiers of the 1st Maryland (Confederate) to catch a glimpse of the fate that awaited the 21st North Carolina. "The fog rising somewhat, a column of the enemy [28th New York] was revealed lying behind a stone wall about three hundred yards in our front, with his right flank resting toward us, and totally unconscious of our close proximity," recollected Washington Hands. "They were apparently intent on watching something before them; presently, to our horror, there emerged from the fog the 21st North Carolina Regiment, altogether ignorant of the ambuscade awaiting. There was nothing on earth we could do to warn them of the danger. Oh, it was a sickening sight to see them thus marching into the jaws of death."[9]

The 46th Pennsylvania and the 5th Connecticut regiments waited until the two lead companies of the 21st North Carolina were silhouetted on the rising ground in front of them before opening fire. Colonel Knipe gave the order to fire first. "We were taken completely by surprise and fell back pell-mell to the foot of the rise on the other companies," confessed a North Carolina private who survived the volley. Mounted on a richly caparisoned brown mare, Colonel Kirkland led the remaining companies up the rise on the run, straight into range of the 5th Connecticut. Said the regimental historian of the 5th: "When they had come on and we had begun to see their flags, the colonel [Chapman] sang out, 'Now boys, up and at them!' The command was obeyed with a will, and we had very good shooting. As we rose up, almost half a mile of butternuts stood way back in a solid mass almost squarely with their flank towards us. It did not seem as if a single bullet of ours, let off into that line, could fail to hit somebody." The 28th New York let go its first volley at about the same time. When the North Carolinians staggered from the effects of the twin volleys, Colonel Chapman ordered Companies A and F, the front units in the regimental column, forward to a three-foot stone wall level with the enemy. He deployed the remaining companies into line, two at a time. Reported Chapman proudly: "The whole regiment then moved to their line and, delivering three well-directed volleys, mowed down the enemy in score, shooting away their flag each time. At the third volley Companies I and B delivered a crossfire by a half-wheel to the right. The enemy broke and ran in confusion." As the North Carolinians fell back, the 28th New York advanced into line on the left of the 5th Connecticut, and the 46th Pennsylvania charged up to the wall on its right. Aligned behind the wall, Donnelly's brigade gave the appearance of an open crescent.[10]

Kirkland waved his regiment back perhaps one hundred yards to the protection of a stone wall that ran parallel to the one that Donnelly held. There the fighting should have ended. But Kirkland's blood was up, and after a fifteen-minute lull he ordered a bayonet charge. The results were inevitable. Said a soldier of the 5th Connecticut: "They rushed up yelling to the wall to come over at us, and a dozen or more of their most zealous leaped on the wall, and one of them even leaped down into the field on our side of the wall, but the firing was so effective that the rest dropped down the other side dismayed, and he too, who had been so adventurous as to come over, dropped down on the hither side of the wall and held up his hand in token of surrender."[11]

The impetuous North Carolinian was lucky to come away with his life; nearly one hundred of his officers and men were less fortunate. Most fell during this pointless charge. Losses in officers were high. The lieutenant colonel was shot through both hips while waving his sword above his head; the wounds were mortal. Regimental favorite Capt. J. C. Hedgecock was shot a half dozen times and left for dead. Capt. John W. Beard of Company F was hit eight times but survived to fight again. Luckily for the regiment, Colonel Kirkland was shot through the thigh and carried from the field before he was able to commit another blunder.[12]

With Kirkland and his lieutenant colonel down, the members of the 21st North Carolina fell back across Abram's Creek. They were able to retire in relatively good order courtesy of the 21st Georgia, which had hurried forward on their right and delivered a volley into the left flank of the 28th New York. Return fire from the left companies of the 28th slightly wounded several Georgians. The New Yorkers wavered, but as the 21st Georgia prepared to charge, the fog settled again over the field, heavier than before and mixed with the thick, sulfurous gunpowder smoke. The combatants were frozen in place, and for thirty minutes not a shot was fired.[13]

Scattered over the ground in front of the 5th Connecticut were scores of dead and wounded North Carolinians, most quiet, and all looking, quipped a Yankee officer, "like bags of shit in a grain field." Colonel Donnelly and his staff stepped over the stone wall to converse with the survivors. In their agony they apparently were accommodating, as General Williams, who chanced upon the scene, said "all expressed regret that they had been fighting against the Union."[14]

Donnelly took little solace in their confessions. Before the fog settled he had counted nine Confederate regimental colors on the hills to his front, all moving toward the east with the evident intention of outflanking him. He shared his fears with Williams, who allowed himself a moment of pride over the appearance of his old brigade: "Every man seemed as cool and cheerful as if preparing for a review; they lay in order of battle behind the crests of hills ready for another attack." But with at least nine regiments opposing them, both he and Donnelly knew the next attack would be unstoppable.[15]

THE MORNING MIST had been lighter, and had parted earlier, on Jackson's front than it had on Ewell's. Riding up the Valley Pike with Gen. Charles S. Winder at the head of the Stonewall Brigade column at daybreak, Lt. Mc-Henry Howard remembered no more than "a slight haze over the country, which the risen sun was dispelling." Winder halted the brigade at Parkins's Mill, near Captain Kurtz's skirmishers, and rode with his staff across Abram's Creek to reconnoiter. They passed around the mill and outbuildings that constituted Milltown and came onto a dirt road leading up a hollow to the west. A plank fence lined the south side of the road, and open ground, rising steeply, protected the north side. Suddenly Federal pickets atop the ridge had the Virginians in their rifle sights. "As we went on this road, the general in front, with a guide or someone, there came several shots from a small hollow or break in the high ground on our right which rattled like stones against the plank fence," said McHenry Howard. "The general put spurs to his horse and got safely past the mouth of the hollow. Next came Captain O'Brien, assistant adjutant general, and myself. We too spurred our horses to get by the dangerous point as rapidly as possible. Two or three shots came, and as I bent my head low to my horse's neck I was astonished to see the cream-colored tail of O'Brien's horse suddenly turn red all over. A bullet had passed through the root. No other harm was done, but the horse went faster."[16]

Winder drew rein beside Jackson, who had ridden as far as Parkins's Mill. To Winder's breathless report of his brush with Yankee skirmishers, Jackson answered simply, "You must take that hill."[17]

Winder prepared to comply. He instructed Colonel Baylor, whose 5th Virginia led the march, to deploy his entire regiment for skirmishing. Behind Baylor's Virginians he placed the Stonewall Brigade in line of battle along the southern bank of Abram's Creek, with the 27th Virginia occupying the left, the 2nd Virginia the center, and the 4th Virginia the right, on the east side of the turnpike. The 33rd Virginia Winder held in reserve. The brigade presented a narrow front. Huge numbers of men had straggled during the march of the day before. The 27th Virginia mustered only 136 rank-and-file members on the morning of the twenty-fifth; the colonel of the 33rd Virginia counted 150 men present. The entire brigade numbered just 1,313 troops.[18]

Sweeping up the steep slope of the ridge Baylor's skirmishers drove off the pickets from Gordon's brigade handily. The remainder of the brigade moved up and took position on the reverse slope. Behind came General Winder with the two Parrott rifles of the Rockbridge Artillery in tow. He told Captain Poague to unlimber on the crest near the old Quaker graveyard, considerably in advance of the infantry.[19]

The brief skirmish on the ridge had not been bloodless. John Worsham of the 21st Virginia recalled meeting one of the casualties of the fight when his regiment reached Parkins's Mill. "He was hatless and had been shot in the head, the blood streaming down his face so freely that the poor fellow could hardly see."[20]

Colonel Gordon reached the battlefield just in time to watch his pickets come running back from the ridge. His absence at dawn had frustrated Colonel Andrews and Major Dwight; now it was Gordon's turn to feel anger as he waited in vain for orders to deploy his brigade. When none came, he directed the 2nd Massachusetts forward to a broken stone wall on one of the lower slopes of Bower's Hill. The 3rd Wisconsin advanced on the left of the 2nd Massachusetts, and the two sections of Battery M, 1st New York Light Artillery, redeployed forward from a knoll to another on Bower's Hill and opened an enfilading fire on Captain Poague's section. Farther to the right a two-gun section of Battery F, Pennsylvania Light Artillery, contributed to the cannonade. Seeing that Poague was badly outgunned, Colonel Andrews waved Companies D and G farther to the right and slightly forward to a second stone wall just two hundred yards from the enemy to get a better angle on the exposed Rebel cannon crews. The men fanned out in a skirmish line. Their fire was unusually accurate, and in a few minutes they scattered the crew of one gun and silenced the second.[21]

Stonewall Jackson's answer to the silencing of Poague's Parrott gun section was to expose more artillery to Yankee sharpshooters. He sent orders for the remainder of the Rockbridge Artillery to take position on the extreme left of the line and directed the batteries of Captains Cutshaw and Carpenter to come up as well—fourteen guns in all. Their limbers with guns and their caissons lined up in column on the Valley Pike between Milltown and Parkins's Mill. Those of the Rockbridge Artillery stood in front, followed by those of Cutshaw, then Carpenter. Campbell's brigade trailed the artillery.[22] Together the batteries set off at a gallop. As the lead limber passed the mill at Milltown, Winder and his staff waved it to the left and onto the dirt road that paralleled Abram's Creek and the southern base of the ridge; the long cavalcade of limbers and caissons were to follow suit.[23]

As a lieutenant in the regular army, Winder had served in the artillery, and he retained a fondness for that arm of the service. To the dismay of McHenry Howard, Winder decided to indulge himself and direct the movements of the batteries Jackson had sent to his support. That exposed him to the shot and shell flying about the ridge. "I remember," said Howard, "a shot or shell passing so close to my head and left shoulder that it seemed to make the blood stir in the shoulder."[24]

With a flair for the dramatic, Winder intended for the three batteries to form on the road beneath the shelter of the hill, wheel limbers to the right, and charge up the ridge, bringing their cannons into position simultaneously and in a straight line. His plan stalled when one of the lead guns fastened itself on a locust post that held open a gate in the lane. The harder the limber horses strained, the tighter the gun became lodged. Captain Poague called for volunteers to cut down the post. A private by the name of Whitt, known for his strength, stepped up. Jerking an axe from a caisson, he began chopping away at the post while drivers struggled to quiet the frightened horses and Poague urged follow-on limbers and caissons to detour over a narrow millrace that ran beside the road. Gun crews were told to lie down behind a protecting embankment to avoid the shells that screeched overhead.

Pvt. Robert T. Barton of the Rockbridge Artillery took in the scene from behind the embankment. "At each lick the axe man grunted, as if playing an accompaniment to the music of his axe. The captain sat still and unmoved upon his horse, and eager faces watched the axe man to see what would happen when the post should fall."[25]

After a while Barton's curiosity got the better of him. Forgetting the danger, he stood up and wandered over to where Private Whitt was working. "Suddenly a strong, rough hand caught me by the neck of my jacket and threw me back over the millrace, saying, 'Lay down, you damn fool.' I fell with my nose in a bunch of mint and, recovering my full sense of danger I lay flat as a snake." When the post finally fell and the horses sprang forward with the gun, Captain Poague yelled out over the din, "*Corporal* Whitt from this hour!" After that the column moved forward like clockwork. Up the hill went the limbered guns, the crews sprinting behind. "We all ran to our places, and the fourteen guns moved up abreast and got in line with the two abandoned guns, and at once the sixteen opened their throats and sought the range of batteries opposite." Poague had run the remaining cannon of the Rockbridge Artillery onto a rise just to the left of the Parrott section; General Winder accompanied Cutshaw's battery into line to the right of the Parrott section. Carpenter's battery unlimbered on Cutshaw's right.[26]

Colonel Andrews's skirmishers sought out the new targets with deadly accuracy. Poague's battery remained the most exposed, and it suffered accordingly. After the battle gunner Lanty Blackford told his father that the carefully aimed shots of the Massachusetts riflemen constituted "by far the hottest and most destructive fire this battery has ever been under." The first man wounded was one of the drivers of his gun. "Just as the piece had been unlimbered and he was putting the limber in position in the rear I noticed him quickly dismount and fall to the rear. The sergeant asked him what the matter was. He exclaimed, 'My arm's broke.' Another man took his place."

The next man hit near Blackford was his good friend and college classmate, Washington Stuart. Stuart had been with the battery only a week and had no regular number. (Members of cannon crews were numbered according to their specific duty on the gun.) As a supernumerary he stood behind the limber waiting to relieve a cannoneer. When the number three man of Blackford's piece became exhausted, Stuart jumped forward to take his place. "Poor fellow, he had not fired the gun once when a minie ball ploughed the side of his face shockingly and he was drawn off, speechless if not senseless, to the rear. Another took his place and our furious work went on." A moment later Blackford glanced to the right and saw his friend John M. Gregory Jr. borne off the field, bathed in blood. "The ball had pierced his arm above the elbow and went round his back, coming out on the other side."

Blackford's attention was drawn to a scream from twenty yards away. "Help here, McKim is not dead yet." Blackford watched McKim carried off, "insensible and almost lifeless, though he lived some hours longer. The top of his head was fractured and furrowed by a bullet. He was just adjusting the primer in the touchhole of the howitzer to which he was number three and was holding the lanyard in his other hand just ready to draw, when he fell backward in his mortal pang." Then Blackford was dealt a near miss. "A solid shot darted right over my head, having first shattered the wheel of my gun, and of course silenced it for the time, and with lightning quickness went through the two lead horses of our limber, within five feet of which I was. The horses were standing a little sidewise, so that the ball transfixed them. The poor beasts made a desperate lunge round to the left (I was on their right) and were quickly disengaged from the harness—just in time to die."[27]

After what seemed an eternity to Blackford and his battery mates, at Winder's behest Poague shifted his fire toward the 2nd Massachusetts skirmishers. Canister raked their line, blasting stones from the wall behind which they crouched and wounding the captain of Company G.[28]

For nearly two hours eight Union cannons, all of them Parrott guns, battled from Bower's Hill with sixteen Confederate field pieces on the ridge west of the Valley Pike. On the east side the ten guns of Courtney's and Brockenbrough's batteries continued to trade salvos with the four six-pounder guns and two twelve-pounder howitzers of Company F, 1st U.S. Artillery, and the two Parrott guns of Battery M, 1st New York Light Artillery, stationed on Camp Hill. From his vantage point on the rise near the Millwood Pike tollhouse, Campbell Brown thought the artillery duel splendid:

Taken altogether there was more of the picturesque connected with this battle than with any I have yet seen. The view was one of singular beauty in itself—the town of Winchester just beneath us in the hollow and extending half-way up the slope of the opposite range of hills, looking as if enclosed in a perfect cup, and only the turnpike leading from it and winding round the base of the hills to indicate where the outlet was.

The distance from the hills on the Front Royal side, which we held with Courtney's and Brockenbrough's batteries, to those opposite held by the enemy was a little over a mile. Hence a good many of their shells and ours burst in the air over the town, and the little expanding globes of smoke made by them, with the two mingled heaps of flame and smoke where the pieces of either side were posted, and a little later the line of little fires from the musketry on the hill beyond, and the burning buildings in the town, seen when the sun had just burst out brightly, formed a beautiful but terrible whole.[29]

Jackson was ubiquitous during the artillery duel. Like General Winder, he was entirely in his element amid the screeching shot and bursting shells. Said the chaplain of the 25th Virginia: "Jackson seemed on this occasion the very personification of the genius of battle as he galloped from point to point and gave his sharp, crisp orders." Riding up to the 33rd Virginia Infantry during the barrage, he yelled to Colonel Neff while pointing to an empty stretch of Bower's Hill: "I expect the enemy to bring artillery to occupy that hill, and they must not do it! Do you understand me, sir? They must not do it! Keep a good look out, and your men well in hand, and if they attempt to come, charge them with the bayonet and seize their guns! Clamp them, sir, on the spot!" And he clenched his fist for emphasis.[30]

Both Winder and Jackson tinkered with the infantry support to ensure that no battery stood alone. Winder moved the 21st Virginia of Campbell's brigade and the Irish Battalion over to the base of the ridge behind the Rockbridge Artillery. He also placed the 33rd Virginia in direct support of Carpenter's battery. Jackson met Colonel Campbell and the 48th Virginia coming down the Valley Pike and escorted them into line on the rear slope of the ridge between Cutshaw's battery on the crest and the 21st Virginia, which was huddled behind the road embankment at the foot of the ridge. The 42nd Virginia took position on the left of the 21st.

Jackson rode forward with Campbell to a hillock ahead of the Rockbridge Artillery to examine the Yankee positions; Colonels Patton and Grigsby accompanied them on foot. A hail of canister and musket balls greeted them. Campbell fell wounded and was carried from the field; Grigsby had a hole shot through his sleeve and cursed the Yankees roundly. Jackson sat calmly on his horse until he had concluded his observations. Command of the Second Brigade passed to Colonel Patton.[31]

Colonel Fulkerson arrived next with the Third Brigade. Sometime during the course of the fight Jackson had given tactical command of the front line to General Winder, and Fulkerson took his orders from him. At the Marylander's direction, he placed the 23rd and 37th Virginia regiments in close column at the base of the ridge to the left of Campbell's brigade. Apparently worried that the detachment of Companies D and G of the 2nd Massachusetts as skirmishers presaged a larger Federal effort to outflank him, Winder ordered Fulkerson to deploy the 10th Virginia on the crest of a dominating hillock a quarter mile northwest of the ridge. Col. E. T. H. Warren accomplished the movement "under heavy fire of shell and rifle balls." Once atop the rise he advanced the members of Capt. Joseph Kaufman's company as skirmishers. The men darted behind rocks and trees and took aim at their Massachusetts counterparts, who were then feeling the first blasts of Poague's adjusted artillery fire. Like Generals Jackson and Winder, Warren traded safety for a better view of the Yankees. "While reconnoitering the enemy's position I drew their fire on me but was protected by Higher Power." Once the 10th was firmly posted on the left flank, Winder sent the 37th Virginia to its support.[32]

On the heels of Fulkerson came Scott's brigade, which for lack of anywhere better to go lined up on the lane behind Campbell's brigade. When Elzey's brigade column reached Milltown a few minutes later, Jackson halted it on the Valley Pike as a tactical reserve.

It was now 7:00 A.M. Not counting Elzey's brigade, Jackson had amassed fifteen regiments on the west side of the turnpike to oppose the four regiments of Gordon's brigade. Clearly it was time to make the weight of superior numbers felt. Again it was Winder who suggested the next move. Recalled McHenry Howard: "General Jackson presently came on the scene and asked how the battle was going on. General Winder told him the enemy ought to be attacked on his (the enemy's) right flank. 'Very well,' said Jackson, 'I will send you up Taylor,' and he rode off."[33]

A short time afterward Howard noticed the Louisianans, with Brig. Gen. Richard Taylor at their head, moving in column along the lane behind the ridge toward the left. Winder left the ridge long enough to point out to Taylor the route his brigade should take to get on the Yankee flank. Jackson, who had sent a staff officer to hurry Taylor along, now caught up with him, and, the young Robert Barton remembered, the two of them and their staffs paused beside his gun to examine the field. "I was close enough to hear the brief conversation between the two generals. The substance of it was that General Taylor should bring up his brigade and prepare, with our infantry supporting us, to charge the men behind the stone fence and on to the batteries in the distance. Turning to the ravine behind us, I saw a column of infantry already on the march towards us, and this was General Taylor's brigade, which was following him."[34]

Taylor had only a moment to study the ground. "There was scarcely time to mark [the] features before the head of my column appeared, when it was filed to the left, close to the base of the ridge, for protection from the plunging fire. Meanwhile the Rockbridge battery held on manfully and engaged the enemy's attention." Taylor suggested that Jackson move to a less exposed place, but he ignored the advice. As Taylor's brigade marched toward the left in column of fours, they passed a gap in the ridge. Spotting them, the Federal artillery adjusted its fire to rake the Louisianans. Several were hit, and instinctively the men ducked their heads. The martinet in Taylor got the better of him, and he barked: "What the hell are you dodging for? If there is any more of it, you will be halted under this fire for an hour!" The effect was instantaneous. Looking "as if they had swallowed ramrods, the men straightened up and closed ranks. But the cursing drew Taylor a reproach from Jackson. "I shall never forget the look of surprise on Jackson's face. He placed his hand on my shoulder, said, in a gentle voice, 'I am afraid you are a wicked fellow,' then turned and rode [off]."[35]

Left to himself, Taylor faced his column to the front and brought it out of the ravine. That occasioned considerable pushing and shoving with the 10th Virginia, as Taylor lacked the room needed to form his entire brigade in line of battle. He threw one regiment in front of the 10th, blocking its field of fire. Warren complained to Fulkerson, who told him to file to the left and form on Taylor's left flank. The 37th Virginia drew up on Taylor's right and slightly to his rear.[36]

For an instant Taylor's thoughts strayed from the approaching carnage. The fog had lifted, and "it was a lovely Sabbath morning. The clear, pure atmosphere brought Blue Ridge and Allegheny and Massanutten almost overhead. Even the clouds of murderous smoke from the guns made beautiful spirals in the air, and the broad fields of luxuriant wheat glistened with dew." Taylor fixed his distracted gaze on a bluebird, "bearing a worm in his beak. Birdie had been on the warpath and was carrying home spoil." Then he returned to the matter at hand. "The proper ground gained, the column faced to the front and began the ascent. As we mounted we came in full view of the army, whose efforts in other quarters had been slackened to await the result of our movement, and I felt an anxiety amounting to pain for the brigade to acquit itself handsomely."[37]

At 7:30 A.M. Taylor's brigade started forward. A gentle swell, two ravines, and a stone wall lay between three thousand Louisianans and the 2nd Massachusetts on Bower's Hill, the only Federal soldiers in their path. As Taylor suspected, all heads had turned toward him. McHenry Howard remembered: "We saw his brigade emerge in a fine line of battle at right angles with the enemy's line." John Worsham said: "General Taylor rode in front of his brigade, drawn sword in hand, occasionally turning his horse, at other times merely turning in his saddle to see that his line was up. They marched up the hill in perfect order, not firing a shot. About half way to the Yankees he gave in a loud and commanding voice that I am sure the Yankees heard, the order to charge!"[38]

Among the Federals, Maj. Wilder Dwight had been the first field-grade officer to discern the impending attack. "I happened to notice one or two mounted officers of the enemy pointing and gesticulating in the direction of our right flank and suggested to Colonel Andrews whether they did not mean to send round a force to flank us. He seemed to think it probable." Dwight rode forward to have a better look. Dismounting he crouched behind the stone wall with the skirmishers from Companies D and G and scanned the horizon for Rebels. He caught sight of Taylor's column passing to the Confederate left at the same moment Cothran's battery spotted it. Andrews told Dwight to report the movement to Gordon, whom the major found astride his mount midway between the brigade front line and the 29th Pennsylvania and 27th Indiana regiments. Gordon blinked. Rather than move at once to counter the apparent buildup, he told Dwight to go back to the wall and count the enemy. Dwight returned to find that two regiments already had passed. Back to Gordon he galloped. Definitely concerned now, Gordon told Dwight to tell Andrews to throw back his right flank while he advanced the 29th Pennsylvania and 27th Indiana along Bower's Hill to Andrews's right.[39]

By then it was too late. Taylor's charging Louisianans easily overwhelmed both regiments. The 27th Indiana had reached the field first. "In much less time than it requires to relate it we were in line and moving by the right flank, in column of fours at a double quick," said the regimental historian. The 27th followed the trace of a ravine up Bower's Hill, on which the 2nd Massachusetts was fighting alone. The first Hoosier killed was a Corporal Michael of Company A. "An immense musket ball struck him squarely in the forehead, opening a hole in his skull an inch in diameter. We were obliged to break ranks somewhat to avoid stepping upon him, as he writhed in the convulsions of death." As they passed over the rise, a stunning panorama of massed men in gray greeted the Indianans "as far as the eye extended. Unquestionably, a year or so later a single glance at such an overwhelming force would have satisfied both officers and men of the stupendous folly of engaging it. But it is well said that new troops do not know when they are whipped. If anyone among us had any thought that the enemy was too strong for us he certainly did not reveal it by any word or sign."[40]

In their eagerness to reach the protection of the stone wall, officers and men forgot the niceties of military formations. Most started for it as fast as they were able to run. Not a few, however, paused to fire before settling in behind the wall. There the men reloaded and fired furiously. "The line officers urged the men vehemently to hurry, but also to be careful to aim correctly," related the regimental historian. Not that there was much chance of missing. Taylor's Louisianans were packed so tightly that even wild shots found their mark. Sgt. Edmund Brown was surprised to see how many Rebels were hit: "A large number were falling down. Some dropped all in a heap, some turned half way round and fell sideways, some fell forward, some backward, some fell prone on the ground, while others caught themselves on their hands. A still larger number were dropping their guns and starting to the rear, most of them clapping both hands to the place where they were hit. It was but a momentary glance, taken while loading, but what it revealed can never be effaced from memory."

Col. Silas Colgrove had little chance to study the effects of his regiment's volleys. No sooner had the 29th Pennsylvania filed past the rear of the 27th Indiana than a troubling sight caught Colgrove's eye: "At about this juncture, and before the 29th Pennsylvania had fired a gun, the enemy's left regiment from the line of battle formed into column and marched left in front until it had flanked the 29th on the right, and then marched by the right flank in column by company with the evident intention of getting in its rear. From the conformation of the ground I was satisfied that this movement, although in plain view of the position occupied by myself, was entirely screened from the observation of Colonel [John K.] Murphy."

Colgrove sent a courier to his fellow regimental commander, who fell back twenty paces. Colgrove then occupied himself with retiring his two right companies to bring them into contact with Murphy's left. As he did so, he realized that the other eight companies were falling back. Colgrove ran toward them (Gordon had issued orders that field-grade officers go into battle on foot, a senseless command that badly hampered their ability to control their regiments); here and there he succeeded in getting a cluster of men to face about and fire. Lt. Col. Abisha L. Morrison appeared and explained that Gordon's aide-de-camp had brought him an order to retreat. Morrison and Colgrove were barely on speaking terms, and the lieutenant colonel had taken it upon himself to give the order.

Colgrove acceded to the inevitable: "I regret to say that the coolness that had marked every action of the regiment in advancing in the face of the enemy and receiving and returning his fire until the time the retreat was ordered was by degrees lost." Colgrove understated matters; an officer in the 2nd Massachusetts observed that the 27th "broke and ran, every man for himself." The Hoosiers had managed three ragged volleys before breaking and had accounted for a fair share of the fourteen Louisianans killed and eighty-nine wounded in Taylor's charge.[41]

The 29th Pennsylvania withdrew on the heels of the 27th Indiana. Its position had been untenable from the start. Colonel Murphy had had no choice but to pull his line back to meet the flanking movement to which Colgrove had alerted him (Murphy said that a bit of late fog arising from the damp ground had blinded him to it). In so doing, he had marched the regiment into a gully—the enemy in front and a rocky extension of Bower's Hill studded with bushes behind. The 29th traded one or two volleys with Taylor's Louisianans, but Murphy knew better than to prolong the hopeless contest. When the Rebels raised a yell—"deafening cheers," recollected Murphy—he gave the order to fall back. The Pennsylvanians clawed their way out of the gully, bullets ricocheting off rocks at every step.[42]

Not everyone heard the order. Pvt. John B. Buchanan of Company A said that his company commander only become aware of it when a man cried out, "Captain, they are all retreating!" Looking around, the captain answered, "Yes, and I guess it is every man for himself, and the devil take the hindmost!" Buchanan saw the head of the Rebel flanking column emerge from a patch of woods. "Here they come," he shouted. "I am going to have a shot at them!" Buchanan and a comrade each squeezed off three rounds, then started for the rear. Buchanan paused to help a man whose pants were caught on a fence. "I pulled the board back and released him, threw my gun over the fence, and just as I got on top a squadron of cavalry rushed past. I waited to see what they were going to do. They formed line as they reached the top of Bower's Hill and commenced firing. A horse came back, and as he passed me I saw a man was dragged with his foot in the stirrup. At almost every jump the horse appeared to kick him." Buchanan resumed his flight. "I jumped down and picked up my gun. Fortunately there was a road opposite, and I took it. Being a good sprinter I soon caught up to the comrade I released from the fence. It was my own brother." Buchanan and his brother escaped, but Taylor's brigade engulfed and captured Colonel Murphy and some two hundred members of the 29th Pennsylvania.[43]

The collapse of the 29th Pennsylvania and the 27th Indiana forced Colonel Andrews to withdraw the 2nd Massachusetts. The regiment got off well ahead of the enemy and in good order, marching rearward in column by companies.

The disciplined ranks of the 2nd suggested a premature withdrawal, and Colonel Gordon collared Andrews with the question, "Why are you falling back?" "I can't help it," replied Andrews, pointing to where his right flank had rested. Gordon understood: "It was true. With his right uncovered, it would have been madness to remain." He told Andrews to move on, then rode away to see that Colonel Ruger pulled back the 3rd Wisconsin, which he did in equally good order.[44]

It took considerable nerve for the soldiers of the 2nd Massachusetts to keep their places in the ranks. "As we passed off the hill the enemy rose on its crest," said Major Dwight. "Their cracking and whistling fire followed us closely. I recollected an unmailed letter in my pocket, and preferring to have it unread, rather than read by hostile eyes, I tore it up as we went down the hill. A few of our men would turn and fire up the hill, reloading as they went on. I delayed a little to applaud their spunk."[45]

Although fired from short range, most of the Rebel shots sailed harmlessly overhead; had it been otherwise, a Massachusetts lieutenant attested, his regiment would have been destroyed. As it was, a good many men fell. Said the lieutenant: "It was cruel to see our poor fellows shot through the back and pitch forward on their faces as we marched down the hill."[46]

The cavalry that had thundered past Private Buchanan and formed atop Bower's Hill behind the recently abandoned position of the 29th Pennsylvania comprised four companies of the 1st Michigan. General Williams was with them. He and the regimental commander tried to fashion a new line of resistance around the troopers, who had drawn rein behind a low stone wall.

Their efforts were futile. The routes of retreat of the 2nd Massachusetts and the 3rd Wisconsin took those regiments too far east of Williams's scratch line for their commanders—who were proceeding under orders from Banks that all units retire to the north side of Winchester for a stand—even to be aware that the line existed. Colonel Ruger ushered the 3rd Wisconsin into town on Braddock Street, then turned onto Main Street near the Taylor Hotel. There the regiment split, both wings emerging from the town intact. Colonel Andrews led the 2nd Massachusetts up Washington Street in relative calm. At one point he called a halt to dress ranks and redeploy from company column to column of fours for the hike through Winchester.[47]

The only troops near enough to answer Williams's summons were those of the 27th Indiana and 29th Pennsylvania, and they were too demoralized to hold a line. "I dashed at them with such of my staff as were with me and made all sorts of appeals to rally them," Williams said. "The men would stop for a while, but before I could get them in line a new batch of fugitives would break all my efforts." As the last of the infantry slipped past him and disappeared into the fenced yards and back streets of Winchester, Williams ordered the 1st Michigan Cavalry to charge Taylor's compact ranks. The troopers leaped the stone wall and formed on the brow of the hill just in time to receive a concentrated volley of 1,500 muskets. The natural consequence of his stupid command appalled Williams: "The air seemed literally to be full of whizzing bullets, which stirred up currents of wind as if the atmosphere had suddenly been filled with some invisible cooling process. The cavalry could do nothing before such an overwhelming force, and it went down in great rapidity. I stopped just long enough to know I could see nothing of value in front." Putting spurs to his horse, Williams galloped down a narrow lane into town.[48]

Northern resistance west of the Valley Pike ended at 9:30 A.M. Winder brought his brigade forward in line of battle in an effort to overtake Taylor and have a chance at the Yankees, but they fled too fast. The inveterate scrounger Lt. McHenry Howard at least got something from the beaten foe: "In passing over where the Federal line had been I observed a fine officer's greatcoat—the long detachable cape with red flannel—lying on the ground, with a little dog on it. I dismounted, routed the dog, and secured it."[49]

The leisurely retreat of the 3rd Wisconsin had confounded Jackson; he had to show the Yankees that they were beaten. Yelling "Forward after the enemy," he ordered Elzey's four regiments down the turnpike after them. Jackson normally was not one for shouting, but on this occasion excitement got the better of him. "Now," he bellowed to his staff while swinging his plain gray kepi in his hand, "Let's shout!" In an instant, recollected Jed Hotchkiss, Jackson galloped off the ridge to take his place at the head of Elzey's column. Raising himself in the stirrups, Jackson urged the infantry to "Press forward to the Potomac." "That was thirty miles away," mused Hotchkiss, "and thirty hours had passed since he or they had rested."[50]

EAST OF THE Valley Pike the fog lifted at 9:00 A.M. It rose "as a curtain," recalled Brig. Gen. Isaac Trimble, "displaying everything, houses and the enemy's troops, in full view in the bright sunshine, as inspiring a battle scene as ever was witnessed."[51] Bradley T. Johnson was determined to be more than a mere witness, declaring as the day cleared: "I shall not wait for orders any longer, but will join that [Taylor's] charge if I live." With the command, "Forward, double quick," he led the 1st Maryland (Confederate) straight for Donnelly's brigade.[52]

General Trimble also wanted decisive action. While the fog yet lay heavy on the field, Trimble had brought forward the 16th Mississippi and the 15th Alabama, so his brigade line of battle extended well beyond Donnelly's right flank. As soon as the mist burned off, he begged Ewell to permit him to advance his brigade in column formation east of Town Run in order first to outflank Donnelly and then to place himself astride the Martinsburg Pike north of Winchester—a mile-and-a-half sprint through wet wheat fields that Trimble was certain his men could make.

Ewell withheld permission pending the return of a staff officer he had sent to confirm the success of Taylor's charge. By the time he returned and Ewell gave Trimble permission, Donnelly had ordered a retreat at General Williams's request. With far less ground to cover, and that by good streets through Winchester, there could be little doubt that Donnelly would reach the Martinsburg Pike first. But Trimble's blood was up, and Ewell let him try. With a yell the 15th Alabama splashed across Abram's Creek.[53]

In his report of the battle, Stonewall Jackson conceded that in negotiating the streets of Winchester, the Federals "preserved their organization remarkably well." But neither he nor any other Southern officer spoke of a most shameful impediment to the enemy's flight—gunfire directed at the Yankees from the windows and doors of homes and shops, much of it by the good women of Winchester.

Union sources, on the other hand, vividly and convincingly described the torment. Muskets, pistols, glass bottles, a pan of scalding water—whatever came to hand was aimed at passing Yankees, particularly stragglers. Women were heard to scream epithets, among the milder of which was "Down with the damned Yankees, kill 'em."

Col. David Strother counted at least twenty shots fired from houses and yards. Drawing rein near a hydrant at which several soldiers had paused to drink, he saw a muzzle flash from a gateway and one of the men fall over in the gutter, mortally wounded. A rapid crackling of pistol shots diverted his gaze down the street in time to see another man drop. While galloping down a side street, General Williams was saluted with a shot from a second-story window that just missed his aide. The lieutenant colonel of the 8th New York Cavalry escaped four pistol shots a woman fired at him from a window, giving rise to a joke among the regiment's officers that their lieutenant colonel was bullet-proof. A correspondent for the *Philadelphia Press* saw a cavalryman who was wounded in the foot stop to rest on the steps of a house. A woman opened the door and asked if he was able to walk. When the man said no, the woman asked to see his revolver. The soldier innocently gave it to her. Holding it to his head, she demanded that he leave her steps. As he limped away, the woman shot him in the back.

Here and there Federals fought back against their civilian assailants. A Corporal Thompson of the 8th New York Cavalry shot the woman who had fired at Colonel Babbitt; Thompson "could see the blood spurt from her breast as the ball struck her, and she fell instantly." Corporals George C. Peoples of the 46th Pennsylvania and James Kearyon of the 27th Indiana later testified that they returned the fire of armed citizens. Cpl. Charles S. Curtis of the 3rd Wisconsin discharged his weapon at a "she-demon" who had shot a man from his company. That night Curtis and his companions swore a "solemn oath to be avenged for the murder of our comrades. As the women of Winchester forgot on the day of our retreat that they were women, so shall we forget when we return. Forbearance in the Valley of Virginia has ceased to be a virtue."[54]

Jackson gave the Federals credit for an orderly withdrawal. Having seen the 3rd Wisconsin and 2nd Massachusetts enter Winchester in good order, he assumed that other Union regiments also had held together well. But the 27th Indiana and the survivors of the 29th Pennsylvania stumbled into town as a mob. As the first regiment of Donnelly's brigade to withdraw, the 46th Pennsylvania quit the field intact and negotiated its way down Market Street without much difficulty. On the other hand, the 28th New York and the 5th Connecticut found themselves in a foot race with Winder's Virginians, who entered Winchester at the same time. Volleys fired from cross streets fragmented both regiments, with a company or two shearing off at each discharge. "As we went scurrying through Winchester the Johnnies were whooping it up in a parallel street," a Connecticut man recollected, "and we were going it neck and neck."[55] General Williams found that it took "great efforts to stop a stampede, especially as the early fugitives had been joined by several unarmed sick from Shields's division, who were scattering alarm with great vigor. These, with a great number of wagons and sutlers and civilians and some army conveyances were whipping and hallooing and creating great alarm." Lt. John M. Gould of the 10th Maine said that a "perfect mob of soldiers, infantry and cavalry" frustrated the efforts of his colonel to form a regimental line across Braddock Street.[56]

Fear that Winchester might be engulfed in flames fueled the panic. A rundown wooden building near the Taylor Hotel went up in smoke when Yankee quartermaster staffers were unable to haul away the stores. After stuffing their haversacks with whatever supplies they could carry, troopers from the 5th New York Cavalry had helped set the structure ablaze. The flames quickly spread to adjacent warehouses and claimed at least two homes on Market Street before Confederate soldiers extinguished the blaze. From the wreckage the victors saved valuable medical stores, along with an ample stock of ammunition and sutlers' merchandise.[57]

Any hope Jackson may have entertained of mounting a close pursuit with his infantry dissolved amid the bedlam in Winchester. Exhaustion claimed whole regiments. Col. James W. Allen had entered town at the head of not only his own 2nd Virginia, but also a good portion of the 5th Virginia. When he reached the railroad depot at the northern edge of Winchester, he discovered that only a handful of men from either regiment had kept up with him.[58] The 1st Maryland (Confederate) made it as far as the Taylor Hotel. There Colonel Johnson detached part of the regiment to help put out the flames that threatened to engulf the place, and uniformed Marylanders joined with civilian men and boys in dragging wagons from the firehouse and passing buckets of water. When a citizen told Johnson that the notorious Porte Crayon was a guest at the hotel, Johnson detailed a company to surround and search the premises. In fact, Strother had escaped just five minutes ahead of the enemy. With Colonel Johnson distracted, those not engaged in firefighting or hunting for Yankee brass wandered off in search of spoils, of which there were plenty. "We found delicacies of every description, sutlers' stores crowded with everything we wanted," Capt. John E. H. Post told his mother, "and as we were unable to pursue the enemy on account of the fatigued condition of our men, we had the benefit of them"[59]

Regiments determined to push on had wrestled with throngs of cheering civilians. Windows were thrown open and long-hidden Confederate banners unfurled. Shouts of "Thank God, we are free—Thank God, we are free once more!" mingled with hurrahs for Jeff Davis and Stonewall Jackson. The filthy aspect of the army went unnoticed in the general thanksgiving. One pretty girl was heard to exclaim, "Oh, you brave, noble, ragged, dirty darlings you! I am so glad to see you." General Elzey told Mary Greenhow Lee it had brought tears to his eyes to hear one old woman bless Jackson and the Confederate army. Women and girls with buckets of cold water and milk and baskets of bread and cakes crowded the pavement, insisting the soldiers pause for refreshments. Some darted in and out of the ranks giving hugs and planting kisses. Among the women, the transition from murder to domesticity was the work of a moment.

Abandoned wagons also proved obstacles to an orderly passage through the town. Many men slipped from the ranks to ransack them. David Earhart of the 4th Virginia supplemented crackers he had accepted from the ladies with a handful of sugar scooped from a burst commissary barrel—the first food he had tasted in twenty-four hours. Artilleryman Randolph Fairfax secured a gum blanket, a Yankee overcoat, a pair of Yankee pants, and a haversack. His haul was typical. "Our troops are loaded with Yankee plunder," he wrote his brother afterward, "and rigged out in Yankee clothes to such an extent that an order had to be issued forbidding them to be worn, for fear that it might give rise to mistakes and lead to firing on our own men."[60]

Most of Jackson's infantry did clear Winchester and try to give chase out the Martinsburg Pike, but in the fields north of town they found only discarded equipment, burning wagons, and a corporal's guard of stragglers. Jackson ordered a halt after five miles, and the Valley army bivouacked at the unheard-of-hour of noon. It was just as well; hardly a man had the strength to do more than lay out his bedroll.

Utterly exhausted himself, Jackson returned to Winchester and secured a room at the Taylor Hotel. Refusing all offers of food, he threw himself across a bed with his clothes, boots, and even spurs on, and was soon fast asleep.[61]

There had been a chance to damage horribly, if not annihilate, Banks's command, and a force on hand—idle and reasonably well-rested—to have done it. The 2nd and 9th Virginia Cavalry regiments, with General Steuart at their head, had passed the morning lounging along the Millwood Pike three miles east of Winchester, while their mounts grazed in nearby clover fields.

As he exited Winchester with two or three artillery batteries and watched Banks's beaten troops stream northward, Jackson reportedly wailed: "Never was there such a chance for cavalry. Oh, that my cavalry was in place." Richard

Taylor agreed: "Past the town, we could see the enemy flying north on the Martinsburg road. Cavalry, of which there was a considerable force with the army, might have reaped a rich harvest."[62]

Needing cavalry, Jackson thought first of Turner Ashby. But the Virginia cavalier was nowhere to be found. With undisguised contempt, Jackson later reported: "I had seen but some fifty of Ashby's cavalry since prior to the pillaging scenes of the previous evening, and none since an early hour of the past night." For three miles Jackson accompanied the Rockbridge and Hampden artilleries down the Martinsburg Pike, pausing with them as they unlimbered to fire a few rounds whenever a good firing position offered itself, and hoping at any instant to see Ashby's troopers appear to give chase. At 10:00 A.M., having lost all hope in Ashby, Jackson told his aide-de-camp, Sandie Pendleton, to find Steuart. He gave Pendleton a simple order for Steuart: the Marylander was to "move as rapidly as possible and join me on the Martinsburg Turnpike, and carry on the pursuit of the enemy with vigor."[63]

Pendleton returned to Winchester. His inquiries were fruitless; no one had seen Steuart. Pendleton next sought out Ewell, under whose command Steuart was acting. He missed Ewell but found the cavalry. Not seeing Steuart, Pendleton spat out Jackson's orders. Flournoy refused to obey; Steuart had ordered Flournoy not to move without him. Galloping another half mile out the Millwood Pike, Pendleton at last came upon Steuart, only to meet with a second refusal to obey Jackson's orders. Steuart was very sorry, but the order must come through his immediate superior, General Ewell. Pendleton was incredulous. Surely Steuart must understand that the order from Jackson was "peremptory and immediate." But Steuart was obdurate and not to be persuaded by a mere lieutenant. In despair Pendleton set off to find Ewell, praying Steuart in the meantime would have the good sense to reconsider.

A two-mile gallop brought Pendleton to Ewell. Campbell Brown watched the young Virginian beg Ewell to order Steuart forward. Brown said that Ewell was "much irritated at this ill-timed scrupulosity" on Steuart's part and "wondered that he had not set off immediately on hearing Jackson's orders." Ewell probably also recognized his own error in not having put Steuart to work himself. Campbell Brown said neither he nor Ewell had realized that Steuart was under Ewell's command, a most unconvincing apology for his chief's negligence.

Whether he had been aware of his responsibilities or not, Ewell now gave Pendleton the oral orders he sought. On his return ride Pendleton found

Steuart with his staff, riding not toward the enemy but rather "slowly after me toward Ewell." Pendleton delivered Ewell's order. "This satisfied him. He rode back to his command, had them mounted, and moved off toward Stephenson's Depot."[64]

From Stephenson's Depot Steuart pushed on halfheartedly as far as Martinsburg, gathering in stragglers and jabbing with part of his force at the Yankee rear guard, but doing little real damage. One attempt to disrupt the Federal retreat near Bunker Hill was almost comical. A group of fifty walking wounded and sick troops, along with a few stragglers, had laid down in a wood to rest when they were suddenly surrounded by twice their number of Rebel cavalry and called upon to surrender. Instead, the Federals grabbed their rifles, fixed bayonets, and drove the enemy troopers out of the timber. So feeble was Steuart's pursuit that General Hatch later doubted that even a single regiment of Rebel cavalry had been in the Union rear. For his part, Steuart considered his command too weak to risk an attack. By the time he reached Martinsburg that was true, as by then Banks had his force well in hand.

Near Bunker Hill, Ashby had joined Steuart with one hundred men of his command—the rest were either too tired, or their mounts too worn out, to take part in a fight. In Ashby's defense, he and his troopers had been in the saddle at least eighteen hours a day for nearly a week. The Southern cavalrymen had to pace their horses more carefully than did their enemy, for whom government animals were generally in good supply. The Rebels provided their own mounts; if a man's horse broke down, he was responsible for finding, stealing, or capturing another.

And where had Ashby been during the battle with the one hundred men left to him? He never offered Jackson a satisfactory explanation, merely saying that he had "moved to the enemy's left for the purpose of cutting off a portion of his force."

That Steuart and Ashby could have accomplished much with their eight hundred men, at least at the beginning of the Federal retreat, is undeniable. Immediately north of Winchester the ground was an open plain, perhaps two miles wide, sloping downward in the direction of Stephenson's Depot. There the Northerners were most vulnerable. Most Union eyewitnesses asserted that the infantry passed over the plain in good order. But with the "artillery, cavalry, and niggers in the advance," said the bandleader of the 3rd Wisconsin, "all was confusion and excitement."[65]

The cavalry and artillery pushed their way to the front regardless of the consequences. Recollected a Wisconsin lieutenant: "Cavalrymen in fright ran over and knocked down foot soldiers, and woe betide the footman who did not get out of the way when the artillery galloped through the throng." The Union infantry marched in three columns. Moving over the fields west of the Valley Pike, the 10th Maine Infantry protected the army's left flank. Gordon's regiments withdrew down the turnpike. Donnelly's brigade marched east of the turnpike and guarded the right flank. Between and behind the columns mingled stragglers and noncombatants.

The apparent orderliness of the infantry in crossing the open ground was deceptive. As General Williams explained, "There is a strange sympathy in courage and in fear, and masses seem to partake of one or the other feeling from the slightest cause." Two or three aggressive squadrons of Rebel cavalry would have been cause enough to tip the balance toward panic. But none came, and Williams and his staff succeeded in restoring order to the stragglers in the first stand of woods north of Winchester. "From this onward to Martinsburg even the leading rabble marched coolly and in quiet," a much-relieved Williams reported.[66]

General Banks also had a hand in rallying the troops. Having expected defeat at Winchester, Banks was mentally prepared for the challenge of the retreat. He moved among the men confidently, and his presence reassured the fainthearted, or at least most of them. The adjutant of the 3rd Wisconsin recorded one sharp-tongued exception: "Banks made an appeal to the soldiery to rally and make a stand 'My God, men, don't you love your country?' he pleaded. 'Yes,' said one, near the writer, 'and I am trying to get to it as fast as I can.' "[67]

Of Banks's success with stragglers and wavering units, Colonel Donnelly wrote afterward: "Confusion and disorder was [sic] not of long duration. General Banks, riding continually among the men, and addressing them kindly and firmly, shamed them to a consideration of their unbefitting consternation. At length, stationing himself and staff with several others across a field through which the soldiers were rapidly fleeing, the men were ordered to stop their flight, were formed into line, and made to march on more in a soldier-like manner."

Lt. Josiah C. Williams of the 27th Indiana put the matter more simply: "After getting a couple of miles beyond Winchester, General Banks succeeded in rallying a good many. The general, making a patriotic little address, with the news of reinforcements coming, made us make a pretty good retreat." Wisconsin lieutenant Julian Hinkley thought General Banks had done "all that lay in the power of any man to bring off his men without loss." Indeed he had, agreed the regimental bandleader: "The retreat was said to be the best ever made during this campaign. All confidence is now placed in our noble commander, General Banks. All now look upon him as the right man for the right place." Without a doubt, a New York correspondent told the homefolk, "General Banks, during the whole of the battle and retreat, showed himself to be a man and a general who cared for his men and worked singly with them. He managed the retreat nobly and has inspired new faith in the soldiers for him."[68]

Banks intended no deceit when he harangued the men with the promise of reinforcements. Train whistles from the direction of Stephenson's Depot suggested to everyone, Banks included, that help was near. That hope was buoyed when, a few minutes later, two squadrons of cavalry cantered up the turnpike. But they belonged to the 1st Maryland (Union) Cavalry, which had escorted the wagons out of Winchester earlier that morning; Banks thought it best not to reveal their identity.[69]

Anticipating a monumental traffic jam when the army and its huge wagon train reached the south bank of the Potomac opposite Williamsport, Banks told Donnelly at Bunker Hill to divert the 5th Connecticut and 28th New York onto a parallel road to the river crossing at Dam No. 4. Both regiments negotiated the remaining fifteen miles to the river without incident.[70]

Banks and his staff reached Martinsburg at 1:30 P.M. The general called a halt until 5:00 P.M., when the last of the army stumbled into town. The rest did more harm than good, said Lieutenant Gould of the 10th Maine, because tired limbs cramped and stiffened. At 2:40 P.M. Banks had sat down at the telegraph office to update Stanton. He gave the secretary an accurate, unadorned summary of the fight at Winchester and an upbeat appraisal of the army's prospects: "The Rebels attacked us this morning at daybreak in great force. Their number was estimated at fifteen thousand, consisting of Ewell's and Jackson's divisions. . . . Our trains are in advance and will cross the river in safety."[71]

After resting briefly at Staub's Hotel, Banks rejoined the retreat. At 5:30 P.M. he wrote a second telegram to the War Department, reporting that a prisoner just captured said that Jackson was to be reinforced for the purpose of invading Maryland by way of Harpers Ferry and Williamsport. Nevertheless, Banks told Stanton, "We [shall] all pass the Potomac tonight safe—men, trains, and all, I think, making a march of thirty-five miles."[72]

At the Potomac that night Banks continued his efforts to boost morale. They were sorely needed. The river at the Williamsport crossing was three hundred feet wide, and recent rains had swollen the ford to a depth of nearly five feet. The descent into the river was exceedingly muddy, and only the strongest animals could resist the swift current. Scores drowned. Only a single scow was on hand to ferry the army across. Banks had the wagon train corralled on the broad, open plain above the riverbank—"in a convenient position for burning, provided such a measure should become necessary," observed a New York lieutenant—and set about ferrying the sick and wounded over first. He did what a good commander should under the circumstances, making himself visible and accessible to the men. Banks offered both words of encouragement and a strong shoulder when necessary.

Praise for his performance was general. "When the teams were crossing the river and getting stuck, horses and mules drowning, he took hold, lifted, and tugged in every way to give aid," attested a New York soldier. A Wisconsin officer said: "General Banks was untiring in his efforts to bring our train safely over, even riding into the water to save mules that had lost their footing and were in danger of drowning."[73]

Reassuring words could go only so far in comforting a defeated army that had retreated thirty-five miles in less than twelve hours. The last of the infantry staggered into makeshift camps near the water's edge at about 11:00 P.M. With regimental wagons corralled, or in some cases lost, food was scarce and a cup of coffee worth its weight in gold. The crossing of able-bodied men began in earnest at 2:00 A.M. "The night, on whichever side of the river it was passed, was very cold," an Indianan recorded. "The writer is willing to put it down in black and white that, all in all, it was the most uncomfortable night he has ever seen. Utterly exhausted, apparently not able to take another step, every joint, muscle, and tendon in his body as sore as a blood boil, an inordinate, sickening craving for food, too much overcome with sleepiness to be able to stay awake, even when standing up or moving around, seemingly on the point of freezing to death, and withal, low-spirited and discouraged, what could add to one's misery?"[74]

Nevertheless, Banks had extricated himself competently from a perilous predicament. If anyone was demoralized by defeat, it was not Banks. One of his first acts on the morning of May 26 was to telegraph Stanton assurances of the army's well-being: "We believe that our whole force, trains and all, will cross in safety. The men are in fine spirits and crossing in good order. The enemy . . . has not made his appearance this morning." At midday the last of the Union army crossed the Potomac. With understandable pride he told the president that afternoon: "The substantial preservation of the entire supply train is a source of gratification. It numbered about five hundred wagons. On a forced march of fifty-three miles, thirty-five of which were performed in one day, subject to constant attack, not more than fifty wagons were lost."

Despite enjoying a four-to-one superiority in numbers, Jackson had not destroyed Banks's army. At Winchester only the 29th Pennsylvania and 27th Indiana had been roughly handled; in Donnelly's brigade, not a single man had been killed. Banks spoke the truth when he reported: "My command had not suffered an attack and rout, but had accomplished a premeditated march of nearly sixty miles in the face of the enemy, defeating his plans and giving him battle wherever he was found."[75]

The losses at Winchester are difficult to calculate. Union reports lumped together casualties incurred at Front Royal, on the retreat of March 24, and at the battle of and retreat from Winchester. Total Federal casualties for the three days were 71 killed, 243 wounded, and 1,714 missing. Many of those listed as missing later turned up, having wandered the Virginia countryside between Winchester and the Potomac River for days. Perhaps 800 were captured at Winchester or gathered up by Confederate cavalry during the retreat—a considerable number, but by no means a crippling blow. For the three days of fighting, Jackson reported casualties of 68 killed and 329 wounded, with just 3 men reported missing. Jackson claimed to have taken 3,050 prisoners, nearly a third being sick or wounded men found in Union army hospitals at Strasburg and Winchester. Of far greater importance than the number of prisoners taken was the seizure of 9,354 stands of small arms, half a million rounds of ammunition, 34,000 pounds of commissary stores, and $125,185 worth of quartermaster supplies.[76]

CHAPTER 23

A QUESTION OF LEGS

For Federal officials in Washington, May 25 was a day of nervous expectation, tinged with panic. At the War Department the morning began with a frantic warning from Banks's aide-de-camp Col. John S. Clark, then at Harpers Ferry. There had been no word from Banks since 7:00 A.M., Clark informed Secretary Stanton, and the last dispatch received told of the army's retreat from Winchester. After enumerating the scant forces on hand—two regiments of Pennsylvania Infantry and fifteen companies of cavalry—Clark advised that, although there were many conflicting rumors, "all agree that the enemy intend to attack Harper's Ferry."[1]

President Lincoln took the news from Harpers Ferry in stride. He telegraphed Secretary Chase, who had not yet left Falmouth, that it appeared Banks had arrived at Winchester on the night of the twenty-fourth and was this morning retreating to Harpers Ferry (Banks was, in fact, retiring toward Williamsport). Jackson and Ewell undoubtedly were in pursuit; not a cause for undue alarm, Lincoln added, but rather for McDowell to press his preparations to cut them off. Concluded Lincoln: "I hope he will put all possible energy and speed into the effort."[2]

Crossing the wires with Lincoln's admonition was a telegram from Chase addressed to Stanton received at 10:15 A.M. It gave the welcome news that Shields's division already had broken camp and was then on the march to Catlett's Station; Rufus King's division would follow as soon as the road was clear. Chase understood both the need for speed and for the generals designated to carry out Lincoln's objectives to have a clear understanding of their orders. "Would not time be saved by bringing General Shields to Washington for consultation?" the secretary of treasury asked Stanton. "His information and judgment are excellent, and his coming would not delay the movement of his division." By all means, answered Stanton, "Bring Shields along with you." Chase then asked if McDowell should command in person or remain at Falmouth. Stanton consulted with the president on the matter, and both agreed that McDowell should remain where he was and "send forward his best commander," a good indication that events in the Shenandoah Valley had not yet unduly troubled them.[3]

Chase's return telegram to Lincoln, received at the telegraph office between 11:20 A.M. and 12:10 P.M., undoubtedly cheered the chief executive. McDowell and his lieutenants were thinking better of the plan to trap Jackson. "General McDowell appreciates, as you do, the importance of the service he is called on to perform. All possible exertion is being made by him and the officers under him to expedite the movement." Chase expected to be back in Washington at 6:00 P.M. accompanied by Shields.[4]

While he awaited new word from the Valley, Lincoln took a moment to catch McClellan up on what had transpired in recent hours and to expand on his reasons for changing McDowell's orders. It appeared, he told McClellan, that Banks was "broken up in a total rout" (which proved to be false). But Lincoln expressed no fear for the safety of the capital and calmly reiterated that he had directed the movements of Frémont and McDowell not to avert a disaster, but rather to "get in the enemy's rear." Lincoln only alluded to a concern for the nation's capital in the concluding sentences of his letter: "Apprehensions of something like this, and no unwillingness to sustain you have always been my reason for withholding McDowell's [corps] from you. Please understand this, and do the best you can with the force you have."[5]

What gave Lincoln and Stanton their only real fright that day were the baleful reports that continued to come in from General Geary, who now had his headquarters at White Plains. They would have appeared fantastic had Geary not seemed so certain of his sources. The drumbeat of doom began at 9:50 A.M. with a telegram to Stanton warning that Confederate forces of indeterminate strength had boxed Geary in from the north, west, and south. That most unreliable of witnesses, a runaway slave, in whom Geary placed absolute faith, assured him that a large Rebel command—whether Jackson's or a new force, his informant could not say—was striking east from Ashby's Gap toward Leesburg.

A Southern army in the Valley strong enough to mount simultaneous thrusts north toward Williamsport and Harpers Ferry and east toward Leesburg would be a matter of the gravest concern. At 1:45 P.M. President Lincoln asked Geary for his "best present impression" of the enemy's strength north of Strasburg and Front Royal, and whether the enemy was "still moving north through the gap at Front Royal and between you and there?"[6]

Not only was the enemy still pouring through Ashby's Gap, Geary hastened to answer, but contrabands also told him that ten thousand Confederate cavalry had suddenly materialized near Warrenton and were thundering down on him.[7]

Trying to give an identity to Geary's phantom foe, Stanton suggested to McDowell that it might consist in part of Anderson's division, which had disappeared from the Fredericksburg front (Anderson actually had been recalled to Richmond). McDowell dismissed the notion. "I hope soon to be able to tell you more precisely where the enemy is. One thing is certain, that whether they left here to join Jackson or not they have not done so yet, and that all the grand masses Geary reports must come from some other place than here. They left here . . . with dread of being attacked."[8]

Neither Stanton nor Lincoln was comforted. During the afternoon of May 25, with no word from Banks and the alarms from Geary growing louder, both grew uneasy. Stanton lost his composure, issuing a ridiculous call for help to thirteen Northern governors that he probably regretted later. The appeal read: "Intelligence from various quarters leaves no doubt that the enemy in great force are marching on Washington. You will please organize and forward immediately all the militia and volunteer forces in your state." More alarming still was the dispatch he sent to the governors of Pennsylvania, Massachusetts, and Rhode Island: "Send all the troops forward that you can immediately. Banks is completely routed. The enemy are in large force advancing upon Harper's Ferry."[9]

Lincoln's unease over Geary's reports and his frustration with McClellan's apparent dithering on The Peninsula found voice in a 2:00 P.M. telegram to McClellan. The possibility that Confederate forces blanketed the country between Warrenton and Winchester caused Lincoln to reconsider the import of Jackson's Valley offensive. He wanted McClellan to remain on the Peninsula and attack—but to do so expeditiously. "I think the movement is a general and concerted one, such as would not be made if [the enemy] was acting upon the purpose of a very desperate defense of Richmond. I think the time is near when you must either attack Richmond or give up the job and come to the defense of Washington. Let me hear from you instantly."[10]

McClellan wrote back at once: "Telegram received. Independently of it, the time is very near when I shall attack Richmond. The object of the movement is probably to prevent reinforcements being sent to me. All the information from balloons, deserters, prisoners, and contrabands agrees in the statement that the mass of the rebel troops are still in the immediate vicinity of Richmond, ready to defend it." McClellan's appraisal of the situation was accurate, but what faith Lincoln placed in it cannot be said, as McClellan often had been wrong in his reading of enemy intentions.[11]

Banks's afternoon telegrams from Martinsburg eased administration fears. "Two of your telegrams have been received," Stanton confirmed to Banks. "They have greatly relieved our anxiety respecting your command." The news from Banks also enabled Lincoln and Stanton to review Geary's messages in a calmer light. The improbability of the scenarios Geary had sketched became apparent. By 8:40 P.M. the secretary of war felt confident enough of the situation to instruct Geary to hold his ground. "The reports from Banks show that he has probably secured himself by falling back from Winchester. Reinforcements have been sent forward. Frémont and McDowell are also under orders to operate against the enemy. McDowell will move toward Catlett's and will support you, so that there will be no occasion for you to fall back any further."

Geary remained dubious. At 12:10 P.M. the next day he warned Stanton that his scouts—evidently the most unreliable in the entire Union army—had reported that Jackson had slipped around Geary and advanced as far east as Middleburg with at least twenty thousand men. "This information is reliable." Twenty minutes later he added: "There are also heavy forces south of me, and I cannot hope successfully to resist the combining elements against me." But the secretary of war had taken Geary's measure, and he passed his latest alarms along to McDowell without comment.

The lamps burned late into the night of May 25 in the White House and the War Department. At 12:40 A.M. Lincoln concluded his circuit of the clock with a correct reading of the day's events to McClellan. "We have General Banks's official report. He has saved his army and baggage and has made a safe retreat to the river, and is probably safe at Williamsport. He reported the attacking force at 15,000."[12]

Outside of official Washington, reaction to Jackson's offensive was largely muted. Some governors responded to Stanton's call with alarming mobilization orders laced with florid verbiage they themselves may or may not have believed. Gov. John A. Andrew of Massachusetts proclaimed: "Men of Massachusetts! The wily and barbarous horde of traitors to the people, to the government, to our country, and to liberty, menace the national capital. . . . The whole active militia will be summoned [and] will march to relieve and avenge their brethren and friends." To the "Gallant Men of Ohio," Governor David Todd announced "the astounding intelligence that the seat of our beloved government is threatened with invasion." Perhaps Todd doubted the danger, as he prefaced telegrams to county military boards with the words, "Astonishing as the fact may be Washington City is in imminent danger." Nonetheless, he added, only men willing to proceed to Washington voluntarily would be asked to do so.

Gubernatorial rhetoric had little parallel in the press. The *Boston Daily Advertiser* reported "ferment" in Boston attributable more to the militia assembling on Boston Commons than to fears for the safety of Washington. The *Philadelphia Inquirer* assured its readers: "Strategic combinations, well made, have doubtless been in a slight degree disconcerted by the hurried retreat of General Banks. . . . But it is very improbable that any permanent damage has been done." In Pennsylvania towns nearer Harpers Ferry, the excitement proved fleeting. The *Chambersburg Valley Spirit* on May 28 reported that Monday, May 25, had been "a day of excitement to a degree not witnessed before during this war. At an early hour the drums were out and large crowds were collected on all the corners. . . . Many of our most patriotic citizens at once commenced getting up volunteer companies to proceed to Washington." But there no longer was cause for alarm. "We do not consider that the rebels have gained any permanent advantage by this little flash of victory for them. It only goes to show the desperation of their cause. . . . They may perhaps again destroy a portion of the Baltimore and Ohio Railroad and burn a bridge or two, but that will be the extent of the injuries before they in their turn are driven back."[13]

In the *New York Times* of May 26, the story of Banks's defeat and Stanton's proclamation was buried on page eight. No alarm was reported in that city, and the *Times* editorialized against overreaction. "The arrival of reinforcements at Baltimore and Washington and the abundant preparations made on every side to prevent the advance of the 'stone wall' hero must inspire confidence that he will do little more damage and be able to hold his advanced post but a few days. The appeal to New York, Philadelphia, and Boston for three regiments each, made this afternoon, is much discussed, and its propriety doubted. It is feared that it will create an undue alarm in the North."

The rival *New York Daily Tribune* took a similar line, observing on May 27 that the men of Banks's army were in fine spirits and ready for revenge. Only the *New York Herald* suggested a serious threat existed to Washington, and that just in its May 26 number.

There had been a flurry of unrest in Baltimore. That had been due not to Confederate sympathizers, of which there were thousands in the city, but rather to popular indignation at the capture of the 1st Maryland (Union) and rumors that Col. John Kenly had been murdered in cold blood after having surrendered.[14]

The streets of Washington were quiet. Press commentary was restrained. The *Sunday Morning Chronicle* of May 25 reported simply that Banks had retired to Winchester, where reinforcements awaited him. Coverage in the *National Republican* was similarly low-keyed. On May 27 the *National Intelligencer* denounced rumors of a Confederate advance on the capital as absurd. According to a *New York Times* reporter in town who had witnessed the frenzy after Bull Run, "The alarm on the night of [May] 25 by no means was as general as it was [then]. We are all surprised, vexed; some of us are a little glad, though, that the enemy is doing something besides everlastingly running away. We don't apprehend any great catastrophe."[15]

In the Union army at Williamsport, fatigue yielded to anger and feelings of betrayal, though there was pride at having escaped from a much larger enemy force. Nearly everyone continued to applaud Banks. "General Banks is a military man of the right stamp," said a Hoosier lieutenant. "The men have unbounded confidence in our noble general," a Wisconsin corporal agreed. "He has but to ride along their front to inspire the men with confidence." "When the country learns fully the history of a retreat made by less than five thousand men, while an enemy of 25,000 moved at the same time on converging roads . . . a retreat which ended in a successful passage of a wide and rapid river . . . this retreat will take its place as a masterly movement," declared the chaplain of the 2nd Massachusetts, "and General Banks, with his gallant little corps, will take high rank in the esteem and affection of the people." In the 28th New York, which had suffered no deaths on the battlefield, the mood was particularly ebullient. "Last night I visited the 28th New York and took dinner in camp," a New York cavalryman recorded on May 29. "They were in fine spirits again, ready to move at a moment's warning." A soldier of the regiment confirmed that opinion: "We found that we had lost only about one hundred men, and all were in the best of spirits to think that we had come out of the scrape as well as we had. We are all ready and willing to go back into Virginia at any time if they will only give us force enough to drive those devils out of the Valley."[16]

Therein lay the rub. Nearly everyone, generals included, thought Banks had been wrongly denied troops. Much ill-feeling was exhibited toward the administration. "It is said that General Banks is to be removed. If this is true I think that it is a cursed shame," a New York infantryman confided to his diary. "Banks has had no chance to do anything. His hands have been tied by orders from the secretary of war. His troops have been taken from him and his requests for reinforcements were disregarded." A New York artilleryman just arrived at Harpers Ferry wrote home: "One thing is certain, there has been a screw loose somewhere, or else General Banks would have had more troops than he was provided with. What he gained and might have held, if there had been no interference, must and no doubt will be gained over again." "I believe I have several times told you that I thought we were in a critical position. If I have not, it was because I did not wish to alarm you," Gen. Alpheus Williams wrote his daughter. "But the War Department seemed determined to strip General Banks of his new command to make new departments and new armies at points where there was no enemy." General Hatch told his father: "There will perhaps some blame attach to General Banks for these disasters; the blame does not belong there, but in Washington, where with no military knowledge the secretary of war has undertaken to carry on a campaign. Our commander, General Banks, is no great soldier, but he is a very good man. I admire him very much."[17]

About the only one not complaining was Banks. "The escape of my command was a miracle. No victory could have produced so profound an impression upon the soldiers or the country. I am very glad that it was well done," he wrote his wife two weeks after Winchester. A Massachusetts congressman informed Governor Andrew confidentially that he had visited the War Department on May 26 and spoken at length with the secretary of war and the president, both of whom lauded Banks's disinterested loyalty:

> Every intelligent man here knew well why it became necessary to withdraw so large a portion of the force under General Banks, whose operations at the time were considered subordinate to the greater movement on Richmond. This must have been a great disappointment to Banks . . . but General Banks comprehended the military necessity that placed him

unexpectedly in a different position and so far from being dissatisfied and complaining of ill usage, I have the highest authority for saying that on this occasion, as at all other times, he followed the orders without hesitation.[18]

WHETHER JOHN C. FRÉMONT would do likewise remained an open question in Washington. To the administration, the march he had been directed to make from Franklin to Harrisonburg looked simple enough. On the map the distance between the two places was forty-one miles, nearly in a straight line over a good turnpike. But for Frémont, the obstacles to the movement Lincoln had demanded were insurmountable. There was no prospect that he would receive either the two hundred wagons he had requisitioned from the quarter-master general of the army, Montgomery C. Meigs, as required to move deeper into Southern territory, or the four hundred horses he had told Lincoln he needed for his cavalry and artillery. Rations remained scanty. "On the eve of another march, I drop you a line," an Ohio soldier wrote his hometown newspaper. "We have been living for the last five days on short rations—one day half-rations, next quarter-rations, and again one-fifth rations." Frémont's supply depot was at New Creek, eighty miles north of Franklin. There were then three hundred wagons in the Mountain Department, of which thirty a day must reach Franklin to provide daily rations to the 13,733 men Frémont reported present for duty in May. The horrid state of the wagon track, made worse by heavy rains, prevented even that meager number from coming up; a correspondent of the Cincinnati Gazette called the route "the most miserable road I have ever traveled." The country around Franklin was destitute of food and forage. An advance on Harrisonburg would prolong an already unsustainable supply line to 120 miles.

Sanitary conditions, particularly in Brig. Gen. Louis Blenker's division, were abysmal. "There are but few ambulances—in one regiment none. In fact, there is not in the whole division more than one-fifth the necessary ambulance transportation," reported the department medical director. "Even for the few wretched vehicles possessed there is a deficiency of animals, and of those they have and call horses, several are little better than living skeletons."[19]

The turnpike between Franklin and Harrisonburg that looked so good on maps was, in fact, a wreck. During the McDowell campaign Jed Hotchkiss had destroyed it at Jackson's behest. Federal scouts found bridges ruined and culverts torn away, boulders rolled onto the road at the passes through Bull

Pasture and Shenandoah mountains, and trees felled across the way for almost a mile along one stretch of the turnpike. There were no side roads worthy of consideration around the obstacles.[20]

The only option open to Frémont, he believed, was to double back northward upon his supply line until he reached Petersburg, where ample stores of rations and forage awaited. From Petersburg he would strike east by way of Moorefield and trust his luck in gaining Strasburg before Jackson slipped back up the Valley. That he might do so without violating instructions seemed to both Frémont and his talented aide-de-camp, Col. Albert Tracy, a career soldier who had seen action in the Mexican War and the Mormon War, a "fair construction" of an order Stanton issued him on May 25. Advising Frémont of Banks's withdrawal toward Harpers Ferry, the secretary of war said: "You must direct your attention to falling upon the enemy *at whatever place you can find him* [italics added] with all speed. You must not stop for supplies, but seize what you need and push rapidly forward; the object being to cut off and capture this rebel force in the Shenandoah." No mention was made of Harrisonburg. Being of more recent date, Stanton's orders took precedence over Lincoln's of the previous day. Confident that he was now "free to choose my line of march," Frémont set out at dawn on May 25 for Petersburg with Blenker's division and Schenck's Brigade over a road knee-deep in mud. Brig. Gen. Robert Milroy was to follow the next day. Frémont would violate Stanton's directive only insofar as he must of necessity stop briefly in Petersburg for supplies.[21]

Overlooked or suppressed in later debate over Frémont's alleged disobedience of Lincoln's Harrisonburg order was a letter dated June 12, 1862, from Brig. Gen. Carl Schurz, whom the president had designated to inspect the Mountain Department after the Battle of Cross Keys. Schurz, a fair man, told Lincoln bluntly: "It is a fact, which admits of no doubt, that when you ordered General Frémont to march from Franklin to Harrisonburg it was absolutely impossible to carry out the order. The army was in a starving condition and literally unable to fight. I have been assured by many that, had they been attacked at Franklin about that time, a number of regiments would have thrown down their arms."[22]

A thirty-mile tramp, punctuated by hailstorms and downpours of cold rain, brought the head of Frémont's column into Petersburg at noon on May 26. Schenck's Brigade arrived first; Blenker's division, encumbered with a long baggage wagon that General Milroy said "they had no skill in getting through the terrible roads," trickled in during the course of the afternoon. Because of

Blenker's delays, Milroy did not reach Petersburg until 8:00 A.M. on the twenty-seventh, just in time to join the remainder of Frémont's army on the second leg of the march.

Frémont lost little time in Petersburg. While there, he directed that all extra baggage—including tents and knapsacks—be left behind. With a resupply of ammunition and five days' cooked rations in haversacks, he brought the army to Moorefield on the evening of May 27.[23]

That night Frémont received as curt a telegram as President Lincoln ever sent to a general in the field. Dated 9:58 P.M., it read: "I see that you are at Moorefield. You were expressly ordered to march to Harrisonburg. What does this mean?"

Frémont answered twice. In his first reply, sent at 6:00 A.M. on May 28, Frémont explained that his troops had been too starved to execute Lincoln's order literally; a line of march farther away from the departmental supply depot would have proved fatal. He thought he had complied with the broad intent of Lincoln's order, adding: "In executing any order received I take it for granted that I am to exercise discretion concerning its literal execution according to circumstances. If I am to understand that literal obedience to orders is required, please say so." Surprisingly, Frémont made no mention of Stanton's May 25 orders.[24]

Both the tone and content of Frémont's message were unfortunate for his case. There had been no room for discretion in Lincoln's order; the president had told him to do this *and* that, not this *or* that. In such instances, army regulations demanded strict adherence to orders. Frémont may have chosen his words more carefully, too, had he known just how angry the president had been when he learned of Frémont's detour. The news had come incidentally to the War Department telegrapher from the military telegraph office in Pittsburg. Lincoln happened to be at the department as Stanton wrapped up his daily council of war. Stanton was at the head of the table with Maj. Gen. Ethan A. Hitchcock and the heads of bureaus seated "in court-martial order along the sides." Secretaries Chase and Seward stood off to one side; President Lincoln reclined on a sofa in the corner. A staff officer interrupted with word of Frémont. Col. George Ruggles, head of the bureau of volunteers, said that "Stanton was furious and took his pen to frame a reprimand. Mr. Lincoln arose from the sofa, came to Stanton's side, placed his finger perpendicularly on the table, and said, 'Write what I say!' " Stanton did so.[25]

Realizing that he had given the impression that he might have gone to Harrisonburg had he simply pushed his men hard—as Lincoln had expected him to—Frémont sent a longer dispatch thirty minutes after the first. He amplified on his supply problems and the desolate state of the country around Franklin, and explained that the road to Harrisonburg was too heavily obstructed to allow passage. He concluded, "We are now moving with the utmost celerity possible in whatever direction the enemy may be found." Legitimate though they were, Frémont's arguments fell on deaf ears. At 1:00 P.M. Stanton telegraphed him that the president directed him to halt at Moorefield and await orders; that there might be no misunderstanding, Frémont was to acknowledge the receipt of the order and the time he received it. Unaware of the natural and manmade obstacles in his path, Lincoln and Stanton were treating Frémont, who was doing his level best to comply with the spirit of presidential orders (there was no way in which he could comply with the letter of his instructions), unjustly.[26]

Stanton's latest message presented Frémont with a dilemma. When he received it he was already ten miles east of Moorefield, having set out from there at daybreak under a pounding rainstorm. Having become literal-minded, Frémont dutifully telegraphed his intention to return to Moorefield the next morning. In the meantime, the army made camp near a hamlet called "Fabius," in a "rough and wild country" and, as the rains ceased and the clouds parted, enjoyed a spectacular view of the Allegheny Mountains they had that morning crossed.[27]

Developments in the Lower Shenandoah Valley caused the president and Stanton to relent. At 4:50 P.M. the secretary of war forwarded Frémont a dispatch from Brig. Gen. Charles S. Hamilton at Harpers Ferry informing the administration that Jackson had halted between Winchester and Charlestown, his troops being "too much fatigued to pursue Banks." That, added Stanton, "probably indicates the true position of the enemy at this time. [The] president directs you to move upon him by the best route you can." Two days earlier Assistant Secretary of War Peter H. Watson, whom Stanton had sent to Harpers Ferry after Banks's defeat as his eyes and ears, had crossed the river and ridden as far as Charlestown without encountering a single Confederate. He expected no attack on Harpers Ferry.

Frémont acknowledged receipt of Stanton's telegram at 7:00 P.M. and assured him the president's order would be "obeyed accordingly." Equally literal-minded, Stanton added a lengthy postscript at 11:00 P.M., voiding the Moorefield order and restating the president's present wishes. "The order to remain at Moorefield was based on the supposition that it would find you there. Upon subsequent information that the enemy were still operating in the vicinity of Winchester and Martinsburg you were directed to move against the enemy. The president now again directs you to move against the enemy without delay." The dispatch ended with the tiresome refrain, "Please acknowledge the receipt of this and the time received."[28]

Frémont now had the discretion he had always expected. But another problem presented itself. His army was used up. The weather had completed the job short rations had begun. "The column crossed one range after another, often amid wild solitudes, and by obscure and difficult roads," an Ohio soldier said. "Rain fell much of the time, and on the mountains it was chilling cold; marching all day, the soldiers, exhausted, threw themselves at night on the wet ground, with no other bed or covering than green pine branches and a single blanket."

That morning the march had been especially brutal. At Moorefield the army had had to ford the South Branch of the Potomac, which the incessant rains had rendered deep and rapid. A cable was stretched across the wide watery expanse and fastened at each end. Then single file the fourteen thousand troops waded across. Remembered another Ohioan: "The water was up to our waist, and it was difficult to prevent our ammunition from getting wet. Some stripped themselves and carried all in one hand above the water while with the other they held the rope. One man lost his britches with twenty-five dollars." Hundreds more lost their last ounce of strength. Nearly a third of Blenker's Germans, disabled and broken-down, were strung out along the road from Fabius back to Moorefield. All were weary, haggard, and nearly starved. After inspecting those who had reached camp, Dr. George Stuckley, the department's medical director, demanded that Frémont grant a day's rest.[29]

While the army bedded down, Frémont's spies and scouts worked overtime. Frémont had brought from his command in Missouri an organization called the "Jessie Scouts," named for his wife. To make up for their lack of knowledge of the region, Frémont employed as spies several men with experience in the Mountain Department. Two were captured near Woodstock before they were able to report Jackson's whereabouts, but enough slipped past his outposts to give Frémont a clear picture of Confederate dispositions. On the morning of May 29 he informed Stanton that his reconnoitering parties reported Jackson's main body four miles below Winchester and his rear guard at Strasburg, with Ashby's cavalry fanned out from Winchester to Harpers Ferry and Martinsburg. He promised to obey the president's order "as promptly as possible."[30]

The president and the secretary of war knew the whereabouts of Jackson;

what they wanted to know was that Frémont would be in place to trap him when McDowell came up. At noon Lincoln telegraphed the Pathfinder a destination and a time to be there: "General McDowell's advance, if not checked by the enemy, should, and probably will, be at Front Royal by 12 (noon) tomorrow [May 30]. His force, when up, will be about twenty-thousand. Please have your force at Strasburg, or, if the route you are moving on does not lead to that point, as near Strasburg as the enemy may be by the same time."

One can imagine Lincoln's ire when he read Frémont's answer. The flesh-and-blood chess pieces far off in the field refused to move as their handlers in the capital demanded. After explaining why he had halted for the day at Fabius, Frémont said that he could not possibly be at Strasburg before 5:00 P.M. on May 31. With commendable restraint, given his limited understanding of matters in Frémont's army, Lincoln told Frémont at 2:30 P.M.: "Yours, saying you will reach Strasburg or vicinity at 5 P.M. Saturday, has been received and sent to General McDowell, and he directed to act in view of it." Then, as if to speed the Pathfinder over the hard mountain road, the president added that the previous night the Confederates had evacuated the important railroad junction town of Corinth, Mississippi.[31]

AS WAS EVIDENT from Lincoln's May 29 telegrams to Frémont, McDowell's column had given a better account of itself over the last four days. Shields's division had had no time since entering McDowell's lines to refit. Most regiments had gone from six to eight months without new issues of clothing, and hundreds of men were barefoot. Artillery horses were weak and underfed, harnesses and traces nearly worn out. No one wanted to return to the Shenandoah Valley. "The men were greatly disappointed," said Colonel Sawyer of the 8th Ohio, "as they had believed they were in full march for Richmond to realize the hanging of Jeff Davis on a sour apple tree, and now to be turned back with faces to the North, and to have to retake the Valley, was really disheartening to both officers and men."

None was more disgusted than General Shields, who made a nuisance of himself with bad-tempered dispatches to the War Department and the White House.[32] But he marched, and marched fast. Leaving Falmouth on the morning of May 26, he reached Manassas Junction that evening. Brig. Gen. E. O. C. Ord's division began to move by water to Alexandria the same day, with orders then to proceed by rail to Manassas Junction to cover Washington from attack by Geary's ghostly enemy. At the junction Shields found nothing but chaos.

"Have arrived," he informed Stanton curtly. "Can get no information. One car here. No wood. Got no axes to cut it with. No one here knows where enemy is. Colonel Geary is retreating they say about twelve miles from here." When that night and the next day passed with no sign of Confederates, McDowell directed Geary to gather up his command of 1,300 infantry and 700 cavalry and march to Ashby's Gap by way of Aldie and Middleburg, at which place Geary had warned the War Department Jackson was lurking. Geary's scouts ranged as far as the gap without encountering a single Rebel.

Meanwhile, Shields had reached his own conclusions. On May 27 he telegraphed McDowell from Catlett's Station: "I think there is no force before General Geary but the cavalry of the mountains. I think the whole is a panic. I want no assistance. My own division is sufficient for present emergencies. General Geary was not, in my opinion, in the slightest danger. I regret the panic that has been created in Washington—that the force that created it was an insignificant one." Pushing on to Geary's former headquarters at Rectortown the next day, he again advised McDowell: "No enemy is to be found in this region, and no enemy approached the place until our troops abandoned it, when a few straggling cavalry came on and, finding nothing to oppose them, burned the bridge between here and Front Royal. I hope no effort will be spared to counteract as far as possible the shameful effects of this shameful retreat."[33]

The absence of enemy contact east of the Blue Ridge calmed lingering administration fears that a push against the capital might be imminent. All effort was now directed toward closing the door behind Jackson in the Lower Valley. At 5:40 P.M. on May 28 Lincoln told McDowell, who had relocated his headquarters from Falmouth to Manassas Junction: "I think the evidence now preponderates that Ewell and Jackson are still about Winchester. Assuming this, it is for you a question of legs. Put in all the speed you can. I have told Frémont as much and directed him to drive at them as fast as possible." His indignation at what he considered Frémont's disobedience of orders still fresh, Lincoln added, "By the way, I suppose you know Frémont has got up to Moorefield, instead of going to Harrisonburg."[34]

With vigor and directness McDowell responded: "I beg to assure you that I am doing everything which legs and steam are capable of to hurry forward matters in this quarter. I shall be deficient in wagons when I get out of the way of the railroad for transporting supplies but shall push on nevertheless." Absolutely, agreed Shields. "All well, and everything going on finely," he wrote

McDowell from Rectortown on the twenty-ninth, promising to set off for Front Royal at 5:00 A.M. the next morning and to be there by evening. McDowell, in turn, directed Ord to march in support of Shields "as rapidly as the means at your disposal will permit" and, as the question was one not only of legs but also of hooves, told Brig. Gen. George Bayard at Catlett's Station to have the cavalry on the shortest road to Front Royal at dawn.[35]

CHAPTER 24

I WAS NEVER SO RELIEVED

IN MY LIFE

Stonewall Jackson was in fine spirits. He spent the evening after the Battle of Winchester visiting with the Graham family, and on the morning of May 26 he sat down to tell his wife the delightful news that "an ever-kind Providence" had blessed the Valley army with twin victories at Front Royal and Winchester. Jackson found the gratitude of the citizenry especially heartwarming. "I do not remember having ever seen such rejoicing as was manifested by the people of Winchester as our army yesterday passed through the town in pursuit of the enemy. The people seemed nearly frantic with joy; indeed, it would be almost impossible to describe their manifestations of rejoicing and gratitude. Our entrance into Winchester was one of the most stirring scenes of my life."[1]

The soldiers of the Valley army had a rare opportunity to reflect on the stirring scenes, as Jackson granted a day of rest and thanksgiving on May 26. A victorious army is a happy army, and amid the general congratulations the toils of the previous week faded. Stonewall Jackson was hailed as a military genius. Letter writing occupied much of the day, and the sentiments Private Waldrop of the 21st Virginia expressed to his father were typical of the praise of Jackson that made its way to the homefolk. "This is one of the most brilliant moves of the war, and Old Jack will be a greater man than ever," declared Waldrop. "We are well satisfied with the result of this trip so far, and though the men have had a hard time I hear no complaining."[2]

In addition to the usual pastimes of letter writing and card playing, a number of Jackson's men amused themselves taking target practice on metal breastplates, thigh protectors, and other assorted pieces of body armor found among sutlers' stores or, if George W. Booth of the 1st Maryland (Confederate) is to believed, stripped off prisoners. Setting the novel items up at various ranges, Southern marksmen tested their stopping power. "At fair range they would turn a revolver ball very well, and a rifle or musket ball if from any considerable distance," observed Booth. "But at close range they were vulnerable to the latter. It has been denied that these doughty warriors wore these appliances, but I can testify to their existence, and moreover, Colonel [Bradley T.] Johnson succeeded in sending one to the rear."[3]

After mailing off his souvenir, Johnson paid a call on Mary Greenhow Lee. He was "full of enthusiasm," she recollected, because he was certain that the victory at Winchester was but the prelude to a conquest of his home state of Maryland.[4]

At least one band of Union prisoners exacted a bit of revenge on their captors. Thinking (wrongly) that they were to be paroled, the captive Federals marched jauntily down Loudoun Street after dark on the twenty-fifth with their escort of Louisiana Tigers. Among them were runaway slaves and, in the arms of a Union officer, a newborn black baby. At the Taylor house General Jackson and his staff were gathered on the portico with a crowd of "gaily dressed ladies," while nearby an army band discoursed the favorite Confederate war tune, "The Bonnie Blue Flag." When the prisoners heard the first strains of the band, they broke into "The Star-Spangled Banner" and drowned out the Southern serenade. The startled Tigers made no effort to suppress the Yankees' patriotic outburst, and the Federals kept singing all the way to their quarters at the railroad depot.[5]

When not escorting prisoners or otherwise engaged, Valley Confederates stuffed themselves with fine food. "I had some nice fresh shad for breakfast this morning that I got out of a Yankee wagon yesterday," James F. Shaner of the Rockbridge Artillery wrote his father, "and I tell you they eat good, for we had not had anything to eat for about two days." Haversacks were emptied of regulation beef and biscuits to make room for potted meats, pickled oysters, lobsters, "genuine" coffee, baked bread, ham, canned fruits, oranges, lemons, and figs—"all kinds of confectionary and various other luxuries," said a Southern chaplain, "to which, even at that date, the Confederacy was a stranger."[6]

Jackson took a moment that morning to inform Richmond of his success. To the adjutant general of the Confederate army, Samuel Cooper, he wrote:

During the last three days God has blessed our arms with brilliant success. On Friday the Federals at Front Royal were routed and one section of artillery in addition to many prisoners captured. On Saturday Banks's main column whilst retreating from Strasburg to Winchester was pierced—the rear part returning towards Strasburg on Sunday, the other part [writing the dispatch himself in longhand, here Jackson penned and then deleted the words "after a short engagement"] was routed at this place. At last accounts Brig. Gen. George H. Steuart was pursuing with cavalry and artillery and capturing the fugitives. A large amount of medical, ordnance, and other stores have fallen into our hands.[7]

To the Valley army Jackson issued a similar proclamation. He thanked the men for their "brilliant gallantry in action and patriotic obedience under the hardships of forced marches," but reminded them that his chief duty was to give thanks to God: "to recognize devoutly the hand of a protecting Providence in the brilliant successes of the last three days, which have given us the results of a great victory without great losses." To give properly the thanks due the Almighty, regimental chaplains were ordered to hold divine service at 4:00 P.M. Jackson chose to worship with the 33rd Virginia.[8]

The Valley army enjoyed a second consecutive day of rest on May 27 as Jackson contemplated just how far north to advance. Absent new orders, Robert E. Lee's directive of May 16 prevailed: If he defeated Banks in battle, Jackson was to "drive him back toward the Potomac and create the impression, as far as practicable, that you design threatening that line." Jackson had accomplished the first clause of Lee's order; it remained for him to fulfill the second. He probably ruled out a demonstration against Williamsport as lacking in drama. Williamsport was too far removed from the Federal capital; better to march toward Harpers Ferry and create the impression that a foray on Washington was imminent. To that end, on the evening of the twenty-seventh Jackson ordered the Stonewall Brigade—less the 2nd Virginia, which had been detached to watch over captured stores in Winchester—to march the next morning on Harpers Ferry by way of Charlestown. As the aim of a strong demonstration toward the Potomac was to cause forces to be stripped from McClellan, Jackson needed to secure his flanks against a Federal counterthrust into the Valley in case the tactic succeeded. Consequently, on the twenty-seventh he ordered the 12th Georgia Infantry of Col. Z. T. Conner, which had fought so well at McDowell, to garrison Front Royal. Jackson gave Conner strict orders to prevent the Federals from securing the bridges over the North and South forks of the Shenandoah. Should Conner be compelled to fall back, the spans were to be destroyed in order to protect Jackson's flank and rear. Taylor's brigade was sent to Berryville to watch the road into the Valley from Leesburg. A detachment of Ashby's cavalry under Captains Edward McDonald and Harry Gilmor remained near Frémont's advance west of the Valley. To guard against an early return of Banks, as well as to secure the considerable stores that the Federals had left behind at Martinsburg, Jackson detached the 1st Maryland (Confederate) to occupy the town.

In the aftermath of the Battle of Winchester, matters of army organization also occupied Jackson's attention. General Taliaferro had returned from sick leave and resumed command of the Third Brigade of the Valley army. Col. John Patton of the 21st Virginia was elevated to command the Second Brigade in place of the wounded John Campbell. And Jackson ordered that those guilty of pillaging during the march on Winchester or after the battle be court-martialed at the earliest opportunity.[9]

Pressing the Federals remained uppermost in Jackson's mind. That this was still the desire of his superiors was confirmed with the arrival on May 27 of Congressman Alexander Boteler, who brought with him orders from the War Department directing Jackson to demonstrate against Harpers Ferry. On the morning of the twenty-eighth, with Winder already on the road, Jackson started Ewell's division for Harpers Ferry. Orders went out that afternoon to the 1st Maryland (Confederate) to quit Martinsburg the next day and rejoin the army.[10]

Had he been able to move on the river town two days earlier, Jackson might have created a panic with minimal effort. A mere show of force on the heights opposite Harpers Ferry might even have induced the Federals to abandon the strategic town. Brig. Gen. Rufus Saxton had replaced Col. Dixon Miles as commander of the garrison on May 26. He found two regiments of volunteers and the unreliable Maryland Potomac Home Brigade, which had a marked aversion to service in Virginia. Reinforcements arrived that night and the next morning in the form of the 78th New York and 109th Pennsylvania and two batteries of artillery, but as late as 9:30 A.M. on the twenty-seventh Col. John S. Clark was reporting to Banks that the seven thousand troops at Harpers Ferry were "badly stampeded." Clark concluded that "immediate steps should be taken to recover morale, which can only be done by moving against the enemy in force." Assistant Secretary of War Peter H. Watson, then at Harpers Ferry, agreed and suggested that Banks retake Martinsburg at once. Banks thought he could be ready to move in two or three days. As yet unsure of his troops, Saxton limited his aggression to a reconnaissance in force on the morning of May 28 by the 111th Pennsylvania, 1st Maryland Cavalry (Union), and a section of artillery toward Charlestown, which was held by two companies of Ashby's cavalry.[11]

Six miles west of Charlestown the Stonewall Brigade heard the low rumble of distant artillery fire. General Winder was at a loss to understand the cause; he had been under the impression that there were no Yankees nearer than Harpers Ferry. Riding "carelessly a hundred yards ahead" of the brigade, McHenry Howard was startled to see a horseman in gray gallop toward him. He recognized the man as Captain Chew. "He reined up and on my asking what was the matter, said the Yankees were at Charlestown," recalled Howard, who expressed disbelief. The Yankees were there alright, countered Chew; he had been visiting family in Charlestown and had narrowly escaped capture. A dozen or so straggling Confederate cavalrymen appeared to confirm Chew's account just as Winder came up.

Deploying his four regiments in line of battle, Winder elected to press forward, showing exactly the sort of aggressiveness that Jackson had come to admire in him. Under cover of a wood a mile west of town, Winder divided his force, sending detachments through the timber toward both Federal flanks. To distract the enemy's attention, he ran forward Carpenter's battery and the Parrott section of the Rockbridge Artillery. A lively artillery duel went on for twenty minutes under a cloudy drizzle before the Union commander, seeing what Winder had in store for him, withdrew toward Harpers Ferry. Winder gave chase to Halltown, within sight of Bolivar Heights, the commanding ground that lay between the Potomac and Shenandoah rivers west of town. Finding the heights well defended, Winder withdrew to Charlestown. Winder falling back met up with Ewell advancing, and together they bivouacked a mile east of Charlestown.[12]

The next day Jackson moved to concentrate his forces. He called up Taliaferro's and Patton's brigades from Winchester and edged the army—less the 12th Georgia at Front Royal—to Halltown, halfway between Charlestown and Harpers Ferry. The 2nd Virginia was relieved of guard duty and hurried forward to rejoin Winder. Saxton became aware of Jackson's approach when a squadron of the 5th New York Cavalry he had sent out to reconnoiter ran into an ambush on the outskirts of Halltown. The New Yorkers rode into range of Capt. A. R. Courtney's battery, posted in timber on the left of the road, without noticing either the guns or their infantry and cavalry support. Campbell Brown was on hand to watch the result, which was decidedly less than hoped for. "Unluckily for Courtney's reputation for sharpness, his fuses were badly cut and he had loaded with shell in lieu of canister," said Brown, "so when after letting them approach within four hundred yards, he opened furiously from his two guns and they scampered back, kicking up between horses and shells a tremendous dust, it turned out that nobody was hurt! Such a chance for killing twenty or thirty men I never saw so thrown away!"[13]

The 2nd Virginia Infantry furnished the only other excitement that day. While waiting for the regiment, Winder had discovered that Loudoun Heights, on the east bank of the Shenandoah opposite Harpers Ferry, was deserted. To occupy them he would have to get a force across the river. There were no boats to be had, but Winder managed a crossing by the novel method of having the soldiers of the 2nd hold onto the tails of cavalry horses as their riders swam them across. In response to Winder's move, Saxton withdrew from Bolivar Heights and took up a nearer line of defense on a height known as "Camp Hill," immediately above Harpers Ferry. He also occupied Maryland Heights with infantry and heavy guns, checking Winder.[14]

Despite disquieting evidence that his ruse may have succeeded too well, Jackson had elected to maintain pressure on Harpers Ferry. Shortly after midnight of the twenty-eighth an elderly civilian had come into Winchester with news from beyond the Blue Ridge. He told Sandie Pendleton that McDowell had left Fredericksburg and that Shields was just a day's march short of Front Royal. The man said he had seen Shields's column on the road and had galloped twelve hours to warn Jackson. Pendleton escorted the man to Jackson in the morning. The general dismissed his story as rumor, but nonetheless urged his chief quartermaster, Maj. John A. Harman, to hurry the removal of Federal stores from Front Royal and Winchester.

News that Jackson deemed more reliable came on the night of May 29 from Captain Gilmor. He reported that Frémont was encamped east of Moorefield, with the evident intention of marching on Strasburg by way of Wardensville. Scouts returning from east of the Blue Ridge also confirmed the advance of Shields. Suddenly the Valley army had become the quarry, rather than the hunter. Four Federal pincers were poised to converge on Jackson; a double envelopment was possible from every direction of the compass. To recapitulate, Jackson's command was deployed as follows: The Valley army and Ewell's division were at Halltown, 12,200 strong. The 2nd Virginia Infantry, 350 strong, was on Loudoun Heights. Taylor's brigade of 3,000 men occupied Berryville. The 12th Georgia, 450 strong, held Front Royal. Ashby with 300 troopers was out on the Wardensville road. Nearest to Jackson's main body were Saxton with 7,000 men at Harpers Ferry and Banks at Williamsport. Reinforcements had swelled Banks's ranks to 7,000 also. At Fabius in the Allegheny Mountains was Frémont with 14,800 men. East of the Blue Ridge on the night of May 29 McDowell had Shields's division of 11,000 troops at Rectortown and Ord's division of 10,000 at Thoroughfare Gap. Brig. Gen. George Bayard was at Catlett's Station with 2,000 cavalry and artillery. Geary had returned to Middleburg with his brigade of 2,000 men. The combined forces of McDowell and Frémont alone were more than double the Confederate strength. Adding Banks and Saxton to the equation placed 52,400 Federals within striking distance of Jackson's 16,300 troops.[15]

ON THE CLEAR and cool morning of Friday, May 30, couriers arrived at Jackson's headquarters intermittently with news of the approach of Shields and Frémont. They also brought word of signs of life at Williamsport, from which Banks already had sent reconnaissance patrols as far south as Martinsburg. Yankee prisoners snatched from the fringes of Frémont's and Shields's columns gave honest estimates of the Federal strength.[16]

Storm clouds gathered as the morning wore on, and Jackson's mood darkened with the skies. The strain of his high-stakes bluff toward the Potomac was beginning to tell on him. His behavior became erratic. After breakfast he cheerfully accepted a call from a delegation of ladies of Charlestown who had come out to pay their respects. Then he rode to the front to check on Winder. He found him and General Elzey astride their horses behind a barn on the Harpers Ferry road, perhaps a mile west of Bolivar Heights. According to McHenry Howard, who eavesdropped on the conversation, Winder told Jackson what he had gathered from civilians regarding the enemy's strength, adding that two citizens had come to him during the night with word, incorrect as it turned out, that Saxton had been reinforced. Elzey interrupted with similar information, adding that the Yankees "had heavy guns on the Maryland Heights." For no apparent reason, Jackson swung into the saddle and snapped, "General Elzey, are you afraid of heavy guns?"

A startled Howard glanced at Elzey. "I saw his cheeks redden, but he made no reply." Just then a courier rode up with a dispatch for Jackson, who read it and, without another word, started for the rear. Howard later assumed the dispatch to have been yet more grim news of Shields and Frémont closing in on Front Royal and Strasburg, nearly fifty miles behind the Valley army. Notwithstanding the trouble brewing in his rear, Howard also said Jackson left both Winder and Elzey with the impression that he intended to roll over Bolivar Heights and storm Camp Hill. "If Jackson had not really intended to go further, certainly he effectually deceived, to the last minute, his own subordinate generals as well as his adversary."[17]

In humiliating one general in the presence of another, Jackson had committed a stunning breach of conduct. But that was not the last of his odd displays. Shortly after dressing down Elzey, Jackson returned to the front. He took up a post on a hilltop near Halltown to watch his cannons shell the handful of Federals remaining on Bolivar Heights. Two Yankee batteries on Camp Hill and the heavy three-inch Dahlgrens on Maryland Heights responded. After watching the artillery duel for a time, Jackson dismounted. Seating himself on the ground at the foot of a large tree behind the nearest Southern battery, he leaned back and went to sleep. Alexander Boteler happened to be on hand. Being something of an artist, Boteler enjoyed sketching the likenesses of Confederate leaders. If Jackson could find time for a nap, reasoned Boteler, he certainly could indulge his hobby. "As he laid there on his back with his arms folded over his breast, his feet crossed like those of a crusader's effigy, and his head turned aside sufficiently to show his face in profile, I could not resist the temptation to make a sketch of him and was busily engaged with my pencil when, on looking up, I met his eyes fixed full upon me." Boteler fared better than Elzey. Extending his hand for the drawing, Jackson said with a smile, "Let me see what you have been doing there." Studying the sketch, Jackson remarked, "My hardest tasks at West Point were the drawing lessons, and I never could do anything in that line to satisfy myself, or indeed," he added with an uncustomary laugh, "anybody else." Jackson paused a moment, then continued: "But Colonel, I have some harder work than this for you to do, and if you'll sit down here now, I'll tell you what it is."

Boteler eased over beside the general. "I want you to go to Richmond for me," Jackson commanded his friend and sometime benefactor. "I must have reinforcements. You can explain to them down there what the situation is here. Get as many men as can be spared, and I'd like you, if you please, to go as soon as you can."

Boteler said he would do whatever he could to help. With a familiarity that none of Jackson's subordinates enjoyed, he insisted, "But you must first tell me, General, what is the situation here." Jackson obliged him. He gave Boteler as full a picture of the situation as he then had, enumerating the strength and location of each of the enemy commands confronting him. "McDowell and Frémont," he concluded,

> are probably aiming to effect a junction at Strasburg, so as to head us off from the Upper Valley, and are both nearer to it now than we are; consequently, no time is to be lost. You can say to them in Richmond that I'll send on the prisoners, secure most, if not all of the captured property, and with God's blessing will be able to baffle the enemy's plans here with my present force, but that it will have to be increased as soon thereafter as possible. You may tell them, too, that if my command can be gotten up to forty thousand men a movement may be made beyond the Potomac, which will soon raise the siege of Richmond and transfer this campaign from the banks of the James to those of the Susquehanna.

Jackson told Boteler to go to Charlestown, where he would find a train at the station with the engine fired up; he was to detach all cars but one and in that car make all possible haste to Winchester. From there he would be furnished transportation to Staunton, where he would take the train to Richmond.[18]

There is an element of the fantastic in Jackson's instructions to Boteler, like his outburst to Elzey—a symptom, perhaps, of growing fatigue and stress. Under the best of circumstances, Boteler would need two days to reach the Confederate capital by the circuitous route available to him. Even if Richmond were inclined to grant Jackson's request, scraping up reinforcements would take considerable time.

And time was something Jackson did not have in abundance. Realizing that he had done all he could at Harpers Ferry, he issued orders early in the afternoon for the bulk of the army to start back to Winchester. Winder was to make a strong feint toward Bolivar Heights that evening to keep Saxton off balance, then cover the rear during the withdrawal. Orders went out for Taylor to retire from Berryville to Winchester. Conner was expected to hold Front Royal until the army had cleared Strasburg, or at least until the captured supplies had been removed from the town.

As the army filed onto the road, the clouds parted and a heavy rain began to fall. In the ranks the men of Jackson's "foot cavalry" instinctively understood that they were being called upon to make another seemingly impossible march. As the Reverend J. William Jones, chaplain of the 25th Virginia, put it, "We entered the lists for a race to Strasburg. I can never forget that march.

'Press forward' was the constant order, and when the troops were well nigh exhausted, word was passed down the column: 'General Jackson desires the command to push forward much further tonight in order to accomplish a very important object,' and every man bent his energies to meet the requirement of our loved chieftain, while the muddy, weary road was enlivened by jest and song and cheers." By late afternoon troops and wagons filled the road from Harpers Ferry for twelve miles.[19]

A dim-witted cavalry lieutenant happened to be the next after Elzey to anger Jackson that day. Watching the procession pass by, he unthinkingly asked Jackson, "Are the troops going back?" "Don't you see them going?" answered an obviously annoyed Jackson. The lieutenant persisted. "Are they all going?" At that Jackson turned to his inspector general and ordered the man arrested as a spy. As the lieutenant stammered an apology and pled his innocence, Ashby arrived on the scene. He convinced Jackson that the lieutenant, although lacking in common sense, was a good officer who meant no harm.[20]

Jackson had lunch at the Charlestown residence of his chief of commissary, Maj. Wells J. Hawks. After eating he decided to take the train to Winchester rather than ride through the rain. Management of the retreat passed to Ewell. Mistakes were frequent No one notified the 1st Maryland (Confederate) of the movement, and the regiment was left behind to fall in with Winder the next day. At one point Ewell's ordnance train took a wrong turn and traveled several miles in the wrong direction. Despite the miscues the army made good time, marching twenty-five miles in ten hours before bivouacking for the night at Stephenson's Depot.

Alexander Boteler had hardly reached the railroad station at Charlestown before Jackson and Sandie Pendleton pounded up through the muck. Boteler was surprised to see them, but not as surprised as he was by Jackson's actions after they boarded the train. "As soon as we took our places in the car, putting his arm on the back of the seat before him as a rest for his head, he fell into a sleep which lasted all the way to Winchester with but one interruption."[21]

The interruption came at Stephenson's Depot. Scanning the countryside with his field glass—perhaps for marauding Yankee cavalrymen—Boteler noticed what appeared to be a single Confederate trooper galloping hard through the rain to intercept the train. Boteler prevailed upon the conductor to stop. The lone rider was Jed Hotchkiss, and drawing rein at the car window he handed a dispatch to Jackson. Hotchkiss waited for orders, or at least a response. None came. "He read it and smiled grimly but said nothing." Jackson shared the contents of the dispatch with Boteler and Pendleton, then tore it up. Dropping the fragments on the floor of the car, he said to the conductor, "Go on, sir, if you please," and then went back to sleep.[22]

That Jackson was able to resume his slumbers was a testimony either to his fatigue or to a sudden return of his customary equanimity. The news Hotchkiss brought could not have been worse. Late that morning the Federals had driven the 12th Georgia from Front Royal. The dispatch, which Col. Z. T. Conner had scribbled from Winchester, read: "General: Just arrived, enemy in full pursuit, unless immediately succored all is lost. Yours Conner."[23]

AT FRONT ROYAL everyone from Colonel Conner down to the lowest private had apprehended danger. On the morning of May 29 Conner had warned his immediate superior, General Elzey, that a prisoner captured the night before at Rectortown had claimed that Shields was en route to Front Royal from Fredericksburg with fourteen thousand troops—an exaggeration of Shields's strength but an otherwise accurate confession. Conner begged Elzey for instructions. "Shall I burn stores on approach of the enemy and come up to the division? Please answer." There was no reply.

Rumors of Shields's approach swirled through the ranks. On the twenty-ninth Pvt. James Griffin noted in his diary that "there came a dispatch the enemy was encamped in eighteen miles of this place advancing on us with fifteen thousand." The same day Shepherd Pryor confided to his wife: "Our regiment is in a good position here, nineteen miles from our main army—to all be captured: I fear the consequences." Even the townspeople knew that trouble was coming. Nineteen-year-old Lucy Buck wrote in her diary, also on May 29, "There is some excitement in town in consequence of the reported advance of Shields."[24]

The Yankees were closer than anyone thought. A small detachment of cavalry had been assigned him, but Conner apparently neglected to push out patrols on the Manassas Gap railroad or the parallel turnpike leading into Front Royal from Manassas Gap—routes that Shields must take to enter Front Royal. His pickets gave him no more than an hour's notice of the enemy approach, and the Yankees, wrote a Georgia soldier about the events of May 30, "were on us almost before we knew it."[25]

The suddenness of the Federal assault was a tribute to the aggressiveness of Shields and hard marching by Nathan Kimball's brigade. General McDowell had promised President Lincoln that Shields would be in Front Royal by noon on May 30, and Shields was determined not to disappoint. At 4:00 P.M. on the twenty-ninth he ordered Kimball to march from Rectortown "immediately; leave your teams and wagons, take only ambulances, ammunition wagons, and provisions, as much as on hand in haversacks."[26]

Two hours later Kimball's command was on the road. An all-night march brought his brigade to the outskirts of Front Royal at 11:30 A.M. Colonel Sawyer led the advance with his own 8th Ohio, two sections of artillery under the personal command of Col. Philip Daum, who at Kernstown had wanted to be in the thick of every scrape, and a squadron of the 1st Rhode Island Cavalry under Capt. William P. Ainsworth.

Nearing Front Royal, Sawyer divided his regiment into two assault groups. He sent Maj. Horace Winslow with half the regiment along the railroad tracks north of Front Royal, while passing with the other half of the 8th Ohio and Ainsworth's squadron around a high hill to halt just in view of the town. Daum led two cannons up the hill. A mile away the camp of the 12th Georgia was plainly visible. There was not the slightest sign of alarm. Sawyer made ready to surround the slumbering Georgians, when "that blockhead Colonel Daum," said cannoneer James Gildea, "warned them by firing two shots into them while we were still a mile off."[27]

The effect was electric. Georgians scattered in every direction. As soon as they abandoned their camp, a mob of civilians—"men, women, and children, colored and white"—rummaged for discarded articles," recollected young Thomas Ashby. Daum's cannonade interrupted their looting. Said Ashby: "While the camp of the 12th Georgia was being ransacked by the people of the village, a piece of artillery was run up without warning on a hill one mile south, and a shell was thrown into the camp. Such running and screaming has seldom been heard. The camp was deserted in the twinkling of an eye."

With the element of surprise gone, Colonel Sawyer waved Ainsworth's squadron forward. As the one hundred Yankee troopers galloped into town from the southeast in column of fours, Colonel Conner departed with one of several wagon trains toward the northwest. Behind him he left the depot and an adjacent warehouse stocked with $300,000 in Federal stores aflame, together with several loaded freight cars. Before retreating, a detail from the 12th Georgia also managed to set fire to the road bridge over the South Fork. But in their haste the Georgians neglected to fire the railroad bridge, an egregious oversight from which the Federals later would benefit. By an eerie coincidence, a violent thunderstorm burst over the town at the same time the depot flames threatened to engulf a fair part of it. For a change the secessionist citizens of Front Royal were glad to have Yankees in their midst. "The Confederates had deserted us and in doing so had threatened the destruction of our village by setting fire to the depot," Thomas Ashby wrote. "But for the rush of the Federal troops, who fought the spread of the fire, and the copious downpour of rain, the place would have been wiped out. Our enemies and the bounty of nature saved us from a general conflagration."[28]

Company C of the 4th Ohio was the first unit to reach the burning buildings. Coming onto the field shortly after Sawyer, Kimball had deployed the 4th to the left of Sawyer's detachment. He sent the regiment through open fields to the left of the turnpike at the same time that Ainsworth charged. The Ohioans hastened into town on the double-quick and headed straight for the conflagration.

Dousing the flames proved a risky gamble. "We removed two carloads of burning muskets from cars and depot buildings," an Ohio private recollected. "Many of the loaded muskets becoming heated, kept up a dangerous fusillade and drove the men from the cars and a burning building." Three locomotives, ten cars, and a large amount of muskets and equipment were saved. The depot and adjoining warehouses burned to the ground, but the fire was contained. Also liberated were several hundred prisoners, among them most of the men of the 1st Maryland (Union) Infantry.[29]

With Conner well on his way to Winchester, Maj. Willis A. Hawkins ordered his men to lay down their arms before Ainsworth's charge. Most refused. Capt. William F. Brown, a grizzled officer commended on later battlefields for "cool daring," took charge. Regrouping on the high, steep ridge between the North and South forks of the Shenandoah, the Georgians released a volley into Ainsworth's eager cavalrymen as they entered the narrow gorge between the river and the ridge after thundering across the bridge. Ainsworth was killed, and seven other saddles were emptied. That ended the Yankee pursuit, but not before Rhode Island troopers had gathered in 128 members of the 12th Georgia, together with two dozen sick and wounded from other regiments who had been convalescing in town.

Pvt. Irby H. Scott was among those of the 12th who escaped. But it had not been easy. Said Scott: "We had to run some distance to save ourselves and retreat to Winchester. A good many of the boys tired down and scattered through the woods, where they were picked up by the enemy's cavalry, some few escaping."[30]

Kimball ordered his brigade to bivouac on the heights west of the South Fork, where they endured a through soaking. "The whole country was flooded," said Colonel Sawyer, "the clouds seeming absolutely to burst in our midst." General Shields came up at 5:00 P.M. with the other brigades of the division. He sent an infantry task force to reconnoiter down the Front Royal road, but a detachment of Ashby's cavalry supported by Chew's battery halted the Federals at Cedarville.[31]

Colonel Conner had escaped from the Yankees only to fall captive to his seeming incapacity for command. That evening Jackson summoned him to give an account of his actions. Entering Jackson's office, the Georgian asked the obvious, "General, I suppose you have heard of my misfortune at Front Royal."

"Yes," snapped Jackson.

"Well General, I did the best fighting I could, but we were overpowered."

"Colonel Conner, how many men did you have killed?"

"I had no men killed, General," replied Conner.

"Colonel Conner, do you call that fighting?" Jackson answered and then dismissed him.

Conner left the room with Jackson's chief commissary officer, Major Hawks. Turning to Hawks, Conner grumbled, "Major, I believe General Jackson is crazy."

Sandie Pendleton emerged from Jackson's office and confronted Conner. "Colonel, consider yourself under arrest."

"Now I know he is crazy," Conner told Hawks.

An order also went out for the arrest of Major Hawkins for cowardice.[32]

WARM, HEAVY RAINS drenched the Lower Valley well into the night of May 30. To Rufus Saxton, who wrestled, so he thought, with Winder for possession of Bolivar Heights, the clash of arms amid nature's tumult was stunning. "The night was intensely dark; the hills around were alive with the signal lights of the enemy; the rain descended in torrents; vivid flashes of lightning illuminated at intervals the magnificent scenery, while the crash of thunder, echoing among the mountains, drowned into comparative insignificance the roar of our artillery." After thirty minutes Winder broke contact. The storm abated near midnight, and the flicker of signal lights was all to show that the Confederates remained near.

At the Taylor Hotel, where Jackson set up headquarters and took lodging, the thunderstorm served only to accentuate the prevailing gloom. Only Jackson seemed immune. That evening Jed Hotchkiss took a moment to scribble in his diary the dire prognosis, "Danger environs the army." Nevertheless, he thought Jackson in remarkably "fine spirits," although he "manifested more anxiety about getting the Stonewall Brigade back to his command in safety than I ever saw him do at any other time."

Jackson called Hotchkiss to his room sometime between 10:00 P.M. and midnight and directed him to ride at once to Charlestown and bring Winder back. Giving the mapmaker his customary advice, "Take no counsel of your fears," Jackson said he would remain in Winchester awaiting Winder as long as possible. Hotchkiss must see to it that the Stonewall Brigade moved with all speed. Impressed with the gravity of the task, Hotchkiss asked Jackson what he should do if he found Winchester occupied before he reached it. "Bring the men around through the mountain," replied Jackson. With those discouraging words on which to cogitate, Hotchkiss set off with a small escort into the pitch-black night.[33]

Alexander Boteler lifted his spirits that night with liquor. Jackson had asked him to wait two or three hours before setting off for Staunton so the general could prepare some important official papers for Boteler to carry along. That suited Boteler; his son had been wounded in the Battle of Winchester and was then lying in the home of a friend. Hurrying to the friend's house, Boteler was delighted to find both his son and his own wife, who had come to Winchester without his knowledge. After lingering as long as he thought permissible, Boteler went to the Taylor Hotel at 10:00 P.M. Before going to Jackson's room, he ordered two whiskey toddies to be brought up after him. When they appeared he offered one to Jackson, who drew back, saying, "No, no, colonel, you must excuse me; I never drink intoxicating liquors."

"I know that, general, but though you habitually abstain, as I do myself, from everything of the sort, there are occasions, and this is one of them, when a stimulant will do us both good, otherwise I would neither take it myself nor offer it to you. So you must make an exception to your general rule and join me in a toddy tonight."

Jackson again shook his head, but nonetheless took the tumbler and began to sip its contents. Setting it down partly emptied, he asked, "Colonel, do you know why I habitually abstain from intoxicating drinks?"

Boteler said he did not.

"Why, sir, because I like the taste of them, and when I discovered that to be the case I made up my mind at once to do without them altogether."[34]

Jackson may be excused for imbibing with Boteler. The Valley army was in a critical situation with little prospect of escape. Shields's division at Front Royal was only twelve miles from Strasburg. Bayard and Ord had advanced to Thoroughfare Gap. King's division, ten thousand strong, had moved up to

Catlett's Station. Frémont at Wardensville was twenty miles from Strasburg. The bulk of the Valley army at Stephenson's Depot was twenty-five miles from Strasburg and the Stonewall Brigade at Halltown nearly twice that distance. The wagons carrying the spoils of Martinsburg and Front Royal were still at Winchester. With them were more than 2,000 prisoners, a burden for a retreating army only seven times larger. An easy march would put Shields with 11,000 men astride the Valley Pike at Strasburg by mid-morning on the thirty-first; Frémont might have his 14,800 up before mid-afternoon. In other words, on May 31 forces double the number of the Valley army could close Jackson's only escape route easily. And then there were Saxton and Banks. Winder's demonstration had placed Saxton firmly on the defensive, but Banks appeared ready to recross the Potomac at any moment. Saturday, May 31, might well prove the day the Valley army ceased to exist.[35]

THERE SEEMED EVERY prospect that both Frémont and Shields would close the pincers on Jackson. On May 30 the Pathfinder had marched his command twenty miles in twelve hours—not a bad record considering the poor state of Blenker's divisions and the heavy rain that dogged the column most of the way. President Lincoln certainly expected Frémont to do his part. At 9:30 P.M. he forwarded him a telegram from Saxton to Stanton indicating that the Rebels were still menacing Harpers Ferry, with the laconic observation, "It seems the game is before you." He offered the same admonition to McDowell.

Shields seemed ready and anxious for the game. He thought Jackson had twenty thousand men, and he told McDowell that evening: "All now depends on activity. Frémont's forces should be pushed forward by direct orders from Washington. If all this be done with activity, the enemy will be captured or cut to pieces."[36]

For all his bluster, Shields failed to follow through with the promised activity. Saturday, May 31, dawned clear and warm. No impediment except for a small body of Ashby's cavalry stood between his division and Strasburg. Somehow Shields got it in his mind that Maj. Gen. James Longstreet's division had come from Richmond to reinforce Jackson and was already in Page Valley. If that were the case, Shields reckoned, marching on Strasburg would expose his rear to attack. Of course, had rumors of Longstreet's approach been true, Joe Johnston would have had scarcely a corporal's guard with which to hold Richmond. Kimball also was nervous. To him, Turner Ashby's paltry command was a "considerable force" that posed a serious threat to his brigade.[37]

Bedeviled by chimera, Shields did nothing all day. In the evening, Kimball took it upon himself to test his assumption of the enemy's strength. It proved wrong. The resourceful Col. Samuel Carroll advanced with his regiment and drove the Rebels off after a brief clash, taking several prisoners and an eleven-pounder cannon. "The enemy having retreated and night having set in," reported Kimball, "Carroll returned to his position."[38]

In the final analysis, responsibility for Shields's inaction rested on the shoulders of Irvin McDowell. He issued Shields no orders to move on Strasburg that day; on the contrary, his communications with the Irishman suggest that he wanted action deferred until Ord's division arrived. Early in the afternoon his chief of staff, Lt. Col. Edward Schriver, informed Shields that "the general is doing everything possible to send forward reinforcements, prepared for the field in every way" and that Frémont was expected to reach Strasburg at 5:00 P.M. But Schriver had no orders for Shields except "Get your division well in hand to go forward to his support." Not go forward to Frémont's support, but be prepared to do so. Nothing more was heard of McDowell or his staff until they rode into Front Royal at 9:00 P.M., having spent twelve hours on the road from Rectortown.[39]

Frémont also came up short on May 31, well short of his promise of the day before that he would be in Strasburg by 5:00 P.M. At that hour his army was slogging its way up the steep western slope of Big North Mountain, the victim of torrential rains that reduced the poor mountain road to paste. It was midnight before the column closed up in the narrow valley between Big North and Little North mountains. Frémont was able, however, to push his advance —two regiments of infantry and a section of artillery under Col. Gustave P. Cluseret—to the west bank of Cedar Creek, just five miles west of Strasburg. While the soldiers of Frémont's army passed a cheerless night in the rain and muck, Frémont and his staff holed up in a broken-down, abandoned farmhouse.[40]

There had been little that day to cheer Stonewall Jackson, except, perhaps, at its end, the knowledge that his army had survived another twenty-four hours. Reveille in the camps around Stephenson's Depot had sounded well before daybreak, but the wagon train and procession of nearly two thousand prisoners and their guard, the 21st Virginia Infantry, delayed their march. The wagon train, which rolled up the Valley Pike in double column, alone stretched seven miles. The first of Jackson's infantry, Taylor's Louisiana Brigade, did not enter Winchester until 8:00 A.M. The mood was somber, among both the soldiers and the populace. As she stood on the pavement passing out food to the men, Mary Greenhow Lee mused: "I could not take in the idea that our soldiers were again leaving us to the Yankees, but they evidently think so, and are so grave about it; they leave us with a fear they had not felt before." And after their murderous antics of May 25, the women of Winchester in particular feared what might follow. "If the Yankees should come here," Lee recorded in her diary, "we will have a far worse time than before."[41]

Stonewall Jackson rode with the vanguard and often beyond. Capt. Edward H. McDonald, whose cavalry company kept close to Frémont's advance, encountered Jackson at midday on the Valley Pike five miles north of Strasburg. Except for two couriers, the general was alone. Behind him the army kept a grueling pace. Fifty minutes of marching filled every hour. Rest periods never exceeded ten minutes. Rumors flew that the Yankees held Strasburg and were awaiting the Confederates in full battle array.

But the rumors proved false, and the Southerners bivouacked for the night in a shallow semicircle along Cedar Creek north of Strasburg. The 21st Virginia halted beside a huge barn near the creek; there they permitted as many prisoners as would fit indoors to take shelter from the rain. Jackson made his headquarters at the George Hupp residence, near the hill of the same name.[42]

Notably absent that night was the Stonewall Brigade, which with the 1st Maryland Infantry (Confederate) had halted at 10:00 P.M. in rain-soaked fields north of Newton, "when flesh and blood could no longer respond to the relentless demand to push on," said George Booth of the 1st. Fellow Marylander Capt. John E. Howard agreed: "Never was I so tired in my life, as I lied down that night in a hard rain to rest my weary limbs and blistered feet. Under no circumstances could any of us possibly have held out."[43]

The officers and men had ample cause for exhaustion. They had marched thirty-five miles on empty stomachs, fully cognizant of their peril and the need for haste. The 2nd Virginia had had it even worse; the men had hiked forty-two miles and had gone two days without rations.

A courier had preceded Jed Hotchkiss on the night of May 30 with orders for the Stonewall Brigade to rejoin the army. The rider reached Winder at midnight. Winder immediately recalled the 2nd Virginia from Loudoun's Heights. "This order," recollected the regimental chaplain, "was executed as rapidly as the dense darkness of that cloudy night would permit." At Charlestown the regiment was reunited with the brigade, and the march resumed at daybreak. The 1st Maryland (Confederate) covered the rear. At dusk the Stonewall Brigade had entered Winchester. With his men straggling fearfully, Winder had found time to take tea with Mary Greenhow Lee and enjoy a song or two with her daughters. By the time the brigade neared Newton, there were more men strung out along the road to the rear than in the ranks. Jackson wanted Winder at Strasburg no later than 7:00 A.M. on May 31, but Winder ignored the command. Snarling to McHenry Howard that he would rather lose his men in battle than on a march, he called a halt to reward the hearty and to allow those who had fallen behind to catch up.[44]

With Winder ten miles north of Strasburg, Shields a similar distance east of the town, and Frémont five miles to the west, on the night of May 31 the safety of the Valley army was far from assured. Despite the obvious hazard of lingering between two Federal forces, Jackson had to hold the road open at Strasburg until the Stonewall Brigade and 1st Maryland (Confederate) arrived. Not overly concerned about Shields, he issued orders during the night for Ashby to picket the roads from Ninevah and Cedarville on the chance that the oddly supine Irishman should venture toward the Valley Pike to intercept Winder. He detached no infantry units in the direction of Front Royal. With the poor showing of Ashby's troopers during the pursuit of Banks's army still fresh in his mind, Jackson directed his cavalry chief to send him status reports every hour on June 1.

The more immediate threat was Frémont, and Jackson took strong steps to thwart his advance. Before midnight he directed Colonel Fulkerson to take his brigade at daylight two or three miles out the Moorefield road and throw out a thick screen of skirmishers to complement McDonald's cavalry. Ewell was to follow with his entire division. The trains under Major Harman, who was so fatigued that Jed Hotchkiss had to help him, were to pass through Strasburg at dawn and halt at Fisher's Hill until further notice. The 21st Virginia with its flock of Yankee prisoners was to follow.[45]

Nature augured a fine day for marching—or fighting. Sunday morning, June 1, began cloudy, but the clouds rolled away early. Bright skies were a welcome change to the weary soldiers of both armies as they rose from their wet bivouacs. The men of the 21st Virginia awoke to a bit of fun at the expense of their captives. As it happened the barn in which the Virginians had allowed the Yankees to sleep was full of hay. "We went to the door and ordered all out; we then called for those that were concealed to come out, or they would be punished when found," Private Worsham remembered. "None came, so some of our men were ordered to go in and see if they could find any. Two or three were pulled out of the hay amidst shouts from their comrades, as well as our men. Then we fixed bayonets and told them we were going to thrust the bayonets into the hay in the entire building. One or two came out, and presently the bayonets began to be used. A few strokes and a man is struck, but fortunately for him not hard enough to hurt him. He and several others then came out."

"We formed line of battle and commenced the march," continued Worsham. "At Strasburg we could see Ewell's division in line of battle on the right of the road, awaiting the advance of Frémont."[46]

Fighting already had begun along the Moorefield road by the time the 21st Virginia and its prisoners shuffled past. First contact came at about 7:00 A.M. as McDonald's troopers fell back before Cluseret's two infantry regiments, which had crossed Cedar Creek at dawn. Colonel Fulkerson arrived at the head of his brigade in time to meet the Federal skirmishers, consisting of two companies each from the 60th Ohio and 8th West Virginia, which "came down the road and through the woods at double quick." Fulkerson deployed a cloud of skirmishers, and the two sides settled into a desultory exchange across a wide meadow.[47]

At 9:45 A.M. Frémont's chief of artillery, Lt. Col. John Pilsen, wheeled two cannons into position near the Union skirmish line and opened up. A Confederate battery responded. From atop Little North Mountain, Frémont and his staff heard the "heavy crack in advance, with the echoes reverberating again and again among the hills, [which] told us of the presence of the enemy," recollected Col. Albert Tracy:

> The general was up at the front full speedily, with his eye glancing and his whole manner indicative of hope and eagerness. A telegram of but a day previous, from earnest friends at Washington, had apprised him that he must find Jackson and fight him, or his chances thereafter for further preferment or reputation were as naught; such indeed are the politics, together with the machinations of the day. Hence as well the more than ordinary manifestation on the part of the general, who was but ripe for the contest to open.[48]

As the artillery duel opened, General Ewell came on the field and assumed command from Fulkerson. Perplexed that Frémont had not pushed the Confederate lines harder, Ewell rode forward to the skirmish line for a firsthand look at the situation. After a few minutes he summoned his ranking brigade commander, Richard Taylor. It was a call Taylor had dreaded; he was feeling terrible that morning, and the Union shelling was only making matters worse. "Whether from fatigue, loss of sleep, or what not, there I was, nervous as a lady, ducking like a mandarin. It was disgusting, and [I] hope no one saw me."

Taylor reported his incapacity to Ewell. "I told him I was no more good than a frightened deer."

"Nonsense!" Ewell answered with a laugh. "'Tis your servant's strong coffee—better give it up."

Returning to the business at hand, Ewell told Taylor: "Remain here in charge while I go out to the skirmishers. They won't advance, but stay out there in the woods, making a great fuss with their guns, and I don't wish to commit myself to much advance while Jackson is absent." With that, Ewell put spurs to his horse and left Taylor with his jangled nerves.

Contriving "to sit my horse respectably" in the presence of Ewell's staff, Taylor heard a "brisk fusillade, which seemed gradually to recede." Ewell returned, a look of bewilderment on his face. "I am completely puzzled," he told Taylor. "I have just driven everything back to the main body, which is large. Dense wood everywhere. Jackson told me not to commit myself too far. At this rate my attentions are not likely to become serious enough to commit anybody! I wish Jackson were here himself!"[49]

General Taliaferro happened to report in from sick leave a few minutes before the artillery opened fire. Jackson greeted him cordially at headquarters. "He insisted that I should rest myself upon his bed and assured me that he had no immediate expectation of collision with the enemy." Taliaferro consented, and Jackson carefully placed the blankets over his recumbent subordinate. "I had not long indulged in this unusual luxury when the not very distant boom of artillery aroused me, and Jackson, hurrying in, directed me to hasten to the menaced front." Jackson remained behind, glued to headquarters by his anxiety for Winder. So absorbed was he in the fate of his old brigade that he forgot the Sabbath. When the customary order for worship services failed to materialize, Chaplain Avirett of Ashby's cavalry, apparently ignorant of the army's peril, went to headquarters to inquire about devotions. "Is this Sunday?" asked Jackson. "It had escaped me: I have been very busy lately." Just then Ewell's guns bellowed another salvo, and, remembered Taliaferro, "the inquiry needed no answer. There was no service that day."[50]

The thunder of the artillery exchange rolled down the Valley Pike. To Winder's haggard men it seemed a sinister omen. They were then near Middletown. No one needed to hurry them. Artilleryman Lanty Blackford said, "We were now pretty well convinced of the true state of the case rendering rapid marching necessary." The mood was somber. "It was a silent and gloomy column that trudged along the turnpike that morning. Officers and men were silent as the grave—occupied all with the same gloomy apprehensions. I fancied that even the gallant General Winder looked chagrined and gloomy," remembered Confederate Marylander Randolph H. McKim. "These anxieties came to a climax when we heard the booming of artillery ahead of us. The men exchanged glances, but no one spoke a word, though the same thought was in every mind, 'We are cut off now—it's all up with us.' "[51]

McHenry Howard happened to be riding a hundred yards ahead of the column when he spotted a group of cavalrymen in front, huddled on horseback near the mouth of the road leading from Middletown to Front Royal. Riding nearer, Howard recognized the dark complexion of Turner Ashby.

Ashby spoke first. "Is that General Winder coming up?" Howard replied in the affirmative. "Thank God for that," sighed Ashby. Shaking Winder's hand warmly when he came up, Ashby said: "General, I was never so relieved in my life. I thought that you would be cut off and had made up my mind to join you and advise you to make your escape over the mountain to Gordonsville."

Together the party rode on a short distance to a point where the Valley Pike offered an unobstructed view of the country as far as Strasburg. Remembered Howard: "We could plainly see the smoke of the discharges of the guns we had heard, seeming to be almost in our front as the turnpike was then running, and we knew that Jackson was holding back Frémont until we got by." To everyone's relief, all was quiet to the east, "where we looked for trouble from an advance by Shields."[52]

At noon the Stonewall Brigade marched into Strasburg. "How different our feelings then!" exclaimed Private McKim. "Our spirits rose; we forgot our fatigue and were ready to sing. What the men said to each other then was of a different complexion—'Old Jack knows what he's about! He'll take care of us, you bet!' From that hour we never doubted him." A dole of rations from captured sutlers' stores, eaten on the march, refreshed the men, as did the contents of a whiskey barrel scavenged near Cedar Creek. "To roll out the barrel, knock out the head, was but the work of a moment, and as the regiment formed again to take up the march, a liberal draught was given to each man."[53]

Winder's close call gave rise to a popular story, developed in the ranks. Some tired wag turned to a comrade and remarked that Jackson was a better leader than Moses. When asked why, the man declared: "It took Moses forty years to lead the Israelites through the Wilderness, while Jackson would have double-quicked them through in three days."[54]

With Winder safe, Jackson hastened to the front. Confirming Ewell's better judgment—Taylor thought Ewell had had to restrain his impulse to lay into Frémont with everything he had—Jackson ordered him and Taliaferro to break contact and retire to Strasburg. Winder would cover Ewell's passage through town from the incomplete hilltop fort that Banks had left behind. From Strasburg the army would march south, its destination for the day the village of Woodstock. Taylor drew rear-guard duty with orders to form his brigade on Fisher's Hill until Winder passed up the pike. The 2nd and 6th Virginia Cavalry regiments, with Brockenbrough's Maryland Battery in support, were assigned to picket the road between Taylor and the enemy.[55]

Disengaging preparatory to a withdrawal is normally a risky endeavor in war. But in this instance no attempt was made to interrupt the Confederate timetable. Frémont had talked a good game to his staff, but at the crucial moment he had lacked the stomach for a fight. Jackson's reputation suddenly loomed large, and a thousand doubts seized him. Had Jackson not whipped Banks just a week earlier? Was it not probable that Jackson outnumbered him, as he had Banks? Where was McDowell? At noon Frémont had most of his command in line of battle, ready and anxious for the word to push forward. Instead, the Pathfinder grumbled excuses. In his diary Colonel Tracy recorded them as though they mirrored his own thoughts. The force they faced, explained Tracy, was likely a rear guard. "But it is possible that, knowing our actually inferior numbers, he may be coming out to fight us. The rear, therefore, is hastened forward and a general halt called upon. And now, with the very important consideration of the refreshment and compact closing up of his columns, the general has determined to make camp."[56]

As if portending Frémont's fate, late in the afternoon black clouds rolled over Little North Mountain. Near sunset the heavens opened with "one of the most violent rainstorms I have ever seen, with really terrible lightning and thunder," reported Frémont, who had suffered more than his share of violent weather on his Western expeditions. First came "sudden, bristly hail," marveled Tracy, who had just sat down in his tent to eat, "and then rain in such masses, and with drops so huge, that we could not so much as keep the tea in our cups. Our plates, with bacon and hardtack, were simply flooded. Tents and flies began to be tossed about, or tumbled over with the wind, the general himself being driven out and forced to take refuge in his ambulance."[57]

The anger of the storm roused Frémont from his lethargy, and he ordered Cluseret, reinforced with two companies of the 4th New York Cavalry under the irrepressible Charles Zagonyi and Col. Philip Figyelmesy, another foreign-born officer of Frémont's staff, to feel his way through the blackness and rain toward Strasburg. Finding the town vacant, Cluseret edged his cavalry screen up the Valley Pike.

At 11:00 P.M. the New York troopers encountered a lone picket from the 6th Virginia Cavalry who, after parleying a bit with Colonel Figyelmesy in the dark, asked to what army he belonged. In answer, Zagonyi bellowed the command "Charge!" and the New Yorkers ran down the picket before he could raise his rifled musket. Twenty yards on they, in turn, stumbled into a booby trap of several strands of telegraph wire stretched across the road. Three riders in the first column of fours were thrown from their horses, but the fourth kept his seat and, drawing his saber, hacked through the wire.[58]

Zagonyi's squadron thundered up the pike in the dark, scattering the 2nd and 6th Virginia Cavalry like chaff. Many of the Virginia horsemen had been asleep in their saddles when the charge came. The noisy Federals so frightened them that they rode over Brockenbrough's battery in their haste to escape. "More than one man," said Campbell Brown, "leaped a twelve-pounder lengthwise." It was another instance of George Steuart's incapacity as a cavalry commander.[59]

Richard Taylor had scarcely settled his men into line along Fisher's Hill when the commotion from the cavalry caught his ear. "Thinking I heard firing to the north, I mounted and looked for the pike. The darkness was so intense that I could not have found it but for the whiteness of the limestone." Taylor collared some troopers galloping rearward. They warned him that they were among the last friendly horsemen on the pike; nearly everyone else already had passed south beyond Fisher's Hill. Close on their heels, they added, was a large force of Union cavalry covering a larger force of infantry.

"This was pleasant," thought Taylor. "Winder's brigade—the last to move— had marched at least four hours since, so that a wide interval existed between us. More firing, near and distinct, was heard, and the command ordered down to the pike, which it reached after much stumbling and swearing, and some confusion. Taylor grabbed two companies and Bowyer's Virginia Battery and started toward the shooting. "The column had scarcely got into motion before a party of horses rushed through the guard, knocking down several men, one of whom was severely bruised. There was a little pistol shooting and saber-hacking, and for some minutes things were rather mixed." The Federals disentangled themselves and galloped headlong back down the pike, stumbling over the abandoned howitzers of Brockenbrough's battery, which in the blackness they had scarcely noticed.

The Yankees took with them eighteen prisoners at a cost of half a dozen wounded, and one officer, a Lieutenant Hawkins, injured in the thigh and captured. Hawkins barely escaped the scrape with his life. A party of angry Louisianans surrounded and were about to bayonet him when Turner Ashby intervened. Ashby detailed some of his own men to build a shelter for Hawkins. The Virginians stayed by him until the Federal cavalry returned the next morning, not leaving him until the Yankee advance had come within shooting distance. Ashby, it seems, had overcome his hatred of officers in blue.[60]

Ashby rounded up enough men to make a respectable pursuit of Zagonyi's squadron until he too was turned back by infantry. Several steady volleys fired into the night from the 60th Ohio cleared the pike of Rebel horsemen. The hoof beats of retreating cavalry receded, and only the drumbeat of heavy rain remained. Muddy from head to foot, wet through every thread of their uniforms, the members of Cluseret's column returned to camp, bringing with them the news that Jackson was in retreat to the south.[61]

For some reason Frémont had elected to telegraph Washington the news of the day prior to Cluseret's return. Not that there was any rush, since all outgoing messages had to be carried by horseback to the telegraph station at Moorefield for transmission. In his impatience, Frémont managed to combine bad news with a touch of humor, telling Lincoln: "A reconnoitering force just in reports the enemy retreating, but in which direction is not yet known. Our cavalry will occupy Strasburg by midnight. Terrible storm of thunder and hail now passing over. Hailstones as large as hens' eggs."[62]

SHIELDS AND MCDOWELL danced the day away in a comic two-step that had begun when Ord's division—now commanded by Brig. Gen. James Ricketts because Ord was sick—failed to complete its march to Front Royal the evening before. Still reluctant to move with only one division at hand, McDowell devoted the first hours after daybreak on June 1 to urging Ricketts's nine thousand men forward. "They were wet, had not tents, and were very much exposed but they got along the best way they could," McDowell later testified to the Joint Congressional Committee on the Conduct of the War. "They kept coming in, in driblets, sometimes in considerable bodies."[63]

The distant thunder of artillery aided McDowell's labors. "We heard firing, and that animated them somewhat, and they began to come in pretty fast."

The exact source of the noise was hard to pinpoint, and McDowell erred in thinking that it came from the direction of Winchester. On that supposition he started Kimball's brigade down the Cedarville road. At 1:00 P.M. two staff officers from Shields's division, who had ridden with a corporal's guard of the 1st Ohio Cavalry toward Strasburg when the firing was first heard, returned to Front Royal to report that they had spotted Jackson's wagon train rumbling south on the Valley Pike. They had not seen the shooting but guessed that it came from the direction of Middletown, and that Banks evidently was pressing Jackson's rear. McDowell naively reported as much to the War Department, which must have sent Stanton into a fit. While Shields's division sorted itself out between Cedarville and Front Royal, McDowell ordered General Bayard out on the road to Strasburg with the nearest available cavalry, the 1st Pennsylvania, and one battalion of the 13th Pennsylvania Reserves under Lt. Col. Thomas L. Kane.

Kane's battalion was a crack outfit. The men were recruited from among the hunters, trappers, and lumbermen of western Pennsylvania and armed with breech-loading Sharp's rifles. The battalion was trained by Kane according to a system of tactics for skirmishers that he had devised in protest against the European tactics that had been forced on American riflemen. His men were nicknamed "Bucktails" for their unique cap-accoutrements, and in terms of stamina and speed they were the equal of most Union cavalrymen.

McDowell had hoped that Bayard and Kane would bag Jackson's wagon train, but instead they found the foothills east of the Valley Pike bristling with artillery and the road filled with infantry. After some warning shells thrown its way, Bayard's detachment fell back across the North Fork of the Shenandoah River (either Ashby had neglected to burn the railroad bridge or Jackson had not thought to have ordered it). McDowell sent out the second regiment of Bayard's Brigade, the 1st New Jersey Cavalry, with orders for Bayard to hang close to the enemy's rear.[64]

Meanwhile, the firing to the west had ceased. Shields had an idea. Jackson evidently had slipped past Frémont and was heading south, most likely with the intention of leaving the Valley at Swift Run Gap to rejoin the army at Richmond. With McDowell's permission, Shields would take his division down Page Valley and cut off Jackson's escape route while Frémont pressed him from behind. McDowell weakly concurred. As he later told Congress: "Shields went off with my consent to Luray, as giving the only chance to effect anything[.] He knew the country, the roads, bridges, etc. better than I did."[65]

At 3:00 P.M. Shields's reunited division set out on the Luray road. To Sam Carroll, the aggressive commander of his Fourth Brigade, Shields gave special instructions. Carroll was to go forward rapidly with four pieces of artillery, less caissons, and some cavalry no later than the night of June 2 in order to burn the bridge across the South Fork of the Shenandoah near Conrad's Store. He was also to select a body of handpicked infantry without baggage to follow close behind as support. "This is the bridge by which Jackson retreated before and by which he will attempt to retreat again, as he can take the cars at Stanardsville for Charlottesville." Carroll should turn command of his brigade over to the next in command and see to the bridge burning himself. "Prepare fagots tomorrow along the road; pile them in your wagons. They can be found in old houses. I hope you have axes and tools along." Returning to a refrain that never seemed to apply to himself, Shields said: "Everything depends on speed. Press horses along the road where it is necessary, leaving your broken-down horses with the owner. Jackson must be overtaken. The burning of the bridge will effect it. You will earn your star if you do all this."[66]

CHAPTER 25

SAVE THE BRIDGE

AT PORT REPUBLIC

On June 2, 1862, the face of war as the citizens of the Shenandoah Valley knew it changed fundamentally. That was the day that Louis Blenker's German rabble began its lawless march up the Valley Pike. There had been occasional pilfering before—a chicken here, a basket of eggs there—but it was usually followed by promises of restitution or at least apologies from officers. Now the plundering was wholesale. The Germans ranged far and wide, robbing and despoiling at will. That thousands left the ranks is evident in the field returns for Frémont's command for June 1, which showed a one-week decrease in troop strength from just over 14,800 to 11,672. "We had a couple of brigades of New York Dutch who seldom marched in ranks but like ravening wolves were in every home near the road," remembered a horrified Ohioan. "After stripping women and children of their clothing as well as of all their proceeds, leaving them entirely destitute of a living, they would kill a cow and get her young. They would gather up young suckling pigs and poultry and stuff them in their haversacks among their crackers and would enter defenseless houses and threaten women with violence, providing they would not give them milk and butter and other things."[1]

Blenker and his subordinate officers winked at the depredations, and Frémont was slow to act against them. General Bayard was embarrassed to be part of Frémont's command. "I am in the Dutch army," he wrote his father after joining Frémont at Strasburg. General Milroy was furious. The mere mention of Blenker's robbers sent him into fits. "The Dutch brigades are composed of the most infernal robbers, plunderers, and thieves I have ever seen. Our army is disgraced by them. They straggle off from their companies and regiments for miles on each side of the road as we march along and enter every house—smokehouse, milk house, chicken house, kitchen, barn, corncrib, and stable—and clean out everything, frequently opening drawers, trunks, bureaus, etc. for plunder, leaving women and children crying behind them," he told his wife. "But no tears or entreaties stop or affect them; the only answer they make is 'Nix forstay.' The officers of these soldiers are to blame for the demoralized character of their soldiers, as they encourage and share in the plunder with them. Such conduct has injured our cause very much, and the name of Blenker's Dutch will be celebrated as vandals. General Frémont has not used the energy he might in trying to stop this disgraceful conduct."[2]

The Germans were not particular about whom they robbed. On June 4 Frémont's chief quartermaster reported, "I have no extra horses, saddles, or bridles, [they] having been stolen by Blenker's division."[3]

There was little to stand in the way of Blenker's thieves. Jackson's army seemed to be on the verge of collapse. The exertions and mental stress of the past seventy-two hours was playing hard on the men, as was the heat and humidity of early June. "The day was uncommonly hot, the sun like fire. Water was scarce along the road, and the men suffered greatly," noted General Taylor. When General Winder, who with the Stonewall Brigade and the 1st Maryland Infantry (Confederate) had taken Taylor's place at the rear of the army, asked him for help to fend off Frémont's advance at one point during the afternoon, Taylor contemplated ignoring the summons. "My men were so jaded as to make me unwilling to retrace the ground if it could be avoided," he said. "Confederate stragglers were picked up in the woods by the scores, and the route was lined with clothing, blankets, broken ambulances, muskets, and articles of equipment left behind by the pursued," remembered an Ohio infantryman.

There was no exaggeration in his claim. General Bayard netted over two hundred prisoners, and Federal infantry gathered in an equal number in his wake. War correspondent Sidney D. Maxwell passed one hundred Rebel prisoners in one short stretch of the road. Lt. James Dinwiddie of Capt. James Carrington's battery wrote home that nearly four hundred men "who dallied on the way, or who could not keep up," fell captive. Colonel Fulkerson told his sister he lost at least forty men from his regiment. "It is not to be wondered at. Many of the poor fellows actually walked much of that weary night [June 1] fast asleep, so worn out and exhausted were they with their terrible duty." And Col. Thomas Munford of the 2nd Virginia Cavalry observed, "Hundreds of our best infantry fell by the wayside." Freed from rear-guard duty, which fell to the 2nd and 6th Virginia Cavalry, Ashby's troopers lent a hand to the foot soldiers. Said Munford: "His steady cavalry, inspired by the indomitable and never weary Ashby, would help them, often taking them up behind them on their horses, or carrying their rifles, or allowing them to hold on and be supported by the stirrups as they limped forward."[4]

Heavy straggling played havoc with unit integrity. "One brigade divided another, and generals and colonels were wandering through the mass in search of their commands," Henry Kyd Douglas recollected. Jackson's patience wore thin, the more so as he had only slept three hours the night before—something of a standard with him since the Battle of Winchester. His "clouded brow and closed lips were ominous," said Douglas, who watched him dress down a frustrated brigade commander.

"Colonel, why do you not get your brigade together, keep it together and move on?" snapped Jackson.

"It's impossible, General; I can't do it."

"Don't say it's impossible," Jackson rejoined. "Turn your command over to the next officer. If he can't do it, I'll find someone who can, if I have to take him from the ranks."[5]

Picking up faltering infantrymen was about all the Southern cavalry was good for on June 2. As a leader of the mounted arm, Brig. Gen. George Steuart was proving incompetent beyond belief. Every attempt at a stand was quickly shattered by the Union cavalry, which under the command of Bayard and a British soldier of fortune named Col. Sir Percy Wyndham, was demonstrating uncustomary dash. Frémont covered the twelve miles between Strasburg and Woodstock in only five hours. So closely did he pursue the Confederates, said Private Worsham of the 21st Virginia, that from his place at the head of the army, guarding Federal prisoners, he could at times plainly see Bayard's cavalry silhouetted on hills to the rear.

After a particularly humiliating rout near Woodstock, in which an entire battery of artillery was nearly lost and the 6th Virginia Cavalry stampeded because Steuart had neglected to orchestrate a passage of lines between that regiment and the 2nd Virginia Cavalry, Colonels Flournoy and Munford sought out Jackson to plead for an immediate transfer to Ashby's command. Jackson acceded that evening. Steuart was relieved and placed in command of the reconstituted Maryland Line, and Ashby was given sole charge of the rear guard.[6]

News of the trouble in the rear had been slow to reach Jackson, who rode near the head of the march column most of the day. Near sunset Jackson was handed a dispatch from Ashby, who had helped rescue Munford and Flournoy from Steuart's bungling, advising him that the enemy was pressing him closely and that, unless he had infantry support, he might lose some of his artillery. At that very moment it began to rain, a torrential downpour that slowed movements to a crawl. "We were three miles at least from Colonel Ashby, and the general wanted to be there at once," said Douglas. "We went at a rushing pace, dashing through the mud and flooded roads. The troops made way and endeavored through the driving rain to raise their usual shout. They looked at 'Old Jack' with his hat in his hand replying to their salute by getting his head drenched in the shower and wondered, 'what has broke loose now?' "

Somewhere along the length of the column they ran into Ashby, who rode "calmly and slowly along the road, encased in innumerable gum blankets and capes and as unconcerned as if there was not an enemy within fifty miles." He said the enemy had stopped for the night. A perplexed Jackson handed him the dispatch that had caused such a commotion. Ashby smiled and said it had gone out at 8:00 A.M.; he had forgotten about it entirely. At once anxiety for Ashby's artillery turned to indignation against the courier. Douglas waited for an explosion of Jackson's wrath. Instead, he turned to his staff and said simply, "a water haul." Bowing to Ashby he rode off to seek shelter for the night.[7] He found it at the Israel Allen residence near Hawkinstown. The army camped in the vicinity of the hamlet, while the wagon train crossed the North Fork and parked on Meem's Bottom until floodwaters forced the wagons to move on. Frémont halted at Woodstock.

Before turning in for the night, Jackson scribbled a few hurried lines to his wife: "I am retiring before the enemy. They endeavored to get in my rear by moving on both flanks of my gallant army, but our God has been my guide and saved me from their grasp." He also wrote to General Johnston, unaware that he had been critically wounded two days earlier at the drawn battle of Seven Pines or that Robert E. Lee now commanded the army before Richmond. "I did not fall back too soon," he explained, "as the enemy's object was obviously to get in my rear, and had I not been in Strasburg yesterday the Federals would have been. We brought off a large amount of medical, ordnance, and other stores, but many have been destroyed for want of transportation, but the most valuable have been saved. I will hold myself in readiness to cross the Blue Ridge should you need me."

Weary though he was, Jackson correctly surmised Shields's intentions. He was not unduly worried about the Irishman, as he knew the rain that made marching uncomfortable on the macadamized Valley Pike would render it nightmarish on the dirt roads of Page Valley. Nonetheless, he sent a detachment of cavalry under Maj. Samuel A. Coyner to Page Valley to burn the White House and Columbia bridges, which would prevent Shields from affecting a junction with Frémont and keep him from heading off Jackson short of Harrisonburg. It also would condemn him to a march of sixty miles over muddy roads to reach a point not over fifty miles distant from the Valley army on its macadam approach. For good measure, Coyner destroyed the bridge at Conrad's Store the following day. It was the last span north of Port Republic by which Frémont and Shields might join forces.[8]

Frémont kept Washington well apprised of his activities on June 2. He wrote first to say that Bayard had joined him. The message went by way of Front Royal, where McDowell added a postscript informing Stanton of Shields's plan to intercept Jackson. The secretary was pleased. "Your dispatches received. We are glad to hear you are so close on the enemy. McClellan beat the Rebels badly near Richmond yesterday. The president tells me to say to you do not let the enemy escape from you. Let us hear from you often." There was no hint of disappointment in the failure of McDowell and Frémont to close the door at Strasburg. Perhaps the president understood that the thunderstorms of the past days were partly to blame. More good news came that afternoon, when Frémont wrote from Woodstock of the hundreds of Rebel stragglers encountered along the road and in nearby fields and forests, adding that "clothing, blankets, muskets, and sabers are also upon the road."[9]

The heavy rains gave bridges added tactical importance. On June 3 Confederate attention was concentrated on destroying the spans along the Valley Pike; that of the Federals on preserving them. Resuming the march at 7:00 A.M., Frémont gained an early advantage in the game. Bayard's cavalry came upon a Rebel detail in the process of breaking up a military bridge that Banks had built across Stony Creek at Edinburg the previous month to replace the civilian bridge Ashby had earlier destroyed. A portion of the planks had been torn up and the center timbers cut, so the structure was partly submerged when the 1st New Jersey cantered up to the bluffs overlooking the bridge. The Confederates were driven off before they could work further mischief. Bayard's troopers found a ford upstream, and Kane's Bucktails "skipped like rope dancers across the shaking beams of the ruined bridge." Ammunition was removed from caissons and wagons and carried across on horseback, and the 1st Maine Light Artillery followed the cavalry across the ford. Within an hour Bayard had resumed the chase. By noon Frémont's main body was across and again on the march.[10]

Federal luck held, and the bridge over Mill Creek, on the outskirts of Mount Jackson, was captured nearly intact. Turner Ashby, who had lingered on the enemy side of the creek, came close to being taken along with the bridge.

Nevertheless, Ashby was in good humor. That morning he had received word of his promotion to brigadier general. Jackson hoped the enhanced responsibility of brigade command would cause Ashby to expose himself less recklessly and perhaps induce him to exercise greater control over his half-disciplined troopers. But the brush at Mill Creek suggested otherwise. When Ashby overtook the army later in the afternoon, Sandie Pendleton took the opportunity to plead with him on Jackson's behalf. A dead brigadier was of no use, Pendleton observed, and Ashby could not long expect to escape death if he continued on his present course. Henry Kyd Douglas said Ashby dismissed Pendleton's concerns with an odd sort of logic. "He did not concur with the general opinion on the subject. He was not afraid of balls that were shot directly at him, for they always missed their mark. He only feared those random shots which always hit someone for whom they were not intended."[11]

Careful Southern preparations denied Frémont the crucial span over the North Fork of the Shenandoah at Meem's Bottom. The task of burning the bridge had been delegated to Capt. Edward H. McDonald of Ashby's command. It was his first detached duty, and McDonald was determined to leave nothing to chance. He had his men stuff the sides and underside of the roof of the covered bridge with straw and dry split wood. From a passing caisson McDonald procured several pounds of powder and a half-dozen shells. These he scattered through the straw, so that the touch of a torch would ignite nearly the entire bridge simultaneously. After the last of Jackson's infantry had crossed, McDonald deployed his men on the friendly side of the river to contest any Yankee attempt to charge the bridge. Behind McDonald's dismounted cavalrymen, artillery and infantry lined up on Rude's Hill to give weight to the defense.

Recrossing the bridge, McDonald waited on the north bank for Ashby's rear guard to come over. Most crossed in a fairly compact body, but a handful remained to challenge the enemy advance, which McDonald noticed was approaching at a brisk trot. "I hurried all the stragglers over except one bolder than the rest, for whom I waited, until the enemy was within pistol shot. As this last man came up, I told him we must ride fast as I wished to fire the bridge." As he turned, McDonald saw that the bridge had been ignited behind him prematurely. "As we galloped we deplored our fate and wondered what to do. The river was swollen and swift, and I knew that if I attempted to swim it in the face of the enemy I would be shot from my horse. The young man with me turned right and went up along the bank. I determined to ride through the burning bridge. As my horse touched the planks the smoke of burning straw and powder blinded me and my horse hesitated, but urged with my spurs he dashed through, while one or two of the shells exploded." From Rude's Hill, a chorus of cheers acknowledged McDonald's good work.[12]

The Valley army made camp between Rude's Hill and New Market. It had rained intermittently throughout the day. "To march at times we have to lock arms to steady each other or fall into the mud," a Mississippi rifleman told his mother. "The road was shoe-mouth deep in mud," recalled Capt. William C. Oates of the 15th Alabama. "My feet were blistered all over, on top as well as the bottom. I never was so tired and sleepy. Several times I went to sleep as I marched at the head of my company, and my orderly sergeant, who was an iron man, would catch me by the arm, shake and call me, 'Captain, Captain!' to arouse me."

Straggling worsened with every mud-splashed step. That night Capt. James K. Edmondson of the 27th Virginia wrote his wife that he had never seen his brigade "so completely broken down and unfitted for service. The march was so heavy that I am satisfied the brigade has lost at least one thousand men broken down, left on the way." James Dinwiddie of the Charlottesville Artillery painted a similar picture for his mother: "We have been on a retreat for five days and an awful time it has been. I never saw so many barefoot men with their feet all swollen and bleeding. Hundreds and hundreds drag along the road."[13]

Rest came hard even at night. New downpours soaked the army. The next day a District of Columbia weather station would record that, in the first four days of the month, northern Virginia had experienced more than 50 percent of the rainfall expected for the entire month during a normal year. "Cooking was out of the question," wrote artilleryman Lanty Blackford, "so hunger was added to our other discomforts. We lay disconsolately, with puddles of water here and there beneath us, about as miserable as outward surroundings could make us." Battery mate Randolph Fairfax agreed. "You have no idea of how completely exhausted our troops are," he told his sister. "In addition to our constant marching our night's rest is so disturbed that we scarcely get more than four or five hours of sleep in every twenty-four."[14]

Jackson was as exhausted as any man; indeed, the lack of sleep and personal fatigue to which he had been subjected worried his staff considerably. Headquarters was pitched in a field outside of New Market, and in the deluge that night the ground on which Jackson's tent was pitched became a creek. Douglas peaked into the tent the next morning to see water "still flowing and various small articles of apparel and furniture floating about like boats." Reluctantly Jackson allowed his staff to prevail upon him to move headquarters to a house in town.[15]

Denied the only means of crossing the North Fork, Frémont bivouacked at Mount Jackson on the night of June 3 and called forward his pontoon train from the rear of the column. Engineers worked through the night and by 6:00 A.M. on the fourth had completed a bridge. Two companies of cavalry and a regiment of infantry crossed before the river began to swell. Within a space of four hours it gained twelve feet. The current grew correspondingly swifter. Driftwood and logs slammed into the pontoons, carrying away planking, and the turbulent waters swamped several boats. As a last resort the ropes were cut, and the bridge swung loose to the northern bank. Artillery was brought up to cover the troops stranded on Meem's Bottom, and Frémont and his staff passed a frustrating day, speculating on the distance the enemy was putting between them. "The whole country is afloat," correspondent Sidney D. Maxwell jotted in his field diary. "So the enemy are now out of harm's way. A heavy smoke has been seen rising in the distance, as if another bridge were burning."

Food, or rather the absence of it, played on the minds of the waterlogged Federals. A similar freshet carried away the bridge over Stony Creek at Edinburg, stranding the army wagon train on the north bank. Blenker's marauding Germans suffered little from the stoppage in supplies, but in better-disciplined units, which had exhausted their three-day issue of rations the day before, the pangs of hunger were making themselves felt. Foraging became commonplace. Farm animals found along the pike between Edinburg and Mount Jackson were slaughtered with the permission of the high command, and enough grain was gathered from neighboring barns, said the regimental historian of the 1st New Jersey Cavalry, "to keep a show of life in the starving horses."[16]

Toward sunset on June 4 the rain slackened and the flood waters began to subside as abruptly as they had crested. Engineers swarmed over the wrecked pontoon bridge, lashing it again to the far bank and completing repairs by mid-morning on June 5.[17]

Jackson had not gained as much of an advantage from the flood as Frémont had feared. He spent a good part of June 4 trying to pinpoint the location of Ewell's brigades and determine the combat readiness of the Valley army. He also gave orders to get two days' cooked rations into haversacks. A false report that Frémont was attempting a flanking movement by bridging the North Fork on the blind side of a ridge west of New Market cost the Confederates much of the afternoon, as Jackson marshaled his scattered forces on high ground overlooking the probable crossing site. The men stood down near nightfall, only to meet with new orders to resume the retreat at 1:00 A.M. on June 5. "Aroused and started at the appointed hour, marched down to the turnpike and stopped in mud and water till day, waiting till the trains passed by," a disgusted soldier of the 16th Mississippi recorded. Another scribbled in his diary, "How far south are we going?"[18]

THAT QUESTION WAS foremost on the mind of Stonewall Jackson as the rains subsided on June 5. There had been no word from Boteler, or from anyone else in Richmond, regarding Jackson's plea for reinforcements. Of more immediate concern was the swollen state near Harrisonburg of the North River, over which Jackson must push his long train of sick and wounded, and of captured Federal arms and equipment. Pioneer troops laboring under the watchful eye of Capt. Claiborne R. Mason, an engineer in civilian life, built boats out of scrap lumber. By nightfall, Jackson's trains were across safely and on their way toward Staunton. The infantry veered off the turnpike and onto the Port Republic road, providing a hint of Jackson's intentions. Narrow and rutted, the clay road proved vexing to the infantry, and nightfall found the army strung out for four miles between the hamlet of Cross Keys and the outskirts of Harrisonburg. Ewell's division camped behind the Valley army; a brigade of one Maryland and three Virginia regiments caballed together, for the hopelessly inept George Steuart brought up the rear of the infantry. Turner Ashby, in command of the rear guard, made camp just beyond Harrisonburg.

A second vexing problem on June 5 was the absence of information on Shields's whereabouts. To obtain it, Jackson had sent Hotchkiss off on the night of the fourth with a flag signalman to ascend Peaked Mountain, as the 1,600-foot-high southern tip of Massanutten Mountain was known.[19]

Not that Shields then posed much of a threat. His march, begun in self-pity,

Peaked Mountain, the southern extreme of Massanutten. (John W. Wayland, *Art Folio of the Shenandoah Valley*, Staunton, Va., 1924)

had degenerated into what one officer dismissed as a "desultory waste of time." Shields's division had covered ten miles on June 1, the first day of its march up Page Valley, and fifteen the second day despite torrential rains and nearly liquid roads. But Shields now despaired of succeeding in the operations he had convinced McDowell to allow him to undertake. On June 2 he bemoaned the sorry state of his command to Secretary Stanton: "We have too many men here, and no supplies. How I will get along I do not know, but I will trust to luck—seize cattle, live on beef—to catch Jackson."[20]

Shields's luck was decidedly bad. On the pitch-black, rain-swept night of June 2, advance detachments of Carroll's brigade marching toward what they assumed to be White House and Columbia bridges instead saw debris floating down the current of the swollen South Fork of the Shenandoah River.

News of the destruction of the White House and Columbia bridges not only dashed Shields's hopes of cutting off Jackson's retreat at New Market, but it also seems to have unhinged him. In relating the loss of the bridges to the secretary of war the next morning, Shields placed his sole hope—which he regarded as a thin one—in finding the bridge at Conrad's Store intact. Then his mind turned to the fantastic. If he continued up the river, he told Stanton, he might find a ford that would bring his division out of the wilderness at Harrisonburg. From Harrisonburg (Shields never mentioned what he hoped to accomplish there), he would face about and march east to Stanardsville and destroy the railroad and depot there, something he could do without having to cross the South Fork. From Stanardsville he promised to push on to Staunton or Charlottesville. Complaining that he lacked a reliable mounted force, Shields vowed that "with good cavalry I could stampede them [Jackson's army] to Richmond. I will destroy their means of escape somehow."[21]

In forwarding Shields's communiqué to Stanton, General McDowell noted laconically: "The amount of all this is that he cannot cross the Shenandoah in time to intercept Jackson. His command is in no condition to go to the places he names."[22]

Everyone from McDowell to the lowest private appeared to be losing confidence in Shields. "This was the strangest campaign of the war," said an Ohio captain. "No march of sixty-five miles presents so continuous a line of varied intentions and halting opinions." An enlisted man observed, "The humblest private could see through and into such a state of affairs and wondered what 'nincompoop' was in command." Discipline suffered as the division was put on half rations the third day out. "All we have to eat is pork and hard bread, in fact we have scarcely tasted anything else," recollected an Ohio soldier. Hoosier Capt. Elijah Cavins told his wife: "The army has become a marauding party, plundering everyone—Union men, women and children as well as Rebels, not leaving anything for them to live on."[23]

June 3 proved no better a day for Shields. That evening President Lincoln had telegraphed McDowell: "Anxious to know whether Shields can head or flank Jackson. Please tell about where Shields and Jackson respectively are, at the time this reaches you." Shortly after midnight McDowell telegraphed that he could only infer the position of Jackson, "as I have nothing on that point from either General Frémont or General Shields." Frémont was near Woodstock; Shields was at Luray with an impassable South Fork of the Shenandoah between him and Jackson.

Before telegraphing McDowell, Lincoln undoubtedly had read Shields's missive dated 4:00 A.M., June 3, in which he boasted of Jackson's imminent destruction while at the same time neglecting to specify how he intended to accomplish it. "My advance last night reached the Shenandoah River to cross to New Market but found bridges burned. We must cross today somehow. We have caught him now[.] Jackson knows I am in his rear, because several fled from here on our approach." (The fleeing party was, in fact, Maj. Samuel Coyner's bridge burners, who were riding comfortably back to the Valley army.) McDowell added by way of comment: "The 'somehow' in which the general is to cross the river today, swollen as it is by the heavy rains, is not so clear, and delay defeats the movement." He had heard nothing all day from Frémont, and his forces—Shields's division in particular—were dangerously low on food. "We are literally from hand to mouth, and may have trouble."[24]

On the morning of June 4, Shields got the answer he had expected: The bridge over Elk Run near Conrad's Store was burned beyond repair. That left only the long, covered span crossing the North River just near its junction with the South Fork at Port Republic. In his telegrams to McDowell that morning, boasting gave way to lamentation: "If it be humanly possible, I will ascend the river, cross it, and take Jackson in the rear. My command are already destitute of everything in the way of shoes, and will soon be destitute of provisions and forage."

Shields did not exaggerate. Forty percent of the division was without shoes and at least 2 percent without trousers. That afternoon he gave up the notion of taking Jackson in the rear, telling Secretary Stanton that high water and muddy roads prevented such a course. Once again, he lost himself in fantasy: "I cannot fight against the elements, but give me bread to keep me alive and they will never leave this valley. Their force is inconsiderable, not, in my opinion, seven thousand. I want hard bread, salt, sugar and coffee. Send me those. I will stampede them down to Richmond if you give me plenty of bread."[25]

The continued downpour blocked the southward movement of Shields's main body over normally insignificant streams. "The ground where we are camped is all afloat," wrote an Ohio infantryman. "Could not move for the creeks are so high. Everything looks dismal."[26]

Except to the erratic Shields. McDowell was sufficiently convinced that the Irishman could accomplish nothing more that he turned back to Fredericksburg with the divisions of Ord and King. Before departing, he asked Shields: "You report the roads beyond Columbia Bridge as being impassable for wagons, and of course for artillery. How then do you propose at this time to get your division to Staunton?" A valid question, but Shields persisted nonetheless. On June 4 he sent Carroll orders to "go forward at once with cavalry and guns to save the bridge at Port Republic." The remainder of his brigade would come up as soon as possible. With the bridge secured, Jackson's only route of escape, reckoned Shields, was by way of Staunton, and to his bridge-saving mission Carroll was handed the Herculean task of pushing his brigade on to Staunton to destroy the railroad depot, train cars, and any other conveyances that might provide Jackson a means of escape.[27]

But escape was the furthest thing from Jackson's mind. Before ascending Peaked Mountain, Jed Hotchkiss had drawn him a map of the neighborhood around Port Republic. Hotchkiss was also summoned to headquarters twice to answer questions about the topography in the vicinity of the village. When Hotchkiss descended Peaked Mountain on the unseasonably cool night of June 5 to report that Shields was bogged down short of Conrad's Store, a delighted Jackson committed the army to a plan he had been contemplating for the past day or two. He would gather his forces at Port Republic, a place of some local importance nestled in the angle formed by the North and South rivers, where they united to become the South Fork of the Shenandoah. The place stood on a plain just a mile northwest of Brown's Gap, an excellent route through the Blue Ridge should Jackson have to leave the Valley. From Port Republic, he could attack the flank or rear of Frémont should that general attempt to march on Staunton. And, of course, the covered bridge over the North River was the only means of communication between Frémont and Shields. But Jackson could not linger at Port Republic indefinitely. No farther to his rear would the tributaries of the South Fork serve as a barrier to Shields, because south of Port Republic their waters were easily fordable, despite the recent rains.[28]

That possibility did not trouble Jackson. He regarded the Valley campaign as over. He considered his move to Port Republic to have neutralized Frémont and Shields, and without reinforcements there was little more he could do offensively in the Valley. Having fulfilled his mission to tie up large enemy forces in the Valley, Jackson suggested to General Lee that his men might be best employed elsewhere, such as at Richmond. "At present I do not see that I can do much more than rest my command and devote its time to drilling."[29]

JUNE 6 BROKE CLEAR and cool, with midday temperatures hovering around seventy degrees. The good weather did little to clear Shields's mind. On the evening of June 5 he had fallen back to Luray with three of his four brigades on the strength of a "vague rumor," as he informed Carroll, that James Long-street's Confederate division was moving against him from Gordonsville by way of Stanardsville. Colonel Carroll, meanwhile, had written Shields the night before that the waters of Elk Run were receding and the stream would be fordable for cavalry by noon of the sixth. He had 150 troopers from the 1st Virginia (Union) Cavalry with his flying column, and if he could receive mounted reinforcements—in particular Company A, 1st Ohio Cavalry—he would be able to "make a dash on Port Republic and save the bridge" on the night of June 6. Shields offered to send him what little cavalry he had, but for the purpose of making a raid on Waynesboro, eighteen miles due south of Port Republic and fourteen miles southeast of Staunton. The town commanded Rockfish Gap, the next crossing of the Blue Ridge south of Brown's Gap. "Can you prepare for a spring on Waynesboro, to burn the bridge, depot, cars, and tear up the railroad, if practicable? If you can cut the road at Waynesboro it will be a splendid exploit and end Jackson." Shields said nothing about the Port Republic bridge, neither repeating his earlier order to secure it nor explicitly retracting it. Shields's latest plan had some merit, but it ignored the sorry state of most of his cavalry, the lack of forage for animals and food for his men, and the fact that three of his four brigades were still at Luray, awaiting a phantom foe.[30]

Shields's state of mind is reflected in an encounter that bugler Samuel L. Gillespie of Company A, 1st Ohio Cavalry, had with him that morning. Gillespie's company of fewer than fifty men was in the saddle at daybreak, but had no clear instructions where to go. The company commander, whose last name and rank happened to be Captain Robinson, the same as the commander of the artillery battery with Carroll's flying column, sent Gillespie to division headquarters to ask whether he should ride south or remain at Luray. Gillespie found the general alone in his bedroom at a private house, with a young slave attending him. Shields invited Gillespie in and to come near, as he was hard of hearing. Gillespie had to repeat his message two or three times before Shields replied:

"Captain Robinson of the artillery?"

"No, Captain Robinson of the cavalry."

"I don't understand. Go downstairs and wait until I come."

As Gillespie reached the door, Shields asked, "Are you one of the Ohio boys?"

"Yes, sir."

"Well, I am glad to see you. Now you are the boys I have been wanting. Go and tell your captain to come on immediately," commanded Shields. "Yes, tell him to come quickly, for I want to see him."

Gillespie left thinking that "the general seemed somewhat childish and was quite deserted by his staff."

Robinson's cavalry received its mission—not to join Carroll, but rather to picket the Stanardsville road against the bogus threat of approaching Rebel masses.[31]

On June 6 the true threat to Jackson would come not from Shields, but from Frémont, and an otherwise inconsequential skirmish with him that day would have broad repercussions for the Valley army.

CHAPTER 26

THE PRESERVATION OF OUR

ARMY DEPENDED ON US

For two days the freshet that had prevented his engineers from throwing a pontoon over the North Fork of the Shenandoah River had tried Frémont's patience. Now on the morning of June 5, just as the floodwaters receded and a pontoon bridge was at last thrown across the North Fork, new problems arose to vex the Pathfinder. His appeal to Irvin McDowell for an explanation of that general's whereabouts and plans of operation brought only a demand that Frémont return Bayard's cavalry and the Pennsylvania Bucktails forthwith. The sole clue of Federal dispositions east of Massanutten Mountain came from McDowell's insistence that Bayard be sent to Shields at Luray.

Sitting himself on a box in a corner grocery store, Frémont scribbled a request to Banks to come to his support. He meant "to push straight through" with or without Banks, though he "much desired" his cooperation. Frémont sent his private secretary down the Valley Pike with the dispatch, which he wrongly addressed to Banks at Front Royal. At that moment Banks was at Strasburg, within a hard day's march of Frémont. His note to Banks elicited simply regret that the lack of supplies and transportation prevented him from joining Frémont.

While Frémont seethed, his troops filed over the pontoon bridge, making ten miles before nightfall and halting near New Market, a town in which, said Northern war correspondent Sidney D. Maxwell, "all are secessionists; the women frowned and the men looked as sullen as they could be."[1]

Frémont had his command on the road before 5:00 A.M. on June 6, another sunny and cool morning, which enabled him to reestablish contact with the Confederate rear guard. Ashby's cavalry made a good show of it, and it was 2:00 P.M. before the Federals occupied Harrisonburg. There Frémont abruptly called a halt and ordered the army to encamp. This was done, said Colonel Tracy, because Jackson's "route [was] for the present uncertain, from the many diverging roads."[2]

Perhaps the general and his staff should have troubled themselves to speak with the locals. The correspondent for the New York Times observed that the "few inhabitants who were not afraid to be seen holding converse with National soldiers stated that it was the avowed intention of Jackson to bear to the left, leaving the turnpike, and make a stand at 'Port Republic,' a little village distant twelve miles."[3]

An impetuous company of the 1st New Jersey Cavalry, in the advance, galloped through Harrisonburg after some of Ashby's men, who seemingly had remained behind a bit too long. As the New Jersey troopers emerged from town onto the open road, they ran into an ambush staged by dismounted Southern cavalrymen hidden behind the stone walls on either side. The company wheeled and made for the rear.

In their place came the remainder of the regiment in column of fours, trotting through town four hundred strong. At the head of the column rode the colonel, English adventurer Sir Percy Wyndham, who allegedly once remarked that he had joined the Union army for the sole purpose of bagging Turner Ashby. Accompanying Wyndham were companies from the 6th Ohio, 4th New York, and 1st Pennsylvania cavalry.

On the outskirts of Harrisonburg Wyndham called a halt shortly before 3:00 P.M. His orders from General Bayard limited him to deploying pickets and vedettes. But a squadron of Ashby's cavalry, drawn up a half mile south of town on the Port Republic road, proved too great a temptation to resist. Wyndham led his mixed command forward, and the Rebels retreated. Wyndham deployed scouts and skirmishers "to feel the pulse of the situation and pick up prisoners," as New York Times correspondent Charles Webb put it. Webb himself learned from a civilian passing by that there were at least a hundred Confederate cavalrymen and several companies of infantry at a crossroads two miles down the road. Webb relayed the news to Wyndham, who said he was reluctant to advance farther without orders. Just then a scout came in and reported the force in question to be merely forty or fifty Rebel troopers and infantry who were too tired to either run or fight. At that Wyndham perked up. "We'll have a little fun then," he remarked to Webb before the bugle sounded "to horse."[4]

With drawn sabers and Wyndham and Webb at the head of the column, the Union cavalcade galloped down the narrow road nearly three miles before reaching the crossroads of which the civilian had spoken. There Webb decided to turn back, "for two reasons, namely: in the first place, my horse was worn out; in the second place the whole thing began to look so much like a trap that I couldn't make up my mind to enter it, and can only wonder how Colonel Wyndham did. But his impulsive bravery led him on."[5]

Wyndham's command continued on until it encountered a line of Confederate cavalry—Ashby's old regiment—drawn up on a ridge just beyond a swampy stream. Wyndham ordered his command to deploy from column into line on a ridge opposite the Confederates. "While the men were still hurrying their wearied horses into the fresh formation," recalled the historian of the 1st New Jersey Cavalry, Wyndham gave the order "Gallop! Charge!" and started down the slope—alone.[6]

On the far ridge 1st Sgt. Holmes Conrad of Company A, 7th Virginia Cavalry, marveled at the sight of a Federal officer charging alone. Drawing his saber, he instinctively set off after the Yankee, only to find after galloping a hundred yards that he too was alone. "I discovered for the first time that none of those who had been with me on the summit of the ridge had attended me in my charge," remembered Conrad. Taking in the fast-closing ground between them, Conrad noticed a dense growth of weeds that suggested a marsh lay in Wyndham's path, while the ground over which Conrad rode was hard and firm. As they simultaneously closed on a sunken rail fence at the bottom of the ravine, and Wyndham's horse began to lose its footing, Conrad seized his advantage. He dropped his saber and drew his revolver. Wyndham's horse was tangled up on the fence, and all the Englishman could do was surrender, but not before terrifying Conrad as "the fiercest looking cavalryman I ever confronted." Wyndham dismounted and walked rearward beside Conrad, all the while cursing the 1st New Jersey for not having followed him.[7]

On the way to Jackson's headquarters, escorted by Henry Kyd Douglas, Wyndham chanced upon Maj. Robideaux Wheat of the Louisiana Tigers. They had fought together under Garibaldi in Italy. "The two, with exclamations of surprise more emphatic than refined," said Douglas, "rushed into the arms of each other and embraced most affectionately, to the infinite amusement of the surrounding soldiers."[8]

Equally if not more amusing to Ashby's troopers and the men of the 6th

Virginia Cavalry, whom Ashby had brought in to the fray, was the ease with which they routed the 1st New Jersey Cavalry and the companies attached to it. Not that the 1st New Jersey had not had a fighting chance. The 7th Virginia cavalrymen had been formed in line with their backs to the enemy and at right angles to the road, "in no position to receive an attack or make one," said Capt. William McDonald. Ashby barked at the regimental commander to move his troops to the rear and attack the enemy. "In order to make the movement the whole command was thrown into disorder but moved in the right direction, all eager to get a chance at the enemy," continued McDonald. "Before we could strike the enemy we had to get over a high rail fence; this accomplished, there was a mad rush for the enemy, who scattered like sheep in every direction." At least four dozen New Jersey troopers were captured, along with three captains and the regimental colors."[9]

Correspondent Charles Webb was on the receiving end of the fleeing cavalrymen. He guided his mare off the road and onto a path in the wood just in time to avoid being run over. "I am sorry to say it, but such an utter rout and demoralization as then ensued I never before witnessed," he reported.[10]

Dusk had settled over Harrisonburg when a lone cavalryman appeared at Bayard's headquarters to announce the disaster that had befallen the 1st New Jersey Cavalry. Bayard set off to consult with Frémont. Unwilling to bring on a general engagement at so late an hour—it was well past 6:00 P.M.—Frémont gave Bayard fresh cavalry but forbade any further advance. As Bayard prepared to picket the Port Republic road with the 1st Pennsylvania Cavalry, Colonel Kane of the Bucktail Rifles interceded to ask for permission to go out and collect the wounded from Wyndham's fight. Bayard told Kane that his request exceeded Frémont's orders. "But to leave poor Wyndham on the field, and all our wounded," remonstrated Kane. "And besides, General, think how such a stampede will dishearten and demoralize the army; let me at 'em, General, with my Bucktails." Bayard yielded to Kane's blandishment. "Just forty minutes, I'll give you, Colonel," said Bayard, pulling out his watch. "Peep through the woods on our left, see what is in them, and out again when the time's up." To keep Kane honest, Bayard rode in his rear with the 1st Pennsylvania Cavalry.[11]

Charles Webb accompanied Bayard. Two miles beyond Harrisonburg they caught sight of Rebel cavalry astride the Port Republic road. Webb watched Kane disappear into the forest to the right of the road: "In go the 150 at an opening in the pines, and the badge they bear on their caps, and from which the battalion takes its name, is soon lost among the green leaves."[12]

Kane deployed his men as skirmishers, and they felt their way through the timber parallel to the road. The Bucktails had gone a mile and a half when one of Bayard's staff officers noticed through his field glass "dark columns of infantry creeping down in the woods." Webb said a cannon could be plainly seen wheeling into position on the road. Bayard yelled at the staff officer to gallop into the timber and recall the Bucktails, said Webb, "but the order is cut short by the rattle of musketry—single shots at first, broadening and deepening into volleys."[13]

The Bucktails had stumbled on two full regiments of Confederate infantry, led by Turner Ashby. He had seen their approach and, galloping back to General Ewell, had asked him for infantry. He also told him that by a certain quick detour through the woods he could take in the flank any enemy column that might venture forth from Harrisonburg. "If you will lend me a good regiment, I will ruin them next time." Ewell instead gave him two of Steuart's regiments, the 1st Maryland (Confederate) and the 58th Virginia, less the brigade commander. Ashby hurriedly explained his plan to Colonel Munford of the 2nd Virginia Cavalry, which he left on the Port Republic road with Chew's battery and his cavalry. "Now Munford," said Ashby, "I'll move the infantry through the woods to your right, so as to take them in the flank and rear. When I get in position, you advance the guns to the next rise in the road, then call in the outpost. Let them move quickly and the Yankees will be sure to charge. I will keep out of view. Let them pass, then when they come within close range, you give them the full charge of the guns and charge with the cavalry." Ashby would come in from the east with the infantry. Ewell elected to go forward with Ashby, in case Ashby ran into more trouble than he could handle.[14]

Ashby had not noticed the nearness of the Bucktails, and the first inkling he had of their presence came from Lt. George W. Booth of the 1st Maryland (Confederate), commanding one of two companies on the skirmish line of the regiment. Ashby insisted that Booth was mistaken, and the lieutenant returned to the skirmish line to await events. Up came the 58th Virginia to the Marylanders' right "with a loud cheer" that "staggering fire" from the Bucktails soon silenced. Hastily seeking cover behind a rail fence and thick underbrush at the edge of a clover field, the Pennsylvanians aimed carefully and took a heavy toll on the 58th. The Virginians, on the other hand, "in their confusion were firing too high to do execution," said Lieutenant Booth, "and if the Bucktails had been in the tree tops, I think it likely they mostly would have been killed." As it was, the 58th crumbled—"gave way and ran back without a moment's notice" was how Col. Bradley T. Johnson of the 1st Maryland (Confederate) put it. At the first fire Ashby, who was riding at the front of the 58th, had his horse shot out from under him. Jumping to his feet and half turning around toward the wavering Virginians, Ashby brandished his pistol or his sword—accounts vary on this point—and ordered a charge. No one obeyed him. Ashby was only thirty yards from the Bucktails' line, and an instant after his empty exhortation he took a fatal bullet. The ball entered his right side just above his hip and came out under his left arm. Ashby uttered not a word after being shot.[15]

As General Ewell bellowed to Johnson, "Charge, Colonel, and end this matter!" the 1st Maryland (Confederate) wheeled its line of battle to the right and slammed into the flank of the Bucktails. Supporting the Marylanders was the 44th Virginia. Meanwhile, the 58th Virginia, which had reformed, traipsed past Ashby's body and held firm.

Perhaps a hundred feet separated the combatants. It had grown dark, but bullets found their marks nonetheless. Bradley Johnson lost 17 of 275 men engaged, and the 58th lost 44 of 200 men engaged before the Bucktails, now reduced to fewer than 60 men, gave way. Left behind was Colonel Kane, sitting against a tree stump with wounds in the leg and chest. The entire fight could not have lasted longer than an hour.[16]

Among the Federal infantrymen bivouacked in Harrisonburg, the evening clash caused scarcely a ripple. General Milroy was mystified that Frémont sent the Bucktails no help. "We were all anxious to go but got no orders," he told his wife. Yet the men seemed confident. "We have got Jackson now. We have him in the jug and all we have to do is to put the stopper in," a civilian heard a squad of Federals boast. True to form, Blenker's Germans cared only for spoils. "The town of Harrisonburg is robbed of nearly everything," a Virginia cavalryman later wrote home. "The marauders entered by force or peaceably every shop and stole everything they could lay their hands on."[17]

In the deepening gloom, Lt. Isaac Coles, whose company of the 6th Virginia Cavalry had been detailed as escort to Ewell, found the general and another officer standing over Ashby's body. Ewell had the officer give him Ashby's rings and other personal effects. After the corpse was laid gently on a gum blanket, four mounted cavalrymen set out for the rear with their tragic burden. As they passed the camp of the 52nd Virginia, a company commander, thinking such a procession odd, asked them who they were bearing. "It is General Ashby," they muttered. "The bearers of the dead were all in tears and so overcome with emotion that they could hardly respond intelligently to the question," remembered Lt. James Bumgardner of the 52nd. Campbell Brown witnessed the same spectacle: "Later in the evening I saw a party of cavalry pass by with Ashby's body, crying, most of them, like children."[18]

A gloom fell over the Valley army as word of Ashby's death spread. Through the ranks there also whirled a sad story that his own troops had accidentally shot Ashby, which may in fact have been the case. Dr. Hunter McGuire examined the body and concluded as much.[19]

In the general mourning, Ashby's shortcomings in discipline and organization were forgotten. Nonetheless, Pvt. Randolph Fairfax of the Rockbridge Artillery thought his death to have been a waste: "It was so unnecessary for him, to expose himself so, especially as he had no business leading infantry, but such was his disposition that I really believe it was a pleasure to him to fight." Battery mate Lanty Blackford was more charitable: "Ashby's death is indeed a grievous loss to us and one which has shorn the cavalry of this army of half its terrors to the enemy." And Thomas G. Penn of the 48th Virginia concluded that "we had lost more by his fall than we had gained during the whole campaign."[20]

High-ranking officers also emphasized Ashby's merits and grieved his loss, both personally and for the sake of the army. "He was the most gallant man I ever saw, and withal a good man," Colonel Fulkerson wrote his sister. "When Ashby was between us and the enemy we felt perfectly secure against any surprise, and he was always on the enemy's heels. They had great fear of him. His place cannot be filled. . . . He had performed more feats of daring and had done more hard and perilous service than any man in the army." Col. William L. Jackson, Stonewall's cousin and a member of his staff, concurred: "He was a great man in his particular line, and his loss cannot well be supplied. I have seen him in battle and he seemed to possess a magnetic influence over his men." General Ewell told Colonel Munford that he had "the highest admiration for Ashby," adding that as a former dragoon he envied the freedom of the mounted arm. He said he would rather have a cavalry regiment than the best division of infantry in the army. "You fellows have some fun," he told Munford, "but I am no better than a darned tin solder. Here I am placed, without orders. Yes, no better than a tin soldier."[21]

Stonewall Jackson learned of Ashby's death while interrogating Sir Percy Wyndham. As the two were conversing, an officer rapped gently on the door and asked to speak privately to the general. Jackson stepped into the hall to receive the messenger's news. Immediately he dismissed Wyndham and locked himself in his room. "As a partisan officer I never knew his superior," Jackson would write. "His daring was proverbial; his powers of endurance almost incredible; his tone of character heroic, and his sagacity almost intuitive in divining the purposes and movements of the enemy."[22]

Irreplaceable or not, Ashby had to have a successor. Jackson chose Col. Thomas Munford as interim commander of the cavalry.

SATURDAY, JUNE 7, BROKE as clear and beautiful as the day before. And unlike the previous evening, there would be no blood spilt now. Frémont spent the day mulling over the situation and closing up his column. He set up headquarters in a stately brick home on the outskirts of Harrisonburg. Colonel Tracy brought in field desks, tables, and clerks and went to work. "Of course, as taken together, both my assistants and myself make some litter, but that does not wholly justify the onslaught of the decidedly high-toned lady of the mansion, who, this afternoon, demanded to know if we were accustomed to bring 'our horses too into people's houses?' "[23]

In the morning Frémont ordered Milroy to collect the dead and wounded from the fight with Ashby and then reconnoiter down the Port Republic road as far as practicable. Milroy proceeded along the road, which he found to be "very bad," to within perhaps a half mile of Cross Keys, when his advance guard ran into Confederate skirmishers posted in the woods northwest of the Union Church, the most prominent feature in the hamlet. Somehow Milroy concluded that the enemy numbered at least 20,000, which he reported. In point of fact, only Ewell's division of 6,620 men was posted in the area.[24]

That evening Frémont called a council of war. Present were brigadier generals Robert C. Schenck, Robert H. Milroy, Henry Bohlen, and George Bayard; Col. Gustave P. Cluseret; and senior staff. Word of Ashby's death had already reached them. It was agreed that Stonewall Jackson had turned to contest Frémont's advance until he was able to cross the bridge over the North River at Port Republic. All concurred in Milroy's estimate of Jackson's strength; scouts had reported even higher numbers. Frémont had a paper strength of 14,050 men, although he later insisted—probably truthfully—that fewer than 10,000 were capable of fighting. "Next," said Colonel Tracy, "it was considered upon what resources, and with what show of strength, we can make our further, and perhaps final demonstration of the pursuit." The council understood that the Union army was in a sorry state, low on supplies, and with both men and horses "pinched, starved, and wearied." Shoes and even shirts were at a premium; nevertheless, it was agreed that only a general engagement warranted a further advance. "But a collision in force being, on comparison of points, held certain, it is resolved to get forward upon the road with the dawn." Frémont accordingly issued orders for a 6:00 A.M. departure on June 8. Whatever his shortcomings as a commander and despite the poor condition of his command, Frémont showed himself ready to fight.[25]

Ironically, at that very moment Secretary Stanton was dictating orders directing Frémont to hold fast at Harrisonburg and to return Bayard's command to McDowell. Orders also were drafted for Shields to rejoin McDowell's corps at Fredericksburg. Like Jackson, President Lincoln and Stanton had concluded that the Valley campaign was over and that further pursuit of an enemy poised to pass through the Blue Ridge at Brown's Gap before anyone could catch him was useless. Neither order reached its recipient until it was too late to prevent what Lincoln's private secretaries called "two unfortunate engagements." McDowell, who was in Washington, asked his chief of staff to repeat the order to Shields at least three times on June 8, but no copy reached Shields in time.[26]

For the Valley army, June 7 offered a much-needed day of rest. "Worn and broken down we present a rare appearance just now, but for all that, our spirit is undiminished and our energy seems never to flag," Lt. James Dinwiddie of Carrington's battery crowed to his mother in a letter he wrote that day. The view from the ranks appeared quite different. Pvt. Lanty Blackford presented a more sober appraisal of the army's condition. To his father, he wrote:

> I would write myself as formerly twice a week but the thing is impossible while General Jackson runs us about constantly as he does. Since April 30, the morning we left Swift Run Gap, sixteen miles from here, thirty-eight days have elapsed. Of these we have been on the march thirty-two days and have marched about 400 miles, an average of twelve-and-a-half miles a day. Much of this has been done in rain, and mud, and over very bad roads. Short rations of food, carrying one's own baggage, and having imperfect shelter from the weather at night (no tents) have greatly enhanced our trials. One of the greatest perhaps is the short allowance of sleep. We have rarely gotten to camp before sundown or near that time, and then the delay about getting rations from the brigade commissariat, and from our own commissary, the cooking of supper and next day's rations, generally kept us up until 10:00 P.M. at least, often later. This difficulty was of course enhanced when, as has been often the case, we have not gotten to our camp until eight, nine, ten, or even eleven or twelve o'clock. The usual time for reveille on a march is 3:00 A.M., so you observe this left but a

brief time for the rest of men broken down by a fatiguing march. Still more was this quantity diminished to those who were unfortunate enough to be on guard, as this always lessens by two and sometimes by four hours the time of rest. Guard duty used to come round not oftener than once a week, but now, owing to our weakness of numbers from death, wounded, and sickness, it comes much oftener.[27]

All told, Jackson had just 11,470 men present for duty that day. Ewell's division made camp southeast of the Union Church at Cross Keys. The 15th Alabama drew picket duty at the church on Ewell's left, to provide the first warning of a Federal approach down the Port Republic road. Jackson's three brigades bivouacked a half mile northeast of Port Republic and the crucial bridge over the North River. The Confederate camp stretched for three miles toward Cross Keys, which in turn was just four miles from Port Republic. Jackson made his headquarters at Madison Hall, a fine residence belonging to Dr. George Kemper at the western edge of the village. Members of the newly formed Charlottesville Artillery were encamped around Jackson's headquarters, and the army trains were parked in a field west of Madison Hall, among them wagons carrying the army's entire reserve supply of ammunition. Only three companies of infantry were in Port Republic itself. Jackson sent two companies of Ashby's former cavalry out on the road from Conrad's Store to give warning of Shields's approach from that direction. In a singular neglect of security, he failed to deploy an infantry covering force east of Port Republic.[28]

Jackson needed rest badly. Sandie Pendleton, who himself was "sadly in need of" sleep, thought the general to be "completely broken down." At dusk a courier interrupted Jackson's rest with news of Milroy's reconnaissance. Jackson ordered up his horse and with his staff conducted a reconnaissance across his own front. At 9:00 P.M. he returned to Madison Hall, issued orders for Ewell for the morning of June 8, and went to bed, unaware that trouble was much closer than he expected.[29]

COL. SAMUEL S. CARROLL, a graduate of the West Point Class of 1856, was a solid officer who could well look after himself and his troops. A strict disciplinarian whose men nicknamed him "Old Brick top," Carroll had arrived at Romney in December 1861 as the new colonel of the 8th Ohio. He struck officers and men as "a dashing officer, anxious to distinguish himself, and above all to qualify his regiment for its duties."[30]

The last thing he needed on the morning of June 7, as he struggled along the miserable road between Conrad's Store and Port Republic, was a verbose, condescending letter from Shields that General Kimball later termed "as insulting an order to as true and patriotic soldiers as ever fought." Shields, who was at Columbia Bridge, had risen at 2:00 A.M. to compose it. "Such is my anxiety that I rise from my bed to write to you." The enemy was in shambles, Shields insisted, and needed only a tap on the flank to "panic-strike them and break them into fragments. No man has had such a chance since the war commenced. You are within thirty miles of a broken, retreating enemy, who still hangs together. Ten thousand Germans are on his rear, who hang on like bulldogs. You have only to throw yourself down on Waynesboro before him and your cavalry will capture them by the thousands, seize his train, and abundant supplies; and yet there is a strange want of enthusiasm in the command."

Shields accused Carroll's subordinates of gross incompetence. "The Germans are not half as well off as you are, but they hang on the enemy without respite. This enemy insulted the capital of your country; he is in retreat; you are within a day and a half of him, and you hesitate. I don't mean you personally, but some of your officers and men. This would be a disgrace. Can this be my boasted Shields's division?" Shields directed that the men march without baggage and that all wagons be returned to Luray at once. Shields informed Carroll that Daum's artillery would start at 5:00 A.M. and Tyler's brigade at 6:00 A.M. to reinforce Carroll. Tyler was not to take command of Carroll's brigade. "I command you both," said Shields. It was hardly an appealing prospect to either Tyler or Carroll to be commanded by a general far to the rear. Shields concluded by directing Carroll to push on with his cavalry, the 7th Indiana, and two cannons so as to reach Port Republic by nightfall and Waynesboro the next day.[31]

Carroll sent back all baggage and incapacitated men and set out. Later that morning, said his acting aide-de-camp, Capt. David Lostutter Jr., Carroll received orders from Shields to burn the bridge at Port Republic, a reversal of his June 4 directive that Carroll "save the bridge." About halfway between Conrad's Store and Port Republic, a second dispatch from Shields arrived directing Carroll not to burn the bridge, "but hold it at all hazards. I saw and read the order myself," said Lostutter. George W. New, the brigade surgeon, said he saw the conflicting orders as well.[32]

What caused the seeming dubiety on Shields's part where the bridge was concerned? A musician from the 7th Ohio thought he knew the answer. The regimental band was serenading Shields at his headquarters on the morning of the seventh when two cavalrymen rode up. One handed Shields a letter. He apparently read it while standing in front of his quarters, then said in a voice "loud and rather sarcastic, 'Frémont thinks he's going to raise hell up there, and I'll show him.'" The implication was that Frémont wanted the bridge burned to prevent Jackson's escape, and out of petty jealousy Shields reiterated his order for Carroll to hold it at all costs. General Kimball substantiated the accusation in a postwar letter, expressing amazement that Shields would order Carroll to "hold the only bridge over which Jackson could possibly escape from Frémont."[33]

Carroll pushed his men hard. In the evening a heavy rain set in, remembered a sergeant of the 7th Indiana, "but we continued to wade through the mud until late in the night, but becoming so wearied and fatigued that to proceed was impossible, we turned into a wooded enclosure to camp for the remainder of the night."

Carroll had halted six miles short of Port Republic, intending to give his men a three-hour rest before closing on the village. Scouts whom Carroll had sent ahead in the rain-swept darkness only heightened his desire to push on. Easily eluding the indolent Rebel cavalry, they returned with an accurate appraisal of the location of Jackson's baggage and ordnance trains and the absence of any force of consequence on the south bank of North River.[34]

At 4:00 A.M. Carroll had his command ready to resume the advance. He led the way with 150 troopers of the 1st West Virginia Cavalry. Accompanying them was Capt. Myles Keogh, whom Shields had sent forward to look after his mounted arm. The troopers were armed with sabers and old flintlock horse pistols, altered to percussion, with portable shoulder stocks—hardly formidable weapons. Moving with the cavalry were the four guns of Capt. Lucius Robinson's Ohio battery. The 7th Indiana followed in close order. Next came the 1st Virginia (Union) Infantry, the 84th Pennsylvania, and finally the habitually unreliable 110th Pennsylvania.[35]

Carroll scarcely could contain his excitement over the prize that awaited him. Orderly sergeant James Gildea of Robinson's battery was mounted beside his captain, awaiting the order to advance, when Colonel Carroll rode up and said: "Captain, my scouts have come in and report that there are no troops over in town except a cattle guard and train; we can cross over and knock [the] hell out of them." Carroll also reiterated his order from Shields not to burn the bridge over the North River.

Off went the cavalry and artillery over the muddy and partly flooded road, parallel to and about half a mile south of the South Fork of the Shenandoah.

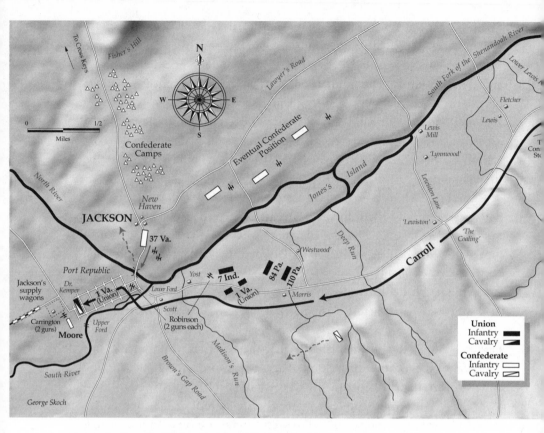

MAP 8. Carroll's Raid on Port Republic, June 8, 1862

The 7th Indiana, many of the men barefoot, struggled to keep up. At 6:00 A.M. Carroll's flying column halted a mile below Port Republic. Protected by an early morning fog and unhindered by enemy pickets, Carroll and Keogh were able to reconnoiter Jackson's dispositions at their ease. Not a single Southern cavalryman had interrupted, or yet reported, their approach. Indeed, said Jed Hotchkiss, most of the two companies that Jackson had sent out to warn of a Federal approach from the east "took to its heels and went off toward Brown's Gap, leaving the river road entirely open." That Ashby's command was worse than useless without its charismatic leader was painfully evident.[36]

The last thing Jackson or his men expected that comfortably cool Sabbath morning—the temperature hovered between sixty and seventy degrees—was an attack. Jackson was still confident that Shields remained bogged down near Luray, and his thoughts on arising in his room at the Kemper house were of worship services and a general tour of the lines. Hotchkiss lay in his tent, "sick with a violent headache, having been exhausted from duty by the general."

Grateful for the respite from the incessant marching and fighting, most Confederates lounged about their camps, writing letters, preparing for religious services, or just relaxing. The men of Capt. James Carrington's untried battery rested in the meadows west of the Kemper house, watered their horses, or put on clean underwear and shirts, their first change of clothing in nearly two weeks. Lieutenant Dinwiddie was sitting on his mess chest reading the Bible. "Our army hoped to rest for several days and prepare for another campaign. With these thoughts, we were lying in our camp," he explained. "A bright sun made all around look beautiful and cheerful," said Capt. Hugh A. White of the 4th Virginia. "We were expecting soon to meet for public worship and to spend the day in calm and holy communion with God and his people." A good many men of the 10th Virginia availed themselves of their campsite near the bridge to go down to the river and wash their clothes and bathe. General Taliaferro, whose brigade rested along the hilltop above, about three-quarters of a mile beyond the bridge, ignored the order for worship services and instead instructed his troops to assemble for inspection. Colonel Fulkerson of the 37th Virginia had just begun a letter. Dr. Hunter McGuire attended to more serious business. He was seeing to the sick and wounded at the Methodist church on Main Street, midway through town. The time was about 8:30 A.M.[37]

Colonel Carroll had completed final preparations for a dash into town. He decided to split Robinson's four-gun battery into two equal sections. One section was to enter the town with the cavalry opposite the center of Port Republic. The second section he posted a mile east of town on a low rise called "Yost's Hill," which afforded a clear field of fire on the covered bridge, standing less than one-half mile away. Advance elements of the 7th Indiana staggered into place behind the hill. Their role, and presumably that of the remaining infantry of the brigade, would be to hold the bridge if the cavalry succeeded in taking it. In case anyone doubted that a fight was at hand, Col. James Gavin of the 7th Indiana galloped back from his conference with Carroll to the head of the regimental column, gave the command to load weapons, then added, "Boys, we are going to have a muss, and somebody will be hurt."[38]

Probably more Confederates and fewer Federals would have been hurt that morning had Carroll not foolishly announced his presence by having the two-gun section with him unlimber in an orchard opposite the middle ford across

South River and open fire on the town before the cavalry was ready to cross. The shots were directed at what the Yankees thought was a guardhouse containing prisoners from Frémont's command; in fact, their rounds struck the steeple of the Methodist church. A horrified Dr. McGuire watched as broken shingles crashed down among the line of ambulances parked outside the church. McGuire at once rode among the drivers, threatening to shoot the first man who decamped. "In order to enforce my commands [I] was using some profane language." While thus engaged, McGuire felt a hand on his shoulder. Turning around, he saw it to be Stonewall Jackson, who with his staff trailing was fast heading up Main Street toward the north bank and safety. Jackson paused in his flight long enough to admonish McGuire, "Doctor, don't you think you can manage these men without swearing?"[39]

Jackson had gotten his first inkling of trouble from three excited troopers who had not fled toward Brown's Gap. Their incoherent ramblings of trouble near Lewiston made little sense, and they were dismissed with orders to acquire more definite information. Sixteen-year-old Henry D. Kerfoot of the 6th Virginia Cavalry galloped up a few moments later with news that Yankee cavalry had fired on him as he made his way across the South River. He had ridden to headquarters at the behest of Capt. Samuel J. C. Moore, whose company of the 2nd Virginia—two dozen men in all—was guarding the Upper Ford of the South River, not quite a half mile from Madison Hall. Kerfoot had served under Moore before transferring to the cavalry, and the captain trusted his word. Jackson greeted Kerfoot's report with skepticism. Without betraying any excitement, he told the young cavalryman simply to "Go back and fight them."[40]

Any remaining doubt Jackson or his staff may have entertained regarding the Federal presence vanished with the first shots from Robinson's guns, and they left Madison Hall in hot haste. Carroll's 150 cavalrymen (one reliable source places the number as low as 115) splashed across the middle ford of South River, rode a narrow slab bridge crossing a millrace on the southern edge of Port Republic, and debouched onto Main Street just minutes after Jackson and most of his staff passed by.

The commander of the West Virginia battalion was not with his men. He had become unhorsed behind a stone building and was "complaining of a sudden illness," so Carroll turned immediate command of the cavalry over to his aide-de-camp, Capt. Earle S. Goodrich. Carroll swam his horse across the South River after the cavalry, and the two cannons trailed.[41]

Colonel Carroll, who appeared to a sergeant of the 1st West Virginia Cavalry as "very anxious to fight someone," made his dispositions rapidly. He cordially greeted Col. Stapleton Crutchfield, Jackson's chief of artillery, who had fallen captive along with Ned Willis of the general staff, an old friend whom Carroll cheerfully offered a drink. Crutchfield was closed-mouthed. From him Carroll learned nothing of the disposition of the Confederate trains or who if anyone defended them. Undeterred, he split his cavalry into two sections, sending two-thirds charging southwest along Main Street in the hope of seizing or at least stampeding Jackson's trains; the remaining third he dispatched to secure the bridge. Carroll sent one cannon, commanded by Sgt. James Gildea, to help guard the North River Bridge. The second piece he placed on Main Street just east of the Methodist church, fronting west. Carroll positioned himself between the two guns.[42]

Events moved with lightning speed. One that did not occur but should have was the burning of the North River Bridge. Despite his orders to the contrary, common sense should have dictated to Carroll its destruction. Afterward a rumor circulated that Carroll had been drunk during the Port Republic raid. That might have been the most charitable explanation for his conduct. Had he burned the expanse, Jackson would have been separated from his ordnance trains and, more ominously, denied a ready means of leaving the Valley by way of Brown's Gap.[43]

Means were certainly at hand for the task. As his limber and gun bounced along Main Street, Sergeant Gildea noticed a large circle of fire in front of a blacksmith shop on the south (Federal) side of the bridge that had been used to shrink wagon tires when the Yankees came into town. "I saw that a good chance to fire the bridge if orders had not prohibited it," said Gildea. "I could have had it in a blaze before Jackson could have got his men up to charge it." Lt. T. H. B. Lemly of the 1st West Virginia agreed: "We could easily have burnt the bridge, as there was plenty of fire in the street at the end of the bridge, where the Rebs were cutting and tightening the tires on some of their wagons." Some West Virginia troopers had begun carrying brands ignited in that fire to the bridge until an officer told them (at least two men claimed it was Carroll himself) to extinguish them.[44]

As it was, Gildea had to content himself with unlimbering and aligning his six-pounder—not pointed directly through the bridge, but rather at a crest perhaps seventy-five yards to the left of it. There a mounted officer made it known by shouts and gestures that he wanted Gildea's gun to cross the bridge. Gildea lowered the elevation screw to get the range of the man, who Gildea concluded was a Rebel. But Captain Robinson rode up yelling, "Don't fire at them. That is our own man." Gildea begged to differ. "It is not our men; they are Rebs." "Well," replied Robinson, "don't fire until I see Carroll." A minute later Gildea heard the colonel shout, "Give them hell, Sergeant." Remembered Gildea: "It was too late. Jackson, supposing that it was his own guns down the road had discovered his mistake and got out of there as quick as possible. When I received permission to fire he was going to the crest of the hill, and I could not get the range quick enough to follow him."[45]

Jackson was having a hard time of it among the bluffs overlooking North River. His hairbreadth escape temporarily robbed him of his characteristic calm. Capt. William T. Poague, whose Rockbridge Artillery rested on the hill nearest the bridge, said he "never saw Jackson as much stirred up at any other time." Lanty Blackford agreed: "Up rode Jackson himself, with more signs of excitement than I ever saw him manifest before. Addressing no one in particular, Jackson's first and only words when he reached the battery were, 'Have the guns hitched up, have the guns hitched up.' As he galloped off to the infantry he shouted 'Have the long roll beat, have the long roll beat.' "[46]

The first infantry that Jackson chanced upon was the 37th Virginia Infantry of Taliaferro's brigade, which may or may not have already started toward the bridge, depending on whether one believes Taliaferro's account of the affair. In either case, the 37th doubled-timed in column to the bluff above the bridge, Jackson riding with them. He broke away long enough to accompany the first of Poague's guns to a wheat field overlooking the river, for a second time snapping an order to Poague to hitch up the rest of his guns immediately, something Poague already had done.[47]

Jackson rejoined the 37th Virginia just as the head of its column came within sight of the bridge. At the right moment, Alexander B. Carrington, the chaplain of the 37th, recalled that Jackson, "with great fire and authority," commanded the regiment to "Fire from column and charge bayonets!" As the men dashed forward, Carrington, who was within a few feet of Jackson, was startled to see his demeanor transformed. He "dropped his reins on the horse's neck, raised his face and both hands to heaven, and engaged in silent prayer."[48]

From the opposite end of the span Sergeant Gildea saw Fulkerson's Virginians stumbling down the hill with their rifles at right shoulder shift. "Without taking aim they brought their guns to the hip and fired down on us. If they had not been excited, I do not think that one of us would have got away. As it was, we suffered some."

Indeed they did. The volley startled the horses, and they ran off with the limber chest. The same volley struck the number three gunner in the forehead as he was placing the friction primer in the gun. He fell into Gildea's arms. Gildea snatched the lanyard from his hand, then passed the man to another member of the gun crew to take him to the rear. Then, looking around, Gildea was shocked to find that the entire squad had run off, except for two men. With them Gildea ran the gun out onto the bridge. Only one friction primer remained. The sergeant and his companions rammed a second charge of canister into the gun. Gildea told the two remaining gunners to "light out"; he would fire the final round. Then he heard the command "Forward, rout step, march" echo from the other end of the bridge and saw the head of Fulkerson's column rush toward him.

Fulkerson feared for his men. "Charging in at one end of a bridge with a cannon yawning in at the other is no very pleasant pastime. But my men went in so well that it elicited the praise of the general [Jackson] and all who witnessed it."[49]

Fortunately for Fulkerson's regiment, Gildea aimed the gun not straight into the bridge but at an angle, "with the intention of weakening the timbers and to ricochet the shots." Then Gildea ran off, the last Yankee to leave the scene, the cavalry having vanished at the first fire from Poague's battery. Speaking of his own final shot, Gildea confessed that "I had no time to see what execution it did."[50]

Fulkerson saw the impact of the canister, which was minimal. One man was killed and two were wounded. As the 37th secured the bridge, Jackson directed the trailing regiment, the 10th Virginia, to lie down on the heights opposite Yost's Hill and pour it on the two Yankee cannons and the 7th Indiana. The range was too great for musket fire to have any effect, but it marked the beginning of a serious change for the worse in Carroll's fortunes.[51]

ON THE SOUTHWEST side of Port Republic, toward which the majority of Carroll's cavalry rode, the Confederates had averted disaster through the efforts of a captain and his twenty-man squad and two seasoned lieutenants of an otherwise green battery of artillery. At the first boom of Robinson's cannon from across the river, panic seized the wagon train, heightened by a stream of frightened townspeople who fled westward to avoid the Yankee cavalry then crossing the millrace on the east side of town.

Lieutenant Dinwiddie painted a poignant picture for his wife of the first moments of the raid as seen from Kemper's Hill, west of Madison Hall. "Such confusion worse confounded I hardly ever saw before, and I have seen and experienced several stampedes. The men however soon became calm, at least those who remained, although some did not stop till they were arrested in Staunton by the provost marshal." Continued Dinwiddie:

> The flight of the Negros and some of our men amused me, but other scenes would have melted a heart of stone. Women and children poured out of town in droves during the cannonade. I met several beautiful young girls with their clothing up around their waists and running for life to the woods and ravines. Mothers with staring eyes, streamed with tears, clasped their little babies in their arms and besought me to take them to a place of safety. I told them not to be afraid and showed them a place out of range and assured them there was no danger. Their looks of gratitude were worth crowns of gold.[52]

At the time he gave them, Dinwiddie's assurances were disingenuous at best. The Charlottesville Artillery was readying itself to join the stampede, not meet the enemy. The first bugle call was to "Limber up in short order," and five of Carrington's guns were speeding westward. Seventeen-year-old Pvt. Leroy Cox was watering his horse in the South River when the alarm sounded. "When I got to camp I found everything in confusion, the men hitching up and a general breaking up of camp. . . . Captain Carrington at once gave orders for the battery to hitch up and fall back up the valley as rapidly as possible. There was a good deal of excitement by this time for the enemy were close upon us, and we were only protected from their view by the depression in the hill we were occupying."[53]

Capt. Samuel J. C. Moore had no intention of running from the fight. At the first hint of trouble he led his squad from its guard post at the Upper Ford of the South River three hundred yards to a perfect defensive position—a stone fence in the northeastern corner of the Kemper yard, near a point where Union cavalry charging down Main Street toward the wagon train would have to veer sharply to the right unless they left the road. Kneeling behind the fence of large limestone rocks, Moore's men would be invisible until they opened fire.[54]

During the wait, Moore moved along his short line of infantrymen, striving to brace them at the nearing sound of pounding hooves. "I told the men to keep cool; not fire a shot until I gave the order, and when they did fire, to take good aim; that the preservation of our army depended on us." Moore, of course, was not exaggerating. Lose his ordnance train, and Jackson would undoubtedly lose any prolonged engagement with either Frémont or Shields.

Around the sharp turn in Main Street south of Madison Hall, the head of the Federal mounted column came into view, the troopers riding four abreast, "moving cautiously." Moore thought he faced more Yankees than he did—his estimate trebled their number to three hundred. At the range Moore desired, his men opened fire, hurling the head of the column back upon the riders to their rear. Moore's squad quickly reloaded, and he led them forward fifty yards to deliver a second volley. At that, the Yankees retreated back up Main Street in dust-caked confusion. Moore hurried his men back to the protection of the stone wall.[55]

While the Federal cavalry regrouped for another dash at Carroll's insistence, an undermanned cannon, a twelve-pounder iron howitzer belonging to Lt. John Timberlake's section, unlimbered beside Moore's men. Timberlake had been about to make for the rear with the rest of the battery when the young Private Cox appealed to him, "Lieutenant, for God's sake don't let us leave without firing a shot. If we do we will be captured." Cox's words had the desired effect. Cox said Timberlake "seemed to grow at least six inches, standing in his stirrups." The lieutenant declared that "I will have my two pieces stay if they are captured," then galloped off to retrieve the gun that had already been moved off. Private Cox, three or four other privates, and a noncombatant barber served the piece without an officer or noncommissioned officer to supervise them.

They did their job well. This time there was no tentativeness to the Yankee approach; they charged around the road bend at a gallop. No one had time to adjust the elevating screw on the howitzer, and the single shot Cox and his comrades fired sailed at least ten feet over the heads of the Federal troopers. But it was enough to frighten them into a second retreat.[56]

As the smoke and dust cleared, Lieutenant Dinwiddie appeared with his two cannons and Timberlake with his second piece. A sheepish Captain Carrington and the Reverend Dabney, who had urged the captain's return, arrived with the last two guns of the battery. These five pieces formed so as to rake the length of Main Street with fire. It took only a few rounds before Colonel Carroll and the Union cavalry quit Main Street and made their way back across the South River, impelled also by the sight of the 37th Virginia bearing down on them from the east. Captain Robinson hurried his second cannon out of town and across the South River behind the fleeing cavalry, only to get the carriage so hopelessly entangled in the timber on the south bank that he was forced to abandon the piece.[57]

There was no immediate safety on the south bank of the river, either for

Carroll's raiders or Robinson's remaining section and the 7th Indiana. Once the town was cleared, Jackson deployed his infantry and artillery along the heights overlooking the South Fork of the Shenandoah and in Port Republic. The Southern guns drove the outmatched section of Robinson's battery off Yost's Hill, and the 7th Indiana followed it in an every-man-for-himself retreat toward the protection of the heavily forested hillsides near Lewiston. Elliott Winscott, a 240-pound raw recruit who could barely keep up with his comrades on the march, found the sudden retreat beyond his capacity. "I lay there on the ground and watched the Rebels march along the hillside on the opposite end. Not a musket shot was fired, as they were beyond range. I arose to my feet, finally, to go and find my regiment, when a cannon shot struck a fence rail in front that sent a sliver that struck me senseless." When Winscott came to, he found the commander of Company E standing beside him. The captain suggested that they take refuge in a nearby barn. As soon as they reached it, a cannon ball ripped the siding of the building just under the eaves. "We concluded that that was no safe place, so we resolved to make the effort to find the regiment, which we succeeded in doing while it lay about three miles back, halted on the roadside, and some of the boys were cooking coffee and hardtack."[58]

Rebel batteries leapfrogged along the heights to follow the Yankee retreat with fire. Carroll's last two regiments—the 84th and 110th Pennsylvania—never fired a shot, but joined in the exodus after closing to within a half mile of Yost's Hill.

Tyler's brigade appeared near Lewiston at 2:30 P.M., during the worst of Carroll's retreat past the gauntlet of Rebel cannons. Tyler's men were unimpressed with what they encountered. Said a member of the 7th Ohio: "Carroll's brigade fell back in not very good order upon our brigade. We came up and found them strung out along the road for four or five miles, very much demoralized." George C. Clouds of the 5th Ohio expressed disgust with Carroll's brigade: "When Tyler's brigade marched toward Port Republic, we saw hundreds of Carroll's men lying along fences in the rear of his command. So many commissioned officers were among them that it looked as though whole companies, if not regiments, had made up their minds that they did not care to take a hand in winning a star for the colonel commanding; or, at least, other hands should run the risk of getting hurt at the bridge. They were cursed roundly by the passing troops of Tyler's brigade as cowards."[59]

Tyler's men had good reason to feel betrayed. They had been awakened well before dawn. Although the brigade was just ten miles in Carroll's rear, it took the unit the better part of the day to reach the front. "We were floundering along through mud and water doing our best to get to the front and lend a hand," said another frustrated soldier of the 5th Ohio. Instead, "all was quiet on our side; the enemy did not seem to care about us so long as we let the bridge alone during the evening."[60]

Challenging Jackson for control of the bridge was the furthest thing from the minds of Carroll and Tyler. In the early evening they held a council of war with their regimental commanders and Colonel Daum. The indomitable German suggested that the two brigades mass their artillery within range of the bridge the next morning and try to batter it down. Tyler, the ranking officer, rejected the scheme out of hand. The subject turned next to the possibility of retreating under cover of darkness to Conrad's Store and await the arrival of the remainder of the division.

That would have been the prudent course of action, particularly as Tyler had no communication with Frémont, and the messages he had received from Shields were hardly encouraging. He sent two couriers to Shields. The first returned with Shields's reply scrawled on the envelope of Tyler's appeal for help—the Irishman promised to "come as soon as possible." But the second courier returned with a note from Shields saying that his men were too weary to move.

Tyler canvassed the council for recommendations. Colonel Carroll advocated an immediate retreat; Colonel Tyler himself was neutral in the matter. But Colonel Daum insisted that the two brigades remain where they were and fight Jackson if he crossed the river. The regimental commanders unanimously concurred with Daum. Tyler's thinking was muddled. Rather than array the eight regiments and three batteries of his and Carroll's brigades behind the fence-lined sunken road from Lewiston to the South Fork (known locally as "Lewiston Lane"), he huddled them "in a strip of woods at the base of the Blue Ridge" a quarter mile northeast of Lewiston and bivouacked, to await what the morning might bring.[61]

CHAPTER 27

I HAVE LOST CONFIDENCE
IN FRÉMONT

While Stonewall Jackson cobbled together units to eject Carroll's 150 raiders from Port Republic, General Ewell on June 8 faced a far more ominous threat four miles to the north: an attack on his three brigades (Richard Taylor was on detached duty with Jackson) by Frémont's entire army. How many men actually made the morning march to Cross Keys is uncertain. Frémont reported his strength at 10,500, which he considered "a liberal estimate of [the] force in hand and for duty." General Milroy thought the number closer to 12,000. Left behind in Harrisonburg was Bayard's cavalry; a lack of horseshoes and hard service had unfitted the command. Even accepting Frémont's lower estimate of his troop strength, he had enough men for the work at hand. Without Taylor, Ewell counted fewer than 5,000 troops present at Cross Keys.[1]

Frémont began his advance on Cross Keys with great precision; units assembled on the Port Republic road and set off at fifteen-minute intervals, beginning at 4:45 A.M. with Cluseret's tiny brigade—consisting of the 60th Ohio and 8th West Virginia—as advance guard. Fifteen minutes later the pioneers and "axe men" followed. The 4th New York Cavalry, which would appear all but invisible during the day's action, swung onto the road at 5:15 A.M. as the lead element of the main body. Brig. Gen. Julius H. Stahel's First Brigade of Blenker's division came next, followed by Milroy, Bohlen's Third Brigade, and Schenck's Brigade. Next came the ambulances and brigade trains. Blenker's

Second Brigade, commanded by Col. John Koltes, brought up the rear at 7:00 A.M.[2]

The march was deliberate. The road was muddy, and both Frémont and Colonel Tracy were convinced that they were about to attack Jackson's entire force, which they calculated at between 16,000 and 18,000 thousand men. Sustaining them were rumors that Shields had arrived near Port Republic and was about to attack Jackson from behind.[3]

The first contact came between 8:00 and 8:30 A.M., when Cluseret's skirmishers, feeling their way down the Keezletown road, encountered two companies of pickets from the 15th Alabama just north of the Union Church cemetery. The remainder of the regiment was formed in line of battle on the left side of the road opposite the two-story brick church. The pickets held their ground just long enough to give Col. James Cantey, commander of the 15th, warning of the Yankee approach, then broke for the rear.

From the main line, Alabamian William McClendon watched the pickets' retreat. "They soon came in sight, passing through the cemetery, frequently taking shelter behind a tombstone long enough to fire and load. The odds were so great against [them] that they came in and took their place in line." Then time seemed to stop. "When the Yankees reached the opening near the cemetery, they halted for a while," McClendon remembered. "A deathly stillness prevailed in our ranks while we were waiting for the Yankees to come [with]in reach, for we were anxious to get a shot."[4]

Colonel Cantey broke the silence. Galloping back from the right of the Keezletown road, where he had been reconnoitering, Cantey bellowed out the command "Cap your pieces," then, "By the right of companies to the rear into column; double quick, march!" Away went the 15th through a succession of wheat fields toward Ewell's lines, which were forming about a mile to the southeast. William McClendon thought Cantey had seen a Federal regiment trying to turn the right flank of the 15th Alabama from the east side of the road, but Capt. William C. Oates of Company G had no idea why Cantey gave the order to retire, reportedly without the men having fired a shot. Oates could see nothing "but a line of skirmishers in hot pursuit, firing upon us and doing some execution." Alabamian B. F. Culpepper remembered the withdrawal as a mad dash for the rear: "One could see the wheat heads flying on either side as we ran. The Yanks could take deliberate aim while we were fleeing. I felt like the frogs in the pond when the boys were rocking them. 'It was fun for the boys, but death to the frogs.'"[5]

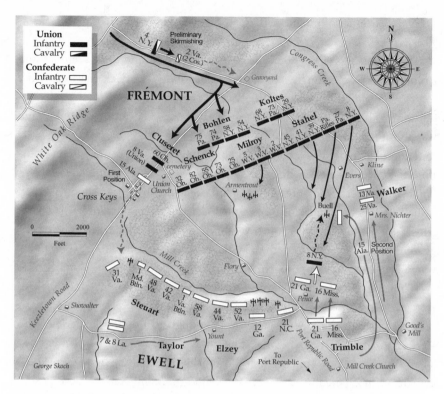

MAP 9. Battle of Cross Keys: Trimble's Attacks, June 8, 1862

The Alabamians' ordeal ended when Capt. A. R. Courtney's Richmond Artillery unlimbered its guns on high ground a mile southeast of Union Church and, with a few well-placed rounds, drove off Cluseret's Federals. The Alabamians rested behind the cannons just long enough to catch their breath, then they were moved to the right of the line to rejoin Trimble's brigade.[6]

Regardless of one's opinion of Cantey's decision making, his engagement with Frémont's advance guard delayed the Federals sufficiently to allow Ewell to position his three brigades at his leisure. The ground he occupied was ideally suited for the defense: a ridge running roughly parallel with and just south of Mill Creek. As Ewell himself described it: "The general features of the ground were a valley and a rivulet in my front, woods on both flanks, and a field of some hundreds of acres where the [Port Republic] road crossed the center of my line, my side of the valley being more defined and commanding the other." Looking at Ewell's ground from the Federal side, Charles H. Webb of the *New York Times* wrote: "The ground in all that region is gently undulating, covered with woods and wheat, or clover fields, alternating with marshy streamlets, ravines, and hollows, interspersed with occasional farm-houses, and a badly frightened people." A *Cincinnati Commercial* correspondent added: "The country is rolling; woods, generally of oak, from the size of a small sapling to a man's body. Occasionally, too, a pine is seen. The ground upon which the battle was fought is a succession of hillocks."[7]

Ewell had his line organized by 10:00 A.M. Steuart's brigade was posted on the left; Elzey's brigade, slightly in rear of the center; and Trimble's brigade, a little in advance of the center on the right. In the center, on a commanding knoll, Ewell posted four batteries—A. R. Courtney's battery, Capt. John A. Lusk's 2nd Rockbridge Artillery, Capt. Charles Raine's Lynchburg Artillery, and John Brockenbrough's Baltimore Light Artillery. The four batteries mustered sixteen guns, placed just behind the crest of the knoll for maximum cover.[8]

Ewell felt comfortable with his dispositions: "Both wings were in woods. The center was weak, having open ground in front, where the enemy was not expected. General Elzey was in position to strengthen either wing." The ground behind the Rebel artillery also was open, which made the men of Elezy's brigade considerably less satisfied with Ewell's arrangements. "Our regiment did not engage the enemy with muskets, but were placed in rear of the artillery to support it," said Irby G. Scott of the 12th Georgia, which the affair at Front Royal and straggling had reduced from 600 to only 175 present for duty. "We lay in an open field just behind the cannon during the whole fight. Solid shot, grape, and bombs seemed like they were raining down upon us during the whole action."

Brig. Gen. Isaac Trimble was unhappy with his position for a different reason. The ridge he was expected to occupy was too heavily wooded to shepherd the men into any semblance of a line of battle. The willful Virginian obtained Ewell's permission to push forward his brigade—minus the 21st North Carolina, which was left behind to support the artillery cluster—nearly a half mile due north to another hillock. The gap Trimble's advance created with the remainder of the Confederate line did not trouble Ewell; he was confident that the artillery could handle any threat that might materialize beyond Trimble's left. Trimble was comfortable with his right, as a "ravine and densely wooded hill" offered tactical security for that flank. Unmanned terrain, no matter how imposing, was no guarantee of safety, so Elzey loaned Trimble two regiments, the 13th and 25th Virginia under the joint command of Col. James A. Walker, to bolster his right on the far side of the "densely wooded hill" of which Trimble spoke.

There could be no doubting the strength of Trimble's new position. A wooden fence ran along the northern edge of the hillock, beyond which two hundred yards of clover and wheat fields intervened between Trimble's elevation and the next belt of timber. To ensure the secrecy of his movement, Trimble had his men crawl up to the fence. When all got in place, the 21st Georgia occupied the left; the 16th Mississippi, the center; and the re-formed 15th Alabama, the right of Trimble's potent deadfall.[9]

Frémont's dispositions displayed none of the ingenuity that marked Ewell's line; neither did he make good use of the ground available to him. Instead, as his brigades came onto the field, he made the fatal mistake of conforming his line of battle to that of Ewell. And unlike Ewell, who posted himself dangerously near the artillery cluster, Frémont passed most of the day in the rear.

His brief appearance at the front was dramatic. Of the opening moments of the fight, as heard from the commanding general's place in the march column, Colonel Tracy recalled:

At about eight the crack of rifles at our front indicated an engagement with the enemy's pickets, while soon the receding of the fire informed us that these were undoubtedly driven in. Then came a muffled detonation above the hills, and through the brush and forest interspersed at our right and left, the sound of heavier guns, and the main body of the enemy's force had been struck and could not be far off. As usual there was a tightening of belts, and a readjustment of knapsacks, blankets, and the like on the part of the men, for a more rapid advance.

Frémont cut a dashing, if somewhat wet and dirty, figure as he hurried forward. "With the general, the staff drove in their spurs and galloped in the direction of the firing at the front. Ambulances, ammunition wagons, guns, caissons, and all, we dashed past, splashing with entire recklessness the pools at this side or that, till arriving behind the point or shoulder of a projecting hill at the right, a halt was had, with the view to a more careful reconnaissance and study of the ground, and the prompt placing in position of troops, as they should arrive."

Frémont went forward as far as the John Armentrout farm, a half mile from Ewell's lines. He and his retinue soon came under artillery fire. The first shell thrown their way plunged "with an emphatic scattering of mud" just in front of Tracy's horse. A second round plowed the earth "within a pace of the horse" of another staff member. Neither round exploded, said Tracy, but "matters were beyond question becoming both exciting and absorbing upon all hands."[10]

By his own admission, Frémont's reconnaissance was perfunctory. Milroy had been talking with him when the shelling started and was amused to see how quickly he and his staff hustled as far to the rear as possible. Frémont felt nearly helpless. "The enemy occupied a position of uncommon strength, commanding the junction of the roads to Port Republic. He had chosen his ground with great skill and was advantageously posted upon a ridge, protected in front by a steep declivity, and almost entirely masked by thick woods and covered fences."

Frémont drew the conclusion that he was heavily outnumbered. "From superiority of numbers his flanks considerably overlapped my own," he later reported. "I was without reliable maps or guides, but from what could be seen I judged that the enemy's right was his strategic flank. I decided, therefore to press him from this side, with the object to seize if possible his line of retreat, and accordingly gave all the strength practicable to my left." How he proposed to outflank a flank that overlapped his own, and that of a foe that by his apparent calculations outnumbered his army two to one, Frémont did not say. On the other hand, a simultaneous attack of all his units might well have rolled Ewell off Mill Creek Ridge, despite the natural strength of the position. So thought Maj. Joseph H. Chenoweth of the 31st Virginia of Elzey's brigade. "I do not like our position," he began to write as the battle opened, "though it is a commanding one, we may possibly have our flanks turned."[11]

Turning the disposition of his forces over to his chief of staff, Col. Anselm Albert, and his chief of artillery, Lt. Col. John Pilsen, Frémont withdrew with the remainder of his staff. Replacing them around the Armentrout house were three batteries attached to Milroy's Brigade. These opened fire at about 10:30 A.M., setting off an artillery duel of perhaps an hour's duration with the four batteries at the Confederate center on Mill Creek Ridge. Besides the three batteries from Milroy's Brigade, within thirty minutes of the start of the barrage, Pilsen had five of his remaining seven batteries in position along what Tracy termed "the crests of a species of intermediate minor elevations, covered at points with brush or timber." Pilsen assumed that they did little execution against a foe "posted in the woods greatly to our disadvantage." Frémont's gloomy assessment of the situation was contagious.[12]

Watching the scene from behind the massed Southern batteries, Campbell Brown thought the Yankee infantry came onto the field "very slowly." Colonel

Albert formed the army line of battle upon Cluseret's tiny brigade, which Courtney's battery had driven back to a point parallel to the Union Church cemetery. Stahel's brigade and the handful of surviving Pennsylvania Bucktails took position on open ground to the left of Cluseret. Bohlen formed his four regiments in double column, closed in mass behind Stahel and Cluseret. Milroy swung into line to the right of what he termed the "three German brigades." Schenck's Brigade formed in echelon to the right of Milroy. Koltes was still on the road from Harrisonburg, well northwest of the action. Frémont's line of battle extended nearly a mile and a half in length.[13]

The lack of a guiding hand at the Federal front was apparent from the start. Stahel opened the action on the left. Not only did he move to the attack before Schenck on the right was even in position, but also he did so with only one of his five regiments. The 39th New York he left behind to support his artillery. Two other regiments, the 41st New York and the 27th Pennsylvania, somehow drifted to the right, "into the timber," leaving only the 8th and 45th New York heading in the direction of Trimble's ambush.[14]

The morning artillery duel at Cross Keys. (Edwin Forbes, *Frank Leslie's Illustrated Newspaper*, 1862)

The 45th New York unaccountably stopped short. Only the 8th New York—548 men strong—trudged into the field shortly after noon, unaware that some 1,400 Confederates, crouched behind a fence in an ideal defensive position, awaited them. The New Yorkers' ignorance of their fate was compounded by the fact that their commanding officer, Col. Francis Wutchel, had neglected to deploy skirmishers. But Wutchel did a wonderful job of maintaining order as the 8th marched across the field, eliciting praise from those who lay in wait to decimate his regiment. A Southern lieutenant said the "Germans came marching across the clover field in beautiful line, carrying their guns at support arms. The colonel, walking backwards in front of them, [saw] that they preserved a perfect alignment just as though they were simply drilling."[15]

Confederate officers made certain that their men held their fire until the New Yorkers were too near to miss. Col. John T. Mercer of the 21st Georgia, toward whom the Yankees marched, sent an order down the regimental line that he would shoot any man who opened fire prematurely.

The members of the 8th New York disappeared briefly into a hollow in front of Mercer's position. As they emerged, "their flag and that of the Georgians exactly confronted each other." Colonel Mercer insisted that his men hold their fire until the Yankees were visible from head to foot, a range of about forty yards. "When the order 'Fire!' rang out from Mercer, a volley from a thousand guns sounded in the air," said a Confederate officer, "and a thousand bullets flew to their deadly work. The poor Germans fell all across each other in piles." The 16th Mississippi and 15th Alabama contributed a deadly enfilading fire on the 8th.[16]

The slaughter stunned the defenders nearly as much as it did the victims. "I will take occasion right here," recorded a soldier of the 15th Alabama, "that I never saw men double up and fall so fast." After the first volley, the smoke from the black-powder muskets hid the New Yorkers from view; James Nisbet of the 21st Georgia climbed the fence to catch a glimpse of the Federals retreating in confusion back through the field. He jumped down to join his regiment and the 16th Mississippi in pursuit. "When we reached their line we saw a most appalling sight. There in the clover lay most of the 8th New York, either dead or wounded, all Germans." The fiasco had cost the regiment 43 killed outright and 134 wounded. Another 43 were captured, some of whom, said a Mississippian, "were eager to see the great 'Shackson.'" With Bohlen's brigade visible on the horizon, Trimble wisely recalled his regiments to protect the fence.[17]

But he was impatient to renew the contest. Scanning the field, Trimble spotted a lone Federal battery—Capt. Frank Buell's Battery C, West Virginia Artillery—a half mile away on the wooded knoll opposite the 16th Mississippi. The battery belonged to Stahel's brigade but had been abandoned by all but the 27th Pennsylvania and the Bucktails, which formed on its right, and the benumbed survivors of the 8th New York, who tried to rally to the left of the artillery. The location of Stahel's other three regiments is unclear, but their almost negligible losses suggest that they were some distance from the action, probably in woods far to the right.

Continuing to fight alone, Trimble "promptly decided to make a move from our right flank and try to capture the battery." Dividing the 15th Alabama into two battalions, the left under Lt. Col. John F. Treutlen and the right under Trimble himself, the general gave orders to the 16th Mississippi and 21st Georgia not to move until the Alabamians had come into contact with the Federal left flank. At that moment both were to charge the Yankees simultaneously.[18]

Matters did not progress as Trimble had calculated. Treutlen's battalion easily brushed aside the remnants of the 8th New York, but was in turn repulsed when it ran up against Buell's battery and the Bucktails. As Captain Oates of the 15th Alabama confessed, "a panic seized [the] command, and it retreated in confusion." Treutlen rallied the men at their starting point.

Obeying Trimble's order to advance as soon as the 15th Alabama made contact, the 16th Mississippi crossed the fence, rushed forward, and kept up a rapid fire as it progressed. Inexplicably, the 21st Georgia did not move with the 16th Mississippi, exposing the 16th's left flank. Col. Carnot Posey thought he detected signs of Buell's battery limbering up to escape—he was mistaken—and pushed his men so quickly to forestall it that he exposed his left rear to a devastating fire from the 27th Pennsylvania. Posey changed front to meet the threat, just in time to receive a Yankee bullet in the chest. His regiment traded volleys with the Pennsylvanians in the smoke-choked woods, neither giving nor gaining ground.

At last the 21st Georgia came up and, with the Mississippians, succeeded in driving off the 27th Pennsylvanians and Bucktails. But the crowning prize, the guns of Buell's battery, eluded the Confederates. The historian of the Bucktails described the battery's escape thusly: "An opportunity seemed to present itself. The artillery belched forth a murderous flood of [canister] and rapidly limbering up, a dash was made by the imperiled battery and its escort toward the Union line."[19]

The line of which the Bucktail spoke was Bohlen's brigade, which had come forward at the request of Stahel to within a quarter mile of the knoll from which Buell's battery and the Pennsylvanians had retreated. Bohlen had four regiments—the 54th and 58th New York and the 74th and 75th Pennsylvania—and Capt. Michael Weidrich's Battery I, 1st New York Light Artillery. Capt. Louis Schirmer's battery of Stahel's brigade took position to the right of Weidrich. No action beyond skirmish fire occurred between Bohlen's regiments and the 16th Mississippi and 21st Georgia, which were regrouping on the captured knoll. But that did not prevent Bohlen from boasting in his report that the 58th New York "met the enemy and drove him back at the point of the bayonet."[20]

The real threat to Bohlen came against his left flank. Trimble with his battalion of the 15th Alabama had linked up with Colonel Walker's two Virginia regiments. The general ordered Walker "to move on my right through the woods and advance on the enemy in line of battle perpendicularly to his line and in rear of the battery." Such a move would render Bohlen's position untenable. But Walker understood his instructions differently. "[General

Trimble] informed me that he was going forward to charge the enemy's battery, and directed me to advance on his right. This I did."[21]

But not to Trimble's satisfaction. When Walker's left crowded the right of Trimble's 15th Alabama battalion, Trimble curtly ordered the colonel to move to the right and keep the Evers farmhouse on his left. That exposed Walker's left flank and brought much of the weight of Bohlen's brigade down upon him. Skirmishers from the 75th Pennsylvania had detected Walker's approach southeast of the Evers farm. Bohlen reinforced the regiment with the 74th Pennsylvania, then ordered both to retire a short distance to give Weidrich's battery "a full sway."[22]

Samuel D. Buck of the 13th Virginia recalled the moment Walker's detachment came under fire on the Evers farm. "Our line was perfect as we moved through a piece of woods. We struck a high fence which we got over, forming as we did so and again we moved up the side of a hill through a wheat field on our left, resting on a fence line leading to a barn. As we rose to the top of this hill, we came face to face with more of the enemy than I had ever seen in one position and with several pieces of artillery, which opened on us with grape, canister, and small arms, which were mowing the wheat about us like a hail storm." Walker's command was in a bad fix. Continued Buck: "Immediately in our front was a very strong post fence which could not be torn down; we could not go forward and would not fall back, and so our only alternative was to stand and take it. Most humbly I do now confess, nothing but pride and a sense of duty kept me from running."[23]

Weidrich's fire was neither as heavy nor as effective as the frightened Sam Buck believed. The New York captain said he fired just "a few rounds in the woods in front by order of General Bohlen." Shortly after the Confederates moved into the wheat field of the Evers farm, the Federal artillery fell silent. Captain Schirmer, whose orders General Blenker had told Weidrich a few days earlier he must obey, suddenly appeared and told Weidrich to limber up for the rear along with his battery, "against my positive order to remain," said Bohlen. Weidrich stopped and fired a few rounds at Trimble's battalion, which had come within range, then reluctantly obeyed Schirmer's order and quit the field.[24]

The departure of the artillery doomed Bohlen's line. The 54th New York had redeployed on the extreme left to help drive Walker's men from their fence line to a body of woods one hundred yards to the right. Despite Walker's retreat, the 74th and 75th Pennsylvania followed Weidrich's battery rearward. The 58th New York fell back as well. The 54th New York was the last to leave the field. All the regiments seem to have retired in good order. After Weidrich's "few shots," said Bohlen, Trimble's battalion fell back "and did not molest us any longer."[25]

Joining the Federal retrograde were the three regiments of Koltes's brigade, which had stood quietly a quarter of a mile behind Bohlen while the fighting raged around the Evers farm. Koltes lost just one man wounded and eight missing in the battle.

Correspondent Sidney D. Maxwell watched Blenker's men emerge from the smoky woods and fields they had lost to Trimble. "There was a lull in the storm. The German regiments begin to come out the same way they went in, retiring in good order to more desirable positions. This quieted the storm." Fellow newsman Charles Webb agreed: "About 3:00 P.M. our troops were seen slowly returning to the position they had occupied in the morning. . . . They retired in perfect order, the enemy showing no signs of pursuing."[26]

Along with the reinvigorated 21st Georgia and 16th Mississippi, Trimble and the 15th Alabama occupied the ground Bohlen had quit. Trimble had much of which to be proud. As General Ewell noted in his report, Trimble had driven the enemy—three Federal brigades—"more than a mile, and remained on his flank ready to make the final attack." Much to Trimble's chagrin, however, there would be no final attack on the left. The battle on that part of the field was over.[27]

WHILE TRIMBLE DROVE Blenker on the Confederate right, in the center the artillery duel that had opened the day's action continued unabated for nearly six hours. The noise was deafening, and the amount of ordnance expended fantastic. Typical was the 12th Ohio Independent Battery of Milroy's Brigade, which from its station near the Armentrout house fired six hundred rounds from its five guns, or one round per gun every three minutes.

But for all the bursting shells and shattered trees that rained down splinters like lances, the damage done both sides was relatively minor. Battery I, 1st Ohio Light Artillery, also of Milroy's Brigade, pushed its guns to within four hundred yards of the five Rebel batteries concentrated on the commanding heights just west of the Beahm house. The battery fought at the edge of a wood line for four hours until its ammunition ran out, then retired with the loss of one man killed and one wounded. The two batteries at the Armentrout house lost one man killed and one wounded between them.[28]

There was suffering enough to go around, but surprisingly, given their superior position, the Confederates endured heavier losses. Massed artillery makes an easy target, as do the men around it. With his brigade hugging the ground in reserve and nothing better to do, General Elzey rode forward of the Southern guns. An exploding shell killed his horse and tore a deep gash in his leg. Later, Steuart went down with a shell fragment that pierced his chest and lodged in his back.[29]

Of unquestionably greater concern to General Ewell personally, if not professionally, was a wound that Capt. Campbell Brown, his future son-in-law, took while delivering messages from his chief near Mill Creek Church up and down the line. As he dashed through the artillery curtain on a late afternoon mission, a shell burst above Brown's head, and a large fragment slapped his shoulder. The blow stunned and unhorsed Brown, numbing his right arm but leaving him otherwise unhurt. Still, when he reported to Ewell, the general noticed Brown's pale aspect and ordered him to the rear for medical treatment. While riding rearward Brown met up with Stonewall Jackson, who had ridden over from Port Republic. Apparently Jackson had no concern over Ewell's ability to handle matters, because after chatting with Brown about the course of the battle he returned with the wounded captain to Port Republic. Ewell and Jackson never saw one another that day. But Jackson did bring with him welcome reinforcements in the form of Taylor's Louisiana Brigade.[30]

No less poignant than the travails of officers were the wounds and deaths that struck down the men in the ranks. Van Buren Clark of the 12th Georgia remembered the fate, perhaps deserved to Clark's way of thinking, of one member of his regiment. Just before the regiment reached the battlefield, a halt was called and the chaplain held a brief service. "While these services were going on I heard from one of our wicked boys the most profane language; it made me shudder," recalled Clark. "I thought at this time, poor fellow, you know not how soon you may be launched into eternity. Sure enough, before the services were fully over, we were called into battle and placed behind a rail fence to support a battery. A few minutes later a cannon ball struck the fence and tore off both legs of our profane comrade."

Lt. Randolph McKim, aide-de-camp to General Steuart, was riding behind the clustered artillery when he saw something he had not witnessed, before or after—two men "absolutely overcome by panic and fear." One was an artilleryman, crouched beneath a caisson and "trembling like a leaf." McKim saw a sergeant ride up and point a pistol at his head, saying: "Come out from under there and do your duty, and you'll have some chance of your life, but if you stay there, by the Eternal, I'll blow your brains out." McKim did not linger

long enough to witness the outcome. But he did see the fate of a second terrified soldier crouching behind a tree. "The next moment came a round shot,
which went through the tree and absolutely decapitated the man!" McKim
came close to losing his life as well, when a round shot plowed through the
head of his horse.[31]

ROBERT MILROY WAS fast losing patience with Frémont's lax management
of the battle. He had demonstrated his go-ahead spirit at McDowell and
would do so again at Cross Keys. Absent orders, Milroy decided about mid-
afternoon to make a go at Mill Creek Ridge. During the artillery duel he
tucked his four regiments—about two thousand men in all—safely in a ravine
near the Armentrout house. When the furious exchange subsided, he rode
forward in search of the "best way of getting my regiments up where they
could use their Enfield rifles." After riding a few hundred yards he came upon
a ravine, really a small drainage ditch, "which could be reached without
exposure," that ran southward and emptied into Mill Creek Bottom. Wheat
grew thickly around the gully, providing the Federals with cover as they advanced but also hiding skirmishers from the 44th Virginia who were deployed
along the base of the ridge.[32]

Milroy had neglected to throw out skirmishers and so was stunned when
the Virginians, lying in tall grass behind a fence, "mowed down the head of my
column by a deadly fire almost as fast as they appeared." The Yankees could
not return the fire, lamented Milroy, as they could not hit what they were
unable to see. Milroy at last wrestled out some skirmishers from his stalled
column, but they could not silence the Virginians. Searching for a place of
safety, as well as a way to flank the Confederates atop Mill Creek Ridge, Milroy
settled on the heavily forested hillside to his right. He sent skirmishers in that
direction and then worked the brigade into something approaching a line of
battle among the wheat, trees, vines, and mucky creek bottom. Milroy's right-
most regiment, the 25th Ohio, lined up opposite Steuart's 1st Maryland (Confederate), which constituted the extreme left of Ewell's line until he hastily
brought over the 31st Virginia from Elzey's brigade to shore up the flank.[33]

Starting up the steep, muddy, and heavily forested hill, Milroy's Federals
stepped into a maelstrom of rifle and renewed artillery fire, the latter from
Brockenbrough's battery, which stood with the 1st Maryland (Confederate).

Milroy was horrorstruck. "I brought up my regiments . . . but a deadly fire
come [sic] out of it and my boys were drop[p]ed by it rapidly." His prized

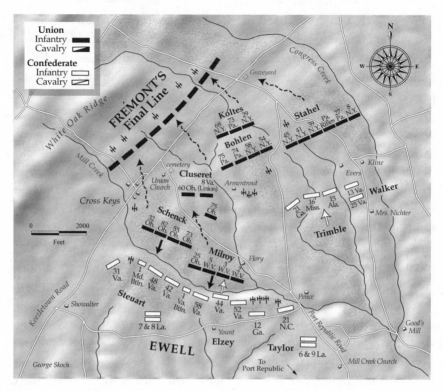

MAP 10. Battle of Cross Keys: Fight in the Center

horse Jasper was hit twice in quick succession. "He reared and plunged and nearly fell with me. I sprung off and saw the blood spurting out of his breast and gave him up for dead."

Directing the fight on foot, Milroy tried to order his regiments still farther to the right. The 25th Ohio seemed to him to be making good progress toward Brockenbrough's battery, and the 1st Maryland Infantry (Confederate) had nearly exhausted its ammunition, when an aide from Frémont dashed up with an order for him to fall back to his first position of the morning. "I was never so astonished or thunderstruck in my life. I could not believe what the Dutchman said and made him repeat it three times." Believing himself on the verge of a stunning success, Milroy felt too ashamed to order his regiments to cease firing and file to the rear. Instead, he had his aides bear the news. Turning his attention to Jasper, Milroy was delighted to find the horse alive and able to hobble on three legs. Milroy led him carefully rearward.[34]

Milroy thought himself poised for victory, but at least one soldier of the 25th Ohio saw matters differently from his perspective in the ranks. "We fought with but little success on either side," Thomas Evans recorded in his diary. But the fight was horrible enough. "The deafening roar of musketry and the loud pealing of artillery. The bursting shells, the whiz of grape and canister. The crushing of timber by the dread missiles mingled with the unearthly yells of opposing forces and the moaning of the dying, and the screams of the wounded. Oh, God, how terrible is war. Here lies a dear comrade bleeding and dying at your side who can just breathe the name of his mother, sister, or wife, and he is gone. How long must man thus strive with man?"[35]

Not much longer, on this day at least. Milroy was pulling his regiments back to their supporting batteries when he saw a sight that infuriated him. "A short distance to the right [was] Schenck's Brigade standing perfectly idle as spectators—thus five regiments [composing] the finest brigade in our army had taken no portion in the battle. Had this brigade been thrown forward on my right to clear the Rebels out of the forest, which they could have done with perfect ease, we could have swept the battlefield like a tempest and captured the whole of Jackson's army. I have lost confidence in Frémont tremendously and so has his whole army."[36]

Robert Schenck was likewise deserving of Milroy's opprobrium. By his own account, Schenck's Brigade—2,138 strong—reached the junction of the Keezletown and Port Republic roads at 1:00 P.M., just as Milroy was forming line of battle a half mile to the east. Schenck broke out of march column and lined up on Milroy's right, with his own right a quarter of a mile east of the Keezletown road. He advanced just far enough to find a good firing position for his two batteries on an open ridge, beyond which the ground was forested.

That was all Schenck accomplished that day. In his report, he attributed his inaction to his ignorance of the terrain and fear that Confederates concealed in the timber south of him were planning to extend their lines and turn Schenck's right; it apparently did not occur to him to test the strength of the Confederate left flank to see if *he* could turn *it*. Timidity got the better of him, and he meekly sent Companies A and F of the 73rd Ohio forward into the woods to skirmish. Milroy already was heavily engaged in his abortive effort to outflank Ewell; that his chances would have improved dramatically had Schenck attacked is certain. Instead, the Ohio skirmishers plunked away at their opposites across Mill Creek until a quiet descended on the woods to their left, indicating that Milroy had broken off his assault. In three and a half hours of skirmishing, Company F lost two killed and one man badly wounded; Company A lost no one. The entire loss in Schenck's Brigade that day was four killed, eight wounded, and four missing.[37]

A portion of Schenck's command in line of battle at Cross Keys. The Armentrout house is on the left. (*Harper's Weekly*, 1862)

In a purely self-serving bit of fiction, Schenck claimed that he was about to advance in strength against the Confederate left when word came for him to retire. When a member of his staff ascertained that Milroy was passing rearward, Schenck said he "had to follow him or be left separated from all the rest of the command." The time, he said, was between 5:30 P.M. and 6:00 P.M.[38]

It was well indeed for Ewell that Schenck remained supine. The only regiment he had been able to spare to extend his left flank was the 31st Virginia, whose soldiers were more interested in dodging Schenck's artillery than fighting. "We remained as silent and quiet as if inanimate while the cannon balls like winged devils were flying around us," said Cpl. James E. Hall of Company H. "I noticed the countenance of the men. Some looked pale but calm, their eyes tranquil. The knitted brow and flashing eyes of others showed the more fiery spirit within." Ewell started the 7th and 8th Louisiana of Taylor's brigade toward the left as well, but they would have arrived too late to be of help in repelling a determined attack by Schenck. Major Chenoweth of the nearby 31st Virginia noted that the firing ceased at precisely 6:13 P.M.[39]

AS DUSK SETTLED over the battlefield and his troops withdrew toward the Keezletown road, Milroy looked up Frémont. He probably gave him a piece of his mind in language unprintable. What he wrote his wife was that he told Frémont he "was very sorry to have to fall back as I could have held my position where I was a month." To this, said Milroy, Frémont expressed surprise and apologized for not knowing of Milroy's dispositions. An astounded Milroy wrote: "[Frémont] has a whole cloud of aides and it was his duty to know everything that was going on in his army when in battle at least."

Frémont knew almost nothing in part because he could see nothing. Correspondent Webb said that the entire day's action was obscured from view, and not merely because of the rising clouds of smoke. Frémont simply was too far to the rear to have any real understanding of what was happening or what opportunities existed. That he also lacked imagination did not help.[40]

What Frémont did know was that a decidedly aggressive Confederate force had chewed up Stahel's brigade and also compelled Bohlen and Koltes to withdraw. The early reversal on the Union left convinced Frémont and his staff that the "Rebels were too many for us."

According to Colonel Tracy and the Pathfinder's report, Frémont was about to renew the contest when a scout appeared with a note from Shields—the first news he had had of Shields's whereabouts in days. It read as follows:

Luray, June 8—9:30 A.M.

Major General Frémont,

Commanding Pursuing Forces:

I write by your scout. I think by this time there will be twelve pieces of artillery opposite Jackson's train at Port Republic, if he has taken that route. Some cavalry and artillery have pushed on to Waynesboro to burn the bridge. I hope to have two brigades at Port Republic today. I follow myself with two other brigades from this place. If the enemy changes direction, you will please keep me advised. If he attempts to force a passage, as my force is not large there yet, I hope you will thunder down on his rear. I think Jackson is caught this time.

Jas. Shields,

Major General, Commanding Division

Shields's dispatch was but another of his remarkable works of fiction. How Shields could have expected twelve cannons to be opposite Jackson's train when in the same message he admitted that Carroll and Tyler's brigades had not yet reached Port Republic defies explanation. And, of course, Shields had no intention of helping them. But Frémont took Shields at his word and acted accordingly. "This was most welcome intelligence," he remembered. "With the certainty now that General Shields was already holding the bridge in force I at once decided to defer until morning a renewal of the battle. My men had been marching and fighting since early in the morning. They were fatigued and hungry and needed rest."[41]

That was a matter of opinion. Sidney Maxwell said "the boys of the center and right had returned reluctantly and sullenly. They wanted to go ahead. They were confident of success and the idea of letting [the enemy] slip when they had their hand upon him they could not brook." Even Bohlen's and Koltes's brigades were eager to take on Trimble again. "They were aching for the encounter," said the reliable Lt. William Wheeler of the 13th New York Battery. The withdrawal order failed to reach his battery, and as Blenker's infantry fell back into a belt of timber, the New York cannoneers found themselves alone between the opposing lines. Nonetheless, said Wheeler, "our men were very cool and collected and only wanted a chance to do something."[42]

So did Trimble. He spent the better part of the evening bombarding Ewell's staff for permission first to make a twilight assault and then, as the hours passed without an answer, a night attack. No word came, and Trimble sulked.

"I was strongly tempted to make the advance alone at night," he proclaimed in his insubordinate report of the battle. But "some scruples in regard to a possible failure" deterred him. Had he had the foresight to demand Taylor, over whom he held date of rank, to join him, "the result would have been reasonably certain without consulting General Ewell."[43]

Trimble received no answer because Ewell was not at his headquarters near Mill Creek Church, but rather in Port Republic consulting with General Jackson. June 8 had been a hard day for Jackson, and at one point the harried general sent Sandie Pendleton to Ewell with the message, "I will keep Shields back if you can hold Frémont in check." By the time Pendleton found him, Ewell was able to answer with confidence, "The worst is over now, I can manage him."[44]

CHAPTER 28

ALL HAS GONE WRONG TODAY

Southern casualties at Cross Keys had been light—only 288 men killed, wounded, or missing (Frémont, by contrast, lost 684). The repulse of Carroll's raid and Ewell's easy victory at Cross Keys rekindled Jackson's natural aggressiveness. That evening his staff assumed that their commander, having dealt Frémont a hard blow north of the South River before Shields had been able to come up with his entire division on the south bank, would use the cover of darkness to "slip out of the trap with his prisoners and stores," as Henry Kyd Douglas put it.[1]

The first inkling that his staff had miscalculated Jackson's intentions came when Maj. John Harman, the chief quartermaster, just returned from leave, received an order to bring wagons back into Port Republic to feed the troops. Harman was astonished, and all present exchanged smiles. Sandie Pendleton said simply, "crazy again." Remembered Douglas, "We were getting used to this kind of aberration, but this did seem rather an extra piece of temerity."[2]

Jackson had his reasons for remaining, which he revealed in his report of the battle filed ten months later. Retreat across the Blue Ridge had never occurred to him. He would leave a covering force to hold Frémont in check and with the remainder of his army attack Shields's two brigades. When the staff officer writing the report asked Jackson why he had chosen to fight Tyler and Carroll instead of Frémont on June 9, he offered several reasons: First, Tyler and Carroll were closer; second, Shields's brigades represented the smaller enemy force; third, Jackson would be nearer his own base of supplies; fourth, from Port Republic the Confederates "had a good way of retreat if beaten" (over the mountains by way of the Brown's Gap Turnpike); fifth, Frémont had an easy line of retreat back to Harrisonburg and then down the Valley Pike if Jackson bested him; and sixth, Tyler and Carroll had a bad road to negotiate if routed. What Jackson lacked was the advantage normally accruing to a force operating on interior lines. As a British student of the campaign noted, "Jackson . . . had too little space between his two battlefields . . . to be able to disregard the one and use his whole force against the other."[3]

The first order of business on the evening of June 8 was to create a means for the Confederate infantry to cross the South River. None of the fords were then shallow enough for foot soldiers to wade. The Stonewall Brigade had camped west of Madison Hall, and Taliaferro's brigade was in the village itself.

Jackson assigned the task of building a temporary bridge to Major Harman, who in turn delegated the job to Capt. Claiborne R. Mason, a sixty-two-year-old engineer who had had much tougher challenges in civilian life. Rounding up his crew of black workmen, known in the Valley army as the "African Pioneers," Mason first prepared the bridge over the North River for burning, then built a new bridge over the South River from a half-dozen farm wagons and loose boards obtained from a nearby sawmill. Pioneers sunk the wagons into the river, one beside the other, then laid the planks, which were particularly long and thin, two parallel across the wagons and between them.

At 4:00 A.M. Mason gruffly informed Capt. Sandy Garber of the general staff: "Sandy, you can go and tell General Jackson that the bridge is done and he can take his folks and his things over." But Mason had no way to secure the planks, and after the first troops crossed two abreast, the planks came loose and began to waiver, compelling follow-on units to tread gingerly.[4]

Garber and Harman rode off in the dark to tell Jackson all was ready. They found him and the rest of the staff asleep.[5]

Jackson slept only briefly that night. A steady procession of high-ranking visitors reported to the commander at the home of Henry B. Harnsberger on the south bank of the South River, a quarter mile due south of Madison Hall by way of the upper ford. At midnight Jackson had summoned Ewell, Munford, and Taliaferro.

Ewell and Munford arrived first. Jackson told Ewell tersely that he was "to move from his position at an early hour on the morning of the ninth toward Port Republic." He added that he planned to attack Tyler and Carroll at first light.

The commanding general's timetable called for Ewell's command to cook rations and cross North River by 2:00 A.M. Trimble with his brigade and Col.

John Patton with the 42nd Virginia and 1st Battalion of Virginia Regulars were to hold Frémont in check and, if hard pressed, retire across the North River and burn the bridge behind them.

Ewell objected to the unrealistic timetable, which, said Campbell Brown, would have had him "ride five miles, get his division withdrawn from the presence of the enemy—within range of their guns—and march five miles, in two hours at night." Jackson relented a bit on the time, but left no doubt that he expected Ewell to move rapidly. Munford he instructed to ascertain at once if the road was open to Brown's Gap, and if so to "place a heavy picket on the road from the gap toward Conrad's Store" and report back "as speedily as possible." It was crucial to Jackson's plan that the Brown's Gap Turnpike be free of Federals, which Munford found it to be.

Whether or not he cared for Jackson's plan, Ewell's opinion of Jackson's generalship had improved dramatically since he was first assigned to the Valley army. As they mounted their horses outside the Harnsberger house, Ewell remarked to Munford: "Do you remember my conversation with you at Conrad's Store, when I called this 'old man an old woman?' Well, I take it all back."[6]

Capt. John Imboden dropped by next. To him, Jackson gave orders to hover on the enemy's left flank with his mule-drawn artillery, which Jed Hotchkiss recalled "was the laughing stock of the whole army. The soldiers chaffed Imboden as he went by, wishing to know which was to do the firing, the mule or the cannon." Imboden's assignment would prove a washout. As Hotchkiss observed: "There was no defile three miles below Lewis[town] where Imboden could get into position to shell the retreating Federals from the spurs of the Blue Ridge with his pop guns."[7]

William Taliaferro appeared well after his midnight summons. He found Jackson "pacing the floor of a small bedroom." Jackson told him that Captain Mason was building a bridge and that he wished Taliaferro to cross it " 'at early dawn,' his favorite expression, for the purpose of attacking Shields." Abruptly changing the subject, Jackson said he would walk awhile in the garden beside the Harnsberger house and invited Taliaferro to sleep in his bed until he returned. Taliaferro thought "his object in seeking the seclusion of the garden was to engage in prayer, unseen by any eye."[8]

General Shields spent the night of June 8 on the march with the two remaining brigades of his division. He preceded his departure with an encouraging note to Carroll, telling him that scouts had reported Frémont at Harrisonburg with twenty-five thousand men and seventy pieces of artillery. After again enjoining Carroll to defend the bridge at Port Republic, Shields closed with a promise to "be with you soon." The receipt of that message at 8:00 P.M. on June 8 had much to do with Tyler's decision to hold his ground. A second message sent at 7:45 P.M. from Columbia Bridge and received on the morning of June 9 clouded matters for Carroll and Tyler. Shields told Carroll that Tyler and Daum were to take up a strong defensive position as close to Conrad's Store as possible. "You are pursued in force," Shields told Carroll, as if he had any way of knowing, "[and] will avail yourself of that position to unite with him. Kimball's brigade is marching rapidly to your support."[9]

Shields's second dispatch implied an intention to advance no farther than Conrad's Store, which led Carroll to suggest that he and Tyler fall back while they still had time. But Tyler clung to the notion that Shields would support him wherever Tyler might be, and so decided to remain at Lewiston.[10]

A hopeful Tyler and a skeptical Carroll rode out at 4:00 A.M. to inspect a picket line that Tyler had thrown forward nearly a mile beyond his cramped bivouac site. The line roughly paralleled Baugher Lane and extended across the Luray road, the only means of egress from the neighborhood of Port Republic. They talked with the pickets, who had had their eyes trained on the North River Bridge. No Southerners had crossed it, they reported, and there was nothing in their front but "a few men in a wheat field." Tyler and Carroll returned to their campsite.

Tyler's pickets had seen no one cross the bridge because by the time they deployed, Jackson had all his army except Ewell's division and the 33rd Virginia, which somehow was left behind on the heights opposite Lewis Mill, across the North River and encamped in and around Port Republic.[11]

The first regiment to cross Mason's ramshackle bridge was the 2nd Virginia of Winder's brigade. The general and his staff rode in the van. It was nearly 5:00 A.M., and the sun was just peeking over the horizon, throwing enough light on the surroundings to reveal a bit of the grim work of the day before. Riding past Yost Hill, from which the 7th Indiana had been driven, McHenry Howard "came to several dead bodies by the roadside, one with the head missing, a few inches of the spinal column projecting above the shoulders, testifying to the effect of our fire yesterday." A private in the ranks commented similarly: "We saw the effects of our fire the day before. Dead and wounded Yankees lay along the road, and the trees and houses were badly torn by the balls."[12]

In an egregious tactical miscue, Jackson elected to commit his forces to battle piecemeal. As Taliaferro put it: "The impetuosity of Jackson had

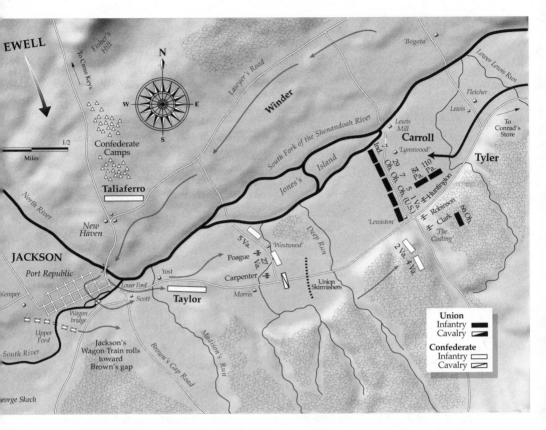

MAP 11. Battle of Port Republic: Opening Moves, June 9, 1862

betrayed him into attacking before his troops were sufficiently massed, which was made difficult by the insufficient means of crossing the river."[13]

After the head of Winder's column had marched about a mile down the Luray road, Jackson ordered him to attack. A few well-placed shells from a section of Joseph Carpenter's battery posted beside the road scattered Tyler's pickets, and Winder began to deploy his four regiments and supporting artillery. He sent Colonel Allen's 2nd Virginia to the right of the road, where woods descending from the Blue Ridge skirted the bottomland, intending to flank Federal artillery massed on a commanding, seventy-foot-high knob three-quarters of a mile away. Known as "the Coaling" because the Lewis family made charcoal there for their blacksmith shops, the "steep, ragged hill, covered with scrub oak underbrush," as one Federal described it, commanded the entire field of battle, from Lewiston Lane to the timberline along Baugher Lane. From it, the rooftops of Port Republic also were visible. One piece from

Robinson's battery, a twelve-pounder howitzer, and six ten-pounder Parrott rifled cannons of Capt. Joseph Clark's Battery E, 4th U.S. Artillery, were arrayed on top of the knob. The five brass ten-pounder rifled pieces of Huntington's Battery H, 1st Ohio, were aligned near the intersection of the Luray road and Lewiston Lane, with a clear field of fire as far as Baugher Lane.[14]

Despite its obvious advantages, the Federal position atop the Coaling was hardly invulnerable. An inconsequential watercourse called "Deep Run" trickled down the mountains in front of the old coal hearth and then parallel to Lewiston Lane. It cut through a heavily wooded ravine to the left of the Coaling. Thick undergrowth rendered the ravine nearly invisible. As a nervous Captain Clark later reported: "Close to the flank was a ravine, beyond which the ground rose rapidly, giving a plunging fire upon our guns, if occupied by the enemy."[15]

A heavy fog obscured the field until 5:45 A.M., and under nature's blanket Winder parceled out his units. He reinforced the 2nd Virginia with the 4th Virginia and the second section of Carpenter's battery to charge the Coaling. Captain Poague's two Parrott guns he placed well to the left of the road in a wheat field in front of Baugher Lane and detached A. J. Grigsby's 27th Virginia to support it, holding Poague's smoothbores in reserve. Winder positioned his remaining regiment, the 5th Virginia, to the left and rear of Grigsby.[16]

At 6:00 A.M. the first artillery shots rang out. The morning was cool and, once the fog lifted, the sky clear. Colonel Carroll had just left his bed at the Lewis house when the shelling commenced. Carroll and his staff remained long enough to join their hosts in morning prayer. "Within five minutes after we arose from our knees," recalled the brigade surgeon, "Rebel cannon balls struck the servants' cookhouse, a frame structure, tearing it to splinters. The Negroes screamed from fright, and all were startled. We left the house immediately and lost the opportunity of breakfasting with Mr. Lewis."[17]

Carroll rode rapidly to find Tyler and urge him to withdraw at once. Tyler declined and instead began to deploy his regiments from the forested foothills northeast of the Coaling into line of battle along Lewiston Lane. The movement resembled a massive left wheel of nearly the entire Federal force. Daum accommodated Tyler by moving three of Clark's and two of Huntington's guns into the wheat field bordering Lewiston Lane a few hundred feet shy of the South River. The 7th Indiana followed and formed between the cannons and the riverbank. A few scattered volleys from skirmishers belonging to the 5th Virginia, which had sidled to the left until its flank rested along the river, compelled the Hoosiers to retire briefly.[18]

The Port Republic battlefield, looking east across the South Fork of the Shenandoah (middle ground) toward the foothills of the Blue Ridge. (Author's Collection)

Next up was the 29th Ohio, which fell in on the left of the artillery. "The sound of fighting quickened our steps," remembered a soldier of Company I. "When orders were received we moved out from where we camped, filing to the right and across the road through the open timber and fields some twenty rods in rear of the 7th Indiana. We halted long enough to pile knapsacks by companies, when the colonel gave orders, 'By the left in battle line!' In order to do this we had to climb over a rail fence."[19]

The 7th Ohio Infantry fell into line on the left of the 29th, the 5th Ohio lined up on the left of the 7th, and the 1st Virginia (Union) Infantry formed beside the 5th Ohio, its left flank resting near the Lewis house. To protect the all-important artillery position at the Coaling, Tyler deployed a company each from the 5th and 66th Ohio in the timber south of the guns. He placed the remaining nine companies of the 66th in reserve directly in rear of the artillery and held the 84th and 110th Pennsylvania regiments "well up into the woods," ready to respond to any emergency around the Coaling. "My entire force was now in position," Tyler later reported. Indeed it was. He had retained no reserves: either Shields would arrive in time to assist him, or he would fight as long and as hard as possible with what he had.[20]

The artillery duel opened poorly for the Federals. Huntington's battery was using Schenkle percussion shells, and the damp weather had so swollen the paper heels on the shells that they could not be rammed into the guns. Men had to pare the shells down with pocket knives. Eventually Huntington's cannons swung into action, and together with Clark's battery and Robinson's twelve-pounder rained shells down on Poague's two Parrott guns exposed in the tall wheat field. "We could see and hear the balls cutting through the wheat," said cannoneer Randolph Fairfax. "But strange to say, we escaped with few casualties." To ensure the preservation of the section, Winder, who was directing the fire himself, split it, sending one of Poague's guns farther to the left.[21]

In the midst of the shelling, Captain Imboden's hapless mule battery provided a bit of comic relief. He had positioned his teams and guns in a ravine two hundred yards behind Poague's Parrotts. "Some of the shot aimed at Poague came bounding over our heads, and occasionally a shell would burst there. The mules became frantic," said Imboden. "They kicked, plunged, and squealed. It was impossible to quiet them, and it took three or four men to hold one mule from breaking away." Imboden was beside himself. "Each mule had about three hundred pounds of weight on him, so securely fastened that the load could not be dislodged by any of his capers. Several of them lay down and tried to wallow their loads off. The men held these down, and that suggested the idea of throwing them all on the ground and holding them there." Just when his "mule circus" was at its height, General Jackson rode up. He paused at the brink of the ravine and said, "Colonel, you seem to have trouble down there." Imboden made a feeble reply, and Jackson said, "Get your mules to the mountain as soon as you can, and be ready to move." Jackson was thinking of pursuit even before the action was decided.[22]

The folly of Jackson's piecemeal deployment, which Winder only compounded, became apparent with the opening shots of the battle. Among the Southern infantry units, first blood was spilled in Colonel Allen's 2nd Virginia, which with the 4th Virginia behind it was struggling through laurel thickets and underbrush in a hopeless mission to overrun the Coaling. Between them the two regiments counted just 494 rank-and-file soldiers, of whom only 177 marched with Allen.

Allen closed undetected to within one hundred yards of the Coaling, there to find the knob cluttered not only with the Union guns but also with three regiments of infantry. Undeterred, he ordered his two left companies to take deliberate aim and fire at the gunners. "Unfortunately," Allen reported, "two chance shots showed our position, and one gun had been brought to bear on us loaded with grape." Allen's first regimental volley drove off the gun crews, but the 66th Ohio came up and opened so heavy a fire that the Virginians were unable to prevent the gunners' return. That doomed the regiment. Said Allen:

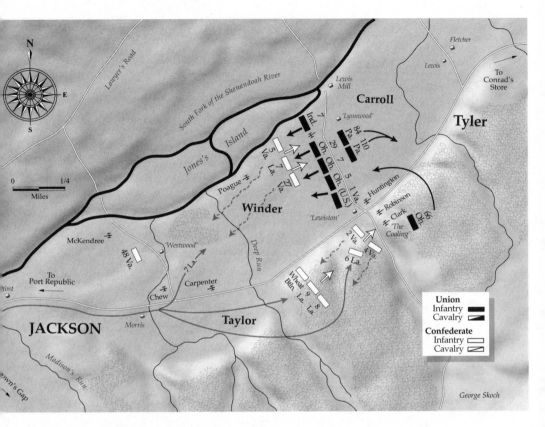

MAP 12. Battle of Port Republic: Winder's Defeat

"They poured in volley after volley of grape on us in such quick succession as to throw my men into confusion, and it was some time before they were reformed." The 4th Virginia formed on Allen's right in time to catch a few rounds, withdrawing in good order with the loss of four men wounded.[23]

Down in the wheat and clover fields between Baugher and Lewiston lanes, Winder subjected the two regiments under his immediate control to a brutal ordeal. For nearly an hour, while the 2nd and 4th Virginia labored to reach the Coaling, the 5th and 27th Virginia stood exposed to fire from the Federal artillery opposite them. Winder wanted to attack, but without additional troops he dared not do more than advance his skirmishers and edge the 5th Virginia forward three hundred yards.[24]

That reinforcements were slow in coming was due to the near chaotic state of affairs in Port Republic. Army wagons clogged the streets, making it hard for infantrymen to reach the makeshift bridge over the South River, which they then had to cross single file. For a time, crossing was halted altogether. It seems that in the middle of the stream the front end of one wagon had been placed beside the rear of another wagon. The resulting discrepancy in height left the ends of the planks without support. When stepped on, the other end rose in the air and dumped the unlucky soldier into the water. A bit of remodeling was done, and Taylor's Louisiana Brigade negotiated its way across the bridge, but then paused to prepare breakfast. Peremptory orders from Jackson brought the Louisianans to their feet, and Taylor started them down the Luray road in column, with Col. Henry B. Kelly's 8th Louisiana as the vanguard.

Waiting for them near the Morris house, alone by Jed Hotchkiss's account, was Stonewall Jackson. Major Dabney told Kelly to report to Jackson for orders, and the commanding general sent him with the 8th and 9th Louisiana and Wheat's battalion through fields east of the Morris house toward the Coaling. Hotchkiss came up just as Taylor appeared with the 6th Louisiana. As the Louisianans approached, said Hotchkiss, Jackson, "pointing with his finger back to General Taylor and bringing his arm around with a sweep from right to left and, pointing to the enemy's battery, said, 'Take General Taylor and take that battery.'"[25]

By "that battery" Jackson meant the artillery concentration on the Coaling. He well understood that the key to the battle lay in seizing the Coaling and turning the Federal left flank. But he also understood that Winder needed help to keep the enemy's attention focused on the plain. While Hotchkiss, who knew the ground thoroughly, led Taylor and the 6th Louisiana "into the forest, which was everywhere a tangle of roads from the coaling operations," Jackson detached Taylor's trailing regiment, Col. Harry T. Hays's 7th Louisiana, to reinforce Winder.

Delighted with the arrival of reinforcements, albeit three hundred men, Winder elected to charge. It was his only alternative. Remaining where he was would only cause more pointless casualties; to withdraw would incur the wrath of Jackson and, of greater immediate importance, imperil the attack of the 2nd and 4th Virginia on the Coaling. Winder placed the 7th Louisiana between the 5th Virginia, which hugged the riverbank, and the 27th Virginia, and at about 8:30 A.M. ordered the line of 1,009 officers and men forward to attack at least twice their number. Poague's two smoothbore cannons and the section of Carpenter's battery that had made an abortive attempt to follow the 2nd and 4th Virginia into the forest followed closely behind the infantry.[26]

Two-thirds of the way across the plain was a rail fence that ran parallel to

Tyler's line. Tall wheat masking them, Winder's men advanced to the fence, harassed principally by the soft, muddy earth beneath their feet and the Federal artillery; the Union infantrymen had been slow in appearing and, once in place, received orders to hold their fire until the enemy was almost upon them. As the Confederates crossed the fence, commands such as that of the colonel of the 29th Ohio—"Aim low, men, and at every shot let a traitor fall!"—rang out along the Union line.[27]

The effect of the first volley was devastating. The 7th Ohio rose up from the wheat in which it had laid, recalled its major, "and delivered its fire. This shower of lead made a fearful gap in the enemy line." Said drummer John SeCheverell of the 29th Ohio: "The entire line poured its leaden hail into the grayclad columns of chivalry, producing fearful slaughter."[28]

The Confederate line shivered but did not break. Retiring behind the fence, the three Southern regiments fell into a savage but inconclusive exchange of fire with the enemy. Losses were heavy, especially in officers. Colonel Hays fell severely wounded, and his lieutenant colonel was mortally wounded. The horse of Colonel Grigsby was shot twice, and Grigsby probably owed his life to having had to dismount and direct his regiment on foot.[29]

Although the Confederates held on for nearly an hour, "amid a perfect shower of balls," said Grigsby, the outcome never was in doubt. Ammunition ran low, and men began trickling rearward. The 7th Louisiana gave way first, having lost 156 men, or nearly half its combat strength. Among the casualties was the regimental color-bearer; with him were lost the colors.[30]

Recognizing their advantage in numbers, the Federals surged over the fence along Lewiston Lane and through the wheat fields toward the fast disintegrating Southern ranks. Shields's meddlesome artillery chief, Colonel Daum, apparently gave the order to charge. Nineteen-year-old Alonzo H. Burton of the 7th Ohio was standing near Daum. An instant before the colonel barked out the command to charge, a ball struck Burton in the mouth, injuring his jaw slightly and loosening several teeth. "I was not going to give up at that, and having loaded my gun sank down on my knees to fire once more when a piece of a shell, which burst by my side, hit me in the right shoulder, disabling me so I could fight no more." Burton stumbled into the woods where he found a doctor, so frightened out of his wits that he had run off, leaving the gathered wounded unattended. Burton seemed fortunate to find four men willing to carry him rearward on a blanket, until a shell burst nearby, "at which they dropped me and took to their heels." Burton struggled to his feet and walked nine miles before finding an ambulance.[31]

Meanwhile, enough Federals were running in the right direction to play hell with Winder's command. Shortly before 8:00 A.M. the 31st Virginia of Walker's (formerly Elzey's) brigade crossed the river and reported to Winder just as the tide turned. He wisely held it in reserve until the shattered remnants of his three regiments cleared the front; they would not regroup until nearly a half mile behind their point of farthest advance. Winder got all his artillery clear of the counterattacking Yankees except one piece of Poague's battery under the command of Lt. James Davis. Davis was fleeing with his cannon when Winder intervened and ordered him to make a stand. It was an impossible order to obey. The 7th and 5th Ohio regiments closed in on the gun in a race to claim it. Limber horses shrieked and tumbled to the ground, and gunners dropped until only Davis and a fraction of his men were left standing. No sooner had he pulled the lanyard on the piece than a bullet felled Davis. The last gunners fled, and the cannon was lost to the 5th Ohio. A man named John "Scotty" Gray—a notorious drunkard—received credit for reaching it first and coercing the dying limber horses to drag it from the field.[32]

At 8:30 A.M. Winder sent the 31st Virginia forward from the Baugher barn to buy time for his troops to rally. The Virginians came up against the 7th and 5th Ohio, both regiments exhilarated by the capture of Poague's gun. The 31st advanced farther than Winder had intended, well into the wheat field beyond Baugher Lane. "Our ardor carried us too far," recollected an officer, and the regiment paid dearly for its impetuosity.

Maj. Joseph H. Chenoweth tried to scribble a few lines home while the regiment marched through the ripening grain. "The ball is open again and we are, from what I see, to have another hot day. . . . I may not see the result, but I think we will gain a victory, though I do not think our men have had enough to eat. I can't write on horseback." Tucking the fragmentary letter into his jacket, Chenoweth dismounted and walked to the front of the left wing of the regiment. Lt. J. French Harding of Company F watched him intently. "As he was advancing up the line, encouraging the men and calling upon them to advance and follow where he led, he was shot, the ball entering just behind his left ear and passing entirely through his head. He fell without a groan, with his sword still in his grasp, pointed toward the enemy."[33]

Plenty fell with him. Of the 226 officers and men who went into the fight, 97 were killed or wounded. One man who survived was a "half-witted" member of Company B named Billy Wright. "When the command was ordered up in the wheat field, [he] had become so frightened by the whistling of the minie balls through the wheat as not to obey the order," said Lt. William R. Lyman.

"He laid still, and when we were driven from the field and the enemy came on, Billy still held his position. He was a cadaverous looking little man at best, and, closing his eyes, Billy let the enemy roll him over and turn his pockets inside out, feigning death among the many actually warm dead bodies around him. The enemy's possession of the field was but of short duration, and when Billy showed up he was boastful of the fact that he was the only member of the regiment who had actually held the field, and he was."[34]

As Winder's units and the 31st Virginia reeled in defeat, the 52nd Virginia of Steuart's brigade—now commanded by Col. W. C. Scott—happened onto the field and tried to squeeze in on the extreme Confederate left beside the mill-race. Crossing Baugher's Lane, it ran headlong into the 7th Indiana and 29th Ohio and was swept from the field in a matter of minutes. One hundred and three Virginians dropped before the 52nd quit the fight. Similarly dispersed near the center of what remained of Winder's line was the 25th Virginia of Walker's brigade. Twenty-nine men were lost, among them Lt. E. D. Camden of Company C, who was seriously wounded. Recalled the lieutenant: "We charged through a wheat field and in crossing near a fence and through some water and mud about half a leg deep I was shot through the shoulder, taking one knuckle and part of my backbone off, and under the jugular vein of the neck. I fell in the water and mud and one fellow by the name of Clayborn Hosey came to me and wanted to take me to the rear, and I said no, go back and fight. I finally went back about one half mile to an old mill."[35]

Winder was making limited progress at best in rallying his troops when help came from an entirely unexpected quarter. Ewell had hurried across the wagon bridge with the first command he found, Scott's brigade. Jackson apparently was responsible for diverting the 52nd Virginia to help Winder, but Ewell—unable to find Jackson—decided to march to Taylor's support with the remaining two regiments of the brigade, the 44th and 58th Virginia. Their route of march took them perpendicular to Winder's line and onto the slopes of the Blue Ridge. As Ewell entered the forest with the brigade, his attention was called to the chaos in the wheat fields. From the foothills he could see Winder's line break and the Federals surge after them until the left flank of the 5th Ohio was nearly at right angles with Scott's regiments. The 5th Ohio constituted the Union left on the plain because the 1st Virginia (Union) had not joined the pursuit.

Without hesitating, Ewell wheeled Scott's troops to the left and made ready to assail the Federal flank. First he called for volunteers to tear down some fences standing between them and the Yankees. That done, he directed Scott to sally forth. Scott's was not a particularly potent force—the 44th Virginia counted no more than 130 men, and the 58th numbered 400. But their unexpected appearance caused the 5th and 7th Ohio to stumble before they changed front to take on Scott. The colonel's tiny command was slaughtered—nearly half the 44th Virginia fell, and 127 members of the 58th were either killed or wounded. Having done what he could to take some of the pressure momentarily off Winder, Ewell withdrew into the timber and resumed his march toward Taylor. The Ohioans saw them off with a loud cheer and then resumed their march on Winder.[36]

Winder had patched together a ragtag line southwest of Baugher's Lane, but it was clearly not strong enough to halt a determined Federal drive. Walker's last two regiments came onto the field, but Jackson—fixated as he was on the Coaling as the key to victory—diverted them from Winder and motioned them along Taylor's path into the wooded slopes of the Blue Ridge. At about the same time Jackson sent orders to Trimble and Patton to quit Frémont's front, hasten to Port Republic, and then burn the North River Bridge behind them.[37]

Shortly after Trimble and Patton pulled out, Frémont marshaled his army for what he presumed would be a renewal of the contest at Cross Keys. Milroy apparently had wanted to open the battle before daybreak. At 1:00 A.M. Milroy awoke his orderly, and together they walked their horses to Frémont's headquarters, so as not to trample on the sleeping soldiers who lined the roads and fields. Milroy found the Pathfinder in his bunk asleep. He expressed his conviction that the enemy was retreating and suggested immediate pursuit. But Frémont rebuffed him, saying: "Hold yourself in readiness to move when ordered. I will notify you when I desire to make a move on the enemy." For a second time Milroy departed Frémont's headquarters in a foul mood.[38]

At daylight, said a soldier of the 25th Ohio, he and his comrades plainly heard the boom of artillery at Port Republic. He commented, "Now we will be called right away." But "we were not called until about 10:00 A.M."[39]

Schenck's Brigade led the way. Officers and men steeled themselves for a fight. The colonel of the 55th Ohio called the regiment into line and announced: "Now boys, we have the hardest work to do today. We are on the center and must do our part well." Lt. Col. Ebenezer Sweeney, commander of the 32nd Ohio, addressed his men in a similar vein. "Attention! Thirty-second Ohio! We are about to move on the enemy, and if there is any hard fighting done today, it will be done by Schenck's Brigade. I will expect the Thirty-second to do its duty. Right face, forward, march!"[40]

But the admonitions of their colonels proved needless. "In a short time we came upon the scene of the previous day's conflict, but to our great surprise no picket was met, no shot fired, and no enemy in sight," an Ohio soldier remembered:

> The Confederate dead, unburied, lay scattered numerously through the woods. Among the enemy's slain I noticed, as we passed along, the body of a young man about twenty years of age who lay where he had fallen, beside a tree. He had been instantly killed by a musket ball striking him in the forehead, and his face was illumined with a happy smile, as though death had been to him a joyous trance. In singular contrast with this in the road a little farther on was the body of an old man, also killed instantly, whose extended hands were clenched, and whose features were distorted as if in a paroxysm of agony and horror.

Continuing on, Schenck's troops came upon the Mill Creek Church, where more scenes of horror awaited them. A private of the 55th Ohio recalled: "Many of the wounded and dying of yesterday's struggle were carried in here and it was filled with suffering. Just behind the building, at an open window, was a pile of arms and legs which the surgeon's knife and saw had helped the shell and bullet to take off. Many of the poor fellows within, undergoing the pain necessarily following such terrible operations were without food. The colonel asked us to divide our crackers with them. The boys hustled out the hardtack lively."[41]

IT WAS IMPERATIVE to Jackson's chances for victory that Taylor overrun the guns on the Coaling before Carroll's Federals were able to press home their attack on Winder's new line, or before Frémont reached the heights overlooking the field of battle and swept the ground with his artillery. But the Louisiana Brigade was having trouble getting into position. Colonel Kelly had set off from the Morris house blind. "I had no guide and was altogether ignorant of the local topography, as were all the officers and men of my command, and the advance was directed solely by the sound of the guns of the batteries upon which we were moving."

Ascending the foothills in front of the Morris house, "covered with a growth of forest trees and thickets of mountain laurel," Kelly somehow managed to form the 8th Louisiana, 9th Louisiana, and Wheat's battalion in line of battle. In that fashion they edged toward the Coaling. With Federal cheers reverberating from the plain below, Kelly reached the crest of the hill over-

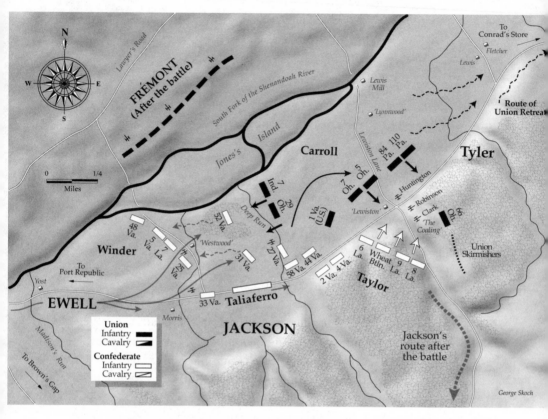

MAP 13. Battle of Port Republic: Fight for the Coaling

looking the Deep Run ravine. At that instant General Taylor arrived with the 6th Louisiana and took command of the movement.[42]

Without any further formalities, Taylor gave the command to charge. From the far side of the ravine the 66th Ohio let go a volley at the Louisianans, which they returned before letting out the Rebel yell and stumbling down the slippery, leaf-caked southern slope of the ravine and up the other side.

Kelly, leading the 8th Louisiana on foot, had the shortest distance to traverse, and those of his regiment nearest him were first among the guns. "By the impetus of the charge over rough ground all formation was lost," recalled Kelly, "and officers and men were all thrown into one unorganized mass." The mass of Louisianans swarmed over the cannons of Clark's battery and Robinson's howitzer with ease. Watching the spectacle from the Luray road, Captain Huntington said the Union artillerymen "made a stout but short resistance, as pistols and sponge staffs do not count for much against muskets and bayonets." Fearful for his own battery, Huntington called forward the limbers to withdraw his cannons.[43]

But the capture of Clark's guns had been too easy. Exultation gave way to agony as canister from Clark's remaining section, which Tyler had hurried over from the right to within two hundred yards of the Coaling, swept the ranks of Louisianans. The 66th Ohio readied itself to counterattack, and the 5th and 7th Ohio broke off their pursuit of Winder, changed front to the left, and hustled toward Lewiston to take the Louisianans in the flank. Also heading toward the fray were the 84th and 110th Pennsylvania, both of which had passed the morning shuttling between the left and right without firing a shot.[44]

As the Federals neared, Lt. Col. William Peck of the 9th Louisiana called out to his men to kill the battery horses to prevent the Yankees from taking away the cannons. The Louisianans obeyed with a will. All over the Coaling horses fell shrieking and jerking in their death throes. Major Wheat drew out his knife and joined in the slaughter, slashing the throats of the horses nearest him until he was "as bloody as a butcher." Others placed their muskets against the heads of the poor animals and fired.

Before long the Federals were upon Taylor's men, and bayonets and clubbed muskets were used liberally. Five color guards of the 5th Ohio were shot down in rapid succession and the colors lost to the Louisiana Tigers. "It was a sickening sight," recalled a Tiger, "men in gray and blue piled up in front of and around the guns and with the horses dying and the blood of men and beasts flowing almost in a stream." Capt. Eugene Powell of the 66th Ohio said "the sight of the captured battery was fearful beyond description. Our gunners were mostly killed at their guns, while the horses had been shot or bayoneted while in their harness."[45]

After perhaps fifteen minutes of close-quarters slaughter, the Ohioans succeeded in bludgeoning Taylor's brigade back into and beyond the ravine. When the Yankees tried to haul off the cannons by hand, Taylor's men cut them down. Only one gun of Clark's battery was removed before Taylor renewed the attack. H. H. Rhodes of the 7th Ohio was one of the men who helped draw off the piece. The wheels of the gun, said Rhodes, were in mud up to the hubs. There were only two horses left to the limber team, and the driver was urging them vainly to yank the piece free of the muck. Rhodes, who had gone into action barefooted, and a comrade who had been shot through the mouth—the bullet having entered one cheek and exiting the other—helped. "I had hold of the right wheel and lifted till I could see stars. My comrade, at the left wheel, each time he lifted the blood would issue from his cheeks like soap bubbles."

Joining Taylor on the left were the 58th and 44th Virginia, running down the Luray road with Ewell in the lead, on foot, cap in hand. The 2nd and 4th Virginia also rallied to Taylor's assistance, and Taliaferro's brigade was rushing up the road from the Morris house. Walker's brigade was advancing behind the Louisianans, but it became so entangled in the thick undergrowth that it never entered the battle.

At 10:00 A.M. Taylor sent his brigade over the ivy- and laurel-choked precipice, through the ravine, and straight at the guns. With Ewell closing in on the Federal left flank and the 2nd and 4th Virginia aligning on Taylor, the Union defense buckled and then broke.

At the same time that the Coaling fell, Winder started the 27th Virginia across the wheat fields, and what remained of the Union line along Lewiston Lane became untenable. Colonel Carroll said he questioned Tyler about the propriety of a withdrawal, but there really was no alternative. It became a race between retreating Federals and pursuing Confederates for the Luray road, the only avenue of escape open to Tyler.[46]

Caught in the maelstrom was Huntington's battery. Two of his three pieces were irretrievably lost, but the Ohio captain had a chance to get one gun, which now stood alone on the road beneath the Coaling, safely away. But two of the drivers of the limber team had been shot from their horses before the piece could be hitched up, and the third could not control the terrified animals, which broke away and dashed off with the limber. Captain Huntington hurried over to the gun crew, telling the chief, "a splendid soldier," to retrieve the team and limber the gun to the rear. "Cool as if on parade, the sergeant turned to obey, when he fell almost at my feet, shot through the heart, and died without uttering a sound." Huntington himself then ran to get the limber, which the driver had brought to rest among some trees. He had to coerce the driver into leaving the cover. "By that time a force had broken out of the woods in our front, and yelling like demons, came pouring up the road, straight for our remaining gun."

The loader stood by the gun, but the man inserting the charge was shot down just as he had put a cartridge in the tube. The loader picked up two canister rounds and rammed them down the tube. The man whose duty it was to fire got the primer in the vent but lost his nerve, dropped the lanyard, and ran. The gunner who stood by the trail ready to help limber grabbed the lanyard and blew a lane in the charging Louisianans that checked their

The climax at Port Republic, as Taylor's Louisianans surge
around Huntington's battery. (Tradition Studios)

onslaught and permitted the gun to be limbered up and saved. Left behind
was Huntington. "My first impulse was to lie down and surrender, as there
seemed to be a very poor prospect of reaching cover with a whole skin. But
having a wholesome dread of Southern hospitality as dispensed at that period,
I concluded to take the chance, and was lucky enough to slip out between the
bullets."[47]

The Federal retreat now became general. The Confederates turned the
captured field pieces on the Coaling against the fleeing enemy, said Colonel
Carroll, "which threw the rear of our column in great disorder, causing them
to take to the woods, and making it for the earlier part of the retreat apparently a rout." Chew's and Brockenbrough's batteries unlimbered to join in the
pounding.

Brockenbrough's battery had rumbled onto the field before the issue was
decided. Brockenbrough sent Pvt. Joshua Davis of the battery to find Jackson

and ask him where he wanted the battery placed. Davis came to "a rather secluded spot, where I found the general alone, seated on his horse, the bridle rein loose on the horse's neck, his cap held in his left hand, and his right hand extended toward heaven in the attitude of prayer." Davis waited quietly until Jackson had finished.

The general glared at him, "Well, sir, what is it?"

"General," Davis stammered, "Captain Brockenbrough of the Baltimore Battery would like your permission to enter the fight, and if permitted, what position should he take?"

Jackson retorted, "Tell him to come into line immediately and take any position he thinks best."

Over on the extreme Federal right, several soldiers of the 7th Indiana escaped by swimming the South Fork and later joining Frémont's command. Wrestling among the foothills of the Blue Ridge, Col. Samuel H. Dunning told his men to head for the mountains as best they could.

S. W. Hart of the 29th Ohio was one of the unfortunate victims of what formerly had been friendly cannons. "As we fell back, [the Rebels] poured canister into our ranks, strewing the fields and road with dead, dying, and wounded. I was wounded in my left hand and shoulder while falling back over the open ground, and my comrades were shot down like blackbirds, some of them being shot after having surrendered." A wounded Hart watched many of his comrades, along with the colonel and his adjutant, take to the mountains, "hoping to flank our pursuers and rejoin our regiments. In that endeavor we simply jumped into a hornet's nest. In every direction all around us were Johnnies, who shouted, 'Halt there. Surrender you damned Yankee.' "[48]

Jackson was alone when the Coaling was taken, just as he had been when Private Davis had encountered him in prayer minutes earlier. As Taliaferro's brigade hustled up the Luray road in column, Jackson waved it after the enemy; Winder's brigade also joined the pursuit. The Confederate infantrymen were tired, and they generally followed the Federals at a respectful distance. After four or five miles they turned over the chase to Munford's cavalry, which had little luck in running down the Yankees. "The secesh cavalry formed for a charge but it was not effective as there was only one road and on each side dense woods," attested James Clarke of the 5th Ohio. "We kept back the cavalry with little trouble." An isolated band of the 29th Ohio formed a square to repel Munford's men.

Campbell Brown concurred in the Yankees' poor opinion of their mounted antagonists. "The Yankees were pretty completely routed, and followed by our cavalry for about three miles, but these halted with exemplary prudence, 'that rascally virtue,' as soon as a single regiment of the enemy showed any signs of standing." Nonetheless, some 450 Yankees were rounded up, together with eight hundred muskets and an abandoned cannon.[49]

The Coaling was a concentrated corner of gore. A member of Jackson's staff was dumbstruck to see so many artillerymen killed in position. "One bright boy, with a brave smile on his fair Northern face, we can never forget. He lay, shot through the heart, with his left arm over the muzzle of his gun, his knees on the ground, and his right hand on the shell he was about to place in the piece, and behind it was the gunner, his body lying over the sight, one eye open, shot in his tracks, and near him one with a broken rammer in his hand." After the war, General Taylor summed up the spectacle with the words, "I have never seen so many dead and wounded in the same limited space."[50]

Back at Port Republic, matters were going Jackson's way as well. Frémont had followed Trimble timorously, allowing him to burn the North River Bridge at his leisure. Colonel Tracy painted a vivid picture of the army's approach to Port Republic: "There appeared in our pathway the sign of wrath and destruction, and a dense and dingy cloud of smoke rose slowly upward towards the heavens. It was the bridge at Port Republic. Who had fired it? Our own, or the troops of the enemy? The question, mentally asked by all, but added an intenser interest to the progress. Now, too, the sound of guns, and high in the air, the bursting shells display their clouds or wreaths of white, and it is evident that a contest is going forward."[51]

All doubt as to who had fired the bridge was removed when Frémont's advance reached the North River shortly before noon and saw the Rebel rear guard in town. Reported Frémont laconically, "Of the bridge nothing remained but the charred and smoking timbers." He had no idea what to do next. Correspondent Charles Webb said: "It was evident, for the first time since I had known him, that General Frémont was surprised, perplexed, and disappointed." Alfred Lewis of the 60th Ohio was nowise disappointed in finding the bridge gone; he left the ranks to make a cup of coffee on the smoldering coals, the first coffee he had enjoyed since the army left Harrisonburg.[52]

Lacking any alternative, Frémont deployed his forces on the bluffs above the South Fork of the Shenandoah, overlooking the late field of battle. It was a dismal sight. Died or dying bluecoats dotted the verdant fields, and the only live members of Shields's command were being hustled rearward by their Rebel captors just half a mile away; so many Federals, remembered correspondent Sidney Maxwell, as to give the appearance of a line of battle. Southern ambulances had begun their grim rounds of retrieving the living of both sides. General Milroy observed "long lines of Rebel baggage wagons filing away for miles in the distance on the other side." Frémont's artillery opened fire, stopping a few of the wagons, said Milroy, by "knocking their teams apart."

But far too many shells fell among the ambulances and wounded, infuriating Jackson. Troops not engaged in the pursuit or under cover of timber also were at risk. Calling Jed Hotchkiss to his side, Jackson asked him about roads leading from the field of battle to Brown's Gap, to which Hotchkiss replied that "the whole plane at the foot of the mountain was intersected by roads that were used to haul charcoal to the old Mount Vernon France at the mouth of the gap."

Jackson ordered Hotchkiss to take the army to the furnace, there to make camp out of harm's way. Jackson, meanwhile, secured quarters at the John F. Lewis residence, near the furnace. He went to bed early that night, but before turning in he telegraphed Richmond in his usual succinct manner: "Through God's blessing the enemy near Port Republic was this day routed with the loss of six pieces of artillery." And to his wife Anna he scribbled a short note: "God greatly blessed our arms near Port Republican [sic] yesterday and today."[53]

That night Jackson's army felt little for which to thank God or General Jackson. Remembered an officer of the 13th Virginia: "We encamped on the side of the mountain where it was so steep we had to pile rocks and build a wall to keep from rolling down when asleep, and to add to our discomfort the inevitable rain began to fall, and the men were wet to the skin. . . . The army had passed through terrible scenes and looked rough and dirty, as well as ragged."

Ewell's division had an especially rough night. With a Virginian's partiality for his own people, Major Harman, charged with quartering the troops, had given Jackson's old division the crown of the mountain and assigned Ewell the slope. When General Taylor saw his camp, on the mountainside at a thirty-degree angle above the road, he swore a blue streak. "The rest of us were more resigned and began to make the best of our unique camp of steepness and darkness," said brigade commissary officer Maj. David Boyd, "but our general only got the madder and cussed the louder." While Taylor fumed, his adjutant found a tree stump and hugged it; "he had some rest, if not much sleep." Taylor's servant spread the general's blankets on wet leaves, with soaked earth and loose stones underneath. Boyd walked down to the road and spread his rubber cloth in the mud beneath a parked wagon. Placing his blanket on top of the cloth, he "had a mattress as soft as a Dutch feather bed, and was sleeping the sleep of the blessed when I was awakened by Taylor's deep voice, calling loudly above the storm for [his] quartermaster. Taylor in his sleep had turned in his steep bed, and he, bed and all, were sliding down the mountain."[54]

Losses may also have been a factor in low Southern morale that night. It had taken Jackson four hours and cost him 816 men to dislodge a force a third his number. Federal casualties were higher due to the large number of captured, and the most reliable figure is 1,002 killed, wounded, or missing.[55]

Jackson's piecemeal deployment of his troops was to blame for his heavy losses. As Campbell Brown wrote home a week after the battle: "Each regiment and each brigade was hurried into the fight as it came up, without being allowed time to form or to collect a large body and make a strong simultaneous attack. The consequence was that when our division came up, three or four brigades having been successively sent against a force of Yankees just strong enough to whip them, our whole force previously engaged was in full retreat from the field having suffered heavily. The whole battle hung on a thread." Even William Allan, among Stonewall's staunchest admirers, agreed that "Jackson's impetuosity had made his victory more costly than it otherwise would have been."[56]

Port Republic arguably was a battle that need never have been fought. Jackson could just have easily burned the North River Bridge and taken his army from Port Republic to the mountains via Brown's Gap Turnpike without a struggle. As one historian observed: "The Valley Army slept the night of June 9 in the same positions it could have occupied twelve hours earlier without the intervening costly battle." And there was no reason for Tyler and Carroll to have sacrificed their brigades. Back in Washington, President Lincoln and Secretary Stanton had concluded that nothing more useful could be done in the Valley, and on June 8—as the Battle of Cross Keys raged—they issued recall orders to McDowell's command, then under the guiding hand of McDowell's chief of staff, Colonel Schriver, at Front Royal, the general having gone to the capital. The president intended to send McDowell's corps and Shields's division with all possible haste to reinforce McClellan in accordance with prior plans. Not realizing he had gone farther, Lincoln that day also directed Frémont to halt at Harrisonburg. Neither order reached its intended recipient in time to prevent the needless loss of life.[57]

GENERAL SHIELDS WAS on hand with his First and Second brigades to rally the shattered remnants of Tyler's and Carroll's brigades as they streamed up the Luray road toward Conrad's Store. Shields had selected a good position to deter further Southern pursuit, a spot where the mountain came close to a bend of the river to form a defile. Tempers were thin when the two commands met, and allegations flew freely. One Ohio lieutenant accused Carroll of riding into Shields's lines inebriated, upon which he made "a ridiculous speech to us trying to throw the blame for his failure on Shields."[58]

The dispirited soldiers of Tyler's and Carroll's brigades were pleased to see Shields, who sat on horseback by the side of the road, offering words of encouragement to the men as they passed. But the disingenuous Irishman was not at all ready to accept blame for the defeat. To a West Virginia infantryman who cried out to him, "All has gone wrong today; we are badly beaten," Shields responded, "My boy, nothing better could be expected of the children when the old folks are not at home." To a captain of the 66th Ohio, he was more direct. After damning the battle as a "bit of folly," he said: "That is not the way that I make war. We have a lot of officers filled with milk-and-water philosophy, who have no idea of war." He might just as well have been speaking of himself—first, for fearing that Longstreet's Southern division lay just over the mountains (a Georgia brigade under A. R. Lawton that had been redeployed from the Deep South to Virginia just days earlier had been diverted toward the Valley, but it is doubtful that Shields knew of its approach); second, for splitting his command in two if he really believed his own dispatches; and third, for sending false promises of help to Tyler the night before the battle.[59]

Little did Shields then know that he had fought his last campaign; that his miserable performance in Page Valley would cause him to be shelved until he resigned from the army in March 1863. But for the moment, most of his division blamed the defeat on Carroll for failing to burn the North River Bridge when he had had the chance; they assumed those had been Carroll's orders, a belief that Shields fueled by telling all who would listen that he had given Carroll peremptory orders to destroy the span.

No accusation against Carroll was too ludicrous. "Colonel Carroll, if he had obeyed orders and destroyed the bridge which he was holding would have pinned them [the Confederates] on the neck of land between the two branches. But he has won for himself the execration of the whole army by ordering the flames to be extinguished three times after it had been set on fire as often," a soldier of the badly mauled 7th Ohio wrote his parents three days after the battle. Said a member of the similarly shattered 5th Ohio: "It was a common opinion that Colonel Carroll disobeyed orders that day; that he tried to hold the bridge instead of burning it, and that he was after a star in so doing."

A thoughtful number saw through Shields's bombast and lies. General McDowell certainly was not fooled. On the morning of the battle he had addressed a sharp note to the Irishman through Colonel Schriver, saying: "It is not clear what is the position of your command, and it is inferred that the force at Port Republic is small. . . . If this be so, the general thinks you have forgotten your instructions not to move your force so that the several parts should not be in supporting distance of each other." Lower-ranking officers also had their doubts. On June 15 assistant surgeon Samuel Sexton wrote in his diary, "Shields is very unpopular in his division, and I hope a better man will succeed him." To his wife three days earlier, Colonel Voris of the 67th Ohio had confided: "We have felt for weeks that we were being led to ruin. We have seriously doubted the sincerity of the commander of the division, and how terribly has this been realized."[60]

CHAPTER 29

THE GAME COCK OF THE VALLEY

June 10 was a miserable day for Jackson's Confederates, hunched on their cramped mountain campsite against a raw wind and steady downpour. The only men to leave the mud-streaked slopes were scouts sent out to monitor enemy movements and members of burial details who roamed the fields and forests searching for dead comrades.

The scouts found little of concern. Frémont had given up any further designs against Jackson. At 3:00 A.M. on the tenth a detachment of Federal cavalrymen dispatched to open communications with Shields returned with the news that Shields was under orders to depart for Richmond. From them Frémont also learned the extent of the debacle at Port Republic, as well as false reports that Jackson had been reinforced. With his own command "weakened by battle and the hardships and exposures of a severe march," Frémont deemed it best to fall back until he could unite with the forces of Nathaniel Banks and Franz Sigel, who had superseded Saxton as commander of the Harpers Ferry garrison, which he then took across the Potomac behind Banks. On June 9 Lincoln had directed Banks to march from Winchester to Front Royal as part of an unspecified "general plan for the Valley of the Shenandoah."[1]

At 8:00 A.M. Frémont's rain-sodden troops turned their backs on the South Fork of the Shenandoah and began their return march to Harrisonburg. Colonel Tracy, for one, was infuriated with the turn of affairs:

> Is it treachery, is it persecution, or possibly a simple indifference, which
> from the first has been deaf to our appeals for the means; which, in the

second place, has left us to ourselves, or avoid connections at moments when everything depended upon a close and vigorous unity, and which now, at the heel of our effort, and with the last remaining chance of success, leaves us away at the front, "in the air," with our force dangerously exposed and at the same time withdraw all cooperation, or hope thereof?

Late in the afternoon the army reached Harrisonburg, and Frémont and his staff established their quarters in a commandeered tavern. There, a frustrated Frémont first learned of Lincoln's instructions of June 8 that he not march beyond that town. It was a "bitter bit of fortune," said Tracy, "that the message had not been issued sooner."[2]

Also at Harrisonburg Frémont found Brig. Gen. Carl Schurz, the fiery antislavery German expatriate whom Lincoln had sent to replace Blenker and report to him on the state of Frémont's army. Schurz reached the town first and got a good look at the soldiers he was expected to whip into shape. "Presently troops began to come in, marching in rather loose order. The men looked ragged, tired, and dejected. I heard a good deal of swearing in the ranks in various tongues, English, German, and Hungarian—signs of a sorry state of affairs." Soon Frémont rode up, flanked by a "troop of neat-looking horsemen," and at once unburdened himself to Schurz. Jackson had been heavily reinforced, he expostulated, rendering Harrisonburg indefensible and making it necessary to retire down the Valley immediately. Schurz listened and then wrote the president his opinion that Frémont lacked self-reliance and resolution, and that the administration needed to "secure concert of purpose and movement, the 'see-saw business,' as it had for some time been going on, wearing out the strength of the army for no useful end."[3]

Before leaving Harrisonburg the unruly Germans, who still remained under Blenker's command, vented their frustration on the citizenry, "committing depredations on the property of our people," a resident reported. "They even destroyed gardens as far as they could."[4]

On the far side of Massanutten Mountain, Shields was having troubles aplenty of his own. He dealt with them in his usual fashion—by lying. Writing from Columbia Bridge at 5:30 P.M., he assured McDowell that he would obey orders to march to Luray. But there he must remain until shoes could be obtained, "about one-third of my command being barefooted and in an exhausted condition." Apart from footwear, he would need two or three days in Luray to recover, his division having been "so overworked that it will take some time to refit it for the field."

In the next breath, Shields had the temerity to tell McDowell that he and Frémont were preparing a combined attack on Jackson for the morning of June 10, "which in all probability must have destroyed him, when peremptory orders reached me, which I did not feel at liberty to disobey." There seemed to be no end to Shields's capacity for mendacity. Colonel Schriver, through whom Shields's work of fiction was routed, added a damning postscript of his own. "The above is a sorry picture of Shields's division, but I do not think it overdrawn." He doubted whether any part of the corps would be fit to take the field in less than a fortnight. "Horses are used up as well as the men," reported Schriver. "The want of discipline and ignorance of the plainest duties are distressing. There is nothing but confusion and disorder."[5]

The skies cleared on June 11. Jackson unleashed Tom Munford's cavalry to nip at Frémont and hurry him on his way, as if the Pathfinder needed any prodding. That night found his army at New Market, from whence it marched to Mount Jackson the next day. Munford put up a fine show of strength and spread rumors, which Frémont accepted as true, that Jackson was behind him with a heavily reinforced army. This "significant demonstration of the enemy," as Frémont called Munford's isolated clashes with his cavalrymen and pickets, along with continued rumors that Jackson had been reinforced to the tune of 35,000 men, sufficed to push Frémont down the Valley to Middletown, where on June 14 he joined Banks and Sigel.[6]

Shields limped slowly over the course of the next week to Front Royal. There he remained until June 21, when, after leaving behind the "sick and foot weary," marched east to rejoin McDowell's command with a division, McDowell told the president, that was "in a bad state morally and materially."[7]

WITH THE WITHDRAWAL of Frémont and Shields from Jackson's front, the Shenandoah Valley campaign was over. Or was it? On June 12 Jackson moved the army back into the Valley, through Port Republic and several miles southwest along the Staunton road. Near a lovely grotto called "Weyer's Cave," Jackson pitched camp and ordered a general cleanup. It was a campsite that all would look back on fondly. Lieutenant Dinwiddie of the Charlottesville Artillery recalled the spot as "one of the most beautiful we have yet camped on. A belt of wood, sloping northward skirts a most charming little stream, as rapid and restless as the times we live in, though taking its rise from a few springs not more than one hundred yards distant. Beautiful fields, covered with the richest grass, are spread out before us. Horses and men, for the present, are enjoying a most delightful repose."[8]

While the men wrote letters home, played cards, bathed, and rested about Weyer's Cave, Jackson was busily formulating an adventure far more daring than anything the Valley army had yet undertaken, a movement similar to the policy he had advocated in the wake of First Manassas. He asked Congressman Alexander Boteler, who had just returned from Richmond on June 13, to travel again to the capital and petition the government to increase his command to forty thousand men to enable him to launch an offensive beyond the Shenandoah Valley and across the Potomac. "By that means," he told Boteler, "Richmond can be relieved and the campaign transferred to Pennsylvania." To his friend, Jackson confided his intention to advance with the utmost secrecy toward the Potomac along the eastern side of the Blue Ridge until he reached a gap in the mountains that would best allow him to get behind Banks at Winchester and crush him, after which he would cross the river at Williamsport. Jackson's twin victories at Cross Keys and Port Republic had lifted his spirits, and Boteler found him "more communicative than I ever knew him to be." Their conversation occurred after dinner, and Boteler promised to leave for Richmond that same evening.[9]

The arrival of Brig. Gen. Alexander R. Lawton's Georgia brigade, the advance elements of which lumbered into Port Republic on June 10, buoyed Jackson's hopes. The next day Lee ordered a demi-division consisting of Brig. Gen. John Bell Hood's Texas brigade and Evander Law's brigade and commanded by Brig. Gen. W. H. C. Whiting to leave for the Valley at once. These reinforcements would swell Jackson's army, badly depleted by casualties and straggling, to eighteen thousand men.

Lee's intentions in reinforcing Jackson were ambiguous. In a message dated June 8, he directed Jackson to "report the probable intentions of the enemy and what steps you can take to thwart them." In the same breath, he added his expectation that Jackson would "make arrangements to deceive the enemy . . . that you may unite at the decisive moment with the army near Richmond." In concluding, Lee enjoined Jackson: "Should an opportunity occur for striking the enemy a successful blow do not let it escape you."

On June 11 Lee informed Jackson that the objective in sending Lawton and Whiting to the Valley was to enable him "to crush the forces opposed to you." But in the same paragraph he told Jackson to move with his main body, including the troops of Lawton and Whiting, toward the Peninsula by whatever means he found most advantageous "and sweep down between the Chickahominy and Pamunkey, cutting up the enemy's communications while this army attacks General McClellan in front."[10]

Boteler arrived in Richmond on June 14 after office hours. He procured a horse and rode first to the home of the secretary of war, who referred him to President Davis. The president, in turn, told him to submit Jackson's request to Lee. Boteler galloped to the commanding general's headquarters.[11]

The Valley congressman found Lee unreceptive to Jackson's entreaty, which Boteler delivered in the form of a letter dated June 13. In the interim Lee had learned from his cavalry commander, Jeb Stuart, who had just completed a ride around McClellan's army on the Peninsula, that the Federal right flank and rear were exposed, offering an excellent chance for Lee to break McClellan's lines of communication and isolate him from his base of operations. For that task, Jackson's reinforced command was essential.[12]

Nonetheless, Lee heard Boteler out "with the kindly courtesy which so eminently characterized his intercourse with everyone." Then he asked Boteler a question that caught him off guard.

"Colonel," Lee began, "don't you think General Jackson had better come down here first and help me to drive these troublesome people away from Richmond?"

Boteler politely tried to dodge the question. "I think," he said, "that it would be very presumptuous of me, General, to answer that question, as it would be hazarding an opinion upon an important military movement which I don't feel competent to give."

"Nevertheless, I'd like to know your opinion," Lee said.

"Well, if I answer your question at all, it must be in the negative."

"Why so?"

"Because," replied Boteler, "if you bring our Valley boys down here at this season among the pestilential swamps of the Chickahominy the change from their pure mountain air to this miasmatic atmosphere will kill them off faster than the Federals have been doing."

"That would depend upon the time they'd have to stay here," countered Lee. "Have you any other reason to offer?"

"Yes," Boteler answered emphatically, "and it's that Jackson has been doing so well with an independent command that it seems a pity not to let him have his own way, and then too, bringing him here, General, will be—to use a homely phrase—putting all your eggs in one basket."

"I see," answered Lee with a laugh, "that you appreciate General Jackson as highly as I myself do, and it is because of my appreciation of him that I wish to have him here."[13]

On June 16 Lee summoned Jackson and his army to Richmond, in a manner as gentle as any order could read. After correctly deducing that Frémont and Shields were in no condition to cause mischief in the Shenandoah Valley, Lee told Jackson: "The present seems to be favorable for a junction of your army and this. If you agree with me, the sooner you can make arrangements to do so, the better." Lee was about to counterattack, and he needed every man he could lay his hands on to drive McClellan from his entrenched positions.[14]

Congressman Boteler and Robert E. Lee were far from alone in their high opinion of Jackson. Indeed, the perceived brilliance of his Valley campaign in general, and the twin victories of Cross Keys and Port Republic in particular, lifted him to the status of a national idol. The *Richmond Whig* declared that he was fast becoming the hero of the war and labeled him the "Game Cock of the Valley." Confessing with humor to the wrong-headedness of their past criticism of Jackson as being "unsound of mind," the editors of the *Whig* said that "since that time he has exhibited not the least symptom of improvement. Within the last two weeks he seems to have gone clean daft. . . . With his foot cavalry at his heels, he has been raving, ramping, roaring, rearing, snorting, and cavorting up and down the Valley, chawing up Yankees by the thousands as if they were so many grains of parched popcorn." Similar praise was heaped upon Jackson in newspapers throughout the South.[15]

After a spring of setbacks, a South starved for victory eagerly imbibed news of the Valley victories. Kate Cummings, an army nurse in Alabama, wrote in her diary: "A star has arisen: his name [Stonewall], the haughty foe has found, to his cost, has been given prophetically, as he proved a wall of granite to them. For four weeks he has kept at bay more than one of the boasted armies." The accolades seemed endless.[16]

Jackson had gained for the South something equally precious—time to improve on the defenses of Richmond, and with it a new lease on life for a Confederacy that in the late spring of 1862 was in its death throes. Nothing Jackson accomplished before Front Royal and Winchester had done more than give sagging Southern morale a temporary boost. But the diversion of McDowell's forty thousand–man command from Falmouth to the line of the Manassas Gap railroad and Front Royal was of the utmost strategic importance. Abraham Lincoln had reacted with commendable calm to news of Banks's discomfiture, and in pulling McDowell from McClellan's support his intention was offensive—to trap Jackson between McDowell and Frémont before the Valley army was able to slip away from the Potomac River southward. But it was a terrible miscalculation, not because the maneuver misfired, but rather because it removed a critical number of troops from what should have been the Lincoln administration's sole strategic goals in the East—the capture of Richmond and with it the destruction of the principal Confederate army. Accomplish those, and Jackson's small Valley force would be inconsequential.

Had McDowell marched south on Richmond, Joe Johnston would have been compelled to strike McClellan's right flank before the two Union forces joined up, an action that probably would have gone against the Confederates. With the weight of McDowell's added numbers, not even one so cautious or so apt to overestimate the enemy's strength as McClellan could have failed to capture Richmond.

Jackson did many things right in the Valley after his stinging defeat at Kernstown. He inflicted approximately 4,000 casualties on the Federals from Kernstown to Port Republic, at a cost of only 2,750 men. But nearly a third of his force melted away during the campaign. Jackson was fortunate that both Frémont and Shields fell back from his front after Cross Keys and Port Republic; a few more days of hard marching or fighting might have used up his army.

Jackson benefited incalculably from a dysfunctional Federal command structure. After April 1, when Lincoln reduced McClellan from the status of general in chief to that of commander of the Army of the Potomac and installed Frémont as commander of the Mountain Department, Frémont, Banks, and later McDowell all reported to and took their orders directly from Lincoln or Stanton. The administration failed to instruct Banks and Frémont to cooperate with one another, and the two Federal forces in western Virginia, often less than fifty miles apart, worked at cross-purposes—Banks struggling to hold his own in the Valley proper and Frémont in the Alleghenies pondering a grand sweep (over impossibly rugged terrain) to eastern Tennessee. From Washington, those fifty miles seemed a deceptively short distance. But to Frémont, who would have to cross some of the most mountainous terrain and march over as wretched a road network as existed in the Eastern theater, the distance rightly appeared daunting.

Brig. Gen. Alpheus Williams vented his frustration at the absence of a guiding hand in a June 16 letter to his daughter. "I am heartsick at the want of common sense in all the management of affairs outside of McClellan's army in Virginia. In this valley it would seem that we are to be the sport of changing policy. . . . We have too many district commands and too many independent commanders."[17]

Three days earlier, during a personal meeting with Stanton, David Strother had expressed the same concern. "I suggested the idea of concentrating the troops under one leader. He replied thoughtfully—'Then Frémont will be in command.' I did not reply except to say that one head was better than many."[18]

Not until it was too late did the president recognize what should have been obvious: on June 8, as Frémont was grappling needlessly with Ewell at Cross Keys, Lincoln wrote his secretary of war: "Richmond is the principal point for our active operation. Accordingly, it is the object of the enemy to create alarms everywhere else and thereby to divert as much of our force from that point as possible" (which is precisely what Jackson had done). Continued Lincoln: "On the contrary, as a general rule we should stand on the defensive everywhere else, and direct as much force as possible to Richmond."[19]

WHERE STONEWALL JACKSON is most open to criticism is in his tactical management of his army once it was committed to battle. His tendency to feed his army into battle piecemeal caused unnecessarily high losses and prolonged some contests longer than was warranted. At Kernstown he deployed his entire force a regiment or two at a time, with the exception of Ashby's cavalry on the right and a single regiment of infantry and a battery of artillery in the center, far to the left of the Valley Pike in a failed effort to turn the Union right flank. Fortunately for Jackson, the acting Federal commander, Col. Nathan Kimball, lacked imagination and conformed his movements to those of Jackson. Had Frederick Lander been alive and in command that day, he could well have been expected to exploit the nearly nonexistent Southern center with Sullivan's brigade. The Valley campaign might have ended before it truly began.

At McDowell, Jackson achieved his objective in preventing Milroy from seizing Staunton with his single brigade, but he allowed Milroy to get the drop on him. While Jackson scanned the mountainous country for a means to outflank the Federals with artillery the next morning, Milroy, who had been reinforced by Schenck's Brigade, hurled four regiments against Jackson's line on Sitlington's Ridge in a classic delaying action. Not only did Jackson abandon his plans for the next day, but he also had to throw nine regiments into the fight to halt the Federal attack, and he lost twice as many men defending high ground than Milroy did in attacking it.

Jackson's piecemeal feeding of units into battle was most apparent—and most costly—at Port Republic. Winder never forgave Jackson the pounding his regiments endured as a consequence.

ALTHOUGH THE PRESS and citizenry were united in their esteem for Jackson after the Valley campaign, within the Valley army itself, opinion remained divided. The consensus was that Jackson had done well—worked miracles even—but at a great cost to his army. Writing from Weyer's Cave, battery commander Capt. Joseph Carpenter told his father: "We have had three days of rest in the last two months—the balance of the time either a forced march or fighting—one or the other. A few more such marches and fights will ruin [Jackson's] old brigade." Lieutenant Dinwiddie told his wife that "we have reason to be thankful, for we are mostly well, though some, a good many indeed, have given way under the exposure of the late marches and have severe attacks of fever and pneumonia. The captain has been quite sick, and Lieutenant Cochran is just entering upon an attack of fever." A North Carolina enlisted man believed Jackson to be "one of the keenest generals in the South, and I know that he is the most successful one, but he his horrible hard on his men." Statistics bear out the strain placed on the army. Fully four thousand men drifted from the ranks during the campaign—some from exhaustion, some to desert (particularly among the drafted men)—double the number killed or wounded in action.[20]

One evening at Weyer's Cave, Winder, Trimble, Taliaferro, and Taylor met to discuss the campaign. Lt. McHenry Howard, who also was present, said that all four generals were of the opinion that Jackson "could not continue to take such risks without at some time meeting with a great disaster."[21]

Even the Reverend Dabney had his doubts. Observing the condition of the men three days after Port Republic, he confided to his wife: "Jackson's great fault is that he marches and works his men with such disregard of their physical endurance. His victories are as fatal to his own armies as to his enemies. With all the rigidity of his character, I think him a poor disciplinarian. He is in too much of a hurry to attend to the physical needs of his soldiers." Dabney was an amateur at war, but even so sound an observer as Charles Winder noted in his diary on June 5 that "Jackson is insane on these rapid marches." Two days after Port Republic, he scribbled: "Oh, how tired I am of this constant movement. Really worn out."[22]

In a letter to his sister written on June 14, Colonel Fulkerson painted a particularly revealing picture of Jackson and his ways, as Fulkerson had come to know them in the Valley campaign:

Our general will certainly not give us much time while there is an enemy to meet. He is a singular man and has some most striking military traits of character and some that are not so good. A more fearless man never lived and he is remarkable for his industry and energy. He is strictly temperate in his habits and sleeps very little. Often while near the enemy, and while everybody except the guards are asleep, he is on his horse and gone, nobody knows where. I often fear that he will be killed or taken. Our men curse him for the hard marching he makes them do, but still the privates of the whole army have the most unbounded confidence in him. They say he can take them into harder places and get them out better than any other living man and that he cannot be caught asleep or taken when awake.[23]

But Jackson was exhausted. His weariness manifested itself in two rancorous encounters with key subordinates. The first was a run-in with his temperamental quartermaster, John Harman. It began the day after Port Republic, when Jackson ordered Harman to collect all small arms left on the field. When Harman offhandedly remarked afterward that many of them appeared to be Confederate weapons, Jackson flew into a rage and told Harman he wanted to hear no more talk of Southerners abandoning their arms. Harman stormed from Jackson's tent and returned with a letter of resignation. "Jackson's mysterious ways are unbearable," he told his brother. "He is a hard master to serve and nothing but a mean-spirited man can remain long with him. God be with us all." The next day Jackson apologized, and Harman stayed on.[24]

The second flare-up was with General Winder. Perceived interference on the part of Jackson with Winder's command during the Battle of Port Republic, along with the commanding general's refusal to grant him leave to go to Richmond (apparently to seek a transfer), caused Winder to submit his resignation on June 13. Richard Taylor interceded on Winder's behalf. To Jackson, Taylor dwelled "on the rich harvest of glory [Winder] had reaped in [Jackson's] brilliant campaign." Taylor's gambit apparently failed. "No reply was made to my effort for Winder, and I rose to take my leave; Jackson said he would ride with me, and we passed silently along the way to my camp, where he left me." That night, Taylor received a note from Winder saying that Jackson had ridden to Winder's headquarters to mend the rift.[25]

A war-weary Jackson wanted nothing better than to be reunited with his wife. On June 14 he wrote Anna: "Our God has again thrown his shield over me in the various apparent dangers to which I have been exposed. This evening we have religious services in the army for the purpose of rendering thanks to the Most High for the victories with which He has crowned our arms, and to offer earnest prayer that He will continue to give us success, until, through His divine blessing, our independence shall be established." In closing, he asked, rhetorically, "Wouldn't you like to get home again?"[26]

Thoughts of home would have to wait. Lee's order of June 16 enjoined Jackson to leave the Valley rapidly and secretly. This Jackson did, true to form. He was even more secretive than usual. Directing Munford to cut off all communications between the lines—he had earlier told his interim cavalry commander to let hints be dropped to bearers of flags of truce that Jackson intended a major offensive down the Valley—he also told him to communicate as little as possible with the infantry. "Instead of sending your dispatches to General Winder," ordered Jackson, "please continue to send them directed to me." He wanted to meet Munford in Mount Sidney at 10:00 P.M. on the seventeenth, undoubtedly to impress upon him the importance of his keeping up a tight screen. "I will be on my horse at [the] north end of the town, so you need not inquire after me. I do not desire it to be known that I am absent from this point [Weyer's Cave]."[27]

Everyone in the Valley army was mystified as to their destination. Campbell Brown wrote his mother on a hot June 17, the same day Jackson was laying the groundwork for leaving the Valley, that he believed the arrival of Lawton's brigade and Whiting's demi-division signified that "the grand battle of the Confederacy will be fought here." Unaccustomed to Jackson's ways, General Whiting, who was with his brigade in Staunton, was furious when Jackson ordered him to headquarters, only to send him back without telling him anything of his plans. It had been a forty-mile round trip. When Whiting returned at midnight, he angrily told his host, John Imboden, "I believe he hasn't more sense than my horse!"

At dawn the next morning a courier arrived with orders for Whiting to entrain his two brigades and travel to Gordonsville. The quick-tempered Whiting exploded anew. "Didn't I tell you he is a fool?" Whiting barked at Imboden. "Doesn't this prove it? Why, I came through Gordonsville day before yesterday!"[28]

What the unexplained orders did prove was that Jackson was on the march east. Shortly after midnight on June 18, the army was awakened; before dawn men were proceeding toward Waynesboro and Rockfish Gap beyond. The day was hot, the road rough and dusty. The ascent of the Blue Ridge offered a grand spectacle. "The road was broad and was likened to a flight of winding stairs," a soldier of the 15th Alabama recollected. "When about halfway to the top I could look up a mile ahead and see the boys in grey marching four abreast, filing around the rugged cliffs, and looking backward and downward, there as far as the eye could reach, I could see the balance of Jackson's corps advancing. The long line of troops . . . with their bright muskets and bayonets glittering in the sun, made an everlasting impression upon my mind, the sublimity and grandeur of which I will never forget."[29]

For many, it was the last time they would cast their eyes on the Shenandoah Valley; others would return with Jubal Early, only to fall in the 1864 Valley campaign. The war rolled east, units were transferred hither and yon, and men died. Stonewall Jackson—who, said Jed Hotchkiss, left the Valley "in fine spirits"—would be mortally wounded eleven months later at Chancellorsville. By war's end, more than one thousand members of his old brigade had been killed, mortally wounded, or had died from disease. The toll fell heaviest on the Valley men, as they served in the brigade the longest.[30]

The evening before he left the verdant Valley for the miasmal swamps of the Chickahominy country, Jackson had written his pastor, Dr. William S. White, a personal letter. Uncomfortable with the fame that had suddenly been thrust upon him, he told White: "I am afraid that our people are looking to the wrong source for help, and ascribing our success to those to whom they are not due. If we fail to trust in God and give Him all the glory, our cause is ruined."[31]

THE OPPOSING FORCES IN THE SHENANDOAH VALLEY CAMPAIGN

MARCH 23, 1862–JUNE 9, 1862

THE UNION ARMY

Forces at Kernstown, March 23, 1862
Brig. Gen. James Shields (w), Col. Nathan Kimball

First Brigade — Col. Nathan Kimball
    14th Indiana, 8th Ohio, 67th Ohio, 84th Pennsylvania
Second Brigade — Col. Jeremiah C. Sullivan
    39th Illinois, 13th Indiana, 5th Ohio, 62nd Ohio
Third Brigade — Col. Erastus B. Tyler
    7th Indiana, 7th Ohio, 29th Ohio, 110th Pennsylvania, 1st West Virginia
Cavalry — Col. Thornton F. Brodhead
    1st Squadron Pennsylvania; Independent Companies, Maryland; 1st West Virginia
      (Battalion); 1st Ohio (Companies A and C); 1st Michigan (Battalion)
Artillery — Lt. Col. Philip Daum
    Battery A, West Virginia Light Artillery; Battery B, West Virginia Light Artillery;
      Battery H, 1st Ohio Light Artillery; Battery E, 4th U.S. Light Artillery

(w) = wounded; (k) = killed

Forces at McDowell, May 8, 1862

Brig. Gen. Robert C. Schenck

Milroy's Brigade — Brig. Gen. Robert H. Milroy
  25th Ohio, 52nd Ohio, 73rd Ohio, 75th Ohio, 2nd West Virginia, 3rd West Virginia;
    Battery I, 1st Ohio Light Artillery; 12th Ohio Battery, 1st West Virginia Cavalry
Schenck's Brigade — Brig. Gen. Robert C. Schenck
  55th Ohio; 82nd Ohio; 5th West Virginia; 1st Battalion, Connecticut Cavalry;
    Battery K, 1st Ohio Light Artillery

Banks's Command, May 23–25, 1862

Maj. Gen. Nathaniel P. Banks

FIRST DIVISION — Brig. Gen. Alpheus S. Williams
First Brigade — Col. Dudley Donnelly
  5th Connecticut, 46th Pennsylvania, 28th New York, 1st Maryland
Third Brigade — Col. George H. Gordon
  2nd Massachusetts, 29th Pennsylvania, 27th Indiana, 3rd Wisconsin
Cavalry — 1st Michigan (five companies)
Artillery — Battery M, 1st New York Light Artillery; Battery F, Pennsylvania Light
    Artillery; Battery F, 4th U.S. Artillery
CAVALRY BRIGADE — Brig. Gen. John P. Hatch
  1st Maine (5 companies), 1st Vermont, 5th New York, 1st Maryland (five
    companies)
UNATTACHED
  10th Maine Infantry, 8th New York Cavalry (five companies dismounted),
    Pennsylvania Zouaves d'Afrique; Battery E, Pennsylvania Light Artillery
    (section)

Frémont's Command, June 1–9, 1862

Maj. Gen. John C. Frémont

BLENKER'S DIVISION — Brig. Gen. Louis Blenker
First Brigade — Brig. Gen. Julius H. Stahel
  8th New York, 39th New York, 41st New York, 45th New York, 27th Pennsylvania,
    2nd New York Battery, Battery C, West Virginia Light Artillery
Second Brigade — Col. John A. Koltes
  29th New York, 68th New York, 73rd Pennsylvania, 13th New York Battery
Third Brigade — Brig. Gen. Henry Bohlen
  54th New York, 58th New York, 75th Pennsylvania; Battery I, 1st New York Light
    Artillery

Cavalry — 4th New York
Unattached Cavalry
  6th Ohio, 3rd West Virginia (detachment)
Advance Brigade — Col. Gustave P. Cluseret
  60th Ohio, 8th West Virginia
Milroy's Brigade — Brig. Gen. Robert H. Milroy
  2nd West Virginia, 3rd West Virginia, 5th West Virginia, 25th Ohio, 1st West
    Virginia Cavalry (detachment); Battery I, 1st Ohio Light Artillery; 12th Ohio
    Battery
Schenck's Brigade — Brig. Gen. Robert C. Schenck
  32nd Ohio, 55th Ohio, 73rd Ohio, 75th Ohio, 82nd Ohio; 1st Battalion,
    Connecticut Cavalry; Battery K, 1st Ohio Light Artillery; Rigby's Indiana
    Battery
Bayard's Brigade — Brig. Gen. George D. Bayard
  1st New Jersey Cavalry, 1st Pennsylvania Cavalry, 13th Pennsylvania Reserves
    (Battalion), 2nd Maine Battery

Shields's Division, June 8–9, 1862
Brig. Gen. James Shields

First Brigade — Brig. Gen. Nathan Kimball
  14th Indiana, 4th Ohio, 8th Ohio, 7th West Virginia
Second Brigade — Brig. Gen. Orris S. Ferry
  39th Illinois, 13th Indiana, 62nd Ohio, 67th Ohio
Third Brigade — Brig. Gen. Erastus B. Tyler
  5th Ohio, 7th Ohio, 29th Ohio, 66th Ohio, 7th Ohio
Fourth Brigade — Col. Samuel S. Carroll
  7th Indiana, 84th Pennsylvania, 100th Pennsylvania, 1st West Virginia
Artillery — Col. Philip Daum
  Battery H, 1st Ohio Light Artillery; Battery L, 1st Light Artillery; Battery A, 1st
    West Virginia Light Artillery; Battery B, 1st West Virginia Light Artillery;
    Battery E, 4th U.S. Light Artillery
Cavalry — 1st Ohio (detachment); 1st Rhode Island (Battalion); 1st West Virginia
    (detachment)

Forces at Kernstown, March 23, 1862
Maj. Gen. Thomas J. Jackson

Garnett's Brigade — Brig. Gen. Richard B. Garnett
  2nd Virginia, 4th Virginia, 5th Virginia, 27th Virginia, 33rd Virginia; Rockbridge
    Artillery; Carpenter's (Allegheny) Battery
Burks's Brigade — Col. Jesse S. Burks
  21st Virginia, 42nd Virginia, 1st Virginia (Irish) Battalion; Marye's (Hampden)
    Battery, Waters's (West Augusta) Battery
Fulkerson's Brigade — Col. Samuel V. Fulkerson
  23rd Virginia, 37th Virginia, Shumaker's (Danville) Artillery
Cavalry — Col. Turner Ashby
  7th Virginia Cavalry, Chew's Battery (Mounted Artillery)

Forces at McDowell, May 8, 1862
Maj. Gen. Thomas J. Jackson

ARMY OF THE VALLEY
First Brigade — Brig. Gen. Charles S. Winder
  2nd Virginia Infantry, 4th Virginia Infantry, 5th Virginia Infantry, 27th Virginia
    Infantry, 33rd Virginia Infantry, Carpenter's (Allegheny) Battery, Rockbridge
    Artillery
Second Brigade — Col. John A. Campbell
  21st Virginia, 42nd Virginia, 48th Virginia, 1st Virginia (Irish) Battalion, Caskie's
    (Hampden) Battery, Cutshaw's (West Augusta) Battery
Third Brigade — Brig. Gen. William B. Taliaferro
  10th Virginia, 23rd Virginia, 37th Virginia, Wooding's (Danville) Battery
ARMY OF THE NORTHWEST — Brig. Gen. Edward Johnson (w)
First Brigade — Col. Z. T. Conner
  12th Georgia, 25th Virginia, 31st Virginia
Second Brigade — Col. W. C. Scott
  44th Virginia, 52nd Virginia, 58th Virginia

Forces in the Operations of May 20–June 10, 1862
Maj. Gen. Thomas J. Jackson

JACKSON'S DIVISION
First Brigade Brig. Gen. Charles S. Winder
  2nd Virginia, 4th Virginia, 5th Virginia, 27th Virginia, 33rd Virginia

Second Brigade — Col. John A. Campbell (w), Col. John M. Patton Jr.

 21st Virginia, 42nd Virginia, 48th Virginia, 1st Virginia (Irish) Battalion

Third Brigade — Col. Samuel V. Fulkerson, Brig. Gen. William B. Taliaferro

 10th Virginia, 23rd Virginia, 37th Virginia

Artillery — Col. Stapleton Crutchfield

 Carpenter's (Allegheny) Virginia Battery, Caskie's (Hampden) Virginia Battery, Carrington's Virginia Battery, Cutshaw's Virginia Battery, Poague's Virginia Battery (Rockbridge Artillery), Wooding's Virginia Battery

SECOND DIVISION — Maj. Gen. Richard S. Ewell

Second Brigade — Col. W. C. Scott, Brig. Gen. George H. Steuart (w)[1]; Col. W. C. Scott

 44th Virginia, 52nd Virginia, 58th Virginia

Fourth Brigade — Brig. Gen. Arnold Elzey (w), Col. James A. Walker

 12th Georgia, 13th Georgia, 25th Georgia, 31st Georgia

Seventh Brigade — Brig. Gen. Isaac R. Trimble

 15th Alabama, 21st Georgia, 16th Mississippi, 21st North Carolina

Eighth Brigade — Brig. Gen. Richard Taylor

 6th Louisiana, 7th Louisiana, 8th Louisiana, 9th Louisiana, R. C. Wheat's Battalion (Louisiana Tigers)

Maryland Line[2] — Brig. Gen. George H. Steuart[3]

 1st Maryland — Col. Bradley T. Johnson

 Brockenbrough's Battery (Baltimore Light Artillery)

Artillery

 Courtney's (Richmond) Battery, Lusk's (2nd Rockbridge) Battery; Raine's (Lynchburg) Battery; Rice's (8th Star) Battery

CAVALRY — Col. Thomas S. Flournoy, Brig. Gen. George H. Steuart, Brig. Gen. Turner Ashby (k), Col. Thomas T. Munford

 2nd Virginia, 6th Virginia, 7th Virginia, Chew's Battery (Mounted Artillery)

---

1. Assigned to brigade command June 2.

2. Attached to Second Brigade June 6.

3. Assigned to command of cavalry May 24.

NOTES

OR   U.S. War Department, *The War of the Rebellion: A Compilation of the Official Records of the Union and Confederate Armies*, 128 vols., series 1, Washington, D.C., 1880–91. *OR* citations take the following form: volume number (part number, where applicable):page number.

PaHS   Historical Society of Pennsylvania, Philadelphia

SHSP   *Southern Historical Society Papers*

SOR   *Supplement to the Official Records of the Union and Confederate Armies*, 100 vols., Wilmington, N.C., 1994. *SOR* citations take the same form as *OR* citations.

TSLA   Tennessee State Library and Archives, Nashville

UNC   University of North Carolina, Chapel Hill

USAMHI   U.S. Army Military History Institute, Carlisle Barracks, Pennsylvania

UVA   University of Virginia, Alderman Library, Charlottesville

VHS   Virginia Historical Society, Richmond

VMI   Virginia Military Institute, Lexington

VPU   Virginia Polytechnic University, Blacksburg

W&L   Washington and Lee University, Leyburn Library, Lexington, Virginia

WiHS   Wisconsin Historical Society, Madison

WRHS   Western Reserve Historical Society, Cleveland, Ohio

WVU   West Virginia University, Morgantown

INTRODUCTION

1 Tanner, *Stonewall in the Valley*, xi.

2 Johnson and Buel, *Battles and Leaders*, 2(2):105.

3 Hattaway and Jones, *How the North Won*, 157.

4 For an excellent discussion of Jackson's transformation, see Robert K. Krick, "Metamorphosis in Stonewall Jackson's Public Image."

5 Mahon, *Shenandoah Valley*, 65–68.

CHAPTER 1

1 Vandiver, *Mighty Stonewall*, 166; Henderson, *Stonewall Jackson*, 122; Kenneth P. Williams, *Lincoln Finds a General*, 1:122, 129.

2 J. William Jones, "Reminiscences . . ., Paper No. 3," 185–89; Dabney, *Life*, 230–31.

3 Robertson, *Stonewall Jackson*, 269.

4 Dabney, *Life*, 186, 234–35; Douglas, "Why Stonewall Jackson Resigned."

5 *OR* 5:881–87.

6 Henderson, *Stonewall Jackson*, 132–33.

7 Malone, *DAB* 10:569–70; Ecelbarger, *Lander*, 19, 130.

8 Ecelbarger, *Lander*, 131–32.

9 Allan, *History*, 13; Kellogg, *Shenandoah Valley*, 34–38.

10 Sauers, *Devastating Hand*, 18; William N. McDonald, *Laurel Brigade*, 25–27; *OR* 12(3):644.

11 Ecelbarger, *Lander*, 134–43; McClellan, *McClellan's Own Story*, 176–77.

12 Robertson, *Stonewall Jackson*, 274.

13 Henderson, *Stonewall Jackson*, 123–24; Mary Anna Jackson, *Memoirs*, 187–88.

14 Henderson, *Stonewall Jackson*, 124.

15 Imboden, "Incidents of the First Bull Run," 238.

16 Mary Anna Jackson, *Memoirs*, 198–99.

17 Ibid., 199; *OR* 5:909.

18 Douglas, *I Rode with Stonewall*, 25; Robertson, *Stonewall Jackson*, 278.

19 *OR* 5:925, 934.

20 Mary Anna Jackson, *Memoirs*, 200.

21 Douglas, *I Rode with Stonewall*, 25–26; James K. Edmondson to his wife, November 5, 1861, Edmondson Letters, W&L; Robertson, *Stonewall Jackson*, 282–83; Mary Anna Jackson, *Memoirs*, 201–2.

CHAPTER 2

1 Wayland, *Twenty-five Chapters*, 5–19, 60; Norris, *History*, 49–50; May, *Port Republic; The History*, 2–3; Julia Davis, *Shenandoah*, 28; Mahon, *Shenandoah Valley*, 1.

2 Julia Davis, *Shenandoah*, 29.

3 Norris, *History*, 54; Wayland, *Twenty-five Chapters*, 62–63, 81–83; Salyards, *Historical Review* 4; Hartman, *Reminiscences*, 45.

4 Julia Davis, *Shenandoah*, 10.

5 Wayland, *Twenty-five Chapters*, 1–9, 50–51; Hess, *Heartland*, 103.

6 Schlebecker, "Farmers," 463, 465–66, 472; Mahon, *Shenandoah Valley*, 133.

7 Colt, *Defend the Valley*, 5; Schlebecker, "Farmers," 464–65, 469; Mahon, *Shenandoah Valley*, 134.

8 Wayland, *Twenty-five Chapters*, 187–92.

9 Ibid., 141, 333–39.

10 Ibid., 307–9; Hess, *Heartland*, 25–26.

11 Hess, *Heartland*, 17–19; Richards, *Winchester and Vicinity*, 66–67.

12 Marshall Diary, March 21, 1862, Oberlin College; Wayland, *Stonewall Jackson's Way*, 76; Marvin, *Fifth Regiment Connecticut*, 69–70; Hess, *Heartland*, 16; William M. Rawlings to his father, December 23, 1861, Rawlings Letters, CWM.

13 Wayland, *Twenty-five Chapters*, 4–5, 188, 399; Summers, *Baltimore and Ohio*, 19.

14 Norris, *History*, 188, 211–12; Colt, *Defend the Valley*, 6–8; U.S. Census Office, Eighth Census [1860], *Population of the United States*, 518; Quarles, *Occupied Winchester*, 2.

15 Richards, *Winchester and Vicinity*, 40, 67–68; James D. Wilson, *Edinburg, 1861–1865*, 10–11.

16 *Manufacturers of the United States*, 603, 606; Ayers, *In the Presence*, 19.

17 Breck, letter to the editor, June 18, 1862.

18 In 1860 the population of the Shenandoah Valley was 147,404, of which 116,601 individuals were white; 4,393, "free colored"; and 26,410, slave. [J. C. G. Kennedy], *Preliminary Report*, 286–88; Quarles, *Occupied Winchester*, 2.

19 U.S. Census Office, Eighth Census [1860], *Population of the United States in 1860*; Hartman, *Reminiscences*, 45; Ayers, *In the Presence*, 19–21.

20 Thomas A. Ashby, *Valley Campaigns*, 20; Ayers, *In the Presence*, 22–24.

21 Phillips, "Lower Shenandoah Valley," 3–6; Quarles, *Occupied Winchester*, 3; Ayers, *In the Presence*, 22.

22 *Staunton Spectator*, November 13, 1860; *Staunton Republican Vindicator*, December 21, 1860; Quarles, *Occupied Winchester*, 3.

23 Phillips, "Lower Shenandoah Valley," 8–9; Quarles, *Occupied Winchester*, 3–4.

24 *Staunton Republican Vindicator*, April 12, 1861.

25 *Staunton Spectator*, April 16, 1861; Cornelia P. McDonald, *Diary*, 14–15.

26 Robertson, *Stonewall Brigade*, 10; *Staunton Spectator*, April 23, 1861.

27 Koiner, letter to the editor, April 20, 1861; Hartman, *Reminiscences*, 49; Wayland, *Twenty-five Chapters*, 97–98; Phillips, "Lower Shenandoah Valley," 96, 125–26.

28 Robertson, *Stonewall Brigade*, 10–17; *Staunton Spectator*, April 16, 1861; William S. H. Baylor, letter to the editor, April 22, 1861; Wert, *Brotherhood of Valor*, 14–18.

29 William S. H. Baylor, letter to the editor, April 22, 1861; Lottie Baylor Landrum, "Biography of Brigadier General William S. H. Baylor," Hotchkiss Papers, LC.

30 Vandiver, *Mighty Stonewall*, 78; Hiden, "Stonewall Jackson," 308–9; Robertson, *Stonewall Jackson*, 122–25.

31 Robertson, *Stonewall Jackson*, 111, 125–26.

32 Tanner, *Stonewall in the Valley*, 27–28; Imboden, "Jackson at Harpers Ferry," 121–22.

33 Mary Anna Jackson, *Memoirs*, 141–42.

34 Robertson, *Stonewall Jackson*, 213.

CHAPTER 3

1 Kearsey, *Strategy and Tactics*, 8–10; Forbes, "Lincoln as a Strategist," 56–57; Tanner, *Stonewall in the Valley*, 36.

2 Quarles, *Occupied Winchester*, 56; *OR* 5:389, 934, 942–43; Boteler, "Jackson's Discontent"; Mahon, *Shenandoah Valley*, 30–31; Phillips, "Lower Shenandoah Valley," 53–54.

3 *OR* 5:937; Allan, *History*, 15.

4 Robertson, *Stonewall Jackson*, 290; Hale, *Four Valiant Years*, 81; Hunter McGuire to Jedediah Hotchkiss, September 22, 1897, Hotchkiss Papers, LC; Thomas A. Ashby, *Life*, 113.

5 McHenry Howard, *Recollections*, 78; Douglas, *I Rode with Stonewall*, 88; Thomas A. Ashby, *Life*, 18–38; Avirett, *Memoirs*, 23–29; Carmichael, "Turner Ashby's Appeal," 148–50.

6 Munford, "Reminiscences," 523–25; McHenry Howard, *Recollections*, 78–79; Douglas, *I Rode with Stonewall*, 88.

7 Avirett, *Memoirs*, 114–15; William N. McDonald, *Laurel Brigade*, 21–23; Carmichael, "Turner Ashby's Appeal," 151–53.

8 Thomas A. Ashby, *Life*, 113–15; *OR* 5:389; Fonerden, *Carpenter's Battery*, 15–16.

9 Charles W. McVicar to Thomas T. Munford, February 24, 1906, Munford Family Papers, DU; Thomas A. Ashby, *Life*, 105–6; Avirett, *Memoirs*, 267–68; Tanner, *Stonewall in the Valley*, 52–53.

10 *OR* 5:977; [Grabill], *Diary*, 14; Fishburne, "Sketch of Rockbridge Artillery," 123.

11 George Baylor, *Bull Run to Bull Run*, 28–30.

12 Allan, *History*, 15–16.

13 Wayland, *Stonewall Jackson's Way*, 49; Mary Anna Jackson, *Memoirs*, 209–10.

14 Robertson, *Stonewall Brigade*, 54.

15 *OR* 5:938–40, 946, 954.

CHAPTER 4

1 "Story of the Illinois Central," 20.

2 Harrington, *Fighting Politician*, 1–3.

3 Ibid., 41–55.

4 Quaife, *From the Cannon's Mouth*, 39–50; John P. Hatch to his father, May 27, 1862, Hatch Papers, LC; Horace Winslow to his family, March 21, 1862, Old Sol-

dier Books, Gaithersburg, Md., catalog 67 (January 1993); H. Melzer Dutton to his mother, May 7, 1862, Dutton Letters, HL; Billy Davis Journal, March 30, 1862, Davis Papers, InHS; Belle Boyd, *Belle Boyd*, 1709; Harrington, *Fighting Politician*, 62–64.

5 Eby, *Virginia Yankee*, 22; Malone, *DAB*, 18:156–57; Hale, *Four Valiant Years*, 120–21.

6 *OR* 5:661–62.

7 McClellan, *McClellan's Own Story*, 192; Kenneth P. Williams, *Lincoln Finds a General*, 1:134; *OR* 5:673, 676–77.

8 Summers, *Baltimore and Ohio*, 101–5.

9 Kepler, *Fourth Regiment Ohio*, 50; Sauers, *Devastating Hand*, 17–18.

10 *OR* 5:638–39, 12(3):644.

11 Kearsey, *Strategy and Tactics*, 18; *OR* 5:693; Summers, *Baltimore and Ohio*, 106; Lamers, *Edge of Glory*, 64–65.

12 *CCW*, 3:162–63.

13 Ecelbarger, *Lander*, 149–50.

14 *OR* 5:943, 965–66; Mary Anna Jackson, *Memoirs*, 218.

15 *OR* 5:935, 938, 964–69; Jefferson Davis, *Rise and Fall*, 1:391.

16 Wessels, *Born to Be a Soldier*, 18.

17 Ibid., 34–35; "An Old Soldier Gone: General Loring Dead after Fifty Years of Military Service," *New York Times*, December 31, 1886.

18 *OR* 5:983–84.

19 Walter A. Clark, *Under the Stars and Bars*, 38; *OR* 51 (2):399–400; Rankin, *37th Virginia*, 18.

20 *OR* 5:975.

21 Walter A. Clark, *Under the Stars and Bars*, 38–39; *OR* 5:979–80, 51(2):405.

22 William B. Taliaferro, typescript reminiscences of Stonewall Jackson, 4, Taliaferro Papers, CWM; Walter A. Clark, *Under the Stars and Bars*, 39; *OR* 5:989.

23 *OR* 5:390, 989; Allan, *History*, 16; Bearss, "War Comes," 164–67; Edward B. Williams, *Rebel Brothers*, 38.

24 *OR* 5:365, 396–97; Charles E. Davis, *Three Years*, 16–17; Bearss, "War Comes," 169–70; Edward B. Williams, *Rebel Brothers*, 38.

25 Allan, *History*, 17; Bearss, "War Comes," 170–71; *OR* 5:687–88, 51:(1):512; Marvin, *Fifth Regiment Connecticut*, 45.

26 Ted Barclay to his sisters, December 21, 1861, Barclay Papers, W&L; Colston, "Personal Experiences," 9–10, Trapner Papers, VHS; *OR* 5:395–96.

27 Colston, "Personal Experiences," 10, Trapner Papers, VHS.

28 Ted Barclay to his sisters, December 21, 1861, Barclay Papers, W&L; Bearss, "War Comes," 171; Frye, *2nd Virginia*, 18–19.

29 Bearss, "War Comes," 171; Colston, "Personal Experiences," 10, Trapner Papers, VHS.

30 Poague, *Gunner*, 13–14; Bearss, "War Comes," 171; Edward B. Williams, *Rebel Brothers*, 39.

31 Colston, "Personal Experiences," 10, Trapner Papers, VHS; Ted Barclay to his sisters, December 21, 1861, Barclay Papers, W&L.

32 *OR* 5:397–98.

33 Kinzer Diary, 13, VHS; John Garibaldi to Sarah A. V. Poor, December 30, 1861, Garibaldi Papers, VMI; Fields, *Grayson County*, 12.

34 Marvin, *Fifth Regiment Connecticut*, 45; John Garibaldi to Sarah A. V. Poor, December 30, 1861, Garibaldi Papers, VMI; Fields, *Grayson County*, 12; Kinzer Diary, 13, VHS.

35 George Baylor, *Bull Run to Bull Run*, 30; Colston, "Personal Experiences," 10; Marvin, *Fifth Regiment Connecticut*, 45. Bearss ("War Comes") maintains that the dam was not breached until 3:00 P.M. on December 20, but the statements of Captain Colston and other eyewitnesses do not support that conclusion.

36 Douglas, *I Rode with Stonewall*, 19.

37 Lyle, "Stonewall Jackson's Guard," 313, Lyle Papers, W&L; [Grabill], *Diary*, [16].

38 Vandiver, *Mighty Stonewall*, 183.

39 Bearss, "War Comes," 175; Marvin, *Fifth Regiment Connecticut*, 49; *OR* 5:399.

40 *OR* 51(1):512.

CHAPTER 5

1 Avirett, *Memoirs*, 135; Kuppenheimer Diary, December 25, 1861, Vigo County Library; John Garibaldi to Sarah A. V. Poor, December 26, 1861, Garibaldi Papers, VMI.

2 Chapla, *48th Virginia*, 14–15, and *42nd Virginia*, 9.

3 Worsham, *One of Jackson's Foot Cavalry*, 54.

4 *OR* 5:1005–8.

5 Digest of General Orders and Letters from the Official Order and Letter Book of General T. J. Jackson, 1, Hotchkiss Papers, LC; Kearsey, *Strategy and Tactics*, 40; John Garibaldi to Sarah A. V. Poor, December 30, 1861.

6 Jackson's draft report of the Romney expedition, dated February 7, 1862, Dabney Papers, UNC; Colt, *Defend the Valley*, 110; Apperson Diary, January 1, 1862, VPU; H. C. Clarke, *Confederate States Almanac*, 2; Kinzer Diary, 15, VHS; Alfred D. Kelly to his mother, January 9, 1862, Williamson Kelly Letters, DU; Pile, "War Story."

7 Abram S. Miller, "Selected Letters," 20; [M. G. Harman], *"Stonewall Jackson's Way,"* 14.

8 Colt, *Defend the Valley,* 110, 112; Richard W. Waldrop to his father, January 12, 1862, Waldrop Papers, UNC; Cozzens, "Jackson Alone," 36.

9 Fishburne Memoirs, 25, Fishburne Family Papers, UVA; Launcelot M. Blackford to his mother, January 11, 1862, Blackford Papers, UVA.

10 Toney, *Privations of a Private,* 27; Kinzer Diary, 15, VHS; Alfred D. Kelly to his mother, January 9, 1862, Williamson Kelly Letters, DU; Lyle, "Stonewall Jackson's Guard," 324, Lyle Papers, W&L; Abram S. Miller, "Selected Letters," 21; Jackson's draft report of the Romney expedition, Dabney Papers, UNC; [Grabill], *Diary,* [18].

11 *OR* 5:1018, 1071.

12 Samuel J. C. Moore to his wife, January 12, 1862, Moore Papers, UNC.

13 *OR* 5:1066, 1071; Tanner, *Stonewall in the Valley,* 69–71; Lyle, "Stonewall Jackson's Guard," 321–22; Kinzer Diary, 15, VHS.

14 Cozzens, "Jackson Alone," 36–37.

15 Charles M. Clark, *Thirty-ninth Illinois,* 27–28; *OR* 5:401.

16 Launcelot M. Blackford to his mother, January 11, 1862, Blackford Papers, UVA; Tanner, *Stonewall in the Valley,* 71; Kinzer Diary, 15, VHS.

17 Charles M. Clark, *Thirty-ninth Illinois,* 32, 51; *OR* 5:400–401.

18 Tanner, *Stonewall in the Valley,* 70–71; Worsham, *One of Jackson's Foot Cavalry,* 57; Charles M. Clark, *Thirty-ninth Illinois,* 32; Richard W. Waldrop to his father, January 12, 1862, Waldrop Papers, UNC; Fishburne, "Sketch of Rockbridge Artillery," 125; *OR* 5:401; [Grabill], *Diary,* [18].

19 Jedediah Hotchkiss to George F. R. Henderson, August 1, 1897, Hotchkiss Papers, LC; J. William Jones, "Old Virginia Town," 19; "Narrative of the Service of . . . Porterfield," 90; Lyle, "Stonewall Jackson's Guard," 321–22.

20 Charles M. Clark, *Thirty-ninth Illinois,* 52.

21 Abram S. Miller, "Selected Letters," 21–22; Walter A. Clark, *Under the Stars and Bars,* 43; White, *Sketches,* 72; Lemley Diary, January 4, 1862, HL.

22 Cozzens, "Jackson Alone," 37.

23 Hooper, letter to the editor, January 6, 1862; Wells, "Annals of the War"; Charles M. Clark, *Thirty-ninth Illinois,* 52.

24 Launcelot M. Blackford to his mother, January 11, 1862, Blackford Papers, UVA; Fishburne, "Sketch of Rockbridge Artillery," 125.

25 Worsham, *One of Jackson's Foot Cavalry,* 58; Alfred D. Kelly to his mother, January 9, 1862, Williamson Kelly Letters, DU; Jackson's draft report of the Romney expedition; Charles M. Clark, *Thirty-ninth Illinois,* 86; Hooper, letter to the editor, January 6, 1862.

26 Abram S. Miller, "Selected Letters," 22; Thomas M. Smiley to his sister, January 10, 1862, Smiley Family Papers, UVA; Charles M. Clark, *Thirty-ninth Illinois*, 36.

27 Jackson's draft report of the Romney expedition; "Charges and Specifications Preferred by Maj. Gen. T. J. Jackson, P.A.C.S., against Col. William Gilham, 21st Regt. Va. Vols.," Jackson Papers, UNC; Allan, *History*, 22; Fishburne, "Sketch of Rockbridge Artillery," 125; Launcelot M. Blackford to his mother, January 11, 1862, Blackford Papers, UVA.

28 Kinzer Diary, 15–16, VHS; Lyle, "Stonewall Jackson's Guard," 325; Apperson Diary, January 4, 1862, VPU; Hite Diary, 66–67, HL.

29 "Charges and Specifications Preferred by Maj. Gen. T. J. Jackson, P.A.C.S., against Col. William Gilham, 21st Regt. Va. Vols."; Jackson's draft report of the Romney expedition; *OR* 5:402–3; Charles M. Clark, *Thirty-ninth Illinois*, 36, 52; Ecelbarger, *"We Are in for It!,"* 5; Hooper, letter to the editor, January 6, 1862.

30 Worsham, *One of Jackson's Foot Cavalry*, 58–59; Jackson's draft report of the Romney expedition; Charles M. Clark, *Thirty-ninth Illinois*, 52–53.

31 Jackson's draft report of the Romney expedition; Randolph Fairfax to his mother, January 9, 1862, Fairfax Letters, Museum of the Confederacy.

32 Baker, letter to the editor, January 6, 1862.

33 Ecelbarger, *Lander*, 161–65.

CHAPTER 6

1 Colt, *Defend the Valley*, 112; William B. Taliaferro, typescript reminiscences of Stonewall Jackson, 5, Taliaferro Papers, CWM.

2 Ecelbarger, *Lander*, 171–73; Wells, "Annals of the War"; Hooper, letter to the editor, January 6, 1862.

3 Taliaferro, typescript reminiscences, 5; Wells, "Annals of the War"; Baker, letter to the editor, January 6, 1862.

4 *OR* 5:391; Samuel J. C. Moore to his wife, January 13, 1862, Moore Papers, UNC.

5 Taliaferro, typescript reminiscences, 5; Quaife, *From the Cannon's Mouth*, 54; Baker, letter to the editor, January 6, 1862; Kinzer Diary, 16, VHS; Colt, *Defend the Valley*, 112.

6 Ecelbarger, *Lander*, 175–76.

7 *OR* 5:694–95.

8 Ecelbarger, *Lander*, 177–78; Allan, *History*, 22–23; *OR* 5:392; Henderson, *Stonewall Jackson*, 145.

9 Kinzer Diary, 16, VHS; [M. G. Harman], *"Stonewall Jackson's Way,"* 14; [Grabill], *Diary* [19].

10 Fishburne, "Sketch of Rockbridge Artillery," 126–27; Fonerden, *Carpenter's Battery*, 17; Launcelot M. Blackford to his mother, January 16, 1862, Blackford Papers, UVA; Robertson, *Stonewall Jackson*, 309–10.

11 Paxton, *Civil War Letters*, 49; Worsham, *One of Jackson's Foot Cavalry*, 60; Carson Memoirs, 20, VHS.

12 Henderson, *Stonewall Jackson*, 146.

13 Fishburne Memoirs, 34–35, Fishburne Family Papers, UVA; Randolph Fairfax to his mother, January 9, 31, 1862, Fairfax Letters, Museum of the Confederacy; Allan, *History*, 25; *OR* 5:392.

14 *OR* 5:404; [Grabill], *Diary*, [19]; Thomas M. Smiley to his sister, January 10, 1862, Smiley Family Papers, UVA.

15 Kepler, *Fourth Regiment Ohio*, 52.

16 X. O. S., "The Battle of Blue's Gap," unidentified newspaper clipping dated October 25, 1905, Elwood Papers, EU; Kepler, *Fourth Regiment Ohio*, 52; Landon, "Fourteenth Indiana," 280; Wayland, *Stonewall Jackson's Way*, 53–55.

17 H. C. Clarke, *Confederate States Almanac*, [1]; *OR* 5:404; X. O. S., "The Battle of Blue's Gap"; Frank Moore, *Rebellion Record*, 4:21–22; Sawyer, *8th Regiment Ohio*, 27–28; Elwood, *Elwood's Stories*, 83.

18 Landon, "Fourteenth Indiana," 281; Sawyer, *8th Regiment Ohio*, 28.

19 Landon, "Fourteenth Indiana," 281.

20 Frank Moore, *Rebellion Record*, 4:22; Elwood, *Elwood's Stories*, 83; Wilder, *Company C, Seventh Regiment O.V.I.*, 20–21; George L. Wood, *Seventh Regiment*, 85; Launcelot M. Blackford to his mother, January 18, 1862, Blackford Papers, UVA; Ted Barclay to his sisters, January 25, 1862, Barclay Papers, W&L; William N. McDonald, *Laurel Brigade*, 35–36; Edward B. Williams, *Rebel Brothers*, 45–46; *OR* 5:404, 435; Allan, *History*, 25.

21 *OR* 5:1026–27, 51(2):435.

22 Robertson, *Stonewall Jackson*, 311; James K. Edmondson to his wife, January 12, 1862, Edmondson Letters, W&L; Allan, *History*, 25.

23 Worsham, *One of Jackson's Foot Cavalry*, 60; Robertson, *Stonewall Jackson*, 310–11.

24 Fishburne, "Sketch of Rockbridge Artillery," 127–28; Colston, "Personal Experiences," 10, Trapner Papers, VHS.

25 Richard W. Waldrop to his father, January 12, 1862, Waldrop Papers, UNC; Samuel J. C. Moore to his wife, January 12, 1862, Moore Papers, UNC.

26 *OR* 51(2):461.

27 Richard W. Waldrop to his father, January 12, 1862, Waldrop Papers, UNC; Kearns Diary, January 14, 1862, VHS; Worsham, *One of Jackson's Foot Cavalry*, 60; Thomas M. Smiley to his sister, January 10, 1862, Smiley Family Papers, UVA.

28 Ecelbarger, *Lander*, 181–83; Quaife, *From the Cannon's Mouth*, 56.

29 Ecelbarger, *Lander*, 183–84.

CHAPTER 7

1 Sawyer, *8th Regiment Ohio*, 29; Ecelbarger, *Lander*, 188, and *"We Are in for It!,"* 19.

2 Kepler, *Fourth Regiment Ohio*, 56; Sawyer, *8th Regiment Ohio*, 28–29; Orville Thompson, *Philippi to Appomattox*, 72; Mathias Schwab to his parents, January 12, 1862, Schwab Letters, CiHS; Landon, "Fourteenth Indiana," 281–82.

3 Ecelbarger, *"We Are in for It!,"* 19.

4 Orville Thompson, *Philippi to Appomattox*, 72; Hart Diaries, 57, University of Wyoming; Elwood, *Elwood's Stories*, 86; S. W. Hart, "Fighting Stonewall Jackson"; Smart, *Radical View*, 1:59–60.

5 Robertson, *Stonewall Jackson*, 311; Digest of General Orders and Letters from the Official Order and Letter Book of General T. J. Jackson, 2, Hotchkiss Papers, LC; Kinzer Diary, 18, VHS; Colt, *Defend the Valley*, 112; Wallace, *5th Virginia*, 21.

6 Ted Barclay to his sisters, January 17, 1862, Barclay Papers, W&L; Cozzens, "Jackson Alone," 74; Launcelot M. Blackford to his mother, January 16, 1862, Blackford Papers, UVA.

7 Cozzens, "Jackson Alone," 74; Algernon S. Wade to his brother, January 18, 1862, Lewis Leigh Collection, USAMHI; Kearns Diary, January 14, 1862, VHS; Pile, "War Story"; Kinzer Diary, 18, VHS; Colston, "Personal Experiences," 10, Trapner Papers, VHS.

8 Allan, *History*, 26–27; OR 5:1039.

9 McDonald Memoirs, 36, UNC; Fishburne Memoirs, 37, Fishburne Family Papers, UVA; Thomas M. Smiley to his aunt, January 15, 1862, Smiley Family Papers, UVA; Colt, *Defend the Valley*, 111; Poague, *Gunner*, 16, 18.

10 Paxton, *Civil War Letters*, 49–52; James K. Edmondson to his wife, January 20, 1862, Edmondson Letters, W&L.

11 William B. Taliaferro, typescript reminiscences of Stonewall Jackson, 5, Taliaferro Papers, CWM.

12 Cozzens, "Jackson Alone," 74.

13 OR 5:1038.

14 Allan, *History*, 27.

15 OR 5:393–94, 1039; Quaife, *From the Cannon's Mouth*, 60; Smart, *Radical View* 1:4; Allan, *History*, 27.

16 Sauers, *Devastating Hand*, xiv, 1–2, 18; Henderson, *Stonewall Jackson*, 147; OR 5:1044, 51(2):1056; Rankin, *Romney Campaign*, 124.

17 Kinzer Diary, 18, VHS; Ted Barclay to his sisters, January 25, 1862, Barclay Papers, W&L; Fishburne Memoirs, 37, Fishburne Family Papers, UVA.

18 Richard W. Waldrop to his sister, January 28, 1862, Waldrop Papers, UNC; Paxton, *Civil War Letters*, 53; *OR* 51(2):461; Robertson, *Stonewall Jackson*, 315.

19 Worsham, *One of Jackson's Foot Cavalry*, 62–63; William F. Harrison to his wife, January 23, 1862, Harrison Letters, DU.

20 *OR* 5:1041–42.

21 *OR* 5:1047–48; Rankin, *Romney Campaign*, 124, 128; Vandiver, *Mighty Stonewall*, 193.

22 Boteler, "Jackson's Discontent."

23 William B. Taliaferro to Robert Y. Conrad, July 11, 1877, Taliaferro Papers, CWM; Taliaferro to W. W. Loring, January 29, 1862, Cook Papers, WVU; Rankin, *Romney Campaign*, 131; Henderson, *Stonewall Jackson*, 151; *OR* 5:1050.

24 William C. Davis, *Jefferson Davis*, 562; Boteler, "Jackson's Discontent."

25 Boteler, "Jackson's Discontent."

26 Douglas, "Why Stonewall Jackson Resigned"; Boteler, "Jackson's Discontent"; J. R. Graham, "Personal Characteristics of General Stonewall Jackson," 3, Hotchkiss Papers, LC; J. R. Graham recollections, found in miscellaneous notes, Dabney Papers, UNC.

27 Ecelbarger, *Lander*, 197; *OR* 5:702–3.

28 Ecelbarger, *Lander*, 203–8; *OR* 51(1):523.

29 Richard W. Waldrop to his father, February 14, 1862, Waldrop Papers, UNC; Lyle, "Sketches," 361–62, Lyle Papers, W&L; Julia Pendleton Allen to Fanny Pendleton, February 11, 1862, Allen Letter, VMI.

30 A. C. Chamberlayne to a friend, March 1, 1862, Chamberlayne Family Papers, VHS; Richard W. Waldrop to his father, February 7, 1862, Waldrop Papers, UNC; White, *Sketches*, 73; Randolph Fairfax to his mother, February 1, 1862, Fairfax Letters, Museum of the Confederacy; Henry Kyd Douglas to "My Dear Miss Tippie," February 10, 1862, Douglas Letters, DU.

31 Randolph Fairfax to his mother, January 31, 1862, Fairfax Letters, Museum of the Confederacy; James K. Edmondson to his wife, February 23, 1862, Edmondson Letters, W&L; Reidenbaugh, *27th Virginia*, 33.

32 *OR* 51(2):461–62; Chase Diary, January 12–19, 1862, HL; Quarles, *Occupied Winchester*, 63; Huckaby and Simpson, *Tulip Evermore*, 29.

33 Chase Diary, various entries from January 12–February 15, 1862, HL; Julia Pendleton Allen to Fanny Pendleton, February 11, 1862, Allen Letter, VMI.

34 *OR* 5:1076, 51(2):466; Lindsley, *Military Annals*, 229; Sperry, "Surrender? Never Surrender!," 152, HL.

35 Vandiver, *Mighty Stonewall*, 195; Douglas, *I Rode with Stonewall*, 26–27; *OR* 51(2):468–69.

36 *OR* 5:1023, 1069, 1086; Julia Pendleton Allen to Fanny Pendleton, February 11, 1862, Allen Letter, VMI; Randolph Fairfax to his mother, January 31, 1862, Fairfax Letters, Museum of the Confederacy; Bean, "Valley Campaign," 333; Hite Diary, 80–81, HL; Thomas M. Smiley to his aunt, February 11, 1862, Smiley Papers, UVA; Chapla, *42nd Virginia*, 11.

37 Vandiver, *Mighty Stonewall*, 196; *OR* 5:712, 1076; Landon, "Fourteenth Indiana," 282; Sandie Pendleton to Turner Ashby, February 19, 1862, Ashby Family Papers, VHS.

38 Ecelbarger, *Lander*, 211–12.

39 Ibid., 216; Hart, "Fighting Stonewall Jackson"; SeCheverell, *Journal History*, 35–36; Landon, "Fourteenth Indiana," 282.

40 Ecelbarger, *Lander*, 224–26.

41 Ibid., 227–28; Sawyer, *8th Regiment Ohio*, 31.

42 Frank Moore, *Rebellion Record*, 4:128; Landon, "Fourteenth Indiana," 283.

43 Spiegel, *Your True Marcus*, 40; Van Dyke, "Early Days," 29.

44 Sawyer, *8th Regiment Ohio*, 31–32; Ecelbarger, *Lander*, 234–35.

45 Landon, "Fourteenth Indiana," 284; David E. Beem to his fiancée, February 17, 1862, Beem Letters, InHS; Sawyer, *8th Regiment Ohio*, 32; Curry, *Four Years*, 235; *OR* 5:406.

46 Ecelbarger, *Lander*, 238–40; [Gillespie], *Company A, First Ohio Cavalry,*, 50; *OR* 5:406; Frank Moore, *Rebellion Record*, 4:128.

47 [Gillespie], *Company A, First Ohio Cavalry,*, 50–51; Frank Moore, *Rebellion Record*, 4:128.

48 Mathias Schwab to his parents, February 17, 1862, Schwab Letters, CiHS; Elwood, *Elwood's Stories*, 88; Haas, *Dear Esther*, 68.

49 Landon, "Fourteenth Indiana," 283–84.

50 David E. Beem to his fiancée, February 17, 1862, Beem Letters, InHS; Van Dyke, "Early Days," 30; *OR* 5:405–7; Frank Moore, *Rebellion Record*, 4:128.

51 *OR* 5:406, 51(1):531.

52 Frank Moore, *Rebellion Record*, 4:127.

53 *OR* 51(1):533.

CHAPTER 8

1 *OR* 5:1083–84; William C. Davis, *Jefferson Davis*, 397–99; Sears, *To the Gates*, 11–12.

2 Kean, *Inside the Confederate Government*, 22–24.

3 Mahon, *Shenandoah Valley*, 50–51.

4 *OR* 5:721–22, 51(1):531; Mathias Schwab to his parents, February 27, 1862, Schwab

Letters, CiHS; Hall, *Diary*, 36–37; Richard W. Waldrop to his father, February 14, 1862, Waldrop Papers, UNC; White, *Sketches*, 77; Bean, "Valley Campaign," 332; J. William Jones, "Reminiscences . . ., Paper No. 3," 185–86.

5 Richard W. Waldrop to his mother, February 21, 1862, Waldrop Papers, UNC.

6 Arnold, *Kalamazoo Volunteer*, 15; Hart Diaries, February 16, 1862, University of Wyoming; Wilson B. Gaither to his sister, February 13, 1862, Gaither Correspondence, CiHS; David E. Beem to his fiancée, February 21, 1862, Beem Letters, InHS.

7 Sears, *To the Gates*, 9–11; Kenneth P. Williams, *Lincoln Finds a General*, 1:138; Forbes, "Lincoln as a Strategist," 65–66.

8 *OR* 5:723, 51(1):529–30; Fishel, *Secret War*, 168.

9 McClellan, *McClellan's Own Story*, 192; Hamilton, "Memoirs of Two Wars," 40, University of Illinois; Kenneth P. Williams, *Lincoln Finds a General*, 1:142.

10 Ecelbarger, *Lander*, 269–70.

11 Andrews, *North Reports*, 253; Francis W. Crowninshield to his mother, February 23, 1862, Crowninshield Letters, Peabody Essex Museum; Arnold, *Kalamazoo Volunteer*, 16; McClellan, *McClellan's Own Story*, 192.

12 Josiah G. Williams to his sister, March 2, Worthington B. Williams Papers, InHS; Hinkley, *Narrative*, 15; Bryant, *Third Wisconsin*, 39.

13 *OR* 5:730–31, 51(1):543; McClellan, *McClellan's Own Story*, 193.

14 Mary Anna Jackson, *Memoirs*, 238–39.

15 Jedediah Hotchkiss to G. F. R. Henderson, May 1, 1895, Hotchkiss Papers, LC; Lyle, "Sketches," 368, Lyle Papers, W&L; Kinzer Diary, 18, VHS; James K. Edmondson to his wife, February 23, 1862, Edmondson Letters, W&L; Sperry, "Surrender? Never Surrender!," 136, HL.

16 Griffith Diary, 66, HL; Chase Diary, 32, HL.

17 Griffith Diary, 66–70, HL.

18 Digest of General Orders and Letters from the Official Order and Letter Book of General T. J. Jackson, 2, and Valley District Letter Book, 26–27, both in Hotchkiss Papers, LC; Mary Anna Jackson, *Memoirs*, 239; Vandiver, *Mighty Stonewall*, 199.

19 Eby, *Virginia Yankee*, 5; Bryant, *Third Wisconsin*, 39–40.

20 Frank Moore, *Rebellion Record*, 4:292; Eby, *Virginia Yankee*, 9; Charles E. Davis, *Three Years*, 38–39; Hinkley, *Narrative*, 16; George H. Hall to "My Dear Emily," March 2, 1862, Hall Letters, University of Washington; Arnold, *Kalamazoo Volunteer*, 16.

21 Hinkley, *Narrative*, 16; Eby, *Virginia Yankee*, 5; Arnold, *Kalamazoo Volunteer*, 17; Bryant, *Third Wisconsin*, 40.

22 Eby, *Virginia Yankee*, 5; Bryant, *Third Wisconsin*, 40.

23 Bryant, *Third Wisconsin*, 40.

24 George H. Hall to "My Dear Emily," March 2, 1862, Hall Letters, University of Washington.

25 Dwight, *Life and Letters*, 230; Quint, *Second Massachusetts*, 100; Mahon, *Shenandoah Valley*, 92.

26 Eby, *Virginia Yankee*, 6.

27 Bryant, *Third Wisconsin*, 40–41; Frank Moore, *Rebellion Record*, 4:292.

28 Quaife, *From the Cannon's Mouth*, 57, 61; Rufus Mead to "Dear Friends at Home," March 4, 1862, Mead Papers, LC; Marvin, *Fifth Regiment Connecticut*, 60–61.

29 Quaife, *From the Cannon's Mouth*, 61; Boyce Journal, 46–47, Boyce Papers, LC; Rufus Mead to "Dear Friends at Home," March 4, 1862.

30 Boyce Journal, 47–49; Augustus Van Dyke to his sister, March 8, 1862, Van Dyke Letters, InHs; Rufus Mead to his brother, March 12, 1862, Mead Letters, LC.

31 Augustus Van Dyke to his sister, March 8, 1862.

32 Charles E. Davis, *Three Years*, 24–26.

33 Hale, *Four Valiant Years*, 106–7.

34 *OR* 5:732, 51(1):544.

35 Marshall Diary, March 1, 1862, Oberlin College; Parmater Diary, 7–8, OHS; *OR* 5:732, 51(1):545–46; Ecelbarger, *Lander*, 277–78.

CHAPTER 9

1 Bean, "Valley Campaign," 333–34.

2 *OR* 5:1087–88; Mary Anna Jackson, *Memoirs*, 239.

3 Army of the Valley Letter Book, 28, Hotchkiss Papers, LC; *OR* 5:1092–93.

4 Samuel Fulkerson to his mother, March 9, 1862, Fulkerson Family Papers, VMI; James K. Edmondson to his wife, March 8, 1862, Edmondson Letters, W&L; White, *Sketches*, 77.

5 Eby, *Virginia Yankee*, 7–8; Voris, *Citizen-Soldier's Civil War*, 35–36.

6 Quaife, *From the Cannon's Mouth*, 62; Brooks Journal, 19, UNC; Kinzer Diary, 19, VHS; Turner Ashby to Judah P. Benjamin, March 17, 1862, Ashby Papers, CHS; James K. Edmondson to his wife, March 8, 1862, Edmondson Letters, W&L.

7 Thomas Nokes to Nathaniel P. Banks, March 8, 1862, Banks Papers, LC; Ecelbarger, *"We Are in for It!,"* 43–44; "Minutes of Evidence of Jacob Poisel, 18 Years Old, a Private of 'Hedgesville Blues,' 2nd Va. Vols., Who Delivered Himself Up to the Pickets of Gen. Williams' Command at Bunker Hill on March 9, 1862," Banks Papers, LC.

8 *OR* 5:745, 51(1):545.

9 *OR* 5:1094–95.

10 Samuel Fulkerson to his mother, March 9, 1862, Fulkerson Family Papers, VMI; [M. G. Harman], *"Stonewall Jackson's Way,"* 38–41; Edward B. Williams, *Rebel*

Brothers, 48–49; Kinzer Diary, 19–20, VHS; Worsham, *One of Jackson's Foot Cavalry*, 64; Chase Diary, 33, HL; Griffith Diary, 72–73, HL; Gates, *Colton Letters*, 92; Sperry, "Surrender? Never Surrender!," 138, HL.

11 Quint, *Potomac and the Rapidan*, 104–5, and *Second Massachusetts*, 69; Quaife, *From the Cannon's Mouth*, 61; Hamilton, "Memoirs of Two Wars," 40, University of Illinois; Sawyer, *8th Regiment Ohio*, 36; Parmater Diary, 8–9, OHS; Powell, "Shenandoah Valley," 1, Sixty-sixth Ohio Infantry Papers, OHS; Allan, *History*, 40–41.

12 Hamilton, "Memoirs of Two Wars," 40–41; Nathaniel P. Banks to "General," March 11, 1862, catalog 125, Abraham Lincoln Book Shop, Chicago; Quaife, *From the Cannon's Mouth*, 62–63.

13 Malone, *DAB* 17:106; Koerner, "General Shields," 974.

14 Condon, *Life*, 45–49; Koerner, "General Shields," 974; "Brigadier General James Shields," *Philadelphia Inquirer*, March 26, 1862.

15 Justin H. Smith, *War with Mexico*, 2, 115–17, 157, 384; Winfield Scott, *Memoirs*, 2, 481; Koerner, "General Shields," 975.

16 Koerner, "General Shields," 975; Malone, *DAB* 17:107.

17 Marshall Diary, March 11, 1862, Oberlin College; Galwey, *Valiant Hours*, 10; John W. Elwood to David Elwood, March 21, 1862, Elwood Papers, EU; Spiegel, *Your True Marcus*, 69–70; Sexton Memoirs, 79, OHS; Parmater Diary, 9, OHS; "Brigadier General James Shields," *Philadelphia Enquirer*, March 26, 1862; Powell, "Shenandoah Valley," 1, and Nathan Kimball to W. H. Brand, November 15, 1878, both in Sixty-sixth Ohio Infantry Papers, OHS.

18 Quaife, *From the Cannon's Mouth*, 63; Hamilton, "Memoirs of Two Wars," 42, University of Illinois; Boyce Journal, 51, LC; Spiegel, *Your True Marcus*, 69; Sawyer, *8th Regiment Ohio*, 36.

19 Kinzer Diary, 20, VHS; Kearns Diary, 27, VHS; Wyatt Diary, 3, CWM; Bean, "Valley Campaign," 336.

20 Mary Greenhow Lee Diary, 2–3, HL; Hale, *Four Valiant Years*, 109; Lyle, "Sketches," 372, Lyle Papers, W&L; Jedediah Hotchkiss to his wife, April 14, 1862, Hotchkiss Papers, LC.

21 Robertson, *Stonewall Jackson*, 332–33; Allan, *History*, 41; Carson Memoirs, 21, VHS.

22 Robertson, *Stonewall Jackson*, 333; Bean, "Valley Campaign," 336–37; Wyatt Diary, 3, CWM; Lyle, "Sketches," 370; Allan, *History*, 41.

23 Lyle, "Sketches," 370; Jones Diary, 1–2, HL.

24 Mary Greenhow Lee Diary, 4, HL.

25 Quaife, *From the Cannon's Mouth*, 63; Ecelbarger, *"We Are in for It!,"* 50; Eby, *Virginia Yankee*, 13–14; Frank Moore, *Rebellion Record*, 4:292; Sawyer, *8th Regiment Ohio*, 36; Boyce Journal, 50–51, Boyce Papers, LC.

26 Quaife, *From the Cannon's Mouth*, 63; Hamilton, "Memoirs of Two Wars," 42,
University of Illinois; Clarke Journal, March 12, 1862, HL; Laura Lee Diary,
March 12, 1862, CWM; Mary Greenhow Lee Diary, 4, HL; Tanner, *Stonewall in the
Valley*, 111.

27 Cornelia P. McDonald, *Diary*, 40–41.

28 Mary Greenhow Lee Diary, 4, HL, and letter to the editor, March 27, 1862.

29 Phillips, "Lower Shenandoah Valley," 133–37; Orville Thompson, *Philippi to
Appomattox*, 83–84.

30 W. F. B., "Letter from the 60th Ohio," *Highland News*, September 4, 1852; Isaac
Panta to his brother, March 14, 1862, Robert M. Panta Papers, InHS; David E.
Beem to his fiancée, March 15, 1862, Beem Letters, InHS; Charles H. Merrick
Diary, March 13, 1862, Merrick Papers, WRHS; Frank Ingersoll to his sister,
March 16, 1862, Ingersoll Letters, InHS; Spiegel, *Your True Marcus*, 74–75;
John W. Elwood to David Elwood, March 21, 1862, Elwood Papers, EU; Hinkley
Diary, March 13, 1862, WiHS; "Charlie" to his brother, March 26, 1862, Lewis
Leigh Collection, USAMHI.

31 Edwin O. Kimberly to his parents, March 17, 1862, Henry Kimberly Papers,
WiHS; Rufus Mead to his brother, March 12, 1862, Mead Letters, LC; Sexton
Memoirs, 78–81, OHS; Brooks Journal, 20, UNC; Stearns, *Three Years*, 58; "Rox-
bury," letter to the editor, March 12, 1862; Clarke Journal, March 12, 1862, HL.

32 George Harman, "Military Experience of James A. Pfeifer," 399–400; Gould,
First–Tenth–Twenty-ninth Maine, 108–9; Anderson memoir, 31, Anderson
Papers, LC; Mary Greenhow Lee Diary, 12–14, HL; Sperry, "Surrender? Never
Surrender!," 147–48, HL.

33 Mary Greenhow Lee Diary, 14–15, HL, and letter to the editor, March 27, 1862;
Quaife, *From the Cannon's Mouth*, 64; Laura Lee Diary, March 12, 1862, CWM;
OR 5:746.

34 Paxton, *Civil War Letters*, 57–58; J. William Jones, "Reminiscences . . . ," Paper
No. 4," 236; Bean, "Valley Campaign," 339.

35 Bean, "Valley Campaign," 338–39; Jones Diary, 4, HL; Kinzer Diary, 20, VHS;
Hale, *Four Valiant Years*, 110.

36 Tanner, *Stonewall in the Valley*, 117–18.

37 Richard W. Waldrop to his father, March 16, 1862, Waldrop Papers, UNC; Strider,
Life and Work of . . . Peterkin, 52; Kearns Diary, March 12, 1862, VHS.

CHAPTER 10

1 Nicolay and Hay, *Abraham Lincoln*, 5:168.

2 Ibid.; Allan, *History*, 42; Basler, *Collected Works*, 5:149–50; Sears, *To the Gates of Richmond*, 17; Dennett, *Lincoln in the Civil War*, 37.

3 Seth Williams to James S. Wadsworth, March 16, 1862; General Order No. 1, First Division, Fifth Army Corps, March 20, 1862; General Order No. 1, Headquarters, Fifth Army Corps, March 20, 1862; and Randolph Marcy to Nathaniel P. Banks, March 14, 1862—all in Banks Papers, LC; Dyer, *Compendium*, 1:300–301; Bryant, *Third Wisconsin*, 43; *OR* 5:748, 750, 12(3):760–61; Hunt, *Colonels in Blue*, 108; Eby, *Virginia Yankee*, 15; Dwight, *Life and Letters*, 215; Allan, *History*, 43.

4 Nathan Kimball to W. A. Brand, November 15, 1878, Sixty-sixth Ohio Infantry Papers, OHS; *CCW*, 3:404; Eby, *Virginia Yankee*, 15.

5 *CCW*, 3:404; Orville Thompson, *Philippi to Appomattox*, 80; [Strother], "Personal Recollections," 183; "Will," letter to the editor, March 22, 1862.

6 [Strother], "Personal Recollections," 183–84; Major S. Davis, letter to the editor, March 21, 1862; Eby, *Virginia Yankee*, 17.

7 Sawyer, *8th Regiment Ohio*, 37–38.

8 Quint, *Potomac and the Rapidan*, 148; Spiegel, *Your True Marcus*, 178; Hinkley Diary, March 31, 1862, WiHS; Curtis Diary, March 30, 1862, Curtis Family Papers, WiHS; Billy Davis Journal, March 20, 1862, Davis Papers, InHS.

9 *CCW*, 3:404; Eby, *Virginia Yankee*, 17; William N. McDonald, *Laurel Brigade*, 38–39; Marshall Diary, March 21, 1862, Oberlin College.

10 Capehart, "Shenandoah Valley . . .: Battle of Kernstown"; Cass, "Valley Campaign"; Sawyer, *8th Regiment Ohio*, 38; *CCW*, 3:405.

11 Sawyer, *8th Regiment Ohio*, 39; Spiegel, *Your True Marcus*, 73; *CCW*, 3:405; Eby, *Virginia Yankee*, 17.

12 *CCW*, 3:405; Sawyer, *8th Regiment Ohio*, 39; Orville Thompson, *Philippi to Appomattox*, 83; Wilder, *Company C, Seventh Regiment O.V.I.*, 24; Dwight, *Life and Letters*, 215; *OR* 12(3):7; Kimball, "Fighting Jackson at Kernstown," 303; Huntington, "Winchester to Port Republic," 304; Marvin, *Fifth Regiment Connecticut*, 73.

13 Hotchkiss, *Make Me a Map*, 4–5; *OR* 12(3):835; Robertson, *Stonewall Jackson*, 335–36.

14 Hotchkiss, *Make Me a Map*, xv–xx, 5–6.

15 *OR* 12(1):380, 12(3):835; Ecelbarger, *We Are in for It!*," 119; Allan, *History*, 44.

16 *OR* 12(1):380–81; Robertson, *Stonewall Jackson*, 338–39; Casler, *Four Years*, 64.

17 Marvin, *Fifth Regiment Connecticut*, 73–74; *OR* 12(1):356–57.

18 *OR* 12(1):348–49; George K. Johnson, "Battle of Kernstown," 5; Sawyer, *8th Regi-*

ment Ohio, 40; Gildea, *Magnificent Irishman*, 15; John H. Elwood, "Fight with Stonewall Jackson 1862," manuscript, n.p., n.d., Elwood Papers, EU.

19 "Jim" to "Brother David," March 22, 1862, Elwood Papers, EU; Covert, "Port Republic," January 1, 1885; Gildea, *Magnificent Irishman*, 15–16.

20 Spiegel, *Your True Marcus*, 84; Voris, *Citizen-Soldier's Civil War*, 39; *OR* 12(1):370; "J. H. J.," letter to the editor, March 26, 1862.

21 *CCW*, 3:409; George K. Johnson, "Battle of Kernstown," 5–6; Clarke Journal, March 26, 1862, HL; Capehart, "Shenandoah Valley . . .: Battle of Kernstown."

22 Nathan Kimball to W. A. Brand, November 15, 1878, Sixty-sixth Ohio Infantry Papers, OHS; Gildea, *Magnificent Irishman*, 16; Marvin, *Fifth Regiment Connecticut*, 74; Myerhoff, "Battle of Winchester"; "J. H. J.," letter to the editor, March 26, 1862.

23 Nathan Kimball to W. A. Brand, November 15, 1878; Ecelbarger, *"We Are in for It!,"* 73–74; *OR* 12(1):357, 372, 12(3):12–13; *CCW*, 3:409, 414.

24 Robertson, *Stonewall Jackson*, 339; Ecelbarger, *"We Are in for It!,"* 74; Tanner, *Stonewall in the Valley*, 120; Allan, *History*, 45; Mary Greenhow Lee Diary, 26, 29, HL; Bean, "Valley Campaign," 341.

CHAPTER 11

1 Spiegel, *Your True Marcus*, 751; *OR* 12(1):350; Allan, *History*, 48; Henderson, *Stonewall Jackson*, 180–82.

2 Sawyer, *8th Regiment Ohio*, 40–41; Spiegel, *Your True Marcus*, 84; Capehart, "Shenandoah Valley . . .: Battle of Kernstown"; Haas, *Dear Esther*, 71; Steen, letter to the editor, March 27, 1862.

3 *CCW*, 3:406, 410; *OR* 12(1)356.

4 *OR* 12(1):369, 385; Sawyer, *8th Regiment Ohio*, 41; Capehart, "Shenandoah Valley . . .: Battle of Kernstown"; Ecelbarger, *"We Are in for It!,"* 82; C. A. R., "Battle of Kernstown," undated newspaper clipping in Hotchkiss Papers, LC.

5 Spiegel, *Your True Marcus*, 84; Voris, *Citizen-Soldier's Civil War*, 40.

6 Frank B. Nickerson to Samuel J. C. Moore, Moore Papers, UNC; *OR* 12(1):68, 385, 389–90; Ecelbarger, *"We Are in for It!,"* 86–87; C. A. R., "Battle of Kernstown," undated newspaper clipping in Hotchkiss Papers, LC; Sawyer, *8th Regiment Ohio*, 41.

7 *OR* 12(1):360, 366, 368, 373, 386, 390; *CCW*, 3:406, 412; C. A. R., "Battle of Kernstown."

8 *OR* 12(1):347, 387, 401, 403, 12(2):836; [Gillespie], *Company A, First Ohio Cavalry*, 55–56.

9 *OR* 12(1):340; *CCW*, 3:406.

10 *OR* 12(1):340, 361, 371; *CCW*, 3:414.

11 *CCW*, 3:410.

12 Nathan Kimball to W. A. Brand, November 15, 1878, Sixty-sixth Ohio Infantry Papers, OHS; *SOR* 1(2):606; Kimball, "Fighting Jackson at Kernstown," 305; *CCW*, 3:406.

13 *OR* 12(1):383, 408; Allan, *History*, 46; Robertson, *Stonewall Jackson*, 340; Worsham, *One of Jackson's Foot Cavalry*, 66.

14 Vandiver, *Mighty Stonewall*, 205.

15 *OR* 12(1):408; Robertson, *Stonewall Jackson*, 341.

16 Worsham, *One of Jackson's Foot Cavalry*, 66; Fishburne, "Sketch of Rockbridge Artillery," 130; Carson Memoirs, 21, VHS.

17 *SOR* 1(2):612, 623, 628, 631.

18 Kimball, "Fighting Jackson at Kernstown," 305; *CCW*, 3:407, 410; Albert J. Myer to Nathaniel P. Banks, April 13, 1862, and W. W. Rowley to Myer, March 26, 29, 1862, both in Banks Papers, LC; *OR* 12(1):340.

19 *OR* 12(1):359, 381, 408; *SOR* 1(2):632–38; Nathan Kimball to W. A. Brand, November 15, 1878, Sixty-sixth Ohio Infantry Papers, OHS; J. H. J., letter to the editor, March 26, 1862; Fowler, "Criticizing Capehart."

20 *OR* 12(1):394–95; *SOR* 1(2):628, 631–32.

21 *OR* 12(1):388, 390–91; *SOR* 1(2):629, 635, 638; Lyle, "Stonewall Jackson's Guard," 391, Lyle Papers, W&L; White, *Sketches*, 79.

22 Lyle, "Stonewall Jackson's Guard," 396; *OR* 12(1):368, 385–86.

23 Fishburne Memoirs, 40–41, Fishburne Family Papers, UVA; Fishburne, "Sketch of Rockbridge Artillery," 130; Lyle, "Stonewall Jackson's Guard," 391; *OR* 12(1):396; Randolph Fairfax to his sister, April 3, 1862, Fairfax Letters, Museum of the Confederacy; White, *Sketches*, 80.

24 Jones Diary, 6, HL; Worsham, *One of Jackson's Foot Cavalry*, 67; *OR* 12(1):398, 401–2.

25 Fonerden, *Carpenter's Battery*, 20–21; *OR* 12(1):405; Kimball, "Fighting Jackson at Kernstown"; Capehart, "Shenandoah Valley . . .: Battle of Kernstown"; J. H. J., letter to the editor, March 26, 1862.

26 *OR* 12(1):395–96; *SOR* 1(2):613–14, 622–23.

27 The unfortunate driver was William H. Byrd.

28 Fishburne Memoirs, 42–43, Fishburne Family Papers, UVA.

29 Worsham, *One of Jackson's Foot Cavalry*, 67.

30 Fishburne Memoirs, 42–43, Fishburne Family Papers, UVA.

31 Bean, "Valley Campaign," 342.

1 *OR* 12(1):394; *SOR* (1)2:614, 624–25, 629, 643–44; Robert K. Krick, "Jackson vs. Garnett," 29.

2 Capehart, "Shenandoah Valley . . .: Battle of Kernstown."

3 Ecelbarger, *"We Are in for It!,"* 118–25; *CCW*, 3:407; *OR* 12(1):347, 350, 352, 357; Nathan Kimball to W. A. Brand, November 15, 1878, Sixty-sixth Ohio Infantry Papers, OHS; Kimball, "Fighting Jackson at Kernstown," 306; Kearsey, *Strategy and Tactics*, 61.

4 Ecelbarger, *"We Are in for It!,"* 121–22.

5 Smalley, "Annals of the War"; Wilder, *Company C, Seventh Regiment O.V.I.*, 24–25.

6 Steen, letter to the editor, March 27, 1862. In his report of the battle, Tyler omitted any mention of the awkward tactical formation with which he approached the enemy, but testimony to its existence from subordinates and common soldiers was legion. Orville Thompson, *Philippi to Appomattox*, 86–87; Wilder, *Company C, Seventh Regiment O.V.I.*, 25; Smalley, "Annals of the War"; Parmater Diary, 9, OHS; SeCheverell, *Twenty-ninth Ohio*, 40; Billy Davis Journal, March 23, 1862, InHS; Young, "Shenandoah Valley"; [Gillespie], *Company A, First Ohio Cavalry*, 63; "Notae," letter to the editor, March 29, 1862.

7 Smalley, "Annals of the War"; Steen, letter to the editor, March 27, 1862.

8 Smalley, "Annals of the War"; *SOR* (1)2:611; [Gillespie], *Company A, First Ohio Cavalry*, 63.

9 Steen, letter to the editor, March 27, 1862; Lawrence Wilson, *Itinerary*, 136; *OR* 12(1):393; Young, "Shenandoah Valley"; Wilder, *Company C, Seventh Regiment O.V.I.*, 25

10 David D. Bard to a friend, March 28, 1862, Civil War Collection, HL; Wilder, *Company C, Seventh Regiment O.V.I.*, 25.

11 Smalley, "Annals of the War."

12 Orville Thompson, *Philippi to Appomattox*, 87.

13 *OR* 12(1):356; Myron Wright to his father, March 25, 1862, *Akron Summit Beacon*, April 10, 1862; Parmater Diary, 11, OHS; McKee, "Correcting Col. Oates"; George D. Lockwood to his mother, March 26, 1862, Lockwood Family Papers, WRHS.

14 Worsham, *One of Jackson's Foot Cavalry*, 67; David D. Bard to a friend, March 28, 1862.

15 Ecelbarger, *"We Are in for It!,"* 139–40; Marshall Diary, March 24, 1862, Oberlin College.

16 Pile, "War Story."

17 *OR* 12(1):395–96; *SOR* (1):2:614–45, 624, 638–39; Jones Diary, 6, HL; Reidenbaugh, *33rd Virginia*, 21.

18 Steen, letter to the editor, March 27, 1862; Lyle, "Stonewall Jackson's Guard," 398–
99, Lyle Papers, W&L.

19 Young, "Shenandoah Valley"; C. Calvin Smith, "Duties of Home and War," 11;
David D. Bard to a friend, March 28, 1862, Civil War Collection, HL; George D.
Lockwood to his mother, March 26, 1862, Lockwood Family Papers, WRHS.

20 Smalley, "Annals of the War."

21 Colston, "Personal Experiences," 11–12, Trapner Papers, VHS; Launcelot M.
Blackford to his mother, April 3, 1862, Blackford Papers, UVA; *OR* 12(1):388–89,
405; Samuel J. C. Moore to his wife, March 26, 1862, Moore Papers, UNC.

CHAPTER 13

1 Kearsey, *Strategy and Tactics*, 25; Sawyer, *8th Regiment Ohio*, 42–43; *OR* 12(1):369–
70, 407.

2 J. H. J., letter to the editor, March 26, 1862, and Gregg, letter to the editor, March
26, 1862.

3 Voris, *Citizen-Soldier's Civil War*, 22–23, 25, 32; Spiegel, *Your True Marcus*, 85;
Ecelbarger, *"We Are in for It!,"* 157.

4 Gates, *Colton Letters*, 95; Ecelbarger, *"We Are in for It!,"* 159; "Will" to the editor,
March 30, 1862; Spiegel, *Your True Marcus*, 85.

5 *OR* 12(1):374; Mathias Schwab to his parents, March 28, 1862, Schwab Letters,
CiHS; Ecelbarger, *"We Are in for It!,"* 162–63.

6 *OR* 12(1):374.

7 Ibid.; Ecelbarger, *"We Are in for It!,"* 179.

8 Fowler, "Criticizing Capehart"; Wells, "Annals of the War."

9 Worsham, *One of Jackson's Foot Cavalry*, 68; Simpson, "Criticizing Capehart";
Craig, "Shields's Division."

10 Fowler, "Criticizing Capehart"; Wells, "Annals of the War." In a postwar account
of the battle, Adjutant Craig claimed that Murray was giving the order to charge,
rather than retreat, when he was hit. Most certainly Craig offered this lie to the
memory of his colonel, whom death had transformed from stooge to hero. *SOR*
1(2):606; Craig, "Shields' Division."

11 E. H. C. Cavins to his father, April 6, 1862, Cavins Papers, InHS; *OR* 12(1):367.

12 Baxter, *Gallant Fourteenth*, 77; Houghton, "Capehart Criticized"; *OR* 12(1):374.

13 Landon, "Fourteenth Indiana"; James H. Simpson, "Criticizing Capehart."

14 Myerhoff, "Battle of Winchester."

15 Schneider, "Winchester"; James H. Simpson, "Battle of Kernstown"; Landon, "Fourteenth Indiana," 286–87; Ecelbarger, *We Are in for It!*," 171–72; Houghton, "Capehart Criticized."

16 Strider, *Life and Work of . . . Peterkin*, 52–53.

17 Worsham, *One of Jackson's Foot Cavalry*, 68; Ecelbarger, *"We Are in for It!*," 176; *OR* 12(1):399, 403; Landon, "Fourteenth Indiana"; James H. Simpson, "Criticizing Capehart."

18 Myerhoff, "Battle of Winchester"; Elijah H. C. Cavins to Nathan Kimball, [1887], Cavins Papers, InHS.

19 *SOR* 1(2):625–26; Allan, *History*, 51; Ecelbarger, *"We Are in for It!*," 174.

20 *SOR* 1(2):645; Ecelbarger, *"We Are in for It!*," 174.

21 *OR* 12(1):395.

22 *OR* 12(1):394, 407.

23 Samuel V. Fulkerson to his sister, April 3, 1862, Fulkerson Family Papers, VMI; *OR* 12(1):409.

24 Smalley, "Annals of the War."

25 *OR* 12(1):409; *SOR* 1(2):610–11.

26 Lyle, "Stonewall Jackson's Guard," 399, Lyle Papers, W&L.

27 Pile, "War Story."

28 *OR* 12(1):389; Frye, *2nd Virginia*, 23; Bean, "Valley Campaign," 343; Frank B. Nickerson to Samuel J. C. Moore, May 10, 1888, Moore Papers, UNC.

29 Worsham, *One of Jackson's Foot Cavalry*, 68; Allan, *History*, 51.

30 Fishburne Memoirs, 43, Fishburne Family Papers, UVA.

31 Ecelbarger, *"We Are in for It!*," 180–86; *OR* 12(1):391–92; *SOR* 1(2):615, 626–30.

32 *OR* 12(1):386, 392–93, 404; *SOR* 1(2):615, 629, 641, 645.

33 *OR* 12(1):351, 374–75, 392; Myerhoff, "Battle of Winchester"; Tanner, *Stonewall in the Valley*, 133–34; Poague, *Gunner*, 18–19.

34 Myerhoff, "Battle of Winchester."

35 Randolph Fairfax to his sister, April 3, 1862, Fairfax Letters, Museum of the Confederacy; Fishburne Memoirs, 43–44, Fishburne Family Papers, UVA; Fishburne, "Sketch of Rockbridge Artillery," 133; Poague, *Gunner*, 19; *OR* 12(1):397.

36 Fishburne Memoirs, 44, Fishburne Family Papers, UVA; Fishburne, "Sketch of Rockbridge Artillery," 133; *OR* 12(1):397.

37 Launcelot M. Blackford to his mother, March 27, 1862, Blackford Papers, UVA; *OR* 12(1):375, 392, 405.

38 Myerhoff, "Battle of Winchester"; *OR* 12(1):372.

39 Frazier, "At Kernstown"; Frank Ingersoll to his sister, March 26, 1862, Ingersoll Letters, InHS.

40 Houghton, "Capehart Criticized"; Schneider, "Winchester"; Landon, "Four-

teenth Indiana," 287; *OR* 12(1):372; Elijah H. C. Cavins to Nathan Kimball, [1887], Cavins Papers, InHS.

41 Frazier, "At Kernstown."

42 Sperry, "Surrender? Never Surrender!," 144, HL; Jedediah Hotchkiss to his wife, March 27, 1862, Hotchkiss Papers, LC.

43 [Gillespie], Company A, *First Ohio Cavalry*, 64–65; Curry, *Four Years*, 236.

44 Colt, *Defend the Valley*, 123.

45 Lyle, "Stonewall Jackson's Guard," 400–401, Lyle Papers, W&L.

46 Casler, *Four Years*, 67.

47 John C. Wade to Ginger Wade, March 26, 1862, Wade Family Papers, VHS.

48 *OR* 12(1):387.

49 Casler, *Four Years*, 67; *OR* 12(1):407.

50 "Scraps from My Haversack, No. 9: Battle of Kernstown," undated newspaper clipping in Hotchkiss Papers, LC; Jackson to A. W. Harman, March 28, 1862, Jackson Papers, VHS.

51 Poague, *Gunner*, 20; "Scraps from My Haversack, No. 9."

52 William F. Harrison to his wife, March 28, 1862, Harrison Letters, DU; Samuel V. Fulkerson to his sister, April 3, 1862, Fulkerson Family Papers, VMI; *SOR* 1(2):627; Randolph Fairfax to his sister, April 3, 1862, Museum of the Confederacy; Avirett, *Memoirs*, 162; Samuel J. C. Moore to his wife, March 26, 1862, Moore Papers, UNC.

53 Gildea, *Magnificent Irishman*, 18.

CHAPTER 14

1 Capehart, "Shenandoah Valley . . .: Battle of Kernstown"; Nathan Kimball to W. A. Brand, November 15, 1878, Sixty-sixth Ohio Infantry Papers, OHS.

2 *OR* 12(1):345, 375.

3 Gildea, *Magnificent Irishman*, 18–19; J. H. J., letter to the editor, March 26, 1862; Marshall Diary, March 24, 1862, Oberlin College.

4 Frank B. Nickerson to Samuel J. C. Moore, May 10, 1888, Moore Papers, UNC.

5 C. Calvin Smith, "Duties of Home and War," 10–11.

6 Cornelia P. McDonald, *Diary*, 50–53.

7 Ecelbarger, *"We Are in for It!,"* 209.

8 Rufus Mead to "Dear Friends at Home," March 27, 1862, Mead Papers, LC; Marvin, *Fifth Regiment Connecticut*, 71; Morse, *Letters*, 47; Dwight, *Life and Letters*, 219–20.

9 Cornelia P. McDonald, *Diary*, 54–56.

10 "Massanhuttan [*sic*]: The Trap Set to Catch Stonewall," *Richmond Dispatch*, June 11, 1862; Bean, "Valley Campaign," 343.

11 Rufus Mead to "Dear Friends at Home," March 27, 1862, Mead Papers, LC; William H. H. Tollman Memoir, Charles Rhodes III Collection, USAMHI; "Charlie" to his brother, March 26, 1862, Lewis Leigh Collection, USAMHI; Ecelbarger, *"We Are in for It!,"* 208–9.

12 Colt, *Defend the Valley*, 124–25.

13 Lyle, "Stonewall Jackson's Guard," 409–11, Lyle Papers, W&L.

14 Quint, *Potomac and the Rapidan*, 119–20; Gordon, *Brook Farm to Cedar Mountain*, 122; Hart Diaries, 69, March 28, 1862, University of Wyoming; Buchanan, "Banks's Advance and Retreat."

15 Gordon, *Brook Farm to Cedar Mountain*, 122–23.

16 Eby, *Virginia Yankee*, 19–20.

17 Ecelbarger, *"We Are in for It!,"* 268–75.

18 Lyle, "Stonewall Jackson's Guard," 414; *OR* 12(3):177.

19 Nathaniel P. Banks to his wife, March 24, 1862, Banks Papers, LC; *OR* 12(3):16–17.

20 *OR* 12(3):16.

21 Kimball, "Fighting Jackson at Kernstown," 308; Robertson, *Stonewall Jackson*, 347; Nathan Kimball to W. A. Brand, November 15, 1878, Sixty-sixth Ohio Infantry Papers, OHS; Quaife, *From the Cannon's Mouth*, 65; Sawyer, *8th Regiment Ohio*, 45; Worsham, *One of Jackson's Foot Cavalry*, 69; [Gillespie], *Company A, First Ohio Cavalry*; Capehart, "Shenandoah Valley . . .: Shields and Jackson."

22 Anonymous, letter to the editor, Mount Jackson, March 28, 1862; Jones Diary, HL.

23 Launcelot M. Blackford to his mother, April 3, 1862, Blackford Papers, UVA; Poague, *Gunner*, 19; Fishburne Memoirs, 471, Fishburne Family Papers, UVA.

24 Hotchkiss, *Make Me a Map*, 9–11.

25 Kimball, "Fighting Jackson at Kernstown," 308; Nathan Kimball to W. A. Brand, November 15, 1878; Anonymous, letter to the editor, Mount Jackson, March 28, 1862; Launcelot M. Blackford to his mother, April 3, 1862, Blackford Papers, UVA; Draft report of Capt. George W. Cothran, March 24, 1862, Banks Papers, LC.

26 Nathan Kimball to W. A. Brand, November 15, 1878; [Gillespie], *Company A, First Ohio Cavalry*, 66; Henderson, *Stonewall Jackson*, 200.

27 Curtis Diary, April 2, 1862, Curtis Family Papers, WiHS; Quint, *Potomac and the Rapidan*, 148; Hinkley Diary, March 31, 1862, WiHS.

28 Morse, *Letters*, 43–44; Gordon, *Brook Farm to Cedar Mountain*, 132.

29 Dwight, *Life and Letters*, 221–22.

30 *OR* 12(3):19–20, 51(1):560.

31 *OR* 12(3):27.

32 Allan, *History*, 54–55; Worsham, *One of Jackson's Foot Cavalry*, 71.

33 *OR* 12(3):840; Jackson to A. W. Harman, March 28, 1862, Jackson Papers, VHS; Kearsey, *Strategy and Tactics*, 52–53.

34 Hotchkiss, *Make Me a Map*, 10–12.

35 Robertson, *Stonewall Jackson*, 348.

36 *SOR* 1(2):618–19; Bean, "Valley Campaign," 344; Robertson, *Stonewall Jackson*, 349; Maury, "General T. J. 'Stonewall' Jackson," 314; Koeniger, "Prejudices and Partialities," 222.

37 G. Campbell Brown, "Reminiscences," 1:35–36, Brown-Ewell Papers, TSLA.

38 Colt, *Defend the Valley*, 130; Jones Diary, 8–9, HL; Launcelot M. Blackford to his mother, April 3, 1862, Blackford Papers, UVA; Bean, "Valley Campaign," 344. For good treatments of Garnett's abortive court-martial, see Koeniger, "Garnett Controversy Revisited," and Robert K. Krick, "Armistead and Garnett."

39 Douglas, *I Rode with Stonewall*, 46–47.

40 Ibid., 47; McHenry Howard, *Recollections*, 75; Robert E. L. Krick, "Maryland's Ablest Confederate," 178–96.

41 McHenry Howard, *Recollections*, 77, 80–81.

42 Ibid., 80.

43 Thomas J. Jackson to A. W. Harman, April 4, 1862, Jackson Papers, VHS.

44 James Shields to Milton S. Lapham, March 26, 1862, and Edwin M. Stanton to Shields, March 30, 1862, both in Shields Papers, Civil War Miscellaneous Collection, USAMHI; Powell, "Shenandoah Valley," 13–14, Sixty-sixth Ohio Infantry Papers, OHS; Hinkley Diary, March 30, 1862, WiHS; Ecelbarger, *We Are in for It!,"* 217–18.

45 Dwight, *Life and Letters*, 217, 226; Gordon, *Brook Farm to Cedar Mountain*, 128; William Wells to his parents, April 2, 1862, University of Vermont; George K. Johnson, *Battle of Kernstown*, 9.

46 Nathan Kimball to W. H. Brand, November 15, 1878, Sixty-sixth Ohio Infantry Papers, OHS; Kimball to James A. Cravens, March 29, 1862, Cravens Papers, InU.

47 *OR* 12(1):342, 361, 375; Ecelbarger, *"We Are in for It!,"* 216.

48 Eby, *Virginia Yankee*, 21.

CHAPTER 15

1 George B. McClellan to Nathaniel P. Banks, April 1, 1862, Banks Papers, LC; Sears, *McClellan*, 170.

2 Sears, *McClellan*, 170–71; Allan, *History*, 56–57.

3 Kenneth P. Williams, *Lincoln Finds a General*, 2:165–66; Sears, *McClellan*, 171; *OR* 12(3):47, 66.

4 Allan, *History*, 57.

5 Basler, *Collected Works*, 5:273; Goldthorpe, "Battle of McDowell," 161–62; Cox, *Military Reminiscences*, 1:198–99.

6 *OR* 12(1):5–6, 12(3):33.

7 Allan, *History*, 55–56; Sears, *McClellan*, 171–73.

8 Paxton, *Civil War Letters*, 60.

9 Gordon, *Brook Farm to Cedar Mountain*, 135; Quint, *Potomac and the Rapidan*, 123–25; Morse, *Letters*, 50–51; Huntington, "Winchester to Port Republic," 308–9.

10 Thomas, *Ashby*, 93; Gordon, *Brook Farm to Cedar Mountain*, 135–36; Eby, *Virginia Yankee*, 25.

11 Gordon, *Brook Farm to Cedar Mountain*, 137; Thomas, *Ashby*, 193; Quaife, *From the Cannon's Mouth*, 70; Horace Winslow to friends, April 3, 1862, Old Soldier Books, Gaithersburg, Md., catalog 64 (September 1992); Powell, "Reminiscences of the War," 1, Sixty-sixth Ohio Infantry Papers, OHS.

12 Morse, *Letters*, 50–51; *OR* 12(1):418.

13 Nathaniel P. Banks to unknown correspondent, April [?], 1862, and James Shields to Banks, Banks Papers, LC.

14 Huntington, "Winchester to Port Republic," 308–9.

15 Hotchkiss, *Make Me a Map*, 25; Bean, "Valley Campaign," 344; Tanner, *Stonewall in the Valley*, 164–66.

16 Jones Diary, April 12, 1862, HL.

17 Marvin, *Fifth Regiment Connecticut*, 84–86; Farrar, *Twenty-second Pennsylvania Cavalry*, 74; *OR* 12(1):426; Haas, *Dear Esther*, 23.

18 Quaife, *From the Cannon's Mouth*, 57; *OR* 12(3):81–83.

19 Quaife, *From the Cannon's Mouth*, 68; *OR* 12(3):74–76; John K. Murphy to Nathaniel P. Banks, April 8, 1862, Banks Papers, LC; Frank Ingersoll to his father, April 4, 1862, Ingersoll Papers, InHS; C. Calvin Smith, "Duties of Home and War," 10; Rufus Mead to his family, April 8, 1862, Mead Papers, LC; Voris, *Citizen-Soldier's Civil War*.

20 Sawyer, *8th Regiment Ohio*, 44–45; *OR* 12(3):94–95.

21 McHenry Howard, *Recollections*, 84; Kimball, "Fighting Jackson at Kernstown," 308; *OR* 12(1):852; Brooks Journal, 28–29; UNC; Douglas, *I Rode with Stonewall*, 49–50; Avirett, *Memoirs*, 172–73; Edward B. Williams, *Rebel Brothers*, 54.

22 Bryant, *Third Wisconsin*, 48; Gordon, *Brook Farm to Cedar Mountain*, 152–53; George D. Lockwood to his mother, April 23, 1862, Lockwood Family Papers, WRHS; Capehart, "Shenandoah Valley . . .: Shields Moves Forward"; Sawyer, *8th Regiment Ohio*, 46; *OR* 12(1):426; Edmund R. Brown, *Twenty-seventh Indiana*, 119.

23 Quaife, *From the Cannon's Mouth*, 69.

24 Huntington, "Winchester to Port Republic," 310; Quaife, *From the Cannon's Mouth*, 69.

25 Bryant, *Third Wisconsin*, 48; Gordon, *Brook Farm to Cedar Mountain*, 155; Boyce Journal, 62, Boyce Papers, LC; Brooks Journal, 29, UNC; Huntington, "Winchester to Port Republic," 311.

26 Dwight, *Life and Letters*, 236; OR 12(1):426–27.

27 OR 12(1):845–51.

28 Pfanz, *Ewell*, 4, 8, 11–12, 99, 136–37.

29 Ibid., 146.

30 Allan, *History*, 61; Hotchkiss, *Make Me a Map*, 26; Jones Diary, 14–15, HL; Henderson, *Stonewall Jackson*, 208–9.

31 William S. H. Baylor to his wife, April 22, 1862, Baylor Correspondence, VPU; Joseph A. Waddell, *Annals of Augusta County*, 469–70.

32 Allan, *History*, 63.

33 Boyce, "Story of the Shenandoah," 246–48.

34 Quint, *Potomac and the Rapidan*, 141; Sexton Memoirs, 111, OHS; Horace Winslow to his family, April 24, May 7, 1862, Old Soldier Books, Gaithersburg, Md., catalogs 39, 45 (May, December 1990); H. Melzer Dutton to his mother, May 4, 7, 1862, Dutton Letters, HL.

35 Hartman, *Life*, 60.

36 Quint, *Potomac and the Rapidan*, 140–41; Sexton Memoirs, 111, OHS; Curtis Diary, April 18, 1862, Curtis Family Papers, WiHS; Hinkley Diary, May 1, 1862, WiHS; Boyce, "Story of the Shenandoah," 244; [Gillespie], Company A, First Ohio Cavalry, 70; Landon, "Fourteenth Indiana," 293; John L. Harding to his parents, May 9, 1862, Harding Letters, InU; Gordon, *Brook Farm to Cedar Mountain*, 156, 166–67; Horace Winslow to his family, May 7, 1862, Old Soldier Books, Gaithersburg, Md., catalog 39 (May 1990).

37 OR 12(1):857–60.

38 OR 12(1):863.

39 OR 12(1):868–69.

CHAPTER 16

1 James K. Edmondson to his wife, April 29, 1862, Edmondson Letters, W&L; Worsham, *One of Jackson's Foot Cavalry*, 74; Jones Diary, 20, HL.

2 Poague, *Gunner*, 21–22; Tanner, *Stonewall in the Valley*, 164–65; Jones Diary, 21, HL; Worsham, *One of Jackson's Foot Cavalry*, 74–75.

3   Tanner, *Stonewall in the Valley*, 152; E. T. H. Warren to his wife, April 24, 1862, Warren Letters, UVA; Murphy, *10th Virginia*, 17; Kaufman Diary, April 22, 1862, UNC.

4   Jedediah Hotchkiss to his wife, April 20, 1862, Hotchkiss Papers, LC; Hotchkiss, *Make Me a Map*, 26–27; Curtis Diary, April 25, 1862, Curtis Family Papers, WiHS.

5   E. T. H. Warren to his wife, April 24, 1862, Warren Letters, UVA.

6   William N. McDonald, *Laurel Brigade*, 51; Avirett, *Ashby*, 176; OR 12(3):880.

7   Avirett, *Ashby*, 176–77; William N. McDonald, *Laurel Brigade*, 51–53; Thomas, *Ashby*, 195, 207–10; McHenry Howard, *Recollections*, 90; Hotchkiss, *Make Me a Map*, 33; OR 12(3):880.

8   Avirett, *Ashby*, 176–77; Thomas, *Ashby*, 195, 207–10; OR 12(3):880. Jackson wrote Lee on the subject on May 5. On April 26, the day after Jackson restored the cavalry to Ashby's command, Sandie Pendleton sent Ashby the following order: "The general commanding directs that you report at once where the enemy's advance is encamped tonight. . . . He also directs that you send at once a party of ten men under an intelligent non-commissioned officer to prepare the Port Republic bridge for burning." Pendleton to Ashby, April 26, 1862, Ashby Family Papers, VHS.

9   OR 12(1):445–46, 12(3):94, 99, 105–7, 51(1):582; Eby, *Virginia Yankee*, 31.

10 Fishel, *Secret War*, 171–72; OR 12(3):94–95, 111–12, 118–19; "S.," "From Shields's Division," *Dayton Weekly Journal*, July 1, 1862; Boyce Journal, 65–66, Boyce Papers, LC; Gordon, *Brook Farm to Cedar Mountain*, 160, 165.

11 Quaife, *From the Cannon's Mouth*, 72–73.

12 OR 12(3):870; Allan, *History*, 65.

13 OR 12(3):872.

14 Allan, *History*, 68–69; Stone, *Letters*, 41–42; Anonymous, letter to the editor, April 21, 1862; Monfort, "From Grafton to McDowell," 12.

15 Allan, *History*, 68.

16 Williamson, "My Service with . . . Jackson," VMI; Allan, *History*, 68; Jedediah Hotchkiss to Hunter McGuire, March 4, 1897, Hotchkiss Papers, UVA.

17 Ewell, "Jackson and Ewell," 30; OR 12(3):877–78.

18 Gill, *Reminiscences*, 50; Booth, *Personal Reminiscences*, 29–30; Harry Lewis to his mother, June 22, 1862, Lewis Letters, UNC; Hands Civil War Notebook, 45–46, UVA; [Riley], *Grandfather's Journal*, 77; Houghton, *Two Boys*, 28; J. William Jones, "Reminiscences . . ., Paper No. 3," 187; Munford, "Narrative," 11, Munford Family Papers, DU.

19 Fishel, *Secret War*, 173; Allan, *History*, 69.

20 Dabney, *Life*, 338–39; Hotchkiss, *Make Me a Map*, 35; Jedediah Hotchkiss to G. F. R. Henderson, May 20, 1895, Hotchkiss Papers, LC; Kaufman Diary, April 30, 1862, UNC.

21 Dabney, *Life*, 339; "Diary of Capt. H. W. Wingfield," 9; William L. Wilson, *Borderland Confederate*, 11; Hotchkiss, *Make Me a Map*, 35–36; Launcelot M. Blackford to his mother, May 1–3, 1862, Blackford Papers, UVA; Algernon S. Wade to his sister, May 3, 1862, Lewis Leigh Collection, USAMHI; Jones Diary, 21–23, HL; Kaufman Diary, May 2, 1862, UNC; Beeler Diary, May 1, 1862, HL; E. T. H. Warren to his wife, May 5, 1862, Warren Letters, UVA.

22 Fishel, *Secret War*, 173, 566; Gordon, *Brook Farm to Cedar Mountain*, 164–65; Jeremiah Sullivan to R. Morris Copeland, 1:00 P.M., May 2, 1862, Alpheus S. Williams to Nathaniel P. Banks, 4:00 P.M., May 2, 1862, and Williams to Copeland, 7:00 P.M., May 2, 3, 1862, all in Banks Papers, LC.

23 Eby, *Virginia Yankee*, 33; *OR* 12(3):122; Nathaniel P. Banks to Schuyler Colfax, May 4, 1862, Banks Papers, LC; *OR* 12(3):129.

CHAPTER 17

1 Woodward, *Mary Chesnut's Civil War*, 444; "Death of Gen. Ed. Johnson," *Richmond Daily Dispatch*, March 4, 1873.

2 Wise, *VMI*, 202–5; Hotchkiss, *Make Me a Map*, 37; Williamson, "My Service with . . . Jackson," VMI; Apperson Diary, May 4, 1862, VPU; Joseph A. Waddell, *Annals of Augusta County*, 470–71; Kaufman Diary, May 4–5, 1862, UNC.

3 Robson, *One-Legged Rebel*, 26–27.

4 McHenry Howard, *Recollections*, 94–95; Hotchkiss, *Make Me a Map*, 38; Launcelot M. Blackford to his mother, May 10, 1862, Blackford Papers, UVA; Murphy, *10th Virginia*, 20.

5 *OR* 12(1):465, 471; Hays, *Thirty-second Regiment Ohio*, 23–24; Paulus, *Milroy Family Letters*, 38; Hotchkiss, *Make Me a Map*, 38–39; Hall, *Diary*, 53; McHenry Howard, *Recollections*, 96–97; George B. Fox to his mother, May 5, 12, 1862, Fox Letters, CiHS; Harding, *Memoirs*, 35–36; Frank Moore, *Rebellion Record*, 5:38.

6 Stone, *Letters*, 46; W. H. T. Squires, "Stonewall Jackson's Victory at McDowell," *Christian Observer*, August 8, 1917; Bean, "Valley Campaign," 356; Goldthorpe, "Battle of McDowell," 182–83.

7 Ladley, *Hearth and Knapsack*, 41; Monfort, "From Grafton to McDowell," 9–10; Anonymous, letter to the editor, April 21, 1862; "Caroms," "From Frémont's Command," *Sandusky Daily Commercial Register*; Schenck, "Notes," 298; *OR* 12(1):137.

8 Schenck, "Notes," 298; *OR* 12(1):141, 147, 462, 465; Frank Moore, *Rebellion Record*, 5:38; George B. Fox to his mother, May 12, 1862, Fox Letters, CiHS; Stone, *Letters*, 46; R. H. H., letter to the editor, May 18, 1862.

9　Thomas W. Higgins to "Dear Al," May 17, 1862, Higgins Papers, BGSU; Gold-thorpe, "Battle of McDowell," 184; Stone, *Letters*, 47.

10　Jedediah Hotchkiss, undated [ca. June 1896] notes on the Battle of McDowell, Hotchkiss Papers, LC; Hotchkiss, *Make Me a Map*, 39; *OR* 12(1):471.

11　Richard L. Armstrong, *Battle of McDowell*, 53–55; Jedediah Hotchkiss, undated [ca. June 1896] notes on the Battle of McDowell; Hotchkiss, *Make Me a Map*, 39; "Diary of Capt. H. W. Wingfield," 9; Williamson, "My Service with . . . Jackson," VMI; *OR* 12(1):483; Stone, *Letters*, 47; Jacob Pinick to "Friend John," May 16, 1862, Pinick Papers, West Virginia and Regional History Collection, WVU; Thomas W. Higgins to "Dear Al," May 17, 1862, Higgins Papers, BGSU; George B. Fox to his mother, May 12, 1862, Fox Letters, CiHS; Monfort, "From Grafton to McDowell," 14.

12　Jedediah Hotchkiss, undated [ca. June 1896] notes on the Battle of McDowell, and Hotchkiss to G. F. R. Henderson, April 18, 1895, Hotchkiss Papers, LC; Hotchkiss, *Make Me a Map*, 39; Williamson, "My Service with . . . Jackson," VMI; *OR* 12(1):471.

13　*OR* 12(1):471, 485; Bohannon, "Placed on the Pages," 116–19.

14　Paulus, *Milroy Family Letters*, 38–39; *OR* 12(1):464–66; R. H. H., letter to the editor, May 18, 1862.

15　John De Hart Ross, "Harper's Ferry," 170; Paulus, *Milroy Family Letters*, 39; Beelman, "It Was the 12th Ohio Battery"; Alvid E. Lee, "Our First Battle," 394–95; *OR* 12(1):468.

16　George B. Fox to his mother, May 12, 1862, Fox Letters, CiHS.

17　Bohannon, "Placed on the Pages," 120; George B. Fox to his mother, May 12, 1862, and to his cousins, May 20, 1862, Fox Letters, CiHS.

18　James G. Rodgers, "The 12th at McDowell."

19　Paulus, *Milroy Family Letters*, 39; *OR* 12(1):466, 483, 485; Harding, *Memoirs*, 36.

20　Richard L. Armstrong, *25th Virginia*, 31; J. K. Boswell to "My Dear Captain," May 14, 1862, George Hay Stuart Papers, LC.

21　Sponaugle, "Recollections."

22　Alvid E. Lee, "Our First Battle," 395.

23　Sponaugle, "Recollections"; Hutchison, "Battle of McDowell," 39.

24　*OR* 12(1):486.

25　*OR* 12(1):466; Harding, *Memoirs*, 36; Ashcraft, *31st Virginia*, 29.

26　*OR* 12(1):483; Samuel V. Fulkerson to his sister, May 16, 1862, Fulkerson Family Papers, VMI; James H. Wood, *War*, 48.

27　H. C. Clarke, *Confederate States Almanac*, 6; Brett Memoir, 10, EU; James G. Rodgers, "The 12th at McDowell"; "The McDowell Reunion," undated newspaper clipping in Hotchkiss Papers, LC; Batts, "Foot Soldier's Account," 96–97; Hutchison, "Battle of McDowell," 39.

28 *OR* 12(1):479, 487; James G. Rodgers, "The 12th at McDowell"; "The McDowell Reunion," undated newspaper clipping.

29 *OR* 12(1):487.

30 J. W. Chandler, letter to his father, May 14, 1862, *Ashland Union*; George B. Fox to his mother, May 12, 1862, Fox Letters, CiHS; *OR* 12(1):469; Hutchison, "Battle of McDowell," 39; Driver, *58th Virginia*, 15–16.

31 Samuel V. Fulkerson to his sister, May 16, 1862, Fulkerson Family Papers, VMI; Monfort, "From Grafton to McDowell," 17; Richard L. Armstrong, *Battle of McDowell*, 72; *OR* 12(1):487; Cammack, *Personal Reminiscences*, 42; Jedediah Hotchkiss to G. F. R. Henderson, April 18, 1895, Hotchkiss Papers, LC. In his memoirs, Hotchkiss said Jackson left him to bring up the Stonewall Brigade.

32 Alvid E. Lee, "Our First Battle," 395; Paulus, *Milroy Family Letters*, 39; *OR* 12(1):467. Except for the German boy, Milroy may have been right in his claim to have removed all his dead. Colonel Williamson of Jackson's staff said he found only one dead Federal when riding over the battlefield the next morning, a boy of fifteen or sixteen years of age, who quite possibly was Alvid Lee's German. Williamson, "My Service with . . . Jackson," VMI.

33 *OR* 12(1):462; Richard L. Armstrong, *Battle of McDowell*, 100–101; Undated notes on Battle of McDowell, Miles Davis Carey Papers, UVA.

34 *OR,* 12(1):473; McHenry Howard, *Recollections*, 98.

35 Williamson, "My Service with . . . Jackson," VMI.

36 Paulus, *Milroy Family Letters*, 40; George B. Fox to his mother, May 12, 1862, Fox Letters, CiHS; *OR* 12(1):461; Stone, *Letters*, 47–48.

37 *OR* 12(1):464 and (2):886.

38 *OR* 12(1):464, 701; Worsham, *One of Jackson's Foot Cavalry*, 80.

39 *OR* 12(2):887–89.

40 *OR* 12(1):701 and (2):887–93.

CHAPTER 18

1 *OR* 12(3):888–89; Tanner, *Stonewall in the Valley*, 452; G. Campbell Brown, "Reminiscences," 1:36, Brown-Ewell Papers, TSLA.

2 Gordon, *Brook Farm to Cedar Mountain*, 164.

3 Dwight, *Life and Letters*, 238–39; Gordon, *Brook Farm to Cedar Mountain*, 164–65.

4 Eby, *Virginia Yankee*, 35.

5 Hinkley, *Narrative*, 22; Morse, *Letters*, 59; Bryant, *Third Wisconsin*, 52.

6   Gordon, *Brook Farm to Cedar Mountain*, 167.

7   Quaife, *From the Cannon's Mouth*, 74.

8   Eby, *Virginia Yankee*, 36.

9   G. Campbell Brown, "Reminiscences," 1:36, Brown-Ewell Papers, TSLA; Pfanz, *Ewell*, 77.

10 R. S. Ewell to T. J. Jackson, May 18, 1862, Jackson Papers, UNC; Pfanz, *Ewell*, 177–78; *OR* 12(3):889.

11 General Orders No. 47, Valley District, May 17, 1862, Polk-Brown-Ewell Papers, UNC; Pfanz, *Ewell*, 178; Hotchkiss, *Make Me a Map*, 46; G. Campbell Brown, "Reminiscences," 1:36, Brown-Ewell Papers, TSLA; Tanner, *Stonewall in the Valley*, 231–32, 452–53; Robertson, *Stonewall Jackson*, 386–87; Allan, *History*, 88–89.

12 Pfanz, *Ewell*, 179; Hotchkiss, *Make Me a Map*, 46.

13 J. William Jones, "Reminiscences . . ., Paper No. 3," 188–89; G. Campbell Brown, "Reminiscences," 1:36, Brown-Ewell Papers, TSLA.

14 McKim, *Soldier's Recollections*, 86.

15 Wayland, *Stonewall Jackson's Way*, 107; Hotchkiss, *Make Me a Map*, 46–47; Edward A. Moore, *Story*, 53.

16 Pfanz, *Ewell*, 179–80; James H. Lane to Thomas T. Munford, January 4, 1893, Munford Family Papers, DU.

17 *OR* 12(1):896–97.

18 Bean, "Valley Campaign," 360; G. Campbell Brown, "Reminiscences," 1:36–37, Brown-Ewell Papers, TSLA; Wayland, *Stonewall Jackson's Way*, 121–22; Tanner, *Stonewall in the Valley*, 237–38, 452; Pfanz, *Ewell*, 180.

19 Bean, "Valley Campaign," 360.

20 *OR* 12(1):897; Pfanz, *Ewell*, 181; Tanner, *Stonewall in the Valley*, 240–41.

21 Joseph E. Johnston to Richard S. Ewell, 2:00 P.M., May 18, 1862, Dabney Papers, UNC.

22 Joseph E. Johnston to Thomas J. Jackson, May 21, 1862, Dabney Papers, UNC; Pfanz, *Ewell*, 181; Imboden, "Jackson in the Shenandoah," 288.

23 William Wells to his parents, May 18, 1862, Wells Papers, University of Vermont; Gordon, *Brook Farm to Cedar Mountain*, 172–73; Rufus Mead to his family, May 20, 1862, Mead Papers, LC; Boyce Journal, 68–69, Boyce Papers, LC; Hale, *Four Valiant Years*, 135.

24 Jedediah Hotchkiss to G. F. R. Henderson, May 1, 1895, LC; Hotchkiss, *Make Me a Map*, 47.

25 Gordon, *Brook Farm to Cedar Mountain*, 173–74.

26 *OR* 12(1):522; Camper and Kirkley, *First Maryland*, 31.

27 Mouat Recollections, PaHS; *OR* 12(1):523; "From Lieutenant Colonel Parham of the 29th"; Bryant, *Third Wisconsin*, 52.

28 Boyce Journal, 69, Boyce Papers, LC.

29 *OR* 12(1):524; Eby, *Virginia Yankee*, 37–38; John P. Hatch to his father, May 20, 1862, Hatch Papers, LC.

30 Hall, *Diary*, 57; Launcelot M. Blackford to his mother, May 22, 1862, Blackford Papers, UVA.

31 Evans, *Confederate Military History*, 2:69; Hands Civil War Notebook, 47, UVA.

32 Taylor, "Jackson," 238–39, and *Destruction and Reconstruction*, 48–49.

33 William L. Wilson, *Borderland Confederate*, 15; Wayland, *Stonewall Jackson's Way*, 122; Taylor, "Jackson," 238–39; Pfanz, *Ewell*, 182; Edward H. McDonald, "Fighting under Ashby," 30; Donohue, "Fight at Front Royal," 132.

CHAPTER 19

1 *Lower Shenandoah Valley 1864, Map II*, Gilmer Collection, VHS; Allan, *History*, 95.

2 Sperry, "Surrender? Never Surrender!," 140, HL; Thomas A. Ashby, *Valley Campaigns*, 122; Eby, *Virginia Yankee*, 36; [George Smith], "The Fight at Front Royal," *New York Times*, May 27, 1862.

3 Hands Civil War Notebook, 48, UVA; McKim, *Soldier's Recollections*, 96–97.

4 Bradley T. Johnson, "Memoir," 53.

5 Hands Civil War Notebook, 48–49, UVA; Booth, *Personal Reminiscences*, 31–32; Gill, *Reminiscences*, 52.

6 Bradley T. Johnson, "Memoir," 53; Hands Civil War Notebook, 49, UVA; Booth, *Personal Reminiscences*, 32.

7 Terry L. Jones, *Lee's Tigers*, 34–36, 249; Booth, *Personal Reminiscences*, 32; John E. H. Post to his mother, June 17, 1862, First Maryland Infantry (Confederate) Papers, MHS; G. Campbell Brown, "Reminiscences," 1:33–34, Brown-Ewell Papers, TSLA; Dufour, *Gentle Tiger*, 170; Bradley T. Johnson, "Memoir," 55.

8 Bradley T. Johnson, "Memoir," 54.

9 Colonel Kenly said the Front Royal fight opened at precisely 1:30 P.M. The historian of the 1st Maryland (Union) placed the time at between noon and 1:00 P.M. Confederate accounts suggest that it opened closer to 2:00 P.M. One officer in Trimble's brigade swore that the first shot was fired at 3:00 P.M. I have accepted Southern calculations of a 2:00 P.M. opening as being more consistent with the time it would have taken the Confederates to march from their May 22 bivouac to Front Royal. "The Battle of Front Royal—Statement of Col. Kenly," *Montgomery County Sentinel*, June 13, 1862; Camper and Kirkley, *First Maryland*, 31; Ellison, "War Letters," 230; Nisbet, *Four Years*, 40–41; *OR* 12(1):702; Dufour, *Gentle Tiger*,

175; John E. H. Post to his mother, June 17, 1862, First Maryland Infantry (Confederate) Papers, MHS; Hands Civil War Notebook, 49, UVA; Bradley T. Johnson, "Memoir," 53–54.

10 George W. Thompson, letter to the editor, May 29, 1862; [George Smith], "The Fight at Front Royal," *New York Times*, May 27, 1862; Allan, *History*, 94–95.

11 George W. Thompson, letter to the editor, May 29, 1862; [George Smith], "The Fight at Front Royal"; Camper and Kirkley, *First Maryland*, 32; *OR* 12(1):536–37, 559; "The Battle of Front Royal—Statement of Col. Kenly," *Montgomery County Sentinel*, June 13, 1862.

12 McKim, *Soldier's Recollections*, 97; Dufour, *Gentle Tiger*, 175; William H. Murray to friend, June 28, 1862, Murray Letters, MHS; Booth, *Personal Reminiscences*, 32.

13 G. Campbell Brown, "Ewell's Division at Front Royal," undated memorandum, and "Reminiscences," 1:37–38, both in Brown-Ewell Papers, TSLA. In the latter account, Brown has Belle speaking to Jackson. See also Douglas, *I Rode with Stonewall*, 60–61, and Robson, *One-Legged Rebel*, 37–38.

14 Thomas A. Ashby, *Valley Campaigns*, 115–18.

15 John E. H. Post to his mother, June 17, 1862, 1st Maryland (Confederate) Papers, MHS; Allan, *History*, 95; *OR* 12(1):564, 725; Hands Civil War Notebook, 50, UVA.

16 *OR* 12(1):556; Camper and Kirkley, *First Maryland*, 34.

17 "From Lieutenant Parham of the 29th"; *OR* 12(1):560–61; Mouat Recollections, PaHS.

18 Fishel, *Secret War*, 175; *OR* 12(1):561.

19 *OR* 12(1):556; Booth, *Personal Reminiscences*, 33.

20 Tanner, *Stonewall in the Valley*, 261–62; Allan, *History*, 95; Hands Civil War Notebook, 50, UVA; Holt, *Mississippi Rebel*, 73.

21 *OR* 12(1):556–57, 506; Camper and Kirkley, *First Maryland*, 35.

22 *OR* 12(1):733.

23 Tanner, *Stonewall in the Valley*, 262; Camper and Kirkley, *First Maryland*, 35–36; *OR* 12(1):557, 560.

24 Holt, *Mississippi Rebel*, 73; Hands Civil War Notebook, 50, UVA.

25 Camper and Kirkley, *First Maryland*, 36; Myers, *Comanches*, 50; Pfanz, *Ewell*, 185.

26 *OR* 12(1):557, 733; *SOR* 1(2):674; Tanner, *Stonewall in the Valley*, 262–63; Coles, "War Reminiscences," 27; Fogelman Diary, May 23, 1862, Fredericksburg and Spotsylvania National Military Park.

27 *OR* 12(1):557.

28 Allan, *History*, 96; Donohue, "Fight at Front Royal," 133–34; Coles, "War Reminiscences," 27.

29 *OR* 12(1):557, 564–65; Camper and Kirkley, *First Maryland*, 37.

30 Hale, *Four Valiant Years*, 149; *OR* 12(1):557; Ammen, "Incident," 431.

31 *OR* 12(1):733–34; Hale, *Four Valiant Years*, 149; Donohue, "Fight at Front Royal," 134; Musick, *6th Virginia Cavalry*, 12–13.

32 *OR* 12(1):562–63.

33 Mouat Recollections, PaHS.

34 *OR* 12(1):565–66, 779.

35 "The Battle of Front Royal—Statement of Col. Kenly," *Montgomery County Sentinel*, June 13, 1862; George W. Thompson, letter to the editor, May 29, 1862; Camper and Kirkley, *First Maryland*, 38–39; Thomas A. Ashby, *Valley Campaigns*, 123–24.

36 Allan, *History*, 97–98.

37 William L. Wilson, *Borderland Confederate*, 15; Edmund R. Brown, *Twenty-seventh Indiana*, 127; Bryant, *Third Wisconsin*, 54.

38 Edmund R. Brown, *Twenty-seventh Indiana*, 127; Bryant, *Third Wisconsin*, 54; Thomas A. Ashby, *Life*, 172.

39 Bryant, *Third Wisconsin*, 54; Thomas A. Ashby, *Life*, 171; William L. Wilson, *Borderland Confederate*, 15; Edmund R. Brown, *Twenty-seventh Indiana*, 127.

40 Bryant, *Third Wisconsin*, 46.

41 Pfanz, *Ewell*, 185–86; Jedediah Hotchkiss to G. F. R. Henderson, May 1, 1895, Hotchkiss Papers, LC.

CHAPTER 20

1 Fishel, *Secret War*, 176; William J. Miller, "Such Men as Shields," 65.

2 Gordon, *Brook Farm to Cedar Mountain*, 190; Beaudry, *Fifth New York Cavalry*, 32.

3 Nathaniel P. Banks to Charles Parham, 5:45 P.M.—May 23, 1862, Banks Papers, LC; Beaudry, *Fifth New York Cavalry*, 32; Eby, *Virginia Yankee*, 38.

4 Curtis Diary, May 23, 1862, Curtis Family Papers, WiHS; George T. Spaulding to his wife, May 26, 1862, Spaulding Correspondence, WiHS; *OR* 12(1):546.

5 Eby, *Virginia Yankee*, 38–39; Edmund R. Brown, *Twenty-seventh Indiana*, 128; E. L. Hubbard to Nathaniel P. Banks, 7:00 P.M.—May 23, 1862, Thomas H. Ruger to Banks, May 23, 1862, and L. Seisler to Banks, 10:00 P.M.—May 23, 1862, all in Banks Papers, LC; John M. Gould to his father, June 2, 1862, Gould Papers, DU; Frank Moore, *Rebellion Record*, 5:62.

6 Gordon's version of events that night, long taken at face value, not only does not square with other accounts or with messages to and from headquarters, but also reflects the arrogance and self-promotion typical of all Gordon's writing. Gordon, *Brook Farm to Cedar Mountain*, 192–95. Most tellingly, in his report of the

battle Gordon confesses to Banks's preparedness, saying: "The precautionary order to pack and send to the rear my brigade and regimental trains was complied with. They started for Winchester at night." *OR* 12(1):614. For a delightful debunking of Gordon's writings, see Edmund R. Brown, *Twenty-seventh Indiana*, 129–30. William J. Miller ("Such Men as Shields," 56) shares in the skepticism of Gordon's truthfulness.

7   Frank Moore, *Rebellion Record*, 5:62, 64; Rufus Mead to his family, May 28, 1862, Mead Papers, LC; Dwight, *Life and Letters*, 252; Richmond, letter to the editor, May 28, 1862; *OR* 12(1):601, 605.

8   Eby, *Virginia Yankee*, 39; Quaife, *From the Cannon's Mouth*, 76–77.

9   Frank Moore, *Rebellion Record*, 5:62; Quaife, *From the Cannon's Mouth*, 77; *OR* 12(1):546, 605.

10 *OR* 12(1):546; John Bigelow Jr., "Jackson's Valley Campaign, 1862," 3, Hotchkiss Papers, LC.

11 *OR* 12(1):525–26.

12 *OR* 12(1):525; Nathaniel P. Banks to Israel Washburn, May 11, 1862, Tenth Maine Infantry Papers, Maine State Archives; Tobie, *First Maine Cavalry*, 31.

13 Hotchkiss, *Make Me a Map*, 48; Brooks Journal, 36, UNC; Quaife, *From the Cannon's Mouth*, 77; *OR* 12(1):551, 566–67, 572, 595, 612; Nathaniel P. Banks to Thomas H. Ruger, 2:00 A.M.—May 24, 1862, Banks Papers, LC; Hinkley Diary, May 24, 1862, WiHS; Boyce Journal, 71, Boyce Papers, LC; Josiah G. Williams to his parents, May 27, 1862, Worthington B. Williams Papers, InHS; Morse, *Letters*, 58.

14 *OR* 12(1):546–47, 573–74, 595.

15 *OR* 12(1):586; William Wells to his parents, May 26, 1862, Wells Papers, University of Vermont.

16 Eby, *Virginia Yankee*, 39; *OR* 12(1):587–88.

17 *OR* 12(1):575, 587; C. S. Douty to R. Morris Copeland, June 14, 1862, Banks Papers, LC; William Wells to his parents, May 26, 1862, Wells Letters, University of Vermont; Tobie, *First Maine Cavalry*, 34; A. C. Spalding to Israel Washburn Jr., June 4, 1862, and John Goddard to Washburn, June 7, 1862, both in First Maine Cavalry Papers, Maine State Archives.

18 Boyce Journal, 73, Boyce Papers, LC; *OR* 12(1):601, 614; Dwight, *Life and Letters*, 252.

19 H. Melzer Dutton to his mother, May 27, 1862, Dutton Letters, HL.

20 Boyce Journal, 72, Boyce Papers, LC.

21 *OR* 12(1):613.

22 Thomas A. Ashby, *Valley Campaigns*, 119–20.

23 Ibid., 119.

24 White, *Sketches*, 84; Dufour, *Gentle Tiger*, 176; Ellison, "War Letters," 231.

25 *OR* 12(1):779. In his report of the Valley campaign, written by a staff officer six

months after the events described, Jackson claimed that he determined on the night of May 23 "with the main body of the army, to strike the turnpike near Middletown, [and] accordingly the following morning General Ashby advanced from Cedarville toward Middletown." In their accounts of the campaign, both William Allan and G. F. R. Henderson accepted Jackson's assertion at face value. But every reliable eyewitness report—from those of Ewell, Trimble, and Hotchkiss to letters and diary entries penned by men in the ranks—disputes this. Tanner does an exceptional job of dissecting Jackson's plans and marches of May 24, and I find myself in agreement with his conclusion that Jackson's pursuit of Banks evolved as the day progressed and Banks's intentions became clearer. Tanner, *Stonewall in the Valley*, 461–70.

26   Tanner, *Stonewall in the Valley*, 267; Pfanz, *Ewell*, 188–89.

27   Jedediah Hotchkiss to G. F. R. Henderson, May 1, 1895, Hotchkiss Papers, LC.

28   G. Campbell Brown, "Reminiscences," 1:39–40, Brown-Ewell Papers, TSLA; Taylor, "Jackson," 242.

29   *OR* 12(1):567, 779; H. C. Clarke, *Confederate States Almanac*, 7; James H. Williams Diary, May 24, 1862, Williams Family Papers, VHS; Tanner, *Stonewall in the Valley*, 268.

30   Tanner, *Stonewall in the Valley*, 268–69; Jedediah Hotchkiss to his wife, May 26, 1862, Hotchkiss Papers, LC; Hotchkiss, *Make Me a Map*, 48.

31   Musick, *6th Virginia Cavalry*, 15; Eby, *Virginia Yankee*, 40; Suppler, "Shenandoah Valley"; Boyce Journal, 75–76, Boyce Papers, LC; Frank Moore, *Rebellion Record*, 5:62.

32   Boyce Journal, 73–74; Brooks Journal, 37, UNC; Quaife, *From the Cannon's Mouth*, 78.

33   Almon M. Graham, "Banks' Retreat."

34   Eby, *Virginia Yankee*, 40.

35   *OR* 12(1):547, 568.

36   Eby, *Virginia Yankee*, 40.

37   Boyce Journal, 75, Boyce Papers, LC; Eby, *Virginia Yankee*, 40.

38   Frank Moore, *Rebellion Record*, 5:62; Marvin, *Fifth Regiment Connecticut*, 94; Edmund R. Brown, *Twenty-seventh Indiana*, 131; *OR* 12(1):547, 578, 595, 613; Boyce Journal, 74.

39   Brooks Journal, 37, UNC; *OR* 12(1):613.

40   Tanner, *Stonewall in the Valley*, 269–70, 465.

41   Hotchkiss, *Make Me a Map*, 48; Jedediah Hotchkiss to his wife, May 25, 1862, Hotchkiss Papers, LC; *OR* 12(1):576, 588–89; Tobie, *First Maine Cavalry*, 34.

42   *OR* 12(1):576; C. S. Douty to R. Morris Copeland, June 14, 1862, Banks Papers, LC; Jedediah Hotchkiss to his wife, May 26, 1862, LC.

43 *OR* 12(1):589–90; Tanner, *Stonewall in the Valley*, 465; William N. McDonald, *Laurel Brigade*, 61; Tobie, *First Maine Cavalry*, 34–35; C. E. Douty to R. Morris Copeland, June 14, 1862.

44 C. E. Douty to R. Morris Copeland, June 14, 1862; *OR* 12(1):548, 590, 567.

45 *OR* 12(1):590–91; Tobie, *First Maine Cavalry*, 35; Douglas, *I Rode with Stonewall*, 61. Douty said his companies fell in behind Collins; Collins said his squadron formed behind Douty. Evidence suggests Douty's version to be correct.

46 John Goddard to Israel Washburn Jr., June 7, 1862, Tenth Maine Infantry Papers, and A. C. Spalding to Washburn, June 4, 1862, First Maine Cavalry Papers, both in Maine State Archives; Tobie, *First Maine Cavalry*, 35.

47 John Goddard to Israel Washburn Jr., June 7, 1862; *OR* 12(1):575–77, 703; Avirett, *Ashby*, 194; Jedediah Hotchkiss to his wife, May 26, 1862, and to G. F. R. Henderson, May 1, 1895, both in Hotchkiss Papers, LC.

48 *OR* 12(1):592; William Wells to his parents, May 26, 1862, Wells Papers, University of Vermont.

49 Jedediah Hotchkiss to his wife, May 26, 1862, Hotchkiss Papers, LC.

50 *OR* 12(1):563, 703, 735, 764; Marvin, *Fifth Regiment Connecticut*, 95; McHenry Howard, *Recollections*, 107.

51 *OR* 12(1):568–69, 582; Brooks Journal, 36, UNC; Henderson, *Yankee in Gray*, 22; William A. Kimberly to his parents, June 23, 1862, Henry Kimberly Papers, WiHS; Eby, *Virginia Yankee*, 53; Taylor, "Jackson," 242.

52 *OR* 12(1):569, 572, 600.

53 *OR* 12(1):581, 586.

54 *OR* 12(1):582.

55 Barton, "Sketch," 5, VHS; *OR* 12(1):764; Jedediah Hotchkiss to his wife, May 26, 1862, Hotchkiss Papers, LC.

56 Taylor, "Jackson," 243–44; Terry L. Jones, *Lee's Tigers*, 79.

57 Brooks Journal, 37, UNC; *OR* 12(1):572.

58 Taylor, "Jackson," 244; Jedediah Hotchkiss to his wife, May 26, 1862, and to G. F. R. Henderson, May 1, 1895, both in Hotchkiss Papers, LC; *OR* 12(1):569, 573, 582; *SOR* 1(2):656–57; Eby, *Virginia Yankee*, 53; William A. Kimberly to his parents, June 23, 1862, Henry Kimberly Papers, WiHS; Foster, "Criticizing Capehart"; Dickenson, "Fifth New York Cavalry," 154.

59 *OR* 12(3):899; Tanner, *Stonewall in the Valley*, 272, 520.

60 Pfanz, *Ewell*,192; Tanner, *Stonewall in the Valley*, 520; G. Campbell Brown, "At Winchester," Brown-Ewell Papers, TSLA.

61 Tanner, *Stonewall in the Valley*, 520; Pfanz, *Ewell*, 192; *OR* 12(1):779, 12(3):900.

62 Gould, *First–Tenth–Twenty-ninth Maine*, 115–16; *OR* 12(1):609; *SOR* 1(2):668; G. Campbell Brown, "At Winchester," Brown-Ewell Papers, TSLA.

63 [Conerly], *Quitman Guards*, 19; [Riley], *Grandfather's Journal*, 80; Hall, *Diary*, 11; Oates, *War*, 97; [McClendon], *Recollections*, 56; Sperry, "Surrender? Never Surrender!," 192, HL.

64 Jedediah Hotchkiss to his wife, May 26, 1862, Hotchkiss Papers, LC.

65 *OR* 12(1):704, 735, 764; Poague, *Gunner*, 22–23; McHenry Howard, *Recollections*, 107.

66 Barton, "Sketch," 5, VHS; Launcelot M. Blackford to his mother, June 7, 1862, Blackford Papers, UVA; Randolph Fairfax to his sister, May 30, 1862, Fairfax Letters, Museum of the Confederacy; Kearns Diary, May 24, 1862, VHS; Henry Roach to his wife, May 30, 1862, Roach Papers, Virginia State Archives; Poague, *Gunner*, 23; McHenry Howard, *Recollections*, 107; Thomas A. Ashby, *Life*, 176–77; Avirett, *Ashby*, 198–99; Jedediah Hotchkiss to G. F. R. Henderson, May 1, 1895, Hotchkiss Papers, LC.

67 *OR* 12(1):704.

68 Douglas, *I Rode with Stonewall*, 62–63.

69 *OR* 12(1):584, 595.

70 Gordon, *Brook Farm to Cedar Mountain*, 206; *OR* 12(1):612, 614; Dwight, *Life and Letters*, 253.

71 Edmund R. Brown, *Twenty-seventh Indiana*, 132–35; Josiah C. Williams to his parents, May 27, 1862, Worthington B. Williams Papers, InHS; Poague, *Gunner*, 23–24.

72 *OR* 12(1):615, 735; McHenry Howard, *Recollections*, 107; Edmund R. Brown, *Twenty-seventh Indiana*, 138.

73 Josiah C. Williams to his parents, May 27, 1862, Worthington B. Williams Papers, InHS; Edmund R. Brown, *Twenty-seventh Indiana*, 138–39; *OR* 12(1):615, 621, 735, 760; Barton, "Sketch," 6, VHS; Frank Moore, *Rebellion Record*, 5:64; Gordon, *Brook Farm to Cedar Mountain*, 207; Graham Diaries, May 24, 1862, BECHS; Dwight, *Life and Letters*, 253.

74 Barton, "Sketch," 6, VHS; *OR* 12(1):743; Jedediah Hotchkiss to G. F. R. Henderson, May 1, 1895, Hotchkiss Papers, LC; Worsham, *One of Jackson's Foot Cavalry*, 84; Harding, *Memoirs*, 39.

75 *OR* 12(1):743, 751, 761; McHenry Howard, *Recollections*, 108.

76 *OR* 12(1):615; Gordon, *Brook Farm to Cedar Mountain*, 209–11; Barton, "Sketch," 6, VHS; William Wells to his parents, May 26, 1862, University of Vermont; Edmund R. Brown, *Twenty-seventh Indiana*, 132.

77 Edmund R. Brown, *Twenty-seventh Indiana*, 132–33.

78 *OR* 12(1):621; Dwight, *Life and Letters*, 254; Morse, *Letters*, 59.

79 Barton, "Sketch," 6, VHS; McHenry Howard, *Recollections*, 108; White, *Sketches*, 86.

80 *OR* 12(1):622; Barton, "Sketch," 6, VHS; Kearns Diary, May 24, 1862, VHS; Dwight, *Life and Letters*, 255–56; Morse, *Letters*, 60.

81 Barton, "Sketch," 6, VHS.

82 Ibid., 6–7, VHS; Kurtz, "Account of the Valley Campaign," 47–48; *OR* 12(1):735, 748; Winder Diary, May 24–25, 1862, MHS; White, *Sketches*, 86; Fogelman Diary, May 24, 1862, Fredericksburg and Spotsylvania National Military Park; Jedediah Hotchkiss to G. F. R. Henderson, May 1, 1895, Hotchkiss Papers, LC.

83 Tanner, *Stonewall in the Valley*, 277.

CHAPTER 21

1 Boyce Journal, 77, Boyce Papers, LC; Marvin, *Fifth Regiment Connecticut*, 96; Gould, *First–Tenth–Twenty-ninth Maine*, 113; John Mead Gould to his father, June 2, 1862, Gould Papers, DU; *OR* 12(1):575; Laura Lee Diary, May 24, 1862, CWM; Chase Diary, 42, HL; Mary Greenhow Lee Diary, May 24, 1762, 110, HL.

2 *OR* 12(1):606, 612–13, 622; Edmund R. Brown, *Twenty-seventh Indiana*, 142–43; Boyce Journal, 77; Brooks Journal, 36–37, UNC; Marvin, *Fifth Regiment Connecticut*, 98; Hinkley, *Narrative*, 23–24; Graham Diaries, May 24, 1862, BECHS; Morse, *Letters*, 60.

3 *OR* 12(1):527, 570; Gould, *First–Tenth–Twenty-ninth Maine*, 119; Huntington, "Winchester to Port Republic," 318.

4 *OR* 12(1):527.

5 *OR* 12(1):549; Quaife, *From the Cannon's Mouth*, 79; John P. Hatch to his father, May 27, 1862, Hatch Papers, LC; Dwight, *Life and Letters*, 256; Allan, *History*, 109.

6 Quaife, *From the Cannon's Mouth*, 79; John P. Hatch to his father, May 27, 1862; *OR* 12(1):549.

7 Blair, *Politician*, 44–45; *OR* 12(3):223–27.

8 *OR* 12(3):215–16.

9 Thaxter, *Sidney Warren Thaxter*, 43; *OR* 12(1):566, 12(3):222–23; Munford, "Narrative," 20, Munford Family Papers, DU.

10 Basler, *Collected Works*, 5:231–32.

11 Ibid., 5:232–33.

12 *OR* 12(3):220.

13 Kenneth P. Williams, *Lincoln Finds a General*, 1:176; Basler, *Collected Works*, 5:233–34.

14 *OR* 12(3):220–21.

15 *OR* 12(3):222.

16 *OR* 12(1):643; Maxwell Diary, May 24, 1862, Maxwell Papers, CiHS.

17 *OR* 12(1):642–43.

CHAPTER 22

1 Dabney, *Life*, 84.

2 Edmund R. Brown, *Twenty-seventh Indiana*, 134; Dwight, *Life and Letters*, 258.

3 Gould, *First–Tenth–Twenty-ninth Maine*, 46.

4 *OR* 12(1):737.

5 Coble Reminiscences, NCSA; Hands Civil War Notebook, 52, UVA; Gould, *First–Tenth–Twenty-ninth Maine*, 46.

6 Pfanz, *Ewell*; *SOR* 1(2):668; Nesbit, *Four Years*, 46.

7 Marvin, *Fifth Regiment Connecticut*, 99.

8 Brooks Journal, 37, UNC; W. L. Foulk, letter to the editor, May 26, 1862.

9 Hands Civil War Notebook, 52–53, UVA.

10 Coble Reminiscences, NCSA; Marvin, *Fifth Regiment Connecticut*, 100; A. Melzer Dutton to his mother, May 28, 1862, Dutton Letters, HL; *SOR* (1):2, 668.

11 Coble Reminiscences, NCSA; Oates, *War*; Marvin, *Fifth Regiment Connecticut*, 101–2; *SOR* 1(2):668.

12 *SOR* 1(2):668–69.

13 Oates, *War*, 98; G. Campbell Brown, "Reminiscences," 1:42, Brown-Ewell Papers, TSLA.

14 Quaife, *From the Cannon's Mouth*, 78–79; Brewster, "Bullet and Shell."

15 Quaife, *From the Cannon's Mouth*, 79.

16 McHenry Howard, *Recollections*, 110.

17 *OR* 12(1):760

18 *OR* 12(1):765.

19 Poague, *Gunner*, 22.

20 Worsham, *One of Jackson's Foot Cavalry*, 86

21 Gordon, *Brook Farm to Cedar Mountain*, 238; Dwight, *Life and Letters*, 29.

22 *OR* 12(1):763.

23 *OR* 12(1):764.

24 McHenry Howard, *Recollections*, 110.

25 Barton, "Sketch," 11, VHS; Poague, *Gunner*, 23.

26 Barton, "Sketch," 11–12, VHS; Poague, *Gunner*, 23.

27 Launcelot M. Blackford to his mother, June 7, 1862, Blackford Papers, UVA.

28 *OR* 12(1):705, 737; Frank Moore, *Rebellion Record*, 5:63.

29 G. Campbell Brown, "At Winchester," Brown-Ewell Papers, TSLA.

30 J. William Jones, "Reminiscences . . ., Paper No. 4," 235; *OR* 12(1):756.

31 *OR* 12(1):705, 737, 764, 766–67; Worsham, *One of Jackson's Foot Cavalry*, 86.

32 *OR* 12(1):736, 772, 775–77; E. T. H. Warren to his wife, May 25, 1862, Warren Letters, UVA.

33 McHenry Howard, *Recollections*, 110.

34 Barton, "Sketch," 12, VHS; McHenry Howard, *Recollections*, 110; Taylor, "Jackson," 245.

35 Taylor, "Jackson," 245–46; Kearns Diary, May 25, 1862, VHS.

36 E. T. H. Warren to his wife, May 25, 1862, Warren Letters, UVA; *OR* 12(1):705, 773, 775, 777.

37 Taylor, "Jackson," 246.

38 Worsham, *One of Jackson's Foot Cavalry*, 87; McHenry Howard, *Recollections*, 110.

39 Dwight, *Life and Letters*, 257–58; *OR* 12(1):616; Gordon, *Brook Farm to Cedar Mountain*, 238.

40 Edmund R. Brown, *Twenty-seventh Indiana*, 145; *OR* 12(1):619.

41 Edmund R. Brown, *Twenty-seventh Indiana*, 146–48, 161–64; *OR* 12(1):619–20, 624; Morse, *Letters*, 61; Terry L. Jones, *Lee's Tigers*, 79.

42 *OR* 12(1):624.

43 Buchanan, "Banks's Advance and Retreat."

44 Gordon, *Brook Farm to Cedar Mountain*, 238–39; *OR* 12(1):622; Frank Moore, *Rebellion Record*, 5:64; Hinkley, *Narrative*, 25.

45 Dwight, *Life and Letters*, 219.

46 Morse, *Letters*, 62.

47 *OR* 12(1):597, 625, 706; Hinkley, *Narrative*, 25; John P. Hatch to his father, May 27, 1862, Hatch Papers, LC.

48 Edmund R. Brown, *Twenty-seventh Indiana*, 149–50; Quaife, *From the Cannon's Mouth*, 81; *OR* 12(1):597.

49 McHenry Howard, *Recollections*, 111; *OR* 12(1):737; Allan, *History*, 129.

50 Jedediah Hotchkiss to G. F. R. Henderson, n.d., and Hotchkiss to his wife, May 26, 1862, both in Hotchkiss Papers, LC; Gordon, *Brook Farm to Cedar Mountain*, 240; Kearns Diary, May 25, 1862, VHS.

51 Allan, *History*, 128.

52 Hands Civil War Notebook, 53, UVA; W. L. Foulk, letter to the editor, May 26, 1862.

53 G. Campbell Brown, "Reminiscences," 1:41, Brown-Ewell Papers, TSLA; Pfanz, *Ewell*, 195; Allan, *History*, 129; *OR* 12(1):606, 611, 795; Oates, *War*, 98; Ellison, "War Letters," 232; Quaife, *From the Cannon's Mouth*, 81; Brewster, "Bullet and Shell"; [McClendon], *Recollections*, 57; [Riley], *Grandfather's Journal*, 80.

54 Charles S. Curtis to his family, June 2, 19, 1862, Curtis Family Papers, WiHS; George T. Spaulding to his wife, May 26, 1862, Spaulding Correspondence, WiHS;

Eby, *Virginia Yankee*, 42; Quaife, *From the Cannon's Mouth*, 82; Anonymous, letter to the editor, May 26, 1862; Dwight, *Life and Letters*, 261; J. V., letter to the editor, May 29, 1862; Frank Moore, *Rebellion Record*, 5:64; Berkey, "Valley's Civilians," 102–5; *OR* 12(1): 550, 585, 608, 613; Quint, *Second Massachusetts*, 89; Lathrop, letter to the editor, May 26, 1862; Boyce Journal, 79, Boyce Papers, LC; John M. Gould to his family, June 8, 1862, Gould Papers, DU; L. D. C. Gaskill, letter to the editor, *Orleans Republican*, June 25, 1862; George H. Nye to his wife, May 26, 1862, Private Collection; H. Melzer Dutton to his mother, May 27, 1862, Dutton Letters, HL; Chase Diary, May 25, 1862, 42–43, HL; Brooks Journal, 38, UNC; Edmund R. Brown, *Twenty-seventh Indiana*, 152.

55 Brewster, "Bullet and Shell"; Edmund R. Brown, *Twenty-seventh Indiana*, 151; Marvin, *Fifth Regiment Connecticut*, 104–5; Morse, *Letters*, 62; Eby, *Virginia Yankee*, 42; W. L. Foulk, letter to the editor, May 26, 1862.

56 John M. Gould to his family, June 2, 1862, Gould Papers, DU; Quaife, *From the Cannon's Mouth*, 82.

57 Boyce Journal, 79–80, Boyce Papers, LC; Dickenson, "Fifth New York Cavalry," 155; John M. Gould to his family, June 8, 1862, Gould Papers, LC; Ted Barclay to his sisters, May 26, 1862, Barclay Papers, W&L.

58 *OR* 12(1):745.

59 John E. H. Post to his mother, June 17, 1862, First Maryland Infantry (Confederate) Papers, MHS; Hands Civil War Notebook, 53, UVA; Booth, *Personal Reminiscences*, 36–37.

60 The order was, in fact, issued that very evening. *OR* 12(3):900; Randolph Fairfax to his brother, May 27, 1862, Museum of the Confederacy; J. William Jones, "Reminiscences . . . , Paper No. 4," 235; W. W. H., letter to the editor, May 25, 1862; Harding, *Memoirs*, 40–41; S. I. Coleman to his mother, May 27, 1862, *Sword and Saber*, catalog 82 (Spring 1996); Apperson Diary, May 25, 1862, UVA; Mary Greenhow Lee Diary, May 26, 1862, 120, HL; Driver, *58th Virginia*, 21; Irby H. Scott to his father, May 26, 1862, Scott Papers, DU; [Riley], *Grandfather's Journal*, 82.

61 Peck, *Reminiscences*, 15; "Diary of Capt. H. W. Wingfield," 11; *OR* 12(1):753, 764, 769; [Riley], *Grandfather's Journal*, 81; J. William Jones, "Reminiscences . . . , Paper No. 5," 273.

62 Taylor, "Jackson," 247; Tanner, *Stonewall in the Valley*, 232; *OR* (1):710; G. Campbell Brown, "Reminiscences," 1:43, Brown-Ewell Papers, TSLA.

63 *OR* 12(1):706.

64 *OR* 12(1):710; G. Campbell Brown, "Reminiscences," 1:43–44, Brown-Ewell Papers, TSLA.

65 *OR* 12(1):606, 706–7; G. Campbell Brown, "Reminiscences," 1:44, Brown-Ewell Papers, TSLA; Winslow, letter to "Dear Eggleston," June 12, 1862; John P. Hatch

to his father, May 28, 1862, Hatch Papers, LC; Thomas A. Ashby, *Life*, 183–84; William L. Wilson, *Borderland Confederate*, 17–18; James H. Williams Diary, May 25, 1862, Williams Family Papers, VHS; Avirett, *Ashby*, 201–2.

66 Edwin O. Kimberly to his parents, June 20, 1862, Henry Kimberly Papers, WiHS.

67 Bryant, *Third Wisconsin*, 69; Quaife, *From the Cannon's Mouth*, 82; Eby, *Virginia Yankee*, 43; Edwin O. Kimberly to his parents, May 27, 1862, Henry Kimberly Papers, WiHS; Bryant, *Third Wisconsin*, 68; *OR* 12(1):584, 597–98.

68 Richmond, letter to the editor, May 28, 1862; Frank Moore, *Rebellion Record*, 5:63; Josiah C. Williams to his parents, May 27, 1862, Worthington B. Williams Papers, InHS; Hinkley, *Narrative*, 27; Edwin O. Kimberly to his parents, June 20, 1862, Henry Kimberly Papers, WiHS; Rufus Mead to "Dear Cousin Aaron," May 30, 1862, Mead Letters, CHS.

69 *OR* 12(1):550–51.

70 *OR* 12(1):606–7; Winslow, letter to "Dear Eggleston," June 12, 1862.

71 Eby, *Virginia Yankee*, 44; *OR* 12(1):528.

72 *OR* 12(1):529.

73 Hinkley, *Narrative*, 28–29; Richmond, letter to the editor, May 28, 1862; Brooks Journal, 38, UNC.

74 Edmund R. Brown, *Twenty-seventh Indiana*, 155; Eby, *Virginia Yankee*, 45; Quaife, *From the Cannon's Mouth*, 83; Gordon, *Brook Farm to Cedar Mountain*, 246; Brooks Journal, 38, UNC; Bryant, *Third Wisconsin*, 69; E. T. Brown to Isaac Butts, June 8, 1862, *Rochester Union and Advertiser*, June 14, 1862.

75 *OR* 12(1):529, 551; Gordon, *Brook Farm to Cedar Mountain*, 246; Nathaniel P. Banks to Abraham Lincoln, May 26—4:00 P.M., 1862, Banks Papers, LC.

76 *OR* 12(1):553–54, 708.

CHAPTER 23

1 *OR* 12(3):234.

2 Basler, *Collected Works*, 5:234–35.

3 *OR* 12(3):228–30; Parmater Diary, 24, OHS.

4 *OR* 12(3):230; Basler, *Collected Works*, 5:235; Kenneth P. Williams, *Lincoln Finds a General*, 1:178.

5 Kenneth P. Williams, *Lincoln Finds a General*, 1:178–79.

6 *OR* 12(3):240–41.

7 *OR* 12(3):233.

8 Kenneth P. Williams, *Lincoln Finds a General*, 1:206; *American Annual Cyclopedia*, 107.

9   Basler, *Collected Works*, 5:236; Kenneth P. Williams, *Lincoln Finds a General*, 5:179.

10 *OR* 12(1):530, 12(3):240, 242. Gallagher ("You Must Either Attack," 6–10) presents a compelling case that Lincoln did not intend for McClellan to break off his Peninsula campaign in response to developments in the Shenandoah Valley.

11 Kenneth P. Williams, *Lincoln Finds a General*, 1:181.

12 Allan, *History*, 121–22; [Gillespie], *Company A, First Ohio Cavalry*, 89.

13 *Chambersburg Valley Spirit*, May 28, 1862; *Boston Daily Advertiser*, May 28, 1862; *Philadelphia Inquirer*, May 27, 1862.

14 *New York Times*, May 26, 1862; *New York Tribune*, May 27, 1862; Andrews, *North Reports*, 254.

15 Tanner, *Stonewall in the Valley*, 301; *New York Times*, May 27, 1862.

16 Graham Diaries, May 31, 1862, BECHS; Josiah C. Williams to his sister, June 9, 1862, Worthington B. Williams Papers, InHS; Charles S. Curtis to his family, June 2, 1862, Curtis Family Papers, WiHS; George T. Spaulding to his wife, May 26, 1862, Spaulding Correspondence, WiHS; Quint, *Potomac and the Rapidan*, 150–51; J. V., letter to the editor, May 29, 1862; H. Melzer Dutton to his mother, May 28, 1862, Dutton Letters, HL.

17 John P. Hatch to his father, May 27, 1862, Hatch Papers, LC; Graham Diaries, May 31, 1862, BECHS; Breck, letter to the editor, May 27, 1862; Quaife, *From the Cannon's Mouth*, 88.

18 S. Hooper to John A. Andrew, May 28, 1862, and Nathaniel P. Banks to his wife, June 7, 1862, both in Banks Papers, LC.

19 *OR* 12(1):30, 12(3):205–6; Jacobs, letter to the editor, June 22, 1862; Tracy, "Frémont's Pursuit," 173–74; Pilsen, *Reply*, 10; Alvid E. Lee, "Battle of Cross Keys," 483; Sidney D. Maxwell to his parents, June 4, 1862, Maxwell Papers, CiHS; "Letter from the 60th Ohio," *Highland Weekly News*, June 5, 1862; Hutchison, "Battle of McDowell," 38; Nachtigall, *75th Regiment Pa.*, 15–16; William J. Miller, "Such Men as Shields," 66–67.

20 *OR* 12(1):11; Tracy, "Frémont's Pursuit," 174; William J. Miller, "Such Men as Shields," 67.

21 Tracy, "Frémont's Pursuit," 166–67, 174–75; *OR* 12(1):11, 644; Evans Diary, May 26, 1862, LC.

22 Basler, *Collected Works*, 5:237.

23 Tracy, "Frémont's Pursuit," 176; Anonymous, letter to the editor, June 21, 1862; Paulus, *Milroy Family Letters*, 43; Frank Moore, *Rebellion Record*, 5:161; Maxwell Diary, May 27, 1862, Maxwell Papers, CiHS.

24 *OR* 12(1):644.

25 George Ruggles to Fitz John Porter, July 28, 1891, Porter Papers, LC; Andrews, *North Reports*, 256.

26 *OR* 12(1):645; Kenneth P. Williams, *Lincoln Finds a General*, 1:190; William J. Miller ("Such Men as Shields," 66–67) shares this view of Frémont's behavior.

27 *OR* 12(1):645, 12(3):249; Maxwell Diary, May 28, 1862, Maxwell Papers, CiHS.

28 *OR* 12(1):646.

29 Alvid E. Lee, "Battle of Cross Keys," 484; Evans Diary, 6, LC; Frank Moore, *Rebellion Record*, 5:161; Tracy, "Frémont's Pursuit," 177; *OR* 12(1):12, 31.

30 *OR* 12(1):647; Fishel, *Secret War*, 178–79; Frank Moore, *Rebellion Record*, 5:161.

31 *OR* 12(1):647–48; Kenneth P. Williams, *Lincoln Finds a General*, 1:190–91.

32 Gildea, *Magnificent Irishman*, 23–24; Powell, "Reminiscences of the War," 5, Sixty-sixth Ohio Infantry Papers, OHS; Sawyer, *8th Regiment Ohio*, 49; Nicolay and Hay, "Lincoln," 132.

33 *OR* 12(3):244–48, 256–57, 269–70, 273; "S," "From Shields's Command," *Dayton Weekly Journal*, July 1, 1862.

34 *OR* 12(1):269.

35 *OR* 12(1):282, 643, 12(3):270.

CHAPTER 24

1 Mary Anna Jackson, *Memoirs*, 265.

2 Richard W. Waldrop to his father, May 26, 1862, Waldrop Papers, UNC.

3 Booth, *Personal Reminiscences*, 35–36.

4 Mary Greenhow Lee Diary, May 26, 1862, 117, HL.

5 Camper and Kirkley, *First Maryland*, 47–48; Richard W. Waldrop to his mother, May 27, 1862, Waldrop Papers, UNC; S. I. Coleman to his mother, May 27, 1862, *Sword and Saber*, catalog 82 (Summer 1996); Nisbet, *Four Years*, 48.

6 J. William Jones, "Reminiscences . . ., Paper No. 5," 273; James F. Shaner to his father, May 26, 1862, Shaner Civil War Letters, W&L.

7 Jackson to Samuel Cooper, May 26, 1862, Pegram-Johnston-McIntosh Family Papers, VHS.

8 *OR* 12(2):563–64; J. William Jones, "Reminiscences . . ., Paper No. 5," 274.

9 Tanner, *Stonewall in the Valley*, 325–26; McHenry Howard, *Recollections*.

10 Henderson, *Stonewall Jackson*, 264; Robertson, *Stonewall Jackson*, 413; John E. H. Post to his mother, June 17, 1862, First Maryland Infantry (Confederate) Papers, MHS; *OR* 12(1):817.

11 John S. Clark to Nathaniel P. Banks, May 27, 1862—9:30 A.M., Banks Papers, LC; *OR* 12(1):262, 639.

12 McHenry Howard, *Recollections*, 112–13; Allan, *History*, 124–25; Boyle, *Soldiers*

True, 29–31; Lemley Diary, May 28, 1862, HL; Launcelot M. Blackford to his mother, June 13, 1862, Blackford Papers, UVA; Fonerden, *Carpenter's Battery*, 22–23.

13 G. Campbell Brown, "Reminiscences," 1:44, Brown-Ewell Papers, TSLA; Allan, *History*, 126; Tanner, *Stonewall in the Valley*, 328.

14 *OR* 12(1):640; McHenry Howard, *Recollections*, 114; William L. Wilson, *Border-land Confederate*, 19.

15 Douglas, *I Rode with Stonewall*, 70–71; Tanner, *Stonewall in the Valley*, 330–31; *OR* 12(3):309; Allan, *History*, 126–27; Henderson, *Stonewall Jackson*, 264, 271.

16 Lemley Diary, May 30, 1862, HL; Hotchkiss, *Make Me a Map*, 49; Edward H. McDonald, "Fighting under Ashby," 32; Munford, "Narrative," 25, Munford Family Papers, DU; Avirett, *Ashby*, 207.

17 McHenry Howard, *Recollections*, 114–15; Hotchkiss, *Make Me a Map*, 49.

18 Boteler, "Jackson in 1862," 164–65; Robertson, *Stonewall Jackson*, 415.

19 Hotchkiss, *Make Me a Map*, 49; J. William Jones, "Reminiscences . . .," Paper No. 5," 274; "Massanhuttan [*sic*]: "The Trap Set to Catch Stonewall," *Richmond Dispatch*, June 11, 1862; Jedediah Hotchkiss to G. F. R Henderson, May 1, 1895, Hotchkiss Papers, LC.

20 Robertson, *Stonewall Jackson*, 416.

21 Boteler, "Jackson in 1862," 165–66; Hotchkiss, *Make Me a Map*, 50; Pfanz, *Ewell*, 200.

22 Boteler, "Jackson in 1862," 166; Hotchkiss, *Make Me a Map*, 50; Jedediah Hotchkiss to G. F. R. Henderson, May 1, 1895, Hotchkiss Papers, LC.

23 Hotchkiss, *Make Me a Map*, 50.

24 Buck Diary, May 29, 1862, HL; Griffin Diary, May 29, 1862, EU; Shepherd G. Pryor to his wife, May 29, 1862, Pryor Letters, GDAH; Bohannon, "Placed on the Pages," 127–28.

25 Bohannon, "Placed on the Pages," 128.

26 Kimball, "Fighting Jackson at Kernstown," 311; Basler, *Collected Works*, 5:251.

27 Sawyer, *8th Regiment Ohio*, 51; Gildea, *Magnificent Irishman*, 24.

28 Thomas A. Ashby, *Valley Campaigns*, 127–28; Sawyer, *8th Regiment Ohio*, 51; Kimball, "Fighting Jackson at Kernstown," 311.

29 Kepler, *Fourth Regiment Ohio*, 67; James Clarke, "Someone Has Blundered," 31.

30 Irby H. Scott to his father, June 12, 1862, Scott Papers, DU; Sawyer, *8th Regiment Ohio*, 52; Thomas A. Ashby, *Valley Campaigns*, 128; Bohannon, "Placed on the Pages," 130; Jones, *Campbell Brown's Civil War*, 365.

31 Kimball, "Fighting Jackson at Kernstown," 311; Sawyer, *8th Regiment Ohio*, 52; Avirett, *Ashby*, 208.

32 Bohannon, "Placed on the Pages," 130–31; Jedediah Hotchkiss to G. F. R Hender-

son, May 1, 1895, Hotchkiss Papers, LC; A. S. Pendleton to Richard S. Ewell, May 31, 1862, Polk-Brown-Ewell Papers, UNC.

33 Hotchkiss, *Make Me a Map*, 49–50; *OR* 12(1):639.

34 Boteler, "Jackson in 1862," 167.

35 Henderson, *Stonewall Jackson*, 265; *OR* 12(3):295.

36 *OR* 12(3):294.

37 Huntington, "Winchester to Port Republic," 322–23; Kimball, "Fighting Jackson at Kernstown," 311.

38 Kimball, "Fighting Jackson at Kernstown," 311.

39 *OR* 12(3):302; Williard Diary, 8, LC; Kenneth P. Williams, *Lincoln Finds a General*, 1:195.

40 *OR* 12(1):1, 13.

41 Henderson, *Stonewall Jackson*, 266–67; Jedediah Hotchkiss to G. F. R. Henderson, May 1, 1895, Hotchkiss Papers, LC; Mary Greenhow Lee Diary, 123–24, May 31, 1862, HL; Worsham, *One of Jackson's Foot Cavalry*, 89; [Riley], *Grandfather's Journal*, 81.

42 Robertson, *Stonewall Jackson*, 419–21; McDonald Memoirs, 45–47, UNC; Hotchkiss, *Make Me a Map*, 50; Worsham, *One of Jackson's Foot Cavalry*, 89.

43 Pfanz, *Ewell*, 201; Booth, *Personal Reminiscences*, 28; A. C. Hopkins to Jedediah Hotchkiss, August 26, 1896, Hotchkiss Papers, LC.

44 A. C. Hopkins to Jedediah Hotchkiss, August 26, 1896, Hotchkiss to G. F. R. Henderson, May 1, 1895, and Hotchkiss to Samuel J. C. Moore, September 8, 1896, all in Hotchkiss Papers, LC; *OR* 12 (1):817; McHenry Howard, *Recollections*, 115–16; Mary Greenhow Lee Diary, 123, May 31, 1862, HL.

45 Henry Kyd Douglas to Turner Ashby, May 31, 1862, Ashby Family Papers, VHS; Allan, *History*, 133; Samuel V. Fulkerson to his sister, June 8, 1862, Fulkerson Family Papers, VMI; G. Campbell Brown, "Reminiscences," 1:45, Brown-Ewell Papers, TSLA.

46 Worsham, *One of Jackson's Foot Cavalry*, 90; Lemley Diary, June 1, 1862, HL.

47 Worsham, *One of Jackson's Foot Cavalry*, 90; *OR* 12(1):14; Samuel V. Fulkerson to his sister, June 8, 1862; "Dixie," letter to the editor, June 5, 1862; Henderson, *Stonewall Jackson*, 268; Frank Moore, *Rebellion Record*, 5:162.

48 Tracy, "Frémont's Pursuit," 180–81.

49 Taylor, "Jackson," 248–49.

50 Avirett, *Memoirs*, 209; Taliaferro, typescript reminiscences of Stonewall Jackson, 5–6, Taliaferro Papers, CWM.

51 McKim, *Soldier's Recollections*, 107–8; Launcelot M. Blackford to his mother, June 14, 1862, Blackford Papers, UVA.

52 McHenry Howard, *Recollections*, 116–17.

53 Booth, *Personal Reminiscences*, 39; McKim, *Soldier's Recollections*, 108.

54 Robertson, *Stonewall Jackson*, 422.

55 Samuel V. Fulkerson to his sister, June 8, 1862, Fulkerson Letters, VMI; A. C. Hopkins to Jedediah Hotchkiss, Hotchkiss Papers, LC; Launcelot M. Blackford to his mother, June 14, 1862, Blackford Papers, UVA.

56 Tracy, "Frémont's Pursuit," 181; Maxwell Diary, June 1, 1862, Maxwell Papers, CiHS; Frank Moore, *Rebellion* 5:161–62; Alvid E. Lee, "Battle of Cross Keys," 485.

57 Tracy, "Frémont's Pursuit," 182; *OR* 12(1):1, 14.

58 Joseph A. Moore, "Shenandoah Valley"; *OR* 12(1):1, 14; Tracy, "Frémont's Pursuit," 182; Frank Moore, *Rebellion Record*, 5:162.

59 G. Campbell Brown, "Reminiscences," 1:46, Brown-Ewell Papers, TSLA; William H. Peck to his mother, June 17, 1862, Peck Family Papers, UNC; Mason Gordon to his mother, June 2, 1862, Gordon Family Papers, UVA.

60 Taylor, "Jackson," 252; Joseph A. Moore, "Shenandoah Valley."

61 Tracy, "Frémont's Pursuit," 183; *OR* 12(1):1, 14; G. Campbell Brown, "Reminiscences," 1:46, Brown-Ewell Papers, TSLA; Alvid E. Lee, "Battle of Cross Keys," 485; "Dixie," letter to the editor, June 5, 1862.

62 Kenneth P. Williams, *Lincoln Finds a General*, 1:197.

63 *CCW*, "Army of the Potomac," 1:265.

64 Ibid., 265; Wallace W. Johnson, "About the Bucktails"; Thomson, *"Bucktails,"* 145–46, 150; Pyne, *First New Jersey Cavalry*, 45; Sawyer, *8th Regiment Ohio*, 62–63.

65 *CCW*, "Army of the Potomac," 1:265–66; Kimball, "Fighting Jackson at Kernstown," 312.

66 *OR* 12(1):316–17; Parmater Diary, 26, June 1, 1862, OHS.

CHAPTER 25

1 Evans Diary, 7, LC; Pilsen, *Reply*, 2.

2 Paulus, *Milroy Family Letters*, 49–50; Bayard, *Life*, 215.

3 Mountain Department Order Book, 73, Sigel Papers, WRHS.

4 Taylor, "Jackson," 253; Sidney D. Maxwell, dispatch to *Cincinnati Commercial*, June 10, 1862, Maxwell Papers, CiHS; James Dinwiddie to his wife, Dinwiddie Papers, UVA; Samuel V. Fulkerson to his sister, June 10, 1862, Fulkerson Family Papers, VMI; Munford, "Narrative," 26, Munford Family Papers, DU; Worsham, *One of Jackson's Foot Cavalry*, 90–91; Alvid E. Lee, "Battle of Cross Keys," 487; *OR* 12(1):15; "Dixie," letter to the editor, June 5, 1862.

5 Douglas, *I Rode with Stonewall*, 78; Robertson, *Stonewall Jackson*, 423.

6 *OR* 12(1):731; Avirett, *Ashby*, 210–11; Hands Civil War Notebook, 58, UVA.

7 Douglas, *I Rode with Stonewall*, 79–80.

8 Mary Anna Jackson, *Memoirs*, 268–69; Robertson, *Stonewall Jackson*, 424; Allan, *History*, 137; *OR* 12(1):15; John Bigelow Jr., "Jackson's Valley Campaign 1862," 8, and J. S. Harnsberger to Jedediah Hotchkiss, July 3, 1893, both in Hotchkiss Papers, LC.

9 Kenneth P. Williams, *Lincoln Finds a General*, 1:197–98; *OR* 12(3):321.

10 *OR* 12(1):15; Thomson, *"Bucktails,"* 152; Pyne, *First New Jersey Cavalry*, 50.

11 Douglas, *I Rode with Stonewall*, 81–82; *OR* 12(1):15–16.

12 Edward H. McDonald, "Fighting under Ashby," 34.

13 James Dinwiddie to his mother, June 4, 1862, Dinwiddie Family Papers, UVA; [Riley], *Grandfather's Journal*, 82; Oates, *War*, 101; James K. Edmondson to his wife, Edmondson Letters, W&L.

14 Randolph Fairfax to his sister, June 7, 1862, Fairfax Letters, Museum of the Confederacy; Launcelot M. Blackford to his mother, June 13, 1862, Blackford Papers, UVA; Robert K. Krick, *Conquering the Valley*, 14.

15 Hotchkiss, *Make Me a Map*, 51; Douglas, *I Rode with Stonewall*, 85.

16 *OR* 12(1):15–16, 652; Tracy, "Frémont's Pursuit," 189–90; Sidney D. Maxwell to his parents, June 4, 1862, and Diary, June 4, 1862, both in Maxwell Papers, CiHS; Alvid E. Lee, "Battle of Cross Keys," 487–88; Pyne, *First New Jersey Cavalry*, 51; Bayard, *Life*, 214.

17 *OR* 12(1):16.

18 Tanner, *Stonewall in the Valley*, 352–53; [Riley], *Grandfather's Journal*, 82; Hotchkiss, *Make Me a Map*, 51; A. Smead to Richard S. Ewell, June 4, 1862, Brown-Ewell Papers, TSLA.

19 Robert K. Krick, *Conquering the Valley*, 20; Taylor, "Jackson," 255; Vandiver, *Mighty Stonewall*, 268; Bradley Johnson, "Fight with Bucktails."

20 *OR* 12(1):255, 12(3):322; Powell, "Reminiscences of the War," 7–8, Sixty-sixth Ohio Infantry Papers, OHS.

21 Winscott, "Fighting Jackson."

22 *OR* 12(3):325–26.

23 Baxter, *Gallant Fourteenth*, 80; Powell, "Reminiscences of the War," 7–8; Kepler, *Fourth Regiment Ohio*, 68.

24 *OR* 12(3):326; Kimball, "Fighting Jackson at Kernstown," 312.

25 *OR* 12(3):334.

26 Parmater Diary, 27, OHS.

27 "Copy of General Shields's Order to Gen. Carroll," Sixty-sixth Ohio Infantry Papers, OHS; *OR* 12(3):335, 340; Joseph Thoburn to Samuel S. Carroll, 4:00 A.M.—June 4, 1862, Sixty-sixth Ohio Infantry Papers, OHS.

28 John Bigelow Jr., "Jackson's Valley Campaign, 1862," 8, Hotchkiss Papers, LC.

29 *OR* 12(3):906–7; Collins, *Battles*, 18.

30 Samuel S. Carroll to James Shields, June 5, 1862, and Shields to Carroll, 11:00
    A.M., June 6, 1862; Parmater Diary, 26, OHS.

31 [Gillespie], *Company A, First Ohio Cavalry*, 87–88.

CHAPTER 26

1   John R. Howard to Nathaniel P. Banks, June 5, 1862, Banks Papers, LC; Tracy,
    "Frémont's Pursuit," 192; Maxwell Diary, June 5, 1862, Maxwell Papers, CiHS.

2   Tracy, "Frémont's Pursuit," 191; Thompson, *"Bucktails,"* 152.

3   Webb, "Overtaking the Enemy."

4   Ibid.; Pyne, *First New Jersey Cavalry*, 52; Morgan, "With Bayard's Brigade."

5   Webb, "Overtaking the Enemy."

6   Pyne, *First New Jersey Cavalry*, 53; Holmes Conrad to Jedediah Hotchkiss, Sep-
    tember 5, 1896, Hotchkiss Papers, LC.

7   Holmes Conrad to Jedediah Hotchkiss, September 5, 1896; "The Death of General
    Turner Ashby," 474; McDonald Memoirs, 54, UNC.

8   "The Death of General Turner Ashby," 474; Dufour, *Gentle Tiger*, 183.

9   McDonald Memoirs, 54–55, UNC; Pyne, *First New Jersey Cavalry*, 56.

10 Webb, "Overtaking the Enemy."

11 Morgan, "With Bayard's Brigade"; Webb, "Overtaking the Enemy"; Thomson,
    "Bucktails," 153.

12 Webb, "Overtaking the Enemy"; Thomson, *"Bucktails,"* 153. Estimates of Kane's
    strength vary between 104 and 150 men.

13 Webb, "Overtaking the Enemy"; Thomson, *"Bucktails."*

14 Thomas Munford to Jedediah Hotchkiss, August 19, 1896, Hotchkiss Papers, LC.

15 Booth, *Personal Reminiscences*, 41–42; Barnum, "Shenandoah Valley"; Hands
    Civil War Notebook, 60, UVA; Bradley T. Johnson, "Fight with Bucktails"; *OR*
    12(1):817; Wallace W. Johnson, "About the Bucktails"; G. Campbell Brown to his
    mother, June 10, 1862, Brown-Ewell Papers, TSLA.

16 Bradley T. Johnson, "Fight with Bucktails"; *OR* 12(1):789; Somerville Sollers to his
    mother, July 30, 1862, and John E. H. Post to his mother, June 17, 1862, both in
    First Maryland Infantry (Confederate) Papers, MHS; Thomson, *"Bucktails"*;
    Hewes, "Turner Ashby's Courage"; G. Campbell Brown, "Reminiscences," 1:47,
    Brown-Ewell Papers, TSLA; Paulus, *Milroy Family Letters*, 44.

17 Micajah Woods to his mother, June 15, 1862, Woods Papers, UVA; Paulus, *Milroy
    Family Letters*, 44; Hartman, *Life*, 62.

18 G. Campbell Brown Reminiscences, 1:47; *Voices of the Civil War*, 119.

19 Vandiver, *Mighty Stonewall*, 517; Samuel V. Fulkerson to his sister, June 10, 1862, Fulkerson Family Papers, VMI; Randolph Fairfax to his sister, June 7, 1862, Fairfax Papers, Museum of the Confederacy.

20 Thomas G. Penn to his brother, June 8, 1862, Green W. Penn Letters, DU; Randolph Fairfax to his sister, June 7, 1862, Fairfax Papers, Museum of the Confederacy; Launcelot M. Blackford to his mother, June 14, 1862, Blackford Papers, UVA.

21 Samuel V. Fulkerson to his sister, June 10, 1862; Thomas Munford to Jedediah Hotchkiss, August 19, 189, Hotchkiss Papers, LC; William L. Jackson to his wife, June 8, 1862, Jackson Letters, West Virginia and Regional History Collection, WVU.

22 Vandiver, *Mighty Stonewall*, 273.

23 Tracy, "Frémont's Pursuit," 192–93.

24 *OR* 12(1):16, 12(3):653; Paulus, *Milroy Family Letters*, 44.

25 Tracy, "Frémont's Pursuit," 192–93; *OR* 12(1):653; Collins, *Battles*, 149; John C. Frémont to Abraham Lincoln, June 12, 1862, Lincoln Papers, LC; "Caroms," "From General Frémont's Command"; Mountain Department Order Book, 77–78, Sigel Papers, WRHS.

26 *OR* 12(1):653, 12(3):354–57; Nicolay and Hay, "Lincoln," 134.

27 Launcelot M. Blackford to his mother, June 7, 1862, Blackford Papers, UVA; James Dinwiddie to his wife, June 7, 1862, Dinwiddie Papers.

28 Robert K. Krick, *Conquering the Valley*, 34–36; Hotchkiss, *Make Me a Map*, 53; G. Campbell Brown to his mother, June 17, 1862, Polk-Brown-Ewell Papers, UNC; James M. Carrington, undated address to Confederate Veteran Association of District of Columbia, 3, Hotchkiss Papers, LC.

29 Robert K. Krick, *Conquering the Valley*, 36–37.

30 Sawyer, *8th Regiment Ohio*, 25–26; Simpson, "Criticizing Capehart."

31 *OR* 12(3):352–53; Nathan Kimball to W. H. Brand, November 15, 1878, Sixty-sixth Ohio Infantry Papers, OHS.

32 Lostutter, "Port Republic"; New, "Criticizing Goodrich."

33 Nathan Kimball to W. H. Brand, November 15, 1878; Rossiter, "Orders Disobeyed."

34 Winscott, "Fighting Jackson"; Robert K. Krick, *Conquering the Valley*, 41.

35 James Gildea to Thomas J. Burke, April 18, 1894, Hotchkiss Papers, LC.

36 Ibid.; Robert K. Krick, *Conquering the Valley*, 42–44, 54; *OR* 12(1):732.

37 May, "Port Republic," May Papers, Harrisonburg-Rockingham Historical Society Collection, JMU; Hotchkiss, *Make Me a Map*, 53; James Dinwiddie to his wife, June 13, 1862, Dinwiddie Papers, UVA; Cox Memoirs, 8, UVA; White, *Sketches*, 88–89; Kaufman Diary, June 8, 1862, UNC; Fravel, "Jackson's Valley Campaign," 419; William B. Taliaferro, typescript reminiscences of Stonewall Jackson, 8–9,

Taliaferro Papers, CWM; Samuel V. Fulkerson to his sister, June 10, 1862, Fulkerson Family Papers, VMI; Hunter McGuire to Jedediah Hotchkiss, May 28, June 12, 1896, Hotchkiss Papers, LC; Robert K. Krick, *Conquering the Valley*, 53.

38 Winscott, "Fighting Jackson"; *OR* 12(1):698.

39 Hunter McGuire to Jedediah Hotchkiss, May 28, 1896, Hotchkiss Papers, LC.

40 Robert K. Krick, *Conquering the Valley*, 65; Samuel J. C. Moore to Jedediah Hotchkiss, May 19, 1898, Hotchkiss Papers, LC; Douglas, *I Rode with Stonewall*, 93.

41 *OR* 12(1):719; Cunningham, "Port Republic"; Lydy, "Battle of Port Republic"; Gildea, *Magnificent Irishman*, 28–29; James Gildea to Thomas J. Burke, April 18, 1894, Hotchkiss Papers, LC; May, "Port Republic," 79, May Papers, Harrisonburg-Rockingham Historical Society Collection, JMU; Goodrich, "At Port Republic."

42 *OR* 12(1):698; Hunter McGuire to Jedediah Hotchkiss, May 28, 1896, and Thomas J. Burke to Hotchkiss, June 4, 1896, Hotchkiss Papers, LC; Willis, "Prisoner's Guard Reversed," 174.

43 Capehart, "Capehart's Rejoinder" and "Shenandoah Valley . . .: Gen. Ashby Killed"; Winscott, "Fighting Jackson"; Galwey Memoirs, LC.

44 James Gildea to Thomas J. Burke, April 18, 1894, Hotchkiss Papers, LC; Cunningham, "Port Republic"; W. J. Brown, "Winchester"; Lemley, "From a First West Virginia Trooper"; George D. Lockwood to his mother, June 4, 1862, Lockwood Family Papers, WRHS.

45 Gildea, *Magnificent Irishman*, 29.

46 Poague, *Gunner*, 26; Launcelot M. Blackford to his mother, June 14, 1862, Blackford Papers, UVA.

47 Poague, *Gunner*, 26; *OR* 12(1):719, 762, 773; Alexander B. Carrington recollections, in miscellaneous notes in Dabney Papers, UNC; Taliaferro, typescript reminiscences, 8–9, Taliaferro Papers, CWM.

48 Alexander B. Carrington recollections, in miscellaneous notes in Dabney Papers, UNC.

49 Samuel V. Fulkerson to his sister, June 10, 1862, Fulkerson Family Papers, VMI; Gildea, *Magnificent Irishman*, 29; Thomas T. Burke to Jedediah Hotchkiss, June 4, 1896, Hotchkiss Papers, LC.

50 Thomas T. Burke to Jedediah Hotchkiss, June 4, 1896, Hotchkiss Papers, LC; *OR* 12(1):762; James H. Wood, *War*, 59.

51 Fravel, "Jackson's Valley Campaigns," 419.

52 James Dinwiddie to his wife, June 13, 1862, Dinwiddie Papers, UVA; Robert K. Krick, *Conquering the Valley*, 81.

53 Leroy W. Cox and Julius S. Goodin to Jedediah Hotchkiss, August 17, 1896, Hotchkiss Papers, LC; Cox Memoirs, 9, UVA; Herndon, "Infantry and Cavalry Service."

54 Samuel J. C. Moore to Jedediah Hotchkiss, May 19, June 18, 1896, Hotchkiss Papers, LC; Robert K. Krick, *Conquering the Valley*, 78.

55 Samuel J. C. Moore to Jedediah Hotchkiss, May 19, 1896; Samuel J. Moore, "Port Republic: How Jackson's Train Was Saved," Moore Papers, UNC.

56 L. W. Cox and J. S. Goodin to Jedediah Hotchkiss, August 17, 1896, Hotchkiss Papers, LC.

57 Cox Memoirs, 11, UVA; Robert K. Krick, *Conquering the Valley*, 105–6; Herndon, "Infantry and Cavalry Service," 173.

58 Winscott, "Fighting Jackson"; Robert K. Krick, *Conquering the Valley*, 114–17.

59 Clouds, "Port Republic"; George D. Lockwood to his mother, June 4, 1862, Lockwood Family Papers, WRHS; Gildea, *Magnificent Irishman*, 32–34; Frank Moore, *Rebellion Record*, 5:112; Parmater Diary, 27–28, OHS; Robert K. Krick, *Conquering the Valley*, 115.

60 James Clarke, "Someone has Blundered," 32.

61 Powell, "New Market, Fredericksburg, and Alexandria" (undated manuscript) and "General Tyler's Statement," September 15, 1878, both in Sixty-sixth Ohio Infantry Papers, OHS; Huntington, "Winchester to Port Republic," 329; Capehart, "Shenandoah Valley . . .: Port Republic"; Frank Moore, *Rebellion Record*, 5:112; Robert K. Krick, *Conquering the Valley*, 277.

CHAPTER 27

1 *OR* 12(1):19, 781; Paulus, *Milroy Family Letters*, 44; Thompson, *"Bucktails,"* 162–63.

2 Collins, *Battles*, 49; *OR* 12(1):19; Tracy, "Frémont's Pursuit," 2:333.

3 *OR* 12(1):19; Frank Moore, *Rebellion Record*, 5:106; Tracy, "Frémont's Pursuit," 2:332; Anonymous, letter to the editor, June 21, 1862.

4 [McClendon], *Recollections*, 64–65; Tracy, "Frémont's Pursuit," 2:333; Culpepper, "15th Alabama with Trimble in the Shenandoah Valley"; Maxwell Diary, June 8, 1862, Maxwell Papers, CiHS.

5 Culpepper, "15th Alabama with Trimble in the Shenandoah Valley"; Oates, *War*, 102; [McClendon], *Recollections*, 65.

6 Robert K. Krick, *Conquering the Valley*, 147; Oates, *War*, 102; Culpepper, "15th Alabama with Trimble in the Shenandoah Valley."

7 Webb, "Gen. Frémont's Command"; *OR* 12(1):781; Frank Moore, *Rebellion Record*, 5:107.

8 G. Campbell Brown, "Cross Keys," Brown-Ewell Papers, TSLA; *OR* 12(1):781.

9 *OR* 12(1):781; Irby G. Scott to his father, June 24, 1862, Scott Papers, DU; Rob-

ert K. Krick, *Conquering the Valley*, 160–65; [Conerly], *Quitman Guards*, 22; Culpepper, "15th Alabama with Trimble in the Shenandoah Valley."

10 Tracy, "Frémont's Pursuit," 2:333.

11 Joseph H. Chenoweth, unsent letter dated June 8, 1862, Chenoweth Papers, VHS; *OR* 12(1):20; Frank Moore, *Rebellion Record*, 5:107; Pilsen, *Reply*, 4; Paulus, *Milroy Family Letters*, 48; Kearsey, *Strategy and Tactics*, 64.

12 Paulus, *Milroy Family Letters*, 44–45; Pilsen, *Reply*, 4–5; Sidney D. Maxwell, dispatch to *Cincinnati Gazette*, June 8, 1862, Maxwell Papers, OHS; Webb, "Gen. Frémont's Command"; G. Campbell Brown, "Reminiscences," 1:49, Brown-Ewell Papers, TSLA.

13 *OR* 12(1):666, 669; Tracy, "Frémont's Pursuit," 334; Paulus, *Milroy Family Letters*, 45; Frank Moore, *Rebellion Record*, 5:107.

14 Robert K. Krick, *Conquering the Valley*, 168.

15 Walter Clark, *Histories*, 2:147; [Conerly], *Quitman Guards*, 22.

16 Walter Clark, *Histories*, 2:148; [Riley], *Grandfather's Journal*, 83; Nisbet, *Four Years*, 52; [McClendon], *Recollections*, 66; Nachtigall, *75th Regiment Pa.*, 16.

17 Lightsey, *Veteran's Story*, 15; [Conerly], *Quitman Guards*, 22; Nisbet, *Four Years*, 53; Robert K. Krick, *Conquering the Valley*, 176–77.

18 Robert K. Krick, *Conquering the Valley*, 183–86; *OR* 12(1):669.

19 Robert K. Krick, *Conquering the Valley*, 186–96; [Conerly], *Quitman Guards*, 22; Nachtigall, *75th Regiment Pa.*, 16–17.

20 *OR* 12(1):669.

21 Robert K. Krick, *Conquering the Valley*, 200.

22 *OR* 12(1):669–70.

23 Buck, *With the Old Confeds*, 35–36.

24 *OR* 12(1):670–71.

25 *OR* 12(1):670, 671–72.

26 Webb, "Gen. Frémont's Command"; Sidney D. Maxwell, dispatch to *Cincinnati Commercial*, June 10, 1862, Maxwell Papers, CiHS.

27 Robert K. Krick, *Conquering the Valley*, 208–9.

28 Collins, *Battles*, 68, 148; John Waddell, "Cross Keys."

29 Collins, *Battles*, 77.

30 Robert K. Krick, *Conquering the Valley*, 230; G. Campbell Brown, "Reminiscences," 1:52–53, Brown-Ewell Papers, TSLA.

31 Van Buren Clark, "Jackson at Cross Keys"; McKim, *Recollections*, 110–15.

32 Paulus, *Milroy Family Letters*, 45–46; Robert K. Krick, *Conquering the Valley*, 219.

33 Paulus, *Milroy Family Letters*, 46.

34 Ibid., 46–47; Hands Civil War Notebook, 82, UVA; John E. H. Post to his mother, June 17, 1862, First Maryland Infantry (Confederate) Papers, MHS; Gill, *Reminiscences*, 59.

35 Evans Diary, 9, LC.

36 Paulus, *Milroy Family Letters*, 47.

37 *OR* 12(1):666; Hays, *Thirty-second Regiment Ohio*, 27; Anonymous, letter to the editor, June 21, 1862.

38 *OR* 12(1):667.

39 Hall, *Diary*, 60; Joseph H. Chenoweth, unsent letter dated June 8, 1862, Chenoweth Papers, VHS.

40 Webb, "Gen. Frémont's Command."

41 *OR* 12(1):21–22; Tracy, "Frémont's Pursuit," 336–37; Pilsen, *Reply*, 7.

42 [Wheeler], *In Memoriam*, 336–37; Sidney D. Maxwell, dispatch to *Cincinnati Commercial*, June 10, 1862, Maxwell Papers, CiHS.

43 Robert K. Krick, *Conquering the Valley*, 268–69.

44 Ibid., 269.

CHAPTER 28

1 *OR* 12(1):644, 785–86; Douglas, *I Rode with Stonewall*, 95.

2 Douglas, *I Rode with Stonewall*, 95.

3 Robert K. Krick, *Conquering the Valley*, 288.

4 Ibid., 289; Jedediah Hotchkiss to G. F. R. Henderson, May 20, 1895, Hotchkiss Papers, LC; [M. G. Harman], *"Stonewall Jackson's Way,"* 19–20; Munford, "Narrative," 32, Munford Family Papers, DU.

5 [M. G. Harman], *"Stonewall Jackson's Way,"* 20.

6 *OR* 12(1):714; Robert K. Krick, *Conquering the Valley*, 283–84.

7 Imboden, "Jackson," 290; Jedediah Hotchkiss to G. F. R. Henderson, May 20, 1895, Hotchkiss Papers, LC.

8 William B. Taliaferro, typescript reminiscences of Stonewall Jackson, 112, Taliaferro Papers, CWM.

9 James Shields to Samuel S. Carroll, June 8, 1862, and Shields to Carroll, 7:45 P.M., June 8, 1862, Sixty-sixth Ohio Infantry Papers, OHS.

10 "General Tyler's Statement," 6, 25–26, Sixty-sixth Ohio Infantry Papers, OHS.

11 Robert K. Krick, *Conquering the Valley*, 279.

12 White, *Sketches*, 90; McHenry Howard, *Recollections*, 126; Jedediah Hotchkiss to G. F. R. Henderson, May 20, 1895, Hotchkiss Papers, LC; Henry B. Kelly, *Port Republic*, 7; *OR* 12(1):740.

13 Taliaferro, typescript reminiscences, 10.

14 *OR* 12(1):696; Robert K. Krick, *Conquering the Valley*, 309; "Gurley" to his parents, June 12, 1862; McHenry Howard, *Recollections*, 127; Gildea, *Magnificent Irish-*

man, 34; Covert, "Port Republic," October 30, 1894; Huntington, "Winchester to Port Republic," 330.

15 Huntington, "Winchester to Port Republic," 330–31; Henry B. Kelly, *Port Republic*, 10.

16 *OR* 12(1):740; Henry B. Kelly, *Port Republic*, 7–8.

17 New, "Criticizing Goodrich"; George D. Lockwood to his mother, June 14, 1862, Lockwood Family Papers, WRHS.

18 *OR* 12(1):696, 699; Henry B. Kelly, *Port Republic*, 10.

19 Rupp, "Captured at Port Republic"; *OR* 12(1):696.

20 *OR* 12(1):696.

21 Covert, "Port Republic," January 1, 1885; Randolph Fairfax to his mother, June 14, 1862, Fairfax Papers, Museum of the Confederacy; *OR* 12(1):741; McHenry Howard, *Recollections*, 127–28.

22 Imboden, "Jackson," 291.

23 *OR* 12(1):745, 747.

24 *OR* 12(1):753; Henry B. Kelly, *Port Republic*, 12.

25 Jedediah Hotchkiss to Robert L. Dabney, July 27, 1897, Hotchkiss Papers, LC; Taylor, "Jackson," 257; May, *Port Republic: The History*, 147; Henry B. Kelly, *Port Republic*, 15–16.

26 *OR* 12(1):741; Henry B. Kelly, *Port Republic*, 12.

27 Henry B. Kelly, *Port Republic*, 13; SeCheverell, *Twenty-ninth Ohio*, 50; George D. Lockwood to his mother, June 4, 1862, Lockwood Family Papers, WRHS.

28 SeCheverell, *Twenty-ninth Ohio*, 50; George L. Wood, *Seventh Regiment*, 121–22; Lindsey, "Battle of Port Republic."

29 *OR* 12(1):741, 753.

30 Henry B. Kelly, *Port Republic*, 12; Collins, *Battles*, 101; Baldwin, "Port Republic."

31 Alonzo H. Burton to his mother, June 11, 1862, Civil War Miscellaneous Collection, USAMHI.

32 James Clarke, "Someone Has Blundered," 32; Parsons, "Port Republic"; Frank Moore, *Rebellion Record*, 5:112.

33 Joseph F. Harding, "Memoir of Major J. H. Chenoweth," 2, Chenoweth Papers, VHS, and *Memoirs*, 44–45; Joseph H. Chenoweth, letter fragment dated June 9, 1862, Chenoweth Papers, VHS.

34 Lyman Memoir, 12–13, Tulane.

35 Richard L. Armstrong, *25th Virginia*, 52; Henry B. Kelly, *Port Republic*, 14.

36 Henry B. Kelly, *Port Republic*, 14–15; Terry L. Jones, *Campbell Brown's Civil War*, 564; Tanner, *Stonewall in the Valley*, 404; Munford, "Narrative," 32, Munford Family Papers, DU; Taylor, "Jackson," 258.

37 Allan, *History*, 204.

38 Work, "An Incident"; Alvid C. Lee, "Port Republic and Lewiston," 590.

39 Ewait, "25th Ohio."

40 Hays, *Thirty-second Regiment Ohio*, 27; Keesy, *War*, 35; Patterson, "Shenandoah Valley."

41 Keesy, *War*, 35; Alvid C. Lee, "Port Republic and Lewiston," 590.

42 Henry B. Kelly, *Port Republic*, 17–18.

43 Ibid., 19; *SOR* 2:673; Huntington, "Winchester to Port Republic," 334; Powell, "New Market, Fredericksburg, and Alexandria" (undated manuscript), 17, Sixty-sixth Ohio Infantry Papers, OHS.

44 Henry B. Kelly, *Port Republic*, 19–20; Powell, "New Market, Fredericksburg, and Alexandria," 17.

45 Powell, "New Market, Fredericksburg, and Alexandria," 18; Terry L. Jones, *Lee's Tigers*, 89; Dufour, *Gentle Tiger*, 187; Rollin L. Jones, "Battery Horses"; Lindsey, "Battle of Port Republic."

46 Henry B. Kelly, *Port Republic*, 25–26; *SOR* 1(2):673; Capehart, "Shenandoah Campaign."

47 Huntington, "Winchester to Port Republic," 333–35.

48 Hart, "From Battlefield to Prison"; Taylor, "Jackson," 259; Parmater Diary, 27–28, OHS; Henry B. Kelly, *Port Republic*, 25–26; Robertson, *Stonewall Jackson*, 444; *OR* 12(1):700; Frank Moore, *Rebellion Record*, 5:112.

49 Houtz, "Affair at Port Republic"; James Clarke, "Someone Has Blundered," 33; G. Campbell Brown, "Port Republic," Brown-Ewell Papers, TSLA; *OR* 12(1):715.

50 Tanner, *Stonewall in the Valley*, 407; [M. G. Harman], *"Stonewall Jackson's Way,"* 21.

51 Tracy, "Frémont's Pursuit," 340.

52 Webb, "Gen. Frémont's Command"; *OR* 12(1):22; Lewis, "How Jackson Escaped."

53 Maxwell Diary, June 9, 1862, Maxwell Papers, CiHS; Paulus, *Milroy Family Letters*, 48; Tracy, "Frémont's Pursuit," 2:341–42; McIlwaine, *Memories*, 194; *OR* 12(1):716; Taylor, "Jackson," 260; Jedediah Hotchkiss to Robert L. Dabney, June 27, 1897, Hotchkiss Papers, LC.

54 Buck, *With the Old Confeds*, 39; David F. Boyd, *Reminiscences*, 15–17; Taylor, "Jackson," 260.

55 Allan, *History*, 205–6; *OR* 12(1):690; Henry B. Kelly, *Port Republic*, 27.

56 Allan, *History*, 207; Tanner, *Stonewall in the Valley*, 411.

57 Tanner, *Stonewall in the Valley*, 409; Kenneth P. Williams, *Lincoln Finds a General*, 1:211–12; *OR* 12(1):655.

58 Galwey Memoirs, 1:30, LC; Voris, *Citizen-Soldier's Civil War*, 61.

59 McKee, "Correcting Col. Oates"; Parsons, "Port Republic"; Covert, "Port Republic," January 1, 1885.

60 John H. Burton to his mother, June 11, 1862, Civil War Miscellaneous Collection, USAMHI; "General Tyler's Statement," September 15, 1878, and Powell, "New

Market, Fredericksburg, and Alexandria," 22, both in Sixty-sixth Ohio Infantry Papers, OHS; Henry B. Kelly, *Port Republic*, 25; Sexton Memoirs, 135, OMS; Voris, *Citizen-Soldier's Civil War*, 60.

CHAPTER 29

1 Basler, *Collected Works*, 5:210; Robertson, *Stonewall Jackson*, 450; *OR* 12(1):656; Tracy, "Frémont's Pursuit," 2:343.

2 Tracy, "Frémont's Pursuit," 2:343–45; Lorenzo Thomas to Nathaniel P. Banks, June 8, 1862, Banks Papers, LC.

3 Schurz, *Reminiscences*, 2:345.

4 Joseph A. Waddell, *Annals of Augusta County*, 477.

5 *OR* 12(3):367–68.

6 Robertson, *Jackson*, 450; Allan, *History*, 207–8; *OR* 12(3):370; "Caroms," "From Frémont's Command."

7 *OR* 12(3):416.

8 James Dinwiddie to his wife, June 18, 1862, Dinwiddie Papers, UVA.

9 Boteler, "Jackson in Campaign of 1862," 172–73.

10 *OR* 12(3):910; Tanner, *Stonewall in the Valley*, 415.

11 Boteler, "Jackson in Campaign of 1862," 173.

12 Tanner, *Stonewall in the Valley*, 419.

13 Boteler, "Jackson in Campaign of 1862," 173–74.

14 *OR* 12(3):913.

15 *Richmond Whig*, June 11, 1862; Tanner, *Stonewall in the Valley*, 414, 559.

16 Tanner, *Stonewall in the Valley*, 414–15.

17 Quaife, *From the Cannon's Mouth*, 96–97.

18 Eby, *Virginia Yankee*, 58.

19 William J. Miller, "Such Men as Shields," 79.

20 A. A. Clewell to his parents, June 16, 1862, Clewell Papers, NCSA; Joseph Carpenter to his father, June 16, 1862, Carpenter Papers, VMI; James Dinwiddie to his wife, June 18, 1862, Dinwiddie Papers, UVA; Tanner, *Stonewall in the Valley*, 429–30.

21 McHenry Howard, *Recollections*, 130.

22 Tanner, *Stonewall in the Valley*, 427, 430.

23 Samuel V. Fulkerson to his sister-in-law, June 14, 1862, Fulkerson Family Papers, VMI.

24 Robertson, *Stonewall Jackson*, 452.

25 Taylor, "Jackson," 260–61.

26 Mary Anna Jackson, *Memoirs*, 283–84.

27 *OR* 12(3):912, 914.

28 Robertson, *Stonewall Jackson*, 455; G. Campbell Brown to his mother, June 17, 1862, Polk-Brown-Ewell Papers, UNC.

29 [McClendon], *Recollections*, 69–70.

30 Wert, *Brotherhood of Valor*, 312–13; Hotchkiss, *Make Me a Map*, 58.

31 Robertson, *Stonewall Jackson*, 457.

BIBLIOGRAPHY

MANUSCRIPTS

Arizona State University, Tempe
    Arizona Collection
        James H. Campbell Letter
Auburn University, Auburn, Alabama
    Benjamin Benner Diary
Bowling Green State University, Bowling Green, Ohio
    Thomas W. Higgins Papers
Buffalo and Erie County Historical Society, Buffalo, New York
    Almon M. Graham Diaries, vol. 1
Chicago Historical Society, Chicago
    Turner Ashby Papers
    Rufus Mead Letter
Cincinnati Historical Society, Cincinnati
    George B. Fox Letters
    Wilson Gaither Correspondence
    Sidney D. Maxwell Papers
    Mathias Schwab Letters
The College of William and Mary, Earl Gregg Swem Library, Williamsburg, Virginia
    Laura Lee Diary
    William M. Rawlings Letters
    William B. Taliaferro Papers
    Asa J. Wyatt Diary

Connecticut Historical Society, Hartford
    Edward F. Blake Papers
    William H. Mallory Papers
Duke University, William R. Perkins Library, Durham, North Carolina
    J. R. Beuchler, "Reminiscences of War between the States"
    Henry Kyd Douglas Letters
    Richard S. Ewell Letter Books
    John M. Gould Papers
    William F. Harrison Letters
    Robert W. Hook Papers
    William Hooke Letters
    Bradley T. Johnson Collection
    Williamson Kelly Letters
    Munford Family Papers
        Thomas T. Munford, "Narrative of Shenandoah Valley Campaign"
    Green W. Penn Letters
    J. W. Preston Letters
    Irby H. Scott Papers
    M. T. Solomon Scrapbooks
East Carolina University, Greenville, North Carolina
    East Carolina Manuscript Collection
        Frank Bisel Papers
Emory University, Robert W. Woodruff Library, Atlanta
    Martin W. Brett Memoir, Confederate Miscellany IV
    John W. Elwood Papers
    John L. Griffin Diary
Filson Club, Louisville, Kentucky
    James William Abert Papers
Fredericksburg and Spotsylvania National Military Park, Fredericksburg, Virginia
    Benjamin M. Blackwell Letter
    Isiah Fogelman Diary
Georgia Department of Archives and History, Atlanta
    Shepherd G. Pryor Letters
Handley Library, Winchester, Virginia
    James W. Beeler Diary
    Lucy R. Buck Diary
    Julia Chase Diary
    Civil War Collection
        David D. Bard Letter
    John Peyton Clarke Journal

H. Melzer Dutton Letters

John H. Grabill Diary

Harriet Griffith Diary

John P. Hite Diary

Francis B. Jones Diary

Mary Greenhow Lee Diary

Jacob H. Lemley Diary

Lewis Collection of 110th Pennsylvania Infantry Papers

Kate S. Sperry, "Surrender? Never Surrender!"

Historical Society of Pennsylvania, Philadelphia

David Mouat Recollections, unpaginated manuscript

Indiana Historical Society, W. H. Smith Memorial Library, Indianapolis

David E. Beem Letters

E. H. C. Cavins Papers

William "Billy" Davis Papers

Jarvis C. Johnson Papers

Samuel V. List Letters

Robert M. Panta Papers

Augustus Van Dyke Letters

Worthington B. Williams Papers

Indiana State Library, Indianapolis

Amory K. Allen Letters

Indiana University, Lilly Library, Bloomington

James A. Cravens Papers

John L. Harding Letters

Frank Ingersoll Letters

James Madison University, Carrier Library, Harrisonburg, Virginia

Margaret Burruss Collection

Harrisonburg-Rockingham Historical Society Collection

George E. May Papers

Knox College, Galesburg, Illinois

Samuel H. Brink Papers

Library of Congress, Washington, D.C.

John E. Anderson Papers

Nathaniel P. Banks Papers

Charles W. Boyce Papers

Thomas Evans Diary

Thomas F. Galwey Memoirs

John P. Hatch Papers

Jedediah Hotchkiss Papers

Abraham Lincoln Papers
Rufus Mead Papers
Fitz John Porter Papers
George Hay Stuart Papers
Joseph C. Williard Diary
Maine State Archives, Augusta
First Maine Cavalry Papers
Tenth Maine Infantry Papers
Maryland Historical Society, Baltimore
First Maryland Infantry (Confederate) Papers
William H. Murray Letters
John E. H. Post Letter
Somerville Sollers Letters
John S. Winder Diary
Museum of the Confederacy, Eleanor S. Brockenbrough Library, Richmond
CSA Soldier Letters Collections
Randolph Fairfax Letters
North Carolina State Archives, Raleigh
A. A. Clewell Papers
Eli S. Coble Reminiscences, unpaginated
Oberlin College, Oberlin, Ohio
Samuel John Mills Marshall Diary
Ohio State Historical Society, Columbus
Alexander Campbell Papers
N. L. Parmater Diary
Samuel Sexton Memoirs
Sixty-sixth Ohio Infantry Papers
Nathan Kimball Letter
Eugene Powell, "Reminiscences of the War: Shields's Division Trotting over
Old Virginia"
Eugene Powell, "The Shenandoah Valley"
Peabody Essex Museum, Philips Library, Salem, Massachusetts
Francis W. Crowninshield Letters
Potter County Historical Society, Coudersport, Pennsylvania
Angelo M. Crapsey Letter
Private Collection
George H. Nye Papers, courtesy of Nicholas Picerno
Rutgers University, New Brunswick, New Jersey
Joseph L. Haines Papers

Tennessee State Library and Archives, Nashville
   G. Campbell Brown and Richard S. Ewell Papers
      G. Campbell Brown, "At Winchester," wartime memorandum
Tulane University, New Orleans
         ——, "Reminiscences of the Civil War, Written in 1867–68," G. Campbell
         Brown Books, 2 vols.
   William R. Lyman Memoir
University of Illinois, Illinois Historical Survey, Urbana
   Charles S. Hamilton, "Memoirs of Two Wars"
University of New Hampshire, Durham
   Barrus Family Collection
University of North Carolina, Chapel Hill
   Southern Historical Collection
      George Brooks Journal
      Robert L. Dabney Papers
      Heartt-Wilson Family Papers
      Thomas J. Jackson Papers
      Joseph F. Kaufman Diary
      Harry Lewis Letters
      William N. McDonald Memoirs
      Samuel J. C. Moore Papers
      Peck Family Papers
      Polk-Brown-Ewell Papers
      Richard W. Waldrop Papers
University of Vermont, Burlington
   William Wells Letters
University of Virginia, Alderman Library, Charlottesville
   Joseph Baer Letters
   Blackford Family Letters
   Launcelot M. "Lanty" Blackford Papers
   Miles Davis Carey Papers
   Leroy W. Cox Memoirs
   James and Bettie Carrington Dinwiddie Papers
   Fishburne Family Papers
      Clement D. Fishburne Journal
      Clement D. Fishburne Memoirs
   Gordon Family Papers
   Washington Hands Civil War Notebook
   Matthella P. Harrison Diary

Jedediah Hotchkiss Papers
McGuffin Family Papers
Smiley Family Papers
E. T. H. Warren Letters
Micajah Woods Papers
University of Washington, Seattle
George H. Hall Letter
University of Wyoming, Cheyenne
Henry Hart Diaries
U.S. Army Military History Institute, Carlisle Barracks, Pennsylvania
Civil War Miscellaneous Collection
John H. Burton Letter
Ireland N. Holman Letter
James Shields Papers
Civil War Times Illustrated Collection
Leonard Schlumpf Diary
Harrisburg Civil War Round Table Collection
Aaron E. Bachman Memoirs
Lewis Leigh Collection
William A. Beam Letter
"Charlie" Letter
Algernon S. Wade Letters
Charles Rhodes III Collection
William H. H. Tollman Memoir
Vigo County Public Library, Terre Haute, Indiana
John Kuppenheimer Diary
Virginia Historical Society, Richmond
Ashby Family Papers
Robert T. Barton, "Sketch of a Battle at Winchester"
Robert P. Carson Memoirs
Miles D. Cary Papers
Chamberlayne Family Papers
Joseph Hart Chenoweth Papers
Joseph F. Harding, "Memoir of Major J. H. Chenoweth"
Jeremy Francis Gilmer Collection
Lower Shenandoah Valley 1864, Map II
Thomas J. Jackson Papers
Watkins Kearns Diary
William T. Kinzer Diary

James H. Langhorne Diary

Patton Family Papers

 Eppa Hutton Letter

 John M. Patton, "Reminiscences of Thomas J. Jackson"

Pegram-Johnston-McIntosh Family Papers

Frederick H. Trapner Papers

 W. B. Colston, "The Personal Experiences of Captain W. B. Colston in the Civil War"

Wade Family Papers

Williams Family Papers

 James H. Williams Diary

Charles C. Wright Recollections

Virginia Military Institute, Lexington

 Julia P. Allen Letter

 Joseph Carpenter Papers

 Fulkerson Family Papers

 John Garibaldi Papers

 Thomas J. Jackson Papers

 Thomas H. Williamson, "My Service with Genl. Thos. J. Jackson," unpaginated manuscript

Virginia Polytechnic University, Blacksburg

 John S. Apperson Diary

 William S. H. Baylor Correspondence

 David Earhart Collection

Virginia State Archives, Richmond

 Robert L. Dabney Papers

 Henry H. Roach Papers

Washington and Lee University, Leyburn Library, Lexington, Virginia

 Alexander T. "Ted" Barclay Papers

 Rockbridge Historical Society Collection

  James K. Edmondson Letters

 John N. Lyle Papers

  John N. Lyle, "Sketches Found in a Confederate Veteran's Desk"

  ——, "Stonewall Jackson's Guard, the Washington College Company, or Imperialism in the American Union"

 Joseph F. Shaner Civil War Letters

Western Reserve Historical Society, Cleveland Ohio

 George D. Lockwood Family Papers

 Charles H. Merrick Papers

 Franz Sigel Papers

West Virginia University, Morgantown
    Roy B. Cook Papers
    James Z. McCheney Papers
    West Virginia and Regional History Collection
        William L. Jackson Letters
        Jacob Pinick Papers
Wisconsin Historical Society, Madison
    Curtis Family Papers
        Charles S. Curtis Diary
    Julian Hinkley Diary
    Henry Kimberly Papers
    George H. Spaulding Correspondence

NEWSPAPERS

Akron (Ohio) Summit Beacon
Alatoona (Pa.) Tribune
Ashland (Ohio) Union
Atlanta Journal
Baltimore American
Bangor (Maine) Daily Whig and Courier
Berkshire Eagle (Pittsfield, Mass.)
Boston Daily Advertiser
Boston Daily Evening Transcript
Boston Saturday Evening Express
Bristol (Tenn.-Va.) Herald-Courier
Chambersburg Valley Spirit
Cleveland Plain Dealer
Daily Evening Bulletin (Philadelphia)
Daily Richmond Enquirer
Dayton (Ohio) Weekly Journal
Highland Recorder (Monterey, Va.)
Highland Weekly News (Hillsborough, Ohio)
Lawrence (Pa.) Journal
Lynchburg (Va.) Republican
Macon (Ga.) Daily Telegraph
Montgomery County (Md.) Sentinel
Mount Vernon (Ohio) Republican

National Tribune
New York Daily Tribune
New York Times
Philadelphia Daily Evening Bulletin
Philadelphia Inquirer
Philadelphia Public Ledger
Pomeroy (Ohio) Telegraph
Orleans Republican (Albion, N.Y.)
Richmond Daily Dispatch
Richmond Dispatch
Richmond Enquirer
Richmond Examiner
Richmond Telegraph
Rochester (N.Y.) Democrat and American
Rochester (N.Y.) Union and Advertiser
Rockbridge (Va.) Union and Advertiser
Roxbury (Mass.) City Gazette
Sandusky (Ohio) Daily Commercial Register
Savannah Republican
Scioto (Ohio) Gazette
Shirleysburg (Pa.) Herald
Staunton (Va.) Republican Vindicator
Staunton (Va.) Spectator
Tiffin (Ohio) Tribune
Valparaiso (Ind.) Republic
Vincennes (Ind.) Valley Advance
Washington County (Pa.) Reporter and Tribune
Wood County (Ohio) Independent

GOVERNMENT DOCUMENTS

[Edwards, J. M.]. *Manufactures of the United States in 1860.* Washington, D.C., 1865.
[Kennedy, J. C. G.]. *Preliminary Report on the Eighth Census, 1860.* Washington, D.C., 1862.
Maine Adjutant General's Office. *Annual Report of the Adjutant General of the State of Maine, for the Year Ending December 13, 1861.* Augusta, 1862.
Supplement to the Official Records of the Union and Confederate Armies. 100 vols. Wilmington, N.C., 1994.

U.S. Census Office. Eighth Census [1860]. *Population of the United States in 1860.*
Washington, D.C., 1861.

U.S. Senate. 37th Cong., 3rd sess. *Report of the Joint Committee on the Conduct of the
War.* 10 vols. Washington, D.C., 1863–66.

U.S. War Department. *The War of the Rebellion: A Compilation of the Official Records
of the Union and Confederate Armies.* 128 vols. Washington, D.C., 1880–1901.

PUBLISHED PRIMARY SOURCES

Adams, Charles R., ed. *A Post of Honor: The Pryor Letters, 1861–63, Letters from Capt.
S. G. Pryor, Twelfth Georgia Regiment.* Fort Valley, Ga., 1989.

Addey, Markinfield. *The Life and Military Career of Thomas Jonathan Jackson.* New
York, 1863.

Allan, William. *History of the Campaign of Gen. T. J. (Stonewall) Jackson in the
Shenandoah Valley of Virginia, from November 4, 1861, to June 17, 1862.*
Philadelphia, 1880.

The American Annual Cyclopedia and Register of Important Events of the Year. New
York, 1862.

Ammen, S. Z. "An Incident of Stonewall Jackson's Valley Campaign." *Southern
Historical Society Papers* 13 (1885): 430–33.

Anonymous. Letter to the editor, March 28, 1862. *Richmond Dispatch*, April 2, 1862.

———. Letter to the editor, May 26, 1862. *Rochester Union and Advertiser*, May 29, 1862.

———. Letter to the editor, June 9, 1862. *Rochester Democrat and American*, June 17,
1862.

———. Letter to the editor, February 28, 1862. *Scioto Gazette*, March 11, 1862.

———. Letter to the editor, April 21, 1862. *Scioto Gazette*, May 13, 1862.

———. Letter to the editor, May 20, 1862. *Scioto Gazette*, June 10, 1862.

———. Letter to the editor, June 21, 1862. *Scioto Gazette*, July 1, 1862.

Armstrong, James H. "General Frémont's Failure." *National Tribune*, October 18,
1923.

Arnold, Delevan. *A Kalamazoo Volunteer in the Civil War.* Kalamazoo, Mich., 1962.

Ashby, Thomas A. *The Valley Campaigns, Being the Reminiscences of a Non-Combatant
While between the Lines in the Shenandoah Valley during the War of the States.* New
York, 1914.

Atwood, Joseph S. "Driving Jackson." *National Tribune*, March 3, 1898.

Avirett, James B. *The Memoirs of General Turner Ashby and His Compeers.* Baltimore,
1867.

Baker, Samuel C. Letter to the editor, January 6, 1862. *Shirleysburg Herald*, January 12, 1862.

Bard, John P. "The Affair at Harrisonburg, Va." *National Tribune*, August 31, 1893.

Baldwin, W. E. "Port Republic." *National Tribune*, September 25, 1884.

Barclay, Alexander T. *Ted Barclay: Liberty Hall Volunteers: Letters from the Stonewall Brigade*. Edited by Charles W. Turner. Natural Bridge Station, Va., 1992.

Barnum, Enoch. "Shenandoah Valley." *National Tribune*, September 24, 1891.

Barow, Henry. "Civil War Letters." *North Carolina Historical Review* 34 (January 1957): 68–85.

Basler, Roy, ed. *Collected Works of Abraham Lincoln*. 10 vols. New Brunswick, N.J., 1953.

"Battle of Kernstown." *National Tribune*, September 8, 1882.

Batts, William. "A Foot Soldier's Account." *Georgia Historical Quarterly* 50 (March 1966): 87–100.

Baxter, Nancy N., ed. *Hoosier Farmboy in Lincoln's Army: The Civil War Letters of Pvt. John R. McClure*. Indianapolis, 1992.

Bayard, Samuel J. *The Life of George Dashiell Bayard*. New York, 1874.

Baylor, George. *Bull Run to Bull Run; or, Four Years in the Army of Northern Virginia*. Richmond, 1900.

Baylor, William S. H. Letter to the editor, April 22, 1861. *Staunton Republican Vindicator*, April 26, 1861.

Bean, W. G., ed. "The Valley Campaign of 1862 as Revealed in Letters of Sandie Pendleton." *Virginia Magazine of History and Biography* 78, no. 3 (July 1970): 326–64.

Beaudry, Louis N. *Historical Record of the Fifth New York Cavalry, First Ira Harris Guard*. Albany, 1868.

Beelman, J. M. "It Was the 12th Ohio Battery." *National Tribune*, February 9, 1917.

Blain, W. I. *A Narrative of My Personal Experiences during the War*. Toledo, Ohio, 1931.

Blair, William A., ed. *A Politician Goes to War: The Civil War Letters of John White Geary*. University Park, Pa., 1993.

Booth, George W. *Personal Reminiscences of a Maryland Soldier in the War between the States, 1861–1865*. Baltimore, 1898.

Boteler, Alexander R. "Stonewall Jackson in the Campaign of 1862." *Southern Historical Society Papers*, n.s. 2, 40 (1917): 162–82.

———. "Stonewall Jackson's Discontent." In *Battles and Leaders of the Civil War*, vol. 6, edited by Peter Cozzens, 102–13. Urbana, Ill., 2004.

Boyce, Charles W. "A Story of the Shenandoah Valley in 1862." *Blue and Gray* 3 (1894): 243–48.

———. *Twenty-eighth Regiment New York State Volunteers*. Buffalo, N.Y., 1896.

Boyd, Belle. *Belle Boyd in Camp and Prison*. New York, 1865.

Boyd, Casper W. "Casper W. Boyd, Company I, 15th Alabama Infantry." *Alabama Historical Quarterly* 23 (1961): 291–99.

Boyd, David F. *Reminiscences of the War in Virginia.* Edited by T. Michael Parish. Baton Rouge, 1994.

Boyle, John R. *Soldiers True: The Story of the One Hundred and Eleventh Regiment Pennsylvania Veteran Volunteers.* Cincinnati, 1903.

Breck, George. Letter to the editor, May 27, 1862. *Rochester (N.Y.) Union and Advertiser,* June 2, 1862.

——. Letter to the editor, June 1, 1862. *Rochester Union and Advertiser,* June 6, 1862.

——. Letter to the editor, June 10, 1962. *Rochester Union and Advertiser,* June 16, 1862.

——. Letter to the editor, June 18, 1862. *Rochester Union and Advertiser,* July 2, 1862.

Brewster, J. H. "Bullet and Shell: How the 5th Conn. And 46th Pa. Stood up at Winchester," *National Tribune,* August 20, 1890.

"Brigadier General James Shields." *Philadelphia Inquirer,* March 26, 1862.

Brown, Edmund R. *The Twenty-seventh Indiana Volunteer Infantry in the War of the Rebellion.* Monticello, In., 1899.

Brown, Edwin F. Letter to Isaac Butts, June 8, 1862. *Rochester (N.Y.) Union and Advertiser,* June 14, 1862.

Brown, Kirk. "Heard Shields Rebuke McDowell." *National Tribune.* July 28, 1904.

Brown, W. J. "Winchester." *National Tribune,* September 22, 1887.

Bryant, Edwin E. *History of the Third Wisconsin Volunteer Infantry.* Madison, 1891.

Buchanan, John B. "Banks's Advance and Retreat." *National Tribune,* April 22, 1926.

——. "On Gen. Banks's Retreat." *National Tribune,* July 29, 1926.

Buck, Samuel D. *With the Old Confeds: Actual Experiences of a Captain in the Line.* Baltimore, 1925.

Burnett, Edmund C., ed. "Letters of Barnett Hardeman Cody and Others, 1861 to 1864." *Georgia Historical Quarterly* 23 (1939): 265–99, 362–80.

Cammack, John H. *Personal Reminiscences of Private John Henry Cammack.* Huntington, W.Va., 1920.

Camper, Charles, and J. W. Kirkley. *Historical Record of the First Maryland Infantry.* Washington, D.C., 1871.

Capehart, Henry. "Capehart's Rejoinder: Gen. Shields at the Bridge at Port Republic." *National Tribune,* August 8, 1889.

——. "Shenandoah Campaign." *National Tribune,* February 13, 1890.

——. "Shenandoah Valley: Operations in Virginia during the Year 1862: Battle of Kernstown." *National Tribune,* March 14, 1889.

——. "Shenandoah Valley: Operations in Virginia during the Year 1862: Shields and Jackson." *National Tribune,* March 21, 1889.

——. "Shenandoah Valley: Operations in Virginia during the Year 1862: Shields Moves Forward." *National Tribune,* March 28, 1889.

——. "Shenandoah Valley: Operations in Virginia during the Year 1862: Gen. Ashby Killed." *National Tribune*, April 25, 1889.

——. "Shenandoah Valley: Operations in Virginia during the Year 1862: Frémont's Inactivity." *National Tribune*, May 2, 1889.

——. "Shenandoah Valley: Operations in Virginia during the Year 1862: Port Republic." *National Tribune*, May 9, 1889.

"Caroms," "From General Frémont's Command." *Sandusky Daily Commercial Register*, June 20, 1862.

Carr, Henry. Letter to his mother, May 26, 1862. *Rochester Union and Advertiser*, May 31, 1862.

Casler, John O. *Four Years in the Stonewall Brigade*. 1906. Reprint, Dayton, Ohio, 1971.

Cass, Samuel W. "Valley Campaign: A Comrade Sides with Capt. Huntington." *National Tribune*, December 19, 1889.

Chandler, J. M. Letter to his father, May 14, 1862. *Ashland (Ohio) Union*, May 28, 1862.

Chilson, Eugene. "Covering Banks's Retreat." *National Tribune*, November 1, 1917.

Clark, Charles M. *The History of the Thirty-ninth Illinois Volunteer Infantry*. Chicago, 1889.

Clark, Van Buren. "Jackson at Cross Keys." *Atlanta Journal*, October 26, 1907.

Clark, Walter A., ed. *Under the Stars and Bars; or, Memories of Four Years' Service with the Oglethorpes of Augusta, Georgia*. Augusta, 1900.

Clarke, H. C. *The Confederate States Almanac and Repository of Useful Knowledge*. Vicksburg, Miss., 1862.

Clarke, James. "Someone Has Blundered: A Federal Writes of Port Republic." Edited by Stephen Davis. *Civil War Times Illustrated* 19, no. 7 (November 1980): 30–33.

Clement, Henry C. "Jackson at the Bridge." In *War Recollections of the Confederate Veterans of Pittsylvania County, Virginia, 1861–1865*, 36–38. N.p., ca. 1965.

Clouds, George C. "Port Republic." *National Tribune*, December 18, 1884.

——. "A Reminiscence of Cross Keys." *National Tribune*, June 14, 1883.

Coles, Isaac. "War Reminiscences of Capt. Isaac Coles." In *War Recollections of the Confederate Veterans of Pittsylvania County, Virginia, 1861–1865*, 22–28. N.p., ca. 1965.

Collis, Charles H. T. "From Gen. Banks's Command." *Mount Vernon (Ohio) Republican*, June 5, 1862.

"Colonel John R. Kenly." *Philadelphia Public Ledger*, May 27, 1862.

[Conerly, L. W.]. *A Historical Sketch of the Quitman Guards, Company E, Sixteenth Mississippi Regiment, Harris' Brigade*. New Orleans, 1866.

"Confederate Monument at Charlottesville, Va.—Tribute to Gen. Ashby." *Confederate Veteran* 5, no. 4 (April 1897): 150–51.

Corlett, William. "Port Republic." *National Tribune*, September 1, 1917.

Covert, J. S. "Port Republic." *National Tribune*, January 1, 1885.

——. "Port Republic." *National Tribune*, October 30, 1894.

Cox, Jacob D. *Military Reminiscences of the Civil War*. 2 vols. New York, 1900.

Craig, Thomas H. "Shields' Division: A Delayed Report of the 84th Pennsylvania at Kernstown." *National Tribune*, November 21, 1889.

Culpepper, B. F. "The 15th Alabama with Trimble in the Shenandoah Valley." *Atlanta Journal*, September 21, 1901.

Cunningham, Francis M. "Port Republic." *National Tribune*, June 2, 1904.

Curry, William Leontes. *Four Years in the Saddle: History of the First Regiment Ohio Volunteer Cavalry, War of the Rebellion, 1861–1865*. 1898. Reprint, Jonesboro, Ga., 1984.

"D." Letter to the editor, March 30, 1862. *Washington County (Pa.) Reporter and Tribune*, April 6, 1862.

Dabney, Robert L. "Stonewall Jackson." *Southern Historical Society Papers* 11 (1883): 125–35.

Danues, C. Z. "Winchester Again." *National Tribune*, September 2, 1918.

Davis, Charles E., Jr. *Three Years in the Army: The Story of the Thirteenth Massachusetts Volunteers*. Boston, 1894.

Davis, Jefferson. *Rise and Fall of the Confederate Government*. 2 vols. New York, 1881.

Davis, Major S. Letter to the editor, March 21, 1862. *Sandusky (Ohio) Register*, April 1, 1862.

Davis, Varina H. *Jefferson Davis: A Memoir by His Wife*. 2 vols. New York, 1890.

"Death of Gen. Ed. Johnson." *Richmond Daily Dispatch*, March 4, 1873.

"The Death of General Turner Ashby, by a Member of Stonewall Jackson's Staff." *The Old Guard* 4, no. 8 (August 1866): 473–78.

Dennett, Tyler, ed. *Lincoln in the Civil War in the Diaries and Letters of John Hay*. New York, 1988.

"Diary of Capt. H. W. Wingfield." *Bulletin of the Virginia State Library* 16, nos. 2 and 3 (July 1927): 7–47.

Dickenson, F. S. "The Fifth New York Cavalry in the Valley." *The Maine Bugle Campaign* 1, Call 2 (April 1894): 147–57.

"Dixie." Letter to the editor, June 5, 1862. *Pomeroy (Ohio) Telegraph*, June 27, 1862.

Donohue, John C. "Fight at Front Royal." *Southern Historical Society Papers* 24 (1896): 131–38.

Douglas, Henry Kyd. *I Rode with Stonewall*. Chapel Hill, 1940.

——. "A Ride for Stonewall." *Southern Historical Society Papers* 19 (1893): 206–12.

——. "Why Stonewall Jackson Resigned." *Philadelphia Weekly Times* 5, no. 21 (July 16, 1881).

Duncan, Russell, ed. *Blue-Eyed Child of Fortune: The Civil War Letters of Robert Gould Shaw*. Athens, Ga., 1992.

Dwight, Elizabeth A., ed. *Life and Letters of Wilder Dwight, Lieut.-Col. Second Mass. Inf. Vols.* Boston, 1891.

Eby, Cecil D., Jr., ed. *A Virginia Yankee in the Civil War: The Diaries of David Hunter Strother.* Chapel Hill, 1961.

Eddy, Richard. *History of the Sixtieth Regiment New York State Volunteers.* Philadelphia, 1864.

Ellison, Joseph M. "War Letters." *Georgia Historical Quarterly* 48 (1964): 229–38.

Elwood, John W. *Elwood's Stories of the Old Ringgold Cavalry, 1847–1865.* Coal Center, Pa., 1914.

Ensley, Philip, ed. *The Civil War Letters of Private Aungier Dobbs.* Apollo, Pa., 1991.

Ewait, John. "The 25th Ohio." *National Tribune,* November 25, 1920.

Ewell, Benjamin S. "Jackson and Ewell: The Latter's Opinion of His Chief." *Southern Historical Society Papers* 20 (1892): 26–33.

Farrar, Samuel Clark. *The Twenty-second Pennsylvania Cavalry and the Ringgold Battalion, 1861–1865.* Pittsburg, 1911.

"The First West Virginia." *National Tribune,* October 9, 1884.

Fishburne, Clement D. "Sketch of Rockbridge Artillery." *Southern Historical Society Papers* 23 (1895): 98–158.

Fonerden, C. A. *A Brief History of the Military Career of Carpenter's Battery.* New Market, Va., 1911.

——. "Carpenter's Battery of the Stonewall Brigade." *Southern Historical Society Papers* 28 (1900): 166–68.

Forbes, Archibald. "Abraham Lincoln as a Strategist: Part 1." *North American Review* 155, no. 428 (July 1892): 53–69.

Foster, James P. "Criticizing Capehart." *National Tribune,* May 2, 1889.

Foulk, W. L. Letter to the editor, May 26, 1862. *Philadelphia Daily Evening Bulletin,* May 29, 1862.

Fowler, Thomas C. "Criticizing Capehart: The Troops That Captured the Stone Wall At Kernstown." *National Tribune,* May 16, 1889.

Fravel, John W. "Jackson's Valley Campaign." *Confederate Veteran* 6, no. 9 (September 1898): 418–21.

Frazier, Lee. "At Kernstown." *National Tribune,* September 26, 1912.

"From Lieutenant Colonel Parham of the 29th." *Philadelphia Public Ledger,* May 27, 1862.

"Further from Valley Mountain." *Macon Daily Telegraph,* January 4, 1862.

Galwey, Thomas F. *The Valiant Hours: Narrative of "Captain Brevet," an Irish-American in the Army of the Potomac.* Harrisburg, Pa., 1961.

"The Game Cock of the Valley." *Macon Daily Telegraph,* June 16, 1862.

Gates, Betsey, ed. *The Colton Letters, Civil War Period, 1861–1865.* Scottsdale, Ariz., 1993.

"General Lander." *Boston Saturday Evening Express*, March 8, 1862.

Gibbon, John. *Personal Recollections of the Civil War*. New York, 1928.

Gildea, James. *A Magnificent Irishman from Appalachia: The Letters of Lt. James Gildea, First Ohio Light Artillery, Battery L*. Milford, Ohio, 2003.

Gill, John. *Reminiscences of Four Years as a Private Soldier in the Confederate Army, 1861–1865*. Baltimore, 1891.

[Gillespie, Samuel L.]. *A History of Company A, First Ohio Cavalry, 1861–1865*. Washington Court House, Ohio, 1898.

Goldsborough, W. W. "How Ashby was Killed." *Southern Historical Society Papers* 21 (1893): 224–26.

Goldthorpe, George W. "The Battle of McDowell, May 8, 1862." *West Virginia History* 13, no. 3 (April 1962): 170–208.

Goodrich, Earle S. "At Port Republic." *National Tribune*, July 11, 1889.

Gordon, George H. *Brook Farm to Cedar Mountain in the War of the Great Rebellion, 1861–62*. Boston, 1883.

Gould, John M. *History of the First–Tenth–Twenty-ninth Maine Regiment*. Portland, Maine, 1871.

[Grabill, John]. *Diary of a Soldier of the Stonewall Brigade*. Woodstock, Va., 1909.

Graham, Almon M. "Banks' Retreat." *National Tribune*, May 24, 1917.

Gregg, James E. Letter to the editor, March 26, 1862. *Sandusky (Ohio) Register*, April 3, 1862.

"Gurley." Letter to parents, June 12, 1862. *Akron Summit Beacon*, June 26, 1862.

Haas, Ralph, ed. *Dear Esther: The Civil War Letters of Private Aungier Dobbs*. Apollo, Pa., 1991.

Hall, James E. *The Diary of a Confederate Soldier*. Edited by Ruth Woods Dayton. Charlestown, W.Va., 1961.

Harding, Joseph F. *French Harding: Civil War Memoirs*. Edited by Victor L. Thacker. Parsons, W.Va., 2001.

Harman, George, ed. "The Military Experience of James A. Pfeifer." *North Carolina Historical Review* 32 (1955): 385–409, 544–72.

[Harman, M. G.]. *"Stonewall Jackson's Way": A Sketch of the Life and Services of Major John A. Harman . . . by an Old Comrade*. Staunton, Va., 1876.

Hart, S. W. "From Battlefield to Prison." *National Tribune*, August 13, 1903.

———. "Fighting Stonewall Jackson." *National Tribune*, October 18, 1927.

Hartman, Peter S. *Life of Peter S. Hartman*. Harrisonburg, Va., 1937.

[Hartzell, Harrison W.]. "From the Eighth Regiment." *Tiffin Tribune*, June 20, 1862.

Haupt, Herman. *Reminiscences of General Herman Haupt*. Milwaukee, 1901.

Hays, E. Z., ed. *History of the Thirty-second Regiment Ohio Veteran Volunteer Infantry*. Columbus, Ohio, 1896.

Henderson, Henry E. *Yankee in Gray*. Cleveland, 1962.

Herndon, John G. "Infantry and Cavalry Service." *Confederate Veteran* 30, no. 5 (May 1922): 172–76.

"He Served His Country Well." *Confederate Veteran* 4, no. 3, (March 1896): 69.

Hewes, M. Warner. "Turner Ashby's Courage." *Confederate Veteran* 5, no. 12 (December 1897): 613.

Higgins, Thomas W. Letter to the editor, May 8, 1862. *Wood County Independent*, May 28, 1862.

Hinkley, Julian W. *A Narrative of Service with the Third Wisconsin Infantry*. Madison, Wis., 1912.

Holt, David. *A Mississippi Rebel in the Army of Northern Virginia: The Civil War Memoirs of Private David Holt*. Edited by Thomas D. Cockrell and Michael B. Ballard. Baton Rouge, 1995.

Hooper, Isaac. Letter to the editor, January 6, 1862. *Alatoona Tribune*, January 16, 1862.

Hotchkiss, Jedediah. *Make Me a Map of the Valley: The Civil War Journal of Stonewall Jackson's Cartographer*. Edited by Archie P. McDonald. Foreword by T. Harry Williams. Dallas, 1973.

——. "Stonewall's Staff." *Richmond Dispatch*, August 9, 1898.

Houghton, William. "Capehart Criticized." *National Tribune*, June 13, 1889.

Houghton, William R. *Two Boys in the Civil War and After*. Montgomery, Ala., 1912.

Houtz, John W. "The Affair at Port Republic." *National Tribune*, February 9, 1911.

Howard, John R. "Frémont in the Civil War." In *Personal Recollections of the War of the Rebellion: Addresses Delivered before the Commandery of the State of New York, Military Order of the Loyal Legion of the United States, Third Series*, 177–95. New York, 1907.

Howard, McHenry. *Recollections of a Maryland Confederate Soldier and Staff Officer under Johnston, Jackson, and Lee*. Dayton, Ohio, 1975.

Huckaby, Elizabeth Paisley, and Ethel C. Simpson, eds. *Tulip Evermore: Emma Butler and William Paisley: Their Lives in Letters, 1857–1887*. Fayetteville, Ark., 1985.

Huffman, James. *Ups and Downs of a Confederate Soldier*. New York, 1940.

Huggins, Herman B. "Letter from the 60th Ohio." *Highland Weekly News*, July 3, 1862.

Huntington, James F. "Winchester to Port Republic." In *Papers of the Military Historical Society of Massachusetts*, vol. 1 of *Campaigns in Virginia, 1861–1862*, 303–35. Boston, 1895.

Hurst, Samuel H. *Journal History of the Seventy-third Ohio Volunteer Infantry*. Chillicothe, Ohio, 1866.

Hutchison, E. M. "The Battle of McDowell: Our Little Band of Heroes." Edited by David Cornelius. *Civil War Times Illustrated* 21, no. 5 (September 1982): 38–39.

Imboden, John D. "Incidents of the First Bull Run." In *Battles and Leaders of the Civil*

War, Grant-Lee Edition, edited by Robert C. Johnson and Clarence C. Buel, 1(1):229–45. New York, 1888.

———. "Jackson at Harpers Ferry." In *Battles and Leaders of the Civil War, Grant-Lee Edition*, edited by Robert C. Johnson and Clarence C. Buel, 1(1):111–26.

———. "Stonewall Jackson in the Shenandoah Valley." *Century* 30, no. 2 (June 1885): 280–93.

J. H. J. [John H. Jack]. Letter to the editor, March 26, 1862. *Sandusky Register*, April 3, 1862.

J. M. R. Letter to his brother, March 19, 1862. *Akron Summit Beacon*, April 10, 1862.

J. V. Letter to the editor, May 29, 1862. *Rochester Union and Advertiser*, June 7, 1862.

Jackson, Mary Anna. *Memoirs of Stonewall Jackson, by His Widow*. Louisville, Ky., 1895.

Jacobs, F. S. Letter to the editor, May 10, 1862. *Ashland (Ohio) Union*, May 21, 1862.

———. Letter to the editor, June 22, 1862. *Ashland Union*, July 2, 1862.

Johnson, B. F. *Bull Run to Bull Run; or, Four Years in the Army of Northern Virginia*. Richmond, 1900.

Johnson, Bradley T. "Fight with the Bucktails." *Southern Historical Society Papers* 10 (1882): 103.

———. "Memoir of the First Maryland Regiment." *Southern Historical Society Papers* 10 (1882): 446–56.

Johnson, George K. *The Battle of Kernstown, March 23, 1862: A Paper Prepared and Read before the Michigan Commandery of the Military Order of the Loyal Legion of the United States*. Detroit, 1890.

Johnson, Robert Underwood, and Clarence Clough Buel, eds. *Battles and Leaders of the Civil War*. 4 vols. New York, 1884–87.

Johnson, Wallace W. "About the Bucktails." *National Tribune*, January 7, 1886.

Jones, B. F. "Battle of Port Republic." *National Tribune*, December 11, 1884.

Jones, J. William. "The Old Virginia Town, Lexington." *Confederate Veteran* 1, no. 1 (January 1893): 18–19.

———. "Reminiscences of the Army of Northern Virginia, Paper No. 3: Down the Valley after Stonewall's 'Quartermaster.'" *Southern Historical Society Papers* 9, no. 4, (April 1881): 185–89.

———. "Reminiscences of the Army of Northern Virginia, Paper No. 4: Capture of Winchester and Rout of Banks' Army." *Southern Historical Society Papers* 9, no. 5, (May 1881): 123–37.

———. "Reminiscences of the Army of Northern Virginia, Paper No. 5: "How Frémont and Shields 'Caught' Stonewall Jackson." *Southern Historical Society Papers* 9, no. 6, (June 1881): 273–80.

———. "Reminiscences of the Army of Northern Virginia, Paper No. 6: "From Port

Republic to the Chickahominy." *Southern Historical Society Papers* 9, nos. 7 and 8 (July–August 1881): 362–69.

Jones, Rollin L. "The Battery Horses." *National Tribune*, June 27, 1889.

Jones, Terry L., ed. *Campbell Brown's Civil War; with Ewell and the Army of Northern Virginia*. Baton Rouge, 2001.

Kean, Robert G. H. *Inside the Confederate Government: The Diary of Robert Garlick Hill Kean*. Edited by Edward Younger. Baton Rouge, 1993.

Keesy, W. A. *War as Viewed from the Ranks*. Norwalk, Conn., 1898.

Kellogg, Sanford C. *The Shenandoah Valley, 1861 to 1865: A War Study*. New York, 1903.

Kelly, Henry B. *Port Republic*. Philadelphia, 1886.

Kepler, William. *History of the Three Months and Three Years' Service of the Fourth Regiment Ohio Volunteer Infantry in the War for the Union*. Cleveland, 1886.

Kimball, Nathan. "Fighting Jackson at Kernstown." In *Battles and Leaders of the Civil War, Grant-Lee Edition*, edited by Robert C. Johnson and Clarence C. Buel, 2(1): 302–13. New York, 1888.

Koerner, Gustav. "General Shields." *Century* 23, no. 4 (April 1887): 973–75.

Koiner, Absalom. Letter to the editor, April 20, 1861. *Staunton Republican Vindicator*, April 26, 1861.

Kurtz, George W. "Captain George W. Kurtz's Account of the Valley Campaign of 1862." In *Diaries, Letters, and Recollections of the War between the States*, 46–48. Winchester, Va., 1955.

Ladley, Oscar D. *Hearth and Knapsack: The Ladley Letters, 1857–1880*. Edited By Carl M. Becker and Ritchie Thomas. Athens, Ohio, 1988.

Landon, William, ed. "Fourteenth Indiana Regiment: Letters to the Vincennes Western Sun." *Indiana Magazine of History* 30 (September 1934): 275–98.

Lathrop, William. Letter to the editor, May 26, 1862. *Rochester (N.Y.) Union and Advertiser*, May 30, 1862.

Lathrop, William. Letter to the editor, June 9, 1862. *Rochester Union and Advertiser*, June 13, 1862.

Lee, Alvid E. "The Battle of Cross Keys." *Magazine of American History* 15 (1885): 483–91.

———. "Battles of Port Republic and Lewiston." *Magazine of American History* 15 (1885): 590–95.

———. "Our First Battle: Bull Pasture Mountain." *Magazine of American History* 15 (1885): 391–96.

Lee, Mary Greenhow. Letter to the editor, March 27, 1862. *Richmond Enquirer*, April 6, 1862.

Lemley, T. H. B. "From a First West Virginia Trooper." *National Tribune*, March 26, 1895.

"Letter from the 60th Ohio." *Highland (Ohio) Weekly News*, May 15, 1862.

"Letter from the 60th Ohio." *Highland Weekly News*, June 5, 1862.

Lewis, Alfred. "How Jackson Escaped." *National Tribune*, February 4, 1904.

Lewis, Samuel E. "General T. J. (Stonewall) Jackson and His Medical Director, Hunter McGuire, M.D., at Winchester, May 1862." *Southern Historical Society Papers* 30 (1902): 226–35.

Lindsey, J. C. "The Battle of Port Republic." *National Tribune*, June 18, 1903.

Lightsey, Ada Christine, [and R. J. Lightsey]. *The Veteran's Story*. Meridian, Miss., 1899.

Long, Andrew D. *Stonewall's 'Foot Cavalryman': Andrew Davidson Long, Company A, Fifth Virginia Regiment*. Edited by Walter E. Long, Austin, Tex., 1965.

Lostutter, David, Jr. "Port Republic." *National Tribune*, January 29, 1885.

Lydy, Alexander. "Battle of Port Republic." *National Tribune*, December 12, 1912.

Magill, Mary T. "Annals of the War: A Battle-Scarred City." *Philadelphia Weekly Times*, July 28, 1877.

Marvin, Edwin E. *The Fifth Regiment Connecticut Volunteers*. Hartford, 1889.

"Massanhuttan [sic]." "The Trap to Catch Stonewall." *Richmond Dispatch*, June 11, 1862.

Maury, Dabney H. "General T. J. 'Stonewall' Jackson: Incidents in the Remarkable Career of the Great Soldier." *Southern Historical Society Papers* 25 (1898): 309–16.

McClellan, George B. *McClellan's Own Story*. New York, 1887.

[McClendon, William]. *Recollections of War Times by an Old Veteran While under Stonewall Jackson and Lieutenant General James Longstreet*. Montgomery, Ala. 1909.

McDonald, Cornelia P. *A Diary, with Reminiscences of the War and Refugee Life in the Shenandoah Valley, 1860–1865*. Nashville, Tenn., 1935.

McDonald, Edward H. "Fighting under Ashby in the Shenandoah." *Civil War Times Illustrated* 5 (July 1966): 28–35.

McDonald, William N. *A History of the Laurel Brigade*. Baltimore, 1907.

McGuire, Hunter. "General Thomas J. Jackson." *Southern Historical Society Papers* 19 (1891): 298–317.

——. "General T. J. Jackson, His Career and Character." *Southern Historical Society Papers* 25 (1897): 91–112.

McIlwaine, Richard. *Memories of Three Score Years and Ten*. New York, 1908.

McKee, Thomas H. "Correcting Col. Oates." *National Tribune*, June 21, 1894.

McKim, Randolph H. *A Soldier's Recollections: Leaves from the Diary of a Young Confederate*. New York, 1910.

McLaughlin, John. *A Memoir of Hector Tyndale*. Philadelphia, 1882.

Merrill, Samuel H. *The Campaigns of the First Maine and First District of Columbia Cavalry*. Portland, Maine, 1866.

Milano, Anthony J. "Letters from the Harvard Regiments." *Civil War: The Magazine of the Civil War Society* 13 (April 1988): 44.

Miller, Abram S. "Selected Letters of Abram Schultz Miller to His Wife, Julia Virginia Miller, Describing Civil War Action in and around Winchester." In *Diaries, Letters, and Recollections of the War between the States*, 20–29. Winchester, Va., 1955.

Monfort, E. R. "From Grafton to McDowell through Tygart's Valley." In *Sketches of War History, 1861–1865: Papers Read before the Ohio Commandery of the Military Order of the Loyal Legion of the United States*, 2:1–21. Cincinnati, 1888.

Monroe, R. J. "Shenandoah Valley." *National Tribune*, April 11, 1889.

Moore, Cleon. "Stonewall Jackson at Port Republic." *Confederate Veteran* 22, no. 11 (November 1914): 511.

Moore, Frank, ed. *The Rebellion Record: A Diary of American Events*. 12 vols. New York, 1977.

Moore, Joseph A. "Campaigning in West Virginia." *National Tribune*, May 9, 1901.

———. "Shenandoah Valley." *National Tribune*, November 5, 1891.

Morgan, F. S. "With Bayard's Brigade." *National Tribune*, June 18, 1925.

Morse, Charles F. *Letters Written during the Civil War, 1861–1865*. Boston, 1898.

Munford, Thomas T. "Reminiscences of Jackson's Valley Campaign." *Southern Historical Society Papers* 7 (1879): 522–35.

Myerhoff, Charles H. "Battle of Winchester." *National Tribune*, July 1, 1886.

Myers, Frank M. *The Comanches: A History of White's Battalion, Virginia Cavalry*. Baltimore, 1871.

Nachtigall, Hermann. *History of the 75th Regiment Pa. Vols*. North Riverside, Ill., 1987.

"A Narrative of the Service of Colonel Geo. A. Porterfield in Northern Virginia in 1861–'2." *Southern Historical Society Papers* 16 (1888): 82–91.

New, George W. "Criticizing Goodrich." *National Tribune*, August 1, 1889.

Newcomer, C. Armour. *Cole's Cavalry; or, Three Years in the Saddle in the Shenandoah Valley*. Baltimore, 1895.

Nicolay, John G., and John Hay. "Abraham Lincoln: A History: Jackson's Valley Campaign and the Seven Days' Battles." *Century* 37, no. 1 (November 1888): 130–44.

———. *Abraham Lincoln: A History*. 10 vols. New York, 1890.

Nisbet, James C. *Four Years on the Firing Line*. 1915. Reprint, edited by Bell I. Wiley. Jackson, Miss., 1963.

Norris, J. E. *History of the Lower Shenandoah Valley*. Chicago, 1890.

Norton, Henry. *Deeds of Daring; or, History of the Eighth N.Y. Volunteer Cavalry*. Norwich, Conn., 1889.

"Notae." "From Shields' Division." Letter to the editor, March 29, 1862. *Lawrenceville Journal*, April 12, 1862.

Oates, William C. *The War between the United States and the Confederacy and Its Lost*

Opportunities, with a History of the 15th Alabama Regiment. 1905. Reprint, Dayton, Ohio, 1974.

Page, John W. "At Port Republic." *National Tribune*, November 3, 1910.

Parsons, H. W. "Port Republic: How We Failed to Reach the Battlefield and Relieve the Wounded." *Ohio Soldier*, August 20, 1887.

Patterson, Newell. "The Shenandoah Valley: Gen. Frémont's Chase after Stonewall Jackson in June 1862." *National Tribune*, January 16, 1919.

Paulus, Margaret B., ed. *Milroy Family Letters, 1862–1863*. Vol. 1 of *Papers of General Robert Huston Milroy*. N.p., n.d.

Paxton, John G., ed. *The Civil War Letters of General Frank "Bull" Paxton, C.S.A.* 1905. Reprint, Hillsboro, Tex., 1978.

Peck, R. H. *Reminiscences of a Confederate Soldier, of Co. C., 2nd Va. Cavalry*. [Fincastle, Va., 1913].

Peterson, Frederick A. *Military Review of the Campaign in Virginia and Maryland in 1862*. New York, 1862.

Pile, George C. "The War Story of a Confederate Soldier Boy, Part 2." *Bristol (Tenn.-Va.) Herald-Courier*, January 30, 1921.

Pilsen, John. *Reply of Lieut.-Col. Pilsen to Emil Schalk's Criticisms of the Campaign in the Mountain Department, under Maj.-Gen. J. C. Frémont*. New York, 1863.

Poague, William T. *Gunner with Stonewall*. Edited by Monroe F. Cockrell. 1957. Reprint, Wilmington, N.C., 1987.

Pope, E. W. Letter to the editor, June 2, 1862. *Rochester (N.Y.) Union and Advertiser*, June 9, 1862.

"Port Republic." *National Tribune*, December 12, 1885.

Pyne, Henry R. *The History of the First New Jersey Cavalry*. Trenton, N.J., 1871.

Quaife, Milo M., ed. *From the Cannon's Mouth: The Civil War Letters of General Alpheus S. Williams*. Detroit, 1959.

Quint, Alonzo H. *The Potomac and the Rapidan*. Boston, 1864.

——. *The Record of the Second Massachusetts Infantry, 1861–1865*. Boston, 1867.

Rawling, C. J. *History of the First Regiment Virginia Infantry*. Philadelphia, 1887.

Reader, F. S. "Frémont at Cross Keys." *National Tribune*, November 8, 1923.

Reid, John G. "Port Republic." *National Tribune*, October 9, 1884.

R. H. H. Letter to the editor, May 18, 1862. *Pomeroy Telegraph*, June 6, 1862.

Richmond, A. S. Letter to the editor, May 28, 1862. *Orleans American (Albion, N.Y.)*, June 8, 1862.

——. Letter to his father, March 30, 1862. *Orleans American*, April 18, 1862.

[Riley, Franklin L.]. *Grandfather's Journal: Company B, Sixteenth Mississippi Infantry Volunteers*. Edited by Austin C. Dobbins. Dayton, Ohio, 1988.

Robson, John S. *How a One-Legged Rebel Lives: Reminiscences of the Civil War*. Richmond, 1876.

Rodgers, James G. "The 12th at McDowell." *Macon Daily Telegraph*, June 24, 1862.

Ross, Charles R. "Old Memories." In *War Papers Read before the Indiana Commandery, Military Order of the Loyal Legion of the United States*, 149–63. Indianapolis, 1898.

Ross, John De Hart. "Harper's Ferry to the Fall of Richmond: Letters of Colonel John De Hart Ross, C.S.A., 1861–1865." Edited by Richard W. Oram. *West Virginia History* 45 (1984): 159–74.

Rossiter, Charles W. "Orders Disobeyed." *National Tribune*, September 2, 1915.

Rowland, Dunbar. *Jefferson Davis, Constitutionalist: His Letters, Papers, and Speeches*. 10 vols. Jackson, Miss., 1923.

"Roxbury." Letters to the editor, March 10–12, 1862. *Roxbury (Mass.) City Gazette*, March 20, 1862.

———. Letter to the editor, March 12, 1862. *Roxbury City Gazette*, March 27, 1862.

Rupp, John. "Captured at Port Republic." *National Tribune*, March 27, 1887.

S. "From Shields' Division." *Dayton Weekly Journal*, July 1, 1862.

Salyards, Joseph. *Historical Review of Shenandoah County, Virginia*. New Market, Va., 1876.

Sawyer, Franklin. *A Military History of the 8th Regiment Ohio Vol. Inf'y*. Cleveland, 1881.

Schenck, Robert C. "Notes on the Battle of McDowell." In *Battles and Leaders of the Civil War, Grant-Lee Edition*, edited by Robert C. Johnson and Clarence C. Buel, 2(1):298. New York, 1888.

Schneider, Joseph N. "Winchester." *National Tribune*, August 12, 1886.

Schurz, Carl. *The Reminiscences of Carl Schurz*. 3 vols. New York, 1907.

Scott, Winfield. *Memoirs of Lieut.-General Scott*. 2 vols. New York, 1864.

Seaman, Elisha B. "At Port Republic, Va." *National Tribune*, November 24, 1910.

SeCheverell, John H. *Journal History of the Twenty-ninth Ohio Veteran Volunteers*. Cleveland, 1883.

Simpson, James R. "Criticizing Capehart," *National Tribune*, May 9, 1889.

Smalley, Virgil E. "Annals of the War: First Battle of Winchester." *Philadelphia Weekly Times*, April 26, 1884.

Smart, James G., ed. *A Radical View: The "Agate" Dispatches of Whitelaw Reid, 1861–1865*. Memphis, 1976.

Smith, C. Calvin, ed. "The Duties of Home and War: The Civil War Letters of John C. Marsh, 29th Ohio Volunteers." *Upper Ohio Valley Historical Review* 8 (1979): 7–20.

Smith, James P. "With Stonewall Jackson." *Southern Historical Society Papers*, n.s. 5, 43 (September 1920): 59–75.

Spiegel, Marcus M. *Your True Marcus: The Civil War Letters of a Jewish Colonel*. Kent, Ohio, 1985.

Sponaugle, George W. "Recollections of George W. Sponaugle." *Highland (Ohio) Recorder*, February 25, 1927.

"Statement of Capt. George Smith." *Philadelphia Public Ledger*, May 27, 1862.

Stearns, Austin C. *Three Years with Company K.* Edited by Arthur A. Kent. Rutherford, N.J., 1976.

Stein, David G. "The Battle of Winchester." *Cleveland Plain Dealer*, April 8, 1862.

———. Letter to the editor, March 27, 1862. *Cleveland Plain Dealer*, April 8, 1862.

Stone, Benjamin F., Jr. *The Civil War Letters of Captain B. F. Stone, Jr., 73rd Regiment, O.V.I.* Edited by Patricia F. Medert. Chillicothe, Ohio, 2002.

"The Story of the Illinois Central Line during the Civil Conflict, 861–65: General Banks." *Illinois Central Magazine* 1 (July 1913): 13–22.

Strickler, Givens. "Liberty Hall Volunteers, Company I, Fourth Virginia Infantry." *Washington and Lee University Historical Papers* 6 (1904): 111–22.

[Strother, D. H.]. "Personal Recollections of a Virginian (Fifth Paper)." *Harper's New Monthly Magazine* 34, no. 200 (January 1867): 172–96.

Suppler, E. M. "Shenandoah Valley, the Experiences of a 29th Ohio Soldier." *National Tribune*, May 16, 1889.

Taylor, Richard. *Destruction and Reconstruction: Personal Experiences of the Late War.* New York, 1883.

———. "Stonewall Jackson and the Valley Campaign." *North American Review* 126, no. 261 (March 1878): 238–62.

Thaxter, Sidney W. Letter to his family, May 27, 1862. *Bangor Daily Whig and Courier*, June 2, 1862.

———. *Sidney Warren Thaxter.* Portland, Maine, 1909.

Thompson, George W. Letter to the editor, May 29, 1862. *Baltimore American*, May 30, 1862.

Thompson, Orville. *From Philippi to Appomattox: Narrative of the Service of the Seventh Indiana Infantry in the War for the Union.* Baltimore, 1993.

Thomson, O. R., and William H. Rauch. *History of the "Bucktails," Kane Rifle Regiment of the Pennsylvania Reserve Corps.* Dayton, Ohio, 1988.

Tobie, Edward P. *History of the First Maine Cavalry.* Boston, 1887.

Toney, Marcus B. *The Privations of a Private.* Nashville, Tenn., 1905.

Tracy, Albert. "Frémont's Pursuit of Jackson in the Shenandoah Valley: The Journal Of Colonel Albert Tracy, March–July 1862." Edited by Francis F. Wayland. *Virginia Magazine of History and Biography* 70, nos. 2 and 3 (April and July 1962): 165–93, 332–54.

Van Dyke, Augustus M. "Early Days; or, The School of the Soldier." In *Sketches of War History, 1861–1865: Papers Read before the Ohio Commandery of the Military Order of the Loyal Legion of the United States*, 5:18–31. Cincinnati, 1903.

Voices of the Civil War: Shenandoah 1862. Alexandria, n.d.

Voris, Alvin C. *A Citizen-Soldier's Civil War: The Letters of Brevet Major General Alvin C. Voris.* Edited by Jerome Mushkat. Dekalb, Ill., 2002.

W. F. B. "Letter from the 60th Ohio." *Highland Weekly News*, September 4, 1862.

Waddell, John. "The Battle of Cross Keys." *National Tribune*, May 7, 1903.

Waddell, Joseph A. *Annals of Augusta County, Virginia, from 1726 to 1891.* Staunton, Va., 1902.

Waller, John. "With Banks from Strasburg to the Potomac." *Blue and Gray* 3 (1894): 194–96.

Walter, William J. "A Louisiana Volunteer: Letters of William J. Walter." *Southern Review* 19 (1933): 78–88.

Ward, Joseph R., Jr. *An Enlisted Soldier's View of the Civil War.* Edited by D. Duane Cummings and Daryl Hohweiler. West Lafayette, Ind., 1981.

Watkins, Sam H. *Co. Aytch: A Side Show of the Big Show.* New York, 1962.

Webb, Charles H. "Gen. Frémont's Command." *New York Times*, June 16, 1862.

——. "From Gen. Frémont's Army." *New York Times*, June 7, 1862.

——. "Overtaking the Enemy." *New York Times*, June 14, 1862.

Wells, Harvey S. "Annals of the War: With Shields in 1862." *Philadelphia Weekly Times*, March 28, 1885.

[Wheeler, William H.]. *In Memoriam: Letters of William Wheeler of the Class of 1855, Y. C.* Cambridge, Mass., 1875.

White, William S. *Sketches of the Life of Captain Hugh A. White of the Stonewall Brigade.* Columbia, S.C., 1864.

Wilder, Theodore. *The History of Company C, Seventh Regiment O.V.I.* Oberlin, Ohio, 1866.

"Will." Letters to the editor, March 22, 30, 1862. *Akron (Ohio) Summit Beacon*, April 10, 1862.

Williams, Edward B., ed. *Rebel Brothers: The Civil War Letters of the Truehearts.* College Station, Tex., 1995.

Willis, Francis T. "The Prisoner's Guard Reversed: Extract from a Letter of Capt. Edward Willis to His Mother." *Southern Historical Society Papers* 17 (1889): 172–77.

Wilson, E. E. "Fighting Jackson." *National Tribune*, July 20, 1899.

Wilson, William L. *A Borderland Confederate.* Edited by Festus P. Summers. Pittsburgh, 1962.

Winscott, Elliott. "Fighting Jackson: The 7th Indiana in the Shenandoah Valley in 1862." *National Tribune*, May 31, 1894.

Winslow, Horace. Letter to "Dear Eggleston," June 12, 1862. *Berkshire Eagle* (Pittsfield, Mass.), July 3, 1862.

Wood, George L. *The Seventh Regiment: A Record.* New York, 1865.

Wood, James H. *The War*. Cumberland, Md., 1911.

Woodward, C. Vann, ed. *Mary Chesnut's Civil War*. New Haven, 1981.

Work, F. M. "An Incident after the Battle of Cross Keys." *National Tribune*, June 10, 1886.

Worsham, John H. *One of Jackson's Foot Cavalry: His Experience and What He Saw during the War, 1861–1865*. New York, 1912.

Wright, Myron. Letter to his father, March 25, 1862. *Akron Summit Beacon*, April 10, 1862.

W. W. H. Letter to the editor, May 25, 1862. *Lynchburg Republican*, May 31, 1862.

Young, William S. "Shenandoah Valley." *National Tribune*, April 12, 1883.

SECONDARY SOURCES

Andrews, J. Cutler. *The North Reports the Civil War*. Pittsburgh, 1955.

Armstrong, Richard L. *Jackson's Valley Campaign: The Battle of McDowell, March 11–May 18, 1862*. Lynchburg, Va., 1990.

———. *25th Virginia Infantry and 9th Virginia Battalion*. Lynchburg, Va., 1990.

Ashby, Thomas A. *Life of Turner Ashby*. New York, 1914.

Ashcraft, John M. *31st Virginia Infantry*. Lynchburg, Va., 1988.

Ayers, Edward L. *In the Presence of Mine Enemies: War in the Heart of America, 1859–1863*. New York, 2003.

Baxter, Nancy N. *Gallant Fourteenth: The Story of an Indiana Civil War Regiment*. Traverse City, Mich., 1980.

Beck, Brandon, and Charles S. Grunder. *The First Battle of Winchester*. Lynchburg, Va. 1992.

Berkey, Jonathan M. "In the Very Midst of the War Track, the Valley's Civilians, and the Shenandoah Campaign," In *The Shenandoah Valley Campaign of 1862*, edited by Gary W. Gallagher, 86–114. Chapel Hill, 2003.

Bohannon, Keith S. "Placed on the Pages of History in Letters of Blood: Reporting on and Remembering the 12th Georgia Infantry in the 1862 Valley Campaign." In *The Shenandoah Valley Campaign of 1862*, edited by Gary W. Gallagher, 115–43. Chapel Hill, 2003.

Carmichael, Peter S. "Turner Ashby's Appeal." In *The Shenandoah Valley Campaign of 1862*, edited by Gary W. Gallagher, 144–73. Chapel Hill, 2003.

Chapla, John D. *42nd Virginia Infantry*. Lynchburg, Va., 1983.

———. *48th Virginia Infantry*. Lynchburg, Va., 1989.

Clark, Walter, ed. *Histories of the Several Regiments and Battalions from North Carolina in the Great War, 1861–65.* 5 vols. Raleigh, 1901.

Clemmer, Gregg S. "War in the Alleghenies: The Civil War on the Parkersburg Pike." *Augusta Historical Bulletin* 15, no. 2 (Fall 1979): 4–19.

Collins, Darrell L. *The Battles of Cross Keys and Port Republic.* Lynchburg, Va., 1993.

Colt, Margaret B. *Defend the Valley: A Shenandoah Family in the Civil War.* New York, 1999.

Condon, William H. *Life of Major-General James Shields: Hero of Three Wars and Senator from Three States.* Chicago, 1900.

Cozzens, Peter. "Jackson Alone." *Civil War Times Illustrated* 40, no. 6 (December 2001): 30–39, 74–76.

Dabney, Robert L. *Life and Campaigns of Lt. General T. J. (Stonewall) Jackson.* Harrisonburg, Va., 1983.

Davis, Julia. *The Shenandoah.* New York, 1945.

Davis, William C. *Jefferson Davis: The Man and His Hour.* New York, 1991.

Driver, Robert J., Jr. *58th Virginia Infantry.* Lynchburg, Va., 1990.

———. *The 1st and 2nd Rockbridge Artillery.* Lynchburg, Va., 1987.

Dufour, Charles L. *Gentle Tiger: The Gallant Life of Roberdeau Wheat.* Baton Rouge, 1957.

Dyer, Frederick H. *A Compendium of the War of the Rebellion.* 3 vols. New York, 1959.

Ecelbarger, Gary L. *Frederick W. Lander: The Great Natural American Soldier.* Baton Rouge, 2000.

———. *"We Are in for It!": The First Battle of Kernstown, March 23, 1862.* Shippensburg, Pa., 1997.

Evans, Clement A. *Confederate Military History: A Library of Confederate States History.* 13 vols. Atlanta, 1899.

Fields, Bettye-Lou. *Grayson County: A History in Words and Pictures.* Independence, Va., 1976.

Fishel, Edwin C. *The Secret War for the Union: The Untold Story of Military Intelligence in the Civil War.* Boston, 1996.

Frye, Dennis. *2nd Virginia Infantry.* Lynchburg, Va., 1984.

Gallagher, Gary W. "You Must Either Attack Richmond or Give Up the Job and Come to the Defence of Washington." In *The Shenandoah Campaign of 1862*, edited by Gary W. Gallagher, 3–23. Chapel Hill, 2003.

Hale, Laura V. *Four Valiant Years in the Lower Shenandoah Valley, 1861–1865.* Strasburg, Va., 1968.

Harrington, Fred H. *Fighting Politician: Major General N. P. Banks.* Philadelphia, 1948.

Hattaway, Herman, and Archer Jones. *How the North Won: A Military History of the Civil War.* Urbana, Ill., 1983.

Henderson, George F. R. *Stonewall Jackson and the American Civil War.* London, 1961.

Hess, Nancy B. *The Heartland: Rockingham County*. Harrisonburg, Va., 1976.

Hiden, J. C. "Stonewall Jackson." *Southern Historical Society Papers* 20 (1892): 307–10.

Hunt, Roger D. *Colonels in Blue: Union Army Colonels of the Civil War, New York*. Atlglen, Pa., 2003.

Jones, Terry L. *Lee's Tigers: The Louisiana Infantry in the Army of Northern Virginia*. Baton Rouge, 1987.

Kajencki, Francis C. *Star on Many a Battlefield: Brevet Brigadier General Joseph Kargé in the American Civil War*. Cranbury, 1980.

Kearsey, A. *A Study of the Strategy and Tactics of the Shenandoah Valley Campaign, 1861–1862*. London, 1953.

Koeniger, A. Cash. "Prejudices and Partialities: The Garnett Controversy Revisited." In *The Shenandoah Valley Campaign of 1862*, edited by Gary W. Gallagher, 219–36. Chapel Hill, 2003.

Krick, Robert E. L. "Maryland's Ablest Confederate: General Charles S. Winder of the Stonewall Brigade." In *The Shenandoah Valley Campaign of 1862*, edited by Gary W. Gallagher, 178–218. Chapel Hill, 2003.

Krick, Robert K. "Armistead and Garnett: The Parallel Lives of Two Virginia Soldiers." In *The Third Day at Gettysburg and Beyond*, edited by Gary W. Gallagher, 93–131. Chapel Hill, 1998.

——. "The Army of Northern Virginia's Most Notorious Court-Martial: Jackson vs. Garnett." *Blue and Gray* 3, no. 6 (1989): 25–30.

——. *Conquering the Valley: Stonewall Jackson at Port Republic*. New York, 1996.

——. "The Metamorphosis in Stonewall Jackson's Public Image." In *The Shenandoah Valley Campaign of 1862*, edited by Gary W. Gallagher, 24–42. Chapel Hill, 2003.

Lamers, William M. *Edge of Glory: A Biography of General William S. Rosecrans*. 1961. Reprint, Baton Rouge, 1999.

Lindsley, John B. *The Military Annals of Tennessee: Confederate*. Nashville, Tenn., 1886.

Lyne, Mrs. William. "Famous Army Horses." *Confederate Veteran* 37, no. 12 (December 1929): 456–57.

Mahon, Michael G. *The Shenandoah Valley, 1861–1865: The Destruction of the Granary of the Confederacy*. Mechanicsburg, Pa., 1999.

Malone, Dumas, ed. *Dictionary of American Biography*. 22 vols. New York, 1943–44.

May, George E. *Port Republic: The History of a Shenandoah Valley River Town*. Staunton, Va., 2002.

McGuire, Stuart. "Hunter Holmes McGuire, M.D., L.L.D." *Annals of Medical History*, n.s., 10, no. 1 (January 1938): 1–14.

Miller, William J. "Such Men as Shields, Banks, and Frémont: Federal Command in Western Virginia, March–June 1862." In *The Shenandoah Valley Campaign of 1862*, edited by Gary W. Gallagher, 43–85. Chapel Hill, 2003.

Murphy, Terrence V. *10th Virginia Infantry*. Lynchburg, 1989.

Musick, Michael P. *6th Virginia Cavalry*. Lynchburg, 1990.

Noyalas, Jonathan A. " 'My Will Is Absolute Law': General Robert H. Milroy and Winchester, Virginia." M.A. thesis, Virginia Polytechnic Institute and State University, Blacksburg, 2003.

Pfanz, Donald C. *Richard S. Ewell: A Soldier's Life*. Chapel Hill, 1998.

Phillips, Edward H. "The Lower Shenandoah Valley during the Civil War: The Impact of War upon the Civilian Population and upon Civil Institutions." Ph.D. diss., University of North Carolina, Chapel Hill, 1958.

Phipps, Sheila. "132 North Cameron Street: 'Secesh Lives Here.' " *Winchester-Frederick County Historical Society Journal* 7 (1993): 52–67.

Quarles, Garland R. *Occupied Winchester, 1861–1865*. Winchester, Va., 1976.

——. *Some Worthy Lives, Mini-Biographies, Winchester and Frederick County*. Winchester, Va., 1988.

Rankin, Thomas M. *Stonewall Jackson's Romney Campaign, January 1–February 20, 1862*. Lynchburg, Va., 1994.

——. *37th Virginia Infantry*. Lynchburg, Va., 1986.

Reidenbaugh, Lowell. *33rd Virginia Infantry*. Lynchburg, Va., 1987.

——. *27th Virginia Infantry*. Lynchburg, Va., 1993.

Richards, L. Adolph. *Winchester and Vicinity*. Winchester, Va., 1953.

Robertson, James I., Jr. *The Stonewall Brigade*. Baton Rouge, 1963.

——. *Stonewall Jackson: The Man, the Soldier, the Legend*. New York, 1997.

Sauers, Richard A. *The Devastating Hand of War: Romney, West Virginia, during the Civil War*. Wheeling, W.Va., 2000.

Schlebecker, John T. "Farmers in the Lower Shenandoah Valley, 1850." *Virginia Magazine of History and Biography* 79 (October 1971): 462–76.

Sears, Stephen W. *To the Gates of Richmond: The Peninsula Campaign*. New York, 1992.

——. *George B. McClellan: The Young Napoleon*. New York, 1988.

Smith, Justin H. *The War with Mexico*. 2 vols. New York, 1919.

Strider, Robert E. L. *The Life and Work of George William Peterkin*. Philadelphia, 1929.

Summers, Festus P. *The Baltimore and Ohio in the Civil War*. New York, 1939.

Tanner, Robert G. *Stonewall in the Valley*. 1976. Reprint, Mechanicsburg, Pa., 1996.

Thomas, Clarence. *General Turner Ashby: The Centaur of the South*. Winchester, Va., 1907.

Vandiver, Frank E. *Mighty Stonewall*. New York, 1957.

Wallace, Lee A. *5th Virginia Infantry*. Lynchburg, Va., 1988.

Wayland, John Walter. *Stonewall Jackson's Way: Route, Method, Achievement*. Staunton, Va., 1940.

——. *Twenty-five Chapters on the Shenandoah Valley, to Which Is Appended a Concise History of the Civil War in the Valley*. Strasburg, Va., 1957.

Wert, Jeffry. *A Brotherhood of Valor: The Common Soldiers of the Stonewall Brigade, C.S.A., and the Iron Brigade, U.S.A.* New York, 1999.

Wessels, William L. *Born to Be a Soldier: The Military Career of William Wing Loring of St. Augustine, Floria.* Fort Worth, Tex., 1991.

Williams, Kenneth P. *Lincoln Finds a General: A Military Study of the Civil War.* 5 vols. New York, 1957–59.

Wilson, James D. *Edinburg, 1861–1865: Civil War Anecdotes and Incidents.* Edinburg, Va., 1982.

Wise, Jennings C. *Military History of the Virginia Military Institute.* Lynchburg, Va., 1915.

INDEX

withdrawal of, to Strasburg, 277–79, 288–89; withdrawal of, to Winchester, 311, 312–13, 315, 320–21, 333; actions of, at Winchester, 341–43, 351, 374; actions of, on retreat to Potomac, 375, 376, 381, 384

Barclay, Pvt. Alexander T. "Ted," 59

Bard, 1st Sgt. David, 180

Barr, Hugh, 200, 315

Barton, Lt. Randolph J., 67, 205, 213

Barton, Pvt. Robert T., 338, 358

Barton's Woods, 168

Bath, Va., 70

Battery C, West Virginia Artillery, 464

Battery E, 4th U.S. Artillery, 482

Battery H, 1st Ohio Light Artillery, 155, 482, 494–95

Battery I, 1st Ohio Light Artillery, 467

Battery L, 1st Ohio Light Artillery, 155, 170

Bayard, Col. George D., 418, 420, 421, 437

Baylor, Col. William S. H., 138, 251, 356

Beard, Capt. John W., 355

Beem, Lt. David E., 117

Benjamin, Judah P., 45, 53, 66, 101

Blackford, Pvt. Launcelot M. "Lanty," 69, 203

Blenker, Brig. Gen. Louis, 238, 384, 420–21

Bloomery Furnace, 108

Bloomery Gap, 108

Blue's Gap, 85

Bohlen, Brig. Gen. Henry, 238, 462

Booth, Lt. George W., 438

Boswell, Lt. J. K., 269, 287

Boteler, Alexander R., 29, 39, 101–3, 396, 400–402, 505, 506, 507

Bounty and Furlough Act, 88

Bowen, Capt. Erwin A., 246–47

Bower's Hill, 349

Boyce, Lt. Charles W., 126, 288, 316

Boyd, Belle, 293, 299

Boyd, Maj. David, 498

Branch, Brig. Gen. Lawrence O'Bryan, 275, 285

Brett, Martin, 271

Bridgford, Capt. D. B., 197

Brockenbrough's Battery, 459, 495

Brodhead, Col. Thornton F., 154, 155, 231, 333

Brown, Maj. A. Campbell, 221, 298, 318–19, 461, 468

Brown, Capt. William F., 405

Brown's Gap, 258

Bryant, Lt. Edwin E., 124

Buchanan, Pvt. John B., 365

Bucktails, 418, 437–38, 439

Buckton Station, 308

Bull Pasture Mountain, 263

Burks, Col. Jesse, 100, 168, 252

Burstenbinder, Col. Otto, 188

Burton, Alonzo H., 487

Campbell, Col. John A., 252, 360

Camp Hill, 350

Cantey, Col. James, 457

Capehart, Henry, 177

Carpenter's (Allegheny) Virginia Battery, 172–73, 176

Carrington, Alexander B., 450

Carrington, Capt. Joseph, 452, 453

Carroll, Col. Samuel S.: background and character of, 155, 160, 216, 239–40, 243, 443; advance of, on Port Republic, 418, 432, 444; raid of, on Port Republic, 445, 447, 448, 453, 455; actions of, at Port Republic, 480, 482; opinions of, after Port Republic, 500

Casement, Maj. John, 180

Casler, Pvt. John O., 206

Cass, Pvt. Samuel W., 150

Casualties: at Kernstown, 215; at McDowell, 273–74; at Front Royal, 307; at Winchester, 377; at Harrisonburg, 439; at Cross Keys, 477; at Port Republic, 499

Cavins, Elijah H. C., 192

Cedar Creek, 24

Cedar Knob, 267

Chamberlain, Maj. Benjamin, 205

Chamberlayne, John Hampden "Ham," 116

Chapman, Col. George D., 353, 354

Charlestown, Va., 122–23, 125

Charlottesville Light Artillery, 452

Chase, Julia, 141, 142

Chase, Salmon P., 146, 346, 378, 379

Chenoweth, Maj. Joseph H., 488

Chesapeake and Ohio (C&O) Canal, 50, 57

Chew, Capt. Robert, 42, 154, 397

Chew's battery, 42, 150, 231, 323, 324; at Kernstown, 154, 155, 161

Clark, Col. John S., 187, 378, 396

Clark, Capt. Joseph C., 151

Coaling, 481

Colgrove, Col. Silas, 333–35, 364, 365

Collins, Maj. William D., 324

Collis, Capt. Charles, 326–27, 328

Colston, Capt. Raleigh, 59

Colston, Sgt. William B., 59, 61, 185

Colton, Lt. Sheldon, 188–89

Conner, Col. Z. T., 266, 403, 406

Conrad, 1st. Sgt. Holmes, 436

Conrad's Store, 245

Conscription Act, 235–36, 250

Cooper, Gen. Samuel, 45

Copeland, Lt. Col. Joseph, 154, 181

Copeland, Maj. R. Morris, 148, 154

Courtney's Richmond Battery, 397–98, 458

Coyner, Maj. Samuel A., 424

Cox, Pvt. Leroy, 452

Craig, Lt. Alfred T., 188

Creighton, Lt. Col. William, 180, 198

Cross Keys, Va., 458–59

Crutchfield, Col. Stapleton, 300–301, 449

Cummings, Col. Arthur C., 170, 197, 251

Dabney, Robert L., 220–21, 258, 326, 329, 349, 453, 486, 510

Dam No. 4, 57

Dam No. 5, 57, 58, 60, 62, 64

Daum, Col. Philip, 150–51, 404, 455, 482, 487

Davis, Lt. James, 488

Davis, Jefferson, 3, 8, 100–101, 106, 115

Davis, Pvt. Joshua, 495–96

De Forest, Col. Othneil, 327, 328, 329, 342

Desertion, 95, 116, 131, 152, 239, 259, 289

Dinwiddie, Lt. James, 447, 453

Discipline: in Jackson's army, 42, 43, 90, 99, 251, 331–32; in Taylor's brigade, 291, 298, 303; in Union army, 48, 87, 233, 420–21, 430

Disease and illnesses, 89, 98, 105, 106, 144

Donnelly, Col. Dudley, 148, 312, 322, 350, 355, 368

Douglas, Maj. Henry Kyd, 222, 241, 254, 299, 332, 436

Douty, Lt. Col. Calvin S., 316, 323, 325–26

Drake, Pvt. S. W., 164

Dunkards, 152, 235, 277

Dunning, Col. Samuel, 85, 87, 107, 242

Dushane, Lt. Col. Nathan T., 298, 301, 305

Dutton, Lt. H. Melzer, 48, 247

Dwight, Maj. Wilder, 124, 218, 224, 337, 350, 363

Echols, Col. John, 176

Edinburg, Va., 26, 27

character of, 99; and Romney petition, 99–100; actions of, at Kernstown, 168, 169–70, 173, 182, 197, 198, 208; actions of, at Winchester, 361; actions of, on retreat, 411, 412, 421

Fuller, John, 109

Funsten, Maj. O. R., 207

Garber, Capt. Sandy, 478

Garibaldi, Pvt. John, 62

Garnett, Brig. Gen. Richard B.: strained relations of, with Jackson, 45, 88–89; actions of, at Kernstown, 168, 173, 177, 182, 196, 199, 200, 208; arrest of, 221–22

Garnett, Lt. Col. Thomas, 65

Garrett, John W., 50

Gavin, Col. James, 447

Geary, Brig. Gen. John W., 288, 343–44, 379, 380, 391

Gildea, Sgt. James, 155, 208, 210, 443, 449, 450, 451

Gilham, Col. William, 66, 72, 77–78, 88

Gillespie, Pvt. Samuel L., 205, 433

Gilmor, Capt. Harry, 396, 398

Glass Farm, 196

Goodrich, Capt. Earle S., 448

Gordon, Col. George H., 148, 214, 231, 233, 277, 279–80, 288, 310; actions of, at Winchester, 350, 356, 363, 366

Gould, Lt. John M., 143

Grabill, Lt. John H., 69

Graham, James R., 44, 138–39

Greenleaf, Cpl. Charles H., 310–11

Gregg, Capt. J. E., 209

Grigsby, Lt. Col. A. J., 176–77, 185, 196, 487

Guard Hill, 292

Hall, Cpl. James E., 116, 289–90

Hamilton, Brig. Gen. Charles S., 134, 137, 140, 148, 388

Hampton, Capt. R. B., 327–29

Hancock, Md., 76

Harman, Maj. John, 133, 217, 411, 477, 478, 498, 511

Harman, Michael C., 84

Harman, Col. William H., 200

Harnesberger, J. S., 241

Harpers Ferry, Va., 120

Harrison, Capt. William F., 99

Harrisonburg, Va., 246, 247

Harrow, Lt. Col. William, 192

Hartman, Peter, 247

Hatch, Brig. Gen. John P., 48, 148, 310, 315, 323–25, 336

Hawkins, Maj. Willis A., 405

Hawks, Maj. Wells J., 207, 402, 406

Higgins, Capt. Thomas W., 264

Hillman's Tollgate, 24

Hotchkiss, Jedediah, 73, 217, 318, 325, 402, 411, 412; background and character of, 152–53; actions of, as chief topographical engineer, 220, 431; special duties of, 252, 256, 287, 385, 407, 428, 486, 498; actions of, at McDowell, 262, 264, 265, 272–73; actions of, during pursuit of Banks, 323, 326

Houghton, Capt. William D., 193

Howard, Lt. McHenry, 223, 273, 332, 367, 397, 399, 414

Hubbard, Capt. E. L., 308

Huntington, Capt. James F., 155, 233, 242

Hyman, Capt. Henry F., 264

Imboden, Capt. John D., 479, 484

Irish Battalion. *See* 1st Virginia Battalion

Jackson, Sgt. A. J., 210

Jackson, Mary Anna, 12, 53

Jackson, Maj. Gen. Thomas J. "Stonewall," 65, 260, 406, 468; as folk hero, 2,

Keogh, Capt. Miles, 445

Kerfoot, Henry D., 448

Kernstown, battle of: strategic impact of, 207–8, 228, 234; Federal leadership at, 226

Kernstown, Va., 159

Keys, Capt. John, 150

Kimball, Col. Nathan: assumes command before Kernstown, 156–57; actions of, at Kernstown, 160, 161, 164–66, 169, 177–78, 187, 189, 192, 209; actions of, after Kernstown, 216–17, 225, 405, 408, 409

Kinzer, Pvt. William T., 62, 98

Kirkland, Col. William W., 330, 332–33, 354

Kitchen, John, 157

Knipe, Col. Joseph F., 353

Kurtz, Capt. George W., 338, 339

Lander, Brig. Gen. Frederick W.: background and character of, 9–10; wounding of, at Edward's Ferry, 11–12; views of, toward Union high command, 12, 52–53, 82, 91, 108; actions of, at Hancock, Md., 79, 81; temper of, 80–81; aggressiveness of, 82, 91, 103, 107, 118; abandons Romney, 92; declining health of, 103–4, 107, 108, 113; actions of, at Bloomery Gap, 110–12; opinions of, 112; death of, 128

Latham, Capt. George R., 264, 267

Lee, Alvid, 269, 273

Lee, Mary Greenhow, 138, 141, 144, 157, 371, 410

Lee, Gen. Robert E., 243, 248–49, 255, 275, 286, 505, 506

Leonard, Col. Samuel H., 58

Letcher, John, 31, 102, 234

Lewis, Col. William D., 79, 181

Lewiston, 258

Lewiston Lane, 455

Lincoln, Abraham, 135, 229–30, 442; role of, in Valley campaign, 3–4, 507–8; relations of, with McClellan, 146–47, 228–29, 379, 380–81; reaction of, to Banks's withdrawal, 340, 344, 378; communications of, with McDowell, 345, 346, 391, 430; communications of, with Frémont, 347, 387, 390

Long, Maj. Richard, 265

Loring, Maj. Gen. William W., 53, 54–56, 66, 69, 73, 75–76, 97, 106

Lostutter, Jr., Capt. David, 444

Louisiana Tigers, 297, 303, 317, 328, 493

Lyle, Lt. John N., 63, 139, 183, 198, 205–6, 214, 215–16

Magill, Mary Tucker, 144

Manassas Gap Railroad, 26

Mann, Maj. O. L., 71

Mapes, Capt. William H. H., 301

Markell, Lt. Arthur S., 132

Marsh, Sgt. Thomas, 184, 211

Martinsburg, Va., 126

Marvin, Edward E., 63

Maryland Line, 282, 423

Mason, Capt. Claiborne, 284, 428, 478

Mason, Col. John, 149, 152, 160, 165, 177

Massanutten Mountain, 18, 21

Massey, Lt. W. A., 268

Matthews, Maj. Joseph, 154

McAbee, H. M., 156

McClellan, Maj. Gen. George B., 113; timidity of, 50, 52, 64, 91; relations of, with Lincoln, 52–53, 146–47, 228–29, 379, 380–81; and Valley campaign, 96, 103, 117, 119–20, 122, 132, 219; Peninsula campaign of, 115, 146–47, 227–28, 344, 345

McDonald, Col. Angus, 40,

McDonald, Cornelia, 141, 211, 213

McDonald, Capt. Edward, 396, 425–26

McDowell, battle of: impact of, 274

McDowell, Maj. Gen. Irwin, 345 346, 379, 391, 392, 409, 417, 418, 419, 501

McDowell, Va., 262–63

McGuire, Hugh H., 122

McGuire, Hunter, 139, 447, 448

McKay, Pvt. George, 183

McKim, Lt. Randolph H., 284, 468, 469

McLaughlin, Capt. William, 57–58, 68, 84, 202, 251

McLean, Col. Nathaniel C., 267, 272

McVeigh, T. J., 131

Mead, Sgt. Rufus, 143

Meem's Bottom, 234

Mennonites, 32, 152, 235, 247

Mercer, Col. John T., 463–64

Middletown, Va., 27

Miles, Col. Dixon, 313

Militia (Virginia), 31, 38, 67, 70, 72, 74, 86, 88, 108, 111–12, 152, 234–35

Milltown, 154

Milroy, Brig. Gen. Robert H., 386, 420, 456; actions of, at McDowell, 262, 263–64, 265, 266, 268, 272, 273, 274, 275; background and character of, 263; actions of, at Cross Keys, 469, 471, 474, 490

Moore, Capt. Samuel J. C., 70, 90, 185, 208, 448, 452

Moorefield, Va., 107

Morrison, Lt. Col. Abisha L., 365

Mouat, David, 306

Mount Jackson, Va., 26

Muhlenburg, Lt. F. D., 71

Munford, Col. Thomas T., 40, 422, 438, 478, 504

Murphy, Col. John K., 364

Murray, Col. William G., 74, 81, 191–92

Myerhoff, Sgt. Charles H., 193, 194–95, 201, 203

Myers, Lt. Frank, 303

Nadenbousch, Capt. John Quincy Adams, 161, 163

Neff, Col. John E., 251

New, George W., 444

New Market, Va., 26

New Market Gap, 21

Newton, Va., 27, 149, 336

Nickerson, Sgt. Frank B., 164, 210–11

9th Louisiana Infantry, 491

9th Ohio Battery, 262

Oates, Capt. William C., 331, 457

110th Pennsylvania Infantry, 79, 81, 181

Opequon Creek, 21, 24

Osborn, Col. Thomas O., 75

Paldi, Maj. Angelo, 154, 322

Parham, Lt. Col. Charles, 301–2, 305–6, 307, 311

Patrick, Lt. Col. John H., 189, 193

Patton, Lt. Col. John M., Jr., 181, 194

Paxton, Maj. Elisha F. "Bull," 59, 84, 95, 98, 144, 207, 230

Peck, Lt. Col. William, 493

Pendleton, Sandie, 116, 129, 171, 175, 234, 254, 299, 372, 402, 476

Perkins, Maj. D. D., 148

Peterkin, Sgt. George W., 145, 194

Pile, George C., 198

Pilsen, Lt. Col. John, 412, 461

Poague, Capt. William T., 61, 201–2, 251, 332, 335, 358–59, 450

Porte Crayon. See Strother, David H.

Port Republic, Va., 26, 257–58, 432

Post, Capt. John E., 294